CHICAGO FURNITURE

CHICAGO

ART, CRAFT, & INDUSTRY

THE CHICAGO HISTORICAL SOCIETY in association with

W. W. NORTON & COMPANY New York / London

FURNITURE

1833·1983

SHARON DARLING

The text of this book is composed in Palatino, with display type set in Goudy.
Composition by the Maple-Vail Book Manufacturing Group. Manufacturing
by The Murray Printing Company. Book design by Christine Aulicino.

First Edition

ISBN 0-393-01818-0

W. W. Norton & Company, Inc., 500 Fifth Avenue, New York, N. Y. 10110
W. W. Norton & Company Ltd., 37 Great Russell Street, London WC1B 3NU

1 2 3 4 5 6 7 8 9 0

To the countless furniture makers whose names do not appear in this book
but whose artistry, skill, and dedication helped make Chicago
one of the great furniture centers of the nation.

CONTENTS

ACKNOWLEDGMENTS

Chicago Furniture: Art, Craft, & Industry, 1833–1983 has been under way since 1976, when Joell Kunath and I began to catalogue the Chicago-made furniture in the Chicago Historical Society's collection. In our efforts to trace the labeled pieces, we searched through documentary material in the Society's library. This in turn led us to some of the manufacturers who had played central roles in the city's furniture industry. From their records and reminiscences it became clear that this was a story that had to be told.

A planning grant from the National Endowment for the Humanities made possible the preliminary survey of available artifacts and research sources, which led to the decision to mount an exhibition and write this book. Later, Harryette and Marcus Cohn of Washington, D.C., and the Chicago Historical Society generously underwrote research trips to Washington, New York, and North Carolina. The project also was funded in part by grants from the National Endowment for the Arts and the Illinois Arts Council.

This work would not have been possible without the encouragement of Harold K. Skramstad, former director of the Chicago Historical Society, and the support of the present director, Ellsworth H. Brown; the trustees; and the members of the Guild of the Chicago Historical Society. Timothy Jacobson, head of publications, made arrangements for publication; James Mairs, Mary Cunnane, Daniel Simon, and Janet Byrne of W. W. Norton & Company were responsible for production.

As always, I am indebted to all my colleagues at the Chicago Historical Society, who helped at every stage, but particularly to Olivia Mahoney, assistant curator of Decorative Arts. Special thanks must also go to Teresa Krutz, registrar; Sylvia Landsman, secretary; Scott LaFrance, curatorial assistant; Roberta Casey, assistant editor; and Janice Soczka and Grant Dean, curator and assistant curator, respectively, of the Printed Collections. Unless otherwise noted, Walter W. Krutz was responsible for photographs of the objects and printed materials.

The project owes much to the devoted efforts of a group of volunteers who gave hundreds of hours to the tedious tasks of searching directories and periodicals, photocopying, and filing. They include Joell Kunath, Sylvia Preston, and Frances Spence. Tita Zeffren located appropriate upholstery fabrics; Cynthia Jones found photographs of Chicago interiors; Betty J. Blum compiled a list of Chicagoans who patented furniture; and Irma Strauss helped research the chapters devoted to art furniture. Anne Stuart Seaton recorded interviews, served as a reader, and helped compile the Appendix. Louis P. Cain III, professor of economics at Loyola University; Tim Samuelson of the Chicago Commission on Historical and Architectural Landmarks; and Anne F. Woodhouse, curator of Decorative Arts at the State Historical Society of Wisconsin, served as readers and offered constructive criticism.

Invaluable assistance was provided by many people connected with the furniture industry, including George Schumann of Sears, Roebuck & Company, who scheduled interviews with various manufacturers; E. C. Snyder, who arranged for the archives of the Chicago Furniture Manufacturers' Association to be transferred to the collections of the Chicago Historical Society; and N. I. and Barton Bienenstock of *Furniture World—Furniture South,* who made their excellent libraries available both in North Carolina and New York. Artifacts, information, and company histories were graciously provided by Carlo Alonzi, Stuart Applebaum, Robert Balonick, Charles Bauer, Douglas Cohen, Morton Cohen, Bruce and Ralph O. Campbell, Burt Fainman, Florence Kruissink Frazer, Morris Futorian, I. H. Hartman, Jr., Meyer S. Kaplan, Philip E. Kelley, Frank Mattaliano, Murray Moxley, Robert Parenti, Abe Rosen, Lawrence K. Schnadig, Francis A. Seng, Jerry Seiff, Marijan Srnak, Manfred Steinfeld, George Stembridge, Jr., Hampton E. Tonk, and Vito Ursini. Special thanks also must go to the relatives and descendants of Chicago furniture makers, who willingly located objects, biographical information, and photographs, including: William F. Christiansen, Mrs. John Erland, Mrs. Lisl B. Ekvall, Mrs. James Eppenstein, Mrs. Abel Faidy, Mrs. Richard Frey, Inez K. Fritze, Mrs. Ethel D. Hintz, Mrs. Wolfgang Hoffmann, Robert Lehmann, Frank Mattucci, Mrs. Jean Sagan, Lorraine Sinkler, Jeane Stiefel, Mary Trimarco, Hazel Kahle Williams, and Violet Wyld. Architects Monroe Bowman, Stuart Cohen, Howard Decker, Paul Florian, Bertrand Goldberg, the late George Fred Keck, William Keck, the late Philip B. Maher, Walter Netsch, Lawrence B. Perkins, Harold Reynolds, Linda Searle, Melvyn Skvarla, Robert Switzer, Stanley Tigerman, John Vinci, L. Morgan Yost; interior designers Norman DeHaan, Richard Himmel, John C. Murphy, Kitty Baldwin Weese, and Marianne Willisch; and industrial designers Henry P. Glass, Nathan Lerner, and E. Raymond Pearson shared their experiences as furniture designers and gave me many leads on whom to interview.

Staff members of various museums, libraries, and business establishments who proved particularly helpful include: William Wright, Mary McKeown, and Rex Battenberg of the American School of Correspondence; Maebetty Langdon, Milo M. Naeve, Daphne Roloff, Pauline Salecka, and John Zukowsky, all of The Art Institute of Chicago; David R. Phillips, Chicago Architectural Photographing Company; Elaine Harrington, Chicago Architecture Foundation; Laura Linard, Chicago Public Library; Irene Roughton, The Chrysler Museum, Norfolk Virginia; William Isaacson, The

Cliff Dwellers Club of Chicago; Laura B. Hoge, Colorado Springs Fine Arts Center, Colorado; Donald Hallmark, The Dana House, Springfield; Victoria Behm, FCL Associates; Donald Kalec, Frank Lloyd Wright Home and Studio, Oak Park; Thomas A. Campbell, Jr., Galena State Historic Site, Galena; Richard R. Stryker, Jr., Grand Rapids Public Museum, Michigan; David A. Hanks, David A. Hanks & Associates, New York; Bill Thompkins, Hedrich-Blessing; John Lindenbush and Jim Stulga, Historic Pullman; Carol Kelm, The Historical Society of Oak Park and River Forest; Karen Indeck, Hokin/Kaufman Gallery; Delecia B. Huitt, Hunter-Dawson State Historic Site, New Madrid, Missouri; Robert V. Hinman, Knoll International; Mary Eisser, The Library of Congress; Mary Doherty, Metropolitan Museum of Art, New York; Terence Marvel, Milwaukee Art Museum, Wisconsin; Rodris Roth and Jennifer Oka, National Museum of American History; Mary S. Hoffschwelle and Patty Dean, Montana Historical Society; Nick Scrattish, Denver office, National Park Service; Margaret DiSalvi and Ulysses Dietz, The Newark Museum, New Jersey; Marilyn and Wilbert Hasbrouck, Prairie Avenue Bookshop; Mary Bartholomew, The Robie House, University of Chicago; Roberta Diemer, Printing and Photographic Services, Smithsonian Institution; George Talbot, State Historical Society of Wisconsin, Madison; David Gebhard, University of California Santa Barbara; Perry Duis, University of Illinois at Chicago; Alan K. Lathrop, Northwest Architectural Archives, University of Minnesota; and Veronica Coyne, Montgomery Ward & Company.

The skills of substantive editor Fannia Weingartner, former head of publications at the Chicago Historical Society, are evident on every page. Her enthusiasm and dedication sustained me through countless drafts and made each phase of the work a pleasure. My husband, Mikell C. Darling, cheerfully spent evenings and weekends photographing and transporting furniture and never ceased to encourage me in my efforts.

CHICAGO FURNITURE

INTRODUCTION

A traveler arriving at the military and fur-trading outpost that was Chicago in 1833 could hardly have guessed that this sparse settlement in an essentially treeless prairie would become the site of one of the most important furniture manufacturing centers in the United States. However, over the next two decades, as Americans began to move westward, Chicago's location at the foot of the Great Lakes and the junction of important rail and water routes would make it both magnet and funnel for immigrants from Europe and the East Coast. Thousands would pass through, but thousands would stay. Many were artisans who brought with them skills in a variety of crafts, including cabinet-making, woodcarving, and upholstering. The availability of these craftsmen combined with technological innovations like steam-powered machinery and the growing Western market to create a furniture empire that would remain in the forefront for some seventy years.

Although many chair- and cabinetmakers were at work in Chicago prior to the Civil War, it was not until 1873 that the city's furniture trade began to assume tremendous proportions. By 1885 Chicago had some 200 furniture factories and led the nation both in the number of employees engaged in that industry and in the amount of its annual production. Sold locally by wholesalers and retailers and through the mail by pioneer mail-order houses, the output of the city's furniture factories was distributed via railroad throughout the United States and touched the lives of rich and poor from New York to California.

Large-scale manufacturing continued into the twentieth century, but by 1900 Chicago had also become known as a center for innovative furniture designs inspired by various aesthetic theories, arts and crafts movements, and the experimentation of the city's innovative architects and interior designers. The result was a renewed emphasis on fine handcraftsmanship not only by individual cabinetmakers but also by some of the larger manufacturers. Although the furniture industry began to decline after World War II, Chicago has retained its role as a furniture design and marketing center until the present day.

This book deals with the chief economic, social, and stylistic factors that influenced the design and production of furniture in Chicago. It considers not only business conditions and technological developments but changes in taste and consumer habits. It examines, as well, the cultural context in which furniture serves both as a functional product and as a symbol of social, economic, and, at times, moral status.

The story is not a simple one, embracing as it does art, craft, and industry. The organization of this book is basically chronological, but within each significant period the furniture makers are treated thematically according to the predominant manner of production. The prime division is between small workshops and large factories. This division was most apparent in the years between 1873 and World War II, the period of Chicago's preeminence in the industry.

Part I concentrates on the first forty years, from Chicago's frontier days in the 1830s to the rebuilding of the city after the Great Fire of 1871. Beginning as frontier craftsmen who combined furniture making with other occupations, Chicago's furniture makers subsequently organized larger manufactories under the stimulus of innovations in technology and transportation. Part II explores the industry's heyday in Chicago, when it served as the primary supplier for America's growing middle class. During this period the adoption of methods of mass production led to specialization, with the result that workshops engaged in general cabinetmaking were increasingly replaced by factories manufacturing a limited range of products, whether upholstered parlor furniture, bedroom furniture, chairs, commercial furniture, or cabinet wares. Part III considers a parallel development, the production of art furniture by a variety of craftsmen for a prosperous and fashion-conscious clientele. Creators and consumers alike were influenced by variations of aesthetic movements of foreign and local origin.

Though mass production and the making of art furniture took place within the same time frame, each was characterized by distinctive features. Furniture made in Chicago factories often lacks identifying labels and tends to reflect the prevailing taste modified for particular markets. The establishments that manufactured these pieces for "the million" are known today through the names of their owners rather than those of their workmen; their customers also remain anonymous.

Although products of the art furniture makers also were often unlabeled, many of these pieces can be identified because they remained in the hands of the families who commissioned them. Executed as works of art, they can be traced to their designers—architects like Adolph Cudell, Frank Lloyd Wright, and Samuel Marx—rather than to their fabricators.

Part IV takes the story of the industry from the end of World War I to the present, noting the city's contributions to modern styling as well as its role as a marketing and distributing center. Although the depression, war, and Southern competition led to the closing of most of Chicago's older factories by the 1950s, a new set of furniture makers appeared on the scene. Engaged in specialty furniture manufacturing, this new generation of entrepreneurs focused on making residential furniture for a regional market or developed their production in response to the growing demand for contract furniture designed for use in public, institutional, and commercial settings. An Epilogue touches on current trends, offering profiles of some of Chicago's most active furniture designers and artist / craftsmen.

Since considerations of space impose the necessity of selectivity, the author has focused on the firms and individuals most heavily documented in records and oral accounts and through examples of furniture. Many others, however, are listed in the directory that follows the Epilogue. Also included is a list of the primary sources on which this work is based. Many of the illustrations show furniture included in the exhibition "Chicago Furniture: Art, Craft, & Industry, 1833–1983" at the Chicago Historical Society from January through August 1984 and then at the Renwick Gallery in Washington, D.C., and the Cooper-Hewitt Museum in New York. Unless otherwise specified, the photographs and graphic materials reproduced in this book are from the collections of the Chicago Historical Society.

FRONTIER FURNITURE MAKERS

1833 - 1851

When lawyer John Dean Caton arrived in Chicago in June 1833, he found a bustling prairie seaport huddled on the marshy point where the Chicago River flowed into Lake Michigan. Lining the riverbanks and three muddy streets, hastily erected wooden shanties, log cabins, and the stockade of Fort Dearborn provided shelter for a transient population of 350. More substantial log structures, some two stories, housed stores and bakeries, a blacksmith shop, a carpenter shop, a tannery, and similar enterprises supplying the necessities of life.

It is in the unpublished version of Caton's reminiscences, begun some twenty years after his arrival in Chicago, that we find one of the few references to Chicago's earliest known cabinetmaker. According to Caton, in 1833 James W. Reed, "the only cabinet maker in town," was working in a small log building on South Water Street adjacent to the south bank of the Chicago River.[1] Caton had vivid memories of Reed, who did double duty as the town constable and happened to be involved in the young lawyer's first case.

Little is known about Reed and no pieces made by him have come to light to reveal his level of skill or the style in which he worked. However, Caton does state that "red cherry timber from Danville [Illinois] was used exclusively by James W. Reed, the cabinet maker."[2] Cherry, a fine-grained, red-brown wood with a golden sheen, was commonly used by country cabinetmakers. Hard yet fairly light, with good woodworking properties, it provided the needed strength for furniture legs and other structural members and also took a fine polish.

With settlers arriving daily and new houses and hotels to furnish, the demand for James Reed's work was undoubtedly steady, for throughout the winter of 1833–34 he repeatedly advertised in the city's first newspaper, the *Chicago Democrat*, for "two or three *journeymen cabinet makers*, to whom good wages will be paid."[3] Simple cupboards and tables and desks and chairs fashioned from cherry or whitewood (tulip poplar) would have provided him with a lively trade; few of Chicago's early residents brought bulky household furniture with them on the long and arduous journey west. After his election as sheriff of Cook County in the summer of 1834,[4] law enforcement must have occupied most of Reed's time, for his place in the local newspapers was soon taken by Clark, Filer & Co., a new firm of cabinetmakers and furniture dealers.

In those advertisements in the *Chicago Democrat* the firm of Clark, Filer & Co. noted that its Cabinet and Furniture Ware House on South Water Street had on hand "a very large assortment of cherry, curl and pin maple, black walnut and mahogany FURNITURE" and promised "CHAIRS, of every description and of the best quality."[5] Although Clark and Filer would have constructed or finished many of the pieces they advertised, some of their merchandise may have been produced by Eastern furniture makers and shipped westward along the Erie Canal to Buffalo and from there by steamboat to Chicago. Listing an array of sofas, sideboards, bookcases, tables, and stands, along with showcases, bedsteads, church furniture, and cribs, the firm's advertisements, worded expressly to attract the attention of newcomers, pointed out that "Families who are emigrating to this section of the country, will do well to call, as they will be supplied on the most reasonable terms."[6] Within a year, however, Clark and Filer themselves had moved on and their riverfront stand had been taken over by a Connecticut-born cabinetmaker, James Rockwell.

Like his predecessors, James Rockwell advertised a "complete assortment" in the weekly newspaper. Although no documents exist to testify to the quality of pieces made in his shop, an advertisement in the June 8, 1835, *Chicago Weekly American* provides some insight into the type of furniture he produced. It lists his stock as "consisting of Sideboards, Secretaries, Bureaus, Commodes, Wardrobes, Lockers, Dressing, Card, Pier, Center and Common Tables, Ottomans, Divans, Crickets, and Foot Stools. Also, a variety of Chairs and Bedsteads, which, with all other articles in his line, will be made after the latest New York and Paris fashions." Business was obviously brisk, for Rockwell's notices included a plea for "a few thousand feet of seasoned lumber, of different kinds, wanted immediately, for which Cash will be paid upon delivery."[7]

Within a year another cabinetmaker, Dennis S. Dewey, arrived in Chicago from the state of New York. Throughout the winter of 1836, Dewey advertised that he wanted to hire "by the middle of April next, 10 Journeymen Cabinet Makers, 5 Chair makers, 1 matterer, 1 cabinet finisher, 1 chair finisher, 4 painters" to assist him in preparing for the seasonal influx of new inhabitants and transients on their way further west. Besides advertising house, sign, and ornamental painting "done to order and in excellent style," Dewey offered Chicagoans an assortment of tables, stands, sofas, and bedsteads manufactured "to order of the best materials and in a superior style" and "mahogany, grecian, fancy and common chairs."[8] Although Dewey stayed in business in Chicago longer than the other early furniture makers, he later moved north to Lake County, where he ran for the office of county commissioner in 1841.[9]

Meanwhile, in December 1839, James Rockwell had sold his business to Augustine S. Bates and Caleb Morgan. Bates, who had come to Chicago in 1836, combined the occupations of cabinetmaking and undertaking. This was not uncommon, especially in rural areas, since much the same skills were needed to build and upholster a coffin as to construct household furniture. Morgan, trained as a cabinetmaker in New Hampshire, arrived earlier that same year.

Bates & Morgan. 199 Lake, 1839–42. **Caleb Morgan.** 199 Lake, 1843–60; 169 Randolph, 1861–64; 239 West Lake, 1864; 209 West Lake, 1865.

Born in New Hampshire, Caleb Morgan (1796–1871) came to Chicago in 1836. Three years later he entered into partnership with cabinetmaker / undertaker Augustine Seymour Bates. When their partnership ended in 1843, Morgan retained the cabinet warerooms. Bates went on to other things; in 1846 he was elected coroner of Cook County, a position he held until November 1851, when he was killed en route to California by Indians near Humboldt, Nevada.

Although no furniture known to have been made by Morgan has come to light, his advertisements indicate that he made "every variety of furniture," including chairs, bedsteads, sofas, tables, and bureaus in styles ranging from Empire to rococo. Morgan's son, Charles, worked as a clerk in his father's shop from 1861 until 1865. In 1866 Caleb Morgan worked as a salesman for J. Beiersdorf, manufacturer of upholstered furniture and possibly one of the new owners of Morgan's former factory.

Advertisement for Bates & Morgan, cabinetmakers and undertakers, from the September 17, 1840, Daily Chicago American.

Moving the cabinet warerooms two doors east from Rockwell's original location on South Water Street to 199 Lake Street, the city's main commercial route, Bates & Morgan kept on hand and manufactured "on short notice" a wide variety of bedsteads, bureaus, settees, and sofas. Also available were chairs in rosewood, mahogany, or "curl maple," painted chairs, and "Fancy" chairs with rush seats.[10]

Bates, who had imported the city's first elegant black-plumed hearse, remained true to his early calling in his partnership with Morgan. Thus the firm advertised, in addition to furniture, "coffins of all sizes and descriptions" and promised, moreover, that "Carriages and all other necessary things for Funerals will be procured and attended to without trouble to the friends of deceased persons."[11]

By 1842 Morgan and Bates had dissolved their partnership, although both stayed in the furniture business. While Morgan remained at 199 Lake, Bates opened a new wareroom a few doors away at 190, continuing to manufacture "every variety of furniture in his line of business," ranging from couches to coffins.[12] By now at least nine other furniture-making establishments were meeting the needs of the city's more than 7,000 residents. These included cabinet shops owned by Dennis S. Dewey, John B.

Weir, G. & R. Tetard, D. A. and E. M. Jones, and David L. Jacobus and chairmaking factories operated by Charles T. Brown, Horatio Cook, Charles Roberts, James McWilliams, and John Phillips. These early furniture makers flourished, aided by infusions of labor and technology from the East.

Just as Americans in the eighteenth century had transformed political ideas imported from the Old World to serve new purposes, so in the nineteenth century they lost no time in adapting the advances of the Industrial Revolution to their own needs. As John A. Kouwenhoven notes in *Made in America*, "As early as 1840 the English author of a *True Guide* to the United States published in London for the British mechanics and laborers who were planning to emigrate, summed up his experience of four years' work and five thousand miles of travel in the new nation by warning that a mechanic from the 'Old Country' should be prepared to meet with 'new and peculiar, if not improved, modes and ideas, and make up his mind also to their immediate adoption.' "[13]

In the 1830s and 1840s Rockwell, Dewey, and others would have had little difficulty attracting skilled workmen to their shops in a thriving frontier town like Chicago. Unhampered by a rigid economic and social structure, the city's cabinetmakers were part of a highly fluid economy characterized by rapidly changing partnerships and sudden rises and declines in fortune. While some went on to establish stable businesses and to become men of considerable wealth, others vanished from the pages of the city directory.

Most early cabinetmakers were from the East, driven from their workshops by the progress of mechanization there. By the 1830s high-speed and high-output machinery was lowering the cost of production and thus broadening the market for furniture. The scope of the market expanded further as a result of the transportation revolution, characterized by the introduction of steamships and railroads. But some artisans resisted the factory system of production, preferring to take their chances by migrating west, where the factory system was not yet established. In the newly opened territories the local market was temporarily protected by the cost involved in transporting bulky and heavy furniture over the long distance from the East, and the migrant cabinetmaker was able to produce competitively priced furniture and earn a sufficient return to remain an independent artisan. Eventually, of course, the new technology would follow labor to the Midwest and, indeed, reach its peak of efficiency there.[14]

Labor-saving machinery encouraged an acceleration in the division of labor and resulted in a significant reduction in cost. This helped transform what had typically been small cabinetmaking shops into sizable factories employing many workers. In practice this meant that rather than one man making a piece of furniture from start to finish, workers with specialized skills concentrated on particular aspects of cabinetmaking and decorating, such as woodturning, ornamental painting, upholstering, carving, or gilding.[15] Increasingly, tables, sofas, and chairs were assembled from a stock of pre-cut interchangeable parts. During slack times a supply of joiner's work, such as chair legs, stretchers, and top rails, would be made in advance

WESTWARD MIGRATION OF LABOR AND TECHNOLOGY

and kept on hand, along with a variety of heavy paper or wooden templates that could be used to reproduce parts quickly for the same or slightly variant furniture forms. This increased efficiency of production and permitted manufacturers to offer in their warerooms a supply of ready-made furniture as well as a variety of items that could be manufactured on short notice and at a lower price than had been possible when each piece was custom made.[16]

Some of the more enterprising cabinetmakers, like Morgan and Bates, soon imported machinery from the East and transformed their modest workshops into manufactories. They did not lack customers for their products; by 1848 the city had 20,000 inhabitants. Famine in Ireland and political unrest in the German states combined to produce a major influx of immigrants to Chicago during this period, bringing at one and the same time more labor and more customers.

The city's phenomenal growth over the next twelve years—by 1860 it had a population of some 100,000—stemmed in large part from its role as a transportation center. In 1848 Chicago became the terminus of the Illinois & Michigan Canal, which connected the Great Lakes and the Mississippi River. That same year the first railroad tracks were laid to the west, soon to be joined by others heading north and south, which, within a decade, would make Chicago the hub of a vast railroad network. Chicago's fine transportation connections in all directions revolutionized the way the city conducted business as well as the kinds of products its workshops and factories manufactured.[17]

WESTWARD MIGRATION OF STYLE

Besides basic skills and a desire for independence, Chicago's pioneer cabinetmakers, chairmakers, and ornamental painters of the 1830s and 1840s brought with them the styles prevalent in Eastern furniture shops, especially those found in New York, Philadelphia, and Boston. Meanwhile, the Eastern furniture makers had taken their cue from abroad.

Inspired by the trend-setting French furniture makers, American manufacturers began to create modern versions of classical Greek and Roman forms freely interpreted from wall and vase paintings found in archaeological excavations. The term "Grecian" was thus applied to chairs and sofas based on antique prototypes, much as it had been used by the famous English cabinetmaker Thomas Sheraton three decades earlier.

If modeled, as advertised, "after the latest New York and Paris fashions," the couches, tables, and bureaus made by James Rockwell and others would have been massive, strongly scrolled or curved forms enhanced by pillar or pedestal supports. Typically constructed with a veneer of mahogany or rosewood over pine, the style permitted the extensive use of locally available wood and allowed a thin layer of highly figured, expensive wood to be glued over the exposed wooden surface.

By the fall of 1834 steam-powered sawmills were in operation in Chicago, and large shipments of white pine imported from the thick forests of Michigan and Wisconsin were arriving at the city's docks and being stored in lumberyards along the southern bank of the Chicago River. The powerful circular saw allowed cabinetmakers to secure twice the amount of veneers from a single block of wood in half the time required by hand-sawing. When thin slices of glowing, coppery-red mahogany or black-veined rosewood were neatly glued over the surface of the cheaper wood, the finished product looked quite luxurious, although it cost but a fraction of what was charged for a similar piece made from solid wood. For the upholstered areas of seating furniture, machine-woven wools were available from the Joliet Woolen Factory, located forty miles west of the city, while, after 1839, practical haircloth and fancier fabrics were brought from the East by steamboats, which arrived every other day during the season when the lake was navigable.[18]

By 1842 furniture in the latest New York and Paris fashion was available in several Lake Street cabinet warerooms, including those of G. & R. Tetard, manufacturers of "French Cabinet work." In *Chicago Democrat* advertisements that featured a classical "French bedstead" with sleigh-shaped head- and footboards and a table with tripod pedestal support, the Tetards indicated that they were "prepared to do all kinds of upholstery" and could manufacture sofas, settees, bedsteads, couches, spring beds, and mattresses "as well and as cheap as in any part of the West."[19] With animal hair and moss covering newly patented coiled springs of iron wire, Tetard's mattresses and spring beds, sofas, and settees offered an entirely new degree of comfort.

The Grecian chairs, scroll-supported tables, and French bedsteads advertised by Rockwell, Dewey, and the Tetards were much in demand as early residents established themselves and set down roots in the new community. By the mid-1830s a number of Classic Revival style public buildings and fashionable residences had begun to replace log cabins. Those possessing the means hastened to construct homes in the manner introduced on the East Coast by Thomas Jefferson, Benjamin H. Latrobe, and others as an architectural style appropriate for the new American republic. Thought to symbolize the dignity, simplicity, and beauty of ancient Greece and Rome, these tiny white painted temples of brick and wood called for equally notable furnishings.[20]

While mahogany-veneered sofas, scrolled tables, and other pieces of Eastern-inspired cabinet ware were undoubtedly produced in large amounts, sizable quantities of simple chairs, low-post beds, paneled wardrobes, and plain chests resembling those made by country cabinetmakers in other parts of the world were also being turned out in cherry, maple, and whitewood. Guided in their work by urban models, country cabinetmakers tended to give individual interpretations to the turnings, carvings, and details found on the more sophisticated and more expensive pieces. An example of this can be found in the crib made by Scotch-Irish cabinetmaker James M. McClure for his children. Passing through Chicago in the late 1820s, McClure followed the Des Plaines River north to more heavily wooded areas, settling near Warren in Lake County, where he worked as a cabinetmaker and undertaker.[21]

Even though the quality and variety of household goods available to Chicagoans increased every year, furnishings found in most of the city's hotels and boardinghouses remained humble at best. When John Dean Caton returned from New York with his bride in 1835, they took up quarters in a small room in the Sauganash Hotel, "fully one-third of which was occupied by the bed. . . . A plain white-wood washstand, with bowl and

Crib of bird's-eye or "pin" maple and walnut made by James McClure for his children in the 1830s.
h: 44" l: 43¾" w: 33¾"
CHS, gift of Conant Wait, 1925

pitcher, a looking glass, a little table, and two new chairs" made up all the other furnishings. Within a year, however, the Catons moved into a house of their own, "abundantly large and well furnished,"[22] probably with some of the chairs, tables, and bedsteads available in local warerooms. One cannot help but wonder if the handsome cherry secretary-bookcase from Caton's home now in the collection of the Chicago Historical Society was produced in Chicago by someone such as James Rockwell or Caleb Morgan, or by one of their journeymen cabinetmakers.

By the end of the 1830s, men trained as general cabinetmakers were still advertising bureaus, secretaries, sideboards, sofas, and similar items based on case or box construction. However, those especially skilled at working with the lathe, the turners, were beginning to specialize in tables, bedsteads, stools, and other furniture, most especially chairs, made primarily from turned parts.

If the chairs illustrated in advertisements placed by Dennis S. Dewey and John B. Weir were typical, many were Grecian, or fancy, chairs.[23] With gently scrolled top rail, straight-turned or gently flaring front legs, and a rush or cane seat, fancy chairs were often painted and decorated in imitation of more expensive models. Frequently highlighted with delicate stripes or ornamented with freehand or stenciled flowers, these stylish yet inexpensive chairs provided a cheerful note in otherwise sparsely furnished rooms. Assembled from an assortment of interchangeable parts, which considerably lowered their cost, fancy chairs could have been made from

Cherry secretary-bookcase made for John Dean Caton ca. 1840.
h: 94½" w: 48" d: 22¼"
CHS, gift of Mrs. Albert J. Beveridge, 1939

Advertisement showing the Lake Street warerooms of John B. Weir (1811–1874) in 1839. Weir worked as a cabinetmaker in Chicago until 1854, when he returned to New York State. From Laws & Ordinances of the City of Chicago, *1839.*

start to finish in Chicago, or assembled from chair parts secured "in the white" from Eastern chair factories such as the one in Hitchcocksville, Connecticut, operated by Lambert Hitchcock, who visited Chicago as early as 1835 seeking orders for his chairs.[24] Massachusetts chairmaker Philander Derby marketed Grecian chairs in Chicago in 1845 while touring the Western states.[25]

Most frequently mentioned in mid-nineteenth-century newspaper and directory advertisements were what were known as Windsor chairs. With back spindles tendoned into a top rail and splayed turned legs pegged directly into a shaped wooden seat, this type of everyday chair was made in all parts of the country. In 1847, for example, James McWilliams, a chair-

and cabinetmaker on **Franklin** Street near Lake, invited prospective customers to "Please observe the sign of the Windsor Chair on the top of the

John Phillips. 27 Franklin, 1843–46; corner Water and Kinzie, 1847–49; near Galena and Chicago Union Rail Road depot, ca. 1850; North Green corner Third, ca. 1857–73; Phillips corner Green, 1874–75.

Phillips & Liebenstein. 7 Superior, 1863–86.

The factory established by John Phillips (1796–1870) was known to produce bedsteads, chamber furniture, and other items, although the primary products were "common" chairs in all varieties. It is not known how, or whether, the factory labeled its products.

Phillips's sons, John, Alexander, William, and James, were associated in various capacities with the business, although the senior Phillips remained sole proprietor. When Phillips died in 1870, he left a substantial estate of $200,000 to be divided in a somewhat peculiar manner. Three-sevenths of the estate went to the town of his birth, Forfarshire, Scotland; one-seventh went to Rush Medical College of Chicago; and the remaining three-sevenths was divided among his four sons. Phillips's sons operated the chair factory under the direction of trustees for their father's estate until 1875, when dissension arose and the plant was sold.

In 1863 Phillips's oldest son, John (1825–1880), having managed several factories in the city, established one in partnership with dealer Henry Liebenstein to manufacture cane- and wooden-seated chairs. Following John's death in 1880, his brother, James Phillips, worked as a salesman for Phillips & Liebenstein until it closed in 1886.

Painted Windsor chair purchased in Chicago in 1843 by William J. Kemper and his bride. Kemper, who was listed in the 1846 city directory as a milkman, was identified as a farmer "north of the city line near Bush" the following year.
h: 32½" w: 17" d: 14½"
CHS gift of Albert J. Freese, 1925

building" in his advertisements in the Chicago city directory.[26] In 1850 the industrial census taker, with but scant attention to spelling, noted that Charles Roberts's Chair Factory on Clinton Street made "450 Gracian" chairs and "500 Winser."[27] The Cheap Furniture Store at 905 State Street showed a low-back Windsor chair, commonly known as a captain's chair, among its merchandise in 1868, along with more expensive chairs of black walnut. As late as 1873 the chair factory of John Phillips claimed "the common wooden-bottomed Windsor chair a specialty."[28]

Although similar in construction to eighteenth-century Windsors, the wooden-bottom chairs made by Chicago chairmakers tended to be simpler and less delicate in line than the earlier models. The top rail was a rectangular, slightly concave board rather than a comb- or bow-shaped rod of bent wood, while the rounded seat had evolved into a squared plank slightly wider in the front than in the rear, with rounded corners and a sharply beveled front edge. A row of round spindles made up the back, with the two end spindles thicker than those in the center and often ornamented with shallow incised lines vaguely reminiscent of bamboo.[29] A typical example is the dark green painted model purchased by Mr. and Mrs. William Kemper in 1843.

Often called plank-bottom or country Windsor chairs, these humble, streamlined Windsors lent themselves to assembly-line production. The chief difference between the plank-bottom and the earlier Windsor was in the degree of elaboration: typically, the classic Windsor had more spindles in its back, a more saddled seat, and more intricately turned legs.

Among those making chairs in Chicago by 1836 were Horatio Cook, Charles T. Brown, Dennis Dewey, and John Weir, but the largest and most successful of the early chair factories was started by John Phillips in 1842. Born into a family of weavers in Forfarshire, Scotland, Phillips made and repaired shuttles for the local weaving mill, becoming an excellent wood-turner in the process. In 1842 he brought his large family to the United States and settled in Chicago. Capitalizing on his skill as a turner, he opened a small shop on Canal Street near Lake, "running a single lathe by foot power." A year later he moved to Franklin Street, adding more advanced power in the form of a "blind old racehorse" ridden "round and round" by two of his sons, John and William, "to keep the lathe in operation."[30] In 1847 he erected a large frame factory building at the corner of Water and Kinzie streets near the Milwaukee Plank Road. By 1850 Phillips's Chair Factory was equipped with a steam engine and employed sixteen men.[31]

The transition from human power to horse power and then to water-powered or steam-powered machinery had been taking place in the older industrialized areas like New York, Philadelphia, and even Cincinnati for some time. However, when it began in Chicago during the late 1840s, mechanization of furniture making proceeded at a very uneven pace. Thus the 1850 Census of Industry showed Phillips's Chair Factory as the only furniture establishment in Chicago powered by steam.

Joseph Shaw, who had arrived from England in 1843 and worked for three different chairmakers in Chicago—James McWilliams, E. M. Jones, and George Brown—reported to Chicago historian A. T. Andreas that during his apprenticeship "all chair work was done by hand, only split and buzz [circular] saws being used by Mr. Jones, and but a few planing mills were here, these being operated by horse power."[32] Shaw recalled that around 1850, when he set up his own chair business, manufacturing methods were still "slow and laborious," for the "age of improvements in wood-turning machinery was just beginning to dawn."[33]

Typical of the rapid evolution from one-man shop to one-horse factory was the experience of German-born cabinetmaker William Niemann. After working for two and a half years for David A. Jacobus, Niemann opened his own workshop in 1847. Recalling that period, Niemann told A. T. Andreas that he had "one boy to aid him in turning the wheel of the single machine he employed." A few years later Niemann was able to acquire a larger "horsepower establishment," followed in 1856 by a move to a still larger factory on Wells Street powered by a 6-horsepower engine that he operated in partnership with Jacob Lauer.[34]

One reason for the uneven pace of mechanization in furniture manufacturing was the cost of machinery. In order to acquire the new technology, people had to have accumulated some money or be in a position to borrow it. Few new arrivals or journeymen cabinetmakers who worked for wages had the means to acquire such capital. Some pooled labor, resources,

William Niemann. Various addresses, 1845–80.
Niemann & Weinhardt. 392–404 North Wood, 1880–90.
Niemann & Weinhardt Table Co. 392–414 (927–945 after 1909) North Wood, 1891–1912.
William Niemann (1821–1886) learned cabinetmaking in Germany before coming to Chicago in 1845. In the following thirty-five years he worked intermittently as a woodturner for David Jacobus and Schultze & Bros., with various partners—Jacob Lauer (ca. 1860), John Uber (ca. 1871), Conrad Lenz and Frederick Herhold (ca. 1876)—and on his own. In 1880 he founded Niemann & Weinhardt with his sons (William Henry and Albert) and son-in-law (Hermann Weinhardt). At first the company manufactured cane-seat chairs, bureaus, whatnots, and cradles, but by 1890, medium-priced tables for homes, offices, stores, and saloons became the firm's mainstay. It also was the exclusive manufacturer of the Russell patent kitchen cabinet. Weinhardt operated the company until 1912, when it closed due to bankruptcy.

Niemann Table Co. Seventy-seventh & Cottage Grove, 1905–30.
In 1905 William Henry Niemann and his two sons founded the Niemann Table Co. In addition to its lines of tables for residences, stores, and restaurants, the company began to manufacture matching chairs in the early 1920s.

and capital and set up partnerships to purchase horses and machines; others relied upon family members or apprentices to power their machinery.

The incentive for expanded production and mechanization was an ever-growing market for the furniture turned out by Chicago's cabinetmakers. A wide and attractive selection of chairs, sofas, and cabinet pieces was available in the city by the fall of 1848, when Henrietta Maria McCormick arrived from Virginia with her husband, Leander, who had come to Chicago to work in his brother Cyrus's newly founded reaper factory. After only thirteen days in the city, Mrs. McCormick was able to write to her sister-in-law, "We are very nicely fixed, and are very much pleased with our new home and friends so far." To help her relatives visualize her new Greek Revival style residence at the corner of Rush and Ohio streets, she continued:

> I have drawn off in a careless manner the plan of this house which I will put in this letter. Our furniture is all new and of the best quality. Beautiful flowered red and green carpet in the chamber and parlor, and when the folding doors are open, the stove in the chamber will heat both rooms. One dozen cushioned mahogany chairs for the two rooms, beautiful bureau in the chamber, and a twenty-four dollar card table in the parlor. I would like to have a sofa and a pretty lamp in the parlor, and think likely we will get them before long.[35]

The art of furniture making in Chicago had come a long way in the course of the previous decade.

CHAPTER 2

STEAM-POWERED MANUFACTORIES

1 8 5 2 - 1 8 7 2

"We have often paused in the railroad depots to notice the immense quantities of furniture accumulating for distribution in the interior, bearing cards of Chicago manufacturers," a *Chicago Democratic Press* reporter noted in the newspaper's annual review of commerce for 1854. That year furniture factories were being "called upon beyond their power to meet the demand" generated by the phenomenal growth of the city and the penetration of railroads into the surrounding territories. With the countryside filling up with new settlers and the old ones "increasing wonderfully in wealth and in wants," the writer expressed the view that there was "probably no other branch of manufacture more inviting at present" than that of furniture making.[1] Responding to the demand, cabinetmakers flocked to the city, increasing the number of sizable factories from thirteen in 1850 to more than twenty-six in 1860.

One of the manufacturers named in the *Chicago Democratic Press* review as "doing a large business" was Caleb Morgan, whose five-story building at 199 Lake was far more impressive than the warerooms that had stood on the site some eighteen years earlier. Following a plan typical of many early nineteenth-century factories, the two lower floors of Morgan's establishment were devoted to sales- and sample rooms, while the upper three provided workspace for assembling, finishing, and upholstering furniture. Employing some forty men, the shop was "engaged principally in the manufacture of chairs and the more expensive kinds of furniture, embracing all the recent styles of pattern, finish, and material."[2] Morgan, like many earlier local producers, was both manufacturer and dealer, selling direct to customers as well as to furniture retailers who purchased goods for resale in their stores in the city and its hinterland.

Other Lake Street manufacturers who had been in business for a decade or so were David L. Jacobus and Thomas Manahan. Arriving from New Jersey in 1843, David Jacobus and his brother, Augustus, started out as looking glass and picture frame dealers. One year later, they formed a part-

D. & A. L. Jacobus. 10 Clark, 1843.

Manahan & Jacobus. 10 Clark, 1844–46.

D. & A. L. Jacobus. 173 Lake, 1847–51.

Boyden & Jacobus. 173 Lake, 1851.

David L. Jacobus. 173 Lake, 1852; factory Jefferson near Lake.

D. L. Jacobus & Bro. 173 Lake, 1853–56.

Jacobus, Steele & Co. 153 Randolph, 1856–57.

D. L. Jacobus & Bro. 182 Lake and 56 North Jefferson, 1857–59.

A native of New Jersey, David L. Jacobus (1816–1884) first appeared in the Chicago city directory in 1843 as operator, with his brother, Augustus Larue (1818–1850), of a looking glass store. In 1844 the brothers formed a partnership with cabinetmaker Thomas Manahan (1813–1884), who had arrived from New York State that year, and began advertising as manufacturers of "furniture made to order in the neatest style." After Manahan left to open his own shop in 1846, the Jacobus brothers continued as furniture manufacturers at 173 Lake. Their factory turned out some of the furnishings for The Tremont House, then Chicago's newest and most elegant hotel. Following the death of Augustus in 1850, David entered into a brief partnership with P. H. Boyden. In 1852 he was joined by his younger brother James.

A number of men who would later become prominent in the Chicago furniture industry worked in the Jacobus factory on Jefferson Street. They included William Niemann, who first found employment there when he arrived from Germany in 1847; Francis Eggleston, a Boston-trained cabinetmaker who served as foreman in 1852; and Jacob Bliss, a cabinetmaker at Jacobus's beginning in 1847 who later went on to found his own company.

nership with Manahan, a cabinetmaker who had just arrived from the state of New York, and became furniture manufacturers. After Manahan opened his own shop in 1847, the Jacobus brothers remained in the furniture business. Although it is not known whether they had been trained as cabinetmakers, it is clear that they were capable businessmen, for by 1850 they were employing thirty workers in their manufactory: turners, cabinetmakers, and upholsterers.

In 1850 Augustus died, but in 1853 yet another brother, James, joined David in the business. Meanwhile, around 1852 the firm had separated its manufacturing from its sales division, erecting a substantial brick factory building on Jefferson Street in the area known as the West Division. This area, west of the point at which the Chicago River bifurcated, eventually became the location for wagonmakers, agricultural implement makers, coopers, and other woodworkers, because it offered ready access to numerous lumberyards and planing mills. The district remained an important center for furniture production throughout the nineteenth century.

David Jacobus and temporary partner P. H. Boyden offered an array of goods, including "rosewood, mahogany, and walnut Sofas, Divans, Ottomans, Centre, Card and Side Tables, Tilht [sic] Tables, Wash Stands, Walnut and Mahogany Bureaus, French, Cottage and Common Bedsteads, Extension Dining Tables, Secretaries, Bronzed Stands, Tables" and "Easy Chairs, Sewing, Gothic, Rocking and Parlor Chairs." They noted confidently, "We flatter ourselves that with our facilities for manufacturing, strict personal attention to business and low prices we may continue to receive the liberal patronage bestowed" on the previous firm of D. & A. L. Jacobus.[3]

By 1856 any potential purchaser wishing to make the rounds of all of Chicago's furniture-making establishments would have had to travel far beyond the central business district. At the corner of Randolph and Wells stood the salesrooms of Daniel P. and Franklin S. Hanson,* whose factory was to be found in the West Division. Employing some sixty workmen and equipped with steam-powered machinery, the Hanson factory turned out large quantities of inexpensive furniture that was "sold all over the West chiefly on credit."[4] On Wells Street, to the north across the bridge, in a predominantly German neighborhood, could be found upholsterers August and George Shiefferstein, cabinetmakers J. H. Schroeder and Conrad Geis, woodcarver John Richler, and countless others who worked in tiny one-man shops in or behind their homes. Over on Clark Street, just east of Court House Square, were the factory of William Toohy, manufacturer of office furniture, and the shops of piano makers Henry Stone and Knauer & Son. On Franklin Street near Randolph stood the new four-story factory of Jacob Strehl, who had arrived from Germany nine years earlier.

During the mid-1850s older craftsmen like Morgan, David Jacobus, and Manahan continued to produce fine cabinetwork and upholstered furniture for the local market, relying upon established reputations and downtown locations to assure themselves of a steady stream of patrons. Newly

---

*As a result of the Panic of 1857 and the depression that followed, the D. P. & F. S. Hanson Company failed in 1860. The factory was later converted into a feed and corn mill called the New England Mills.

organized companies, however, often opened salesrooms on Lake, Randolph, or other busy streets, though they located their factories west, north, and south of the business district close to the river and lumberyards in less developed areas, where land was more abundant and cheaper. Almost without exception, the factories erected between 1852 and 1856 supplemented the basic hand-, foot-, or horsepowered woodworking machinery with labor-saving circular saws or turning lathes powered by steam.[5] The new firms directed their attentions toward producing large quantities of inexpensive furniture as cheaply and as quickly as men, machinery, and the expanding westward market would allow.

Typical of these new enterprises was the firm of Ferris & Boyd, which located its showrooms on Lake Street and its factory on Van Buren. The machinery in the latter, so the 1854 *Democratic Press*'s review of commerce reported, required "an engine of fifteen horse power, and the increase of their business compelled them to add forty feet of shafting within a few months." The firm was said to employ "constantly about fifty men, while their machinery does the work of twenty-five or thirty hands." Like the output of most of the modern factories, the picture frames and furniture made by Ferris & Boyd tended to be "rather more in the common and useful line, than the luxurious and expensive."[6] By using less expensive woods like whitewood and pine, and by keeping carving and detailing to a minimum, that firm could produce great quantities of furniture at a much lower cost than could artisans like Morgan or Manahan.

A year later, following up on the fortunes of the firm, the *Press* reported that the factory was now equipped with a 25-horsepower engine and that the number of employees had increased from fifty to eighty. Sales of the company's "plain and common articles of furniture" and looking glasses and picture frames, had increased during the year from $50,000 to $80,000.[7] Like William McLaughlin and Joseph Glass, who were also in the frame business by 1860, Ferris & Boyd enhanced many of the wooden forms with thin layers of gold leaf or gilt to create the elegant golden pier and mantel mirrors sought by the owners of fine homes, hotels, and business houses. In the meantime, another branch of mass furniture making had been developing at a similar pace.

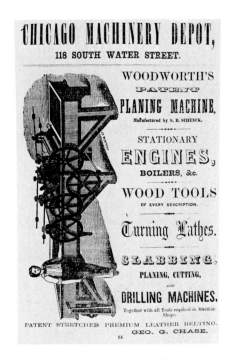

In this advertisement for the Chicago Machinery Depot, a mechanic stands next to a Woodworth planer capable of smoothing a surface thirty inches wide. From Chicago City Directory, 1855–56.

BEDSTEADS

With the exception of elaborate hand-carved versions, bedsteads, like chairs, proved particularly suitable for factory production, since they could be constructed using interchangeable parts. Consisting of a headboard, footboard, two side rails, and a series of plain wooden slats, bedsteads were basically an assemblage of flat boards, turned spindles, and ornaments joined to create a simple rectangular form. With the use of a lathe, a variety of identical turnings could be achieved in spool, bobbin, vase, knob, or ring shapes. Moreover, the various parts could be crated unassembled or "knocked down" ("K.D.") for easy shipment by railroad car or canal boat. Throughout the West, from Chicago to California, settlers in city and country provided a steady market. Whether housed in cottage, hotel, or log cabin, even the poorest settler aspired to a bed.

Among the first to apply steam-powered woodworking machinery in

STEAM POWER
BEDSTEAD
MANUFACTORY,
Corner Green and Fulton Streets, West Division.

CITY & COUNTRY TRADE
Can be supplied with
BEDSTEADS IN ALL THEIR VARIETY,
AT
WHOLESALE OR RETAIL.

All orders for
TURNING
PROMPTLY EXECUTED.

Being prepared with
POWER, STOCK & MACHINERY,
To answer any demand, I flatter myself that I can
EXECUTE ORDERS
In the above line
A LITTLE CHEAPER
Than any other Factory in the City.
ELISHA CLARKE.
Corner Green and Fulton Streets.

Elisha Clark turned spindles and ornaments for cabinetmakers and carpenters in addition to making bedsteads. Advertisement from Udall & Hopkins' Chicago City Directory, 1852–53.

the manufacture of bedsteads was Elisha Clark,* a New York-trained chairmaker who had arrived in Chicago in 1835. After a year, Clark and his wife moved to Lake County, where they farmed for seven years before returning to Chicago in 1843. Reestablishing himself as a cabinet- and chairmaker, Clark used hand- and foot-powered machinery until 1852, when he opened the Steam Power Bedstead Manufactory on the corner of Green and Fulton streets in the West Division, not far from the terminus of the Milwaukee Plank Road. The new factory was equipped with circular saws and turning lathes.[8] Advertising in the city directory that year, Clark announced that "City and Country Trade can be supplied with Bedsteads in All Their Variety at Wholesale or Retail" and that "all orders for turning" would be promptly executed. "Being prepared with Power, Stock & Machinery, To answer any demand," Clark proudly claimed, "I flatter myself that I can Execute Orders In the above line A Little Cheaper Than any other Factory in the City."[9] When Clark died suddenly the following year, the factory was taken over by his son, Augustus B. Clark, and Benjamin F. Adams, who continued to produce bedsteads. By 1856 the firm had changed its name to Adams & Clark and employed sixty men, making it the largest of three factories in the city devoted primarily to bedsteads, of which it turned out 18,000 that year.[10]

Next in size was the Eagle Bedstead Factory, operated by Henry Chapman and Levi Atwood in conjunction with Chapman's sash, door, and blind factory south of the business district at State and Taylor streets. Taking advantage of the steam-powered saws and planing machines already owned by the mill, Chapman & Atwood's factory employed fifty-six men and manufactured $20,000 worth of bedsteads after only five months of operation. Another new steam-powered factory owned by Charles W. Patten employed twenty men producing bedsteads and chairs on the corner of North Avenue and Clark Street in the heart of the North Side German neighborhood.[11]

Beginning in 1857, the Milwaukee Avenue factory of Louis Schultze manufactured a general line of furniture but specialized in "common bedsteads and chairs for the million."[12] In 1860 the Wilson Avenue chair factory of John Schuyler, equipped with a 10-horsepower steam engine and employing twenty men, produced 800 bedsteads and 18,000 chairs, consuming 230,000 feet of black walnut, cherry, and whitewood and twelve barrels of varnish. Dividing the value of that year's output by the number of pieces produced, the price of the bedsteads averaged five dollars and the chairs averaged fifty cents each.[13] If, as the industrial census indicated, wages of furniture workers averaged twenty dollars a month, these bedsteads and chairs were well within the reach of the average Chicagoan.

Less numerous but selling for about the same price were the bedsteads produced by those who still relied upon hand- or horse-powered woodworking tools. Described as a "turner" in the 1860 directory, Robert George had two employees and made cherry and black walnut bedsteads. John Poehlmann and Conrad Geis, both located on Blue Island Avenue, made

*The name is spelled as both Clark and Clarke in the city directories. Clark occurs more frequently.

bedsteads in addition to a variety of bureaus, desks, and tables using cherry, oak, whitewood, and black walnut.[14]

If the bedsteads pictured in the city directory advertisements placed

by Chicago manufacturer and importer Shearer, Paine & Strong in 1859 accurately represent those sold in Chicago, many were of a type designated as "Elizabethan" or "Cottage."[15] With head and foot composed of spiral or ball-turned spindles tendoned into a straight or curved top rail, these factory-made beds were considered a modern interpretation of furniture made during the reign of Queen Elizabeth I of England. Still popular were sleigh beds with scroll-shaped rails in the "Modern Grecian" or French style.

EXPANDING MARKETS

Soon after Chicago's potential as a central distribution point and market became evident, ambitious Northeastern and Midwestern furniture manufacturers established wholesale or retail branches in the city and hired local men to act as their agents. Although styles continued to emanate from New York City, several of the branch houses that were to have the greatest impact on the Chicago furniture industry had their origins in Boston and Cincinnati. With markets in those more established areas leveling off and used furniture markets developing, some of these manufacturers began to look for expanding markets. Chicago, with its booming economy, was an obvious place to try.

One of the first to open a branch in the West was Shearer & Paine of Boston, whose agent, William W. Strong, set up a showroom on Canal

Street in 1856. To capture the local trade, Shearer, Paine & Strong delivered goods free of charge within the city and promised to pay particular attention to packing and shipping "goods for the country."[16] Deliveries were

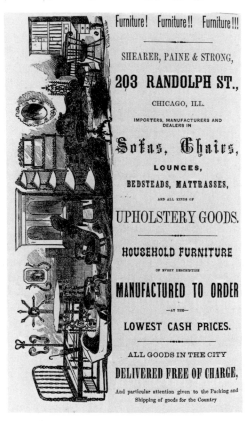

Furniture! Furniture!! Furniture!!!

SHEARER, PAINE & STRONG,

203 RANDOLPH ST.,

CHICAGO, ILL.

IMPORTERS, MANUFACTURERS AND DEALERS IN

Sofas, Chairs,

LOUNCES,

BEDSTEADS, MATTRASSES,

AND ALL KINDS OF

UPHOLSTERY GOODS.

HOUSEHOLD FURNITURE

OF EVERY DESCRIPTION

MANUFACTURED TO ORDER

—AT THE—

LOWEST CASH PRICES.

ALL GOODS IN THE CITY

DELIVERED FREE OF CHARGE,

And particular attention given to the Packing and Shipping of goods for the Country

Furniture made in Chicago was sold alongside pieces imported from the Eastern states by Shearer, Paine & Strong. From D. B. Cooke & Co.'s Chicago City Directory, 1860–61.

made by wagon, with Strong always on the lookout for sturdy horses that could be secured in exchange for furniture.[17]

Strong also served as intermediary for shipments of Boston-made furniture passing through Chicago on its way to the company's southern branch in New Orleans, Louisiana. Arriving by steamer in Chicago, Shearer & Paine's furniture crates would be loaded on to railroad cars or canal barges for eventual trans-shipment to Mississippi River steam packets destined for New Orleans.[18]

In 1861, when the Civil War put a halt to Shearer & Paine's shipments, Strong used the large profits he had derived from furniture sales and real-estate investments to purchase the business of veteran cabinetmaker David Jacobus, who remained with the new firm of W. W. Strong as a salesman for several years. By 1870, backed by the good will of his millionaire father-in-law, Philo Carpenter, Strong was employing more than fifty hands in the production of elegant chamber and parlor sets, lounges, easy chairs, and mirrors. Retaining hand- and horse-powered equipment in the factory acquired from Jacobus on Jefferson Street, Strong relied upon fine craftsmanship, exotic woods and finishes, and fine silk fabrics to create unique and expensive furnishings for sale in his stylish Randolph Street store.[19]

A second Chicago manufacturing firm that started out as a retail branch of a Boston company was the one founded by Charles Tobey. Leaving the family farm in Cape Cod, Massachusetts, to enter the more lucrative mercantile business, Tobey began by working as a salesman in a Boston furniture store. In 1855, at the age of twenty-one, he caught "the fever" and left for the West. On the train to Chicago, he met an agent for a Boston furniture company and made arrangements to represent the firm in Chicago. When the Boston firm failed a year later, Tobey was left with a small rented store on Lake Street and a promissory note for his unpaid wages. Borrowing $1,000 from a relative, he was able to continue operations on his own account, buying stock at sunrise and selling it by nightfall in a shop so small "that when he made a sidewalk display the store proper was empty."[20] Tobey took his brother, Francis B. (Frank) Tobey, into partnership. Buoyed by another loan, the firm of Charles Tobey & Brother managed to survive the Panic of 1857 and the three years of depression that followed by buying up the stock of the stores that failed. In the economic upsurge following the outbreak of the Civil War, the Tobey brothers did a large and profitable business.

In 1865, having joined forces with Chicago furniture manufacturer F. Porter Thayer, Charles Tobey acquired part-ownership of Thayer's factory on the corner of Jefferson and Randolph streets. Tobey's skill as a salesman and his reputation for "indomitable perseverance," combined with ownership of one of the city's larger manufactories, enabled the firm of Thayer & Tobey to secure large contracts for hotel furniture, "fitting up" most of the city's new hotels, including the entire Grand Pacific, the Sherman House, the Tremont House, and some of the rooms in the Gardner and the Palmer House.[21] Clearly by now Charles Tobey enjoyed the highest reputation as a manufacturer and dealer in "every description of rich, medium and plain furniture" and the name "Tobey's" had become "almost as familiar to fine houses throughout the city as those of their occupants."[22] By 1868 the firm was able to build a large new store on State Street, following the lead of Potter Palmer, who had purchased extensive frontages along the street and built a large hotel and department store there.

One of Charles Tobey & Brother's best known customers during the 1860s was Mary Todd Lincoln, wife of President Abraham Lincoln, who had gone to the White House in 1860 from Springfield, Illinois. After her husband's assassination in April 1865, Mrs. Lincoln moved to Chicago to be near her son, Robert Todd Lincoln, who had recently joined the law firm of Scammon & Lincoln. The following year Mrs. Lincoln enlisted the aid of Frank Tobey to furnish her home on West Washington Street.

Most notable of the various furnishings, which cost "something over 7,000 dollars,"[23] that Mrs. Lincoln purchased in 1866 from the Tobey brothers was a rosewood parlor suite composed of settee, méridienne, chairs, and matching table. Upholstered in expensive French silk, the suite was distinguished by laminated rosewood frames elaborately curved, pierced, and carved in a style made famous by New York cabinetmaker John Henry Belter. While Tobey's made the most of having such a well-known client, the fact remains that they did not make the suite but merely upholstered it for Mrs. Lincoln.

Shearer, Paine & Strong. 203 Randolph, 1856–60.
W. W. Strong Furniture Co. 203 Randolph, 1861–70; 353–59 West Randolph, 1871–78; 193–97 Wabash, 1879–84.
John H. Thayer. 193–97 Wabash, 1885–97.

Chicago's premier furniture dealer and manufacturer during the 1870s, W. W. Strong specialized in elaborate high-grade furniture and expensive upholstered items for residences, hotels, and public buildings. A retailer as well as a manufacturer, the firm did an extensive business, importing marquetry, panels, furniture, and accessories from as far away as France, Austria, China, and Japan.

In 1878, when the company experienced financial problems, management was taken over by one of the owners, W. Solomon. William W. Strong went into the real-estate business with his father-in-law, Philo Carpenter, while another partner, T. Allen French, left to become a furniture designer for John A. Colby. John H. Thayer later advertised as a furniture agent at the Wabash Avenue address.

When shown a photograph of the suite by Robert Todd Lincoln's secretary some forty-one years later and asked if his firm had made it, Frank Tobey responded that he remembered it well because "it was the most

Charles Tobey's new store on State Street in 1868–69.

elaborate and highest-priced set which his firm had up to that time, turned out, the woodwork having been made by a factory in Cincinnati, and the fabric having been imported from Paris."[24] Although Tobey positively identified the parlor suite as the one supplied by his company, the manufacturer of the suite's rosewood frames remains unidentified.

Since no labeled furniture known to have been made in the Tobey & Thayer factory has been found, one can only assume that some of the firm's tables and chairs were similar to those shown in a *Chicago Tribune* advertisement placed forty-four years later to emphasize the durability of the company's products.[25] Featured were an intricately carved table with satyr supports designed and made for iron and steel baron Seneca D. Kimbark in 1868 and a Rococo Revival style armchair made for Kimbark three years earlier. This armchair resembled those of the parlor suite supplied to Mrs. Lincoln in 1866.

CHICAGO FURNITURE

Although Chicago factories promised furniture "in the latest fashion," it was not uncommon for Chicago's affluent families to furnish the most important rooms of their houses with furniture made in New York or Boston. Around 1856, for example, clothier and dry goods merchant Tuthill King furnished the double parlor of his impressive new five-story row house in Terrace Row* on Michigan Avenue with an elegant thirteen-piece pierced and carved rosewood suite from the shop of John Henry Belter. About the same time a less elaborate set in what has come to be known as the Rosalie[†] pattern was purchased from Belter's shop by the family of hardware and iron merchant William Blair, whose residence stood nearby.[26] Since there appear to be no bills of sale or family records, it is not known whether the New York- and Boston-made furniture was purchased in the East or through importer/dealers in Chicago, such as Charles Tobey & Brother or Shearer, Paine & Strong.

Although the *Daily Democratic Press* review of trade for 1855 assured its readers that it was "no longer necessary to send East after handsome furniture" because "Chicago's manufacturers turn out the most substantial and luxurious that can be desired, and at a cost much less than Eastern prices, including transportation,"[27] large amounts of imported furniture continued to be sold in and shipped through Chicago. In 1860, for example, receipts at the Chicago Custom House indicated that 40,055 bedsteads, 839 packages of Chair Stuff (upholstery, stuffing, perhaps even frames), six pianos, and 20,000 pounds (10 tons) of furniture had arrived by lake. Added to this were 792 pounds (10.4 tons) of furniture delivered via canal and 486,160 pounds (243 tons) by railroad. In contrast, shipments from

Pine washstand with turned legs made by Marsh Bros. in the 1860s.
h: 33½" w: 33" d: 17"
Private Collection
Photograph by Abramson-Culbert
Studio

Chicago consisted of 42,000 pounds (21 tons) sent by canal, and two lots and 503 packages leaving by lake.[28] Unfortunately, no figures for exports by railroad were available.

*Located on the block where the Auditorium Building now stands.
†Named "Rosalie" because the carved floral and fruit ornament relates to that on the parlor suite at Rosalie, Natchez, Mississippi.

From the 1850s through the 1860s, "square and boudoir" pianos and melodeons arrived from manufacturers in Boston and New York to be sold in Piano Forte Ware Rooms like those of Reed & Watkins, "agents for the Western states." Local production had begun, too, albeit on a very small scale, to provide for entertainment and leisure. That year, the city's first piano manufacturer, Knauer & Son, made eight rosewood pianos.[29] Five years later, the firm produced twenty-eight pianos, while its new competitors, John Preston and Henry Stone, each made twenty. The pianos were "all sold in and about the city."[30]

That same year, 1855, the new Dearborn Street factory of R. G. Greene, employing twenty workmen, turned out 300 melodeons.[31] Relying upon air drawn through reeds using a bellows to produce sound instead of the more complicated strings and action found in pianofortes, melodeons were far simpler to make than pianos and therefore could be sold at a much lower price. Often called "the piano's little country cousin," attractive rosewood melodeons resembling small square pianos could be installed in the family parlor or local church for as little as $100, a fraction of the price of a piano.[32]

Many Eastern melodeon manufacturers followed a common practice of the day by supplying unlabeled melodeons to dealers who then sten-

Rosewood melodeon with "W. W. Kimball" handwritten on one candle-stand and "1867" on the inner mechanism.
h: 37¾" w: 30" d: 20"
CHS, gift of Don Pebbles, 1976

ciled their own names upon the instruments. Thus the names and reputations of leading Chicago melodeon and piano salesmen such as William Wallace Kimball or Julius Bauer were far better known than those of the manufacturers. By the mid-1860s Kimball and his agents could claim approximately one-fourth of the total sales of some 15,000 reed organs made by American manufacturers, encouraging Kimball to open his own factory in Chicago in 1879.[33]

Another new enterprise was the manufacture of billiard tables and accessories for use in private homes and the city's many gambling establishments. In 1857 billiard table manufacturers John M. and Joseph Brunswick sent their brother, Emanuel, to Chicago to serve as agent for their pioneer Ohio manufactory.* By July 1859 J. M. Brunswick & Bro. had opened a branch office and salesroom at Brunswick's Billiard Hall at the corner of Clark and Washington streets. "Fitted up in a most magnificent style," the

Scientific billiard players at a stylish table manufactured by J. M. Brunswick & Bros., 1864. From Halpin's Chicago City Directory, 1864–5.

hall contained fifteen of their celebrated patented tables and claimed to be "the finest resort and place of amusement" in the city.[34]

By 1864 the firm had opened a factory on Randolph Street to supply the city's "scientific Billiard Players," both men and women, with a variety of stylish tables ornamented with scrolled aprons and carved cabriole legs.[35] A year later, in 1865, the Chicago Billiard Table Manufactory was opened by Rudolph Kleeman, George Stephani, and Henry Monheimer on South Water Street to manufacture what were known as pigeonhole, Jenny Lind, and Combined Dining and Billiard tables in addition to the standard models. In 1867 Adolph Zeller established a billiard table manufactory on South Canal with showrooms on Washington Street, followed in 1871 by the opening of another factory, this on State Street, by Emanuel Brunswick. No longer in partnership with his brothers in the J. M. Brunswick & Bro. Company, Emanuel also operated "the finest billiard hall on the continent, on Washington Street, opposite the Court House" by 1873.[36]

UPHOLSTERED PARLOR FURNITURE

By 1870 improved distribution and the continuing influx of immigrants combined to swell the number of potential clients for furniture within Chicago alone to almost 300,000—to say nothing of the additional population in the surrounding areas—and the number of furniture factories to more than fifty. Whereas only 212 men had been employed in furniture making in the city in 1860, this figure had risen to 1,126 by 1870.[37] While increases were seen in all branches of cabinetmaking, most notable was the appearance of new factories engaged exclusively in the production of upholstered parlor furniture.

Typical of the rise from struggling entrepreneur to prominent furni-

*The J. M. Brunswick & Bro. Company was founded in Cincinnati, Ohio, in February 1847.

ture manufacturer was the career of Henry S. Carter. Born in New Hampshire, Carter worked as a cabinetmaker before moving to Chicago in 1856 and establishing "the only wholesale parlor furniture factory in the city" on State Street. Although he was considered a skilled workman, Carter's business remained small until after the Civil War, when he formed a partnership with Colonel George C. Joslin, a wholesale furniture dealer based in Keene, New Hampshire. Two years later, in 1866, Carter acquired own-

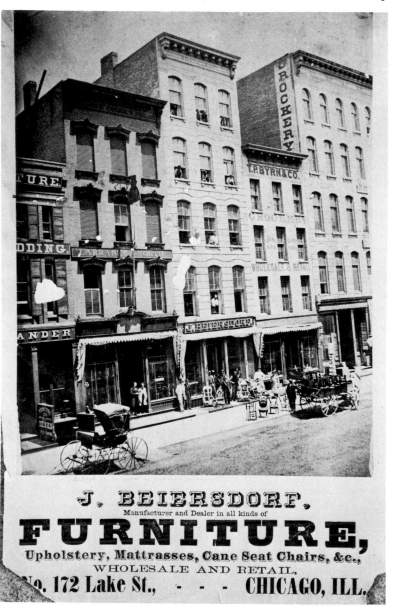

J. Beiersdorf's salesrooms at 172 Lake Street ca. 1867. Upholstered chairs and unupholstered frames are being delivered from the factory.

ership of the company, which produced a variety of upholstered parlor suites, easy chairs, lounges, and rocking chairs. By 1870 H. S. Carter & Co. employed thirty men in its showrooms and factory and had become the second largest producer of upholstered parlor furniture in the city.[38]

CHICAGO FURNITURE

Another "rags to riches" story was that of Jacob Beiersdorf, a Bavarian-born Jewish cabinetmaker who left Europe because of religious persecution. Immigrating to Chicago in 1854, Beiersdorf worked for cabinetmakers Sternberg & Isadore for one year before entering into partnership with Henry Buschmeyer. Leasing a small factory, Beiersdorf and Buschmeyer took orders for counters, desks, and other cabinetwork, executing the "first fine mahogany work in Chicago."[39] Following Buschmeyer's retirement in 1858, Beiersdorf moved five times, finally settling in 1866 in larger quarters at 172 Lake Street. Here he sold and manufactured upholstered parlor suites, easy chairs, and lounges primarily, with the aid of pioneer cabinetmaker and upholsterer Caleb Morgan, who came to work as a salesman for Beiersdorf following the demise of his own business in 1866.

A year before moving to the Lake Street location, Beiersdorf, in partnership with George Sugg and George W. Lozier, had purchased another factory on Canal Street. Operating under the name of the Northwestern Furniture Manufacturing Company, the new factory supplied Beiersdorf's shop and other local upholstered furniture manufacturers with wooden frames in addition to making a general line of bedchamber furniture and tables.

By 1870 Carter and Beiersdorf found themselves in competition with a number of other Chicago factories specializing in the production of upholstered furniture for the main sitting room or parlor. Among these were the firms of Henry Liebenstein & Co.; J. F. Rapp; McCabe & Wilkins; Lee Nelson; C. C. Holton & Co.; McDonough, Price & Company; and Schiefferstein & Bros. In many instances the companies combined furniture upholstering with mattress making, since both required the same basic raw materials—primarily springs, curled hair, and moss.

Firms engaged in upholstering and mattress making tended to employ large numbers of low-salaried women and youths under sixteen. In the industrial census of 1870, C. C. Holton listed five men, three women, and four children as employees; McDonough, Price & Company paid wages to fifteen men, three women, and seven youths. Similarly, more women and youths than men were employed by E. A. Jacobs and A. B. Fiedler, owners of the two factories devoted to making the cords, tassels, and fringes used to trim upholstered pieces.[40] As in textile mills of the period, youths and women were often employed to tend the looms and winding machines used in weaving the assorted trims. The elaborate fringes and tassels then in vogue were formed, twisted, and tied by hand.

Judging from the average value of the parlor sets, lounges, and chairs finished by Chicago manufacturers in 1870, much of their production consisted of low- and medium-priced goods of the type advertised for sale by local dealers or sold through agents in other Midwestern cities. That year, the 75 sofas completed in the factory of J. F. Rapp had an average wholesale value of $39.33, while lounges (daybeds) averaged $18.00 apiece. McCabe & Wilkins made 10 parlor sets, worth an average of $100 per suite, in addition to individual sofas and chairs. The shop of Schiefferstein & Bros., listing only 2 employees, upholstered 100 parlor sets with an average value of $85.00 and 37 lounges averaging $17.00 each. All these pieces were covered in conservative, long-lasting fabrics like terry, rep, Brussels carpet, and haircloth.* Only the manufactory of W. W. Strong, which made expensive high-style parlor sets in addition to other forms of furniture, listed silk as fabric for upholstery.[41]

While labeled examples are exceedingly rare, trade catalogues indicate that parlor furniture reflected the two prevailing styles of the day, rococo and Renaissance. Characterized by curvilinear frames highlighted with delicate scrolls and carved fruits, foliage, or shells, the rococo or "modern French" style was considered high fashion. Made in a variety of designs ranging from expensive versions elaborately pierced and abundantly carved (like those associated with the shop of John Henry Belter) to simpler examples with molded rails and relatively little carving (like those made in Chicago), rococo furniture was particularly favored for parlors and ladies' boudoirs.

In contrast to the graceful rococo, furniture in the Renaissance style was generally straight in line and heavy in proportion. Bold carvings, pediments, cartouches, raised and shaped panels, incised lines and other motifs commonly employed in architectural design frequently occur as ornament on the otherwise rectilinear shapes, as do carved garlands, medallions, and human and animal heads.

Typical of the moderately priced upholstered products available from Chicago manufacturers was the rococo style parlor suite upholstered in black haircloth purchased by the George Hanselman family in the summer of 1871. Like other standard sets, it consists of seven pieces: a "tête," or sofa; a large easy or gentleman's chair; a smaller-sized easy or lady's chair; and four armless side chairs. With black walnut frames enhanced by a simple scroll of carved leaves, the sofa and armchairs feature plain seats and comfortably tufted backs, while the side chairs have oval balloon-frame backs.

Hanselman, who was listed in the 1870 city directory as a porter for Swain, Barnard & Co., wholesale liquor dealers, acquired the parlor set for his frame cottage at 11 Hammond Street (now 1814 Orleans Street) on the city's Near North Side. According to family tradition, the parlor furniture was purchased from a local German-speaking furniture maker whose name began with an "S."[42] This could have been the shop of A. Schieferstein & Bro. at 439 State Street; but it could also have been another shop employing German workmen, since by 1870 Germans constituted 20 percent of Chicago's population and predominated in the furniture industry.

Tufted rococo sofas with high arched backs, shown in the ads of Caleb Morgan as early as 1847,[43] peaked in popularity during the 1860s. In the 1870s, however, black walnut variations of the style were still a popular choice for medium-priced furniture in Chicago and other Midwestern cities. In 1874, for example, the catalogue of McDonough, Price & Company showed simple "parlor suits" with plain molded frames similar to the Hanselman set, as well as ones with frames enhanced by crests of carved fruit

---

*Terry cloth was similar to velvet with the looped pile left uncut; rep had a surface closely-ribbed or corded; Brussels carpet was a tightly woven wool carpet characterized by uncut loops; haircloth was a stiff, wiry fabric with a weft of hair, especially horsehair, and a cotton, linen, or wool warp.

Seven-piece parlor suite with walnut frames and black horsehair upholstery purchased by Mr. and Mrs. George Hanselman in 1871. Notified of the approach of the fire on October 8, 1871, Hanselman, like many other Chicagoans, buried his most valuable household goods in a large pit in his backyard. The parlor suite survived the fire, although the family's house was destroyed.
Settee, h: 40" w: 68" d: 30"
CHS, gift of June Hanselman, 1975

or foliage. Prices varied with the grade of the frames, whether "full molded" or plain, and according to the quality of the fabric coverings, with silk terry and haircloth costing a few dollars more than wool terry or rep.[44]

The George Hanselman cottage at 11 Hammond Street (now 1814 Orleans Street) as it was rebuilt after the 1871 fire. Mrs. Hanselman and her daughter are on the front porch.
June Hanselman

SPECIALIZATION

During the 1860s growing competition among the large number of furniture manufacturers, combined with continuing technological change and growth of the market, encouraged many firms to limit their production to a certain type of furniture (parlor, chamber, dining room, church, or office) and gear the grades of goods produced to certain wholesale or retail markets. At the same time, advances in woodworking technology and the greater availability of steam power and machines encouraged the production of those products that made the best use of the specific types of machinery on hand.

In 1870, according to the census of industry, the most mechanized furniture factories were still those devoted to the production of bedsteads and chairs—the simplest types of furniture to make. Operating steam-powered manufactories engaged primarily in the making of bedsteads were John F. Koenig, whose firm produced 1,000 bedsteads that year in addition to tables; Otto and John Nottelmann, whose production included cradles; Francis Kron, who also made sideboards; Rohn & Bro., who manufactured "bedsteads of every variety, style and price"; and Anton Matuska, who supplemented bedchamber suites with wardrobes. The factories of Charles Tarnow, F. Mayer & Co., and Pries & Wichman turned out walnut and cottage chamber suites. Machinery listed by the above companies in the 1870 industrial census consisted of plain, circular, and scroll saws, turning lathes, shapers, and borers.[45]

Matching pieces of bedroom furniture (chamber suites) were not commonly made by local manufacturers until the early 1860s. Charles Tarnow, a German cabinetmaker who immigrated to Chicago in 1855, is credited by A. T. Andreas with being the first to introduce "French bedsteads and suites of local manufacture" in 1863.[46] At the time, a typical suite consisted of a bedstead, a bureau, a commode or washstand, a small table, and four chairs. For larger bedrooms the group could be expanded to include a matching nightstand and a towel rack. Among Chicago manufacturers black walnut was the favored wood for bedchamber furniture, followed in popularity by cottage sets whose painted surfaces disguised a variety of less expensive woods.

Owning the most equipment and employing the most hands were the chair manufacturers. In 1870 the factory of John Phillips, the city's oldest in this line, had a work force of seventy and claimed "40 different machines." The chair factory of Phillips & Liebenstein, established in 1863 by Phillips's son, John, and furniture dealer Henry Liebenstein, listed fifty-six standard machines, which reduced the cost of production while increasing the number of chairs its seventy-six workers could make.[47]

Other well-equipped new firms included the Chicago Chair Factory, where workers produced black walnut chairs, and the Herhold Johnson Chair Factory, which made bureaus, washstands, and chairs. With the exception of Philip Loehr, whose one-man shop produced chairs with the aid of one lathe, all of the large chair manufacturers employed sizable numbers of youths aged sixteen or under. At Phillips & Liebenstein, for example, forty-six men and thirty youths made up the work force, while John Phillips employed twenty youths in addition to fifty men. At the Herhold Johnson Chair Factory, youths outnumbered men thirty to twenty-eight.[48] While some of the youths were undoubtedly apprentices who would work their way upward to more responsible positions as they gained experience, others were destined to remain semiskilled machine tenders for the remainder of their lives as factories grew in size and individual jobs became increasingly specialized.

By 1871 the success of the furniture makers was typical of the growth and prosperity being enjoyed by manufacturers of a large variety of products. Less than forty years after its incorporation, Chicago was a thriving center of commerce and industry. Already the city's handful of cabinet and chair factories had been transformed into a Goliath of steam-powered manufactories employing hundreds of men. Then tragedy struck.

Constructed primarily of wooden boards and shingles, the city's structures had been under threat of destruction by fire since they were built. In the fall of 1871, following a hot and dry summer, the hazard was particularly

THE FIRE OF 1871 AND RECOVERY

strong. On Saturday evening, October 7, fire broke out in the West Division between Canal and Clinton streets. Fanned by wind, the flames spread from wooden shacks to lumberyards, factories, planing mills, and coalyards on the bank of the river. Scarcely had residents recovered from the fire of the seventh when, on the night of the eighth, another fire broke out on the West Side. Destroying everything in its path, the new fire swept eastward across the river and gradually ate its way south and north. By the time the flames slowly died out on the following day, almost the entire business district was a smoldering ruin.

Few of Chicago's most prominent furniture houses remained untouched by the fire. Jacob Beiersdorf; W. W. Strong; McCabe, Wilkins & Spaulding; J. Koenig; C. C. Holton & Co.; Schultz, Gobel & Co.; J. M. Brunswick & Balke; Emanuel Brunswick; and Phillips & Liebenstein—all located in the heart of the city or on the Near West, South, and North sides—were among those who lost everything. More fortunate were Thayer & Tobey and H. S. Carter & Company, whose factories survived, and McDonough, Price & Company, whose showrooms were saved. The only well-known furniture manufacturer to escape the conflagration totally was A. L. Hale & Bros. Keeping a large force at work day and night, that firm was busy "coining money" in its West Side factory, *Cabinet Maker* reported in December 1871.[49]

Although many businesses, goods, and residences had been consumed by the fire, the city's transportation network remained relatively unharmed, making it possible for the materials and goods needed to rebuild the city to be imported without delay. This, combined with the fact that much of the West Side remained intact, enabled manufacturing and commerce to resume almost immediately. Thus, before the ashes had cooled, relief was under way and businesses began to reopen.

Within a week, many furniture men were back in business. With much of the loss from their State Street store covered by Eastern and foreign insurance companies, Thayer & Tobey reopened immediately in their factory on West Randolph at Jefferson and on the following day "took an order for the furniture for the West side Sherman House."[50] Henry Carter, in Boston buying goods by the twenty-eighth of the month, resumed manufacture of his recently patented bed lounge in his undamaged factory on Jefferson and Lake.[51]

Patent model for a portable table registered by David M. Reynolds on November 8, 1870. Seven thousand similar tables were produced by Reynolds's factory shortly after the 1871 fire.
h: 6" l: 11⅜" w: 5¼"
CHS, purchase, 1981

W. W. Strong, who had lost his factory and his showroom, immediately secured the use of a building and hurried off to the Boston furniture market to order goods after arranging for the construction of a new factory on West Randolph Street. When the new factory was completed only four weeks later, work began on an elegant salesroom on Wabash Avenue, which, like State Street, became one of the most fashionable retail areas after the fire.[52] John Koenig, burned out on South Wells Street, immediately began erecting a new building on North Green Street and had "the wheels of industry again running in three weeks after the fire."[53] Showing the same spirit, David M. Reynolds, whose toy factory on State Street had been destroyed, "started again the next day and took an order for 7,000 relief tables, which were manufactured and delivered forthwith."[54]

Not all the furniture makers fared as well as Tobey, Strong, Koenig, and Reynolds. In spite of the fact that many had purchased fire insurance, at least half of the insurance companies could not pay because of the vast number of claims made on them as a result of the fire. Unable to secure financing elsewhere, many small shops never reopened. Other manufacturers struggled for years, determined to rebuild their factories, reestablish their credit ratings, and regain their former standing within the community.

Typical was the plight of Jacob Beiersdorf, who, during his eleven years in Chicago, had risen to become a factory owner and had established a reputation for "industry and honorable dealing." Although insured for $20,000, he recovered no more than "5 cts on the dollar" after the fire and was forced out of business. During the summer of 1872, Beiersdorf finally secured a loan from the National Bank of Illinois, which enabled him to resume business the following fall. Not until March of 1874 was he able to pay his creditors in full.[55]

Despite its initially disastrous effect, the 1871 fire would prove the prelude to a period of unprecedented boom for manufacturers of all kinds and for the furniture industry in particular.

FURNITURE FOR "THE MILLION"

1873-1917

I N T R O D U C T I O N

All of Chicago's manufacturing industries received a boost from the 1873 Inter-State Industrial Exposition, which celebrated the city's remarkable recovery from the fire and displayed to the world the great strides in material and cultural progress made by Chicago and the Northwest. Held from September 25

The Inter-State Industrial Exposition Building in 1873. From Illustrations of Greater Chicago.

to November 12, 1873, in a magnificent glass and iron building erected for the purpose along the lakefront from Adams to Jackson streets,* the exposition drew attention to the city's industrial, agricultural, and artistic achievements

*The present site of The Art Institute of Chicago.

through exhibits of products as diverse as terra-cotta chimney caps and fashionable parlor furniture.[1] In conjunction with the celebration, Savillon S. Schoff prepared a publication, *The Glory of Chicago—Her Manufactories,* which provided brief biographical sketches of the majority of the city's manufacturing establishments and detailed their progress since the fire.[2]

Prominent among the displays of manufactures in wood were the products of Chicago's furniture manufacturers. *The Inter-State Exposition Souvenir,* a guidebook issued in conjunction with the exposition, presented the work of a host of these manufacturing concerns, from that of W. W. Strong and Emanuel Brunswick & Co., who had been well established before the fire, to the products of the Empire Parlor Bedstead Company, which had been in business only a year before the exhibition. Conspicuous were the manufacturers of multi-purpose furniture, which would become highly popular in the course of the next decade.

At this stage the furniture makers of Chicago ranged from large establishments like Thayer & Tobey, A. L. Hale & Bros., and A. H. Andrews & Co., employing from 150 to 250 workers and using machinery undreamed of in 1833, to one-man shops like those owned by Robert Galle and Rudolph Weidemann, still primarily handicraft operations resembling the ones operated by Chicago's earliest cabinetmakers. During the next three decades this variety of workshops would persist, but the balance would tip in favor of large factories, growing mechanization, and increased specialization. Thousands of pieces in an astonishing variety of shapes and styles were turned out, with revivals of Elizabethan, rococo, Renaissance, Egyptian, Second Empire, and other historically inspired furniture appearing alongside unornamented, strictly utilitarian pieces.

An excellent example of the Victorian penchant for revival styling was the new Palmer House that rose like a phoenix out of the ashes of the old hotel and opened in the fall of 1873. Distinguished by mansard roofs, huge dormer windows, and columns and statuary, the exterior of Potter Palmer's magnificent hostelry was strongly influenced by recent additions to the Louvre in Paris. Inside, thirty-four varieties of marble, frescoed ceilings, gas chandeliers, massive mirrors, and costly furnishings fostered the boast that the Palmer House was the "largest and best furnished hotel in the world."[3]

Luxurious and "almost royal," the furniture of the Palmer House was executed in "an entirely new and novel style." As the *Palmer House Illustrated* explained: "There are rooms furnished in the style of the old Egyptians; parlors designed from the sumptuous age of the luxurious Romans; while the modern French styles, as well as the English, have also their representatives. In this regard, the parlors, halls and dining saloons are a museum of art, taking the visitor back through the ages, and recalling to mind his knowledge of history."[4]

Only two blocks from the great Inter-State Industrial Exposition Building, the new Palmer House boasted 200 rooms, a dining hall to seat 1,000, and a barber shop whose marble floor was inlaid with silver dollars. Demolished in 1925, it was replaced by its current namesake.

Spectacularly frescoed, marbled, mirrored, and draped in satins and velvets in the latest French style, the Grand Parlor did not belie its name. Even more intriguing was the Egyptian Room, "designed and wrought out wholly by the W. W. Strong Furniture Co., of this city."[5] Visitors could learn as much from studying the room as from a visit to the Berlin Museum, claimed the booklet. Indeed, they could learn even more, for, as the author noted, "we cannot believe that the ancients knew how to upholster as well as the skillful workers who made these wonderful chairs and covered them with satins and lace."[6]

Equal in size and rivaling the Egyptian Room in magnificence were the State Parlours and Bridal Chambers. "Cheery and bright," the mammoth rooms displayed "rich and costly" furniture inlaid with floral marquetry set beneath a ceiling frescoed with "cupids and doves, wreaths of flowers and filmy veils of lace." The bed was an awesome creation of ebonized and gilded wood surmounted by "a canopy in the French style."[7] Beneath the canopy, a pair of gilded figureheads flanked a high, crested headboard. A pair of pedestals at the foot of the bed served as back corner supports for the sofa that formed the footboard. A special design from the factory of W. W. Strong, the bed was part of a suite that included an elaborate dressing case, a writing desk, and table (all inlaid with marquetry), and richly upholstered chairs in a variety of designs.

By 1873 the Thayer & Tobey Furniture Company had executed similarly elaborate furnishings for the Grand Pacific Hotel, as had A. L. Hale & Bros. for the

One of the bridal chambers at the Palmer House. From The Palmer House Illustrated, *1876.*

Sherman House and the Briggs House.[8] In fact, visitors to the Inter-State Industrial Exposition were invited by A. L. Hale & Bros. to visit the company's showrooms "in order to see where all the furniture in the great Chicago hotels came from, and where so many of our private citizens have obtained the sumptuous and luxurious furniture in their residences."[9]

Many undoubtedly took advantage of Hale's offer, for the Palmer House, the Grand Pacific, and the city's other great hotels seemed the epitome of splendor—the American equivalent of Europe's royal palaces. But unlike the old-world castles, they could be enjoyed by anyone who entered their doors or paid the price of a room.

Following the Great Fire, ornate and costly furnishings similar to those commissioned by the hotels could be found in many of the spacious drawing rooms and salons of the new French-style row houses and mansions being built throughout the city. In the large, high-ceilinged rooms of some of the wealthy, furniture of walnut or rosewood with gilt tracings, immense wall mirrors reaching from ceiling to floor, and massive cabinets of ebony and gilt inlaid with marquetry panels made an impressive display among thickly tufted chairs and sofas covered with silk or velvet.

Far more common, however, were the plainer parlors and sitting rooms of the moderately well-to-do. Arranged on a floral Brussels carpet, black walnut sofas and chairs upholstered in serviceable terry, rep, or haircloth surrounded a center table topped with marble or draped with cloth of blue or cherry-colored vel-

vet. Easels, hassocks, small tables to hold bouquets or photographs, wall
pockets to hold Valentines or bits of sewing, lounges for reading or resting, a
patent rocker, and a parlor organ often completed the cozy scene.

*Dressing table from a bridal suite at
the Palmer House, 1873.
h: 129½" w: 68" d: 21¾"
CHS, purchase, 1979*

While variations in size, scale, ornamentation, and cost visibly differentiated
the drawing rooms of the rich from the parlors of the middle class, their owners shared the widely held belief that decoration reflected not only the family's

financial standing but also its moral values. As *Industrial Chicago* pointed out in 1891, "Great moral results follow from people's houses being pretty as well as

Desk made by W. W. Strong for a Palmer House bridal suite, 1873.
h: 90¾" w: 36½" d: 21¾"
CHS, purchase, 1979

healthy."[10] A "beautiful" home became a social ideal, the object of sentiment, and a criterion of status. Within this context, furniture came to play a dual role. Not only did it serve the family's physical needs, it was considered a reflection of the father's economic success, the mother's cultural achievements, and the couple's aspirations for their children.[11]

By the second half of the nineteenth century, the increasing numbers and growing affluence of the middle class—or "the million," as authors of the day were wont to call them—provided the primary market for the building trades and for the manufacturers of household furnishings. The increase in the ranks of those able to afford more than the barest necessities combined with a growing sophistication of taste to create an unprecedented market for furniture and other household articles. By 1883 the Chicago-based *Inland Architect & Builder*

Table top inlaid with colored woods from a bridal suite in the Palmer House, 1873.
l: 50½" w: 29½"
CHS, purchase, 1979

According to The Land Owner, *in 1873 W. W. Strong's new store on Wabash Avenue contained "probably the most elaborate and costly stock of fashionable furniture ever displayed in Chicago," with many of the items incorporating pieces of elaborate marquetry imported from overseas.*

could claim: "Manufacturers are vying with each other in the production of beautiful shapes, and the West with her supply of material is not lacking in men of enterprise and genius, who keep even pace with the demand of the times, and with artistic talent and mechanical skill shape the furniture that make our homes the center of the world, the haven of rest, and the place of comfort."[12] Centrally located and well equipped, Chicago's furniture manufacturers were in an ideal position to supply the needs and wants of the million.

In the section that follows, chapter 3 offers an overview of the dynamics of the furniture industry in Chicago from around 1873 until America's entry into

Drawing room in the home of a prosperous Chicagoan, Frederick Tuttle, at 2022 South Michigan Avenue, showing sofa and chair from a rosewood parlor suite purchased from the W. W. Strong Furniture Company in the late 1870s.
The Newark Museum

Parlor or sitting room in the home of Samuel Starkweather Gardner at 190 Warren Avenue in the 1880s.

World War I in 1917. The next six chapters deal with developments within various specialties, including upholstered furniture; patent furniture; bedroom furniture; chairs; commercial furniture; and plain and fancy cabinet wares.

THE DYNAMICS OF THE INDUSTRY

1 8 7 3 - 1 9 1 7

The development of a mass market in America proved particularly favorable to the furniture industry, which found itself filling a growing volume of orders for domestic, commerical, and institutional customers.[1] Technological innovations in a variety of fields made it possible for the industry to take full advantage of this growing market. On the one hand, advances in methods of production enabled manufacturers to turn out a large volume of attractive furniture at medium prices; on the other, it enabled them to advertise and distribute their goods at reasonable cost.

In 1870, with a total population of about 300,000, Chicago claimed 59 furniture factories employing 1,126 workers. Within a decade the city's population had risen to around 500,000. During this same period the number of furniture factories had tripled while the number of employees and the value of goods produced had quadrupled. By 1895 Chicago counted 276 concerns engaged in the manufacture of furniture and allied goods, employing 28,000 men; some 12,500 of these worked for firms making upholstered goods.[2]

By 1880 only New York and Philadelphia surpassed Chicago in the total value of furniture produced. By 1895, however, Chicago was in first place, producing furniture worth $4,000,000 more than New York's output and twice the value of the production of Grand Rapids, Michigan.[3] In 1886, comparing Chicago with other American furniture manufacturing centers, A. T. Andreas wrote:

> Chicago in 1870 manufactured about one-half as much furniture in value as Cincinnati, one-third as much as Boston and Philadelphia and one-sixth as much only as New York. In 1880 the census returns show that Chicago was in advance of all other places excepting New York; but in 1885 the footings show that Chicago marches to the front both in the number of employees, and in the amount of the annual product. In parlor furniture especially, Chicago leads the world, the annual sales of upholstered goods and frames equaling those of New York, Boston and Cincinnati combined.[4]

Chicago's meteoric rise was due to a combination of fortunate circumstances. In addition to being centrally located, the city's furniture makers

had access to abundant raw materials, expanding markets, and plenty of willing workers. These advantages were evident by 1878, when the local correspondent for *American Cabinet Maker* wrote:

> Not alone in enterprise and go-a-head-a-tive-ness is the Chicago manufacturer blessed, but he has every facility at hand for the furtherance of his plans and aims. . . . He has the advantage, first of all, of vast forests of lumber almost at the very door of his workshop, so cheap has transportation by the network of railroads become, as well as superior navigation facilities, and not only this but labor is an important item. . . . The advantages in this line are not in the mere fact that mechanics work for less than elsewhere, for the mechanic can well afford to work cheaper, when it is considered that our average mechanic is able to own his own cottage and the land on which it stands at an exceedingly low valuation.

Moreover, the trade journal noted, Chicago manufacturers were "favored with a broad extent of territory, radiating thousands of miles in all directions and rapidly filling up with an industrious population."[5] Waves of settlers passed through the city, continuing westward to Nebraska, Kansas, and the Dakotas, as well as to outlying territories north and south. Thousands more stayed on in Chicago. In 1898 the city's population pushed past the one million mark, making Chicago the nation's second largest city.

Among the circumstances favoring the industry was the fact that, during the same period, Chicago became the country's most important livestock market and the largest meat-packing complex in the world. The industries that developed as a consequence provided local manufacturers with a bountiful supply of glue, hair, feathers, leather, and other materials. The stockyard purveyors used "everything but the squeal," as a wit had it. Indeed, some went so far as to make novelty furniture out of animal horns.

A variety of subsidiary industries was well established by 1884. Three large firms supplied the cured feathers, and three others provided the curled

Map showing locations of furniture factories in the 1880 American Cabinet Maker. Courtesy of *Furniture World*

hair used by mattress makers and upholsterers. Nine firms made spring beds and cots, five made woven-wire mattresses, and others produced coiled-wire springs. The litany goes on. Two factories made tassels, fringes, and other trimmings used in finishing parlor furniture, clothing, and carriages. Seven firms, among them J. V. Farwell and Marshall Field & Company, dealt in wholesale upholstery goods, importing their fabrics directly from Europe. Five firms provided veneers and cabinet woods; four, cabinet hardware; others, glue and varnish. Two factories made coffins and four sold undertaking supplies to furniture dealers who were also undertakers.[6]

Factories making furniture were scattered through every ward of the city. As early as 1877 *American Cabinet Maker* identified the locations of the different specialties as follows: "Chicago has that peculiar feature of its kindred manufacturers being located together in certain districts. The chair factories are on the northwest side, while chamber furniture manufacturers are principally settled in the southwest side. Frame makers are on the north side, while manufacturers of upholstered furniture are more scattered."[7] Following a pattern begun in the 1850s, new factories tended to locate away from the central business district in areas closer to raw materials and transportation facilities (like the West Division) or near their major sources of labor (like those clustered in the German neighborhood on the city's Near North Side).

By the 1880s most cabinet and chair manufactories were to be found west of the central business district in the West Division. In an industrial belt separated from downtown by the Chicago River, large and small furniture factories congregated in close proximity to sawmills, foundries, marble works, tanneries, and workshops making other lumber-based products such as wagons, boxes, barrels, and agricultural implements. Here they had easy access to numerous railroad depots, as well as to the docks and lumber district.

Northwest of the business district, factories were concentrated in three major regions. The first, a thirteen-block area of manufacturing establishments and commission houses, was bounded by Carroll Avenue, North Canal Street, West Randolph Street, and Elizabeth Street. The second was located around the intersection of West Chicago Avenue and North Halsted Street. And the third was to be found along that part of Milwaukee Avenue that formed a major artery in the largely German-speaking area of Chicago.

There were two additional concentrations of furniture factories on the southwest side of the city. Many were located in a wide corridor (bounded on the west by Green Street and on the east by South Canal) that ran parallel to the railroad tracks lining the west bank of the south branch of the Chicago River. A second cluster had grown up in the vicinity of Blue Island Avenue, a major thoroughfare that connected the West Side industrial district with the lumberyards lining the south branch of the river.

Most workers lived close at hand. The unmarried ones found inexpensive lodgings in workingmen's hotels and boardinghouses scattered among the factories. Others walked to work from nearby residential areas filled with frame cottages that had been built up on the periphery of the industrial district. Prosperous factory owners also lived nearby, building fine houses in Logan Square or Wicker Park on the West Side or in Lincoln Park on the Near North Side.

While the 1871 fire had caused great hardship and suffering, it also generated a city filled with newly built factories equipped with the most modern machinery, usually powered by steam. Chicago factories could turn out goods more cheaply than their competitors on the East Coast, where facilities were much older and where the work force was being steadily depleted by the departure of skilled craftsmen drawn by the promise of greater opportunities in the West.

Furniture manufacturers in general benefited from new technological developments that reduced the cost of production. After the Civil War, inventors perfected a variety of shaping and finishing machines that speeded the basic procedures of cutting, planing, turning, boring, and sanding wood. Others reduced the cost of ornament by making it easier and faster to cut veneers or carve wood. By the early 1880s it was possible to cut burls into veneers so thin that they resembled sheets of paper. First adopted by manufacturers of organs, pianos, and sewing-machine cabinets, these "paper veneers" were soon put into use in factories making all types of household furniture.[8]

Other machines encouraged "the art of carving by steam power."[9] Introduced after the Civil War, simple "spindle shapers" with rotating metal burrs were gradually replaced by carving machines with whirling knives that could cut four replicas of a three-dimensional hand-carved model at one time. By the 1890s even cheaper "carvings" could be obtained using drop-carving or embossing machines that used a die mandrel of forged steel to impress bas-relief patterns on flat or slightly curved surfaces like the ones commonly used on the backs or seats of chairs.

Although the carving machine introduced in the 1890s could turn out eight duplicates at a time, it did not precipitate widespread unemployment among the carvers, as they had feared. From the Furniture Worker, *April 10, 1902.*

Since hand-carving was a particularly slow and costly process, carving machines were quickly adopted by Chicago manufacturers who were mass producing medium- and low-priced furniture. "The new carving machines are coming into use in Chicago at about two a week," *Trade Bureau* reported in 1888, when carved furniture was at the peak of its popularity and local factories were running at full speed.[10]

In 1891, when a new machine capable of carving eight duplicates simultaneously was about to be put on the market, the hand-carvers—at that time the highest paid workers in the industry—were apprehensive about the effect this would have on their jobs. The manufacturers responded by pointing out that machinery had "in the main worked no hardship to this deserving class of men, owing to the rapid extension of the demand for carved furniture, popularized by the cheap price at which the new machines have enabled manufacturers to place it on the market."[11]

Technology similarly reduced the amount of hand labor and the cost of materials, making soft, comfortable seating furniture affordable just when "the million" could aspire to have a parlor. After the Civil War, numerous patents had been taken out on various components used in upholstering. Chicago's many metalworkers proved particularly adept at developing variations on the helical wire springs used in making furniture and mattresses. As the demand for upholstered parlor furniture grew, machines were developed for speeding up the unpleasant tasks of cleaning, sorting, and baling the various animal hairs, moss, and tow used in stuffing mattresses and upholstered pieces. At the same time, the introduction of improved high-power looms in the textile industry continued to reduce the price of cloth while increasing the variety of weaves and textures available to the consumer.

Introduced late in the 1890s, the Novelty Tufting Machine could mechanically tuft the backs and seats of couches and carriage seats in far less time than any upholsterer could do the job by hand. Promising uniform, perfect, and durable tufts, advertisements for this machine pointed out that the device could be operated by youths at a saving of 50 to 70 percent of the wages paid to journeymen upholsterers.[12] Other machines offered mechanical methods of sewing ruffled and button bands onto inexpensive couches.

As new machinery was perfected, it became possible to use woods previously considered unsuitable for making furniture. By the end of the century, hard-to-work woods like ash and birch were being used for factory-made furniture, an article in *Furniture World* explained, "partly because timber of the sort long used in furniture making has become scarce, partly because modern machinery makes it possible to work woods that in earlier times could not be profitably worked."[13] Woods such as aspen and sycamore, considered especially troublesome because they warped easily, could be used now due to the availability of steam-heated drying kilns that seasoned the wood rapidly.

While mahogany and walnut remained the favorites for fine furniture, other woods rose and fell in popularity in accordance with their availability and cost. After American black walnut became scarce in the late 1870s, manufacturers turned to abundant, cheaper woods such as birch, elm, gum, and oak. To make these lighter woods resemble the more fashionable dark-toned ones, however, they stained birch to resemble mahogany and finished red gum a nut brown to create "Circassian" walnut. Oak, butternut, and maple were often finished to reveal their handsome grain and attractive golden-brown colors.

Despite the adoption of waste-reducing machinery and new methods of finishing surfaces, the cost of the wood suitable for furniture making increased steadily due to the denuding of forests in the Great Lakes states. By 1912, when much of the lumber was being imported from the heavily timbered Southern states, hardwood cost twice as much as it had in 1900.[14] In reaction to this steady escalation in the cost of wood, several manufacturers turned to producing office, bedroom, and novelty furniture out of iron, steel, and brass in the late 1890s. Others wove willow, rattan, and reed into furniture, while still others created unique pieces using bamboo, twigs, and as mentioned earlier, animal horn. Factories increasingly specialized to produce certain types and grades of furniture, with the bulk of the household furniture production falling into the low and medium price range, and expensive goods limited primarily to church, hotel, office, saloon, and other special furniture.

During the last quarter of the century, several companies became sizable commerical enterprises, employing hundreds of men in plants within the city as well as in branch factories or warehouses located in other states. A few, like A. H. Andrews & Co., J. S. Ford, Johnson & Co., and S. Karpen & Bros., expanded the scope of their businesses so as to increase their control over each step of production, from the purchase of timberland to insure themselves of a ready supply of lumber to the acquisition of exposition buildings in which to display and sell their products. Jacob Beiersdorf and Wendelin Seng organized subsidiary businesses to supply their firms and other manufacturers with metal springs or hardware fixtures.

Conversely, entrepreneurs in allied industries occasionally became furniture manufacturers when their machinery or by-products made that feasible and profitable. For example, tinware manufacturer Adams & Westlake made metal bedsteads, while butcher supplier Wolf, Sayer, & Heller turned cattle, deer, and elk horns into fancy parlor chairs and novelties. In addition, countless millworkers, picture frame makers, and fireplace mantel makers created all kinds of wooden furniture, while basketmakers handwove chairs and other furnishings.

While the size of the average factory increased, the range of products each one produced narrowed, reflecting the capabilities of its machinery and the particular skills of its workmen. "The business has become specialized," the editor of *Furniture Worker* reported in 1899. "While formerly manufacturers made a little of everything in the line of furniture, they now confine themselves to the manufacture of a few articles, frequently but one, but turned out in the greatest variety of styles. Their entire attention being given to these, they can turn them out in large quantities at greatly reduced prices."[15] Thus specialization benefited not only the producer but the consumer, who ended up paying less.

Filling the huge demand for parlor furniture, 43 of Chicago's 187 factories in 1884 made upholstered couches and chairs. Of these firms, about half made pieces from start to finish, while the other half made only the

SPECIALIZATION

wooden frames. In addition, 47 factories made wooden cabinet ware, 30 created "fancy" cabinet ware and picture frames, 10 specialized in com-

A cabinetmaker finishes a sofa frame in the Tobey & Christiansen Cabinet Co. in 1906. From About Tobey Hand-made Furniture *by Oscar L. Triggs, 1906.*

mercial furniture, 5 manufactured rattan and reed goods, and 4 made only chairs.[16] Within these broad classifications, some factories made only bureaus, tables, or office desks, while others specialized in folding beds or piano stools.

In the larger factories, specialization and mechanization went hand in hand with assembly-line production. Contrary to widely held assumptions, mass production required more, rather than fewer, workers. This was conclusively shown in 1899 when an exhaustive study comparing hand and machine labor was published by the U. S. Commissioner of Labor. After computing the labor, time, and cost required to make dozens of manufactured products, the commissioner concluded that "the number of employees under the machine method is greater than under hand, the cost per total is far less and the average rates of wages are as high, and, in some instances, higher than under the old methods."[17]

This was demonstrated in one of several case studies abstracted in *Furniture Worker*, which compared the 1860s and 1890s methods of making twelve oak bookcases (each 3'7" by 5'5"):

Under the hand method two men were employed, working 12 hours per day, receiving $1.50 per day. Under the machine method 24 different persons were employed in the manufacture of similar bookcases, each working 10 hours per day. The total time consumed under the hand method was 654 hours, whereas under machine methods only 157 hours and 14.4 minutes was required. The total cost under the old method was $81.75; under machine methods this was reduced to $25.30.[18]

However, responding to the fact that the use of "machine methods" reduced the amount of skill the workers were required to bring to their jobs, *American Cabinet Maker* in 1871 warned that the assembly line was "fraught with evil as it encourages the superficial education of the artisans themselves."[19] By 1877 the trade journal was even more despondent about the situation, noting, "The state of the trade at the present time is not one that fosters the skill of the cabinet-maker although it does that of the machinist."[20]

American Cabinet Maker was not the only party concerned with the state of the trade. The workers themselves saw mass-production methods as reducing the value of specialized skills and hence reducing their status and wages in the furniture industry.

WORKERS AND MANUFACTURERS

Continuing a tradition set by Chicago's earliest furniture makers, most factory owners and workers were recent immigrants to the city. But, unlike the city's pioneer cabinetmakers, who came primarily from the northeastern United States, men of this new generation tended to be of foreign birth with experience acquired through apprenticeships completed in their native lands or in older Chicago factories. In 1870, 13 percent of the city's total population had been born in Ireland and 20 percent had come from various principalities in Germany. Large numbers of newcomers from the British Isles and Scandinavia also swelled the work force, creating a city in which one of every two citizens had been born outside the United States.

Germans, who made up the single largest ethnic element in Chicago's population between 1873 and 1917, also predominated in the various branches of the woodworking trades, from house construction and interior finish to furniture making and the manufacture of pianos and organs. By the 1880s most manufacturers who had achieved some prominence in the industry were first-generation Germans or Bohemians from the wooded provinces of the Austro-Hungarian Empire. They were most likely to rise from being employees to being employers if, in addition to their accomplishments as craftsmen, they had managerial and sales skills. In many cases, the second generation of foreign-born manufacturers—sons and nephews—also went into the furniture business, but they usually started in managerial and sales positions rather than at the bench.

Until the passage of the restrictive immigration quotas in 1921, the most skilled workers continued to be drawn from among foreigners arriving from countries with strong woodworking traditions like Germany or Scandinavia, where workmen had to serve long apprenticeships before they were allowed to enter the trade. In America, a fluid social structure and increasing mechanization discouraged the apprenticeship system. Moreover, many young people were unwilling to spend years working for low wages, while employers were reluctant to invest money in training youngsters at a time when experienced workers were plentiful and boys and girls under sixteen could be hired at low wages to do the unskilled work.

In an effort to control and regulate conditions in the furniture industry, both workers and manufacturers organized, the German furniture workers as early as 1855, when they formed the Cabinet Makers Society of Chicago. They did not have really effective representation, however, until 1872, when Furniture Workers' Union No. 1 was organized. An item in the German-language paper *Vobote* on July 1, 1876, reported union meetings in six separate sections of the city, each organized around a different language group.[21] By 1886 the union claimed 2,429 members in Illinois and was active in securing wage increases and insurance benefits.[22]

Meanwhile, in 1872, local manufacturers decided to form a Furniture Manufacturers' Exchange, to serve several purposes. One was to coordinate information on credit ratings to avoid losses incurred by manufacturers through the defaulting or dishonesty of some retailers. The second may well have been to provide self-insurance for an industry highly vulnerable to loss by fire. Inevitably, however, one of the group's main functions came to be that of representing manufacturers' interests in negotiations with workers.

Eventually represented by a number of unions organized according to specialties—the Carvers' Union, the Upholsterers' Union—as well as by the more comprehensive Furniture Workers' Union, many workers were drawn into the radical politics that gathered strength in Chicago in the aftermath of the depression of the mid-1870s. Some of the foreign-born workers had brought socialist and anarchist ideas with them. Others became radicalized in the course of such upheavals as the Railroad Strike of 1877, which spread to Chicago from the East and eventually involved workers from many industries in violent confrontation with police and militia.[23] Unresolved in the following decade, social unrest in Chicago would come to a head in the Haymarket Affair of 1886, when a demonstration in favor of the eight-hour working day came to a bloody conclusion.[24]

This red silk flag made in the 1870s was carried by members of Furniture Workers' Union No. 1 in demonstrations for the eight-hour day, including the one that culminated in the Haymarket Affair of May 4, 1886. It was later given to the Chicago Historical Society by the Brotherhood of Carpenters and Joiners, Local No. 7, with which the furniture workers had amalgamated in 1917.
Photograph by Scott Hyde

One of the principal issues dividing American employees and employers in the 1870s, the workers' demand for an eight-hour day generated intense passion on both sides. In 1879 it had been one of the chief demands in a strike called by Furniture Workers' Union No. 1; the following year, a National Eight Hour Committee was organized in Chicago. In 1884 the Federation of Trade and Labor Unions of the United States and Canada, meeting in Chicago, resolved that as of May 1, 1886, eight hours would constitute a day's work.[25] But transforming the resolution into reality proved difficult, since employers were determined to maintain the status quo despite a spate of strikes. In its issue dated April 24, 1886, the industry's publication, *Trade Bureau,* noted: "It is reported from Chicago that the furniture factory of F. Mayer & Co. was closed by the proprietors rather than accede

Located at 804–14 Hawthorne, the Tonk Manufacturing Co. began by making fancy cabinet ware, then narrowed its scope but expanded its output to become the country's largest manufacturer of piano stools.
Mr. and Mrs. Hampton E. Tonk and Family

to the demands of the workmen who wanted an advance of 20 per cent in wages and an eight hour day. Between 275 and 300 men are idle in consequence. They are all members of the Furniture Workers' Union."[26]

The same publication reported a lockout at A. H. Andrews & Co., purely on the eight-hour issue. The upholsterers went further in their demands:

> At a meeting of furniture manufacturers in Chicago Tuesday evening a communication was read from Upholsterers' Union No. 1 demanding an increase of 20 per cent on piece work, and also stating that ten hours' pay would be demanded for eight hours' work. After a full discussion of the question it was unanimously declared that in view of the present state of the trade, the light demand for goods, and generally unsettled condition of prices, it was entirely inexpedient to comply with any demand which contemplated a reduction of hours or an increase of wages.[27]

What had been a strike in the industry acquired more widespread connotations after May 4, when in the course of the pro-eight-hour-day rally at Haymarket Square a bomb was thrown into a group of policemen and workingmen, precipitating a riot that led to the death of one police officer and a civilian and the wounding of sixty-six officers and twelve others.[28] The tragic conclusion to the Haymarket meeting and the subsequent reaction to it ended any hope the striking furniture workers might have had of securing their demand for an eight-hour day. In an item headed "Hours and Wages," the *Trade Bureau* of May 22, 1886, reported: "The question of labor is being rapidly solved all over the country by the men returning to work on the old basis of ten hours. The movement to adopt the short day schedule in furniture factories has failed, and the workers recognize the fact."[29]

An account of a parlor furniture manufacturers' meeting the following month, reported by the same publication in its June 12 issue, explains why the Chicago workers stood little chance of gaining their objective:

> A number of the firms had already secured workmen from other cities, and had also employed a number of young men apprentices, who were learning the business very rapidly and would soon be able to do excellent work and turn out as much work as older hands. Not the slightest indication of weakening was manifested on the part of the manufacturers, who stated that as the spring trade was now over and many orders had been canceled, they could just as well afford to remain as they were as to attempt to start up with a full force of men in anticipation of fall orders.

However, the parlor furniture manufacturers indicated that "if the men concluded to return to work on the old terms all the feeling engendered by the strike would be absolutely forgotten, and the men could come back with as much freedom as though nothing unpleasant had occurred. . . . The manufacturers will not, they said, make terms with any union or association, but every individual workman may return, and all will be treated fairly by their employers."[30]

Employees of the Tonk Manufacturing Co. in 1893. Many of the workers were under sixteen years old. The use of cheap, unskilled labor was common in the furniture industry.
Mr. and Mrs. Hampton E. Tonk and Family

Further attempts to establish the eight-hour day in the industry during the next few years also proved unsuccessful, as an item in the May 31, 1890, issue of the *Trade Bureau* made clear. "Chicago stated that union shops work nine hours and non-union shops ten hours." The same article also reported that the average wages in Chicago were "thirty cents an hour."[31]

Wages were a continuing source of grievance. In its November 10, 1898, issue the *Furniture Worker* published an abstract of figures collected by the Department of Labor on the rise and fall of wages in skilled trades in the United States, Great Britain, France, and Belgium between 1870 and

Dear Sirs:-

You are hereby notified that on and after May 1st, 1906, we, the Wood Carvers of the City of Chicago, do hereby make the following demands:

On and after said date the rating system shall take effect; the minimum wage scale for carvers employed by all furniture manufacturers shall be 30¢ per hour, except carvers working on samples or machine patterns, who shall be rated at a minimum of 35¢ per hour. Further, all carvers shall be rated above said minimum according to their merits.

Robt. McCrae
President.

Jno. Brannan
Cor. Secy.

The woodcarvers were among the best paid—because they were among the most skilled—of the workers in the furniture industry. Nevertheless, they frequently went on strike.
CHS, gift of the Chicago Furniture Manufacturers' Association, 1978

1898. Summarizing the portion of the report that dealt with furniture workers, the article noted:

> An analysis of the tables of the prices of labor as arranged by the labor department shows that the men who make the furniture, understood to come within the cabinetmaker's province, are not, in the first place, paid a high rate of wages, and that in the second, this rate has varied only slightly within the last twenty-eight years. . . . In 1870 a cabinetmaker could make on an average $2.14 a day in any of the larger cities of the United States. The next year he received an increase of 9 cents a day. In two years after, his wage had fallen to $2.11 ½ a day, which was the lowest sum paid him for a day's work in the twenty-eight years since 1870. From that year his earnings gradually increased until in 1892, he was being paid $2.47 ½ a day for his work. The next year a decline set in, and in 1898 he is receiving $2.29¾ a day.[32]

While wages did not go up during this period, falling price levels, in fact, led to a 60 percent increase in real wages for furniture workers—that is, in the amount they could buy with their pay.[33] The statistics published in *Furniture Worker* did not take this into account, appearing only as raw figures that showed minimal progress.

Even before the setback of 1886, some workers had decided to assume control of working conditions by forming cooperatively owned factories, to be run on an eight-hour-day schedule. Following the strikes of 1877, three such cooperatives—the Chicago Furniture Frame Company, the Chicago Parlor Set Manufacturing Company, and the Northwestern Parlor Suit Manufacturing Company—were organized to produce upholstered furniture.[34] After the strike of 1879, the Chicago Furniture Workers' Association was organized to make chamber sets and bookcases by cabinetmakers formerly employed in the factories of A. H. Andrews & Co. and Brunswick & Balke Co.[35] Of these, only the Northwestern Parlor Suit Manufacturing Company was still in business by 1890. Most of the others had disbanded as their members left the cooperatives to produce furniture on their own.

Meanwhile, the manufacturers, organized in 1872 by Henry S. Carter as the Furniture Manufacturers' Exchange, had engaged in a variety of activities to benefit members. This included agreements among the manufacturers setting minimum prices to insure a stable market, as well as keeping records concerning the financial reliability of retailers and manufacturers.[36] In 1888, to protest against freight rate increases and to counteract the growing strength of the furniture workers' union, manufacturers formally organized the Chicago Furniture Manufacturers' Association, electing parlor furniture manufacturer John Schoen president. The Association also hired a salaried secretary.

Supported by dues and yearly assessments based on the number of workers employed by each manufacturer, the association kept its members abreast of pending legislation, negotiated with union leaders, and represented members in hiring strike breakers, maintaining a Labor Fund with which to pay them.[37]

FACTORY TO CONSUMER

From the 1870s onward most of the furniture produced in Chicago factories was sold on a wholesale basis to retail furniture dealers, interior decorators, and contractors, who then resold it to the public. Small manufacturers, who sold primarily to regional buyers, often set up sample rooms in a

Salesmen—or drummers, as they were called—found that their sales improved substantially if they could show potential customers photos of the products they were selling. From Salter & Bilek, Chicago, ca. 1885.

corner of their factory where customers could examine the goods and bargain with the owner. Others sold their products on consignment through commission agents or "jobbers" like William R. Schick, who operated the Chicago Furniture Manufacturers' Sales Rooms and issued catalogues displaying the furniture of many different makers. Many more relied upon traveling salesmen, commonly called "drummers," who traveled from town to town calling on shopkeepers and taking orders for the manufacturers whose lines they represented.[38]

Delivering frames made in the Doetsch & Bauer factory ca. 1908.
Mr. and Mrs. John Erland

Since the size and bulk of furniture prohibited the transportation of full-size samples, most drummers carried photographs displaying the pieces in each line. Early on, manufacturers learned the value of good photographs as a means of selling their products. Although a few roving photographers went from factory to factory, most Chicago manufacturers had to haul their samples to the studio of one of the "commercial photographers" who had located in the city's downtown business district by the early 1880s. This was also safer, since the ignition of the powder used in photography could easily set their wood-filled and sawdust-laden factories on fire.

Early in the 1870s, when steam presses began to lower the cost of printing, many manufacturers started to issue annual or semiannual catalogues filled with wood engravings or lithographs illustrating their furniture lines. A few firms, like chamber furniture manufacturers Sugg & Beiersdorf and F. Mayer, published large lithographed broadsides. In 1879, for example, F. Mayer supplied potential customers with a handsome poster illustrating its bedsteads and tables, accompanied by "a catalogue of unusual mechanical excellence of upwards of 50 pages, the representations being of unusual size."[39] One year earlier, the catalogue of parlor furniture manufacturer McDonough, Price & Company had been filled with brightly colored chromolithographs printed by the same process as the celebrated Currier & Ives prints.

As the mail-order market grew, catalogues were mailed out more frequently, accompanied by price lists. Some manufacturers published supplements featuring a particular item, such as folding beds or office desks. Some went even further—by 1897, the firm of S. Karpen & Bros. was issuing a monthly magazine called *Upholstered Furniture* to show off its myriad patterns.[40]

This advertisement from the April 1879 Furniture Trade Journal *stresses the "low rates of freight" for which unassembled furniture could be shipped.*

As competition increased, specialty furniture manufacturers began to publish elaborate catalogues that were sent all over the country.

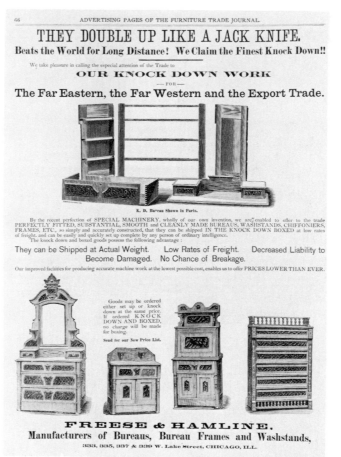

Cheaper and faster printing also encouraged the proliferation of weekly or monthly trade papers devoted to various aspects of the furniture business. Manufacturers of expensive furniture caught the attention of architects and decorators by advertising in *Inland Architect* or *Decorator and Furnisher*, while wholesale manufacturers reached those in the retail trade by publishing illustrations of their products in *American Cabinet Maker* (later *Furniture World*), *Furniture Worker*, and *Upholsterers' Journal*. At various times a *Daily Furniture Journal* and three weekly trade papers—*American Furniture Gazette* (which became *Furniture Journal* in 1908), *Western Furniture Trade*, and *Furniture Herald*—were published in Chicago. Several other publications maintained offices in the city.

Although catalogues and drummers were successful in reaching small dealers in outlying districts, most furniture buyers were eager to see the products for themselves before placing large orders. As early as 1878, efforts were under way to bring full-size samples to western furniture dealers. That year, for instance, a Pullman Palace car divided into showrooms was placed on the Chicago & North Western Railroad for the exclusive use of furniture drummers. "This car is an experiment," *American Cabinet Maker* explained. "It is intended to make stops of a day or two at advertised points, the drummer having the privilege of his section of the car in which to

Parlor furniture advertised by H. S. Carter & Co. in the Western Furniture Gazette, *August 1876.*

View from the Auditorium Tower on Michigan Avenue ca. 1895, showing furniture exhibition buildings along Michigan and Wabash avenues and the nearby tracks and terminal of the Illinois Central by the edge of the lake.

display his goods."[41] Manufacturers soon discovered, however, that it was both cheaper and more convenient to lure potential buyers to Chicago.

Between 1873 and 1891 retailers and wholesalers alike could display their furniture each fall in the Inter-State Industrial Exposition Building. When it was announced that this building would be torn down to make way for the 1893 World's Fair, manufacturers sponsored a spectacular exposition in July of 1891. Modeled after ones being held in Boston, New York, and Grand Rapids, it became a semiannual event. The source of continual rivalry between Chicago and Grand Rapids, its closest competitor, the Chicago expositions soon outdrew all other regional markets. Not to be outdone, Grand Rapids furniture manufacturers mounted extensive advertising campaigns promoting both their city and their products.

Expositions proved so successful in furthering sales that in the 1890s local manufacturers formed the Chicago Furniture Exposition Association to sponsor markets in July and January each year. Reorganized as the Chicago Furniture Market Association in 1909, the group publicized the biannual showing of merchandise and also published the "Chicago Order Book," a buyer's guide listing each manufacturer's location and products.[42]

At the time, manufacturers displayed their samples at their factories or in showrooms in several independently owned exposition buildings located along Wabash and Michigan avenues in the vicinity of the Illinois Central Railroad station. Two of the largest were the Chicago Furniture

The institution of installment buying greatly expanded the market for furniture.
CHS, gift of I. H. Hartman, Jr.

Exposition Building, opened in 1896 by chair manufacturer J. S. Ford, Johnson & Co. at 1433 Wabash Avenue, and the Chicago Furniture Exchange at 370 Wabash Avenue. By 1900 other large buildings in the area had been converted to use as showrooms by S. Karpen & Bros., Heywood Bros. & Wakefield, and the National Parlor Furniture Company.[43]

A huge Chicago Manufacturers' Exhibition Building, erected at 1319 South Michigan Avenue by real-estate developer James A. Pugh, offered some two hundred furniture manufacturers from various parts of the country an opportunity to display their samples year-round. The year 1912 saw the opening of the National Furniture Exchange of Chicago, a mammoth building at Twenty-second Street and the lakefront. Illinois Central tracks ran right into the building, relieving manufacturers of the burden of having their samples hauled to and from the station.

Many believed that expositions benefited the retail dealer and consumer more than the producer, since the introduction of new patterns twice a year raised costs and reduced profits. As *Furniture Worker* explained, frequent changes necessitated "the constant employment of expensive designers, the frequent issuing of new catalogues, the sacrifice in the disposition of previous styles, generally to auction houses, and the overloading of dealers' stocks."[44]

To make up for increased expenses, manufacturers were forced both to increase their productivity and to sell more goods. One of the chief means of stimulating sales was the adoption of the installment plan of payment. This enabled storekeepers and customers to purchase furniture with a small down payment, followed by regularly timed installments. Other manufacturers worked out arrangements with mail-order houses, whereby local catalogue dealers like Sears, Roebuck & Company, Montgomery Ward & Co., and the Hartman Furniture Company became large buyers of cheap and medium-priced goods. Attractively illustrated in thick catalogues soon christened "wish books," and seemingly inexpensive, mail-order furniture proved irresistible to thousands of rural buyers, much to the distress of the merchants in nearby towns.

In an effort to combat increasing sales to Chicago mail-order houses, retail dealers banded together in the early 1900s to pressure manufacturers not to sell to these houses. By then, Sears, Roebuck & Company and several other large catalogue dealers had acquired an interest in several factories and had exclusive marketing arrangements with numerous others. However, retailers did succeed in persuading a great many wholesale manufacturers to sell their furniture only through retail outlets and not directly to consumers.

While retailers fought mail-order houses and, later, department stores, wholesale manufacturers attempted to cope with the rising cost of raw materials, labor, and freight as well as with increasing competition. In an effort to stabilize prices, manufacturers in various branches of the industry began to organize themselves into associations or trusts to fix prices. By the end of 1899, local manufacturers had formed the Western Iron and Brass Bed Manufacturers Association, the Chicago Parlor Furniture Manufacturers Association, the Chicago Parlor Frame Mfrs. Association, the National Association of Chamber Suit and Case Work Manufacturers, and the Northwestern Table Association. Among the largest of the new confederations was the United States Chair Company, which counted many of Chicago's largest chair manufacturers among its members.[45] After 1907, interest in associations of this type cooled when Federal courts, enforcing the Sherman Antitrust Act of 1890, began to prosecute and heavily fine firms active in the "school furniture trust," which allegedly controlled 80 percent of the school desk and church pew business in the United States.

Prior to World War I, when nearly all furniture moved between cities by rail, the rates charged by railroads and forwarding agencies for shipping and handling furniture were critical for both manufacturers and retailers. Since rates were determined by volume—that is, by the number of railroad cars used rather than by the number of items shipped—it was in the interests of the manufacturers to consolidate their shipments. They were helped in this by forwarding agents who gathered together the products of the different manufacturers and repacked them into what were known as "mixed," or "pool," cars, to secure the cheaper carload rates.

By 1909 at least six Chicago forwarding firms were competing to perform this service. But instead of benefiting the manufacturers, the existence of so many forwarders often delayed shipment, sometimes for as long as six months, since each forwarder held his cars until they were full. To eliminate such delays and the trouble they caused, members of the Chicago Furniture Manufacturers' Association organized their own pool car consolidator, the Chicago Furniture Forwarding Company, and agreed to channel all of their shipments through this one agency.

Securing sheds at Sixteenth and Jefferson streets and hiring men, horses, and wagons, the Forwarding Company began operation early in 1910. Nonmember manufacturers in Chicago and factories located outside the city could use the facilities for the same fees as members, sharing the benefit of cheaper carload rates while reducing the costs and risks involved in transit.[46] This company remains in business today.

UPHOLSTERED PARLOR FURNITURE

CHAPTER 4

1873-1917

By the 1880s over half the output of Chicago's furniture factories consisted of upholstered parlor furniture. In 1879 *American Cabinet Maker* noted, "Chicago has acquired a reputation for cheap goods."[1] But by 1884, when *American Furniture Gazette* devoted its Fall Extra to the "Furniture Interests of Chicago," the editor could call attention to the "immense strides" made in the quality of the city's parlor goods:

> Formerly the finer grades of parlor furniture were exclusively "custom work" and made only to order, the classes of goods made at wholesale being mainly of medium and cheap grades. As the great bulk of consumers require mainly goods of the latter grades as a matter of course, they make up most of the production, but a heavy business is also done in the goods alluded to, many of the leading retail houses in all parts of the country buying all their upholstered goods without exception in Chicago. The traveling salesmen in this line visit every nook and corner of the country, and so excellent a reputation has Chicago parlor furniture that it sells very largely in cities like New York and Boston where are located the principal competing manufacturers.

Questioning why large quantities of Chicago-made frames and upholstered goods were increasingly shipped eastward, where they lost their competitive edge, the editor conceded that the answer lay "in the unusual aggressiveness of Chicago merchants," who did not hesitate to ship their goods "to the remotest quarters of the Union."[2]

During the 1880s some forty Chicago companies were classified as manufacturers of parlor furniture. Of these, approximately one-half were upholsterers who "manufactured" furniture by supplying stuffing, springs, and fabric. With the exception of a few firms like H. S. Carter & Co. and S. Karpen & Bros., which produced parlor furniture from start to finish, the remaining firms specialized in frames.

FRAME MAKERS

Ricke & Herrmann. 265 Division,
1862–67.
Henry Ricke. 1868–71.
H. Ricke & Co. 1873–74.
S. Ricke & Co. 1875–80.
Bruschke & Ricke. 1880–86.
Bruschke Furniture Co. 1886–89.

Listed in the 1860 city directory as a
carpenter, Henry Ricke teamed up with
William Herrmann in 1862 to make
frames for parlor furniture in a factory
on Division Street. After Ricke's death
the company was headed by his wife,
Sophie, who operated the factory with
the help of foreman Charles Bruschke.
He became the owner following her
death (ca. 1886).

Several patents for furniture designs
were granted to Bruschke & Ricke. By
1885, when its novel Good Luck line of
horseshoe-shaped gout stools and parlor frames attracted considerable comment, the firm had abandoned
medium-grade parlor frames and was
making mahogany and rosewood mantels, parlor frames, and even some
chamber furniture. In the 1880s
Bruschke & Ricke used paper labels to
identify their products.

By 1886 at least nine large factories were engaged in making parlor furniture frames in Chicago. Of these, two of the largest, Sugg & Beiersdorf and
H. S. Carter, had been founded before the fire. Most of the others were
established after 1877, when demand soared after prosperity began to return
to the agricultural regions surrounding Chicago following four years of
depression.

Made from hard, nonsplitting woods like walnut, cherry, ash, and
birch, most frames were sold "in the white" to manufacturers who upholstered the forms and finished the exposed wood in their shops. Others
were "finished to order" by the manufacturers for jobbers or retailers who
wanted special patterns or frames that they could keep on hand ready to
upholster for customers. New frame patterns were offered twice a year, in
the fall and in the spring, and in a wide variety of grades and price ranges.
Price depended upon the type of wood, the complexity of the carving, and
the kind of finish applied to the frame. Parlor sets and lounge frames dominated production, although the manufacture of lodge and church chairs,
student chairs, rockers, and footstools increased steadily as the city's population grew.

The largest factory devoted solely to making frames was that of Joseph
Zangerle, an Austrian-born cabinetmaker who had arrived in Chicago shortly
after the 1871 fire and had set up shop in a barn on Halsted Street between
North and Clybourn avenues with his brother, Peter. The brothers used
horse power by yoking a small pony to a long bar attached to the shaft that
operated their machinery; the pony turned the shaft by circling it continuously. In the afternoon, the same animal pulled the wagon used to deliver
the frames. Eventually ten Austrian artisans were employed by Zangerle,
who, like the majority of Chicago furniture makers, worked at the bench
alongside his men when he was not superintending shipping, keeping books,
and attending to sales and bill collections.[3]

By 1876 Zangerle's business had prospered sufficiently to enable him
to erect a four-story brick building at the corner of Dayton and Weed, where
he employed 50 men and a designer. By 1884 the Zangerle Manufacturing
Co. employed 160 and was the largest frame-making establishment in the
city. Zangerle goods were "as familiar in New York as in Chicago" and
were shipped "to England, to Australia, and as far south as civilization and
parlor furniture are consistent with each other."[4] However, poor health
forced Zangerle to retire from business and, deciding to return to Austria,
he sold the factory to the firm of Hafner & Schoen, which operated it until
1892.

In 1892 Zangerle returned to Chicago and in partnership with George
Peterson, a former employee, purchased the Northwestern Parlor Suit
Manufacturing Co., whose factory on Clybourn Avenue had been making
frames since 1879. Noted for designs that were "numerous and in good
taste," the Northwestern Parlor Suit Co. had recently expanded its four-
story brick factory to house new machinery "for cabinet makers and machine
men" and had added a spacious finishing room.[5] Reorganized as Zangerle
& Peterson in 1892, the firm produced parlor frames until it was purchased
by a larger firm, the Wells-Gardner Electronics Corp., in 1974.

Not far from the Zangerle factory on the city's North Side was the large establishment of S. Ricke & Company, specializing in wholesale parlor frames. Employing 120, the Ricke factory was unique during the 1870s in that it was owned by a woman, Sophie Ricke. Widow of cabinetmaker Henry Ricke, who had founded the firm in 1868, Mrs. Ricke operated the company under their own name from 1875 until 1880, when manager Charles Bruschke became co-owner and the firm was renamed Bruschke & Ricke. Like most frame producers, S. Ricke & Co. supplied the Western trade with carloads of frames shipped K. D. as well as assembled and ready for upholstering.[6] In 1881 *Trade Bureau* announced that the firm was making some of the most expensive frames in the market and enjoying "a very large trade, especially in the East."[7]

Long-lasting, though far smaller than Zangerle or Ricke's factory was the operation conducted by Herman Z. and his son, Herman W., Mallen. Arriving from Massachusetts in 1873, Herman Z. Mallen started a table factory in a small one-story building on Wentworth Avenue. Herman worked beside him for a while, "until the boredom of scraping and sanding table tops by hand was too much" and led him to resign.[8] After trying his hand at undertaking and carpentry, he went to the north woods of Wisconsin, where he worked in the lumber camps until 1876. At that point he decided to go into the furniture business for himself and returned to Chicago.

Approaching Charles Tobey at Thayer & Tobey, young Mallen secured an order for fifty black walnut parlor suites, for which he would be paid "$45.00 a suite." Armed with Tobey's order, Mallen purchased lumber on credit and arranged to cut the stock in a local planing mill.[9] His father agreed to let him assemble the frames in his table factory. Working together, the two Mallens completed the order and began an arrangement whereby father and son made parlor furniture under the name of H. Z. Mallen & Co. In 1898 the father retired, but under Herman W. Mallen's direction the company continued operation until 1911, when it added an upholstery division and began producing complete sets of parlor, library, and hall furniture.[10]

While most frame factories relied upon the practical skills and business acumen of one individual, at least three companies organized after the strikes of 1877 were cooperatives owned by the workers. One of these, the Illinois Furniture Company, remained in operation at the corner of Indiana (now Grand) and Kingsbury streets for at least ten years. The second firm, the Chicago Parlor Set Manufacturing Company, was organized in August 1877 by eleven men who were "all practical workmen."[11] A third cooperative enterprise, the Northwestern Parlor Suit Manufacturing Company, was headed by August and Robert Hausske and later by Joseph Doetsch before being purchased by Joseph Zangerle in 1892.[12]

Other companies manufacturing parlor frames included Stampen, Lee & Co.; Herman Barth & Co.; Ketcham & Rothchild; the Chicago Parlor Frame Works; and Poths & Co., succeeded by the Continental Manufacturing Company in 1888. Cabinetmakers operating frame factories included Anton Dietsch, William Gifford, Nils Jacobson, C. C. Holton, Zola Green, and John E. O'Mara. By 1903, when the Columbia Parlor Frame Company and the Western Parlor Frame Company had joined their ranks, Chicago was calling itself the "Parlor Frame Market of the World."[13]

Joseph Zangerle & Co. 663 North Halsted, 1871; 665 North Halsted, 1872–74; 25 Weed, 1875–78; 25–53 Weed, 1879–82.
Zangerle Manufacturing Co. 25–53 Weed, 1883–88; 99–103 Weed, 1889; 125 Weed, 1890.
Zangerle & Peterson Co. 687–701 (2172 after 1909) North Clybourn, 1892–1914; 2146 North Clybourn, 1915–72; 2701 North Kildare, 1973–74.

Joseph Zangerle (1847–1910) came to Chicago from the Tyrol in Austria in 1860, worked for various firms, and in 1871 began making parlor frames and patent rockers in a small shop on the city's North Side with his brother, Peter. By 1879 the number of cabinetmakers in the shop had grown from 10 to 115, making it the largest frame factory in Chicago.

In 1887 Zangerle returned to Austria, selling the business to William H. Hafner and John A. Schoen, wholesale upholsterers and former officers in the company. Hafner later sold out to Schoen, who in 1890 sold the factory to the Bush and Gerts Piano Company.

Returning to Chicago in 1892, Zangerle combined forces with George Peterson (1852–1933), whom he had employed as a woodcarver and designer, to purchase the bankrupt Northwestern Parlor Suit Manufacturing Co. Acquiring the company's five-story factory, the new firm manufactured parlor frames in all price ranges. After 1910, when Zangerle's son, A. Arthur (1882–1959), became president, the company added lines of wooden tables, desks, and other novelty furniture. Following his retirement in 1950, the firm became a division of the Wells-Gardner Electronics Corp., which until 1974 used the facilities to make radio cabinets.

Although cabinetmakers and upholsterers were equal partners in the production of upholstered furniture, frame makers were "the advance contingent of the trade," since they brought out new designs.[14] While the upholstery often caught the eye of dealer or homemaker and actually sold the piece, it was the wooden frame that determined its overall configuration and thus its style. Advertisements in *American Cabinet Maker* reveal a striking similarity among frames produced in Chicago and those made in Cincinnati, Grand Rapids, and New York. One is impressed, however, both by the number of Chicago advertisers and by the variety of designs they were making available in the late 1870s.

By 1878 frames in styles designated as French, Grecian, Eastlake, Queen Anne, and Turkish prevailed in advertisements, although catalogues issued by local manufacturers reveal that graceful rococo frames introduced at least a decade earlier were still available for conservative clientele. Rectilinear sofas, lounges, and chairs in a simplified Neo-Grec idiom were produced by most Chicago frame makers, who advertised them as "Grecian" or "French." Made of black walnut rather than ebony or rosewood, French parlor set and lounge frames were topped by crests of flattened palmettes, scrolls, or roundels, and occasionally by the carved bust of a goddess or warrior. Chairs and sofas were supported by sturdy-looking vase-shaped front legs, while lounges had scrolled bracket feet. Some sofas featured divided backs; others showed upholstered ovals or squares in the center surrounded by molding or openwork. Panels of highly polished ebonized veneer provided a touch of contrasting color on seat rail and crest, while incised lines followed the angular contours and created scrolls, palmettes, curlicues, flowers, or fanciful geometric motifs.

Queen Anne lounge with original brown plush upholstery. The frame is identical to one shown in the 1881 catalogue of Joseph Zangerle & Co.
h: 36" l: 70" d: 26"
CHS, gift of Suzanne Swift, 1969

English-inspired frames identified as Queen Anne were distinguished by rows of short turned spindles inset in the crest rail or supporting the arm rests. Grecian designs included lounges with scrolled backs and arms or chairs with X-shaped legs based on designs of Roman curule chairs. Increasingly popular as the eighties progressed Turkish frames were intended for overstuffed pieces that revealed woodwork only at base and legs. What were known as Egyptian frames bore a close resemblance to those with scroll-sawed fretwork labeled Japanese. Often ebonized with conventionalized designs traced or incised in gilt, both featured geometric motifs meant to recall the Orient or any faraway place. With the exception of exotics like Turkish and Egyptian, distinctions among the patterns were so subtle that most of the parlor furniture shown in frame makers' advertisements, if found today, would be categorized as Eastlake, a style extraordinarily popular in Chicago by 1876.

By the mid-1870s, frame makers were quite familiar with the design theories of English architect Charles Locke Eastlake, whose publication *Hints on Household Taste, Upholstery, and Other Details* (1868) was intended to serve as a practical guide to home furnishing and offered specific advice on the selection of every kind of household article from furniture and wallpaper to clothing and jewelry. A true believer in the value of good craftsmanship, Eastlake praised the simplicity, functionalism, and honesty of construction that he viewed as characteristic of medieval buildings and furnishings and advocated a return to these principles.[15]

Although *Hints on Household Taste* was readily available in Chicago, few manufacturers followed Eastlake's dictates precisely, preferring instead to add to frames what they took to be Eastlakian details. "In Chicago . . . the place is deluged with imperfectly-made imitations of medieval work, called 'Eastlake' furniture," wrote the city's correspondent for *American Architect and Building News* in the spring of 1876. "I can only say, Heaven save them, if Eastlake should come over here, and see such abominations! The berating which he gave the London shopkeepers would be nothing to it."[16]

While truer interpretations of Eastlake's teachings appeared in the warerooms of a few manufacturers, many continued to produce a wide range of frames distinguished primarily by their novelty. Reviewing the new patterns introduced in the spring of 1878, the editor of *American Cabinet Maker* noted: "Fantastic miracles of ugliness are the prevailing fashion in furniture. On closer inspection it will be seen that the present century has been a period of rapid oscillations of thought and feeling of which the mixed up Neo-Grec, Queen Anne and Eastlake imitations are merely the latest phase." A year later, in the spring of 1879, noting the addition of Louis XVI, Flemish, and Renaissance to the repertoire of styles, a writer for the same periodical playfully observed that manufacturers "do not confine themselves to strictly one style, but often combine the peculiarities of two or three different styles in one piece of furniture—making what a dealer laughingly calls the American Renaissance."[17]

PARLOR FURNITURE MANUFACTURERS

Better known to retail dealers and jobbers (the middlemen who bought from the manufacturers and sold to the retailers) were the firms that specialized in the upholstering of parlor furniture. Typically employing from 1 to 125 workmen, small upholstery shops and factories were scattered throughout the city in predominantly residential neighborhoods. Other, usually larger, operations could be found on the city's Near North Side, as well as southwest of the business district in the vicinity of South Canal Street.

Unlike frame makers, whose mobility was hampered by bulky woodworking machinery and the necessity of a power source, upholsterers could set up shop with a minimum of equipment. As long as they could find a large, well-lighted space, they could begin business with a tack hammer, a webbing stretcher, an assortment of curved and straight needles, shears, ripping tools, and skewer pins. Trestles or benches to support the work, a worktable for cutting fabric, a sewing machine for seams, and a hair-picking machine to loosen and fluff stuffing materials completed the well-equipped workshop.

Continuing a well-established tradition that still holds true today, most of Chicago's successful parlor furniture manufacturers started out in small shops. If they possessed basic skills, they could make a modest living. Those who had the winning combination of skills, marketing ability, and energy—and were blessed with good luck as well—went on to establish sizable factories employing several hundred workers in the mass production of parlor goods.

During the 1880s the largest concentration of parlor furniture manufacturers could be found on South Canal Street. Jacob Beiersdorf, a leading retail dealer and manufacturer for many years, erected a large five-story brick building in 1882 and gave up retailing to devote his entire attention to manufacturing parlor furniture (see page 29). Two blocks away was Gannon & McGrath's large four-story factory, employing about 100. Established in 1878 by Thomas J. Gannon and James J. McGrath, the firm made a medium grade of goods "very popular with the northwest and western trade." Across the street from this firm was the new four-story headquarters of The Hafner & Schoen Furniture Co., whose origins went back a decade to 1873, when the firm had been established by Wendelin Seng and William Hafner.

Located in the same area of Canal Street, between 1879 and 1881, R. Deimel & Bros. chose a site on Wabash Avenue for its imposing brick, stone, and terra-cotta building, completed in 1883. Brothers Rudolph, Joseph, and Simon Deimel had begun manufacturing parlor furniture together in 1877. By 1884 the factory employed an average of 275, who produced "everything coming under the head of upholstered furniture," from frames noted for originality to upholstery distinguished by "handsome and novel effect."[18] It turned out that some of the Deimels' success was due to questionable business practices, a matter that came to public attention when the firm declared bankruptcy in 1890. Nevertheless, in 1891 Rudolph and Joseph Deimel resumed business as the National Parlor Furniture Co.

Prominent among Chicago parlor furniture manufacturers whose careers could be considered "typical of what American opportunity has done for energetic, thrifty" immigrants[19] was Solomon Karpen, a cabinetmaker and upholsterer who, with his brother, Oscar, founded S. Karpen & Bros. in the summer of 1880. Born in Posen, Germany, Solomon and Oscar had been brought to Chicago in 1872 by their father, Moritz, a third-generation cabinetmaker, along with their seven brothers. Before leaving Germany,

Solomon, the oldest son, had been trained in his father's shop. In Chicago he was apprenticed to an upholsterer, while Oscar worked as a finisher in a local furniture factory.

The employees of R. Deimel & Bros. photographed with some of their products in the 1880s.
CHS, gift of the Chicago Furniture Manufacturers' Association, 1978

In 1880, when Solomon was twenty-two, the two young men began making upholstered furniture in the basement of a building at the corner of Milwaukee Avenue and Tell Street, not far from the family's home on Emma Street. In 1883 they relocated their growing factory and showroom in two loft spaces on West Lake Street. By 1887 they had secured a spacious showroom on Wabash Avenue and a new factory building was under way at the intersection of Wood and Ellen streets near Wicker Park on the city's Northwest Side. Brothers Adolph, Isaac, William, Benjamin, Michael, and Leopold had joined the firm, so that in 1894, when the youngest brother, Julius, began to work in the factory, all nine Karpens were engaged in the family business.

Looking back to these early days some fifty years later on the anniversary of the firm's founding, Isaac Karpen recalled the simplicity of their first equipment and related how, lacking money for a wagon, "their own strong backs and sturdy legs had to serve as the vehicles to carry their sample lines of furniture to the photographer."[20] At the time, Isaac was serving as foreman of the upholstery shop, while Oscar supervised the making of frames. Solomon attended to the buying of raw materials, William kept the books, Adolph specialized in sales, and Julius took care of credit and correspondence at the factory. Leopold supervised the city trade, while Michael was a "commercial traveler" representing the company in the northern and southwestern states.[21]

S. Karpen & Bros. 204–5 Lake, 1883–86; 42 South Canal, 1887–88; 298–304 Wabash, 1889–91; 154–55 Michigan, 1892–09; Twenty-second and Union (became 636 West Cermak), 1910–52.

From 1900 to World War I, Karpen offered a wide range of mission chairs and sofas, along with overstuffed parlor suites, folding bed lounges, Morris chairs, and Art Nouveau, colonial, and various period adaptations. After 1914, when Karpen acquired the former Ford Johnson plant, the firm employed prison labor to hand-weave rattan and reed furniture in that plant's premises in Michigan City, Indiana. During the 1920s the firm introduced a line of wooden Windsor adaptations that included not only chairs but day beds and breakfast-room suites.

In addition to upholstering parlor furniture, S. Karpen & Bros. manufactured church and lodge furniture and seats for streetcars and buses. Karpen goods were priced in the medium to high range, although after 1910 medium-priced offerings prevailed. From 1897 on, Karpen pieces were identified by metal tags bearing the name and accompanied by a Certificate of Guarantee.

As the original Karpen brothers died or retired from the business, the firm shrank and became less active in the industry. In 1952, when S. Karpen & Bros. was in the hands of a liquidator,

By aggressively adopting the most efficient woodcarving and upholstering machinery and by resorting to innovative advertising, displays, and shipping techniques, the Karpens transformed their operation from a tiny basement workroom into "the largest factory in the world making upholstered furniture" in just twenty years.[22] Truly leaders in the industry, they introduced machines and procedures that not only kept Chicago in the forefront in production but aided in revolutionizing the entire furniture industry.

Realizing that quantity production rested upon the efficient use of machinery, the Karpens and their workers not only tested every new woodworking machine and mechanical appliance that came on the market but also devised new ones. In 1899 the firm was among the first to install A. Freschl's Novelty Tufting Machines to quickly complete the backs and seats of less expensive couches. Noting that they could be operated by boys, *Furniture World* claimed that one such machine could take the place of twenty-five skilled workmen.[23] By 1899 the firm controlled the patents for the tufting machine and had sold "shop rights" to seventeen other manufacturers.[24]

In 1900 two Karpen employees, Frank Streich and Charles L. Rurks, invented a spindle machine that could carve eight duplicates at one time. S. Karpen & Bros. not only put the machine to use in its own factory but set up a separate enterprise, the Universal Automatic Carving Machine Company, to produce and sell it, advertising it as the "greatest labor saving device ever invented in wood-working machinery."[25]

Karpen's decorating, tufting, and carving machines substantially reduced the cost of labor while increasing production. They also made possible such a wide range of styles and products that the firm truly deserved its motto, "Makers of New Patterns."[26] By 1901 illustrations in the company's monthly catalogue ran the gamut from low-priced couches to ornately carved and gilded Art Nouveau and Louis XVI creations, aptly described as the "most expensive and daring designs ever attempted in carved furniture in America"[27] (see page 195).

While convinced of the necessity of using the latest labor-saving machinery, the Karpens made a conscious effort not to sacrifice quality for speed and tried to keep the morale of their workers high. Speaking to members of the Chicago Furniture Manufacturers' Association in 1897, Adolf Karpen chastised his fellow manufacturers for "appealing to the pocketbook too much, and not enough to the eye and soul. He said there was too much cheapness in the construction of furniture nowadays, and not enough of the ideal and artistic."[28] In their own factory the Karpens employed both staff and free-lance designers and concentrated the skills of their workmen on those processes best done by hand, such as joining, finishing, spring setting, and upholstering.[29]

The Karpens' manufacturing plant and salesrooms were also organized along the most modern industrial lines. In 1897, when the firm moved into a new plant covering six acres between Twenty-first and Twenty-second streets, Union Street, and the river, its mammoth facility was praised as a model of efficiency. Although it resembled one large structure, the factory was actually composed of three closely connected buildings, each of which housed a different stage of its operations: woodworking, upholstering, and shipping. Resembling a railroad freight house, Karpen's shipping room had a spur of the Chicago, Burlington & Quincy Railroad running the entire length of the shed. Within that space, workers could load thirteen cars with furniture at one time. The facility not only served the factory but functioned as a clearinghouse for "mixed cars" filled with furniture from Eastern and Midwestern manufacturers destined for dealers in the West. Within only six months after the scheme was put into operation in 1899, some 400 cars had been loaded.[30]

To house its main offices and showrooms, the Karpen family purchased the old Richelieu Hotel on Michigan Avenue in 1896 and transformed it into the Karpen Building. Displaying its own goods on the first

the Schnadig Corporation bought the name and plant facilities. The firm continues to use the Karpen name on one of its lines of upholstered furniture.

The nine Karpen brothers in 1888. From The Trade Bureau, *March 10, 1888.*
Library of Congress

two floors, the Karpens rented the upper stories to other furniture manufacturers to use as showrooms. In 1918, when the Standard Oil Co. acquired this property, the showrooms were moved to the new Karpen Building on Wabash Avenue at the corner of Eighth Street.

In 1900 S. Karpen & Bros. became the first upholstered furniture manufacturer in the wholesale trade to appeal directly to the consumer. To create an identity, the company advertised heavily in such leading homemaker magazines as *Ladies' Home Journal, Good Housekeeping, Vogue, Saturday Evening Post,* and *Harper's Bazar,* calling attention to its solid construction, quality workmanship, and moderate price. To prove that each piece was "honestly constructed of dependable material throughout," the firm supplied a Certificate of Guarantee stressing its use of sound lumber, strong springs, and fine American fabrics.[31] To reinforce the guarantee, a metal nameplate bearing the words "Karpen Guaranteed Upholstered Furniture Chicago" was attached to the frame of each piece. This trademark proved a most effective form of advertising, fellow manufacturers later recalled, for it "compelled national interest in their products and absolute confidence in the integrity of their house."[32]

An equally well-known manufacturer of parlor goods, Peter E. Kroehler, founder of the Kroehler Manufacturing Company, possessed an aptitude for accounting and an extraordinary talent for promotion. Before the age of forty, he had transformed the Naperville Lounge Company from a firm making overstuffed couches in an abandoned Naperville skating rink into a modern corporation operating factories in Illinois, New York, and Ohio. During the 1890s, when he worked his way from manager to president of Naperville Lounge, Kroehler specialized in supplying couches for use as giveaways with orders of Wrigley chewing gum or Quaker Valley silver plate. After devising a short-cut method for tufting Turkish couches, he sold them at the unheard-of price of six for $25, earning the nickname of "Six-for-a-Quarter Pete" among those in the industry. By 1902 skillful maneuverings and quantity sales had allowed him to buy out his partners and create a new firm, selling half-interest to one of his largest customers, Sears, Roebuck & Company. Just twelve years later Kroehler contracted to buy back Sears's half-interest, paying the mail-order firm forty times its original investment.[33]

FRAME STYLES AND FABRIC COVERINGS

Since few examples of upholstered seating furniture attributable to specific factories have survived from the late nineteenth century, it is necessary to examine the catalogues issued by manufacturers to see the parlor furniture of which Chicagoans were so proud. Illustrated with woodcuts, the catalogues contain an amazing assortment of styles and patterns. Here Eastlake, Turkish, Half-Turkish, Egyptian, and French vie with Queen Anne "têtes" and chairs, all available in a choice of plain or striped terry, plush or coteline, leather or haircloth, tapestry or carpet. Faced with this splendid array, one can easily understand why some chose to furnish each room in their house in a different style.

At first glance, few of the upholstered pieces appear to have much in common with one another. But closer examination reveals that they are, in fact, variations on several basic styles, for beneath the often profuse ornamentation, standardization was the rule. Often one parlor frame varied from another only in the type or amount of ornament applied at the arm or crest rail. It was up to the upholsterer to provide the final form—through stuffing, fabric, and trim—to create the illusion of choice so important to the house furnisher, and vital in selling the product.

Chicago manufacturers excelled in this area, creating extraordinary surface interest through the use of a variety of upholstery techniques rarely used today. Backs were channeled, piped, pleated, or tufted in patterns resembling diamonds, half-diamonds, or stars. Wide, rich bands of pleated "ruffling" edged seats, arms, and backs; soft, twisted cord with the appearance of rope called attention to curves and contours. Splashy floral carpet or gaudy striped terry emphasized the practicality of lounges, while wide panels of colorful Berlin wool embroidery drew attention to the sloping lines of easy chairs designed for ladies.

As early as 1871 an article on "Style" in *Cabinet Maker* recommended that fashionable folk order parlor suites but "have no two pieces alike." Instead, "have two sofas—one long enough for reclining, the other a little confidante for two—and choose four easy chairs of various shapes and sizes, for people of different sizes, instead of the regulation for two armchairs and four straight-backed uncomfortable ones."[34] Yet the regulation seven-piece parlor suite persisted until the end of the century—perhaps due as much to its social role as to fashion. In design and in use, the parlor suite enforced social distinctions and constituted a diagram of the middle-class Victorian family. While the focal point, the sofa, embodied the principle of sociability, the large armchair—the gentleman's chair—reflected the dominant position of the father. Like the mother in the family, the daintier lady's chair served as an intermediary between the largest chair and the group of smaller offspring.[35]

By the mid-1870s a wide variety of "odd" chair and ottoman frames and upholstery matched or complemented the standard seven-piece set. Corner chairs with low backs and arms forming a right angle (destined, of course, to sit in corners) could be found in a variety of shapes and finishes, as could window chairs, which featured low, rounded backs ideally suited for bay window alcoves. Large and comfortable, student or easy chairs with sloping backs and wide seats were designed for reading or relaxing in parlor, sitting room, or library. Conversation chairs were two seats coupled on an S-plan so that sitters shared the same chair yet faced in opposite directions. As McDonough, Price & Company's 1876 catalogue suggested,

Walnut chair frame with carved dog's-head arms made by Joseph Zangerle & Co.
h: 39½" w: 29¼" d: 22¾"
CHS, given in honor of Theodore Tieken by his daughter, Nancy B. Tieken, 1980

Closeup of the carved dog's head on the chair frame from Joseph Zangerle's factory.

"Dog Head" student chair with a walnut frame and plush upholstery made in Chicago in the early 1880s.
h: 38¼" w: 28¼" d: 20½"
CHS, gift of Elizabeth May, 1980

"It is in style, taste and comfort to have odd chairs any place in the house, particularly in the parlor and sitting room."[36]

Joseph Zangerle offered something for every taste and pocketbook in his 1881 *Illustrated Catalogue,* with eight models of student chairs ranging from a plain one with only a touch of incised carving on the seat rail to an elaborate one with curule legs and sloping arms elaborately carved with acanthus leaves and a wooden tassel.[37] Medium priced but very appealing was "Student Chair, No. 3," featuring arm supports playfully carved in the form of beagles' heads with soulful eyes and protective collars. Obviously popular in its day, Zangerle's "Dog Head Chair" and its numerous variations are among the few easily identifiable examples of Chicago-made seating furniture commonly found in the Midwest today.

Two rare parlor furniture catalogues issued by McDonough, Price & Company and its successor, McDonough, Wilsey & Co., and printed using chromolithography, reveal the striking color combinations common on Chicago-made furniture of the late 1870s. As the company's 1876 *Book of Illustrations* made clear, "Combinations of Clarets and Crimsons, Browns and Blues, Browns and Scarlets, and Drabs and Blues are very handsome, and in taste." Illustrating this, one "large and extra fine suite" displayed a covering of gray haircloth trimmed in scarlet; another was "covered with purple terry, and trimmed with purple plush, with black and gold gimp and cord." For those restrained by conservative taste or restricted by limited means, "a very nice, cheap suite, with veneered polished panels" looked quite handsome done up in black or gray haircloth edged with Vandyke gimp.[38]

Haircloth (and imitation haircloth for cheaper sets) remained a com-

Some of Chicago's stockyard purveyors used cattle horns to create novelty furniture like this chair.
h: 48¼" w: 42½" d: 19"
Clifford and Susan Haka

mon upholstery fabric for medium-grade parlor furniture until the end of the century. By the early 1870s, however, it had been abandoned by the fashionable, who preferred the softer, richer fabrics like plush, terry, and cashmere, that had become available in a variety of brilliant colors. But colors in the West remained subdued, with darker ones like seal brown, claret, olive drab, and purple prevailing. This was due more to "local causes" than to style. As *American Cabinet Maker* explained in 1876: "The smokey atmosphere which surrounds Chicago and the excessive amount of soft coal that is burned, are causes which make everything that is the least exposed blackened and soiled. Upholstered furniture being of those goods which are of a necessity liable to this exposure is made with the darker colors and the shades that this soot which permeates everything cannot so badly affect."[39]

It was around the same time that another by-product of Western enterprise—the horns of cattle, buffalo, and elk—began to be used by the Tobey Furniture Company to form the legs, arms, and backs of upholstered parlor furniture. In 1876 a parlor sofa and chair with seats upholstered in maroon plush and frames constructed from the horns of Texas longhorn cattle caused considerable comment at Chicago's industrial exposition.[40] By 1881 Tobey had become "well known as manufacturers of chairs formed of cattle's horn."[41] Two years later, a reporter from *Inland Architect and Builder* expressed delight at seeing innovative horn furniture displayed among the more familiar-looking household goods. "Everything is antique, or copies the antique," he wrote, "excepting those chairs with polished horn for backs, and they are as modern as the Texas cowboy and as inimitable."[42]

Only a few months later, in the fall of 1883, a particularly original suite was exhibited by Tobey or another local manufacturer. "A curious set of furniture, in which the hide, horns, forelocks and fetlocks of Hungarian steers were variously utilized, was exhibited recently by one of our art

Upholstered parlor furniture available from J. R. Sheridan & Co. between 1886 and 1888.

CHICAGO FURNITURE

firms; the silken locks became fringes, the polished horns arms and legs, while the hide formed a very ornamental upholstering, with its silver-grey and black hair."[43]

No longer a novelty by the early 1890s, horn furniture was manufactured in great quantity by Wolf, Sayer & Heller, suppliers of butcher's equipment at the corner of Fulton and Peoria streets. Here, in addition to "Meat Market, Sausage Room and Packing House Outfits," workers produced an incredible variety of "ornaments and novelties in horn goods" in the form of clock holders, hall racks, footrests, tables, and parlor furniture.[44] Built primarily for exhibition and for sale to Easterners, furniture made of buffalo, deer, elk, and Texas cattle horns became increasingly popular as an evocation of the spirit of the Old West, designed to summon up visions of buffalo hunts and cattle roundups.

By 1876 overstuffed, or Turkish, seating furniture was commonly found among the tightly tufted models of parlor furniture. Upholstered "all over" with none of the wood frame showing, it was often covered with Turkish rugs, brocatelles (a form of brocade), crushed or plain plushes, or raw silk. Backs and arms were heavily tufted, deep fringe often hung from the base of the frame to the floor, and tassels dangled from armrests or each corner of the back. Exotic in form, covered with gaudy fabrics, and beguilingly soft, this furniture was meant to suggest the decadent luxury of Turkish palaces and harems, so imaginatively portrayed by writers and painters of this period.

The unprecedented comfort and resiliency inherent in such furniture was due to helical wire springs. Used since the mid-nineteenth century, spiral springs of iron (and later of tempered steel) were placed between the webbing foundation and the stuffing to produce a softer seat than could be

Upholsterers completing parlor furniture in the store of retail dealer John M. Smyth in 1892. From John M. Smyth's Town Market, *1892.*

created by using only hair, moss, or other padding. During the 1880s the use of spiral springs, deep tufting, and luxurious fabrics increased to such a degree that the frame was reduced to a support system with little if any wood showing.

Less expensive parlor furniture, like that available from J. R. Sheridan's factory on Lake Street between 1886 and 1888, imitated the style of the seventeenth-century upholstered hall furniture at Knole Park, Kent, in England, which had been illustrated in Eastlake's popular *Hints on Household Taste*. Sheridan's large printed broadside, offered in lieu of a catalogue, depicts a wide range of richly upholstered "smooth, reliable made goods" whose rectilinear form is emphasized by horizontal bands of upholstery in contrasting colors and patterns.[45] Shallow button tufting appears on the arms and crests of some of the suites and odd chairs, although the majority show smooth upholstery. Novelty printed and textured fabrics and trims rather than expensive, hand-tied tufts create surface interest. Designed for those who sat in the parlor—by choice or for lack of a separate sitting room— standard suites now included "one sofa, one large patent rocker, one easy chair, and four side chairs."[46] The rocker referred to was one of a growing number of pieces of patent furniture that were to fill the catalogues and homes during the last three decades of the nineteenth century.

PATENT FURNITURE

1873-1917

In 1878 the proliferation of folding lounges, patent rockers, and unusual combinations emanating from Chicago's furniture factories caused the *Trade Bureau*, a New York-based paper covering the furniture and upholstery industry, to comment: "Chicago is possessed of very many unique things, but probably the power of her citizens to devise and construct remarkable affairs is the most wonderful. Inventive genius is not an exclusive Yankee qualification, unless it be admitted that the original race which bears that name extends throughout the entire country. And so Chicago is pretty sure to furnish its quota to the records and revenue of the Patent Office."[1]

Between 1870 and 1900, when patent furniture was in its heyday, some 1,200 Chicagoans were granted patents for furniture or furniture-related items by the U. S. Patent Office.[2] Some of the inventions, like Robert N. Barger's Combined Folding Bed, Billiard Table, and Settee (1892), Joseph Cardona's Combination Table, Bathtub and Washtub (1886), or Frederick Brown's Patented Electromagnet Therapeutic Chair (1890) probably never made it into large-scale production.[3] Others, like Beiersdorf and Bunker's platform rocker spring, Henry Carter's folding lounge, or Andrews's folding parlor beds, were produced by the thousands, perhaps even the tens of thousands.

Both practical and pretentious, comfortable yet contrived, patent furniture was, according to Siegfried Giedion's *Mechanization Takes Command*, "the furniture of the engineer," designed to meet the needs and wants of a growing middle class confined in the limited quarters of an urban environment. In his pioneering study of nineteenth-century patent furniture, Giedion stressed the portability, adaptability, and comfort inherent in patent furniture, attributing its development to "anonymous engineers" who approached furniture design from an entirely new point of view.

Patent furniture consists of types evolved by the middle brackets for their own urgent needs. Wealthy people had no call for a lounge convertible into a cradle, or a bed convertible into a wardrobe. They owned both the space and the means to satisfy their needs in other ways. The patent furniture arose, in America at least, from the demands of an intermediate class that wished, without overcrowding, to bring a modicum of comfort into a minimum of space. The chair that converts into a lounge, the bed that converts into a wardrobe, the bedroom that converts into a living room, were more naturally and more thoughtfully suited to the two or three rooms of the rising middle-class than was the heavy furniture of the ruling taste.[4]

The idea of convertible furniture was not new; folding beds, chair-tables, and fold-up chairs had been in use for centuries. But during the last half of the nineteenth century, multi-purpose furniture was new to the middle class, which was buying it for the first time.[5] The production of patent furniture proved an important phase in the development of Chicago's furniture industry. Moreover, it was one that benefited both the industry and the quality of everyday life in the home and in the workplace.

One of the first pieces of furniture to undergo improvements was the rocking chair, whose cumbersome arc-shaped rockers were replaced by a base or supporting frame. By rocking in place using a variety of coiled spring mechanisms, it saved wear and tear on carpets and walls. Made by the same manufacturers who produced upholstered parlor furniture, platform rockers resembled easy chairs and featured fashionable frames and fabrics.

Comfortable and practical, platform rockers—as can be seen from the decorating manuals of the day—clearly met the needs of "the million." But alas, as *Beautiful Homes* (1878) indicated, "the million" could least afford them. "These patent rocking-chairs are far too expensive to be purchased by the "million" who most require them, consequently they are never seen save in the houses of the wealthy. . . . We would say, though, to every woman who can possibly raise the amount of money required for it, to purchase one of the patent rocking-chairs (for her sitting-room at least), for she will find it money well spent."[6] Rockers may not have been within the reach of all, but Chicago manufacturers were working hard to remedy the situation. That year, the local representative of *American Cabinet Maker* called attention to the fact that "The variety of patent rockers are still on the increase and the country is literally flooded with good, bad, and good-for-nothing rockers."[7]

Chicago, endowed with a host of practiced upholsterers, mechanics, and tinkerers, contributed its share to the patent rocker craze that reached a peak in the 1880s. Nearly every parlor furniture manufacturer offered some form of "patent" platform rocker. These were either entirely of the manufacturer's invention or incorporated, through a licensing agreement, some part or mechanism devised by someone else.

As Siegfried Giedion pointed out in *Mechanization Takes Command*, between 1850 and 1890 "America takes the lead and raises patent furniture to a stature never approached in Europe. . . . Toward 1860, in pace with the growing activity of invention, an overwhelming rush sets in that culminates, within a decade, in a high degree of technical proficiency."[8] During the 1870s, in particular, all manner of springs and mechanisms were developed to connect the rocking frame to the stationary base. The devices that proved successful were often based on very simple solutions, such as the one patented jointly by Chicagoans Jacob Beiersdorf and William I. Bunker in 1879.

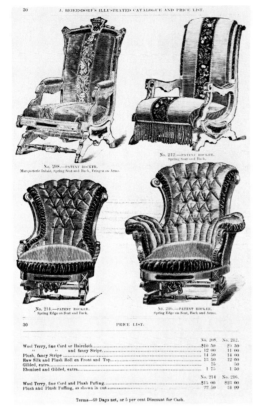

Patented spring for platform rockers marketed by Jacob Beiersdorf and William Bunker. From American Furniture Gazette *Fall Extra 1884.*

Patent rockers from J. Beiersdorf's Illustrated Catalogue and Price List *for 1879.*

Beiersdorf and Bunker's B & B Patent Platform Rocker Spring was "an alarmingly simple coiled spring which attached at its top to the rocking frame and at its bottom to the platform base at the pivot point between the two pieces of the platform rocker."[9] In fact, it was so simple and so successful that Beiersdorf, the parlor furniture manufacturer, and Bunker, the inventor, lost no time in organizing the Rocker Spring Company as an adjunct to Beiersdorf's Wabash Avenue factory to market the springs to other furniture manufacturers.

By 1882 advertisements placed by the Rocker Spring Company claimed that B & B springs were already in use "on more than 60,000 Platform Rockers." The advertisements explained: "These springs measure two and one half inches in diameter, are made of the best oil tempered steel, are practically one piece, easily put on any Platform Rocker, and will not SING or SQUEAK, being perfectly mute; they are so simple that they cannot get out of order, and are nearly indestructible."[10] By the fall of 1883 the company had introduced a two-coil Double Patent Spring designed for Turkish rockers, and sales of their standard spring had reached a "Victorious 350,000!"[11]

In addition to being a partner in the Rocker Spring Company, Jacob Beiersdorf supervised the J. Beiersdorf Company, which manufactured upholstered furniture until 1884. He also served as president of Sugg & Beiersdorf, manufacturers of chamber and parlor furniture, until 1887. William I. Bunker, a practical mechanic who, by 1899, held some sixty patents for rocking chair attachments, springs, and bicycle gears, served as presi-

The B & B patent rocker spring enabled the arc-shaped chair base to rock on a stationary platform.
CHS, gift of Jane Dunham, 1981

Workmen in W. Seng and Co.'s factory in 1894. Owner Wendelin Seng (wearing suit) is seated at left in the front; his son, Frank (in vest), is standing in the center.
Francis A. Seng

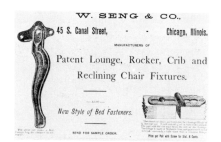

W. SENG & CO.
45 S. Canal Street, - - Chicago, Illinois.
MANUFACTURERS OF
Patent Lounge, Rocker, Crib and Reclining Chair Fixtures.
—— ALSO ——
New Style of Bed Fasteners.
SEND FOR SAMPLE ORDER.

W. Seng & Co. Clybourn & Halsted, 1872; 26–28 Chicago, 1873–75.
Seng, Schoen, & Co. 292 State, 1876–78; 265–67 South Canal, 1879–83.
W. Seng & Co. 224 East Washington,

dent of the Rocker Spring Company and later founded the Bunker Saddle Company, which produced seats for bicycles.

Platform rockers and folding lounges also attracted the attention of upholsterer Wendelin Seng, who, with his sons, founded W. Seng & Co., advertised as "Machinists to the Furniture Industry." Born in Prussia, where he had been trained as a weaver, Seng had migrated to Chicago in 1856. After working as a laborer for a year, he became an upholsterer and mattress maker, building up a sizable business by the 1870s.

Intrigued by the mechanics of adjustable furniture, Seng in 1872 patented a cast-iron leg for folding bed lounges,[12] which he incorporated into his Patent Extension Bed Lounge. Around the same time he developed an Adjustable Summer Rocking Chair, which, displayed alongside his bed lounge at the first Inter-State Industrial Exposition, received special notice in the *Souvenir* booklet.

CHICAGO FURNITURE

This chair rocks on a framework which is immovable upon the floor. The bottom of the chair rests upon a bellows, from which is attached an air tube, the same running up the back of the chair and over the head of the occupant, who, when engaged in rocking, is gently fanned without exertion, as the rocking inflates the bellows and from which the air escapes through the tube and is used for the purpose already stated. To a close observer the chair only presents the appearance of an ordinary luxurious upholstered parlor rocker, all the novelties being entirely out of sight.[13]

When shortly after the exposition John Schoen joined Seng and his partner, William Hafner, in the manufacture of parlor furniture, Seng began to devote more and more of his time to the production of iron hardware for the company's popular patent lounges and rocking chairs. In 1877 Hafner and Schoen took over the daily operation of the factory, while Seng set up a small company to produce mechanisms for a variety of patent furniture, to which he soon gave his entire attention. By then, it seems, local manufacturers had discovered that it was cheaper to buy furniture fixtures from Seng than to make them in their own shops.

Seng worked in a series of small workshops until 1887, when he was joined by two of his sons, Wendelin and Julius. W. Seng & Co. then moved into a spacious factory on South Canal Street. In 1892, when ill health led the senior Seng to retire from business, leadership of the firm passed to his oldest son, Frank J. Seng, who had worked as a bookkeeper at Sugg & Beiersdorf for the previous five years. By then the foundations had been laid for a family concern that would continue to make iron (and eventually steel) fixtures for the furniture industry until 1973, when it was bought by Hoover Universal.

Beginning in the 1870s, middle-class Chicagoans could not only rock in the sitting room and parlor but could also recline in one of the myriad adjustable chairs offered to the public. Sophisticated versions of the folding chair, adjustable chairs allowed one to sit up, lean back, lie flat, elevate or lower one's feet, and return to a sitting position. This was accomplished by the use of ratchets, levers, concealed legs, or other patent mechanisms. The simple, inexpensive construction of adjustable chairs, first developed for invalids, doctors, or barber chairs, made them suitable for mass production.

At first these adjustable chairs were all similar in construction. Before long, however, manufacturers developed a whole series of variations designed to meet the needs of particular professions. In 1867, for example, Theodore A. Kochs of Chicago patented a simple tilting barber chair equipped with an adjustable headrest and a back that pivoted on an angle base, allowing a person "to sit up straight while having the hair dressed, or lean back while being shaved."[14] A separate footrest, resembling a kneeling bench, provided support for the feet. Constructed of wood, the frame was distinguished from other patent barber chairs by elegant swan-shaped armrests. A manufacturer of barber supplies, Kochs supplied frames for the chair to local upholsterers and furniture dealers, who offered them in a variety of sturdy upholstery fabrics, among them Brussels carpet, haircloth, and mohair plush. Obviously popular, they appeared in the catalogues of the Chicago firm of Eastman & Wilkins and other manufacturers

1878–86; 11–13 South Canal, 1887–96. *The Seng Company.* 86–90 East Ohio, 1897–1900; 47–51 (1450–68 after 1909) Dayton, 1901–73.

Wendelin Seng (1828–1896), founder of the company that became the "machinists to the furniture industry," began making metal mechanisms for furniture shortly after the Great Fire. He soon held numerous patents for the devices used on rocking chairs, folding lounges, reclining chairs, extension tables, and other pieces. Specialties included hinges and legs for folding lounges, forerunners of today's sofa-bed, swivel supports for office chairs, and springs for platform rockers, reclining chairs, and mattresses. Later the firm introduced metal bed rails, emphasizing its hygienic and constructional superiority over wooden slats, and added all types of metal parts used in furniture making and allied industries.

After Wendelin Seng retired, the company was headed by son Frank J. Seng (1869–1946), and then by grandson Francis A. Seng. In 1912 The Seng Company joined with the Kroehler Manufacturing Co., S. Karpen & Bros., and Pullman Couch Company to form the Davenport Bed Makers Association to advertise and promote the sale of this product, which, redesigned in the 1950s, remains a popular item today. For many years, the firm published *Seng Furniture Facts* annually and a monthly trade bulletin, *Good Fixtures.*

In 1973 the 100-year-old firm was sold to Hoover Universal. At the time, the Seng company employed 500 and operated factories in Chicago; High Point, North Carolina; Los Angeles, California; and Litchfield, Kentucky.

Barber chair with swan's-head armrests and footrest patented and manufactured by Theodore A. Kochs during the 1870s.
Chair, h: 45" w: 27" d: 32"
Footrest, h: 26" w: 17" d: 26"
CHS, purchase, 1960

Wilson Adjustable Chair patented by George Wilson in 1870–71.
National Museum of American History

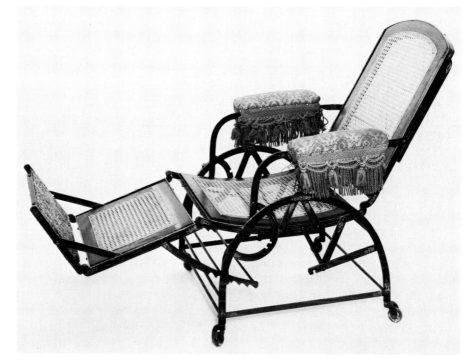

until the 1890s, when the design was superseded by chairs mounted on a column that permitted them to both recline and revolve.

By the end of the 1870s, adjustable chairs designed for invalids were being turned into furniture for use in the home through the addition of decorative upholstery and an ornamental frame. Chicago's three most successful manufacturers of reclining chairs—George Wilson, DeBert Hartley, and George F. Child—did just that, combining the manufacture of parlor

Reclining chair with walnut frame and original horsehair upholstery patented by F. W. Lange in 1869.
h: 39¼" w: 23" d: 43" (open)
Mrs. Ethel D. Hintz

and invalid chairs "for comfort in health or sickness."[15] One of the first to adopt the principles underlying the design of the invalid chair to furniture for everyday was Wilson, who, in 1870 and 1871, patented two variations of a folding chair whose angular frame was composed of interlaced iron straps riveted together to form a back, seat, and footrest. Two semicircles of iron supported the seat and allowed the chair to rock or swing; optional wheels permitted the chair to roll. Rivets, which worked as hinges, adjusted the back and footrest, which could be set at ninety-degree angles or lowered to the same plane as the seat. A single lever allowed the occupant to control the mechanism without rising from the chair.[16] Known as the Wilson Adjustable Chair, it was available inset with cane or "upholstered in striped terry and reps" with armrests encircled with fringe.[17]

Wilson exhibited his chair at the 1873 Inter-State Industrial Exposition in Chicago and again at the 1876 Centennial Exhibition in Philadelphia, promoting its ability to assume six different positions and form "a chair for the parlor, for the invalid, and for the sick . . . revertible to a lounge, a bed, and a child's swinging crib."[18] By 1873 he had set up a factory and had established retail branches in major cities to market his chairs. In Chicago, Wilson, Pierce & Co. and the Wilson Adjustable Chair Co. sold the chairs in 1873. After 1875 (by which time Wilson had moved to New York) parlor reclining chairs continued to be manufactured by the firm of Wilson & Bayless, along with a variety of "physicians', surgeons' and gaenecological [sic] chairs."[19]

Similar in overall appearance to the Wilson chair but using an elegant wooden frame, the rocking, reclining, and easy chair patented by DeBert Hartley in 1883 also had wide appeal. Between 1883 and 1898 the Hartley Reclining House Chair was produced in large number by the Hartley Mfg. Co. and occasionally by other manufacturers as well. However, the chair was only one of Hartley's many "furniture specialties," which included revolving bookcases, reclining lounges, and a combined dresser and commode.

Also introduced in the 1880s, the George F. Child Adjustable Parlor Chair combined the best features of the platform rocker and the reclining

Reclining chair patented by DeBert Hartley in 1883. From American Furniture Gazette *Fall Extra 1884.*

H. S. Carter. Various locations on State, 1856–61.

Joslin & Carter. 206 East Lake, 1865–66.

H. S. Carter & Co. 226–28 Lake, 1867–68; 195–97 Lake, 1869–71; 29–31 Jefferson, 1872–95.

Carter patented and manufactured numerous folding lounges and patent chairs, which he marketed with great success to retailers and upholsterers around the country. In 1877 the *Upholsterer and Carpet Reporter* described the firm as the only one in Chicago manufacturing parlor furniture complete in all its details. At the time, some forty workers concentrated on making frames, while another thirty completed the upholstery.

In 1884 a report noted that "recent innovations in trade, competition and slow collections brought about collapse" of H. S. Carter & Co. However, the firm was purchased by a Mr. Wilson, a brother of one of Carter's partners, who operated it under its previous name.

chair, and was, according to its inventor, "the most complete Adjustable Chair made."[20] By making a series of simple adjustments, the sitter could lean back, elevate his feet, lie flat, or rock. Made with various modifications, it was "suitable for parlor use or library, as well as for invalids and physicians' office use."[21] The chairs were manufactured by the George F. Child Adjustable Parlor Chair Co. from 1886 until 1897, when the name of the firm was changed to the Chicago Chair and Wheel Company and the line expanded to include wheel chairs and tricycles.

Like platform rockers and reclining chairs, the patent folding lounges introduced in the 1870s combined the talents of upholsterer, frame maker, metalworker, and engineer. A form of couch with a low back and a headrest at one end, the lounge was suitable for use in parlor, sitting room, dining room, library, or hall. Given the furniture makers' penchant for novelty, and Chicago's growing population, it is not surprising that many manufacturers turned their attentions to developing lounges that converted into beds. And there was a ready market, as the practical Mrs. C. S. Jones acknowledged in *Beautiful Homes:* "It is frequently a great accommodation to have in sitting-room or library some opportunity of arranging an *impromptu* bed; indeed, either in living room, *boudoir,* or library, a tasteful lounge so constructed as to admit of being changed into a bed, is a real comfort."[22] The columns of *American Cabinet Maker* verified this trend, noting the widespread demand "among poorer folks" for bed lounges that served as "a bed at night and a seat by day."[23]

One of the first Chicagoans to patent a workable bed lounge, or folding lounge as it was commonly called, was Duncan Forbes, a Scotsman. First listed in the city directory as a ship's carpenter in 1861, he entered the retail furniture business two years later. Together with another furniture manufacturer, Jeremiah E. Wilsey, Forbes patented a bed bottom spring and a bed bottom in 1866. Two years later he drew on this experience to develop a folding lounge.[24]

The patent model for Forbes's lounge, now in the collection of the National Museum of American History, reveals that, like most of the folding lounges patented by Chicagoans, the seat concealed a folded mattress. When the seat was flipped over and supported by hinged metal legs, it formed a bed. Perhaps recalling his days aboard ship, Forbes built a wide drawer underneath to provide storage space.[25]

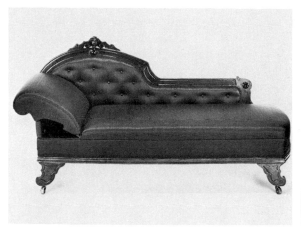

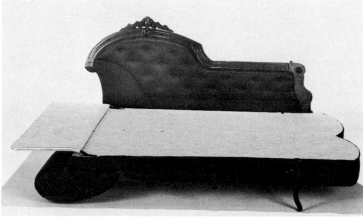

Folding bed lounge patented by Henry
S. Carter in 1871.
h: 37" w: 70" d: 24"
CHS, by exchange with the Evanston Historical Society, 1981

Carter's patent bed lounge opened to reveal a mattress.

As early as the spring of 1871 Henry S. Carter reported that his newly patented "spring bed lounge" had "achieved a remarkable success" both in the Western states, where sales were "very extensive," and in the local market, where they were selling "at the rate of twenty per day." The *Cabinet Maker* described Carter's Patent Lounge as having "none of the awkward or ungainly appearance that affect many of these articles." It followed the same principle as Forbes's lounge, except that when the seat was pulled out, the "spring bolster" at the elevated end of the lounge dropped down to the floor, "making a very firm substitute for a leg."[26]

A prominent manufacturer of upholstered furniture since 1856, Carter offered seventy-eight patterns of lounges by 1877, when he added Carter's Patent Rocker to his line.[27] The finer grades of Carter's Patent Lounge included a woven-wire mattress to support a thin foldable mattress of moss or curled hair. The 1876 prices of his folding lounges upholstered in terry, haircloth, or carpet ranged from $14 to $26.[28] Since "frames in wood" were available for only $4.50, labor and upholstery materials were clearly the primary factors determining cost.

Lounges almost identical to Carter's were advertised in the catalogue of the Union Wire Mattress Company, which had been using power machinery to make wire mattresses in Chicago since 1874. In fact, the frames might even have been supplied by H. S. Carter & Co., for only a short time earlier, the *Cabinet Maker* had noted that Carter was putting in additional machinery "to enable them to make lounge frames a specialty."[29]

Others who patented and manufactured bed lounges during this period included James W. McDonough (1866), Frederick Fischbeck (1868), William Lotz (1868), Charles H. Hildreth (1872), Thomas J. Gannon (1874), John A. Schoen (1875), Charles Wetzler (1877), Anton N. Hornug (1879), William Ott (1884), and Amos Stronk (1885).

One of the most unusual lounges incorporating the folding principle was the Combined Sofa and Bath Tub offered in 1883 by Bruschke & Ricke, manufacturers of parlor frames. The seat of this elegantly swagged and fringed lounge opened to reveal "a full-sized Bath Tub," while the bolster

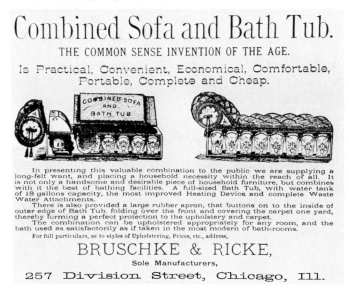

rolled back to uncover a water tank and heater. Called "the common sense invention of the age," the sofa-tub was advertised as "practical, convenient, economical, comfortable, portable, complete and cheap." In addition to attachments for filling the tub and heating and draining the water, it came with "a large rubber apron" that buttoned onto the outer edge of the tub and spread out "covering the carpet one yard."[30] In an era when most Midwesterners lacked indoor plumbing, this complete lounging/ bathing facility must have had special appeal. However, an oft-told tale among furniture manufacturers reveals that the success of the combination was short-lived. It seems that the gas-fired water heater had a tendency to ignite the combustible lounge, setting it, the bather, and the house afire.[31]

Equally clever but far more practical were the patent folding beds offered in a variety of sizes and disguises. Designed for use in the parlor, the exterior of a parlor folding bed looked like another piece of furniture—a bookcase, wardrobe, sideboard, or desk. The bed was created by flipping the false hinged front forward and down to form the frame and unfold the hidden mattress. The great attraction of these folding beds was that they took up so little space and allowed multiple uses for the room in which they were placed.

Though not low priced, the parlor folding bed was advertised as an economical solution to some of the problems associated with urban living. As the Empire Parlor Bedstead Company's brochure explained its invention had been "called forth by the social conditions of the times." The writer went on to say that "high rents, small houses, over-crowded tenements, and a constantly increasing population, together with the tendency to economize, constitute potent reasons for its introduction to the public."[32] Summarizing its merits in 1872, *Chicago Magazine* agreed, "Saves room, saves rent, and enables all to live genteelly in one or two rooms."[33]

Among the first to introduce parlor folding beds were David A. Titcomb and Elbridge A. Pratt, who together founded the Empire Parlor Folding Bedstead Company in 1872. The bedsteads, which were exhibited at

Portable bed with woven-wire mattress made by the Union Wire Mattress Company during the 1890s. The wooden frame is stenciled UNION WIRE MATTRESS CO./CHICAGO/WAGNER PATENT NOV. 18, 1899.
h: 17" w: 29¾" l: 73½"
CHS, purchase, 1980

Bookcase style parlor folding bed shown in the Illustrated Catalogue *of the Empire Parlor Bedstead Co. in 1875.*

the Inter-State Industrial Exposition the following year, came in six different styles representing "an elegant book case, dressing case, wardrobe, sideboard, etagere, or desk, adapted to parlor, library, dining-room, office or store." Available in single, three-quarter, or double widths, the parlor folding bedsteads ranged in price from $25 for the Plain Style (which resembled a simple cabinet) to $100 for the fanciest Wardrobe Style, augmented with "octagon corners, veneered panels, elaborate brackets and drop handles, with Mirror doors."[34] To stimulate sales, Titcomb & Pratt made the bedsteads available "to such as desire it on monthly payments,"[35] thus joining a number of manufacturers and dealers in pioneering the sale of furniture on the installment plan during the years of economic recession that followed the Panic of 1873.

Improvements in spiral springs and the invention of machines for coiling, twisting, and interlocking wire yielded increasingly elastic and lightweight mattresses. By 1868 springs in the form of a mesh of interwoven wire were being employed to create mattresses for steamer berths, sleeping cars, and hospitals, as well as for use in folding lounges and folding beds for the home. By 1884 several firms had been founded to manufacture these new "woven-wire" mattresses, including Ames & Frost, E. Yeoman, and the Union Wire Mattress Co. At the latter manufactory 100 workmen were employed in the production of "Union" folding beds and in operating the steam-powered wire-weaving machines developed by D. O. Powers, president of the company.[36]

The ease with which Boyington's chiffonier could be converted into a bed is illustrated in this advertisement from the Furniture Trade Journal, *April 1879.*

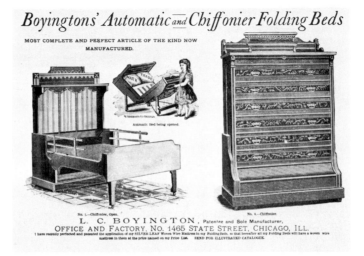

During the 1880s the incorporation of woven-wire mattresses combined with the influence of Charles Eastlake's advocacy of simplicity led to refinements in parlor folding beds that made them lighter in weight, easier to operate, and plainer in appearance. The Boyington Folding Bed Company offered a line of Queen Anne and Eastlake style chiffonier, writing desk, wardrobe, bookcase, and bureau folding beds that could be moved from room to room without being disassembled, did not rumple the bedclothes when closed, and featured woven-wire mattresses with a central spring support guaranteed not to sag. The beds had been developed and patented by Levi C. Boyington (brother of the well-known Chicago architect W. W. Boyington), who applied mechanical skills developed as a carpenter and bridge builder to the problems of spring and folding beds.[37] Within a decade Boyington introduced five variations of the parlor folding bed, finally developing what he declared to be "the most perfect bed in the market today. Anybody can handle or adjust it, and it is made and sold cheaper than any other folding bed of its character and style." *American Furniture Gazette* reinforced Boyington's claim by describing its reception at the 1884 Inter-State Industrial Exposition. "Mr. Boyington is exhibiting his bed at the Industrial Exposition. It attracts crowds, and every woman who sees it open and shut, don't shut up talking about it, till she gets 'Hubbie' to go and order one. The bed, folded or open, is a handsome piece of furniture, an ornament to please the eye, and an object to rest the body."[38] Boyington's factory employed fifty workmen in the production of forty-eight different styles of folding beds that were "the perfection of all improvements in their line" and "sold at a price within the reach of all."[39]

One of A. H. Andrews & Co.'s patents—to the left, a desk, and to the right, the bed that folds out of it.
National Museum of American History

"Upright beds" similar to Boyington's "with double ventilation and practical wardrobe attachments" were turned out at the rate of ten beds a day by the People's Folding Bed Company, organized in 1884.[40]

Folding beds resembling mirrored wardrobes and slant-front writing desks also were produced in large numbers for hotels, boardinghouses,

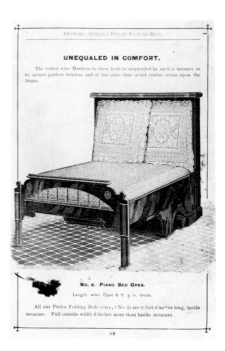

The Piano Folding Bed as illustrated in A. H. Andrews & Co.'s ca. 1890 catalogue of folding beds.

and college dormitories by A. H. Andrews & Co., a firm specializing in school and office furniture. For home use Andrews recommended its Etagere-Top Bed fitted with shelves to hold ornaments or the functional Book-Case Bed that contained a small but usable writing desk. But the ideal parlor bed was undoubtedly Andrews's Parlor Folding Piano Bed, which combined the cachet of an upright piano with the economies of an upright bed. Complete with keyboard, fake foot pedals, and "rosewood piano finish," the Parlor Piano Bed provided the household with an aura of culture during the day and a bed to accommodate visiting relatives at night.[41]

BEDROOM
FURNITURE

CHAPTER 6

1 8 7 3 - 1 9 1 7

Like all of Chicago furniture manufacturers, factories specializing in case goods, tables, and chairs benefited from the city's central location and excellent distribution facilities. But the two specific advantages that underwrote their success were the availability of cheap lumber from nearby Michigan, Wisconsin, and Indiana, and the abundance of skilled cabinetmakers, woodcarvers, and turners from Germany, the Austro-Hungarian Empire (especially Bohemia), and Scandinavia.

In 1884 *American Furniture Gazette* reported that thirty-three of the forty-seven factories making cabinet ware in Chicago specialized in the production of bedsteads, bureaus, washstands, wardrobes, and other forms of chamber furniture. Among these were three of Chicago's largest furniture factories, each employing some three hundred workers, as well as about a dozen other factories whose work forces averaged a hundred employees. Nearly all made an assortment of items, offering their products in matching suites and supplementing their lines with a variety of tables, bookcases, or sideboards. Some introduced as many as fifty new patterns a year, although the average was closer to twenty.[1] Some of the smaller firms made only one line, specializing in bedsteads or case pieces such as bureaus and washstands.

Pieces made in small factories were often designed by the owners, while large factories frequently retained designers or architects expressly for this purpose. By 1884 Chicago chamber furniture had reached a respectable level of sophistication, according to *American Furniture Gazette*.

Many of the leading houses employ trained and skilful [sic] designers, and the standard of designing is very high, while in construction, finish and general excellence, Chicago-made chamber furniture has won a reputation of the very best. The sales in this line are growing very rapidly and there is not a city, town or village in America where chamber furniture made in Chicago does not find its way.[2]

BEDROOM FURNITURE

95

Frank Mayer & Co. 331–33 South
Canal, 1866–71; 302–14 South Clinton,
1872–87.
*Turk & Voss Furniture Manufacturing
Co.* 319–29 South Canal, 1888–92.

During the 1860s and 1870s Frank
Mayer made bedsteads in partnership
with John A. Kirchner. When a fire
destroyed their factory in 1881, Mayer
rebuilt with Joseph A. Turk, and the
firm began to make complete suites of
chamber furniture. The work force
numbered nearly 250. When Mayer
died, the May 15, 1886, *Trade Bureau*
reported that the North-Western Furniture Manufacturers' Association had
passed a resolution noting that "with
no help or advantages besides his
hands and his head he had worked his
way up to that of a leading furniture
manufacturer." Turk and John H. Voss
continued to produce chamber furniture until 1892.

For fifteen years one of the city's largest chamber furniture factories
was owned by two brothers, Henry A. and Emory A. Clark, who had
established a branch of their Philadelphia factory in Chicago shortly after
the 1871 fire. Operating as Swan, Clark & Co. between 1872 and 1878, the
firm specialized in walnut and painted cottage style chamber sets in "a
medium grade for the million."[3] These they shipped at the rate of three
carloads a week to Philadelphia, pioneering the practice of shipping Chicago-made furniture to the East.[4] In 1878, the Clark brothers' partnership
agreement with B. C. Swan expired. After the business had been advertised for sale, the Clark brothers bought out Swan's share, keeping both
the Philadelphia and Chicago factories.

From 1878 until 1887 the Chicago factory was supervised by Emory
Clark, who expanded its production to include bookcases, sideboards, and
a variety of roll-top desks. Clark Brothers & Co.'s spacious and efficient
complex on Robey Street (now Damen Avenue) near Blue Island Avenue
provided for each step in the production of furniture, from the delivery of
logs at their own dock on the Chicago River to the loading of the finished
pieces on a railroad spur that ran on the Blue Island Avenue side of the
factory. Uncut logs were delivered to the factory sawmill, to be cut into
boards. These were moved along an internal rail system to the lumber shed,
or kiln, where they were seasoned. The main building was divided into
various areas. Assuming that the placement of equipment in this factory
followed the usual layout, the machinery used to cut furniture components
would have been located on the ground floor, while the assembling and
finishing would have taken place on the upper levels away from the flying
sawdust.

The main source of power for operating the machinery was steam,
which was generated by a 150-horsepower engine. The excess, or "waste,"
steam was used to heat the building and to season the lumber in the drying
shed. Unlike some Chicago furniture manufacturers who sold their products directly from their factories, Clark Brothers & Co. operated showrooms in the central business district for the convenience of out-of-town
buyers who arrived in Chicago primarily by train.

Equal in size to Clark Brothers & Co. was the firm of Sugg & Beiersdorf
on South Canal Street, where, by 1876, "two hundred workmen were
engaged exclusively in the manufacture of chamber suites." Established in
1867 by cabinetmaker George Sugg and parlor furniture manufacturer Jacob
Beiersdorf (see page 29), Sugg & Beiersdorf was, according to *Cabinet Maker*,
one of the first Western manufactories "to reach out boldly for the California and Pacific Coast trade," and by 1876 could claim well-established markets in San Francisco, Salt Lake City, Denver, and much of New Mexico.[5]
By 1882 the company had introduced nearly nine hundred patterns of
chamber suites, wardrobes, desks, sideboards, and cradles in walnut or
maple.[6]

Similar chamber sets and lounges, plus an assortment of inexpensive
tables and étagères, were made by F. Mayer & Co., whose huge factory
stretched westward from South Canal Street to Clinton Street, just south
of Harrison Street. One of the three largest chamber furniture manufacturers in the city, the firm was operated by Bavarian-born cabinetmaker Frank

Mayer, who in 1862 had arrived in Chicago from New York with "no friends and a bare capital of $200."[7] First in partnership with George Sugg and then John A. Kirchner, Mayer was co-owner of the company with Joseph Turk in 1886, when it employed 300 workers.[8]

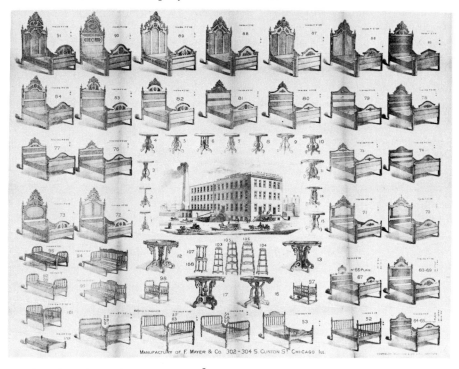

Another firm showing "considerable enterprise in the manufacture of walnut chamber furniture and cottage bedsteads" by 1877 was that of J. Koenig & Co. at the corner of North Green Street and Pratt Street (now Huron).[9] The owner, John Koenig, had been active in the furniture business since his arrival from Germany in 1854. By 1880, when his firm was producing more than 175 patterns of chamber sets, cribs, and tables in walnut and ash, Koenig employed sixteen. In addition to standard items the company made spool-turned patent lounges that could be expanded to form a bed, patent extension tables complete with compactly created leaves, and the McLean Patent Crib, which, like the platform rocker, rocked in place with a "noiseless, lateral, reciprocating, rocking motion."[10]

Others offering a full line of chamber furniture in addition to a wide variety of sideboards, bookcases, and desks during the 1870s included Albert Rauch, whose factory was located at the corner of West Chicago Avenue and Green Street for more than twenty-five years; John Monzel, a woodcarver who made parlor suites as well as chamber furniture in his State Street factory; Pries, Lohse & Co., who manufactured walnut chamber sets at 203 West Twenty-first Street; and Louis Schultze, operator of the Northwestern Furniture Factory on Milwaukee Avenue. Bostelmann & Ladenberger offered chamber sets in walnut, mahogany, and cherry after 1874, while Anton Matuska made chamber furniture before specializing in folding beds. Horn Brothers, founded in 1876 by John C. Horn, formerly a carver at Sugg & Beiersdorf, and his brother, Jacob, a skilled turner, made chamber furniture in Chicago for many years.

In 1877 the painted and enameled cottage style chamber furniture exhibited by manufacturers Donnelly & Barnes "received its share of admiration, from the country people especially" at that year's Inter-State Industrial Exposition.[11] After 1878, all kinds of chamber furniture was made in the factory of Christian E. Jorgenson, a "practical mechanic" who had learned his trade in Denmark before emigrating to Chicago in 1872.[12] During the 1880s additional factories were organized by H. Halvorson, Balkwill & Patch, Olbrich & Golbeck, Louis and Frederick Oberbeck, Christian and Henry Molter, and Albert, Charles, and Herman Hanke.[13]

Bureau from a suite of painted cottage furniture in the Galena, Illinois, home of Ulysses S. Grant, purchased from the W. W. Strong Furniture Co. of Chicago ca. 1870.
U.S. Grant Home, Illinois Department of Conservation
Photograph by J. D. Quick, Galena

Typical of factories making only one form of chamber furniture were those operated by Iver Doe, Freese & Hamline, and August Wichman, all founded in 1868. Working at 274 North Green Street, Iver Doe specialized in making bureaus. John D. Freese and L. M. Hamline produced bureaus, washstands, and medium-grade chamber suites in ash, oak, walnut, and maple. By 1879 the company offered all of its products "knock down and boxed," ready for assembly upon arrival. Advertising in *Furniture Trade Journal* that year, the firm noted that its "improved facilities for producing accurate machine work at the lowest possible cost" enabled it to offer lower prices and to produce "perfectly fitted, substantial, smooth and cleanly made" bureaus, washstands, and dressers that could be "easily and quickly set up complete by any person of ordinary intelligence."[14] Shipped K.D. and compactly crated, furniture was less likely to break during shipment and was cheaper to transport because it took up less space.

Also suitable for shipping in crated form were the walnut bedsteads produced in some twenty varieties in the West Fourteenth Street factory of

August Wichman. A woodcarver who—following his arrival from Germany in 1864—had worked for several years in the chamber furniture factory of Charles Tarnow, Wichman employed about forty men in the making of bedsteads noted for "good workmanship, fine finish and great durability."[15]

Unlike his fellow manufacturers, Wichman was slow to mechanize. Early in 1879 *American Cabinet Maker* called attention to the fact that Wichman did "not have a longing to manufacture all of the bedsteads that go out of Chicago" and commented: "The visitor to his factory will observe a novelty not seen in every factory of the present day. While steam is generally used as a motor, Mr. Wichman clings to the horse and his machinery may be said to be propelled by just "three horse power" which are fed on hay and oats in preference to wood and coal."[16] In 1884 *American Furniture Gazette* reported that Wichman's "designs are not so elaborate as those seen in chamber furniture factories of large pretensions, but they are neat and tasteful and take well." The article described Wichman as "a genial, hearty man, having no malice for his adversary, and exceeding great charity for his customers."[17]

CHAMBER FURNITURE STYLES

Since few labeled examples of Chicago chamber furniture survive, one must rely on trade cards, illustrated catalogues, and advertisements for a view of the furniture manufactured within the city during the last decades of the nineteenth century. From these materials it becomes clear that the pieces produced by the different firms resembled each other to such an extent that it is almost impossible to attribute any one of them to a single manufacturer. As in the production of parlor furniture, all of the makers of cabinet ware tended to use the same technology and materials. Moreover, because they catered to the popular taste, they all followed the styles of the day.

During the 1870s most of the bedroom furniture made in Chicago manufactories was in a style known as Renaissance. Ornate and massive, chamber sets were made out of rich dark woods such as walnut or mahogany. Headboards of bedsteads were crowned with heavy arched pediments and elaborate central crests, complemented by arched footboards, corner posts with finials, and side rails flaring upward at each end. The liberal use of roundels and turned wooden ornaments such as urns, finials, and drops produced extravagant contours, while burl veneer panels with beveled edges or incised geometric patterns created dramatic shadows on glossy varnished surfaces.

Monumental in appearance and eclectically ornamented, Renaissance chamber furniture echoed in wood the classical and picturesque architectural details found on the façades of fashionable French-inspired buildings constructed throughout Chicago just before and after the 1871 fire. Not only did the style recall an age of wealth and opulence, but, like the lavish furnishings of Chicago's great hotels, it symbolized the tremendous progress inherent in the American way of life, which permitted the common man to "sleep like a king." As Harriet Spofford wrote in *Art Decoration Applied to Furniture*, published in 1878: "There is no worthy or industrious, however humble, citizen of this country, out of all its millions, who has not his comfortable bed and his clean sheets, and who cannot enjoy his

Mahogany bedstead in the Renaissance Revival style, with carvings of fruit on the crest of the headboard, made for the Geraghty family during the 1870s. h: 8'9" w: 65" d: 6"
CHS, gift of Mr. and Mrs. Maurice P. Geraghty, 1980

rest as luxuriously to his body, if not as delightfully to his eye, as any of the old feudal nobles could."[18]

Typically, a chamber set consisted of three pieces: a bedstead, a chest of drawers, and a washstand. Headboards of bedsteads tended to be higher and more ornate than their footboards. On moderately priced beds, headboards averaged between four and six feet in height; on expensive models, seven feet was the common height, although many topped eight feet. Double beds were the norm, although single beds were coming into vogue. In 1877, for example, *American Cabinet Maker* noted that Sugg & Beiersdorf had introduced "a number of new patterns of single bedsteads in maple with imitation French veneer panels" and went on to comment: "Single bedsteads are coming into popularity instead of the large nuptial bed. They are placed side by side and are more healthy than the former."[19]

The chest of drawers, or bureau, was a wooden case enclosing three or four drawers topped by a mirror whose frame was equal in height and similar in design to the headboard of the bed. On expensive suites, the bureau was often replaced by a "dressing case" with a larger, longer mirror. Combining the functions of a chest of drawers and a long mirror, a dressing case was, according to *Beautiful Homes*, "a great comfort in a ladies' dressing-room."[20]

The washstand was a simple box composed of a drawer over a pair of doors, topped by a splashboard of wood or marble. The less expensive chamber sets featured washstands and bureaus with wooden tops; the medium- or higher-priced ones had marble tops cut to order at the local marble works. Matching towel racks, small tables, and commodes to hold washbasins and chamber pots were available to expand the set.

French bedsteads and other walnut chamber furniture shown in Louis Schultze's *Illustrated Catalogue* issued in 1875 and also pictured on a large broadside circulated by F. Mayer & Co. demonstrate the wide range of patterns that manufacturers could obtain using what has been described as the "additive" approach in composition and decoration.[21] On the least expensive model, superimposed boards formed simple arched headboards and footboards to which were glued simple decorations such as a plain roundel or a pair of flat veneered panels. A crest of carved leaves attached to another bed of the same basic design would produce a slightly more expensive model, as would the addition of another board to increase the height of the headboard. Yet other patterns would be created with the addition of molded pediments to head- and footboards, carved ornaments to side rails, a pair of finials to corner posts, or a larger or more elaborately carved crest. Since each of these elements called for a correspondingly greater expenditure of labor and material, the price increased accordingly.

With the exception of the foliate crests and carvings, which had to be executed by hand, each bed was a compilation of interchangeable parts produced with the aid of labor-saving machinery and assembled and finished using assembly-line procedures. Since a machine capable of doing fine three-dimensional carving had not yet been perfected, furniture crests and ornaments in a variety of shapes and sizes were turned out by woodcarvers employed in the factory or purchased in lots from one of the local carving establishments.

Within Chicago, at least four woodcarvers—Albert H. Wiser, D. W. Bosley, John Kraus, and Max Tonk—operated shops that specialized in supplying the local furniture factories with wooden carvings and ornaments in all styles, shapes, and sizes. One of the best known of these carvers was Tonk, who established a small carving factory at 87 West Lake Street in 1873. Here an impressive array of walnut ornaments naturalistically carved to resemble clusters of leaves, festoons of fruit, or graceful scrolls could be ordered for various uses: as handles for drawers, crests for bedsteads, or decorative accents for mirrors, picture frames, or coffins. Also available were turned and carved finials for bedsteads; draped urns for hearses; and engraved backpieces and arms for couches. "To fill up the chinks" between orders, Tonk and his five workmen made parlor shelves

Side detail from the headboard of the Geraghty bedstead.

or "brackets," along with an assortment of piano stools, drum sticks, and fifes for sale to local musical instrument dealers.[22]

Throughout the 1870s most of the medium and better grades of chamber furniture made in Chicago were constructed from American black walnut, a dark wood widely used for furniture, gun stocks, and other exacting work because of its strength and stability. Its abundance in neighboring Indiana and Ohio meant that Chicago manufacturers could get it at a good price. Rich-looking and substantial, black walnut furniture was most often purchased by members of the middle class who wanted well-made furniture that was both serviceable and stylish.

As a result of the widespread preference for American black walnut and the huge increase in furniture production between 1870 and 1880, this wood became increasingly scarce and expensive as the decade wore on. By 1878 supplies in the older Midwestern forests had been exhausted and lumbermen were stripping the forests of southern Arkansas and Tennessee. Since transportation greatly increased the cost of walnut, manufacturers of medium-grade furniture turned to less expensive, locally available woods such as cherry, maple, and ash, which they stained or "ebonized" in an attempt to satisfy the demand for darker, more exotic woods.[23]

The high cost of walnut suites was revealed by a reporter who visited the showroom of the Tobey Furniture Company in 1883. "Here is a chamber set, made of solid walnut and veneered with the most beautiful of walnut burl," he told the readers of *Inland Architect and Builder*. "Eleven hundred dollars is the price, and fit for the palace of royalty, or, what perhaps is more to the point, of a 'bonanza king.' "[24]

Around 1880, red and white oak were introduced for use in furniture making and in the production of "interior finish," as the making of stairways, mantels, and woodwork was called. A hardwood with a distinctive grain, red oak took a high polish yet was soft enough to work easily. White oak was prized for the beautiful grain displayed when quarter-sawn. Little-used by the woodworking industry before walnut became scarce, oaks still stood in large stands throughout southern Illinois, Indiana, and other Midwestern states.

Mahogany, the wood for which walnut had first been used as a substitute, began to return to favor for finer merchandise. "We are observing every day mahogany work peeping out at us from the retailers' stock. . . . As the months go by we find another and still another piece manufactured from this beautiful wood offered for sale to the Chicago public," the local correspondent for *American Cabinet Maker* observed in 1876. By November 1880 he could report: "The great increase in demand for Mahogany shows most conclusively that this wood is rapidly becoming popular. Mahogany chamber suits [sic] in particular are back in demand."[25] Describing furniture for sale at the Tobey Furniture Company in 1882, a writer for a local architectural journal commented: "[F]ashion is again changing and reverting to 'old mahogany.' The forests of Yucatan and Central America are full of this beautiful wood and the new railroads which are opening up Mexico to commerce will certainly bring this and other beautiful and now costly woods to our markets at prices within the reach of all."[26]

Horn Bros. Manufacturing Co. 272–80 North Sangamon, 1876–83; 281–91 (1144 after 1909) West Superior, 1884–1933.

Both skilled woodworkers, John C. Horn and his brother, Jacob M., worked in Chicago furniture factories for several years before founding Horn Bros. Manufacturing Co. in 1876. John served as president, while Jacob took charge of the factory. In 1882 the company employed fifty; a decade later the size of the work force doubled. At first, Horn Bros. manufactured center tables as well as chamber furniture. In 1885–86 it patented several folding lounges. By the 1890s the firm was advertising numerous patterns of cheap and medium-priced bedroom suites, in addition to dressers, sideboards, and music cabinets. Bedroom furniture continued to be made until 1933, when the company went bankrupt and forfeited all of its stock to the First National Bank of Chicago.

Walnut bureaus and washstands in the 1875 *Illustrated Catalogue of Louis Schultze.*

Elaborately carved mahogany dressing case made in W. W. Strong's factory during the 1870s.
h: 8'1½" w: 43" d: 21"
Mr. and Mrs. Thomas Meyer

The use of light-colored and delicately figured woods such as pale yellow poplar, yellowish brown butternut (also known as white walnut), curled and birds-eye maple, and golden brown oak coincided with the introduction of new, simpler styles advocated by the English reformers of taste. By 1875 Eastlake furniture in chestnut, white oak, and butternut was being exhibited at the Inter-State Industrial Exposition by a few avant-garde Chicago manufacturers.

By 1877 Eastlake and Queen Anne chamber sets in walnut or maple appeared alongside standard Renaissance sets in Chicago manufacturers' catalogues as well as in their showrooms. Like Eastlake-inspired furniture, Queen Anne-styled pieces represented a mood rather than a concise arrangement of parts. At the time, there appears to have been considerable confusion as to what constituted Queen Anne. "We have been unable to

Walnut chest with burl panels made by John Christian Lilleskau, foreman of the chamber furniture factory of Iver Doe in the 1880s.
h: 42" w: 43" d: 20"
Mrs. Arthur B. Carlson, Jr.

find in any of the older text books any reference to the 'Queen Anne Style' as now practiced," the *Builder and Wood-Worker* reported in 1880. "During the life of that esteemed lady [Queen Anne], the prevailing style of architecture was vastly different from that which now goes by her name. . . .

We fail to see, however, in any of the ancient examples of this reign, any of the spindles that are so conspicuous, and seem to be the trade-mark of the style that now bears the good queen's name."[27]

Using local woods and standard woodworking machinery, manufacturers continued making boxy, marble-topped bureaus, washstands, and dressers. But, instead of heavy foliated crests and other applied carvings, panels of shallowly carved leaf-and-flower forms, incised geometric lines, or a band of saw-tooth or scalloped carving appeared at the tops of case pieces. Glove boxes and other appurtenances disappeared from the tops of bureaus; round metal rings or rectangular brass backplates replaced leafy carved pulls on chests of drawers; veneer panels lost their curves and became oblong or square. Since Eastlake did not offer suggestions for wooden bedsteads, manufacturers modified the standard high-backed form to conform in outline and ornament to the new-style case pieces so as to produce compatible suites.

Photographs illustrating furniture carvings available from the shop of Max Tonk in the 1870s.
Mr. and Mrs. Hampton E. Tonk and Family

Within a decade, "square style" Eastlake and Queen Anne bedsteads dominated the market. In 1881, when the Tobey Furniture Company secured the contract for furnishing the Florence Hotel in the town of Pullman, it supplied dozens of oak chamber sets in a modified Eastlake style.[28] By 1887 *The Illustrated Catalogue of Furniture Manufactured by F. Mayer & Co.* showed only Eastlake-inspired designs, ranging from a modest maple bedstead with a neatly ornamented headboard four feet tall to an elaborate walnut model whose headboard topped six feet and displayed richly burled walnut panels, geometrically engraved side posts, and triple rows of saw-tooth carving.[29]

By the early 1880s, when nearly every factory was busy producing Eastlake or Queen Anne designs, the showrooms of John A. Colby, W. W.

Bedstead from Eastlake chamber suite made for the Florence Hotel in Pullman by the Tobey Furniture Company in 1881. Named after George M. Pullman's daughter, Florence, the hotel was built to house visitors to the Pullman Palace Car Company.
h: 72" w: 60" l: 84"
Historic Pullman Foundation

Strong, Charles Tobey, and other firms catering to the carriage trade had already begun to show other styles. At the Tobey Furniture Company, for example, a visitor reported in 1883, "the fashion has all gone to light and graceful house furniture."[30] By the 1890s not only had tastes and styles begun to change, but Chicago chamber furniture manufacturers were facing stiff competition from local manufacturers of brass and iron beds.

METAL BEDSTEADS

Metal beds for institutional use had been made in Chicago by the Chicago Iron Bedstead Mfg. Co. as early as 1864, and from the 1870s onward by the Union Wire Mattress Company. However, it was not until after 1883, when the Chicago physician Dr. Henry Gradle shared Louis Pasteur and Robert Koch's experiments in bacteriology with the American public, that the manufacture and sale of metal bedsteads became a lucrative business. Fear of disease and infection through microbes lurking in thick plush draperies, dusty carpets, and the crevices of deeply tufted and heavily ornamented furniture prompted many homemakers to streamline their households by introducing lightweight curtains and shades that let in the sunshine, rugs that could be taken up and beaten, and bedsteads and other furniture made from iron, brass, or steel. "The microbe is to-day one of the most active promoters of genuine household art," Helen Campbell wrote in *House Beautiful* in 1899, acknowledging the role of the germ theory of disease in ending "the era of strange bewitchment of wood."[31]

The growing acceptance of metal household and office furniture, plus the introduction of the less expensive Bessemer process for producing steel,

encouraged many local metalworkers to begin manufacturing iron and brass beds in the late 1880s. Calling attention to the great variety of such bedsteads available in Chicago by 1899, *American Cabinet Maker & Upholsterer* commented: "The demand for these goods is growing with startling rapidity, as their use from a hygienic point of view is apparent to the dullest mind, consequently their manufacture and sale is one of the features of the trade."[32] By 1909 *Furniture* magazine was pointing out: "Chicago can claim credit for the first real American style brass and iron beds, and today there are more beds made within a radius of one hundred miles of Chicago than are made in any other spot in the world."[33]

Between 1890 and 1907 the largest manufacturer of metal bedsteads in Chicago was the Adams & Westlake Company, a firm well known for its production of hardware, stoves, and railroad supplies. Organized in the 1870s by James McGregor Adams, John Crerar, and William Westlake, the company's extensive factory on the city's Near North Side was equipped with its own foundries for casting iron and brass. Early in 1890 the company took heed of the growing demand for metal bedsteads and introduced its first brass beds. By 1893 it advertised as "the largest American manufacturers of brass bedsteads," stressing that bold and novel designs, good materials, substantial construction, and high-quality finish made their product superior to all others on the market.

There is no line of brass bedsteads made in this or any other country, which can stand the close inspection that may be given ours. They may be taken apart, which is something almost impossible with other makes, and when so

Adams & Westlake Company. 110 West Ontario, 1874–1959; Oakbrook, 1959 to the present.

Manufacturer of lanterns and other hardware specialties for the railroad and shipping industries, Adams & Westlake took advantage of its extensive metalworking facilities to manufacture Adlake bicycles and brass and iron bedsteads between 1880 and 1907, when demand for these products was at a peak. By 1893 the company operated one of the largest bed manufactories in the country, turning out more than 100 different designs with a variety of Adlake finishes. Production ended in 1907, when sales began to decline.

J. McGregor Adams served as president of Adams & Westlake from its inception in 1874 to his death in 1904. He was succeeded by Ward W. Willits, who headed the firm until 1937. The company manufactured metal products for the transportation industry in Chicago until 1927, when it moved its factory to Elkhart, Indiana. In 1959 the administrative offices were transferred to Oakbrook, Illinois, when the firm became a subsidiary of Midwest Management.

apart, every piece may be carefully examined. The solid brass mounts and knobs, and castors, will bear examination, as also the lacquered surface of the entire bed.[34]

The fact that Adams & Westlake's beds featured interchangeable parts and could be easily dismantled proved a boon to furniture dealers who shipped by rail. The sturdy castors were solid brass. Other parts were made of brass-plated Bessemer steel. To retain its luster, the brass was coated with a high-grade English "hot-process" lacquer that allowed the bed to remain shiny with only a wipe of a cloth. "Adlake beds," *Furniture Journal* noted, set the "standard by which all other beds were measured."[35]

About fifty designs ranging from simple four posters to elaborate fabrications of canopies and curlicues were made in brass by the company, with some fifty more available in iron. While brass beds were coated with lacquer, cheaper iron beds were painted with several coats of enamel. White was by far the most popular color, although Adams & Westlake's iron beds also came in moss green, bronze, antique Japanese copper, Roman gold, and a high-gloss Adlake finish resembling that used on bicycles made by the firm.[36] In 1893 the gleaming brass and iron beds drew the admiration of visitors to the 1893 World's Columbian Exposition; in 1896, when "the silver question" pervaded politics, the firm drew attention to its products

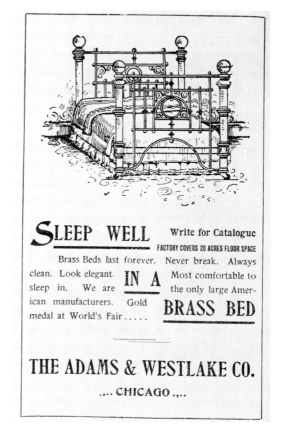

Advertisement for "Adlake" beds in the Chicago Furniture Manufacturers' **Classified Directory** *of 1895.*

by featuring "apt and timely" silver-plated bedsteads at that summer's expositions in Chicago and Grand Rapids.[37]

By the end of the 1890s at least five new firms had joined Adams & Westlake in manufacturing metal beds, among them Davis, Horwich, &

Steinman; the Art Bedstead Company; and the Kimball & Chappell Co., organized in 1897 by Charles H. Kimball and J. Dixon Chappell, two former employees of Adams & Westlake. By 1899 another new company, Miller Hall & Son, was employing 235 people in its factory at Taylor and Rockwell streets, turning out 1,000 iron beds a day. Specializing in iron beds trimmed with brass and porcelain, the company made some 150 patterns, offering about twenty new models each summer.[38] Metal beds were also sold in the city by the Acme Spring Bed Company, whose beds and "Acme" Hygienic Couch and chairs were manufactured in Milwaukee, and by the Northwestern Wire Mattress Co. (later Simmons Mfg. Co.), whose offices were located in Chicago but whose factories were in Kenosha, Wisconsin.

The brass and iron bedstead business remained strong in Chicago until America's entry into World War I, when metals were rationed and many foundries were put to use producing goods for the war effort. By then, however, Adams & Westlake had ceased to make beds, having withdrawn from the furniture business in 1907 in order to concentrate its efforts on the production of metal parts for an even more promising product—the automobile.

CHAPTER 7

CHAIRS FOR ALL OCCASIONS

1 8 7 3 - 1 9 1 7

In 1884 nearly 2,000 workers toiled daily turning out undreamed-of quantities of chairs in local enterprises ranging from handicraft operations to highly mechanized factories. The largest firms specialized in making wooden chairs, while the smallest fabricated what was known as wickerwork.

Advertisement from the August 1876 Western Furniture Trade *illustrating products made by A. P. Johnson & Co.*

Walnut rocking chair with cane back and seat of the type made by A. P. Johnson & Co. in the 1870s.
h: 34" w: 21½" d: 31"
CHS, gift of Benjamin Ayer Fairbank and Kellogg Fairbank, 1955

WOODEN CHAIRS

Unlike the manufacture of parlor furniture and cabinet ware, which was carried on by numerous entrepreneurs in premises ranging from one-man workshops to sizable factories, the production of wooden chairs in Chicago came to be dominated by two large firms. One was headed by Frederick Herhold, the other by Andrew P. Johnson.

Low-back Windsor chair from the home of Joseph Shaw, a cabinetmaker who emigrated to Chicago from England in 1843. Shaw later combined cabinet-making with farming in the village of Jefferson.
h: 29½" w: 20" d: 20"
CHS, gift of the Estate of Joan Shaw, 1981

Rocking chair with turned spindles made by the Herhold Chair Company, ca. 1910.
h: 37" w: 19¾" d: 18⅞"
Teresa and Walter Krutz

Ironically, the two enterprises shared a common origin in the firm of Herhold, Johnson & (Adolph) Borgmeier, founded in 1868. Located in a small frame building at the corner of Third (West Erie) and Green streets, just a short distance from the large factory of pioneer chairmaker John Phillips, the new firm made chairs, bureaus, and washstands. The three partners had purchased the business from Ole G. Thompson and his partner, John Crawford, who had been making cane seat chairs there since the early 1860s.

According to Chicago historian A. T. Andreas, Herhold had completed his apprenticeship in cabinetmaking in his native city of Hanover, Germany, and had come "to Chicago direct" in 1851, bringing with him his widowed mother and "exactly fifty cents."[1] An experienced chairmaker, Herhold found work with John Phillips, and eventually also worked for Thayer & Tobey and its successor firm, the Tobey Furniture Company. For a brief period in 1859, he went into business for himself, making chairs in a little shop located at the rear of a building on West Erie Street. Lack of capital forced him to return to working in the shops of other Chicago furniture makers until he joined Johnson and Borgmeier in 1868.

Andrew P. Johnson (born Jearager), a native of the town of Voss in Norway, had migrated with his family in 1850 at the age of fifteen. One of twelve children, he worked on the family farm until he was twenty, when he went to Beloit, Wisconsin, to learn the carpenter's trade. Two years later he became a contractor. In 1861 he moved to Chicago and shortly thereafter enlisted in the Union army. He returned to Chicago in 1865, after the end of the Civil War, having in the meantime changed his name to Johnson. He worked as a carpenter until 1868, when he was offered the opportunity to join Herhold and Borgmeier in the furniture business.[2]

By 1879 an advertisement in *Furniture Trade Journal* noted that A. P. Johnson & Co. was manufacturing "over 200 varieties of wood and cane seat chairs, bureaus, washstands."[3] At the time, the company employed an average of 200 workers, including 100 full-time chairmakers and 40 youths under sixteen.[4] By 1883 the factory (renamed the Johnson Chair Co.) was turning out 3,500 chairs and rockers a week.[5]

Workers of all ages, including a large number of boys under sixteen, at the Johnson Chair Co. ca. 1890.
Mrs. Richard Frey

In the late 1860s, when Herhold, Johnson & Borgmeier started their business, they advertised "all kinds of wooden and cane seat chairs."[6] The successor firm, A. P. Johnson & Co., specialized in hoop-back chairs with thick plank seats as well as maple rockers with oval cane backs and rounded cane seats. Later, having become distributors for the New Haven Folding Chair Co. of Connecticut, the Johnson Chair Co. added walnut folding chairs upholstered with floral carpet to its line.[7]

After selling his share of the Green Street factory to the Johnsons in 1874, Frederick Herhold went into business with chairmaker Conrad C. Lenz at the corner of West Erie and Carpenter streets. Shortly afterward, he sold his interest to cabinetmaker William Niemann and organized the Northwestern Lead and Oil Company. Two years later he withdrew from active participation in that enterprise and rejoined Niemann, Lenz & Co.

in making cane and wooden-seated chairs. In 1880 Herhold bought out his partners and renamed the firm F. Herhold & Co.

When Herhold acquired the business in 1880, it employed an average of seventy-five chairmakers.[8] Only three years later, under his energetic leadership, the work force had nearly doubled and, according to Chicago promoter Jonathan Land, one small building had increased to four "fitted with every kind of improved machinery known in this branch of business for the accurate and swift production of 143 different styles in cane and wood seat chairs, the capacity of the works being 1,500 chairs daily."[9] By 1885, Herhold employed 170 workers; a decade later, more than 400 were employed in the factory. By this time, two of Herhold's sons had joined the business. Frederick, a bookkeeper, took charge of the office details, while his brother William, who had learned wood turning in the family establishment, served as superintendent of the factory.[10]

Despite the immense variety of chairs available to the public, the Chicago correspondent of *American Cabinet Maker* reported in 1879 that "demand in the Northwest and South has been for the genuine old-fashioned wood seat painted chair."[11] Typical of chairs being produced by factories throughout the United States, this type consisted of a bowed wooden back inset with plain or vase-shaped ring-turned spindles, a contoured plank seat, turned legs tapering at each end, and one or two front stretchers that repeated some of the turnings found on the back spindles. Sturdy, practical, and cheap, these "common" chairs were suitable for kitchens, dining rooms, bedchambers, factories, or offices—indeed for any use that called for a serviceable, if not particularly stylish, chair. As in other branches of furniture making, the prudent use of materials, the application of machinery, and the adoption of assembly-line procedures allowed Chicago's largest chairmakers to flood the market with cheap but functional chairs.

After 1888 both the Johnson Chair Co. and F. Herhold & Sons offered chairs whose backs and seats featured low-relief floral or pictorial patterns that had been "pressed" into the wood using an embossing machine. Equipped with a hot steel die that impressed a design on the thin wooden panel, a single embossing machine could produce a design that simulated carving thirty times faster than a man could carve the same pattern by hand. Around 1890 a new "twist machine" or spiral molder came onto the market and chairs began to feature an abundance of specially twisted spindles and stretchers. Similarly, in 1893 Herhold's factory began using a newly invented "stretcher and sawing machine" that had the capacity to automatically turn out 20,000 chair stretchers a day.[12] Equipped with modern machinery that was most efficient when producing large quantities of inexpensive goods, it was no surprise that Chicago's largest chairmakers endeavored to produce—in the words of F. Herhold's advertisements— "chairs and rockers . . . for everybody, everywhere, in largest variety, handsomest styles and lowest prices."[13]

But not all Chicago chairmakers immediately adopted the latest machinery and styles. Throughout the 1880s, maple rockers with high cane backs and scrolled arms, walnut cottage chairs with bracket arms, and "Grecian" chairs that were heavier, plainer versions of the classical models made in Chicago a half-century earlier were still available from the shop of

Herhold, Johnson & Borgmeier. 233–35 North Green, 1868–70.
Herhold, Johnson & Co. 233–35 North Green, 1871–74.
A. P. Johnson & Co. 233–35 North Green, 1875–82.
Johnson Chair Co. 233–35 North Green, 1883–1908; 1898 West North, 1909–48.

Born in Norway, Andrew P. Johnson (1835–1907) grew up in Boone County, Illinois. After being trained as a carpenter for some years in Wisconsin, he came to Chicago in 1861 and worked for a construction corps during the Civil War. He joined forces in 1868 with Frederick Herhold and Anton and Adolph Borgmeier to buy out Thompson & Crawford's small chairmaking business. Johnson later bought out Anton Borgmeier and Herhold, forming A. P. Johnson & Co. in 1875.

At first the firm's output included bureaus and washstands, but the demand for chairs was so great that by 1883 it was producing the latter exclusively and changed its name to Johnson Chair Co. By the turn of the century the company employed more than 500 workers and advertised 1,000 patterns of office and dining chairs in more than 400 styles. In 1899 the Johnson Chair Co. produced the chairs used to furnish the United States House and Senate, including an elaborately carved mahogany chair for the vice-president.

In 1907, when A. P. Johnson died, his brother, Nels, became president of the Johnson Chair Co. From the 1920s on, the company made only office chairs. Nels's son, Walter, and Andrew's sons—Joseph, Arthur, and Olaf—were all involved in the firm. In 1947 Walter, Arthur, and Olaf bought up most of the company stock. A year later they sold the company to Helene Curtis. The Johnson Chair Co. trade name was sold to the Gunlocke Co. of Wayland, New York, which manufactured chairs under the Johnson name and maintained a showroom in Chicago until 1979.

Francis F. Eggleston, a chairmaker since 1852.[14] Similarly, classic cane and wooden-seated chairs remained the stock in trade of Joseph Shaw, who made chairs on the city's West Side from 1848 until his retirement in 1893.[15] At the same time, "all classes of wood-seat chairs and rockers and maple cane chairs and rockers" continued to be produced in the chair factory of Phillips & Liebenstein until 1886.[16] The pioneering firm of John Phillips, which had begun to make chairs in the 1840s, continued in business until 1884.

Fashionable patent folding chairs were occasionally shown in the advertisements of Chicago chair factories, yet none of the manufacturers claimed these as their own, instead referring to their firms as agents for various Eastern manufacturers. One of the most important agents in the city as well as one of the largest chair manufacturers in the country was J. S. Ford, Johnson & Co., whose headquarters and warehouses were in Chicago but whose products were manufactured in Indiana and Massachusetts. Organized in 1872, the firm was jointly operated by Ford & Johnson, manufacturers of chairs in Michigan City, Indiana, and Philander Derby, who operated one of the nation's largest chair factories in Gardner, Massachusetts.

An early conglomerate composed of several partners and representing several factories, J. S. Ford, Johnson & Co. was the outgrowth of a furniture-making business founded in Columbus, Ohio, in 1861 when John Sherlock Ford contracted for the labor of thirty-five convicts and trained them to make chairs. In 1865 Ford was joined in business by Henry W. Johnson, a former schoolteacher and Civil War veteran who shortly afterward became his brother-in-law. Three years later Johnson took over active management of the company—renamed Ford & Johnson—and moved the factory from Ohio to Michigan City, Indiana, in response to an invitation from civic leaders who were eager to attract industry to the small town located thirty-five miles southeast of Chicago. Attracted by Michigan City's lakefront and railroad connections, Ford & Johnson selected a site in the town with an eye toward making nearby Chicago the company's future distributing point.[17]

Ford and Johnson realized this goal in 1872 when they joined with chairmaker Philander Derby to purchase the assets of Stoll & Barnes, a furniture jobbing house in Chicago specializing in the sale and distribution of chairs. With F. J. Barnes (formerly of Stoll & Barnes) and Derby joining as partners, Ford and Johnson organized a new enterprise, called J. S. Ford, Johnson & Company, to serve as an outlet for chairs manufactured by the Ford & Johnson factory in Michigan City as well as for goods manufactured in the Massachusetts factory of Philander Derby & Co. Yet another partner in this venture was Reuben H. Hitchcock, who had at one time worked as a traveling salesman for Ford & Johnson.

In 1881 Ford & Johnson opened a second factory in Michigan City, the Hitchcock Chair Company, to produce fine chairs for office and residential use. The older factory, meanwhile, concentrated on the production of commercial seating furniture for railroad depots, churches, billiard halls, and summer resorts. By 1886 more than 100 people worked for the Hitchcock Chair Company, while more than 500 "operatives" produced chairs in the original Ford & Johnson factory. Eighty were employed in the office and warehouse of J. S. Ford, Johnson & Co. in Chicago, while seven salesmen stayed "on the road."[18]

Office chair made by J. S. Ford, Johnson & Co. used by George M. Pullman at the Pullman Palace Car Works.
h: 38" w: 23" d: 22"
CHS, gift of C. W. Bryan, Jr., 1959

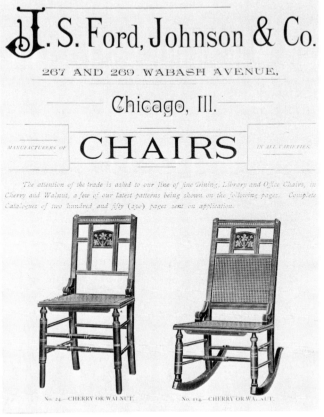

Interchangeable parts allowed J. S. Ford, Johnson & Co. to offer more than 3,000 patterns of chairs by 1884. An efficient distribution network carried the firm's products to every part of the United States. From American Furniture Gazette *Fall Extra 1884.*

During the mid-1880s J. S. Ford, Johnson & Co. offered more than 3,000 varieties of chairs, rockers, and cradles ranging from old-fashioned "Grecian chairs and rockers" to fashionable "folding rustic settees."[19] Of these, nearly 400 patterns of office, dining, railroad, and rocking chairs emanated from the Michigan City factories alone. When added to the folding chairs, rattan and reed goods, lawn goods, and office chairs supplied by other manufacturers, the array could easily have made up what *American Furniture Gazette* claimed was "probably the most varied assortment offered by any one house in America."[20]

While chair manufacturers offered many patterns, variations among them were often very slight. Pattern no. 10, for example, with backs, splats, legs, and stretchers identical to those of Pattern no. 9, might feature a cane seat while no. 9 had a wooden one. No. 11 might be identical to no. 10, except for the addition of a bit of carving, a panel of veneer, or a different arm, slat, or crest rail. It was by this kind of manipulation of interchangeable parts that J. S. Ford, Johnson & Co. could legitimately boast that it manufactured "everything in the line of chairs and embracing some three thousand varieties."[21]

Except for the chairs from the Michigan City factories, which were sold exclusively through Chicago, goods from J. S. Ford, Johnson & Co.'s large Chicago warehouse were shipped to the East as well as to the West, with Philander Derby & Co. and J. S. Ford, Johnson & Co. exchanging and selling "mutually."[22] As furniture jobbers, the company handled the packing and loading of goods on railroad cars for customers outside of Chicago, often combining furniture ordered from other Chicago manufacturers with ones from their company for shipment further west.

The largest city with manufacturing facilities and rail connections close to the western frontier, Chicago became a primary supplier of furniture to Far Western states during the last quarter of the nineteenth century. For example, 1880s and 1890s photographs of interiors of homes in Helena, Montana, and of ranch houses like the one owned by Conrad Kohrs, "King of the Cattlemen," in Deer Lodge Valley reveal an abundance of factory-made furniture of the kind being produced in Chicago at the time.[23] And indeed, bills, receipts, and letters now in the Montana State Historical Society confirm the fact that large quantities of bedding, furniture, and decorative accessories were purchased in Chicago and shipped westward to Montana by rail. By the early 1870s goods shipped from Chicago to Montana or Idaho could be expected to arrive twenty days ahead of those being shipped from St. Louis, a previous source of supply.

WICKERWORK

In marked contrast to the city's larger cabinet ware and chair factories, where steam-powered machinery screeched and howled, were the smaller establishments in which workers transformed long, flexible fibers of rattan, reed, or willow into various kinds of "wicker" furniture. Here employees skilled in the techniques of basketmaking created fanciful wicker superstructures over prefabricated wooden frames.

Highly pliable switches from willow trees had been used for centuries to make baskets and various types of furniture. In Chicago, the first references to a wicker furniture industry appeared in the 1860s. By 1873 five manufacturers—William Pottle, John Lehmann, A. Gill, George J. Schmidt, and Tillmann & Frederick—were offering full lines of willowware, including chairs, cribs, work stands, and ferneries. All of the factories were small, employing an average of five workers. The manufacturers attributed the limited size of their operations to the paucity of willow. Although willow trees were native to Illinois, most of the shoots used in manufacturing had to be shipped from Kentucky (where basketmaking was a thriving industry) or imported from Germany (with manufacturers paying an import duty of 35 percent of the cost of the material). Forced to rely on inadequate and expensive sources of raw material, willowware manufacturers tried to encourage local farmers to meet their needs. "If farmers in this State would cultivate a few acres of basket willow," they told writer S. S. Schoff in 1873, "they would make more money than from a whole field of wheat."[24]

The report of a representative from *American Cabinet Maker*, who visited the Chicago willowware factory of William Pottle in 1877, suggests that

Willow and rattan chair made ca. 1870 by William Lehmann, a basket weaver who emigrated from Germany in the 1850s.
h: 41" w: 28" d: 16½"
CHS, gift of Robert Lehmann, 1983

farmers had heeded Schoff's advice. "The growing of willow ready for the manufacture is itself a prominent industry and because of stiff competition in the industry is now sold at a remarkable reduction in price."[25] Admiring the "neat and tasty warerooms" of William Pottle, the correspondent commented: "The manufacture of willowware has increased to a remarkable extent, and the many articles now produced are artistic and durable and afford a relief to the sameness in furniture which now prevails."[26]

In 1873 Charles W. H. Frederick of Tillmann & Frederick, probably responding to the difficulty of finding a steady and inexpensive supply of willow in Chicago, began to experiment by combining the long, elastic canes of rattan (a climbing palm native to tropical Asia) with switches of willow to weave chairs. A tough, reedlike vine that grows to a length of some five hundred feet, rattan has a glossy outer bark, known as cane, which has long been used in weaving backs and seats. However, the inner pith, called reed, had not been put to use until the 1840s, when it began to be employed in the construction of frames for hoop skirts and later in the making of furniture. Unlike rattan, which was water-resistant and could only be lacquered, reed could be easily painted or stained. Both were extremely strong and pliable and, after soaking or steaming, could be woven or formed into intricate shapes.

One of the first Americans to use rattan in the mass production of furniture was Cyrus Wakefield of Boston, who in 1844 began importing rattan and cane from Canton, China. In 1855 Wakefield established a fac-

The materials used to weave wicker furniture lent themselves to a variety of airy and fanciful designs. From American Furniture Gazette, *April 1885.*
Hazel Kahle Williams

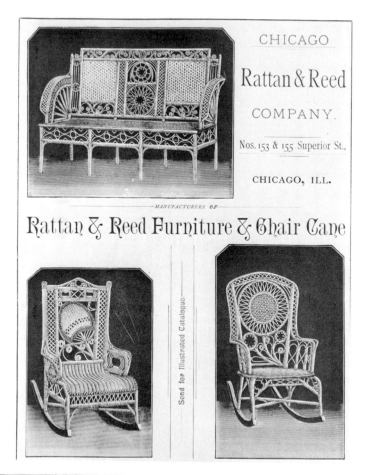

Locally made rattan chair and workstand in the bedroom of Mrs. Charles Walker at 392 LaSalle early in the 1890s.

tory in South Reading (later Wakefield), Massachusetts, where rattan was split into cane and reed using water power (and eventually steam), and then combined with willow to make whimsical rococo style furniture. During the 1840s Levi Heywood, a manufacturer of chairs in Gardner, Massachusetts, had invented a machine for bending wood, as well as "a combination of three machines for splitting, shaving, and otherwise manipulating rattan."[27] Later, one of his employees developed a power loom that could weave cane into continuous sheets, and "an automatic channeling machine that could cut a groove around the wooden seat of a chair, thereby allowing the edges of this "sheet cane" (as it has come to be called) to be pressed into the groove and fastened tight by means of a triangular-shaped reed called "spline."[28] Around 1875 Heywood Brothers & Company, then the largest manufacturer of wooden chairs with cane seats and backs in the country, began producing rattan and reed furniture. By then, however, wicker furniture was already being made in several large factories in New York City as well as in cities as far west as Chicago.

C.W.H. Frederick, the creator of "the first rattan chair ever manufactured in Chicago,"[29] had been apprenticed to a willowware maker in Beloit,

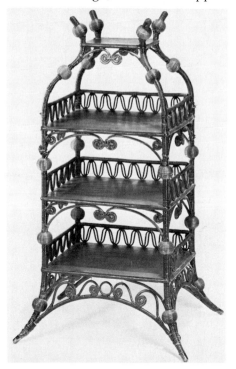

Rattan and reed were steamed, then twisted while moist to create the elaborate swirls and arabesques in this Heywood & Morrill chair made ca. 1899. h: 42" w: 19½" d: 25"
CHS, gift of David A. Hanks in honor of Mrs. A. Loring Rowe, 1977

Heywood & Morrill wicker whatnot enameled black and maroon, made between 1886 and 1896. h: 38" w: 21½" d: 12"
Jane Dunham

Wisconsin. In 1864, at the age of seventeen, he moved to Chicago, where he went to work making baskets and other willowware in the factory organized just a year earlier by George Bildhauser and Matthias Tillmann. After

Wakefield Rattan Company Robey near Blue Island, 1887–96.
Heywood and Morrill Rattan Co. 146 West Washington, 1888; 1251 West Taylor, 1889–96.
Heywood Brothers and Wakefield Company. 464 South Washtenaw, 1897–1901; 1302 (2653 after 1909) Harvard, 1902–20.
Heywood-Wakefield Co. 2653 Arthington, 1921–39; showroom: American Furniture Mart, 1924–63; Merchandise Mart, 1964–82.

Heywood & Morrill Rattan Co. was the Western branch of Heywood Brothers & Company, whose main factory was in Gardner, Massachusetts. The firm established a factory at Washington and Union streets in 1884, constructed a new building at Taylor and Rockwell streets four years later, and in 1897 merged with its rival, the Wakefield Rattan Company, which also had operated a rattan factory in Chicago since the mid-1880s. The resulting Heywood Brothers & Wakefield Company was, at the time, the country's major importer of rattan and the largest manufacturer of cane and reed products.

In Chicago the company made baby carriages in addition to rattan furniture. It added wooden opera chairs to its products after 1906, as well as a variety of chairs designed for use by children. In 1926 the Heywood-Wakefield Co. employed 5,000 people in 7 factories and 13 warehouses located in various parts of the country. When the depression forced the firm to consolidate its interests, the Chicago factory was closed, although the Arthington Street building remained in use as a warehouse for the next seven years. The company filed for bankruptcy in 1982.

the fire of 1871 destroyed the factory, Bildhauser withdrew and the company was reorganized as Tillmann & Frederick. The partners began making willow furniture in 1871 and two years later added rattan. When the partnership dissolved in 1880, both continued on their own.

By 1884, reflecting the growing acceptance of rattan and reed furniture, Frederick's firm had become the second largest wickerware manufacturer in the city. His work force had grown from two to thirty and, according to *American Furniture Gazette*, produced "800 articles" made of rattan, reed, and willow that year in Frederick's factory on Kinzie Street.[30] In addition Frederick operated a successful wholesale business that supplied other furniture manufacturers in the area with rattan imported from the East Indies.

The largest rattan and reed furniture factory in the city was the Chicago Rattan & Reed Company, organized four years earlier by William Pottle, Jr., and Henry V. Pierpont as a successor to the willowware company founded by Pottle's father in 1861. In 1882 Pottle and Pierpont "at once opened direct communications with the East Indies to secure a constant supply of rattan" and "put into operation the ingenious machines required in splitting rattan" in their factory at the corner of Sedgwick and Erie streets.[31] By 1886 the business had expanded so rapidly that the firm moved into a larger building on Superior Street, where 100 workers turned out 140 patterns of rattan and reed chairs and rockers. As *American Furniture Gazette* pointed out, most of the Chicago Rattan & Reed Company's products were sold to buyers in the West, since they could save on freight by buying in Chicago.

In the mid-1880s, when wicker furniture was at the height of its popularity, the country's two largest manufacturers of rattan and reed furniture—the Massachusetts-based firms of Wakefield Rattan Company and Heywood Brothers & Company—found it necessary to establish branch houses in Chicago in order to compete effectively with the large rattan and reed furniture factories that had sprung up within the city and had begun to monopolize the lucrative Western markets. Many years later, in a speech commemorating the 125th anniversary of Heywood Brothers, Richard N. Greenwood related how the two rival firms went about locating sites in the city:

> Both wanted a Chicago plant and warehouse. In spite of their competing interests, they decided to establish a joint manufacturing enterprise there. Representatives of both firms met in Chicago for the purpose of finding a suitable building. The first day's search was fruitless, so it was decided to renew the quest the following day. The next morning, however, the Wakefield men left early, found a plant and informed the Heywood representatives that the building was so satisfactory that they would purchase it independently and operate it themselves. After the resulting storm subsided, Henry Heywood and Amos Morrill of Heywood Brothers and Company found a plant to their liking, which was to be the Chicago factory and warehouse until 1930. It is safe to assume that competition was keener than ever during the years following this Chicago episode.[32]

During their early morning search, the Wakefields had discovered the large chamber furniture factory of Clark Brothers & Co., on South Robey

Street (now Damen Avenue) near Blue Island Avenue. The two parties negotiated a suitable agreement as a result of which the Wakefield Rattan Company moved into its spacious Chicago factory toward the end of 1887.[33]

The building found by Henry Heywood and Amos Morrill was located at the corner of West Washington and Union streets. For the next two years, the Heywood & Morrill Rattan Co. made chairs there under the supervision of George A. Ellis, a salesman familiar with the Western territory, and James S. Piper, an employee from the Gardner, Massachusetts, factory. In 1888 George H. Heywood was sent to Chicago to manage the new branch and under his supervision a new factory was built on vacant prairie lands on the city's West Side at the corner of West Taylor and Rockwell streets.[34]

In Chicago, as in the country as a whole, the 1880s were the golden age of wicker. Catering to the public's demand for novel and "artistic" furniture as well as to a growing fashion in things associated with the Ori-

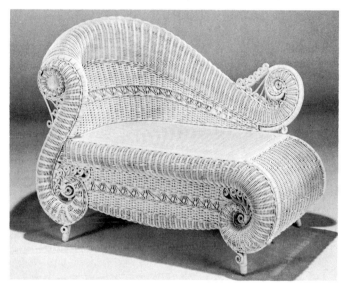

Made in the Chicago factory of Heywood Bros. and Wakefield Company during the 1890s, this rattan settee was later sprayed with enamel.
h: 33" w: 42" d: 21"
CHS, gift of the Estate of Evelyn Marie Stuart, 1970

ent, manufacturers took full advantage of the nature of rattan, reed, and willow to create designs that proved practical as well as stylish. Since rattan itself came from the Far East, manufacturers capitalized on its foreign origin by weaving Japanese fans, latticework, arabesques, or diaper (repeated diamond shaped) patterns inspired by the art and architecture of the Orient into the backs of wicker chairs.

In 1884, for example, an advertisement placed by C.W.H. Frederick in *American Furniture Gazette* showed a wicker rocking chair with a Japanese fan set in the back encircled by airy criss-cross latticework; a second rocker displayed a square of fine spiderweb caning surrounded by curlicues and interlocking loops of reed.[35] In the same publication, chairs offered by the Chicago Rattan & Reed Company featured backs inset with horseshoes, hearts, or diamonds caned with a common but intricate pattern resembling tiny six-pointed stars. Other chairs featured hollow serpentine arms, interlocking loops and lattices, roundels, and spirals. All of the wooden structural members, with the exception of rockers and the rims of the seats, were tightly wrapped with rattan, and all had cane or woven seats. Although the advertisements made no mention of color, wicker furniture made at

the time was either left in its natural state, lightly varnished, or painted in such colors as Pompeian Red, Cherry, Ebony, or Bronze. Because it could take stain or paint, reed was much more commonly used than rattan.

Toward the end of the 1880s, Chicago's wicker manufacturers began to join forces. By February 1888 C.W.H. Frederick had sold out to the Wakefield Rattan Company and was serving as manager of the latter company's Chicago branch.[36] In 1897 the Wakefield Rattan Company merged with its old rival, Heywood Brothers & Company, creating a new organization called the Heywood Brothers and Wakefield Company.

This merger of Chicago manufacturers may have been hastened by the sharp drop in the prices of rattan goods that occurred when a wickerworks was opened at Joliet Prison, some thirty miles southwest of Chicago. The flood of cheap prison-made chairs drew the wrath of Chicago rattan manufacturers, who lobbied unsuccessfully to have legislation passed prohibiting the sale of these goods on the open market. By 1914, when fire destroyed the prison workshop, it was estimated that 60 percent of the prisoners at Joliet were employed making chairs.[37]

While wooden and wicker chairs were being produced in large quantity and variety by well-established factories for use within the city and on the western frontier, a completely different set of companies was turning out highly popular lines of furniture destined for use in the country's new "commercial" buildings.

COMMERCIAL FURNITURE

CHAPTER 8

1873 - 1917

While the majority of Chicago furniture manufacturers took advantage of the rapidly growing residential market, others specialized in meeting the demands of the city's commercial, educational, and religious enterprises. The tremendous expansion of the city's industrial and commercial base, combined with the growth of the population between 1871 and 1893, led to a building boom that has never been equaled in Chicago's history. In the space of twenty-two years, Chicagoans put up 98,838 buildings, including 110 churches and 346 schools.[1]

The most important structures built during this period, however, were office buildings. After 1882, ten-, twelve-, and eventually, twenty-story "skyscrapers" dominated the Loop, as the city's central business district had come to be called. These new-style buildings were massive in scale and incorporated the latest technological innovations. Typically they sported sparsely ornamented façades of brick, terra cotta, and glass usually supported by steel-frame construction.

Inside these new buildings, hydraulic elevators carried workers and materials from floor to floor. Electric light supplemented the natural light let in by what became known as "Chicago windows," large windows with fixed center panes flanked by movable sashes designed to let in air as well as light.[2] In 1891, commenting on what they called the new "commercial style," the authors of *Industrial Chicago* accounted for its widespread appearance in the heart of the city as follows: "The requirements of commerce and the business principles of real estate owners called this style into life. Light, space, air, and strength were demanded by such requirements and principles as the first objects and exterior ornamentation as the second."[3]

The designers of furniture for use in these new types of structures tended to work within the same set of principles that had guided their architects. Modern business practices, public education, and a growing population created new design criteria. Form followed function and utility

A. H. Andrews & Co. 82 Washington, 1866–71; 119–121 Washington, 1872; 156–170 Mather, 1873–82; 195 Wabash, 1883–96; Twenty-second and Fiske, 1897–1909; 1100 West Twenty-second, 1910–ca. 1936; 1114 West Cermak, 1935–45; 4005 West Irving Park, 1965–66.

During the late nineteenth century A. H. Andrews & Co. was the largest furniture factory in Chicago, employing 500 workers in 1886 and operating branch factories in New York, Michigan, and Indiana. Andrews was involved in all aspects of manufacturing—from owning lumberyards to operating warehouses—and produced a wide range of products that included furniture, interior finish, and accessories like globes and books.

Specialized departments catered to outfitting offices, banks, schools, churches, and residences, supplying all of the furniture and interior woodwork as well as architectural elements like metal hardware and stained glass. Important commissions included the design and manufacture of furniture and interior finish for the Illinois Trust & Savings Bank, Chicago (1897); the Administration Building at the 1893 World's Fair; the Court House and Post Office, Philadelphia (1883); the Texas

counted for more than ornamentation. For example, desks designed for the modern office incorporated an abundance of drawers and pigeonholes for storing and filing ledgers and correspondence, as well as generous writing surfaces, and "roll" or cylinder-shaped tops (often called "curtains") that could be closed and locked to insure privacy when the owners were away from their desks. Special desks with indented tops or pull-out ledges were designed to accommodate typewriters. Surfaces were smooth and plain. Ornamentation, when it appeared, was unobtrusive, relegated to drawer fronts and side panels.

Chairs too were designed to meet particular needs, with special models being made for typists, clerks, telephone operators, or general office workers. A hybrid between a rocker and a revolving chair, the desk or "office" chair featured a seat that swiveled on a stationary tripod base, allowing its occupant to lean forward or backward or turn to face a visitor. In contrast, the typewriter chair revolved but did not tilt, since the typist's major requirement was a resilient support for the spine and the freedom to reach left and right.[4] School desks, opera chairs, railroad seats, and bank furnishings developed in the same way, reflecting the adaptation of standard forms to increasingly specialized needs.

By the 1880s several large Chicago firms were engaged in making furniture designed to meet the needs of offices, schools, and churches. One of the oldest of these, the Sherwood School Furniture Company, had been established in 1856. Between 1867 and 1871 Henry M. Sherwood patented designs for school desks and for a folding seat suitable for church, hall, or garden[5] and was awarded a prize for school furniture at the Vienna International Exposition of 1873.[6]

Such firms generally worked under contract to design and manufacture large quantities of given items for a business or institution. This was true, for example, of Stotz, Woltz & Co., which operated a large factory on Illinois Street between 1863 and 1893. Both founders of the firm had come from Germany and had begun by working for some of Chicago's pioneer cabinetmakers. Woltz, who had arrived in 1847, served an apprenticeship with John Harrison and then worked in the shops of Jacob Strehl, the Cook brothers, and Caleb Morgan. Stotz, who had arrived in 1854, was employed by March Brothers and Charles Tobey.[7]

Prior to the 1871 fire, Stotz and Woltz manufactured all kinds of furniture; afterwards, they specialized in custom-designed commercial furniture and interior woodwork for fine residences. By 1883, 100 "skilled mechanics" worked in their factory, making bank, office, store, church, and lodge furnishings. Often under contract to the government to execute the interiors of large public buildings, they had just completed the counters, screens, and fixtures for the Customs House in Chicago[8] and had been commissioned to furnish the Customs House under construction in St. Louis, Missouri.

The largest firm engaged in the manufacture of commercial furniture—and also the largest furniture enterprise in general in Chicago during the 1880s and 1890s—was A. H. Andrews & Co., founded by Alfred H. Andrews in 1865. A native of Hartford, Connecticut, Andrews had moved to Chicago in 1857 and had become a salesman for the Sherwood School

Furniture Company. Eight years later he organized A. H. Andrews & Co., leasing an office in the Crosby Opera House and acquiring a factory at the corner of Washington and Jefferson streets where he began to manufacture school furniture.

State Capitol (1888); and the Chicago Public Library (1897). A. H. Andrews & Co. identified its products using metal tags (desks, cabinets, etc.) and paper labels (custom furniture and wood-work), or by casting its name as part of the design (school desks).

Starting in 1894, the company's fortunes took a turn for the worse. Bankruptcy and failure in 1895 caused reorganization in May 1896, with A. H. Andrews & Co.'s merchandise, lumber, and good will being sold to Merle & Heaney Mfg. Co. The following year a fire destroyed the company's warehouse. Alfred Hinsdale Andrews (1838–1914) continued to be listed as president of the company through the year of his death. After 1933, A. H. Andrews & Co. made only bank furnishings.

Advertisement showing the variety of products available from A. H. Andrews & Co. by 1873. From Rebuilt Chicago, *1873.*

In 1870 Andrews was joined by Herbert L. Andrews (relationship unknown), who, two years earlier, had patented a school desk incorporating a simple and efficient method of joining the folding seat to the desk standard that allowed the seat to fold noiselessly and not strike against the back of the seat.[9] Put into production in six sizes as the Triumph school desk, it featured a curved wooden back and "Gothic" style cast-iron supports on the sides of the desk. This desk was first exhibited at the Inter-

Oak and cast-iron school desks made by A. H. Andrews & Co., used in St. Michael's Catholic School, 1620 North Hudson, from 1910 through 1978.
h: 30¼" w: 24" d: 32"
CHS, gift of St. Michael's School, 1978

State Industrial Exposition in Chicago in 1873. Displayed again at the 1876 Centennial Exposition in Philadelphia, the desk won an award for "Strength, Durability, and Good Form."[10] Four years later Andrews claimed to have sold "over 50,000 school desks yearly, for the past three years," including $50,000 worth to the Chicago public schools.[11]

By 1873 Andrews had added maps, globes, blackboards, erasers, and other supplies necessary for equipping schoolrooms to its line of products. To "feed the brain as well as feast the eye," the company later began to operate a publishing house, furnishing works of history and political science in a profusion that, according to the *Inland Architect and Builder*, "astonished the cynics who call this an age of triflers."[12]

Adapting the principle used in making folding school desks, Andrews added a department to manufacture "opera" chairs with folding seats and perforated wood or upholstered backs for use in auditoriums, theaters, and other meeting places. In 1879 Andrews supplied the new Chicago Music Hall with opera chairs equipped with tilting backs as well as with racks underneath the seat to hold gentlemen's top hats.[13] Similar chairs were eventually installed in the McVickers, Hooley's, The Schiller, The Columbia, and other Chicago theaters and in the Metropolitan Opera House and numerous theaters in New York City. Around 1889 the company received "the largest single contract ever awarded in this country for opera chairs" when it was chosen to fabricate some 4,000 folding seats for the Auditorium Theater then under construction on West Congress Street.[14]

The firm also began to manufacture other kinds of furniture. Its 1876 catalogue indicated that Andrews was capable of furnishing an entire church—"including the Pews, Pulpits, Altar, Chairs, Stained Windows,

Interior of the Illinois Trust & Savings Bank, Chicago, outfitted by A. H. Andrews & Co. in 1897.

Communion Tables and Service, Bells and miscellaneous conveniences, and the entire furnishing of the Sabbath School Room, Vestry and Pastor's Study."[15] By 1879 it had acquired the rights to the Burr Patent Parlor Bed, which folded into a writing desk, dressing case, bureau, or bookcase.[16] *Marquis' Hand Book of Chicago* for 1885 claimed that nearly 100 of these celebrated folding beds were in use in the Palmer House alone.[17]

From folding chairs and church outfitting, A. H. Andrews moved into the realm of interior work, opening branch houses in New York, Philadelphia, and Boston to satisfy "all the varied wants of court houses and other public buildings, also interior woodwork of first-class dwellings."[18] The company's catalogue by 1886 included 100 patterns of office desks; office chairs upholstered in leather or cane; revolving top store stools "in endless variety"; bank and office sofas and lounges; and settees and desks especially designed for use in railroad offices and stations.[19]

In addition to woodwork and furniture, Andrews supplied original designs in metal, stained glass, wall decorations, and draperies. Grilles, gates, partitions, hardware, and other metalwork required in completing every aspect of architectural or furnishing commissions came from the company's own brass and wire departments, while stained glass and wall decorations were created by artists employed by the firm or hired on contract from one of the local glasswork or decorating studios. By 1882 A. H. Andrews & Co. had supplied all of the furniture for the new post office in

Hartford, Connecticut, and for the Customs House in Chicago, and had completely furnished fourteen courtrooms, seven clerks' offices, the law

library, and the reading room in the new Cook County Court House being completed at Clark, Randolph, LaSalle, and Washington streets.[20]

At its peak in the mid-1880s A. H. Andrews & Co. was a diversified manufacturing empire that comprised seven branches of furniture making and encompassed all aspects of production and ownership from timber supplies and fabrication of subsidiary products to branch offices for sales and shipment. Four large factories—three in Chicago and one in Mishawaka, Indiana—employed more than 500 people, including draftsmen, carvers, cabinetmakers, and finishers, along with a variety of clerical workers and salesmen.[21] For administrative purposes, manufacturers were divided into seven distinct departments: school and office desks; globes and other school apparatus; opera chairs; church fittings; bank fittings; fine brasswork fittings; and folding beds. Organized as a subsidiary of the firm in 1884, the Andrews Lumber Company owned large tracts of timberland in northern Arkansas and supplied all of the lumber used in the parent firm's various manufacturing divisions.[22] Similarly, A. H. Andrews & Co. owned and furnished "to a vast clientage" the Noyes Process for kiln-drying lumber and served as agents for the Electro-Pneumatic Valve System, an electric thermostat developed to maintain a uniform temperature within large buildings so as to save fuel and prevent furniture and woodwork from cracking.[23]

To complete the interiors of fine residences, Andrews offered wood fireplace mantels and furniture "designed to order," staircases, wood paneling, and entire reception halls that could be installed locally or shipped prefabricated in railroad cars to be assembled thousands of miles away.

Oak altar made in 1897 by A. H. Andrews & Co. for the Grand Army of the Republic Hall in the Chicago Public Library (now the Cultural Center). The carved panels depict the Battle of Bull Run and the encounter between the Monitor *and the* Merrimac. *Wood carvers generally applied full-size drawings on which the main lines were perforated to the wood, then hit them with a chalk bag to transfer the main outlines.*
h: 42" w: 96" d: 47"
Chicago Public Library Cultural Center

Today, few interiors known to have been executed by Andrews have survived the ravages of urban renewal in the Chicago area. One can, however, still view the splendid oak-paneled stair hall made by A. H. Andrews & Co. for Craigdarroch Castle in Victoria, British Columbia, Canada. Completed in 1889, the large Norman-towered "castle" was commissioned by Scottish-born coal millionaire Robert Dunsmuir, who named it after the home of Scottish heroine Annie Laurie. It had been designed by the architectural firm of Williams and Smith, Portland, Oregon, which commissioned A. H. Andrews & Co. to fabricate the Great Hall in Chicago and then had it shipped west by railroad.[24]

Closer to home, Andrews executed the interior finish and special furniture for the Chicago Public Library at Washington Street and Michigan

Avenue erected in 1897. Still to be seen in the Grand Army of the Republic Memorial Hall are massive built-in exhibition cases and a central altar/podium hand-carved on all sides with scenes from the Civil War. The carving was done under the supervision of Julius Fritze, a German woodcarver who was foreman of A. H. Andrews & Co.'s carving shop from the late 1880s through 1908.[25]

Since the first Inter-State Industrial Exposition in 1873, when the firm displayed a parlor table inlaid with 85,000 pieces of wood, A. H. Andrews & Co. had taken great pride in the skill of its workmen in executing marquetry. While the company's line of parquet flooring provided examples of this art in the form of a utilitarian product, the company's craftsmen also created more exotic pieces of marquetry as presentation offerings to mark special occasions or for display at exhibitions. For example, to commemorate the Republican National Convention held in Chicago in 1884, at which James G. Blaine was nominated the party's presidential candidate, A. H. Andrews & Co. presented a gavel "made of wood from every State and territory in the Union including Alaska" with a handle made from the old Charter Oak tree of Hartford, Connecticut.[26] The gavel's whereabouts are unknown, but the walnut podium upon which it was pounded, also made

Carving crew at A. H. Andrews & Co. taking a lunch break in 1897. Foreman Julius Fritze is standing in the office doorway in rear.
Inez K. Fritze

by A. H. Andrews & Co., has long been in the collection of the Chicago Historical Society. Used in 1880, 1884, and 1888, the podium bears inscriptions recording the nominations of James A. Garfield, James G. Blaine, and Benjamin Harrison.

Something of a departure from its wooden furniture was the line of metal furniture that A. H. Andrews & Co. was manufacturing by 1892. This included office and other chairs, stools, easels, and tables made of twisted strands of iron and advertised as "Elegant, Indestructible, Cheap."[27]

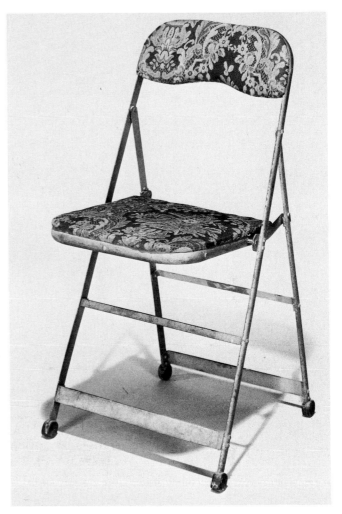

These wire chairs were made by A. H. Andrews & Co. for use in restaurants, hospitals, and factories.
Colorado Springs Fine Arts Center

Metal folding chair with tapestry upholstery made by the Royal Metal Manufacturing Company ca. 1920.
h: 34" w: 15"
CHS, gift of Mrs. Dewey A. Ericson, 1971

The chairs and tables were used primarily in restaurants, factories, and hospitals, where sanitation was of prime concern. By then, similar twisted-wire products were being made by piano stool manufacturer Max Tonk and the Royal Metal Manufacturing Company. A metalworking firm organized in 1888 by Joseph Salmon, a former vice-president of the Chicago Architectural Iron Works, the Royal Metal Manufacturing Company began early in the 1890s to create airy chairs, shoeshine stands, mirror frames, and tables whose contours resembled those of furniture produced in bent wood by Austrian furniture maker Michael Thonet. By 1907 the firm offered

Royal Metal Co. 106–08 Oakley, ca. 1897–1900.

Royal Metal Manufacturing Co. 34–36 West Washington, 1901–4; 42–44 South Clinton, 1905; 1817–19 Dearborn, 1906–11; 2318 South Western, 1912–17; 1100–40 South Michigan, 1923–39; 175 North Michigan, 1940–57; Merchandise Mart Plaza, 1958–62. Factory located in Michigan City, Indiana, after 1920.

Joseph Salomon organized the Royal Metal Co. after working for several years at the Chicago Architectural Iron Works. The company produced a wide range of metal furnishings, including chairs, stools, tables, mirrors, and folding chairs, all intended for office, industrial, or commercial use. Some of the products were made of twisted wire; others were molded metal. Joseph Salomon's nephew, Irving, took over as president in 1928.

Thorson & Tollakson. 27 North Jefferson, 1875–78; North Lincoln corner West Kinzie, 1878–82; 17 Armour, 1883.
Central Furniture Manufacturing Co. 37–41 Armour, 1884–86
Central Manufacturing Co. 37–41 (454–56 after 1909) Armour, 1887–1929.
Central Desk Co. 454–56 Armour, 1930–ca. 1968.

such a wide variety of bent-iron products, steel folding chairs, and swiveling iron-based store stools that *Furniture Journal* commented, "Their line is probably the most complete on the market, embracing everything known to 'Stooldom.'"[28]

While companies like A. H. Andrews and Tonk Mfg. continued to diversify their line of products, several smaller firms took advantage of the steadily increasing demand for various kinds of office desks. One of the largest of these was the Chicago Desk Manufacturing Co., whose factory at Peoria and Kinzie streets employed eighty workers by 1887.[29] Organized eight years earlier by Lars L. Skielvig and John H. Minges, the firm shipped nearly all of its output to customers located outside of the city. At Nineteenth and Blackwell streets, thirty patterns of "flat-top, slope-top, standing and cylinder desks" in walnut and cherry were manufactured by Simmen & Sebastian. Both former employees of Sugg & Beiersdorf, John Simmen had worked as a designer and carver at the firm for five years before setting up his own factory in 1883. His partner, Bavarian-born cabinetmaker Michael Sebastian, remained a major stockholder and secretary of Sugg & Beiersdorf, where he had worked since 1868.[30]

At the Central Manufacturing Co. on Armour Street more than fifty patterns of desks and bookcases were being made under the direction of Norwegian cabinetmakers Soren Thorsen, Thore Tollakson, and Nils Arneson. Founded as Thorson & Tollakson in 1875, the firm was shipping goods to such distant places as San Francisco and New York by 1884.[31] Nearby, A. Petersen & Co. produced sixty-seven varieties of desks finely finished with veneer panels, incised lines, and an abundance of pigeonholes. A pioneer in the export trade, A. Petersen claimed by 1899 to send a carload of desks "abroad every two weeks, the greater portion going to London, some to Germany, Norway, Sweden, Denmark, Finland, and even South Africa."[32]

Cylinder desks were a specialty of R. T. Hambrook, whose factory made a general line of church, school, office, and residential furniture. In 1873, S. S. Schoff reported, Hambrook was manufacturing a desk "unsurpassed" in elegance of design that was "also furnished with a lock of peculiar construction (for which a patent has been applied for)." One double turn of the key "unlocked every drawer and pigeon-hole, both inside and outside the desk, as well as the cylindrical slide."[33]

While the great majority of cabinetmakers prided themselves on the large number of patterns they offered, at least two manufacturers were content to develop, patent, and produce one type of product only. One such "useful invention" was the wood and cast-iron stand designed for holding heavy dictionaries manufactured by its inventor, LaVerne Noyes. Establishing his own factory in 1879, Noyes built up "a very large connection among the wholesale booksellers" for his patent dictionary holders by 1887.[34]

Another specialized company was T. E. Gordon & Son, which made "vertical cylinder desks," whose rounded tops, instead of rolling inward, "hinged out to a horizontal position even with the base of the inside case forming a wide and roomy space for writing." To use every inch of space,

Poulsen & Johnson, like most of the city's desk manufacturers, offered desks for both commercial and home use. From American Furniture Gazette, *April 1885.*

Born in 1847 in Norway, where he was trained as a cabinetmaker, Soren Thorson emigrated to Chicago in 1870. After spending several years as a journeyman, he worked in partnership with Thore Tollakson between 1875 and 1884, making office and library desks and bank and office fixtures. In 1884 a trade journal noted that Thorson & Tollakson had been succeeded by the Central Furniture Manufacturing Co. and that the new firm employed more than 100 Scandinavian workers, producing roll-top and flat-top desks and office furniture.

In 1905, when Nils Arneson was the company's president, A. E. Strand's *A History of the Norwegians of Illinois* noted that the Central Manufacturing Co. employed "more than six score expert artificers in wood." Alf Normann (1872–1956) headed the firm from the early twenties through about 1952. After World War II the company employed twenty to thirty workers manufacturing medium- to high-priced office furniture in walnut, mahogany, and oak.

Alf Normann's son, Chester, was president in 1961 when the firm was sold to Vincent Ford and Casimir Bogdan. While about 70 percent of the company's production remained the same, modular office furniture and custom office work became more important. In 1964–65 the name was changed to Central States Furniture Co.

the inside of the top was divided into pigeonholes of all sizes to hold letters or stationery, while the base opened out to reveal even more drawers, pigeonholes, and bookracks. Described as "an inventive genius" by *American Cabinet Maker*'s visiting representative in 1878, Gordon had turned his attention to the production of furniture specialties "for the use and convenience of mercantile men in their offices and counting rooms," which combined "all the qualities of convenience, room and comfort as well as looks."[35]

Chicago's phenomenal expansion soon attracted the attention of outside entrepreneurs as well. In 1886, for example, three of the largest manufacturers of commercial furniture whose factories were located in other cities—the American Store Stool Company, Thomas Kane, and Wm. H. Foulkes & Co.—located their headquarters within two blocks of one another on Wabash Avenue. At 246 Wabash Avenue, store, bank, and office furniture and fittings were sold through the Chicago branch of the New York-based American Store Stool Company. Next door, fifty clerks employed by Thomas Kane took orders for church, school, and office furniture manufactured by the Racine Furniture Manufacturing Co. of Racine, Wisconsin.[36] In the next block, Wm. H. Foulkes & Co. served as an outlet for the products of the Richmond Church Furniture Works, as well as for Wooten's Patent Office Desks, wooden fireplace mantels, and ceramic tiles.[37]

Smaller companies that manufactured office and store fixtures in Chicago included the U. S. Desk & Office Fitting Co., which operated factories at Calhoun Place and on Sloan Street (now Crystal); the firm of Mikkelson & Bendtsen, engaged in general jobbing in office furniture and tables, counters, and signs for stores; and Weber Brothers, organized in 1882 to manufacture store fixtures.[38] Yet another was the Amberg File & Index Co., founded by William A. Amberg, who had developed the system of flat letter filing now in universal use in 1868. After 1870 his company made wooden filing cabinets and storage units to order.[39]

A wide variety of church pews, pulpits, and chairs was available through manufacturers' catalogues, although many large congregations preferred to have their churches outfitted with furnishings especially designed to complement the interior of the building. By 1886 two manufacturers—Sebastian Buschert and Valentine Gramer—were active in this branch of cabinetmaking, kept busy by the steady demand for furniture and altars for the many churches then under construction in Chicago and the areas further west.

Buschert, for example, employed "ten hands, selling throughout the country by advertising and through the missionary fathers." Described by A. T. Andreas as an artist "who makes his own designs," he had come to Chicago in 1866, when, at the age of seventeen, he began an apprenticeship as an ornamental carver in the shop of his uncle, Anton Buschert, the city's pioneer manufacturer of church furniture.[40] Also German born, Valentine Gramer employed fifteen workmen and, like his rival, made his own designs for Catholic churches located throughout the western United States.[41]

When Chicago's furniture manufacturers were tallied in 1891, they totaled 257, a marked increase over the 59 recorded in 1870. Approximately 30,000 were employed in various branches of the industry, compared with 1,126 workers 22 years earlier.[42] To celebrate the amazing growth of the industry, Chicago manufacturers began to make plans to be represented in the World's Columbian Exposition originally scheduled to take place in their city in 1892. However, as mentioned earlier, "another and prior opportunity arose for them to display their enterprise" in 1891.[43]

When members of the Chicago Furniture Manufacturers' Association heard that the lakefront building that had housed the Inter-State Industrial Expositions since 1873 was to be demolished, they "determined that it should go out in a blaze of glory" and planned a colossal furniture exhibition to serve as a preview for the larger exhibition of 1893.[44] With this in mind, they organized committees to oversee finance, space allotment, rules and regulations, decorating and entertainment, advertising and transportation.

Oak and cast-iron dictionary stand patented and manufactured by LaVerne Noyes in the 1880s.
h: 39½″ w: 21⅛″
CHS, gift of Mr. and Mrs. Larry Boeder, 1983

Walnut slant-front desk made by John Christian Lilleskau while employed as foreman at the Central Desk Company in the 1880s.
h: 61″ w: 31″ d: 17½″
Hazel Kahle Williams

The executive committee, headed by fancy cabinet ware manufacturer Frank Wenter, mailed out 50,000 invitations to friends and furniture dealers around the country.

The Chicago Furniture Exposition opened on July 6, 1891, and ran for one month. It featured 105 exhibitors, including 11 from Rockford. Illinois, and Wisconsin. Covering 240,000 square feet of floor space, striking displays of varnish, woven-wire mattresses, woodworking tools, feathers, and furniture fixtures were interspersed with exhibits of Chicago-made furniture. Office desks, bookcases, and library furniture were displayed by large firms such as the Chicago Desk Manufacturing Company and the Central Manufacturing Company, as well as by smaller firms such as Hans Poulsen, A. Peterson, and A. J. Johnson & Co.

Two entire "art rooms" were filled with hall trees, china closets, and other fancy furniture from the factory of Frank Wenter, while Turkish chairs and lounges made by the Hafner & Schoen Furniture Company covered an area totaling 3,500 feet. A. Matuska, Sugg & Beiersdorf, J. F. Balkwill & Co., and A. H. Andrews & Co. displayed parlor folding beds; Louis F. Nonnast, J. P. Wolf & Co., and Niemann & Weinhardt exhibited tables. Quarter-sawn oak chamber sets were featured by Olbrich & Golbeck, L. M. Hamline, and J. F. Balkwill; Adams & Westlake, a Chicago metalworking company, introduced its new line of brass and metal beds. J. S. Ford, Johnson & Co., F. Herhold & Sons, and the Johnson Chair Company showed a great variety of chairs, while parlor furniture was displayed by the National Parlor Furniture Co., August Hausske, and S. Karpen & Bros.

As plans for the World's Columbian Exposition became known, Chicago's furniture manufacturers had reason to be pleased at their enterprise in holding the 1891 exposition. It turned out that so little space had been allocated to American-made furniture that the major companies in several of the centers of furniture manufacture—Grand Rapids, Indianapolis, and Rockford—decided to display their products in combined exhibits. The upshot was that individual firms were able to show only one or two samples of their finest work. In the *Official Catalogue* of the 1893 fair, thirty-two Chicago firms were listed as exhibitors in the Manufacturers' Building, with products ranging from the billiard tables of Brunswick-Balke-Collender Company to barber chairs by Theo. A. Kochs and school and office furniture from the factories of A. H. Andrews & Co.[45]

Among the award winners from Chicago were the Tonk Manufacturing Co. for piano stools and S. Karpen & Bros., whose Turkish parlor suite was awarded a prize for excellent workmanship in upholstery of overstuffed furniture.[46] Upholstered in leather and elaborately tasseled and fringed, the suite was tufted on back, seat, and double armrest and outlined with bands of puffing. Following suggestions appearing in *American Cabinet Maker & Upholsterer*, Solomon Karpen had obviously succeeded in creating "the highest art in design, and the most perfect workmanship and finish which his establishment has at command."[47]

Though not known to be a prize winner, J. S. Ford, Johnson & Co. was richly represented at the Columbian fair through the 54,000 chairs ordered for the dedication exercises. To complete the order in time for the

·1893·

TONK MANUFACTURING CO'S EXHIBIT AT WORLD'S FAIR, CHICAGO.

Tonk Manufacturing Co. spared no expense to make a fine showing at the 1893 World's Columbian Exposition.

Blue ribbon won by Tonk Manufacturing Co. for its display at the 1893 World's Columbian Exposition.
Mr. and Mrs. Hampton E. Tonk and Family

opening, the company was forced to subcontract work to the Johnson Chair Co. and F. Herhold & Sons of Chicago, as well as to several Wisconsin firms. "It was no small task to get this large number of chairs in place," *American Cabinet Maker & Upholsterer* reported. "All of them but the best ones were put together in the building, a force of men being occupied doing this part of the work for ten days."[48]

COMMERCIAL FURNITURE

Oak piano stool by the Tonk Manufacturing Co. of the type shown in the firm's display at the World's Columbian Exposition.
h: 17½" d: 14¼"
Mr. and Mrs. Hampton E. Tonk
and Family

Throughout this ordeal, Chicago furniture manufacturers received nothing but praise from their colleagues. "The furniture interests of Chicago have a very large interest to represent to World's Fair visitors. Their output last year represented $24,000,000. It will be greater this year. . . . It can be said, however, that the Chicago manufacturers have in no respect been clamourous, or disposed toward selfishness in the matter of their participation in the furniture display at the Fair. They are Chicagoans and their action and attitude, I can truthfully say, have been thoroughly in keeping with the broad spirit manifested by Chicago in building the Fair."[49]

*Walnut piano stool with plush uphol-
stered seat made in the Tonk factory.
h: 17½"*
CHS, purchase, 1976

Max Tonk. 87–91 West Lake, 1874–77;
87 West Lake and 37 North Jefferson,
1878–80; 87 West Lake and 24 North
Jefferson, 1881–82; 804 Hawthorne,
1883–84.
Tonk Manufacturing Co. 804 Hawthorne, 1886–1902; 2028–32 Clybourn,
1903–18; 1960 Lewis, 1920; 1912 Lewis
(renamed Magnolia in 1937), 1921–62.

Born in Berlin, Germany, Max Tonk
(1851–1914) moved with his family
from Newark, New Jersey, to Chicago
in 1857. As a youth he learned to carve
in the factory owned by his uncle,
Julius Bauer, manufacturer of pianos
and organs. Tonk opened his own
carving shop in 1873 to supply the
carved wooden ornaments then used in
abundance on furniture and coffins. He
soon began making carved and scroll-
sawn wall brackets and a line of piano
stools. From the 1880s through the
1920s the company manufactured
swivel stools and, later on, benches for
use with pianos and organs, as well as
twisted-wire chairs, music cabinets,
and music racks. During the 1890s it
made wooden Old Hickory bicycles. In
1932, when the depression reduced the
demand for piano benches, it turned to
producing tables and other novelty furniture.
    After Max Tonk's death, the com-
pany was headed by his son, Percy A.
Tonk (1890–1967), and later by his
grandson, Hampton E. Tonk, and
granddaughter, Doris A. Tonk.

CHAPTER 9

CABINET WARES: PLAIN AND FANCY

1873 - 1917

Stadtfeld & Wolf. Van Buren, SW corner Franklin, 1871; 96 Beach, 1872; 69 Beach, 1873–75; 398 South Canal, 1876; 351 South Canal, 1877–83.
J. P. Wolf & Co. 351 South Canal, 1884–97.
Chicago Table Works. 351 South Canal, 1898; 750–60 Throop, 1899–1904.

The table factory founded by Matthias Stadtfeld and John Peter Wolf was one of the largest and best known in Chicago during the 1870s and early 1880s. In 1884, when Stadtfeld left the firm, the company's sixty workers continued making tables under the name of J. P. Wolf & Co. After Wolf's death in 1895, Michael Brand ran the company until 1899. A year later the *Furniture Worker* noted that Chicago Table Works was "toning up the line of goods" and catering to a better trade. At that time, it employed thirty to thirty-five men. On February 10, 1904, a fire destroyed the factory.

In 1878 the authors of *Beautiful Homes* advised their readers that the "inevitable" center table that once stood firmly in the middle of the parlor had been replaced by several small tables standing around the periphery of the room. Mentioning just a few of the possible shapes and sizes, they noted that "the methods of embellishing these elegant little affairs are *ad infinitum.*"[1]

In Chicago, furniture makers offered a host of tables in a variety of shapes and sizes. While thousands were made by firms producing chamber furniture, thousands more were turned out by manufacturers specializing solely in the production of tables. One of the first firms in Chicago to make tables exclusively was Stadtfeld & Wolf, established in 1868 by Matthias Stadtfeld, an expert in scroll sawing, and John Peter Wolf. A rare sixteen-page *Illustrated Catalogue of Stadtfeld & Wolf's Center Table Manufactory* from the mid-1870s demonstrates the variety of their manufactures: square or oval walnut Renaissance style center tables in thirty-six patterns; plain kitchen tables with poplar tops and hardwood legs; walnut drop-leaf breakfast tables; ash or walnut extension tables with additional leaves; five styles of hatracks; and four types of whatnots, two with scroll-sawn supports, two with turned pillars. The introduction noted that goods could be shipped either "set up" or "K.D. boxed," indicating a well-established wholesale mail-order market.[2]

In 1879 *American Cabinet Maker* reported that Stadtfeld & Wolf's factory was "running full blast," noting that the firm had "a larger business than ever" partly due to a recent order from California for "1,000 feet" of "leaf extension tables." "The popularity of their extension tables," the trade paper commented, "is largely due to their patent leg arrangement for unscrewing the legs thus enabling the tables to be shipped knock down." Commenting on the progress of the firm one year later, the periodical noted that Stadtfeld & Wolf now employed "sixty men in the manufacture of 43 different styles of marble top tables."[3]

Center tables and whatnots similar in appearance and price to those made by Stadtfeld & Wolf were produced by Rudolph E. Pohle and H. F. Klopp, two "young persevering gentlemen" who worked in a "snug little

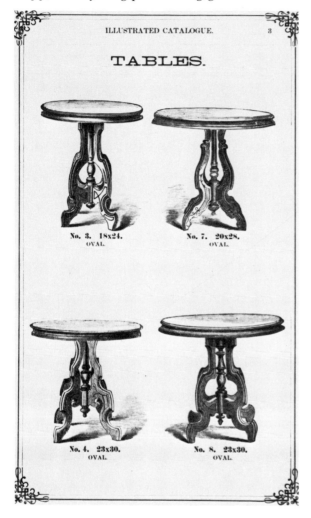

Pages from Illustrated Catalogue of Stadtfeld & Wolf's Center Table Manufactory *issued ca. 1875.*

Walnut table with marble top, burl veneer panels, and turned center support made by Stadtfeld & Wolf in the 1870s.
h: 28¾" w: 18⅛" d: 14⅛"
CHS, purchase, 1979

factory" at 316 South Clinton Street.[4] Born in Chicago of German parents, Pohle began an apprenticeship at the age of thirteen in the shop of chamber furniture manufacturer John Koenig, where he was trained as a woodcarver. Two years later, in 1869, he began working for Butzow Brothers (manufacturers of cylinder desks and center tables) during the day and studying bookkeeping and design at a commercial college in the evening. At seventeen he began working as a cabinetmaker in the table factory of Stadtfeld & Wolf, where he was soon promoted to foreman of the factory and superintendent of the shipping room.[5] Here Pohle remained until 1876, when he and Klopp pooled their capital and accomplishments.

Starting out in a twenty-by-sixty-foot room, Pohle and Klopp worked hard and saw their factory grow steadily. Three years later, when Pohle purchased his partner's share of the business, the work force had increased

Mahogany center table made at the factory of Rudolph E. Pohle ca. 1885. Ornamented with veneered panels and carved roundels, the base supports four carved pots of flowers.
h: 29½" w: 30½" d: 22"
CHS, purchase, 1971

Pohle & Klopp. 316 South Clinton, 1877–1879.
R. E. Pohle & Co. 316 South Clinton, 1880–83; 313–17 South Clinton, 1884–97; 306 and 308 South Clinton, 1897.

Rudolph E. Pohle (b. 1854) operated one of the largest table factories in Chicago in the 1880s and early 1890s and manufactured center, pillar, and extension tables in addition to hall trees and whatnots. Although a large advertisement for the company appeared in an 1897 trade journal, no listings appear in the Chicago directories after that year. Pohle is listed variously as a laborer and a manager through 1913. In 1898 *American Cabinetmaker & Upholsterer* mentioned that W. A. Giffert, successor to R. E. Pohle & Co., had gone out of business.

from only two to twenty. By 1883, when Pohle moved across the street into a new factory embracing some 15,000 square feet, fifty workmen were employed in "the largest table factory in Chicago."[6] Commenting on the firm in 1884, *American Furniture Gazette* noted that "Mr. Pohle designs and manufactures as many tables as any other man in the business west of New York" and claimed that "his work, his factory, himself are now living active testimonials of industrial prosperity."[7]

Illustrations of tables appearing in *American Cabinet Maker* and in his catalogues indicate Pohle's preference for rectangular center and side tables in his personal interpretation of the Eastlake, Queen Anne, and Gothic styles. Shown are tables with wooden tops or frames for marble tops, and aprons edged with saw-tooth or volute bands and flat, stylized carving. Legs were often joined at the base by stretchers whose intersections were topped by a finial, a turned support, or a garden of carved sunflowers.[8]

By the end of the 1880s one of the largest table factories in the city was supervised by pioneer furniture maker William Niemann. A Chicago cabinetmaker since 1845, Niemann had been foreman at Louis Schultze's Milwaukee Avenue furniture factory from 1865 until 1875, when he joined Conrad O. Lenz and Frederick Herhold in operating their chair manufactory on Erie Street. After fire destroyed the chair factory in 1880, Niemann built a new factory at 392 North Wood Street, taking into partnership his sons, William Henry and Albert, and his son-in-law, Hermann Weinhardt. In this new enterprise, the senior Niemann designed the furniture and supervised the factory, while William Henry took over the shipping department and Albert worked as a turner in the machine shop. Hermann Weinhardt, who had spent nine years as bookkeeper for silversmiths Juergens & Anderson, ran the office and kept track of sales.[9]

During the first year of operation, Niemann, Weinhardt & Co. made walnut and maple cane seat chairs along with bureaus, washstands, and cradles.[10] These items were soon discontinued, however, in favor of inexpensive whitewood kitchen and dining-room tables and a line of center

French-style side table with brass mountings made in the factory of Louis F. Nonnast from a design by John Christian Lilleskau ca. 1910.
h: 29½" w: 16" d: 16"
Hazel Kahle Williams

tables, wardrobes, and baby cribs.[11] "Substantial, reliable goods," not fancy tables, became the hallmark of the company. Production was geared to "goods which are intended for actual hard usage and hence are built honestly and substantially, with as neat an outline as is compatible with their make-up."[12] By 1884 Niemann, Weinhardt & Co.'s factory, including lumberyards and kilns, covered ten lots. *American Cabinet Maker* could claim that the company's table factory had "the largest business of any in the United States."[13]

In 1888 Niemann's younger son Albert left the company organized by his father, half-brother, and brother-in-law to join his brother, Henry C.

Neimann, and August Horman in organizing a rival table factory, H. C. Niemann & Co. Located on North Rockwell Street, the new firm produced medium and cheap grades of extension and parlor tables, stands, wardrobes, and cupboards.[14]

Workmen at the table factory of Louis F. Nonnast & Sons, 1025 North Halsted, ca. 1915. Emery Nonnast, son of the founder, is seated in the first row, fifth from left. To his left is John Christian Lilleskau, foreman and designer from 1895 until 1923.
Hazel Kahle Williams

Nonnast & Luchs. 27 North Jefferson, 1878–79.

Louis F. Nonnast. 25–27 North Jefferson, 1880–88; 254–64 North Green, 1896–1908; 935–1025 North Halsted, 1909–13.

Louis F. Nonnast & Sons. 935–1025 North Halsted, 1914–31.

A German who came to Chicago in 1865, Louis Frederick Nonnast (b. 1848) specialized in making tables of all kinds as well as hall trees, fancy chairs, and curio cabinets. In 1899 *American Cabinet Maker* described the company as "the largest manufacturer of hall trees and tables in the country." A decade later *Furniture Journal* cited 75 types of library and director's tables in addition to the firm's 100 patterns of dining-room tables.

At the turn of the century the company employed 150 workers and a full-time designer, John C. Lilleskau. Advertisements indicate that Nonnast was the "sole manufacturer" of Peerless and Royal extension tables, which contained a special sliding device patented by Nonnast and Wilhelm Tesar in 1900.

Nonnast's factory was sold in 1903 to the Chicago & North Western Railway Co. to make way for a new passenger station. The new factory on Halsted Street covered three acres and featured separate buildings for a power plant, pumphouse, veneer house, and lumber sheds.

Other table manufacturers included Framke & Sievers, a partnership composed of Reinolds Framke and August Sievers, Jr., whose factory employed seventy-five workmen in 1886;[15] Schuebert Bros., a company manufacturing center tables, hall trees, and cradles distinguished by an abundance of finials and drops;[16] and A. W. Ovitt & Co., which made wooden refrigerators and ice, grocery, and beer boxes in addition to Bent's Patent Fall & Folding Leaf Extension Table and other furniture "specialties."[17]

At the corner of North Sangamon Street and Austin Avenue (now Hubbard Street), Norwegian cabinetmakers employed by Peterson & Oveson produced center, library, and parlor tables for sale to local wholesale furniture houses.[18] Another Norwegian cabinetmaker, Paul Olaison, was making tables at 19 North Page Street (now Hermitage Avenue). Also on the West Side, Danish cabinetmaker Louis Hanson and his employees were at work producing hall furniture, mirrors, and parlor and library tables. By 1909 Hanson employed 500.[19]

Working in a large factory building at 27 North Jefferson, where several cabinetmakers shared a steam engine and woodworking equipment, Louis F. Nonnast made tables and hall stands for eleven years before moving into his own factory on North Green Street in 1889. Nonnast's staff of 150 workmen created 55 patterns of hat racks and 55 types of extension tables by 1899, when *American Cabinet Maker & Upholsterer* commented that "his line is extensive, of excellent repute regarding pattern and finish, and he has an abundant stock to choose from."[20]

In striking contrast to the large tablemaking factories was the Dearborn Street shop of Bert L. Chapman, where "rustic" stands and easels were assembled from oddly shaped tree branches between 1890 and 1893.

Label on twig stand by Bert L. Chapman. After making rustic furniture for three years, Chapman became a salesman in 1894.

Rustic stand fabricated by Bert L. Chapman ca. 1892. Painted black and gold, the twigs support a red plush-covered top.
h: 29" w: 15" d: 15"
CHS, gift of Merle Glick, 1983

Held together with tiny nails and painted black with touches of gold, the mass-produced but distinctive-looking side tables, flower stands, and easels were popular for use on porches and in conservatories, where they elicited memories of shady woods and rural crafts now largely lost to city dwellers.

FANCY CABINET WARE

During the 1870s a new branch of cabinetmaking emerged as many manufacturers turned to producing highly decorative easels for holding paintings, stands for supporting statuary, paintings, or floral bouquets, and wall furniture like wallpockets, cabinets, or shelves. In fashionable modern homes, numerous small tables and shelves (or brackets) were needed to hold the books, photographs, and bric-a-brac commonly found in parlor, chamber, sitting room, or hall. By 1884 Chicago had thirty factories specializing in such fancy cabinet ware.

Niemann & Hallman. 333 North Woods, 1887.

Niemann & Horman. 952 North Rockwell, 1880–89.

H. C. Niemann & Co. 954–64 (1801 after 1909) Rockwell, 1890–1929.

Chicago-born Henry C. Niemann manufactured tables in partnership with Clement F. Hallman and August Horman before organizing H. C. Niemann & Co. in 1890. Over the next thirty-nine years the firm manufactured inexpensive and medium-priced parlor, library, extension, café, and kitchen tables, as well as stands and cupboards. In the mid-1920s it began to offer chairs in patterns to match its dining tables.

In 1900 an article in *Majestic Chicago* noted that Niemann's factory was "equipped with all the latest machinery and mechanical appliances, driven by a fifty-five horse power steam engine, all giving employment to a large force of skilled operatives" and claimed that the firm sold its furniture throughout the United States and Great Britain. At the time, H. C. Niemann was manager of the firm, while Albert Niemann served as factory superintendent. A third partner, Caspar Landgraf, was described as a native of Saxony.

The great proliferation of ornamental and inexpensive fancy wares reflected new trends in home decoration as well as in the increasing availability of easily operated woodworking machinery. Especially important was the scroll saw, or fret saw. Equipped with a narrow ribbonlike blade for cutting curved or irregular shapes, the scroll saw could make cuts in the interior of a flat piece of wood without having to cut through the outer edge. Large steam-powered scroll saws had been widely used in factory production for decades, but the introduction of inexpensive foot-operated or hand-held scroll saws early in the 1870s proved a boon to woodworkers and homemakers alike. As Henry T. William and Mrs. C. S. Jones explained in 1878 in their book *Beautiful Homes:* "The invaluable 'bracket' saws, carving and ornamenting tools, which are now to be procured for so small a sum, place household decoration, indeed the complete furnishing, within the means of everyone, and where any member of the family with sufficient strength can use one of the finer foot power scroll saws, we should say that it were money well invested to secure one of these never failing sources of satisfaction and pleasure."[21]

Reiterating a fundamental premise—"Cheap luxury *is* easily obtained in this day by any woman who possesses the use of hands and head"—the authors explained in great detail how, with small saws and carving tools, ladies could "find it a most pleasurable occupation to fashion all the lighter articles of household decoration and light fret-work panels for even heavy furniture."[22] With this in mind, Williams, who was also the publisher of the Williams Household series, used the back pages of *Beautiful Homes* to advertise *Ornamental Designs for Fret-Work, Scroll Sawing, Fancy Carving and Home Decorating* (containing over three hundred patterns), as well as small, cheap bracket and fret saws available by mail.

Similarly, Arthur Hope's *A Manual of Sorrento and Inlaid Work for Amateurs,* published in Chicago in 1880, contained detailed instructions and patterns for a host of items.[23] The effectiveness of such advertisements is demonstrated by the phenomenon upon which John A. Kouwenhoven remarked in *Made in America,* namely, that "the sale of jigsaw blades leaped from a few thousand a year to about five hundred thousand a month" within two years after the Philadelphia Centennial.[24]

It was a period in which a homemaker's success might well be judged by the quality and arrangement of "the thousand little felicities in shape of a pretty bracket here, an artistic gem of picture, statuette, or bust,"[25] to quote Williams and Jones. Harriet Spofford, author of *Art Decoration Applied to Furniture* (1878) shared this philosophy, telling her readers that "a few moments' observation in the drawing room of any family will usually give much information concerning the grade of that family's culture by nothing more than the character of the bric-a-brac to be seen there."[26]

By this time hundreds of wall pockets, cabinets, pedestals, stands, and brackets were available in Chicago from Frank Wenter's manufactory on West Washington Street. Called a "young man of energy and enterprise" by *American Cabinet Maker,* Wenter was known for producing "good work at low figures." Shortly after opening his business in 1872, Wenter began "experimenting with machines and shapes" that would reduce the time required to produce cabinet ware while increasing the number of patterns he could offer. By 1877 *American Cabinet Maker* reported: "The carving which figures so prominently in fancy furniture is turned out with amazing speed as three carving machines are in operation besides five hand carvers. The

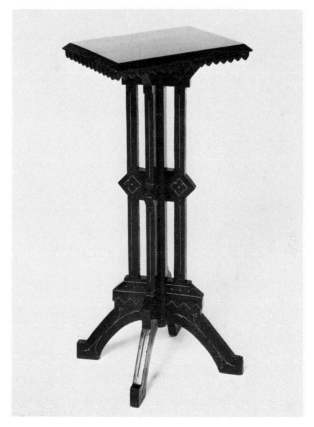

Ebonized stand in what was known as the Anglo-Japanese style.
h: 32½" w: 15" d: 10¼"
CHS, gift of Mary Pat Hough Green, 1978

Ebonized easel with gilt detailing from a set of some eight pieces of novelty furniture purchased from Field, Leiter & Co. for the Richland Center, Wisconsin, home of Lura Bailey Gonsalves between 1873 and 1881.
h: 76¾" w: 21½" d: 6"
CHS, gift of Mary Pat Hough Green, 1978

machines do the rough work and shaping—the hand carvers do the finer work."[27]

   The carving machines used in Wenter's shop could have been spindle shapers, simple machines that came onto the market in 1876. Equipped with metal burrs mounted on the end of a rotating metal shaft, spindle carvers were used to cut geometric patterns and small-scale irregular shapes.

Louis Hanson Co. 126–32 North Curtis, 1895–1909; 1500 North Kostner (Forty-fourth before 1914), 1909–ca. 1950.

Arriving from Denmark in 1865, Louis Hansen (1843–1923) found employment in woodworking operations in Maine and Boston. After a few years he changed the spelling of his name to Hanson. Around 1870 he went to work for Chicago's Goodwillie & Goodwillie, the city's leading manufacturer of wooden boxes, picture frames, and moldings. After the 1871 fire he became a partner and in 1874 the owner of the firm.

In the mid-1890s Hanson expanded to include the production of barber chairs and furniture. A decade later, having sold his barber shop interests to Emil J. Paider, he made only furniture, specializing in such hall items as trees, racks, chairs, and mirrors. Following World War I the firm produced bedroom suites as well as desks and tables.

Hanson admitted his three sons—Martin, John, and Louis, Jr.—to the firm in 1903. By 1923, when he died, they had gradually taken over their father's duties. During the 1930s the company made radio cabinets as well as bedroom furniture. Orders for war goods kept the factory operating during World War II.

They might also have been early versions of the direct-copying or multiple-carving machines commonly used in furniture factories today. An adaptation of the pantograph tracing device, these machines were equipped with sharp, rotating knives and a stylus. When the operator guided the stylus over the surface of a hand-carved model, the knives roughed out identical copies. Simple carvings of uniform contour such as those commonly found in incised work could be executed quickly and efficiently, although complex designs like busts or leaves required too many adjustments for the use of the machine to be cost-effective.[28]

Equipped with such time-saving machinery, Wenter's thirty workmen were able to turn out an amazing variety of fancy cabinet ware ornamented with three-dimensional carvings of deer, elk, and birds. Among the most popular items were cheap and medium-priced "boquet stands" [sic] or small tables designed for holding vases of flowers. Extensively advertised in the *Furniture Trade Journal* and *American Cabinet Maker*, the tables had round tops about a foot in diameter held aloft by a turned spindle or an asymmetrically curved support, which in turn was supported by a tripod of angular legs. The top rims of simple Eastlake stands were ornamented with scallops of slender metal chains. On fancier stands, carved eagles with outspread wings or miniature deer-head trophies perched atop each leg or upon a tiny ledge that jutted out from the central pedestal.[29]

These, of course, were but a few of the 110 patterns offered by Wenter in the fall of 1879, when *American Cabinet Maker* dubbed him "the champion manufacturer of fancy cabinetware of the West." Wenter's work force had more than doubled by then—going from thirty to seventy—and he found himself with "more work than he has the room."[30]

In 1880 Wenter moved his operation into "fine and roomy quarters" on Van Buren Street. Four years later, his work force having increased to 135, he moved again, this time into a larger brick factory at the corner of Fourteenth and Canal streets, close to many of the other leading furniture manufacturers. Describing Wenter's new factory in 1884, *American Cabinet Maker* called it "a model of factory architecture" designed for "efficient and economical production."

> The machine rooms occupying the lower floor are models of convenience, light and airy with windows on four sides, and with every convenience for economical handling. The second floor is occupied by the office and cabinetmakers, the third floor is given over to the finishers and the fourth floor is used as a stock-room. In a three story addition forty feet square on the ground floor is located the engine and boiler rooms and shaving-vault, shut off from the main building by a fire wall and iron doors; in the second-story of this wing are the carvers, while the third floor is a fine sample-room, communicating with the office by a handsome oak stairway. The office itself is a pleasant room fronting Fourteenth Street, neatly fitted up in hard woods, with glass screen partition and private office. An extension in the rear gives ample accommodation to the shipping department and adjoining is a large detached lumber dryer. There is also plenty of yard room for lumber storage.[31]

Successful in his business, Wenter became a man of some influence in the city and in 1891 was appointed a member of the commission charged with overseeing the drainage of the Sanitary and Ship Canal. Increasingly absorbed by other interests, he ceased to manufacture cabinet ware in 1895.[32]

Wall furniture, footstools, and fancy tables were also manufactured by Mueller, Gloeckler & Co. between 1871 and 1882. Located on the city's Near North Side, the company was owned by Charles Mueller, a former furniture dealer, and Charles Gloeckler, a woodcarver who had come to Chicago from Massachusetts. From the beginning, the company was known

Walnut footrest with plush upholstery of the type made in Mueller, Gloeckler & Co.'s fancy cabinet ware factory ca. 1885.
h: 18¼" w: 20½" d: 10¼"
Private Collection

for "elaborately carved" black walnut shelves ornamented with ebonized patterns and incised lines traced in gilt.[33] By 1876 the firm offered 492 different items executed in black walnut, including footrests with upholstered tops, smoker's stands, bamboo work, and Eastlake brackets. According to *American Cabinet Maker*, the factory used walnut exclusively because it provided a "better ground work for illumination."[34]

By the mid-1870s the growing popularity of fancy cabinet ware had prompted Max Tonk, manufacturer of furniture carvings on West Lake Street, to increase the number of parlor brackets and shelves that he offered in his line. In November 1877, for example, *American Cabinet Maker* reported that Tonk and his men had been "quietly at work through the summer months preparing new designs and new goods" for the upcoming holiday season, when, the reporter noted, fancy cabinet ware could be counted on to meet "the general demand for something cheap and showy and at the same time useful."[35]

Described as being "remarkably artistic and of the very best finish," Tonk's new goods consisted primarily of intricately carved and pierced brackets composed of vines and scrolls made by workmen adept with the scroll saw and carving machine. Tonk was particularly proud of an excellent new "finish" he had developed that stained common hardwood to look like rosewood, enabling him to sell "rosewood" brackets at greatly reduced prices.[36]

In addition to brackets, Tonk offered five styles of piano stools to complement the mass-produced pianos and organs that had begun to appear in middle-class parlors. All featured swivel seats of a "square serpentine shape" screwed into a turned support with a large wrought-iron screw. The simplest stool was supported by three legs stained to imitate rosewood. More elaborate models, available in imitation rosewood or walnut, showed legs paneled and mounted with turned ornaments, and a seat "ornamented with veneer panel, and neatly engraved." The same seat and

Selection of brackets from the catalogue issued by Max Tonk ca. 1876.
Mr. and Mrs. Hampton E. Tonk and Family

SIDE BRACKETS.

leg arrangement appeared on Tonk's most celebrated stool, a "neat and tasty" model with a comfortable-looking upholstered back. "This is a most excellent stool," *American Cabinet Maker* commented in 1877, noting that it was in "universal favor with the Chicago piano dealers."[37]

A major outlet for Tonk's piano stools and possibly the catalyst behind this enterprising idea was Tonk's uncle, Julius Bauer, one of the most successful piano and organ manufacturers in Chicago. A native of Berlin, Bauer had emigrated in 1849 to New York City, where he opened a music store. Eight years later he moved his business to Chicago and was, as the papers said, "an immediate success." Not long afterward he persuaded his brother-in-law, William Tonk, who was living in Berlin, to come to Chicago to help him supervise this growing business. Bauer's nephew, William Tonk, Jr., eventually entered the firm's employ as a bookkeeper. The latter's brother,

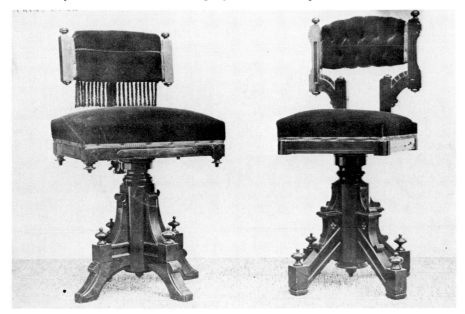

Photo from ca. 1880 used by salesmen to sell piano stools made in Max Tonk's factory.
Mr. and Mrs. Hampton E. Tonk and Family

Max Tonk, worked as a carver in the piano factory until 1873, when, at the age of twenty-one, he opened his own carving shop.

Another Chicago manufacturer of fancy cabinet ware was Salter & Bilek, located at 40 North Union Street in 1886. The firm had been established seven years earlier by George W. Salter, a former furniture salesman who had migrated from England, and Stephen Bilek, a Bohemian-born woodcarver who had been the foreman in Frank Wenter's factory from 1873 until 1879. Employing forty-five "skilled and experienced artisans," Salter & Bilek specialized in parlor stands, music portfolios, and brackets in walnut or "ebony and gilt," with incised geometric ornamentation, all "conveniently made for shipping" throughout the United States.[38] In contrast, nearly all of the fancy work made at the factory of Keller & Co. was sold within the city through large wholesale houses. Employing fifteen workers, the factory was owned by Edward A. Keller, a designer and woodcarver who had come to Chicago from Ohio shortly before the 1871 fire, and J. C. Wartenweiler, a native of Switzerland, who had worked as a woodturner in Chicago since 1867.[39]

During the 1880s fancy cabinet ware—or artistic furniture, as it was sometimes called—was also made by Dean & Company, manufacturers of "decorative furniture in bamboo and hardwood";[40] Frank B. McAvoy and Edward Roos, whose factory also made curtain poles and cornices; and the Lutwyche and Leuty Manufacturing Company (later Barnhart & Hunt), which produced ebonized novelty wares with Japanese and Eastlake detailing.

Particularly adept at marketing small-scale fancy cabinet ware was E. J. Lewis, a manufacturer of "handsome and salable goods" at 65–67 West Washington Street. By 1884 Lewis had developed "assorted packages" of walnut tables and brackets especially designed to appeal to small-town and country furniture dealers. Two different packages of tables were available, as well as a variety of brackets, which, *American Furniture Gazette* explained, were neatly boxed and contained "from one to four dozen brackets of some

Mahogany table with sphinx supports carved by Max Tonk in the 1880s. An identical design appeared at the base of Tonk's most "artistic" and expensive piano stool.
h: 29¼" w: 21½" d: 21"
Mr. and Mrs. Hampton E. Tonk and Family

particular grade, five grades of brackets ranging from 12½ cents to $1.00 being put up this way."[41] After 1887, when E. J. Lewis's "plant, stock and good will" were acquired by Edgar S. Boynton, the standard walnut line was supplemented by Japanese-inspired cabinets and brackets with asymmetrical shelves and engraved cranes, or ornamented with Eastlake motifs or Queen Anne spindles.[42]

Although the production of frames and fancy cabinet ware continued unabated well into the twentieth century, forms and fashions underwent considerable changes. In the spring of 1883, when *American Furniture Gazette* devoted a special issue to Chicago, it was clear that "the era of the jig-saw" was over.[43] Comparing the modern interiors of 1883 with those common a decade earlier, the *Gazette* explained that the fashionable living room was now French in inspiration, while the library, dining room, and hall followed the contemporary English mode in decoration. Deep-toned libraries, dining rooms with richly tiled fireplaces and elaborate built-in sideboards, and entrance halls so large "as to become virtually reception rooms" were becoming common in middle-class homes under construction throughout the city and in such suburban areas as Hyde Park, Beverly, Evanston, Oak

Cover of fancy cabinet ware catalogue issued by Edgar S. Boynton ca. 1890.

Park, and Riverside. Electric lighting, oak woodwork, and stained-glass windows were other amenities mentioned in the *Gazette*'s "hasty glance at a few specimens of modern work" that characterized the "new Renaissance" in household decoration taking place in the Chicago area.[44] "All the furnishing and decorations are more carefully considered. Stiffness is banished; and all gross and offensive coloring—the old striped papers of our ancestors, the French Rococo bedstead of ten years back, and the ponderous structures of Eastlake have been supplanted by papers and furniture eminently beautiful and human."[45]

In these Chicago interiors of the late nineteenth century, open fireplaces were considered essential, especially the dining room and hall. In the dining room, the *Gazette* explained, a glowing wood fire contributed "vastly to the general comfort, and to the imagination and repartee of a dinner conversation." In the hall, it symbolized warmth and protection and served as "a refuge for chilled bodies and snow-dazed eyes."[46] Besides being symbolic, fireplaces and expanded halls provided an excuse for a host of new furnishings. Built-in or high-backed hall seats resembling the old-fashioned "settle" made an appearance, along with long, narrow tables, large leather-upholstered hall or "reception" chairs, and heavily carved boxes or chests "similar to those used in medieval households for storing linens and other stuffs."[47]

In addition to new designs, the increased use of hall furniture encouraged the resurrection of many an old heirloom, including tall case clocks, sofas, chairs, and spinning wheels. As the author pointed out, "the fashion of using these possessions of our ancestry has discovered for many a purely modern family a previously unsuspected antiquity, exactly as the destruction wrought by the fire of 1871 was the first intimation to the closest of friends of many Chicago families that possessed rare collections of books and works of art."[48]

By 1883, antique furniture made in America, England, or on the Continent during the seventeenth, eighteenth, and nineteenth centuries had begun to appear in parlors alongside new furnishings designed to recall the spirit of the Middle Ages, the decadent luxury of the Ottoman Empire, or the artistry of Japan. This move toward eclecticism would persist in the coming decades, as is clear from the following statement by a Chicago furniture salesman published in the *Trade Bureau* in 1889:

> Taste is now gravitating toward the antique . . . and designers are busy working over Romanesque, Renaissance, Louis XIV, and Colonial patterns. We adapt and unite the different styles, just as modern architects combine different styles of architecture, and many of our most pleasing effects are obtained this way. The popular fad keeps up within the leading strings of the antique, and so far as this requirement is met we are free to make as many violations or combinations of art principles as we choose.[49]

The many forms that resulted from the designers' "many violations and combinations" ran the gamut from Gothic to Romanesque to colonial. Yet within this backward-looking era could be found the seeds of new movements in design that, by the early twentieth century, would begin to revolutionize the look and construction of American furniture.

ART FURNITURE

1873-1917

I N T R O D U C T I O N

In the period between the 1873 Inter-State Industrial Exposition and America's entry into World War I in 1917, the decorative arts flourished in Chicago as architects, designers, and craftsmen experimented in a variety of idioms. Although thousands worked in factories making furniture for "the million," a small but highly influential number of Chicagoans designed and crafted custom pieces—often one of a kind—for a more affluent clientele. Regardless of the style—Modern Gothic, Art Nouveau, Arts and Crafts, mission, or Prairie—each piece represented a conscious effort on the part of the designer to create an original or, at the least, a new interpretation of a traditional style. Handmade by men and women who revered and perpetuated the art of fine woodworking, the resulting products merit the appellation of "art furniture."

Students of this dynamic and productive era run the risk of confusing the various influences reflected in the work of Chicago's furniture designers and producers. Indeed, a number of historians have treated the several design philosophies as one, encouraged in this simplification by the fact that the same people were active in more than one of these movements. For example, Joseph Twyman and the Tobey Furniture Company produced and promoted both Art Nouveau and Arts and Crafts furniture, while simultaneously manufacturing colonial and other period reproductions. Frank Lloyd Wright was both a founder of the Chicago Arts and Crafts Society and a leader of the Prairie school of architecture. And, although the University of Chicago's Professor Oscar Lovell Triggs never made a piece of furniture himself, he was nonetheless highly influential as a founder of the Industrial Art League and the many furniture-making enterprises that it fostered. Because of the large number of people and theories involved, each chapter in this section explores a different approach to furniture design and production and describes the work of its chief practitioners.

The architect/designers responsible for the creation of Modern Gothic furniture in the 1870s are discussed in chapter 10, while their successors at the turn of the century, the Prairie school architects, are described in chapter 15. Although their furniture looked quite different, both generations of "radical" architects shared a similar philosophy and created unique furniture whose designs evolved in concert with their progressive theories of architecture. Their contemporaries who worked in the eclectic and historic styles are treated in chapters 11 and 12.

Chapters 11 through 14 deal with the makers of furniture, who also worked in a variety of styles and expressed diverse views on their art. In addition, chapters 11 and 12 discuss the many custom shops, interior decorators, woodcarvers, and special firms producing custom furniture. Furniture handcrafted by individuals and cooperatives working under the aegis of the Arts and Crafts movement is described in chapter 13, while mission furniture—the mass-produced version of the Arts and Crafts and Prairie styles—is treated in chapter 14. Furniture designed in the Prairie style is covered in chapter 15.

Not only were many developments in furniture making taking place simultaneously, but certain key notions, phrases, and words appear again and again in the writings and pronouncements of those designing, making, and reviewing furniture. Since only a few of the designers and manufacturers wrote down their theories or recorded their work, much of our information comes from exhibition and sales catalogues, periodicals like *House Beautiful, Inland Architect,* and *Craftsman,* or trade journals like the *Furniture Worker* and *American Cabinet Maker & Upholsterer.*

Keeping in mind that theory and practice do not always come together, it is nevertheless important to realize that the ideas of English social critics John Ruskin and William Morris influenced Chicago intellectuals throughout this period and helped shape the work both of those who looked to the past for inspiration and of the avant-garde who looked to the future. As these ideas became part of the general culture, they influenced the sellers and buyers as well as the designers and makers of furniture.

MODERN GOTHIC: THE SEARCH FOR TRUTH AND BEAUTY

1 8 7 3 - 1 8 8 0

In the spring of 1865 *New Path*, a bold little journal published in New York City, devoted a series of articles to "Our Furniture; What it Is, and What it Should Be."[1] As might be expected, a survey of the furniture of the day revealed other objects utterly devoid of "even the commonest principles of good design." In their stead, contributors to the journal proposed "modern" furniture, made according to what they saw as the "true" principles of construction that had guided the makers of furniture during the High Gothic phase of the Middle Ages.

These admirers of High Gothic believed that during that era, architecture and the arts had reached the height of perfection, in part because metal, wood, glass, and stone had been allowed to express their inherent beauty rather than being tortured into unnatural shapes or imitated by other materials. Moreover, so went the theory, medieval carvers gloried in their handiwork, drawing their inspiration for ornament from the "real" world of nature. This happy state could be recaptured and truth and beauty returned to art if consumers and manufacturers alike would only follow a "new path." Indeed, furniture makers could lead the way. In the words of the journal: "When the cabinet makers begin to look with some reverence on their trade, and to design wooden articles as if they were not ashamed of their being wood, they will find themselves capable of doing better work than they have ever done, and, thereafter, they will daily do better. They will then have good precedents to go upon, as well, for they will be surprised to find that they are producing Gothic furniture."[2]

The editors and publisher of *New Path*—which appeared erratically between May 1863 and December 1865—were members of the Association for the Advancement of Truth and Art, founded in 1863 by eight devotees of John Ruskin. Believing that "the primary object of art is to observe and record truth, whether of the visible universe or of emotion," they maintained that painting and sculpture realized their potential most fully when integrated with architecture.[3]

Members of the Association referred to themselves as Realists, or Gothic revivalists, rather than Pre-Raphaelites like their English counterparts. Reformers rather than copyists, they looked back to the twelfth and thirteenth centuries for guidance in revitalizing the art of their own day. They urged a return to a single style of architecture that gave equal attention to the interior and exterior of a building. The same held for the furniture and accessories placed in the interior.

In the surge of rebuilding and expansion of the post-Civil War era, many of the Association's founders went on to make their mark in a variety of fields. Russell Sturgis became a prominent architect, teacher, and critic; Clarence Cook, editor of *New Path*, became the art critic for the New York *Tribune* and author of *House Beautiful,* an influential domestic guide; while Charles Herbert Moore became the first director of the Fogg Museum of Art in Boston. Englishman Thomas C. Farrar, a painter and the moving spirit behind the founding of the Association, returned to England, while architect Peter Bonnett Wight, who recorded the Association's history, left New York for Chicago in 1871. In this new locale he soon found another band of Gothic revival enthusiasts, with whom he collaborated to revitalize the decorative arts, particularly furniture making.

MODERN GOTHIC IN CHICAGO

The Chicago proponents of the Gothic revival were influenced not only by the writings of John Ruskin but also by the works of French architect and theorist Eugene Emmanuel Viollet-le-Duc. Responsible for the restoration of some of France's most important medieval buildings—including Sainte Chapelle and Notre Dame de Paris—Viollet-le-Duc was a proponent of what he called "rational architecture." An architect, he maintained, should not just copy the masterpieces of the past but should first analyze them, make his own synthesis, and then apply the principles thus derived to solving his own architectural problems.[4] Within this framework, he advocated the use of new materials and technologies to create a scientific architecture that would meet the needs of modern civilization.

Viollet-le-Duc's publications, especially the ten-volume *Dictionnaire raisonné de l'architecture française du XIe au XVIe siècle* (1854–69)* and his *Dictionnaire du mobilier français de l'époque carolingienne à la Renaissance* (1858–75),† helped fuel the enthusiasm for Gothic architecture both on the Continent and in the United States. The *Dictionnaire du mobilier* was particularly important to students of the decorative arts because it provided detailed drawings and descriptions of the metalwork, stained glass, and furniture made during the medieval period. Thus Viollet-le-Duc provided models as well as a theoretical framework for the disciples of the Gothic revival, among them a group of architects working in Chicago during the 1870s.

These architects included William LeBaron Jenney, whose invention of the steel frame introduced the era of modern skyscraper construction in the 1880s; Peter Bonnett Wight, who later pioneered the use of fireproof construction materials; Daniel H. Burnham, architectural impresario and

*"Comprehensive dictionary of French architecture from the 11th to the 16th century."
†"Comprehensive dictionary of French furniture from the Carolingian era to the Renaissance."

chief of construction for the 1893 World's Columbian Exposition; and Burnham's partner, John Wellborn Root, whose Rookery and Monadnock
buildings established his reputation before his untimely death in 1891. Other
practitioners of Modern Gothic in Chicago were architects John Addison,
George R. Clarke, Frederick W. Copeland, August Fiedler, and Asa Lyon,
and craftsmen James Legge and Isaac E. Scott. Of these, Jenney and Wight
were the key figures, since several of the other men began by working in
their offices or by executing their commissions.

Peter Bonnett Wight (1838–1925) had been summoned to Chicago two
weeks after the Great Fire by architect Asher Carter. In 1872 Wight sent to
New York for John Wellborn Root, who became chief draftsman in the
newly established firm of Carter, (William H.) Drake & Wight. A few months
later the young Daniel H. Burnham, previously an employee of Loring &
Jenney, joined the firm. Between the fall of 1871 and Carter's retirement in
1873 the firm completed more than fifty buildings, including several in
what Wight later referred to as a " 'commercial' Gothic style."[5]

Although William LeBaron Jenney (1832–1907) had been educated in

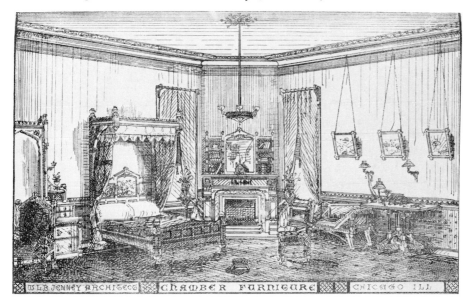

*Design for chamber furniture by
W.L.B. Jenney published in the September 2, 1876,* American Architect
and Building News. *A note indicated, "this furniture was executed in
Chicago on special order."*
The Art Institute of Chicago

Paris and Wight in New York, both had fallen under the spells of Ruskin
and Viollet-le-Duc prior to their arrival in Chicago. Like many idealistic
architects of their day, they wanted to help develop "a true national style"
of architecture that would be suited to the climate, needs, and tempera-
ment of the American people. In the words of Jenney, Americans "had
joined the English in their endeavor to modify the early English gothic so
as to adapt it to modern requirements."[6]

While both Jenney and Wight had worked briefly in Chicago prior to
1871, the Great Fire must be credited with changing the course of their
careers. A native of Massachusetts, Jenney had studied engineering at the
École Centrale des Arts et Manufactures in Paris during the 1850s, then
stayed on to work abroad. He returned to America following the outbreak

of the Civil War and enlisted in the Union army. Jenney went on to serve on the engineering staffs of Generals Grant and Sherman, attaining the rank of major-general. Eventually he returned to Chicago and in 1868 opened an architectural office there. He had few commissions until 1871, when restoration of the fire-gutted business district led to a demand for engineers and architects. Skilled in both areas, Jenney became a leading figure during the city's reconstruction.[7] Sharing a similar outlook, Jenney, Wight, and a circle of friends set out to emulate medieval modes of construction and designed furniture with a decidedly Gothic look.

"CONSTRUCTIVE" FURNITURE

The design and construction of Modern Gothic furniture was based upon a series of principles derived from studying furniture made during the thirteenth century in England, France, and Italy. In some case, knowledge came from first-hand study of extant examples or illuminated manuscripts to be found in Europe. More often, however, it was gleaned from publications like Bruce J. Talbert's *Gothic Forms Applied to Furniture* (London, 1867), Henry Carey Baird's *Gothic Album for Cabinet Makers* (Philadelphia, 1868), the *Furniture Gazette,* or Viollet-le-Duc's comprehensive works on the decorative arts and architecture.

In England, architects like Augustus Welby Pugin, William Burges, Alfred Waterhouse, and William Butterfield and artists like Edward Burne Jones and William Morris had been designing furniture based on medieval prototypes since the 1850s. Leading exponents of the style in America were architects James Renwick, Jr., designer of the first Smithsonian Institution building, and Alexander Jackson Davis, who designed Gothic furniture for the many villas, college buildings, and churches for which he served as architect prior to the Civil War.[8]

Following the medieval style of using mortise and tenon joints in furniture making, the nineteenth-century proponents of the Gothic style eschewed the use of glue and nails on the ground that these were unnatural materials, different in character from "natural" wood. Wood was cut so that its grain would be visible through the full length of the pieces, as in quarter-sawn oak. In the same way, they emulated their medieval forebears by leaving visible all the joinery like dowels and pegs and by emphasizing the constituent planking and trestles. Since wood was liable to shrink when used in wide pieces, case goods were made from beveled planks set within a square frame that made allowance for this natural phenomenon. Further, they ornamented their furniture with rich carving, taking advantage of inset wooden panels larger and thicker than strength demanded. Plants and animals were the principal and most valued decoration.

One of the principal tenets of the Gothic revivalists was that "the ornament all grows out of and exhibits the construction"; and another, that "the adaptation of the ornamentation to the nature of the material is as universal and as beautiful as the adaptation of the ornament to the structure."[9] It was from these principles that Wight and his associates derived the term "constructive furniture." In an article entitled "Concerning Furniture," in *American Architect and Builder*, Wight summarized the adaptation of medieval principles to modern furniture design. "The structure is not to be denied or concealed by the decoration; glue is to be used as an aid to, and not instead of, framing; veneering is disallowed except in panels; straight-grained woods are not to be cut or 'shaped' into such wanton curves, especially in the bearing members, as will interfere with their natural strength."[10]

Although not as prolific a writer as Wight, Jenney expressed similar views and added a few suggestions of his own. Within a house, carving was to be confined almost entirely to the furniture and mantels, where it could be seen and appreciated. Furniture was to be "superior" to the woodwork.[11] But, in general, "There is but one rule that is safe to follow," he maintained. "The house should be one harmonious whole from turret to foundation stone."[12]

It is not known when Jenney first began to design furniture. However, he was putting his basic rule into practice by the spring of 1875, when the *Chicago Tribune* reported: "Mr. George B. Clarke and Mr. W. L. Jenney are doing a great deal of designing in English Gothic furniture. These designs are specifically designed to suit the style of architecture and fittings of the houses, and the designs become the property of the owners just as the plans of the house. Mr. Jenney has at present orders of this character amounting to upwards of $5,000. The designs even extend to metalwork, such as door hinges, many of the patterns being unique and beautiful."[13]

Special furniture like Wight's, Jenney's, and Clarke's was most frequently commissioned for libraries, dining rooms, or bedchambers. These rooms where some of the most important familial rituals took place were furnished in keeping with their symbolic significance. The dining room, where the family gathered three times a day, came close to being "the heart of the house."[14] The library, where one was mentally uplifted by communing with minds that once "had swayed the world,"[15] served as the inner sanctum for quiet pursuits. Rarely discussed in terms of function in the domestic guides, yet always subject to considerable interest, was the bedchamber, with its bittersweet associations with marriage, birth, and death. On a more mundane level, these three rooms called for furnishings made primarily of wood, rather than upholstery, and thus allowed greater opportunity for originality of design and the creation of furniture that would complement the interior finish of the room.

For all three rooms, Modern Gothic furniture was considered particularly appropriate; for libraries, its somber lines and heaven-pointing spires encouraged meditation. In dining rooms, tables and chairs displayed strength and solidity through richly grained surfaces, foliated columns, ebonized details, and oversized mortise and tenons. In the bedchamber, crocket-topped canopies and insets of tile and carving focused attention on the bedstead.

POPULARIZING MODERN GOTHIC

In the fall of 1875, the Art Committee of the Inter-State Industrial Exposition, assisted by Wight and Jenney, organized a display of "artistic furnishings and house-fittings" to promote the latest trends in Household Art and provide "lessons in good taste."[16] In organizing the exhibition, an article in the *Art Journal* explained, "the committee was led to believe that the exhibition of the large quantity of medieval furniture which had accumulated in private hands, together with contributions from the Chicago artisans, would lead to good results."[17]

When the exhibition opened, a large pavilion designed by Wight stood near the center of the exposition hall. Surrounded by a raised platform displaying architectural details, the interior featured six courts and a central passage. On one side, three completely furnished model rooms—a bedchamber, dining room, and library—had been installed. On the other side, chairs, bookcases, and other furniture were displayed amid pottery made at the new Chicago Terra Cotta Works, carpets and parquet flooring, and brilliantly colored wallpapers designed by English architects William Burges, Charles L. Eastlake, and William Morris. One set of decorative wallpapers, all in two-dimensional stylized floral patterns, had been designed by Wight and printed by local wallpaper manufacturer John J. McGrath. Except for the rugs and some of the wallpapers, "everything contained in the exhibition was of original design, and manufactured in Chicago."[18]

Concerned by the absence of artistic fittings for people of moderate means, a writer for the *Chicago Tribune* nevertheless praised the exhibition's success in illustrating the importance of household art and of making "good use of common things." Admitting that most people would not care to furnish an entire house in the Modern Gothic style, even if they could afford it, the writer acknowledged the propensity of many families to lavish extra care and expense on a single, special room. If anything elaborate was to be attempted, he recommended that they seek an architect's assistance. "Chicago is fortunate in possessing a considerable number of excellent designers, whose names may be found attached to the articles exhibited here," the *Tribune* writer noted.

> Some of them make a practice, if it is desired, of fitting a house throughout with furniture, carpets, curtains, etc., at a contract price, usually a separate price for each room. The connection of the architectural profession with the subject of household taste is well shown in the room devoted to drawings and designs, where there are plans not only of the outside and inside of houses, but of a variety of chairs, tables, bureaus, and other articles of domestic use. These drawings, often very artistic in execution, show just how a good designer goes to work to make a fine piece of furniture and furnish the connecting link between the artist and the maker.[19]

Since the Art Committee had had only one month to mount the household section, there had been no time to prepare a detailed catalogue. As a result, most of the participants in the 1875 Household Art exhibition remain anonymous. Fortunately, however, an article entitled "Household Art in Chicago" written for the *Art Journal* described and illustrated what the author considered to be the five finest examples of furniture in the exhibition.[20]

The selection comprised three cabinet pieces and two chairs, all designed by Chicago architects. One of the chairs was a leather-upholstered library armchair with pointed crest rail pierced by a trefoil motif. It had been designed by John Addison, who was in Chicago supervising the reconstruction of the Second Presbyterian Church for New York architect James

Renwick, Jr.[21] The designer of the second chair was not mentioned, although the carving on this high backed oak "pulpit or altar chair" was attributed to Isaac E. Scott.

Among the cabinet pieces, a solid chestnut sideboard with simple paneled doors on base and cupboard designed by August Fiedler featured a gabled top and seven stylized finials. A second sideboard, this one designed by Asa Lyon, featured a bay front, inset with a carved relief panel depicting a swan gliding among cattails.[22] The "chef-d'oeuvre of the collection" was a large butternut and white holly bookcase designed by Frederick W. Copeland. Consisting of a wide central section of four open shelves over a paneled cabinet, the bookcase was flanked by a pair of shelved porticoes whose steep, sloping roofs were carved in a pattern resembling tiles. Inlaid panels of stylized leaves and flowers formed a cornice and ornamented

Carved bookcase designed by Frederick Copeland on exhibition at the 1875 Inter-State Industrial Exposition. It was executed by Isaac E. Scott.
Chicago Architecture Foundation

each door. Except for Fiedler's sideboard, all of the pieces illustrated had been executed by the talented Chicago woodcarver Isaac E. Scott.

Although Household Art did not receive a special pavilion at the Inter-State Industrial Exposition of 1876, Modern Gothic furniture was exhibited by several local manufacturers. On a raised platform hung with red curtains, A. Fiedler & Co. displayed a dining-room set of oak. A. H. Andrews

& Co. exhibited a "very fine carved oak sideboard, with clock in the upper part, in the Gothic style," designed by architect Albert Fehmer, along with a fireplace mantel, bookcases, and chairs in the same style and "equally good in design."[23] Specialists in ecclesiastical commissions, Fehmer and his partner, Cuthbert W. Laing, advertised their services as architects and designers of art furniture in A. H. Andrews & Co.'s *Guide to Church Furnishing*, published in 1876.

Another custom manufacturer, R. W. Bates & Co., showed a "massive and costly Gothic bedroom set in ebonized wood relieved slightly with gold and color." Decorated in oil colors on gold grounds "in the Japanese manner," it had been painted by Frederick N. Atwood, a respected Chicago wall decorator and mural painter. For Reed & Sons, a firm of Chicago piano agents, Wight's former assistant, John W. Root, had designed a "constructive medieval case" for an upright piano.[24] Two artistically carved white holly end panels constituted its sole ornamentation.

Receiving the most praise, however, were the Patent Gothic Star Chairs exhibited by Frederick W. Krause, a local cabinetmaker and machinist who had begun as a maker of shoe lasts and had turned to making "constructive chairs" only a year earlier. In Wight's words:

> He is, I believe the only manufacturer in the country who makes constructive chairs at wholesale, and nothing else. He is doing just what Eastlake said the furniture-makers ought to do, but despaired of their ever doing it,—trying to bring constructive furniture within the reach of persons of moderate means, and putting it into direct competition with the trash turned out all over the land. To this end he employs machinery in its manufacture to the largest extent practicable, and makes large quantities of each kind at a time. . . . Though his designs are not the best, his construction is unquestionable.[25]

Patented in August 1875, Krause's Gothic or Eastlake "Star" chairs were made of oak or maple in styles suitable for use in parlor, dining room, church, or school. Some were upholstered in leather, but most had cane seats and backs. In the center of each narrow, pointed back was a distinctive open trefoil, or "star." Legs were either square-turned or plain with a few notches. Arched brackets appeared where seats joined legs; mortise and tenon construction was visible wherever wood intersected wood.

In a tiny pamphlet probably printed to accompany his display of chairs at the 1876 Philadelphia Centennial, Krause explained that his chairs were

> made durable by returning to medieval joinery, accomplished by the aid of machinery, constructed especially for their manufacture, in every way solid and substantial, showing the honest construction in the tenons and key which hold them together, not relying entirely upon the glue-pot for strength, but using glue only to add to their stability. The basis of the design being all straight, the wood is all cut with the grain, showing the beauty of the woods, discarding all senseless curves.[26]

Wight, who was impressed by Krause's work, may well have hired him to execute chairs for special commissions. However, for the elaborate cabinetwork or special carving, Wight, in common with most other Chicago architects, turned to individuals like Isaac Scott or August Fiedler. For the large-scale or multiple constructions needed to furnish a large house, library, or club, they often took their designs to commercial furniture man-

Cover of the catalogue issued by Frederick W. Krause in 1876.

One of ten walnut Gothic Star chairs with upholstered seats purchased by Edwin H. Galloway for his home in Fond du Lac, Wisconsin, in the late 1870s. h: 37⅝" w: 17½" d: 16½" Galloway House and Village, Fond du Lac County (Wisconsin) Historical Society

ufacturers like A. H. Andrews & Co. or D. M. Swiney & Bro. Since these manufacturers owned specialized machinery and employed large numbers of workers, they could be counted on to execute furniture quickly and at competitive rates. Moreover, they were already accustomed to making furniture with plain surfaces and "constructive" joinery.

MANUFACTURING MODERN GOTHIC

Among the designer/craftsmen working in Chicago during the 1870s, Isaac Elwood Scott was one of the best known. A native of Pennsylvania, he had worked as a carver in Philadelphia during the late 1860s. Although his employer remains unknown, it is likely that Scott worked for a cabinet shop specializing in executing architects' designs, for after arriving in Chicago in 1873, he immediately established a partnership with architect Frederick W. Copeland. An advertisement in the *Lakeside Directory* for 1874–75 referred to Scott & Copeland as "Designers, Carvers, and Art Wood WORKERS" and encouraged prospective clients to "refer by permission to W.L.B. Jenney, G. R. Clarke, H. S. Jaffray and Drake & Wight, Architects."[27] By 1876 Scott was listed alone, this time as a "designer." During this period he was also employed as a modeler of terra cotta ornament and sculpture at the Chicago Terra Cotta Works.

Since two pieces executed by Isaac Scott—the sideboard designed by Asa Lyon displayed at the 1875 exhibition and another designed by Jenney—have panels featuring a swan carved in the same unusual manner, it is possible that a new type of "Art woodcarving" described as "indigenous to Chicago" in the *Art Journal* should be attributed to Scott. Likening the technique to that of cameo cutting, the *Art Journal* explained in 1876 that this new process involved:

> the decoration of wooden panels by placing successive layers of different kinds of wood together, and carving away the several strata, preserving form as well as outline, and thus securing from the different materials the same effects obtained in cameo-cutting. . . . After the panel is prepared, the artist has only to draw and to carve, and is not troubled with any mechanical processes. The effects produced, especially when holly and ebony are used, are somewhat like cameo-work, for gradations are secured, not only by the form of the carving, but by reducing the outer layers to such thinness as to show the colour of the wood which is under, through the outer layer. Colour and gold have been added to these panels with good pictorial effect.[28]

While the small sideboard designed by Lyon may no longer exist, the cabinet portion of the large sideboard designed by Jenney and executed by Scott reveals the quality of this work. Inset with cameo-carved panels each depicting different birds and animals, the piece features bands of low-relief stylized floral carving and slender hand-wrought metal hinges. At the base it is signed: "W.L.B. Jenney, Archt., Scott—.M. [aker]." (See color plate.) A sketch for an almost identical cabinet piece drawn by Jenney and published in the 1880 *American Cabinet Maker* indicates that the missing top was a massive mirrored affair surmounted by an arched pediment and flanked by side panels inset with carved tiles.[29]

Describing this "beautiful and unique production," *American Cabinet Maker* noted that it was to be executed in mahogany and that the cherry panels should be veneered first with black ebony and then with a very thin layer of white holly before being carved. "These panels soon grow to look like ivory work," the writer noted, "and if skillfully treated are very beautiful."[30]

During the eleven years that Isaac Scott lived in Chicago, he executed furniture, woodwork, and fireplace mantels, gave woodcarving lessons, designed interiors, modeled terra cotta, and worked briefly as an architect. In 1876 he carved the interior ornament and made furniture for stockyard magnate John B. Sherman's house, located on Prairie Avenue. The first important commission entrusted to the fledgling firm of Burnham & Root in 1874, the Sherman house had an interior "in entire accord with the exterior" and was finished "in keeping with the architecture." Burnham and Root had both served as draftsmen in Wight's office before becoming partners in 1873 and were identified as "professed Gothic men" in the *American Architect and Building News*'s report of this commission. In the same article, Scott was referred to as "a self-trained carver, who may be claimed as a native product of Chicago," referring perhaps to the development of his talent after his arrival in the city rather than to his place of birth.[31] In 1877, when the Art Committee of the Inter-State Industrial Exposition arranged for the loan of a large collection of ceramic bric-a-brac, Scott, by then also an accomplished ceramicist, arranged the installation and made "its appropriate and tasteful cases."[32]

Between 1876 and 1883 Scott's most loyal clients were Mr. and Mrs.

Walnut davenport desk made by Isaac Scott for the John J. Glessner family in 1879.
h: 46½" d: 25" w: 30"
Chicago Architecture Foundation, gift of Mrs. Charles F. Batchelder

John Jacob Glessner. Attending the 1875 Inter-State exposition, the Glessners had "noticed this furniture particularly and bought some of it," their daughter Frances later recalled, "then contacted Mr. Scott and ordered more furniture to go into the new house they had just bought in Chicago."[33] An executive at International Harvester, John Jacob Glessner had purchased a house at 261 West Washington Boulevard (now 952 West) for which he and his wife commissioned a walnut bookcase similar to the one displayed by Scott & Copeland in the household art exhibition. The first of many pieces to be executed for the Glessners, the bookcase initiated a friendship with Scott that lasted nearly fifty years.

The numerous pieces Scott later designed and executed for the Glessner family included a library table, bookcase, chamber furniture, and a desk. When Frances Glessner was born, Scott created a finely carved crib. For the family's growing print collection, he provided uniquely carved frames. A master of many crafts, he designed jewelry and textiles for Mrs. Glessner, taught the children how to draw and carve, and planned a gardener's cottage and playhouse for the Glessners' summer home near Littleton, New Hampshire.

The furniture pieces designed by Scott for the Glessner family are all rectilinear in form and distinguished by superbly executed carving. Earlier pieces, such as the bookcase and library table of 1876, are clearly Modern Gothic. Later pieces like the crib made in 1878 and the Glessners' chamber set, reflect the subtle influence of Queen Anne styling, especially in the bands of well-turned spindles.

Master bedroom in the home of John J. Glessner at 216 West Washington, ca. 1879. The bedstead, dresser, and crib were all executed by Isaac Scott. Chicago Architecture Foundation, gift of Mrs. Charles F. Batchelder

In 1887, when the Glessner family moved into a massive granite residence at 1800 Prairie Avenue designed for them by Boston architect H. H. Richardson, their highly-prized Scott furniture and ceramics were transferred to this new setting and placed amid handsome William Morris wallpapers, fabrics, and rugs. By then, however, Scott had moved on to New York and, later, Boston, where he worked as an interior designer and taught art.

Since Isaac Scott was listed only as a "designer" at various addresses during the 1870s, it is likely that he rented space in other people's furniture factories rather than maintaining a permanent workshop of his own. In some instances, he appears to have relied upon others to make the basic pieces that required little carving: "Ordered small bookcase, Scott's design, but he had it made by Fiedler, cost $70," wrote Mrs. Glessner in her journal on May 26, 1876.[34]

August Fiedler, another furniture maker who executed only custom designs, had arrived in Chicago from New York early in 1874. The first year he was in partnership with architect John W. Roberts, then, in Decem-

Crib made by Isaac Scott for Frances Glessner in 1878.
h: 51" l: 65" w: 40¼"
Chicago Architecture Foundation, gift of Mrs. Charles F. Batchelder

ber 1875, he organized A. Fiedler & Co. From the first, A. Fiedler & Co. was known for furniture of the highest quality. In 1876, for example, when a mantel, sideboard, and chairs made by the firm were exhibited at the Inter-State Industrial Exposition, *American Cabinet Maker* praised the display and claimed that the company's furniture ranked "equal to anything we have seen in Chicago."[35] A small booklet published by the firm in 1877 listed forty-eight clients, nearly all members of Chicago's social elite.

In this booklet, entitled *Presented by A. Fiedler & Co., Designers and Manufacturers of Artistic Furniture,* Fiedler expressed gratitude to patrons and friends who had shown faith in his undertaking: "The increase in our business," he wrote in the preface, "assures us that our efforts have not been in vain, and that the experiment of establishing a manufactory of *really good and artistic* furniture, in Chicago, has been appreciated by the advancing culture of our metropolis and the West."

Going on to expound his design philosophy, Fiedler explained that "furniture is to a great extent inseparable from the inside wood-work of

Design for a library included in a booklet published by A. Fiedler & Co. in 1877.

the rooms'' and advocated that homeowners exclude the interior finish from the carpenter's contract so that it could be made to complement the furniture.

Unlike many of his colleagues, Fiedler advocated the use of different styles in different rooms "in order to avoid the monotonous effect invariably produced by the fanatic apostles of the so-called Eastlake and Modern Gothic." He was referring, one assumes, to wholesale furniture manufacturers and not to architects like Wight and Jenney, who were listed among his patrons. He indicated that to avoid monotony, "articles of luxury" such as easels, brackets, and cabinets should incorporate Moorish, Byzantine, or Japanese motifs. Fiedler concluded his essay by pointing out, "With discrimination and judgment, it need cost no more to make your house beautiful than it has cost to make it ugly."[36]

As mentioned earlier, several manufacturers of commercial furniture also executed furniture for Chicago architects. Among these, the four best known for their art furniture commissions were A. H. Andrews & Co., L. G. Fairbank & Co., R. W. Bates, and D. M. Swiney & Bro. Like most large factories specializing in interior finish, A. H. Andrews & Co. regularly executed furniture following architects' designs. By 1877, however, the firm had hired Luther W. Crosby, a Boston furniture designer, to create special designs, including all of the furniture shown in a model library exhibited at that year's exposition. Although the style of this ebony and gold ensemble remains to be discovered, at the time *American Cabinet Maker* assured its readers that it was "characterized by excellent taste."[37]

Similarly, L. G. Fairbank & Co. furnished an Eastlake dining room and Modern Gothic library and bedchamber with furniture "from their regular stock" at the 1877 exhibition. According to *American Cabinet Maker*, the library furniture was finished in ebony and gold, while the chamber set was made of silver-gray maple "with panels of natural flowers" on a black ground. The overall effect was "very pleasing" and unpretentious, "not over-reaching the popular taste."[38] Formerly secretary of the W. W. Strong Furniture Company, Lemuel J. Fairbank had operated the Novelty Cabinet Works with cabinetmaker Henry F. Rickenberg in 1875 and 1876. On his own by 1877, Fairbank continued to make "artistic" wooden goods including furniture, mantels, and doors until 1882.

Gothic-styled furniture and mantels were also displayed at the 1876 Inter-State Industrial Exposition by Richard W. Bates, a designer and manufacturer of custom furniture and interior fittings. A native of Massachusetts, Bates worked in Chicago first as a draftsman at the F. Porter Thayer & Co. furniture factory from 1868 until 1870, after which he and John Westworth together advertised as "Designers and Carvers." Two years later they had changed their designation to furniture manufacturers.

In partnership with several others during the early 1870s, Bates manufactured custom-designed cabinetwork for the Pullman Palace Car Company until about 1874, when he began executing artistic furniture "from special designs" for local residences, churches, and public halls.[39] In 1875 Bates executed the interior decorations and "Eastlake-Gothic" style furniture for the Chicago Literary Club, located in the American Express Building, for Wight.[40] The following year he and the Novelty Cabinet Works outfitted the interior of the new Chicago Club House designed by architects Treat & Foltz in the Modern Gothic style.[41]

Descended from a family of Irish woodcarvers, Dennis M. and Edward E. Swiney, proprietors of D. M. Swiney & Bro., had served apprenticeships in Boston before migrating to Chicago in 1865. Having established a manufactory on Kinzie Street, they specialized in making cabinet furniture for offices, banks, public buildings, and libraries. By 1873 they were advertising "the latest and most artistic styles of furniture for private and public rooms" in the *Lakeside Directory* and offering "unsurpassed" manufacturing facilities.[42]

In 1874 D. M. Swiney & Bro. executed a Modern Gothic paneled bedstead and mirrored dressing case designed by Peter Wight for Eliphalet W. Blatchford, a prominent Chicago lead manufacturer. Around the same time, the Swineys had Wight design some chamber furniture to be made and sold by them. One piece, a bedstead to be done in walnut or mahogany, had a tall, gabled headboard with incised ornament, roundels, and griffins. A lady's dressing case, the sketch for which included the notation "made to suit the trade," was even more elaborate.[43] Although there is no proof that these pieces were ever made, one cannot help but speculate whether they were part of the "magnificent chamber-set, also of special Gothic design, and very excellent design, too" that caught the eye of a *Tribune* reporter at the 1875 exhibition.[44]

Sometime in 1874 E. W. Blatchford commissioned Wight to design and decorate a large and elegant house to replace his North LaSalle Street home, destroyed in the 1871 fire. To be located on the same site, the new house was to be called "Ulmenheim," German for "home under the elms." Completed in the fall of 1876, the residence drew considerable attention "not only on account of its size" but because of "the novelty of its design and construction." In a modified Gothic style with details "of Neo-Grec," its exterior was highlighted by colorful ceramic tiles and four carved stone tympana on which stylized tableaux of flora and fauna depicted the four seasons. The interior was "throughout in harmony with the constructive manner of the exterior," while the furnishings were "designed for the places in which they are to go."[45]

For the hall and library of the Blatchford house, Wight designed several slat-backed oak and chestnut settees with loose, upholstered cushions. Simple yet comfortable, the settees harmonized in line and detail with the maple and butternut bookcases lining the library walls. Near the top of each bookcase, philosophical sayings such as "Nature—the Art of God" and "Footprints in the Sands of Time" painted in polychrome and gold identified the types of books in each case.

For the dining room, Wight created a rectangular oak table with a complex trestle support distinguished by ebonized foliated columns and large, exposed mortise and tenon joints. It was accompanied by a matching case to hold the table's multiple leaves and eighteen dining chairs. The latter were ornamented only by narrow horizontal ebonized bands and "con-

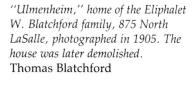

"Ulmenheim," home of the Eliphalet W. Blatchford family, 875 North LaSalle, photographed in 1905. The house was later demolished.
Thomas Blatchford

structive" joinery similar to those illustrated in Bruce Talbert's *Gothic Forms Applied to Furniture*, published a decade earlier.

More elaborate were the Modern Gothic sofa, hanging cupboard, and table for the parlor. Made of maple and butternut, the pieces displayed inset panels with conventionalized floral carving, spires and arches, and geometrical detailing that repeated motifs decorating the interior of the house. In the bedrooms, elegant rectilinear suites of white maple were inset with brilliant ceramic Minton tiles imported from England or with cameo-carved ebony and holly panels.

Although none of the Wight-designed furniture is signed with the names of its makers, Blatchford family records indicate that pieces for "Ulmenheim" were made by A. H. Andrews & Co. and D. M. Swiney & Bro. A

Dining room of "Ulmenheim" in the late 1870s. The dining table, chairs, and stencil decorations were designed by Peter B. Wight.
Thomas Blatchford

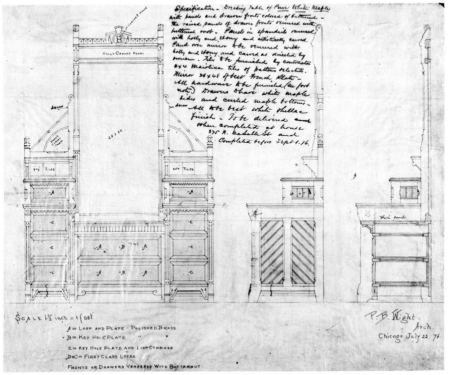

Elevation and section of dressing table prepared by Peter B. Wight for the E. W. Blatchford family in July 1876. The specification reads: "Dressing table of Pure White Maple *with panels and drawer fronts colored of butternut—The raised panels of drawer fronts veneered with butternut [illegible]. Panels in spandrils veneered with holly and ebony and artistically carved. Panel over mirror to be veneered with holly and ebony and carved as directed by owner. Tiles to be furnished by contractor 4 x 4 Maiolica tiles of patterns selected. Mirror 26 x 48 of best French Plate. All hardware to be furnished (see foot note). Drawers to have white maple sides and curled maple bottoms. All to be best white shellac finish. To be delivered when completed at house 875 North LaSalle St. and completed before Sept 1.76."*
Burnham Library, The Art Institute of Chicago

diary kept by E. W. Blatchford's son, Paul, records visits to both factories in mid-August 1876. On August 17 the youngster reported that he and his father "drove up to Swinneys [*sic*] then over town to Mr. Wights." On the eighteenth, after visiting Andrews's factory, where he and his father had stopped that day as well as two days before, he wrote, "it is wonderful to see the advances they had made."[46] Notations on sketches for the furniture now in the Wight collection at The Art Institute of Chicago indicate that the manufacturers were instructed to deliver the furniture to the LaSalle Street house by September 1.

Oak dining-room chair with ebonized bands from "Ulmenheim."
h: 35¼" w: 20" d: 20½"
The More Collection

Butternut wall cabinet with inset floral carvings of cherry designed by Wight for "Ulmenheim."
h: 42" w: 32½" d: 23⅜"
The More Collection

Despite commissions from the Blatchfords, Glessners, and other affluent Chicagoans, custom-designed Modern Gothic furniture had reached the apex of its popularity by 1876. After this it quickly became passé. Introduced as an alternative to constantly changing styles, it too had become "a style." As soon as popularized versions of Modern Gothic forms covered with ornament that bore no relationship to the construction began to proliferate in manufacturers' showrooms, architects and their clients began to lose interest in this style of furniture.

In January 1877, reviewing furniture displayed at the Philadelphia Centennial, a writer for *American Architect and Building News* indicated that the better art furniture manufacturers had already begun to abandon Modern Gothic in favor of the Queen Anne style, whose picturesque details could be seen in Norman Shaw's British Building at the fair.

> The Gothic revival in America . . . . has found its imitators among the furniture manufacturers who only give us part of the shell and none of the kernel of the nut. This has proved so disgusting to people of taste and judgment, that a very few of the conscientious manufacturers like Herter of New York, and Fiedler and Bates of Chicago, have taken up the Queen Anne style, freely treated, and worked on constructive principles. . . . This last movement cannot fail to produce good results.[47]

Cherry and butternut hall table with trestle base from ''Ulmenheim.''
h: 29½" diam: 38"
The More Collection

Unlike Modern Gothic with its crockets and spires, the Queen Anne style offered a more fanciful vocabulary to the furniture designer and a more delicate and appealing configuration to the homeowner. But, while spires and buttresses disappeared, many pieces retained the medieval construction techniques revived by Modern Gothic and the conventionalized ornamentation advocated by Dresser, Eastlake, Morris, and Viollet-le-Duc.

It is unlikely that the movement would have had widespread appeal, even if architects had continued to design Modern Gothic furnishings, and if manufacturers had copied them exactly. As *American Cabinet Maker* explained in 1877, many Americans found ''the ecclesiastical caste'' of the style ''inappropriate for modern furniture.'' ''Anyone of a religious turn of mind might find pleasure in a bedstead that suggested the stall of a cathedral and perhaps would relish the devotion it could excite,'' the editor wrote, ''but the majority of buyers appreciate bedsteads for their own uses and attach little sentiment to such objects.''[48]

As the economy began to recover after several years of depression, and as the pace of building again began to assume frenetic proportions, Jenney, Wight, Burnham, Root, and other progressive architects of the Chicago school turned their attention to solving the engineering and design problems inherent in developing a new "commercial" style of architecture adapted to the needs of a booming city. By 1886 John W. Root would refer to the Modern Gothic episode as the "Victorian-Cathartic—as too true to be good and too good to be true." In his words, "It came upon us all in the time of our virgin innocence when architecture seemed the vale of pure Arcadia, and Ruskin was its prophet."[49] However, Root retained his interest in art, designing tiles and wallpaper and serving as first president of the Chicago Art Guild, an organization founded by artists and decorative designers in 1882.[50]

Remaining adamant in his hatred for Queen Anne style furniture, Jenney too found inspiration in other styles, namely Italian Renaissance and Romanesque. "However much we may feel the loss of our Gothic that promised such great things . . . the architects and builders have made steady progress," he wrote in 1883. By then, schools in Boston, Ann Arbor, and Paris had given the city "many well-trained young men," Jenney said, adding, "our population has grown rich; the land in the business centers of our great cities has so increased in value that we cover every square inch of it, and build heavenward."[51]

A short-lived phenomenon, Modern Gothic nevertheless left a legacy of some imaginatively conceived and finely crafted pieces that will continue to serve as landmarks in the history of Chicago furniture design. At the same time, it established a tradition of furniture that harmonized not only with other interior furnishings but with the buildings that housed them.

SPECIAL DESIGNS FOR "THE SIFTED FEW"

1 8 8 0 - 1 9 1 7

During the 1880s and 1890s, Chicago acquired the look and manners of a great metropolis but still retained much of the bustling energy of a place recently emerged from the frontier. Visiting the city in 1888, journalist Charles Dudley Warner was quick to observe that social life in Chicago was "as unformed, unselected, as the city—that is, more fluid and undetermined than in Eastern large cities."[1] Chicago's wealthier citizens became increasingly cosmopolitan, however, as they traveled in the United States and Europe. Their children, often schooled on the Eastern seaboard, polished off their education with a year's travel abroad, while honeymooners and octogenarians alike filled their homes with artworks, furniture, and trinkets acquired on an obligatory Grand Tour.

As in many American cities during the Gilded Age, wealth and the culture it could buy became indices of social standing. The list of names in *The Elite Directory* grew longer as the number of Chicago's rich increased. Castellated mansions chock-full of grandiose furnishings provided the setting for costly entertainments attended by extravagantly dressed men and women. Indeed, they provided first-hand evidence of "conspicuous consumption" for the University of Chicago's economist Thorstein Veblen, author of the controversial social critique *The Theory of the Leisure Class* (1899). But Veblen failed to mention the contributions of many of these same figures to civic and cultural causes. Within a decade of the 1871 fire the reconstructed city could boast of museums, libraries, opera houses, and a fine orchestra, as well as an abundance of elegant mansions.

Some of Chicago's most palatial homes could be seen on Michigan Avenue south of the business district. Two blocks east was Prairie Avenue, known locally as "the sunny street that holds the sifted few."[2] There, on the six blocks between Sixteenth and Twenty-second streets, stood more than fifty mansions, including those of railroad magnate George M. Pullman, piano manufacturer W. W. Kimball, farm implement maker John Jacob Glessner, meat packer Philip D. Armour, financier Clarence Buckingham, and dry goods merchant Marshall Field. Other elegant residences were to be found on Grand Boulevard and Drexel Avenue.

The Near North Side, soon to be termed the Gold Coast, boasted Potter Palmer's "mansion to end all mansions."[3] Close by were the palatial homes of members of the McCormick family, while a number of splendid

The 1800 block of Prairie Avenue ca. 1900, with the home of piano manufacturer W. W. Kimball in the foreground.

Residence of Potter Palmer on Lake Shore Drive shortly after it was built in 1885.

edifices could also be found clustered around the landmark Water Tower. On the West Side, handsome residences lined West Jackson Boulevard, West Washington Boulevard, and Ashland Avenue. Shady streets radiating from the green squares of Union and Garfield parks sported impressive brick, stone, and wooden houses owned by captains of industry, finance, and commerce. In the "garden suburbs" of Kenwood, Hyde Park, Riverside, Oak Park, and Evanston that encircled the city stood the fine homes of Chicago businessmen who commuted to the city daily by railroad.

Emulating French châteaux, German Schlösser, Swiss chalets, Gothic castles, and Renaissance palaces, the mansions, clubhouses, and public buildings erected by Chicagoans between 1880 and 1918 tended to be monumental in scale and rich in material. Whether scaled-down replicas or mélanges of several styles, the buildings commonly incorporated architectural details based on antique prototypes. Often built to house "collections" of art, books, or household furniture, these fanciful recreations symbolized wealth, power, and cultural achievement. They reflected the era's fascination with history and art and at the same time provided a comforting, if wholly romantic, link with the ruling classes of the past.

The creation of such impressive edifices called for the employment of numerous contractors. Often, the exterior of the building was the work of one architect—like the prestigious revivalists Richard Morris Hunt of New York or Adolph A. Cudell of Chicago—while the floor plan, woodwork, and other details were designed by a second, "interior" architect. Once the interior was finished, a decorator took over, selecting or fabricating appropriate murals and ceiling paintings as well as textiles, stained glass, furniture, and decorative accessories.

Corner of drawing room in the residence of commission merchant William Taylor Baker, 2255 Michigan Avenue, in the 1880s.
Mrs. Charles H. Brown

Chicagoans who wanted to live in the style of a German baron, a French duke, or an English lord, but did not choose to import their furnishings from Europe, had no trouble finding the proper accouterments close to home. By the 1880s, custom-made furniture that harmonized with the fashionable historic revival interiors could be bought from local decorators, cabinetmakers specializing in interior finish and fireplace mantels, and professional woodcarvers. By the end of the century, furniture made "from special designs" in a variety of expensive woods was the mainstay both of exclusive custom shops operated by Chicago's most prestigious furniture retailers and of a myriad of small carving shops.

After 1877, when art furniture first appeared as a category in the city's *Lakeside Directory,* a number of cabinetmakers, carvers, and former carpenters also offered their services as designers and makers of custom work. Jacob S. Bast, a carpenter and contractor, made artistic furniture in his North Clark Street shop, advertising as a "Designer and Manufacturer of UNIQUE FURNITURE, in Walnut, Ebonized or Fancy Woods."[4] By 1881 he had added "genuine antiques" and reminded readers of the *Elite* directory that his establishment was "An Interesting Place to Visit."[5] William D. Boyce, formerly a billiard table manufacturer and foreman at R. W. Bates & Co., advertised art furniture made "From Architects' Designs and Original Drawings," while woodcarver John F. Martens offered artistic furniture, frames, and interior decorations "made to order under guarantee of thorough workmanship, From My Own or Architects' Designs."[6] Others making furniture to order by the end of the 1870s included cabinetmakers Bennet Doak, John C. Proteau, and Frederick Diez, who worked in partnership with Simon Strahn, Joseph H. Thain, and Frank Peters, consecutively. Simon Strahn joined Richard C. Foster in 1883 in founding the Decorators Supply Co., a firm specializing in wood and plaster ornamentation that continues to serve Chicago architects to this day.[7]

By the mid-1880s a few furniture designers had begun to work on a free-lance basis, selling designs to manufacturers or architects as well as to individual clients. After 1884, for example, Kies & Fromm prepared sketches for woodcarving and furniture, contracting by the piece, the room, or the entire building. Trained in Berlin and Paris as a cabinetmaker, Nicholas Kies had been a designer for chamber furniture manufacturer C. E. Jorgensen & Co. before joining Fromm in 1884. An experienced woodcarver, George Fromm had worked for the New York firm of Pottier & Stymus before migrating to Chicago in 1877. In Chicago, he had worked with August Fiedler, James Legge, Cudell & Meissner, and Tomlinson & Carsley before accumulating the requisite capital and contacts to risk becoming a free-lance designer.[8]

By 1893 small firms such as The Grazeo Designers offered sketches and working drawings for furniture, mantels, and household furnishings to individuals, architects, and manufacturers.[9] Similarly, E. J. Knapp and E. A. Lloyd were among a growing number of free-lance furniture designers who prepared sketches and detailed drawings for "the trade," providing small manufacturers with unique designs while sparing them the expense of a full-time designer.[10]

INTERIOR DECORATORS

As in earlier decades, some of Chicago's more fashionable citizens turned to New York or Boston designers and manufacturers for high-style home furnishings. The George M. Pullmans, Potter Palmers, and Cyrus McCormicks, to name but a few, hired prestigious Eastern firms such as Herter Brothers, Tiffany & Co., and L. Marcotte & Co. of New York, or A. H. Davenport & Co. of Boston, to decorate their houses with costly woodwork, frescoes, stained glass, tapestries, and furniture. By 1886 Herter Brothers and Tiffany operated branches in Chicago, helping set the standards by which artistic interiors were judged and sparking lively competition among the many decorators who had opened shops in the city during the 1870s.

But Chicago boosters were not to be outdone. "Whenever New York artists have been brought into contact with Chicago men, the latter have shown the better taste, the better arrangement of harmony and color, the evener tone and the more skillful, original and artistic ornamentation," boasted the Chicago correspondent of the monthly publication *American Carpet and Upholstery Trade* in the fall of 1890. Noting that "the West has become educated up to a healthy taste for real art, and it has the money to gratify this taste," he illustrated this claim by pointing to the fact that the celebrated interior of the new Auditorium Building designed by Louis H. Sullivan had been executed almost exclusively by local talent.[11]

In 1890, when the Auditorium Building opened to the public, Mitchell & Halbach and Healy & Millet were two of Chicago's best-known decorating firms. The founders of both had started out as painters of murals, stencils, and frescoes early in the 1880s. Gradually expanding their scope to include complementary textiles, wallpapers, stained glass, and woodwork, they soon began to design and execute furniture.

Trained as decorative painters, Otto William Mitchell and Frederick A. Halbach had expanded their business to include complete interiors after successfully decorating Chicago's City Hall in 1885. By 1891 they had created "designs for everything" installed in the interiors of the Hotel Metropole and Spaulding's jewelry store and were at work remodeling the interior of Marshall Field, Jr.'s mansion at 1919 Prairie Avenue. "They have made studies for the wood work, gas fixtures and electric lighting, furniture, leather, wood floors, carpet as well as their decorations, plastic ornamentation and stained glass," reported *Industrial Chicago*. "All the work is executed under their supervision, and when completed this will make one of the most artistic as well as magnificent residences in this city."[12]

Also executing fine cabinetwork and wooden mantels in conjunction with exquisite frescoes and stained glass was the firm of Healy & Millet, probably Chicago's most celebrated interior decorating establishment of the 1880s and 1890s. The son of renowned Chicago portrait painter G.P.A. Healy, George P. Healy had met his partner, Louis J. Millet, while both were studying architecture at the École des Beaux Arts in Paris. Following their graduation in 1879, the two men moved to Chicago, where, over the next eighteen years, they decorated the interiors of churches, residences, theaters, and clubs with stenciled walls, stained glass, and specially designed furniture. Much of their best work was done in conjunction with the architectural firm of Adler & Sullivan. Louis H. Sullivan had been a fellow student of Healy and Millet's in Paris.[13] In addition to his success as a decorator, Millet developed an enviable reputation as an instructor in architecture and design at the School of the Art Institute of Chicago between 1886 and 1918.

In the 1880s Adolph A. Cudell (1850–1910) started a new trend by manufacturing furniture for the interiors of houses he had designed. Born and educated in Aix-la-Chapelle, France, Cudell had migrated to Chicago in 1873. By the late 1870s he had designed a number of large residences, including the mansarded Cyrus Hall McCormick mansion (1875–79) on Rush Street, and Aldine Square (1878), a French-inspired complex of row houses overlooking a picturesque landscaped lagoon on Chicago's South Side.

In 1881 Cudell purchased half-interest in a factory on South Jefferson Street in partnership with a German cabinetmaker, Robert F. Meissner. While Cudell created designs for furniture and fine interior finish, Meissner supervised the factory, which, at times, employed as many as 140 men.[14] When Meissner retired in 1885, his interest was purchased by Alfred A. Lehmann, son of Chicago brewer Frederick Lehmann, and the firm was renamed Cudell & Lehmann. Reviewing the lineage of the company in 1886, historian A. T. Andreas noted that Lehmann's "business ability and Mr. Cudell's architectural and inventive talents comprise a most advantageous combination." He went on to report that "the work of the firm on some of the principal public buildings and residences of the city and State has gained it a high reputation for exceptional work."[15]

At the time of Andreas's writing, Cudell & Lehmann were completing two residences for brewer Conrad Seipp, formerly Lehmann's father's partner and owner of one of the largest breweries in Chicago. In the city, Cudell was supervising the construction of a stylish residence at 3300 South Michigan Avenue; for the family's country sojourns, he was designing a large, rambling Queen Anne cottage on Lake Geneva in Wisconsin. Still owned by Seipp's descendants, the summer house is furnished with dining-room and library furniture designed by Cudell and made in his factory.

After Lehmann withdrew from the firm in 1889, his share was acquired by Cudell's new partner, August Blumenthal. When Cudell and Blumenthall dissolved their partnership two years later, the factory was taken over

The residence of Conrad Seipp at Thirty-third Street and South Michigan Avenue, ca. 1893.

Mahogany library table designed by Adolph Cudell for the home of Conrad Seipp and executed by Cudell & Lehmann ca. 1886.
Table, h: 2'6" w: 6'2" d: 2'11"
Mrs. William F. Petersen

Mahogany chair executed by Cudell & Lehmann for the home of Conrad Seipp ca. 1886.
h: 42" w: 22" d: 22"
Mrs. William F. Petersen

by the latter, who operated it until 1896. One of the more colorful figures involved in furniture making, Cudell was described by architect Richard E. Schmidt, who had begun his career in Cudell's office, as "a handsome man with black hair in Apollo-like ringlets, and as a draughtsman of ability with a meticulous technique."[16] Writing some thirty years after Cudell's death, in 1941, architectural historian Thomas Tallmadge noted that "many places of entertainment on the North Side took pride in the possession of various pieces from the hand of Cudell, obtained in his later years as payment in kind."[17]

CUSTOM SHOPS

At the same time that interior decorators began to offer furniture, prominent furniture retailers like John A. Colby & Sons, Wirts & Scholle, and the Tobey Furniture Company began adding drapery, wallpaper, and interior design departments to their stores. Like their competitors, they produced furniture and cabinetwork in "special designs" following sketches created by architects, interior decorators, or the company's own designers.

Sketch of a reception hall designed and furnished by John A. Colby ca. 1890. The delineator was Alexander Hompe. From Auditorium, *ca. 1890.*

Maple side chair purchased from Wirts & Scholle by Julian Rumsey ca. 1874. h: 41⅜" w: 20¼" d: 18⅞"
National Museum of American History

Two of the leading furniture houses, John A. Colby & Sons and Wirts & Scholle, were spin-offs of a partnership formed in 1869 between John A. Colby and Jacob C. Wirts. The latter, who had come from Ohio in 1865, had been a grocer before becoming a furniture manufacturer. In 1879 Colby, backed by a wealthy lumberman, bought out his partner and organized John A. Colby & Co. In the meantime, Wirts teamed up with Henry E. Scholle, a cabinetmaker from Cincinnati, to form Wirts & Scholle.[18]

Intricately carved cherry dining-room table from the Jackson Boulevard home of Henry Lee Borden made by the Tobey Furniture Company in the 1880s.
h: 29⁹⁄₁₆" w: 53¾" d: 53¾"
The Metropolitan Museum of Art, gift of Mrs. Frank W. McCabe, 1968

Opening a store on Wabash Avenue, Wirts & Scholle were primarily furniture dealers, although they also manufactured upholstered furniture and made Williams patent folding beds. Among their customers early in the 1880s was Julian A. Rumsey, a former mayor of Chicago, who purchased a set of Renaissance style dining-room chairs for his home at 313 Huron Street (now 40 East). Later one of Rumsey's ten children, Eliza Voluntine, recorded the provenance of the chairs in her memoirs, *Recollections of A Pioneer's Daughter* (1936). "Some of the furniture for the house was made in New York by Herter and Company," she wrote, but "the dining room furniture was made by Werts and Sholle [*sic*] in Chicago."[19] The Rumseys' spacious dining room had been "finished in curled maple, the table and chairs to match, eighteen of these making an imposing array."[20]

After the 1879 reorganization, Colby hired designer T. Allen French, who for many years had been superintendent and part-owner of the W. W. Strong Furniture Company. Taking charge of Colby's special order department in April 1879, French was "prepared to furnish original designs and estimates on all works to order."[21] French remained with the firm only two years, but with his appointment, Colby established the precedent for employing first-rate designers and craftsmen that the firm would follow into the twentieth century.

Louis XV style mahogany center table carved by Otto Andersen, chief carver in the Tobey & Christiansen Cabinet Company, in the 1890s. A birthday gift from Wilhelm F. Christiansen to his wife.
h: 28½" w: 28" d: 28"
Family of William F. Christiansen

During the 1880s John A. Colby & Co. served as a training ground for some of the Midwest's finest furniture designers and future manufacturers, including George Franklin Clingman, John E. Brower, Charles P. Limbert, and A. W. Hompe.[22] When French left the firm he was succeeded by Clingman, a talented young designer who had been in Colby's employ since 1879. The son of one of Chicago's pioneer tailors, Clingman had attended business college and worked as a bookkeeper before going to work for Colby at the age of twenty-one.[23] After working for John A. Colby for ten years, Clingman left in 1888 to become the head designer at the Tobey Furniture Company. Colby, meanwhile, hired John E. Brower, who, at the time, was designing Tobey's special-order furniture. Also a native Chicagoan, Brower had worked as a "detailer" for designer/craftsman Isaac E. Scott (see page 166) and for mantel manufacturers Keller, Sturm & Ehman before joining Tobey in 1884.[24]

When Brower left for Grand Rapids in 1890, his replacement at John A. Colby & Sons was Alexander W. Hompe, a designer who had worked as a draftsman in an architect's office before joining the firm around 1888. While working at Colby's, Hompe created interiors with an airy, spacious look and designed clean-lined furniture with a minimum of carved ornament. During the 1890s he too was drawn to Grand Rapids, where by 1906 he had become president of the Royal Furniture Company.[25]

Colby's major rival, the Tobey Furniture Company, had been manufacturing commercial and residential furniture since the 1860s (see page 23). After 1875, however, when vice-president Frank B. Tobey took over daily operation of the firm, his "cultured taste" began to be reflected in "high-art improvements" in the company's furniture. During the early 1880s Tobey added departments to sell mantels, tiles, wallpapers, and draperies and enlarged the special-order department. "In all lines of artistic furni-

Details of carving by Otto Andersen.

ture, the company takes precedence," A. T. Andreas pointed out in 1886, noting that the Tobey Furniture Company was "the first to introduce model apartments ready furnished, for inspection and selections of furniture."[26]

In September 1888 Charles Tobey died and the presidency of the firm passed to his brother, Frank B. Tobey. That December, to secure the services of Wilhelm F. Christiansen, an excellent Norwegian cabinetmaker who had been superintendent of John A. Colby & Sons' factory, Tobey invited Christiansen to become his partner in a subsidiary company, the Tobey & Christiansen Cabinet Company. From then until his death in 1918, Christiansen supervised the factory on Churchill Street where he and approximately thirty workmen made the high-quality, expensive furniture that placed the Tobey Furniture Company in the top rank of American furniture makers.

Like much of the custom furniture produced in Chicago at the time, the special pieces custom-made by Tobey in the 1880s and 1890s were nei-

Parlor in the home of Wilhelm F. Christiansen at 389 Courtland Avenue, ca. 1900.
Family of William F. Christiansen

ther signed nor labeled. This means that they can be attributed to the firm only if accompanied by a bill of sale or if they can be found in one of the company's advertisements in newspapers or magazines. Nevertheless, Tobey's output of custom furniture in the latter part of the century is known to have been considerable. A note in *Furniture World* (successor to *American Cabinet Maker*) provides some clues to the quantity and quality of the work available from designer "George Clingman's pet department" during the summer of 1900. "The finest furniture made in this country, if not in the world, is made by this company in its own factory and for stock. A very large room is devoted to this furniture, and it will surprise many to know that the stock at present on the floor will inventory between $40,000 and $50,000. The finest figured mahogany lumber is used, and the articles are mostly plain, but one does not often see such magnificent cabinet work. The construction and workmanship are perfect."[27]

In the summer of 1898 the company had begun to identify such pieces as Tobey Hand-Made Furniture and was promoting them through advertisements and booklets that stressed the uniqueness of their designs, the high quality of their woods, and the handicraft aspects of their production.

French-style mahogany chair made in the Tobey & Christiansen Cabinet Company in the 1890s.
h: 39" w: 20½" d: 20½"
Family of William F. Christiansen

Mahogany pier mirror with carved frame made in the Tobey & Christiansen Cabinet Company ca. 1890.
h: 83" w: 26" d: 12"
CHS, gift of Lorraine Sinkler, 1970

Made from highly figured wood—mahogany, curly birch, or bird's-eye maple—the pieces were assembled using framed drawer panels, hand-made dovetails, and very little glue. They were then finished by hand, the process taking from four to five weeks for each piece. Among the country's first manufacturers to brand its furniture with an identifying trademark, the Tobey Furniture Company took advantage of the reputation it had established locally to promote its special furniture throughout the country.[28]

The distinctive qualities of Tobey design, according to promotional literature, were "simplicity and consistency, with the best principles of art."[29] The forms relied upon classic lines and hand-carved details for their beauty, while construction techniques followed those traditionally practiced by fine cabinetmakers: "That which survives in literature, art, music, design is only the best, and from the best surviving examples of household furniture we take the models for Tobey hand-made furniture,'' the company pointed out in 1900.[30] By not confining themselves to any one time, place, or period,

Footboard from a mahogany Dolphin pattern chamber suite made by the Tobey Furniture Company for Mr. and Mrs. Henry Tifft, 1322 (was 492) North Dearborn Street, ca. 1905. Labeled Tobey Hand-Made Furniture. h: 29" w: 58" l: 67"
CHS, gift of Mrs. Dillon Randall Brown, Mrs. Rawson Goodsir Lizars, and Mrs. Donald Neath Clausen in memory of Mr. and Mrs. Henry Tifft, 1973

Tobey's designers worked to create pieces that would not be quickly out-dated. The advertisements for Tobey's handmade art furniture stressed its hand-wrought construction, beautifully grained woods, and other features not found in mass-produced furniture.

In 1905 the Tobey Furniture Company opened a store in New York City, on West Thirty-second Street near Fifth Avenue, which sold only Tobey Hand-Made Furniture and was staffed with designers who would create custom pieces. This new store, the company's advertisements noted, would "afford opportunity for people in that part of the country to become acquainted with our Hand-Made Furniture—to see at close range the harmony, sound principles of construction and natural beauty of finish which distinguish furniture which bears the name of Tobey."[31]

Although George Clingman occasionally designed furniture while serving as the store's manager and chief buyer, many of the pieces emanating from Tobey's Chicago workshop between 1898 and 1904 were the work of Joseph Twyman. An Englishman who had come to Chicago in 1870, Twyman had earlier promoted the latest English styles in household art while managing the large wallpaper establishment of John J. McGrath between 1873 and 1885. Under Twyman's direction, McGrath's had acquired a reputation as the place to buy trend-setting papers imported from England and France. By the early 1880s, for example, the firm carried English reform style wallpapers designed by Bruce J. Talbert, Christopher Dresser, Walter

Crane, E. M. Pugin, Owen Jones, and William Morris, as well as a number of private patterns especially designed for McGrath's by architects John W. Root, Russell Sturgis, Peter B. Wight (see page 162), and Twyman himself.[32] After McGrath's closed in 1885, Twyman worked as a free-lance decorator until he became head of Tobey's interior decorating department in 1898.

Elongated dolphins flank the writing compartment of this desk from the Dolphin chamber suite made by the Tobey Furniture Company.
h: 53½" w: 45⅞" d: 22"
CHS, gift of Mrs. Dillon Randall Brown, Mrs. Rawson Goodsir Lizars, and Mrs. Donald Neath Clausen in memory of Mr. and Mrs. Henry Tifft, 1973

While many of the pieces designed by Tobey's "corps of artists" were plain almost to severity, Joseph Twyman's furniture often featured elaborate hand-carved details, including scrolled floral supports or large claw feet. Made primarily from mahogany, the pieces exhibited French-inspired rococo scrolls and foliage as well as forms and details found on eighteenth- and early nineteenth-century English and American furniture. "What people want at present in furniture is what was in vogue one to two hundred years ago," Twyman told a *House Beautiful* reporter in 1899. "It is these classic, ever-living pieces of furniture that afford inspiration to the decorator and designer. It is our mission to begin where these articles leave off, and so modify them that they will exactly fit into our present mode of life."

Pointing out that it was "ridiculous to use *precisely* the same styles of furniture that were in fashion two centuries ago, because our life is different," Twyman expressed his belief that, in the twentieth century, there

Frank B. Tobey (1833–1913), ca. 1906, sitting in a chair made in his factory. From About Tobey Furniture *by Oscar L. Triggs.*

The work force at the Tobey & Christiansen Cabinet Company, ca. 1906. Wilhelm Christiansen, with arms folded, is seated in the center of the second row. His sons, Rolf and William, are seated in the front row, at left end and third from left. Carver Otto Andersen is in the front row, second from left.
Family of William F. Christiansen

should be "a vigorous effort after originality based on the best things that have been done in the past."[33]

A youthful advocate of Gothic Revival who had become a self-proclaimed disciple of William Morris, Twyman confessed to an affinity for colonial or Old English styles. Simple in material and pure in line—and made by craftsmen who used their hands rather than machines—colonial furniture, for many designers, answered "every requirement of the Morris and Ruskin school."[34] Nevertheless, Twyman found it expedient to design furniture whose forms appealed to the buying public. Like many successful designers, he was able to create handsome designs working within various vocabularies, achieving a harmonious effect from the final interplay of

Dining room in the original Montana Governor's Mansion in Helena showing furniture purchased from the Tobey Furniture Company ca. 1900.
Montana Historical Society, Helena

Oak corner table made for the Montana Governor's Mansion ca. 1900. Labeled Tobey Hand-Made Furniture.
Montana Historical Society, Helena

well-proportioned forms, figured woods, finely carved details, and meticulous construction.

Despite Twyman's preference for English styling, the Tobey Furniture Company also did a thriving business reproducing Louis XIV, XV, and XVI furniture. As Chicago's *Interior Decorator* explained in 1894: "The most distinctive evidence of "high fashion" that we have observed lately has been the revival of the French styles of furniture, the periods of the Empire, of Henry II and of the Louis having all received much attention. The *façon* Louis XV has naturally been the greatest favorite, as affording the most scope to the designer and craftsman, but this style is not to be attempted unless the cost is of little account."[35] Intricately carved and therefore costly, Louis XV-inspired furniture was particularly popular with Tobey's affluent clientele, according to Wilhelm Christiansen's son, William, who had been trained in his father's shop and designed Tobey furniture from 1908 until 1927. At the time that young Christiansen joined the design department, stock pieces of Tobey Hand-Made Furniture occupied half of the store's fourth floor. The other half was the design studio, where customers discussed their special needs with the designer. Once the client made his selection, the designer produced detailed scale drawings of the piece and sent it to the factory for the workers to follow.[36]

In 1901 the Tobey Furniture Company introduced a number of designs that echoed the exuberant curvilinear lines and organic forms embodied in

Mahogany Art Nouveau card table with swirling leaves decorating the base made by the Tobey Furniture Company ca. 1910.
h: 29¾" w: 36" d: 18¼"
The Chrysler Museum at Norfolk, Virginia, gift of Walter P. Chrysler, Jr.

the distinctive Art Nouveau furniture then being shown in France and Belgium. Promoted as "the new art" at the Paris Exposition of 1900, Art Nouveau furniture represented a break from academic tradition, an attempt on the part of a small group of architects and designers to create a new style whose forms were derived from nature rather than based on historical precedent. Tobey's "New Art" line, executed in fine mahogany, included

Mahogany sideboard with ebony and holly cameo carving designed by W.L.B. Jenney and executed by Isaac Scott ca. 1875. Describing Modern Gothic furniture designed by Jenney, the Chicago Tribune noted in 1875: "A new style of paneling has been devised which is very striking. . . . the designs are fanciful arabesque patterns, with central figures of conventional shape."
Dr. and Mrs. Herman Kelly Sutton

Detail of left side of Jenney sideboard. The round panels depict Jack Horner and "Symon Fishing" above carvings of a peacock and a parrot.

Detail of door of Jenney sideboard showing cameo-carved swan and hand-wrought hinges.

Desk made by W. W. Strong Furniture Co. for a Palmer House bridal suite, 1873.
h: 90¾" w: 36½" d: 21¾"
CHS, purchase, 1979

Oak desk with inset panels of contrasting burl displayed by Lladislaus Zdzieblowski (1857– 1929) at the 1893 World's Columbian Exposition.
h: 75" w: 56" d: 56"
Private Collection

Queen Anne lounge with original brown plush upholstery. The frame is identical to one shown in the 1881 catalogue of Joseph Zangerle & Co.
h: 36" l: 70" d: 26"
CHS, gift of Suzanne Swift, 1969

Mahogany framed armchair with oak leaves, made by the Tobey Furniture Company ca. 1906.
h: 41" w: 28" d: 31"
Mr. & Mrs. Wistar Morris III
Photograph by Abramson-Culbert
Studio

Oak dower chest made by Madeline Yale Wynne for Bertha Bullock on the occasion of her marriage to William R. Folsom in 1900.
h: 25½" w: 39" d: 22"
Glenn C. Hjort

Dining room in the home of Frank Lloyd Wright, Oak Park, after restoration in 1981 to its 1909 appearance.
The Frank Lloyd Wright Home and Studio Foundation
Photograph by Sadin / Kurant

Fiber rush furniture made in the Chicago factory of Heywood-Wakefield Co. ca. 1926. The pieces are painted chartreuse highlighted with woven diamonds and braid of black and orange.
CHS, purchase, 1978
Photographs by Abramson-Culbert Studio

AT LEFT:
Armchair and footstool, both with original floral cotton upholstery.
Chair, h: 39½" w: 30¾" d: 32"
Footstool, h: 17" w: 23½" d: 24¾"

BELOW LEFT:
Side table.
h: 24¼" w: 20¼" d: 9½"

BELOW CENTER AND RIGHT:
Desk and chair.
Desk, h: 34½" w: 29"

Skyscraper style furniture designed by Abel Faidy in 1927 for the Charles and Ruth Singletary penthouse at 1244 Stone Street, Chicago.
CHS, purchase, 1977
Photographs by Abramson-Culbert Studio

Settee upholstered in burgundy leather with an ebonized and natural wood frame.
h: 47½" w: 49¼" d: 28½"

Dining table of veneered maple with ebonized banding. The leaves fold upward to lie flat on the table's surface.
h: 20¾" l: 66" w: 40"

LEFT:
Armchair upholstered in leather.
h: 35" w: 26½" d: 32¼"

BELOW LEFT:
Dining chair with leather upholstery.
h: 49½" w: 18¼" d: 20¾"

BELOW RIGHT:
Armchair from dining suite.
h: 55½" w: 21⅝" d: 22"

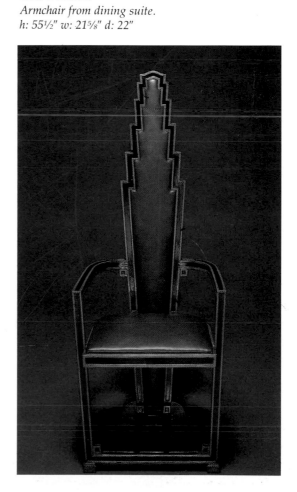

Modern Chromsteel furniture designed by Wolfgang Hoffmann for The Howell Company in the mid-1930s.
CHS, Decorative Arts Fund, 1981

Prototype settee with its original striped cotton velour upholstery made in the company's model shop ca. 1934. It was later produced in modified form. h: 30" w: 50" d: 32½"
CHS, Decorative Arts Fund, 1981
Photographs by Abramson-Culbert Studio

Armchair with its original black and gold leather upholstery, ca. 1935. h: 30" w: 30" d: 32½"
CHS, Decorative Arts Fund, 1981
Photographs by Abramson-Culbert Studio

Living room of Chicagoan Laurie Kaufman showing furniture designed by Jon Cockrell in 1982.
Hokin / Kaufman Gallery.

a Drawing Room Suite comprising tables with supports of swirling leaves, and chairs and sofas whose curvilinear frames were accented with bursts of naturalistic foliage. According to *Furniture World*, the pieces were exact reproductions of those shown at the Paris Exposition.[37]

Mahogany framed armchair carved with oak leaves, made by the Tobey Furniture Company ca. 1906. h: 41" w: 28" d: 31"
Mr. and Mrs. Wistar Morris III
Photograph by Abramson-Culbert Studio

French Art Nouveau furniture, displayed in the Palace of Decorative Arts at the 1900 Paris Exposition, had also attracted the attention of Chicago furniture manufacturer Solomon Karpen. Returning to Chicago, Karpen brought out a new line of French-inspired Art Nouveau parlor suites that were offered to the public in the spring of 1901. The most intricate of the suites, described in the company's promotional material "as the most artistic and beautiful example of this school of decoration ever produced," used a climbing rose as its chief motif, with the vine twining upward around its curved frame to "bloom in a burst of glory at the top and center of each piece."[38] In the midst of the bloom swirled a female dancer resembling Illinois's own Loie Fuller, who had performed at the 1900 Exposition. Using flowing silks and theatrical lighting to create novel dance routines in which she transformed herself into a lily or a butterfly, Fuller came to symbolize many aspects of the dramatic new style. Another suite featured a simpler floral theme "detailed on an outline of a pure Louis XVI style."[39]

In 1904 a six-piece Art Nouveau suite especially made to be shown at the Louisiana Purchase Exhibition in St. Louis captured the Grand Prize for upholstered furniture. Inspired by the blossom of the Catillya [sic] orchid, this suite consisted of a sofa, easy chair, side chair, ottoman, elongated divan, and a table, all heavily carved. As with other Karpen Art Nouveau pieces, customers could have the frames executed in solid Cuban mahogany or covered with gold leaf.[40] Truly for "the sifted few," the pieces were very expensive, with the gilded lily-carved Grand Prix Suite priced at $850 in 1906, a sum equal to more than a year's salary for a typical furniture factory worker.[41]

Karpen's Art Nouveau parlor furniture was innovative both in design and in construction. As the *Furniture Worker* noted:

> The main idea in the design is to imitate nature as nearly as possible. For instance, the foot of a settee will be carved to appear like the trunk of a tree cut off just where the roots branch off from the body, and the same natural idea will be carried out, up the leg of the piece, and the branches of the tree will spread in graceful curves up the arm and over the back of the settee. Or, perhaps, it will be a grape vine that twines itself about the legs, arms and back of a piece of parlor furniture.[42]

Unlike Tobey's pieces, whose details were completely hand-carved, S. Karpen & Bros.'s intricate parlor frames were executed using the company's newly patented Karpen Automatic Carving Machine. To make the highly detailed frames of the Art Nouveau line, a sculptor first modeled the entire framework in clay. A plaster cast was then made from the clay model to be used as a pattern to guide the spindle shapers on the multiple carving machine. Fine details and finishing were completed by the company's "army of hand carvers."

Solomon Karpen, George Clingman, and Joseph Twyman were not alone in their appreciation of well-made cabinetwork and well-executed ornamentation. By the turn of the century, Chicago was in the midst of a renaissance in woodcarving as artisans employed by millwork, mantel making, and carving shops turned out handsomely detailed interiors and furniture distinguished by abundant and intricate carving.

HAND-CARVED FURNITURE AND PERIOD REPRODUCTIONS

CHAPTER 12

1880-1917

"Even the least costly bit of carved furniture receives a great deal more hand work than is ordinarily supposed," an article in the *Furniture Worker* explained in 1900. Pointing out that even the most sophisticated carving machines were manipulated partly by hand, the writer went on to estimate: "Chicago has probably 5,000 artists in wood carving working in the various furniture factories. At the rows of benches one sees old men and boys side by side, working away with chisels and saws and tiny polished tools at sofa heads and chair arms, which are very much nearer real art than many an ambitious student gets with brush and paint."[1] The large number of European-trained carvers in Chicago made possible the production of hand-carved furniture, mantels, and woodwork at reasonable cost, while the fashionable architectural styles and a building boom provided unprecedented amounts of work. Although the majority of carvers were employed in furniture factories, others worked for firms making mantels and millwork or in one of the specialized carving shops. Some worked on furniture that was highly original or individualistic, others carefully replicated the handwork of their predecessors.

MILLWORKERS AND MANTEL MAKERS

Perennial efforts to harmonize furniture with a building's interior woodwork or "finish" prompted the city's millworkers and fireplace mantel manufacturers to apply their woodworking skills and equipment to the production of artistic furniture. By 1883, for example, the Goss & Phillips Manufacturing Company, the city's oldest producer of sashes, staircases, and doors, had begun to "make a specialty of modern architecture and decorations" and the requisite sideboards, cabinets, and hall furniture.[2] At the Inter-State Industrial Exposition that year, the company exhibited a pair of rooms—an entrance hall and a parlor—completely outfitted with staircase, woodwork, and furniture to demonstrate its skill and versatility.

Newer, but equally diverse in its production, was the firm of Tomlinson & Carsley, organized in 1882 by millworker Isaac Tomlinson and Francis M. Carsley (who had been superintendent for ten years at A. H. Andrews & Co.). Operating a large factory that employed 140 men, the company specialized in "fine interior finish" and made furniture from special designs created by Luther F. Crosby, another former Andrews employee. By 1883, when the company had been in business just over a year, Tomlinson & Carsley had "fitted up . . . a great number of the most beautiful houses in Chicago."[3] The next year, the firm made all of the furniture and interior fittings for the residence of shoe manufacturer Mason D. Wells, just completed by architects Wheelock & Clay at the corner of Michigan and Twenty-sixth Street. As the following description from the *Inland Architect and Builder* makes clear, the process of "fitting up" such an artistic interior required considerable coordination among the various contractors. "The interior is finished in natural woods, manufactured by the interior finishing firm of Tomlinson & Carsley, the designs for which, as well as for the furniture, were made by Luther F. Crosby, who, in conjunction with the decorator, Mr. Abner Crossman, and the tapestry artist who furnished all the tapestries and upholstering, carpets, etc., Mr. G. W. Haskins, united in the work of producing the artistic and harmonious interior."[4]

A woodcarver at work in the Tobey & Christiansen Cabinet Company in 1906. From About Tobey Handmade Furniture *by Oscar L. Triggs.*

Interior decorator Abner Crossman—who was in partnership with George R. Lee at that time and, after 1893, with J. F. Sturdy—specialized in original frescoes for walls and ceilings. George W. Haskins supplied elegant textile furnishings. Although known primarily as painters, both Crossman & Lee and G. W. Haskins operated workshops where furniture, mantels, portieres, and other furnishings were manufactured.

Custom-made furniture was also manufactured by the Henry Dibblee Company, one of the city's largest suppliers of fireplace mantels, grates, and tiles. Founded by Henry Dibblee, a real-estate salesman and brother-in-law of Marshall Field, the company specialized in iron products until the early 1880s, when wooden mantels with surrounds of ceramic or mosaic tiles began to supersede iron in popularity. Shifting its emphasis from metal to wood, the firm offered a large selection of custom-made mantels, imported huge quantities of English ceramic tile, and began to make matching furniture.

In 1886, when Dibblee retired, the company was purchased by its energetic manager, Anson S. Hopkins, who persuaded several prominent Chicago businessmen to become stockholders in the firm. Among these were O.S.A. and A. A. Sprague of Sprague, Warner & Co., A. C. Bartlett of Hibbard, Spencer, Bartlett & Co., and Charles Hosmer Morse of Fairbanks, Morse & Co., who became president of the firm by 1888. In addition to having important social connections, the Henry Dibblee Company employed "one of the best designers in the United States" (who remains tantalizingly anonymous) and claimed in 1891 to be the largest importer of English tiles in America.[5]

In addition to custom mantels, the Henry Dibblee Company offered artistic sideboards and dining-room, hall, and library furniture in complementary designs. By 1891 the firm had furnished mantels, mosaics, and tiles—and in some instances, furniture—for the Pullman Building; the Auditorium Hotel, Theatre, and Office Building; the Dearborn Street Station; and numerous Chicago hotels and restaurants. By then, according to *Industrial Chicago,* many of the city's architects had begun to use the services of designers employed by manufacturers. As the publication explained:

> Many of our best architects with their rapidly increasing business find commission work does not compensate them for the time required in preparing designs and details for such parts of the interior as the mantels, sideboards, bookcases and in many cases fine pieces of furniture, and appreciating the effort of this company in employing a designer conversant with the requirements, are very glad to turn over such items to the company to design and execute. In all such cases the general character and feeling of the architect's plans is adhered to, and these designs when adopted are not duplicated for any one else.[6]

In 1895 the Henry Dibblee Company was succeeded by the Chicago Interior Decorating Co., which continued to make furniture from in-house or free-lance designs in addition to executing murals and installing ceramic tiles.[7]

"Ordered furniture from special designs" and "high-art wooden mantels" were also manufactured by the firm of Rickenberg & Clarke, organized by Henry F. Rickenberg (formerly co-owner of the Novelty Cabinet Works) and businessman Henry F. Clarke in 1884.[8] Employing about fifty men, this company furnished several offices in the Board of Trade and by 1886 had outfitted a number of residences, including that of piano manufacturer W. W. Kimball on Michigan Avenue. Similarly, H. V. Wagner & Co. manufactured furniture and mantels and sold tiles, stained glass, and brass goods in its shop on Wabash Avenue, while the Ehman & Simon Mfg. Co. created High-Grade Mantels and furniture in its factory at the corner of Fulton and Elizabeth streets.

Like other contractors for interior finish, John Blackwell Rees, who specialized in stairs and handrails, also made special furniture. In 1893, for example, when Welsh settlers in America planned a festival for poets and

The griffin, symbol of Wales, and the eagle, as represented in the Illinois state flag, are carved on the back of the Bardic Chair.

Oak Bardic Chair carved by John Blackwell Rees for the 1893 World's Columbian Exposition.
h: 52" w: 24" d: 19½"
Mrs. Peter Crawford

musicians, known as an Eisteddfod, to be held at the World's Columbian Exposition, Rees, a Welshman by birth, offered to make the chief prize—a Bardic Chair. Carved with dragons and other mythological symbols, the chair displayed the carving skills that Rees had learned from his father, a cabinetmaker/undertaker, before leaving Wales. But, alas, the Welsh authorities refused to give the Eisteddfod their blessing and so the event never took place. Returned to Rees, the chair became a treasured family heirloom.[9]

CARVING SHOPS

By the early 1880s several Chicago woodcarvers advertised as "architectural sculptors," offering to execute details on the interiors or exteriors of buildings, carve furniture, or create models from clay or wood for use in casting metal or plaster. Such multi-purpose carving shops were operated by James Legge, one of the city's most sought-after craftsmen until his death in 1890; Theodore Mack, who operated a studio at 13 North Union Street (between Randolph and Lake Street); and Gustave Behm, who worked on the city's North Side between 1887 and 1926. Woodcarver Emanuel Kopriwa began executing elegant mahogany furniture by 1887. In 1907 the *Furniture Journal* noted that Kopriwa had had "many years of experience as a designer and woodcarver and modeler, and has made a specialty of high class work for furniture, pianos, organs and interior finish."[10] His son, also named Emanuel, continued the manufacturing operation through the 1930s.

Trade card of carver Joseph Dux.
CHS, gift of Timothy Samuelson

Oak chest carved by Leopold Belli in 1892. A scroll on the front is inscribed "1892/OHIO/MAX." Written on the base of the piece is "L. G. BETTI—2956 COTTAGE GROVE AVE."
h: 31" w: 49" d: 23"
Clouia Rath and George Joosten

Leopold Betti, a designer and carver, specialized in architectural work in his shop on Cottage Grove Avenue from 1888 until 1903. Even more specialized was the New York and Chicago Carving Company, whose manager, Thomas V. Brooks, created to order "show figures" for circuses, ships, and steamboats and supplied the region with gaily painted cigar-store Indians.[11]

Two of the largest firms were operated by Joseph Dux and Gensch & Hartmann. A Philadelphia native who moved to Chicago in 1880, Dux employed forty skilled designers, modelers, sculptors, and carvers in his studio by 1899. Describing the shop that year, the editors of *Majestic Chicago* wrote, "Mr. Dux superintends all their labors and executes a general line of designing, modeling and carving in stone and wood and ornamental plaster work, and the most artistic, effective results are attained in every instance."[12]

Employing thirty-five to forty-five men in its studio at 47–49 West Lake Street (near Clinton Street) in 1899, the firm of Gensch & Hartmann had been organized in 1891 by Herman Gensch and John Hartmann, two German woodcarvers who had worked in Chicago since 1884.[13] In addition to manufacturing building ornamentation, Gensch & Hartmann made special furniture, some of which was displayed in a furniture exhibit at the 1893 World's Fair. Praising the display, *Interior Decorator* commented that it "would almost deserve a place in the Palace of Fine Arts, so artistic are the designs and execution and so delicate the carving."[14] A year later two examples of this work, a rococo toilet table and an Italian Renaissance pedestal, were shown at the annual exhibition of the Chicago Architectural Sketch Club alongside hand-carved furniture made by John A. Colby & Sons, the Tobey Furniture Company, and cabinetmaker and designer Fortunato Visconti, who specialized in antique furniture reproductions.[15]

Mahogany desk and chair carved by Gustav F. Behm (1856–1926) and presented to Albert H. Pick on the occasion of his marriage to Gertrude Frank in 1892.
Desk, h: 64" w: 48" d: 25¾"
Chair, h: 43" w: 19" d: 24"
CHS, gift of Mrs. Albert Pick, Jr., 1978
Photograph by Abramson-Culbert Studio

Because of their complexity and cost, furniture pieces made by woodcarvers tended to be one of a kind, often created to commemorate an anniversary, battle, or other special event, or to stand in an entrance hall or chancel. Suites were most often commissioned for dining rooms, where chair backs, table bases, and sideboards showed the carving to the best advantage and offered an opportunity to display the owner's initial, crest, or favorite motif. As a group, pieces tended to be ornate and heavy, a reflection, perhaps, of the Old World training of most of the city's woodcarvers.

Although many woodcarvers did not sign their work, pieces known to have been made by Chicago artisans indicate the variety of their output. As mentioned earlier, Isaac Scott executed a wide range of household furnishings, ranging from simple picture frames to ambitious bookcases and desks (see page 166). Others, like Gustav Behm, were often called upon to create highly ornamental presentation pieces, such as the desk and chair presented to hotel supplier Albert Pick on the occasion of his marriage in 1892. Ornamented with relief profiles of Shakespeare, Goethe, and Schiller,

Detail of Behm desk showing bust of William Shakespeare.

the desk was accompanied by a chair whose wooden seat had been carved to resemble leather.

A simpler desk made by Polish cabinetmaker Lladislaus Zdzieblowski, an employee of the Pullman Palace Car Company, also features portraits of legendary figures. On the cabinet doors, George Washington faces Thaddeus Kosciusko, Polish patriot and commander of American troops during the Revolutionary War. According to family tradition, Zdzieblowski's work was exhibited at the 1893 World's Fair. For his family's use, Zdzieblowski made side chairs and tables inlaid with delicate mother-of-pearl and marquetry, following a practice popular in Chicago in the 1890s.

Other pieces made in Chicago reflected the Victorian passion for collecting mementos or "relics" associated with famous people, places, or events. Occasionally carvers were called upon to use wood taken from historic trees or buildings to make exceptional furniture. A striking example is a whimsical armchair made from logs taken from the second Fort Dearborn, the military post erected in 1803 and rebuilt in 1816 on the site that became Chicago. Carved by an anonymous Chicagoan for dry goods merchant Levi Z. Leiter, the chair features cattle-head finials and a bear peeking over its crest rail. Indian motifs and eagle arm rests recall the city's frontier days.

Colby & Wirts. Various addresses, 1869–78.

John A. Colby & Co. 217 State, 1879–84.

John A. Colby & Sons (name changed to **Colby's** in mid-1940s). 217 State, 1885–90; 148 Wabash, 1891–1910; 29 South Wabash, 1911–15; 129 North Wabash, 1916–66; 129 East Chestnut, 1974 to the present.

One of Chicago's oldest furniture retailers, Colby's is the descendant of a furniture and auction house founded in 1869 by John A. Colby (1833–1909) and Jacob C. Wirts.

After 1879, when Colby bought out Wirts, he established a factory to produce special furniture. There is some confusion about the beginnings and location of this factory, since Chicago directories list only the retail address until 1901 and company records have been destroyed. A Colby advertisement in 1894 lists 85–89 Henry Street. However, a 1901 *Chicago Tribune* article stated that the factory (which employed 100 and supplied the store with three-quarters of its furniture) had been located at 44 North Elizabeth since 1886. During the 1890s the company advertised "Interior Woodwork Made to Order" in addition to custom furniture. It also made curtains and draperies, including the large embroidered and appliquéd curtain for the stage of the Auditorium Theatre completed in 1889.

John A. Colby had been joined in business by his sons, Henry C. and Edward A., in 1881. By 1913 all three had died and the company was sold to Gustavus, Henry B., and Fred Babson of Chicago and Adam W. Crawford of Lincoln, Nebraska, who became president of the firm. The company closed its furniture factory, whose work force had dwindled to only ten craftsmen, during the 1920s.

Typical of carved dining-room furniture is a set made at the turn of the century for the Astor Street residence of Charles F. Clarke, vice-president of the Hibernian Bank. Each piece of the set—a round dining table, sideboard, and six chairs—is ornamented with a naturalistic fruit motif. Meandering grape vines encircle the table top, while clusters of grapes emphasize

Ebonized side chair with frame inset with mother-of-pearl and abalone made by Lladislaus Zdzieblowski in the 1890s. "The fashion of inlaying parlor chairs with mother-of-pearl-marquetry is now at full tide here," the Furniture Worker *noted on July 10, 1898 h: 35½" w: 14¾" d: 16¼" Private Collection*

Oak armchair with leather upholstery made from logs secured from Ft. Dearborn for Levi Z. Leiter ca. 1880. h: 55" w: 30" d: 25" CHS, gift of Thomas Leiter, 1941

the curving contour of the sideboard. A different fruit is featured on the crest of each chair. Family tradition maintains that the furniture was made

*Table with chip-carved frieze of grapes
and leaves and lion's-paw feet.
h: 30" d: 65"*
CHS, gift of the Estate of Mrs.
Charles F. Clarke, 1978

*Side chair with leather upholstery
carved with melon. Each of the six
chairs features a different motif.
h: 45½" w: 19" d: 18"*

by a German woodcarver whose shop was located on Clark Street. The
directories show several German woodworkers on that street at the time
but it is not known which one of them executed this commission. While
these woodcarvers were engaged in producing original work, there were
others who specialized in fine reproductions.

*Mahogany dining-room suite made for
the Astor Street home of Charles F.
Clarke ca. 1890.*
CHS, gift of the Estate of Mrs.
Charles F. Clarke, 1978

PERIOD REPRODUCTIONS

Throughout the 1890s and into the twentieth century accurate reproductions and "adaptations" of antique prototypes remained in vogue and provided a stable livelihood for the city's corps of woodworkers and "high art" furniture makers. Indeed, several small furniture factories founded prior to World War I limited their work almost entirely to the production of period furniture emulating colonial or European styles. Some produced composites that combined elements of many styles; others prided themselves on their accurate reproductions of antique models.

While imitations of European furnishings summoned up visions of royalty and wealth, the revival of colonial, or Georgian, styles reflected a sentimental desire to return to America's "good old days," when life was simpler and people nobler. As Chicago's *Fine Arts Journal* proclaimed, "The Colonial type of furnishing and interior decoration might well be termed the classic style of America, for while handed down from the thrilling and romantic period of our earliest history, its characteristics are simplicity, elegance, and grace."[16] The colonial revival, whose origins predated the Centennial of 1876, represented a growing interest in the preservation of antiques as well as the celebration of Americanism as a counter to the increasing numbers of foreign-born in the population. Between 1895 and 1914, close to 13 million immigrants entered the United States, giving rise to fears that the traditional character of American society was being undermined. Many Americans formed patriotic societies and supported what they perceived as indigenous architecture, arts, and crafts in order to preserve American ideals.[17]

Ironically, colonial style furniture had little to do with genuine colonial American furniture. As furniture designer W. L. Kimerly, writing in 1917, would point out in *How to Know Period Styles of Furniture,* many pieces were based on French forms prevalent early in the nineteenth century. "Probably the most popular type of modern Colonial today is the one derived from the Empire style. The brass ormolu mounts of the Empire have been discarded and the classical features retained and from this has come a distinct American period style."[18] Most often executed in mahogany, colonial style case pieces were characterized by classical columns, carved or plain; S-shaped scrolls; and lion's-paw or scroll feet. Chairs were usually variations of the popular Windsor type.

One of the first Chicago concerns to specialize in colonial reproductions was John A. Colby & Sons, whose factory on North Elizabeth Street was making revival designs as early as 1894 (see page 184). In 1899 the company announced that it had been running its factory "to the fullest limits for several months, and the superb results can be seen in our showrooms." At the time, the firm was promoting Colby's Reliable Furniture, advertising its mahogany sofas, dining tables, writing desks, and four-poster beds as "exact reproductions of the best existing types of rare Colonial masterpieces." Not only did Colby's pieces have graceful curves and fine upholstery, they were "made better than the original" and "cost only one-half as much."[19]

By 1900 designer William F. Halstrick was offering *House Beautiful* readers handmade reproductions of antique Dutch chairs "solidly built on the true

Advertisement for furniture made by John A. Colby & Sons in House Beautiful, *November 1900.* The Newberry Library

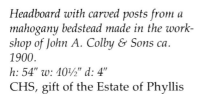

Headboard with carved posts from a mahogany bedstead made in the workshop of John A. Colby & Sons ca. 1900.
h: 54" w: 40½" d: 4"
CHS, gift of the Estate of Phyllis Healy, 1977

colonial lines" in his shop on Van Buren Street, while the Storey Furniture Company advertised a "quaint and handsome" Windsor Arm Chair that was "a faithful reproduction of one of the Mayflower patterns," with a rocker to match.[20] The largest firm to successfully produce colonial style seating furniture, the Colonial Chair Company, was started in 1906 by two Scandinavian furniture makers, Claus O. Krabol and L. B. Johnson. Krabol had worked as a mechanic in the A. H. Andrews factory following his arrival in America in 1878, while Johnson had been a woodcarver and chair designer since 1874.

Carved furniture also became the mainstay of the Chicago Wood Carving Company in 1914, when the firm's new owner, Danish cabinetmaker H. C. Filstrup, shifted production from turned wooden spindles for carpenters and cabinetmakers to "specially high-grade and artistic furniture."[21] Four years later Filstrup, who had headed the cabinet shop for musical instrument maker Lyon & Healy, told historian J. Seymour Currey that the expensive parlor, dining-room, and bedroom furniture being made by his thirty-five skilled woodworkers was intended to "appeal to connoisseurs and others who demand the best in artistic conceptions and fine workmanship."[22]

CUSTOM SHOPS

Beginning in the 1890s several Chicago furniture retailers and department stores, including A. H. Revell and Marshall Field & Company, as well as a number of interior decorators, established custom shops to make furniture in both period and modern styles. Marshall Field & Company, for example, began making its own frames and upholstering parlor furniture in the 1880s. The store sold few cabinet pieces until 1896, when its buyers began purchasing ''modern'' furniture and ''carloads of Morris chairs'' from Midwestern manufacturers to sell alongside Shaker chairs brought from Mt. Lebanon, New York, and antiques imported from France.[23]

The firm was doing a brisk business in colonial, English, and French Salon furniture by 1902, when it began selling the plain oak pieces made by Gustav Stickley's United Crafts (see page 235).[24] Around this time the store hired Art Institute graduate Frederick C. Walton as a furniture designer and opened its own custom shop. By 1912, when Field's advertised ''special pieces executed in our own cabinet shop'' in *Architectural Record*, the store was executing pieces on a contract basis for local architects and interior designers in addition to making the furniture designed by its own staff.[25]

Many of the designers and furniture makers employed by Marshall Field & Company later established their own businesses in Chicago. In 1916, for instance, Frederick C. Walton joined another Field's employee, Charles Watson, in founding the new firm of Watson & Walton, in the Garland Building. Eight years later, when Richard Boaler became Watson's

Showroom of Watson & Boaler, 722 North Michigan Avenue, in the 1920s. Watson & Boaler

partner, the firm was renamed Watson & Boaler and moved into new premises at 722 North Michigan Avenue.[26]

The first home furnishings dealer to locate in what soon became the city's most fashionable shopping district, Watson & Boaler was widely known as a purveyor of ''magnificent things.'' The firm specialized in European antiques and "faithful reproductions," often importing entire rooms of pine or oak paneling from Europe and reassembling them in its store to provide a setting for its furniture compositions. One such room, removed from a French chateau after World War I, came complete with the autographs of

Pretzel chair, a reproduction of an Italian Empire armchair made by Watson & Boaler ca. 1950.
h: 30" w: 24" d: 20"
Watson & Boaler
Photograph by
Abramson-Culbert Studio

Colonial style mahogany side table made by W. K. Cowan ca. 1918.
h: 26" d: 18"
Mrs. C. Phillip Miller

the doughboys who had been billeted there. After the war, the company operated its own custom shop, where craftsmen executed furniture in both period and modern designs (see page 272).[27]

By 1918 Rudolph Hasselgren, W. K. Cowan, and David Zork, three highly regarded interior designers, operated custom workshops specializing in the production of period furniture. Hasselgren, who had been head of John A. Colby & Co.'s interior design department in the 1880s, had joined with William C. Moulton in 1897 to found R. Hasselgren & Co. In 1911, when new owners took over the firm, it was renamed Hasselgren Studio, and a showroom was opened on Michigan Avenue. Headed by John P. Scharff, the firm specialized in furnishing large suburban houses through 1937.

A graduate of the Chicago Manual Training School, William Kennett Cowan (1869–1928) had studied architecture in the office of Henry Ives Cobb before serving as superintendent of sanitary work at the 1893 World's Fair, where he was in charge of designing and installing all the plumbing and appurtenances. After the fair, he turned his talents to designing special furniture, organizing the firm of W. K. Cowan & Co. in 1894.[28]

In 1899 Cowan opened a salesroom in the newly renovated Fine Arts Building to display the colonial and Empire-style furniture being made in his workshop on North State Street. Working only in solid mahogany, the company specialized in "correct copies" of historic American furniture, such as George Washington's desk and Martha Washington's sewing table, in addition to pieces made after Cowan's own designs.[29] That year, in *House Beautiful*, W. K. Cowan discussed the growing appreciation for "things colonial" and his making of reproductions.

> When we obtain an authentic old piece we make an exact copy of it in every detail, not adding a single line or curve. This duplication gives a large group of people the benefit that otherwise would be confined to one individual. And these reproductions, I am glad to say, are exceeding popular. Our own factory is running at its fullest capacity, making exact copies of old Sheraton, Chippendale, and Hepplewhite pieces, and doubtless other firms are doing the same thing. These modern copies are made of carefully selected mahogany, and veneered with the finest crotches, so that when finished they are exact duplicates in appearance and in reality of the original specimens.[30]

By 1906, furniture made in Cowan's workshop was being shown alongside decorative accessories and antiques imported from Europe. By then he had expanded beyond the colonial styles to install a series of "correct specimen rooms in all the best periods" in the Cowan Galleries in the Fine Arts Building.[31] Within ten years of its introduction, Cowan furniture was being made in some six hundred patterns in a new factory at Lake Shore Drive and Ohio Street that, according to company literature, covered floor space equivalent to seven times the area of a city block. Patterns included "exact replicas" of Queen Anne, French colonial, Chinese Chippendale, and Hepplewhite style chairs, tables, desks, beds, and sewing tables modeled after antiques imported from Europe or purchased along the Eastern seaboard. A 1909 advertisement explained some of the qualities that contributed to its wide appeal. Cowan Mahogany Period Furniture, it noted, "is based solely upon original models of the best periods in furniture history—each model a collector's piece—and yet the number of patterns is so large and varied that you may furnish a home entirely with it, thereby, insuring a harmony of result impossible by any other plan."[32]

Operating along similar lines, and appealing to the same class of customers, was the David Zork Company, a retail and manufacturing enterprise founded in 1915 by one of Cowan's employees. A native of St. Louis, David Zork (1875–1957) served as general manager of W. K. Cowan & Co. for ten years before going into business for himself. Opening a shop on North Michigan Avenue, Zork sold antique furniture and reproductions made specifically for his shop as well as imported decorative accessories until 1957. For many years the manufacture of period reproductions at the firm's subsidiary, the Zork Mfg. Co., was under the supervision of Frank Joseph Wagner, a Hungarian art furniture maker who had joined the firm in 1919.[33] Interviewed by *Furniture Journal* in 1921, when he had just opened

W. K. Cowan & Co. 111 North State, 1896; 121–23 North State, 1897–99; 203 Michigan, 1900–2; 245 North Wells, 1903–4; 203 Michigan, 1905–10; 525 Ohio, 1909; 484 East Ohio, 1910; 460 East Ohio, 1911–16; 318 South Michigan, 1911–12; Lake Shore Drive and Ohio, 1920–21.
Cowan Cabinet Co. 410 South Michigan, 1922–23; 844 Rush, 1924–26; 243 South Wabash, 1927.

Organized by Scottish cabinetmaker William Kennett Cowan (1869–1928), W. K. Cowan & Co. manufactured mahogany and walnut reproductions and adaptations of colonial and Empire furniture. These were sold alongside antiques purchased in the South and in Europe and "hangings, papers, and various stuffs for use in the decorative and upholstering arts." Catalogues indicate that Cowan produced a wide range of novelty furniture, including "Martha Washington sewing tables" and "Independence gate-leg tables."

an impressive new store, Zork was quoted as saying: "I go to a great deal of expense and trouble to get exquisite little things used in the home. . . . to have what the other stores have not, and to bring that about we bring

Cane adaptation of Chinese Chippendale chair with hand-painted frame made in the custom shop of David Zork ca. 1916.
h: 34" d: 17½" w: 22¼"
James L. Bohenstengel

David Zork Company . 1029 South Wabash, 1914–1915; 7265 South Michigan and 1018 South Wabash, 1916; 201 North Michigan, 1923–44; 205 North Michigan, 1945–50; 846 North Michigan, 1951–56; 840 North Michigan, 1957.

David Zork (1875–1957) worked as a salesman for H. E. Scholle & Company and later served as general manager for W. K. Cowan & Co. for ten years before founding his own company in 1914. Variously listed as an antique dealer and interior decorator and dealer in reproductions and antiques, Zork remained in business until his death.

The Zork Mfg. Co., located at 1509 North Halsted Street, was managed for many years by Joseph Wagner, an "art furniture builder" from Hungary. Reproductions of antique furniture and special pieces were created for sale in Zork's shop and for Midwestern interior decorators. Examples of pieces made in Zork's shop, which were identified with metal tags and occasionally were signed and dated, can be seen in Akron, Ohio, at Stan Hywett Hall (a house built in 1912–15 for F. A. Seiberling, founder of the Goodyear Tire and Rubber Company), now maintained as a museum.

furniture from every country in Europe . . . which we have to 'Americanize' for use here."[34]

Equally well known for his ability to adapt the work of eighteenth-century English craftsmen to twentieth-century taste and scale was Johan C. Tapp (1888–1939), a Dutch designer and cabinetmaker who had emigrated from Holland in 1914. After serving as foreman of Marshall Field & Company's cabinet shop, Tapp joined John De Wilde and William Wallace in organizing Tapp, De Wilde & Wallace in 1920. Although they experimented with modern designs and offered some "ensembles in the French style," the firm's reputation as one of the city's premier furniture makers

was based on pieces that exactly duplicated an existing piece—like a Chippendale, Hepplewhite, or Sheraton chest or chair—or were scaled-down, modern-day interpretations of such classic pieces. "Whatever adaptation he made was done for the purpose of making the various pieces more useful in present day homes," one writer explained, noting that Tapp "never attempted to 'embroider' on the work of the masters of the golden age of furniture design."[35]

Signed by Tapp, each piece of English or French reproduction furniture made in his Arcade Place factory was expertly constructed from the finest woods and carefully hand-finished. "Mr. Tapp developed an extremely beautiful antique finish which gave his furniture a feeling of mellowness and age," a newspaper reporter noted, adding, "it is hard to tell some of his pieces from originals of the eighteenth century which have been carefully preserved."[36] Operated after Tapp's death in 1939 by his partner Vernon Jannotta, Tapp, Inc., was sold in 1941 to new owners, who moved the business to Wisconsin.

Tapp furniture was sold through the company's showrooms in Chicago, New York, and Los Angeles. Among the popular creations were such twentieth-century innovations as coffee tables and magazine holders incorporating details copied from Louis XIV, Regency, or Chippendale furniture. Similarly, bedroom furniture included beds with head- and footboards modeled after Chippendale chair-backs. Sheraton-style drum tables with inlaid leather tops were popular for living rooms. In all of these cases, the characteristic features of each stylistic period had been gracefully interpreted so that Tapp's pieces, scaled to the smaller dimensions of modern rooms with lower ceilings, blended effectively with antique, reproduction, or modern furnishings.

"We cannot do better than to accept the standards of other times, and adapt them to our uses," wrote interior decorator Elsie de Wolfe in her

Watson & Walton. 58 East Washington, 1916–23.

Watson & Boaler, Inc. 722 North Michigan, 1924–54; 712 North Rush, 1954–69; John Hancock Building, 1870–80; 154 West Hubbard, 1981 to the present.

Now the oldest interior design firm in Chicago, Watson & Boaler has responded to numerous changes in fashion and taste since its founding by Charles Watson and Frederick Walton, both employees of Marshall Field & Company.

Richard Boaler became Watson's partner in 1924, and during the next three decades the company established an enviable reputation for merchandising and manufacturing quality furniture. In addition to importing fine European antiques and wall paneling, Watson & Boaler maintained its own drapery workroom and a cabinet shop for making, upholstering, and refinishing furniture until the mid-1950s. Hundreds of chairs, tables, and cabinets, usually original but sometimes adapted from antiques, were made in their custom shop on East Ohio. Wooden pieces were branded with the firm's name; upholstered furniture was identified with woven labels.

Albert Hagmayer, creator of the firm's modern gallery in the 1930s, designed furniture for the shop and was the first to import the now classic Hans Wegner chair from Denmark. Other well-known staff members included Madam Cecile Coverly and

influential guide, *The House in Good Taste,* in 1913. "We have not succeeded in creating a style adapted to our modern life," she continued. "It is just as well! Our life, with its haste, its nervousness, and its preoccupation does

John C. Murphy, who joined the firm in 1946 and became its president five years later. Architect Glenn E. Craft succeeded Murphy as president of the firm in 1977. The geographic scope of the firm's work ranges from Beverly Hills to the Bahamas and in size from the Inland Steel Building to a tiny elevator foyer in a cooperative apartment building.

Mahogany chest of drawers made by Johan Tapp ca. 1936.
h: 51" w: 36" d: 20¾"
Mr. and Mrs. Murray Moxley

not inspire the furniture makers."[37] On the eve of the Great War, this attitude was shared by many Chicagoans, who continued to find reassurance in colonial or European-inspired architecture and furnishings. But by 1913, one could also find in Chicago a substantial number of homemakers, architects, decorators, and furniture makers who were rebelling against this adulation of antique styles.

CHAPTER 13

THE ARTS AND CRAFTS MOVEMENT

1889-1917

At the very time that opulent furnishings filled the increasingly palatial houses of Chicago's rich, a reaction in favor of smaller, simpler homes was already gathering strength. As early as 1893 interior decorator Katherine Morse pinpointed a trend toward simplicity that suggested that Americans, particularly women, were once again ripe for reform:

> We had a few years of "art" wallpapers, "art" furniture, "art" draperies, wherein much that was good enjoyed favor impartially with much that was bad. Our houses were weeded out, however, and we learned that beauty was not dependent on expense. . . . The Japanese-Eastlake-Morris-Cook influence has made women think for themselves, and moved the more cultivated and self-reliant among them to act upon the principle that their home is as individual a possession as their wardrobe, and may as honestly express their personal taste and convictions. . . . In this matter of furnishing we must bear in mind that upon utility must all ideas of decoration and ornament finally rest, and that an over-dressed house is, were that possible, in worse taste than an over-dressed woman.[1]

The ideal interior was now to be achieved through elimination rather than accumulation. Morse summarized: "The secret of success is the absence of all second-rate ornamentation, the fewness of decorative objects, the genuine utility and simplicity of every article, and the unbroken color harmonies."[1] Advocacy of this stance was taken up by architects, decorators, and educators, who spread their message throughout Chicago via lectures, correspondence courses, exhibitions, and publications sponsored by the Central Art Association and similar "betterment" societies.[2]

The manufacturers of home furnishings quickly became aware of this new trend. "Of late quite a change has been apparent in the popular taste concerning household furniture," reported the *Furniture Worker* in the spring of 1898. "Furniture makers have been kept busy designing straight-backed chairs, massive sideboards, tables, tabourets, cabinets, such as were in use

300 years ago. This new style, or rather this revival of old style, is expensive, but none the less fashionable for that."[3] For inspiration, designers turned not only to the Middle Ages but to the colonial period, considered the "golden age" of American craftsmanship. Forms used by seventeenth- and eighteenth-century English, Dutch, and Spanish settlers in the New World inspired a host of chairs, chests, and tables characterized by simple lines and fine hand-carving.

By 1898 furniture of this type was being made in Chicago by craftsmen working alone or in cooperative workshops, by students in manual training classes, and by a few custom furniture manufacturers whose designers or owners had come under the influence of an English-inspired philosophy of betterment known as the Arts and Crafts movement. While each craftsman interpreted and adapted this imported philosophy to meet his particular needs, the fundamental principles of the movement prevailed.

The philosophy of the Arts and Crafts movement developed in reaction to what were perceived as the highly undesirable consequences of industrialization: the dehumanization of the worker and his loss of pride in the product. While the lot of the worker drew the attention of some reformers, the proliferation of shoddy mass-produced goods elicited the protest of others.

Those chiefly responsible for developing the theoretical foundations of what became the Arts and Crafts movement in England were three nineteenth-century writers and social critics: Thomas Carlyle, John Ruskin, and William Morris. While each brought a different perspective to the movement, all were concerned with the inhumanity of machine production and its demoralizing effects on the worker. As one Chicago proselyte explained: "Carlyle announced the doctrine, Ruskin elaborated the system, and Morris gave the first practical example."[4]

William Morris (1834–1896) gave dignity to the crafts by becoming both a practitioner of the applied arts and operator of a successful commercial venture. In 1861 he established the firm of Morris, Marshall, Faulkner & Co. (later Morris & Co.), endeavoring to put the principles of medieval craftsmanship into practice by infusing old forms with a modern spirit. Morris spent years perfecting wallpaper and textile patterns, which were then hand printed using hand-carved wooden blocks. He mastered the art of tapestry weaving, dyed wool with his own hands, and learned to weave and tuft rugs in his workshops at Merton Abbey. Among the most popular products of Morris & Co. was what became known as the Morris chair. When he founded the Kelmscott Press in 1890, he designed his own typefaces and hand printed his books on handmade paper.

Next to William Morris, the English practitioner who would have the greatest influence on the movement as it came to be translated in Chicago was Charles R. Ashbee (1863–1942), an architect, industrial designer, and social reformer. In 1888, inspired by Morris's combination of social theory and crafts, Ashbee had launched the Guild and School of Handicraft at Toynbee Hall, in London, the original settlement house established four years earlier in one of that city's worst slums. Like his mentor, Ashbee embraced handicraft as a way of restoring dignity to the worker. Con-

THE ENGLISH ARTS AND CRAFTS PHILOSOPHY

vinced that craft and industry could exist together, he contended that some form of guild system or "model workshop" could be established to meet contemporary industrial needs.

Putting this theory into effect in 1902, Ashbee moved the Guild and School of Handicraft to the rural Cotswold community of Chipping Campden. This offered an idyllic, healthy setting for its workers, but the cost of transporting the Guild's products to market and competition from imitation "handmade" goods forced the liquidation of the venture in 1908. Ashbee visited Chicago in 1900 and 1908; by then, however, his work was already familiar to Chicagoans who had called on him in England or had seen his work displayed at The Art Institute of Chicago or at Hull-House as early as 1897.[5]

In 1888, the same year that Ashbee started his guild, the newly organized Arts and Crafts Exhibition Society in Britain held its first exhibition in London, coining the phrase "Arts and Crafts." Both the Exhibition Society, which began to exhibit abroad, and the magazine *The Studio*, which began publication in 1893, contributed to the growing prestige of British design and helped to spread it to other countries. By October 1896, when William Morris died, organizations dedicated to the production and promotion of arts and crafts were active in Scotland, Belgium, Germany, Austria, and Scandinavia. One year later an Arts and Crafts Society was founded in Chicago. The second such group in America, it followed the founding of a Boston society by only a few months.

The principles of the British Arts and Crafts movement found a sympathetic audience in Chicago among those already involved in the campaign for cultural and social reform in the city. By this time the products of William Morris, Walter Crane, Charles Ashbee, and other exponents of the movement had made their way to Chicago, and publications like *The Studio, International Studio, Ladies' Home Journal,* and Chicago's own *House Beautiful* kept American readers abreast of the latest creations and theories of British and Continental designers. But the most direct link between the British movement and Chicago were two American women, Jane Addams and Ellen Gates Starr.

THE CHICAGO ARTS AND CRAFTS SOCIETY

Hull-House as it looked ca. 1910.

In 1888 Jane Addams and her college friend Ellen Gates Starr had returned from a visit to England full of enthusiasm for the accomplishments of the Arts and Crafts crusaders there. Following Ashbee's lead, Addams and Starr opened a settlement modeled after Toynbee Hall in the old Hull mansion on South Halsted Street in a crowded immigrant neighborhood on Chicago's Near West Side. Though not a crafts practitioner herself, Jane Addams became one of the most influential advocates of the American Arts and Crafts movement and set out to adapt its tenets to the special needs of the immigrant population. Like many Chicago reformers, Addams regarded hand craftsmanship as a regenerative force rather than as a practical alternative to an increasingly mechanized society. Convinced of the uplifting influence of artistic surroundings, Ellen Gates Starr sought to bring beauty into the lives of her neighbors by establishing an art gallery, organizing exhibitions, forming reading groups, and teaching art classes. Eventually Starr became a bookbinder.

From the first, local craftsmen were encouraged to show their work in conjunction with annual art exhibitions held at Hull-House. By the late 1890s, carpentry and metalworking classes were being taught in a small workshop under the supervision of two residents: George M. R. Twose, a young English architect who served as secretary of the settlement, and Frank Hazenplug, staff artist for publisher Stone & Kimball and a graduate of Chicago's Art Institute. Two evenings a week Twose and Hazenplug, architect Augustus Higginson and his wife, Frances, and Homer and Isadore Taylor taught neighborhood boys and girls the use of tools and the rudiments of carving, cabinetmaking, and metalworking. "Many of the scholars are employed during the day in uncongenial occupations, and they all are more than enthusiastic over their woodwork," reported the *Chicago Inter-Ocean* in 1898.[6] By 1902 these classes had developed into the Hull-House Shop, where a team of instructors and students produced furniture, textiles, and metalwork for sale to the public.[7]

Miss Addams and Miss Starr's dual commitment to art and social causes and the activities held at Hull-House drew many supporters to the settlement. A center for the free exchange of ideas as well as a charitable organization, Hull-House became a social and philosophic force of considerable power in the Chicago community, bringing together artists, educators, politicians, and the city's social elite for discussions of topics as diverse as vegetable gardening and Ruskin's socialism. In time, Hull-House became headquarters for a number of small groups and societies, including the Chicago Arts and Crafts Society, which was organized there on October 22, 1897.

Prompted by Jane Addams, the Chicago Arts and Crafts Society brought together a small band of men and women who made "beautiful things with their own hands" or designed things to be made by others.[8] The enthusiastic founders included painter Ralph Clarkson, metalsmiths Madeline Yale Wynne and Florence Koehler, bookbinder Ella R. Waite, professors Charles Zueblin and Oscar Lovell Triggs, and designers Frank Hazenplug, Ida J. Burgess, Edith Sheridan, Louise Anderson, and Frances Higginson. Architects included Allen and Irving Pond, Augustus Higginson, George Twose, and Frank Lloyd Wright.

Adopting a constitution, members of the Society pledged "to cultivate in its members, and through them in others, a just sense of beauty," especially in the design and production of utilitarian articles. They intended to "consider the present state of the factories and the workmen therein, and to devise lines of development which shall retain the machine in so far as it relieves the workman from drudgery and tends to perfect the product." They insisted, however, "that the machine no longer be allowed to dominate the workman and reduce his production to a mechanical distortion." In addition, members promised to encourage handicraft by promoting manual training and art education, by holding exhibitions, and by founding workshops.[9]

The Society's announcement that it would hold its first exhibition in March 1898 in conjunction with the Chicago Architectural Club drew a host of new converts. By the time the show opened, the Society had 127 members. It was clear that men and women committed to the principles of the Arts and Crafts movement had been at work throughout the city for some

time. As one reporter noted: "No sooner did it become noised about that such an exhibition was to be held, than new members of the society and interesting exhibits were found on all sides. It seemed as if in many directions people had been working in their own way and almost in secret, until the society found them out and brought them together. . . . It would be indeed flattering to the pride of Chicagoans should the present small beginning be the forerunner of a 'Chicago school.' "[10]

Despite a small beginning, the Society's first exhibition was impressive. In the Art Institute galleries, 540 handcrafted objects—matte glazed pottery, hand-wrought copper, embroidered textiles, silver jewelry, hand-painted porcelains, and leatherbound books—complemented drawings and photographs displayed by members of the Chicago Architectural Club.

"The furniture, owing to its massiveness, probably attracted the most attention on first entering the rooms," wrote the reviewer for *Arts for America*. Mentioning the simple oak settles, tables, and mirror frame exhibited by Frances and Augustus Higginson, the writer added approvingly, "the carving is deep and vigorous, without the over-finish which is frequently a fault with woodcarvers."[11] "Mr. Higginson is the carpenter," the *Furniture Worker* reported, "the carving is largely the work of Mrs. Higginson, who is also the designer, evolving most of the interesting, Celtic-like patterns out of her head."[12]

Several chairs and a hanging cupboard, made after an old Norwegian model and decorated with burnt and painted designs, revealed the skill of Fredericka Schmedling. A quaint, substantial cedar chest with exterior of dark stained oak, carved by Vibe K. Spicer following his wife Anna's design, was ornamented with "a bold graceful pattern" and "huge iron hinges" that combined to impart "a charming air of comfort and mystery."[13] Louise Anderson and Jeannette Kittredge showed settles, tables, chairs, screens, and boxes. Cabinetmaker George Dole, who inlaid his furniture with light woods or metal, displayed a hall clock, chests, and tables. Ida J. Burgess exhibited a screen ornamented with "fire etching," or pyrography (in which designs were burned onto the wood surface with a red-hot stylus), while the Hull-House Shop sent an oak chair and a bookcase designed by Twose and executed by students. A decorative folding screen painted with a scene from "Alice in Wonderland" designed and executed by Frank Hazenplug for *House Beautiful* publisher Herbert S. Stone drew praise as "one of the most interesting exhibits in the room."[14]

"ARTS AND CRAFTS" FURNITURE MAKERS

The Chicago Arts and Crafts Society's next four annual exhibitions featured a similar assortment of furniture: sturdy pieces made for sale by students in the Hull-House shops or local craft guilds; carefully executed furniture made for their own homes by Augustus Higginson and George Dole; and simple, medieval-looking pieces designed or executed by professional crafts workers like Louise Anderson, Ida Burgess, Jeannette Kittredge, or Julia M. Bracken. While limited in number, the selection accurately represented the types of furniture makers who first became active in the Arts and Crafts movement: architect/designers, manual arts students and instructors, hobbyists, and women. While each had espoused the movement for different reasons and while their products varied considerably, all shared the desire to change the way furniture looked by participating in the process of making it.

Like many of his English counterparts, architect and Hull-House resident George Twose concentrated on the practical aspects of good design and the actual making of furniture. Augustus Higginson, also an architect, lived the Arts and Crafts philosophy by designing his own house in Winnetka and then making all of his own furniture.[15] However, most practicing Chicago architects, like Frank Lloyd Wright and his contemporaries, tended to look upon furniture as an integral part of architecture and considered their work as decorative art rather than handicraft. Accordingly, they showed their furniture and decorative designs in the annual exhibitions at the Art Institute sponsored by the Chicago Architectural Club rather than in the exhibits of the Arts and Crafts Society.

Given the Arts and Crafts movement's emphasis on "honest craftsmanship," it was not surprising that many found the philosophy appealing. Public school teachers, manual training instructors, and others concerned with progressive education soon joined the Arts and Crafts crusade. During the last two decades of the century, Chicago industrialists, realizing the benefits to be gained from better-trained and self-reliant workers, supported such schools as the Chicago Manual Training School (later part of the University of Chicago) and both the Armour Institute of Technology and the Lewis Institute (which merged to become the Illinois Institute of Technology). Although these schools were concerned chiefly with giving training in engineering, mechanics, and industrial design, they also offered courses in drawing and woodworking in the belief that "a boy's hands ought to be trained no less than his brains."[16]

During the 1890s the influential Central Art Association campaigned vigorously on behalf of the teaching of "art industries" in the public schools. The Association stressed the value of the crafts both as a means of self-expression and as a source of livelihood. But its members did not reject the realities of industrialization. "The era of machinery is with us, and there is no use in deploring the fact," the Association's bulletin, *Arts for America*, declared in 1897. "It is much wiser for us to put modern tools into the hands of those made competent through perfect training than to wish for a return of old-time methods."[17] By then, many high schools were adding courses in woodworking, sewing, metalworking, and other practical skills to balance purely academic programs. Progressive educators like John Cotton Dana and Felix Adler in the East and Francis Parker and John Dewey in Chicago advocated the teaching of handicrafts for their cultural and social significance as well as for sheer enjoyment. By 1910 three out of every four Chicago high schools were equipped for manual training and superintendent Ella Flagg Young was urging that industrial and household arts classes be extended to include children below the seventh grade.[18]

Such courses and numerous publications encouraged woodworking as a hobby as well as an occupation. After 1901, for example, furniture maker Gustav Stickley's magazine *The Craftsman* supplied simple designs suitable for use in home workshops and manual training classes. Closer to home, faculty members at Bradley Polytechnic Institute in Peoria published instruction books through the Manual Arts Press. Beginning around 1909, the Popular Mechanics Press in Chicago developed a whole series of small handbooks on how to make arts and crafts furnishings. The three-volume *Mission Furniture: How to Make It* by H. H. Windsor provided detailed drawings and step-by-step instructions for constructing furniture with simple tools and inexpensive equipment.[19]

Women were drawn to the crafts for practical and aesthetic reasons. "A girl who does not marry, or desires to earn her living needs some stated occupation," wrote Katherine Louise Smith in 1899 in an article on "Women in the Art Crafts" in *Brush and Pencil*.[20] She explained that not only was art a profession "open to women," it was a calling in which women could excel. Not all women could become portrait painters or sculptors, but they could apply their considerable artistic skills to "some branch of manufacture" such as carving, needlework, interior design, or the making of jewelry, pottery, or stained glass. Since the home was women's "proper sphere," it was natural for them to seek advancement through careers associated with the creation of home furnishings—now made profitable as well as fashionable under the guise of arts and crafts.

Oak slant-front desk made by Henry Larson in manual arts class at Highland Park College in 1915.
h: 43¾" w: 24⅜" d: 18¼"
Robert and Margaret Chainski

This oak patent rocker, whose frame was chip-carved by Cara Swenson, was displayed at the World's Columbian Exposition in 1893.
h: 38" d: 27" w: 23½"
Mr. and Mrs. J. Anzalone

After 1886, when Louis F. Millet began to teach "decorative designing" at the Art Institute, women outnumbered men in his classes.[21] While many women applied their skills along traditional lines based on needlecraft or painting, large numbers also ventured into new areas such as metalworking, pottery making, or stained-glass making. Some learned to carve wood or to create unusual designs using pyrography; a few hardy souls became furniture makers. In 1903, praising Millet's success in preparing students for employment, Art Institute director W.M.R. French pointed out: "the graduates are found in mercantile and manufacturing establishments all over Chicago and in the West, making designs for stained glass, wallpaper, rugs, jewelry, carpets, metal work and decorative work of all kinds."[22]

When graduates of Millet's decorative design classes formed an alumni association in 1902, they attempted to gain more recognition for local and regional craftsworkers by organizing a major arts and crafts exhibition at the Art Institute. The showing drew such an impressive turnout that the Institute agreed to host an Art-Craft exhibition each year. Later referred to as exhibitions of Applied Arts, these yearly displays incorporated the work of Chicago Arts and Crafts Society members and brought national recognition to many local craftsmen.

Woodcarving as an occupation was promoted as early as the 1870s, when women were being encouraged to create all types of household art under the aegis of the Chicago Society of Decorative Art. Founded in 1877, the Society trained needy women to support themselves by providing free classes in needlework, painting, and woodcarving and by maintaining a salesroom where the women's work could be sold.[23] Between 1882 and 1884, woodcarving classes were conducted by furniture maker Isaac E. Scott (see page 166), who volunteered his services.

In most cases, female woodcarvers confined their work to small cabinets, chests, or picture frames, applying surface decoration to wooden forms secured from professional cabinetmakers. A few were more ambitious. As early as 1879, for example, *American Cabinet Maker* reported that Mrs. Christian Olenson, who had learned cabinetmaking and carving from her father, had designed and produced nearly all of the furniture in her house. According to the correspondent, the furniture was "all handsomely carved and deftly put together . . . in a style that would be envied by a majority of people in much better circumstances in life." Mrs. Olenson was described as being "36 years of age, tall and straight, fair, pleasant and determined."[24]

Less strenuous and far more popular among women were such methods as "chip-carving" (in which various-sized notches and hollows were cut away with a hook-bladed knife) and pyrography. In 1893, for example, pyrography was combined with more ambitious carving to decorate bookshelves, cabinets, tables, and other furniture exhibited by the female students of the Chicago Atheneum Wood Carving School in the Woman's Building at the World's Columbian Exposition.[25] By 1901 the technique was widely used to create striking effects on furniture and leather.

Probably the best known female furniture maker in Chicago at the turn of the century was Louise C. Anderson, a craftsworker for several years before the founding of the Chicago Arts and Crafts Society. Noted for her fine appreciation of color and form, Anderson worked equally well in wood or metal, relying for effect on "harmonious combinations of these two materials rather than on decoration."[26] "She does no carving and has almost given up pyrography," noted the *Furniture Worker* in 1898, "but, by the combination of leather or metal, or both, with wood she obtained some very effective results."[27]

That year Miss Anderson showed a stark, rectangular armchair made from black oak boards with a leather seat at the Arts and Crafts Society's exhibition. For the display in 1900, she fashioned a corner desk of weathered oak that consisted of a triangular cabinet over a triangular work surface. "She attributes her inspiration to the furniture of the old Spanish missions," a visitor from *House Beautiful* wrote regarding the desk, "but it is nevertheless a very original piece of work." The writer continued: "In her artistic house on Rush Street it stands firmly in the corner, temporarily holding some of her copper bowls. Near it is a big oak table, frank in every line, and by its side a sturdy broad-backed oak chair. . . . A fruit dish of carved black walnut, low in design, with a border of leaves and great copper handles, is among her new ventures . . . she has a nursery cupboard with low shelves for toys, with gay Walter Crane pictures fastened back of the small glass doors, and a rabbit screen for small people that is a positive delight."[28]

Woodworker Madeline Yale Wynne was also a master of many media. The daughter of a miniature painter who invented the Yale lock, Madeline Wynne was a middle-aged widow when she moved to Chicago in 1893 to manage the household of her brother, Julian Yale. A talented metalsmith, she was best known for the "revelations of color" she achieved by enameling silver and copper.[29] Active in literary and artistic circles in both Chicago

Cover of dower chest made by Madeline Yale Wynne. Heavy wrought-iron hinges divide the design and frame the carved figure of the Virgin above a heavy cross of iron.
Glenn C. Hjort

and Boston, Mrs. Wynne was a regular contributor to *House Beautiful* and even wrote a popular short story, "The Little Room," whose title was later adopted as a name by a number of Chicago writers, artists, and architects who organized an informal group in the 1890s.

In her studio in the Tree Studio Building, Mrs. Wynne employed her skills in metalworking, carving, and painting to produce a series of much-publicized bridal chests early in the century. Inspired by the antique bridal chests she had seen at the historical society in Deerfield, Massachusetts, where she lived six months of the year, Mrs. Wynne's chests were strong rectangular boxes made of well-seasoned oak. "The wood is carved on the front and ends in a bold and simple pattern, the chief decoration being reserved for the top," wrote Chicago poet Harriet Monroe in *House Beautiful*, describing a chest made for Bertha Bullock. Inside the lid Wynne had painted a "beautiful decoration in greens and blues and whites—a conventionalized spray of lilies against broad mountain passes, toning from green through distant blues to the lighter blue of the sky."[30] (See color plate.)

Other chests made by Wynne displayed hand-wrought copper panels inset with iridescent abalone shell. Miss Anderson and Mrs. Wynne sold their work through their own studios; other craftsworkers relied upon exhibitions or salesrooms sponsored by organizations such as the Chicago Arts and Crafts Society or one of the many crafts shops and guilds that had opened in and around the city.

While many craftsmen worked alone in home workshops or rented studios, a number of the city's Arts and Crafts furniture makers chose to pool talents and resources by forming firms, guilds, or cooperatives modeled after those founded earlier by William Morris or Charles Ashbee. One of the first, The Krayle Company, was organized in 1899 by several of Chica-

GUILDS AND COOPERATIVES

Krayle Company products, described as "Hall-seat by Julia Bracken, Cupboard by Mrs. Krycher, Chair by Miss Burgess," were shown in House Beautiful, *December 1900.*
The Newberry Library

go's most talented young artworkers. Renting a workshop in the Tree Studio Building, the group produced decorative sculpture, stained glass, furniture, leatherwork, and other items useful in beautifying a home. Headed by Ida J. Burgess, the original members included sculptor Julia M. Bracken, metalworker Christia M. Reade, graphics designer Elizabeth Krysher, portrait painter Carl Lindin, and Harvey White. A talented painter whose murals had decorated the Illinois Building at the 1893 World's Fair, Ida Burgess specialized in integrating mural painting and interior design.[31]

When the group first organized, the English-looking furniture designed by Ida Burgess and Julia Bracken elicited much attention. In 1899, for example, a journalist who had visited the group reported that Miss Bracken was just finishing a large settee "decorated with strange Egyptian designs in burned and stained wood."[32] The following year, Burgess used a similar technique to decorate some redwood chairs, described by a *House Beautiful* writer as "simple in line and with a slight decoration in fire-etching."[33] Reflecting the group's multiple talents, desks executed by the versatile Burgess often featured carvings by Julia Bracken and copper hinges or handles hand-wrought by Christia Reade. By 1902 The Krayle Company, having opened a salesroom in the Marshall Field Annex, was known for its fine selection of tooled leathers; hand-bound books and custom bookplates; hand-beaten silver, copper, and brass jewelry; bowls; and lighting fixtures.[34]

Possibly encouraged by the success of The Krayle Company, two Art Institute graduates, D'Arcy Gaw and Mary Mower, joined architect Lawrence Buck to organize The Crafters in the fall of 1901. Opening a studio in Steinway Hall, the three prepared designs for wall decorations, furniture, electric and gas fixtures, and other household items, living up to their motto: "Houses made beautiful in an inexpensive way."[35] According to another Art Institute alumna, Bessie Bennet, The Crafters, using inexpensive and simple materials, in 1902 supplied "the fittings for an entire room, wall decoration, furniture and floor coverings in good taste, without indulging in a high priced article of any kind."[36] Although D'Arcy Gaw left Chicago two years later, Lawrence Buck and Mary Mower continued work as The Crafters through 1906.

Kitchen of the Craftsman's Guild on Michigan Avenue showing Arts and Crafts furniture and foodstuffs made by the cooperative.
Perry Duis

Several of the new crafts ventures were located in suburban settings, where fresh air, sunshine, and the absence of urban congestion proved particularly invigorating to the idealistic men and women who rejected factory production and city living in favor of handicraft and "the simple life." On the North Shore, for instance, workmen at The Skokie Shop were creating "very picturesque and substantial furniture in a nice airy barn on the banks of the stream from which it derives its name." By March 1902, they were turning out weathered oak tables, chairs, desks, and music cabinets in addition to "original books with especially designed type, handmade paper and odd covers" for sale in their Chicago salesroom.[37]

Claiming almost as many members as the Chicago Arts and Crafts Society was an association called The Skylight Club, with headquarters in the large loft of an old barn in Madison Park, in the South Side's fashionable Kenwood community. A fellow craftsworker described the group in 1902: "Several architects, brimming with new ideas for construction and interior decoration, form a solid background for their fellow crafts workers, who create novelties for wall decoration, illustration of books, art nouveau, jewelry and lamps, leather hangings, not to mention the miniature, etching, basket weaving and modeling interests."[38]

Another South Side cooperative, the South Park Workshop Association, maintained a workshop at 5835 Kimbark Avenue. Members paid an annual five-dollar membership fee to use the shop and its woodworking and bookbinding equipment.[39] In nearby Hyde Park, The University Guild operated handicraft shops at 5001 Lake Park Avenue from 1901 until 1903, when the operation was reorganized in Longwood, Illinois.

North of the city, in the suburb of Evanston, Edwin F. Brown set up the Windiknowe Shop in 1900 in the boathouse of his wooded lakeside estate and outfitted it with lathes, furnaces, and other equipment used for woodwork, ceramics, and printing.[40] Farther north, in Highland Park, the Craftsman's Guild made "straight line animal toys" and children's furniture, which it sold through its salesroom and restaurant on Michigan Avenue in downtown Chicago.[41]

At Longwood and Lockport, Illinois, the combination of handicraft and agriculture recalled the medieval concept of a community of craftsworkers in an unspoiled countryside. In the spring of 1902 George L. Schreiber, formerly with the University Guild, organized the Longwood Art Industrial and Stock Company in Longwood, a community south of Chicago. Turning an old church into a workshop, Schreiber equipped it for making furniture, pottery, textiles, and metalwork. "Flax was also grown in the gardens, surrounding the workshops," *House Beautiful* reported in 1906, "and classes were held, both for adults and young people who came from long distances, and boarded in the vicinity during the summer months."[42]

In rural Lockport, southwest of the city (near Joliet), Edward F. Worst, supervisor of manual training for Chicago's elementary schools, not only made simple oak furniture for his bungalow but helped needy Swedish women to become self-supporting by organizing them into a village cooperative that built its own looms and wove household linens using locally grown flax. These products, along with hand-dipped bayberry candles, were marketed through Chicago handicraft shops through the 1920s.

Another manual arts instructor, Louis S. Easton, turned his attention to making furniture. Born in Half Day, a small farming community north of Chicago, Easton had graduated in 1890 from the Bloomington (Illinois)

Normal School. There he had also met his wife Jane, sister of Elbert Hubbard.[43] A former Chicago soap salesman who styled himself the American equivalent of William Morris, Elbert Hubbard had become a convert to the

Oak drop-leaf table with cane side supports made by manual arts instructor Edward F. Worst ca. 1910.
h: 23¾" w: 23⅜" d: 8¾"
Mr. and Mrs. William Worst

Oak table with folding legs made by Edward F. Worst for his home in Lockport ca. 1910.
h: 27¼" d: 27"
Mr. and Mrs. William Worst

Arts and Crafts cause after meeting Morris at the Kelmscott Press in 1894. The following year Hubbard set up the Roycroft Press in East Aurora, New York, and began publishing a little magazine, *The Philistine*, and a series entitled *Little Journeys* to the homes of famous people, including Chicago meat packer Philip D. Armour. In the artistic community that grew up around the charismatic Hubbard, straight-lined, unadorned furniture was made as early as 1899, when visitors began to order duplicates of pieces being made for use in the Roycroft Inn.

Easton's sturdy furnishings reflected the same principles that inspired his brother-in-law. During the early 1890s Easton taught manual training at Lemont (Illinois) High School, becoming principal in 1893. With the help of "a few wealthy men he organized classes of poor boys and taught them, with success, to make useful and beautiful things with their hands."[44] Later, moving to Austin, a community on the city's West Side bordering Oak Park, Easton spent his evenings designing and making oak furniture for use in his own home.

Shown in the 1902 Arts and Crafts Exhibition at The Art Institute of Chicago, Easton's furniture—settles, chairs, a desk, and a buffet—was described by a *House Beautiful* writer as "fine, strong pieces stamped with the unique device, 'Easton-Austin.' "[45] *The Sketch Book*, a student publication, also found Easton's work appealing. "For practical purposes and lasting qualities the Easton furniture is most commendable. A writing desk for a lady is very sturdy and simple with two shelves on one side where one's necessary books may be stowed without interfering with the usual desk room. Some very good settees for hall and bedroom uses, and chairs of every type make up an interesting collection."[46]

Just as Easton's work began to attract public attention his health started to fail. Seeking a milder climate, he and his wife moved to Pasadena, California, during the winter of 1902–3. After a year of rest, Easton built a home for his family and furnished it with angular handmade furniture. When he had finished, he hung out a shingle offering "Bungalows and Furniture" and launched a new career designing and building some twenty-five houses in the Pasadena area. They frequently included Easton-made bookcases, settles, desks, and buffets built into the walls.[47]

Also exhibiting new-style furniture for the first time in 1902 were G.W.E. Field and R. G. Work, who called their partnership The Craftery and whose furniture designs bore a resemblance to those of Scottish architect Charles Rennie Mackintosh, who worked in Glasgow. "The forms of the pieces exhibited by the craftery [sic] are most original and verge on the fantastic," claimed *The Sketch Book*, calling particular attention to a tall case clock "in weathered oak with inlays of colored glass" and "a work table of graceful form with needations [sic] in green and blue." Also mentioned were some green-toned oak pieces designed by Frederick O. Seymour, son of publisher Ralph Fletcher Seymour, which included a large desk, a library table, a clock, and a "Skokie chair" made by students in The Skokie Shop and the Quisisana workshop in La Porte, Indiana.[48]

Both the Skokie and the Quisisana shops had been fostered by the Industrial Art League, an organization founded in 1899 by Oscar Lovell Triggs, professor of literature at the University of Chicago. Biographer of America's poet of democracy, Walt Whitman, Triggs worked tirelessly on behalf of "the democratization of art." The League, which claimed 400 members in 1903, sponsored manual training classes and supported such model workshops as the Longwood Art Industrial and Stock Company, the Quisisana Shop, The Skokie Shop, and the South Park Workshop. Organized along the lines of medieval craft guilds, each group consisted of members "banded together to make money incidentally, but with the firm principle deeply rooted to make it by placing the best possible product on the market."[49] Although metalwork and pottery were also made, the specialty of the shops was "furniture, colonial and modern."[50]

Another influential offspring of the Industrial Art League, the Bohemia Guild, founded in 1902, in turn organized an experimental School of Industrial Art and Handicraft under the direction of sculptor Julia Bracken, bookbinder Gertrude Stiles, and printer Fred W. Goudy. Housed in the artists' studios in the Academy of Fine Arts on Wabash Avenue, the school operated workshops and a salesroom where apprentices learned bookbinding, woodcarving, pottery making, and other crafts and sold their productions to the public. Among the first articles produced by the Guild were plaques and prints commemorating the "great industrial prophets" Carlyle, Ruskin, and Morris. Guild members also designed and printed a handsome book, *Chapters in the History of the Arts and Crafts Movement*, written by Oscar L. Triggs.[51]

Like other projects initiated by Triggs, the Bohemia Guild reflected his belief that the lot of the worker could be improved only by changing the nature of work and restructuring the social system. As he wrote, "The eight-hour day is no solution of the labor problem. . . . The real solution is in so changing the character of work that it becomes a pleasure."[52] Although highly productive, the Bohemia Guild discontinued its work in 1904 when the Industrial Art League disbanded. By then, its founders claimed, their original goals had been attained and their cause was being carried forward by a new Art-Craft Institute supported by local manufacturers, businessmen, and educators, as well as by the widespread adoption of manual training in the public schools and by the growing number of independently owned crafts shops. Controversy concerning the League's founder, Oscar L. Triggs, also contributed to the demise of the organization.

Triggs, who had been asked to leave the University of Chicago early in 1904 in the course of an academic freedom dispute provoked by his political views, had gone on to edit *To-Morrow*, a journal of socialist protest, and to found the People's Industrial College, a socialist university whose faculty and students would live according to the theories of William Morris.[53] Organized with the help of banker Parker H. Sercombe and labor lawyer Clarence S. Darrow, the People's Industrial College was to be "a practical school and home for *Industrious People* of all ages." Its curriculum would consist of "common sense" courses in the arts and sciences and practical experience gained through activities such as cabinetmaking, agriculture, and beekeeping. Teachers and pupils were to do "at least four hours of useful work with their hands each day" and design, construct, and furnish the shops and cottages to be built on the 300 acres of land in Saugatuck, Michigan, donated to the university. To raise money for the undertaking, supporters made furniture, bound books, and beat metal in their workshop at East Twentieth Street.[54] No buildings were ever constructed, however, and the project as envisioned seems to have been abandoned, since Triggs moved to California in 1907.

Despite all this activity, no Chicago furniture makers showed their work in the Art Institute's Arts and Crafts Exhibition in 1903. Instead, Gustav Stickley, a craftsman from upstate New York, had the stage all to himself. Remarked a surprised *House Beautiful* writer: "With the exception of Gustav Stickley, who sends nearly a roomful of furniture bearing the usual hallmarks—which are sterling, by the way—there is not a table, chest, or chair. We miss the Quisisana, the Stokey [sic], and the Easton pieces. Have our local craftsmen changed their occupations, or have they, like Mr. Easton, moved to California, and gone to building bungalows?"[55]

The writer had guessed correctly. From then until the applied arts exhibitions ceased in 1921, few pieces of furniture appeared among the handicrafts. As early as 1903 some of the Arts and Crafts furniture makers had begun to change occupations. By then the best-known women furniture makers—Louise Anderson, Christia Reade, Julia Bracken, and Madeline Yale Wynne—had abandoned wood for metal, stained glass, or clay, and were producing more profitable jewelry and household accessories. While there was a steady and growing market for handmade goods, demand tended to be for smaller, less costly items that had a distinctly handcrafted look.

Both Artistic and Useful

℄ We are prepared to receive your orders for bookbinding, leather work and artistic products from our wood and metal working shops.

℄ We offer especial inducements in the way of actual co-operation to those who can "do things" with their hands.

Address

People's Industrial College

76 E. 20th Street, CHICAGO, ILL.

Advertisement for furniture made by the People's Industrial College in 1905. From To-Morrow, March 1905.

The furniture-making guilds, cooperatives, and associations likewise reached a peak of activity and began to fade away. Even though the furniture they had made tended to be high priced, it sold well. But the cost of raw materials and the expense of transporting the bulky goods into the city often ate up the craftsworkers' meager profits. A skilled craftsman could earn more money making furniture in one of Chicago's factories, which by this time had begun to manufacture similar-looking pieces.

At the same time, not all craftsmen found joy in their work. Free-thinking individualists of the type attracted to such idealistic groups often found it difficult to surrender their independence and abide by majority rule. Some lacked skill and persistence; others grew bored or were tired out by the hard physical work. When asked about the status of the arts and crafts in 1902 Art Institute director W.M.R. French replied, "Within a part of our community it [arts and crafts] is at present a fad, and its votaries are often enthusiasts who find much difficulty in working together."[56]

Hobbyists and students continued to make simple Arts and Crafts style oak furniture for their own use, one piece at a time, until the early 1920s. But, soon after the turn of the century, production of Arts and Crafts furniture in Chicago began to be dominated by two types of professional furniture makers with two very different markets in mind. On the one hand, a small number of craftsworkers and custom shops created high-style, often unique, pieces for a select clientele. On the other hand, a large number of manufacturers turned out great quantities of medium- and low-priced "straight-lined" furniture expressly for the retail and mail-order businesses.

MISSION FURNITURE: "CASTING OFF OF THE SHACKLES OF THE PAST"

1 8 9 5 - 1 9 1 7

In 1898, reporting on a recent meeting of the young Chicago Arts and Crafts Society, *House Beautiful* noted that "a spirited discussion took place as to whether the public taste or the manufacturer's obduracy was most to blame for the shocking commercial furniture in all the large stores, and the fact that it is almost impossible to purchase, for example, a really good chair for a small sum of money." A local furniture manufacturer present at the

British author Arnold Bennett (left) and Chicago writer Hamlin Garland seated on mission furniture in the Cliff Dwellers Club, November 1911. Cliff Dwellers Club of Chicago

meeting pleaded his case, pointing out that customers often passed up good models, like rush-bottom chairs with plain colonial backs, in favor of "oak chairs upholstered in pink worsted and decorated with stamped carving."[1] Society members responded by resolving to educate consumers as to the merits of well-designed and well-made furniture.

Simple, sturdy furniture, they emphasized, need not be expensive. To prove this, Society members completely furnished a model tenement apartment with "good cheap articles" for a 1900 Art Institute exhibition sponsored by the Improved Housing Association. "Foolish, bad color and objects with meaningless line have been eliminated," a *House Beautiful* writer explained, describing the inexpensive factory-made furniture and utensils that outfitted the two rooms constructed by the Chicago Architectural Club.[2] Although such displays did little to improve the "usual crude taste of the tenant," they encouraged middle-class homemakers to simplify their furnishings and to appreciate better goods. They also helped convince furniture manufacturers that there was a market for plain, clean-lined furniture.

Middle-class Americans were also the targets of advertising campaigns conducted by Gustav Stickley, a New York furniture maker who became the chief spokesman for the American movement, and the Tobey Furniture

Advertisement for Tobey's New Furniture from House Beautiful, *November 1900.*
The Newberry Library

Company, which was to become the city's leading retailer of Arts and Crafts style furniture. In 1900 the paths of the two crossed when the Tobey Company introduced Stickley's New Furniture to the public.

The Tobey Furniture Company was one of the first American retailers to aggressively market factory-made Arts and Crafts furniture using modern advertising techniques and brand-name identification.[3] As early as 1898 advertisements placed in newspapers and homemaker magazines had stressed the chaste lines, fine woods, and careful workmanship that characterized Tobey Hand-Made Furniture, and pointed out that "no veneers, no machine carving or stamped ornaments are used in its construction."[4] By the spring of 1900 the company offered a line of squarish "Mission"

THE NEW FURNITURE

Chas. Tobey. 294 State, 1856–57.
Chas. Tobey & Bro. 72 State, 1858–64;
87–89 State, 1865–69.
Thayer & Tobey Furniture Company.
87–91 State, 1870–71; 195–99 State,
1871–74.
The Tobey Furniture Company. 195
State, 1875–87; 96 Wabash, 1888; 100
Wabash, 1889–1911; 33 North Wabash,
1911–26; 200 North Michigan, 1926–39;
121 South Wabash, 1939–54.
Tobey & Christiansen Cabinet Company. 36 (2041 after 1909) Churchill,
1888–1930.
For nearly a century the Tobey Furniture Company was one of Chicago's
premier furniture retailers and manufacturers. A list of the company's customers would read like a roll call of

furniture designed by George F. Clingman, promoting it as "an unconventional style for unconventional people, admirably suited to rest and sunshine."[5] A few months later, in October 1900, Tobey introduced the New Furniture, a large collection of oak pieces whose original designs, clean lines, sturdy construction, and moderate prices were intended to appeal to practical, modern-thinking consumers in the new century. Like the Art Nouveau designs introduced by Tobey the following year (see page 194), the New Furniture represented an attempt by furniture designers to develop original designs that were not imitations of traditional, historical models.

Headlined "Furniture As An Educator," and heavily laced with Arts and Crafts rhetoric, Tobey's advertisements for the New Furniture stressed the originality of its designs and the absence of curves and ornament. They explained:

> The New Furniture belongs to a school of design almost unknown in this country, but it is understood and in great esteem in Europe at this time. Much of the furniture shown at the Arts and Crafts Exhibition in England and shown at the Glasgow School of Design, finds its motive from the same source, and the late William Morris worked largely along these lines. It is a departure from all established styles, a casting off of the shackles of the past—the only influence being the present.
>
> It is *angular*, *plain*, and *severe*. Such ornament as it bears is incut carving after what is known as the Nancy method . . . something from nature, a flower or a leaf, as its motive, and all the carving is in bold line, but unlike the impressionist style of painting.
>
> It is but a beginning—the first slight harvest in this new field of furniture. Now that it has met with success, nothing will hinder its development. New pieces—pieces hitherto impossible to find—are being made, and it will be our constant endeavor to produce a variety of furniture that will be thoroughly practical, not too good for daily use, moderate in price, in demand by people of culture and taste, and that will help to make life better and truer by its perfect sincerity.[6]

The New Furniture consisted of some seventy-five tables, chairs, stools, settees, tabourettes, and desks stained "Tyrolean green," "gun metal gray," or gray-brown "Weathered Oak." All had a dull wax finish. Several of the plant stands and tables featured practical tops inset with ceramic tiles made by the Grueby Faience Company of Boston. Some of the chairs and benches had rush seats; others loose leather cushions or Spanish leather seats held in place with large oxidized nails. One Gothic-looking library table was supported by a trestle with "slot and pin" construction so "genuine," promotional copy explained, it would "delight the soul of Ruskin."[7]

A few forms clearly reflected the recent work of Scottish and English furniture designers; some emulated Japanese models; others recalled pieces found in the old Spanish missions of California. These sources of inspiration were easily identified, since the pieces carried such names as Tom Jones Drink Stand, Yokohama Plant Stand, and Bungalow Library Table. The Tobey Furniture Company labeled each piece with its name and the phrase "The New Furniture," encircled by twigs.

Although similar to some of the pieces being produced in Tobey's factory, the New Furniture was the work of Gustav Stickley. One of five brothers active in the furniture business, Gustav Stickley and his younger brother, Leopold, had made eclectic and colonial revival style furniture in Eastwood, a suburb of Syracuse, New York, during the early 1890s. In 1898, after seeing the work of the leading English, Scottish, and French designers while on a tour of Europe, Gustav began to experiment with designs, techniques, and finishes to create an easily manufactured version of the modern furniture that would appeal to the average American.

Gustav Stickley's new furniture was first offered to dealers at the Grand Rapids Furniture Exposition of July 1900. There it was seen by George F. Clingman, manager and chief buyer for the Tobey Furniture Company, who purchased nearly the entire lot and worked out an exclusive agreement for marketing the new designs. With the exception of some Elizabethan-looking pieces with ball-turned legs (which were probably not purchased by Clingman), items shown in Tobey's catalogue entitled *The New Furniture* the following October were identical in name, design, and dimensions to those pictured in Gustav Stickley's own catalogue of the same name.[8] Even Stickley's order numbers had been retained, with Tobey adding a "3" in front of each number to identify the line.[9]

The New Furniture proved popular from the start. In October 1900, the same month that this furniture was put on the market by Tobey, *House Beautiful* illustrated some of the pieces and praised the "endeavor to place honest workmanship within the reach of the masses." Calling it "sensible furniture," Margaret Edgewood noted its charming medieval quality, its pleasing color tones, and its simple, straightforward shapes. "This furniture comes at an opportune time," she wrote, enthusiastically declaring that "the day of cheap veneer, of jig-saw ornament, of poor imitations of French periods, is happily over."[10]

While the New Furniture was clearly a success, the arrangement between Gustav Stickley and the Tobey Furniture Company was not. By December 1900 Stickley had severed his connection with the company and also his partnership with his brother Leopold. In a new shop in Syracuse, a trade paper noted, he was busy making goods "on simple lines and so solidly made as to be almost indestructible."[11] Labeling his products "Craftsman" furniture, he began, with the help of family and friends, to formulate an optimistic philosophy based on the theories of Ruskin and Morris. Meanwhile, Leopold and J. George Stickley organized a shop in Fayetteville, New York.[12] Since advertisements for the New Furniture continued through 1901, it is possible that the original contract with the Tobey Company was fulfilled by Leopold Stickley, with pieces supplied by the L. and J. G. Stickley enterprise, called the Onondaga Shops after the county in which it was located.[13]

By the end of 1901 the energetic Gustav Stickley had reorganized his workshop into a semicooperative called the United Crafts and had started to mark his products with his own name and trademark; he had patented a chair and two tables; and he had put out three issues of a new monthly magazine called *The Craftsman*. Subtitled *An Illustrated Monthly Magazine for the Simplification of Life,* the magazine, as well as Stickley's catalogue, promoted his "structural" Craftsman designs as "democratic" furniture ideal for solid, hard-working Americans living simple, honest lives.[14]

prominent Chicagoans and Americans and include presidents, governors, and mayors.

The founder of the firm, Charles Tobey (1831–1888) operated a branch store for a Boston furniture dealer in Chicago for a year before opening his own business. In 1857 he was joined by a brother, Francis (Frank) Bassett Tobey (1833–1913), who later became his partner.

The Tobey brothers became manufacturers as well as dealers in 1870 when they formed a partnership with F. Porter Thayer. In 1875 the Tobeys purchased Thayer's interest, and in 1876 the company received considerable publicity when it secured the contract to furnish the Centennial Hotels in Philadelphia. In 1881 Tobey furnished the Chicago residence of banker Samuel M. Nickerson and outfitted the Florence Hotel for railroad magnate George M. Pullman.

After Charles's death in 1888, Frank became president of the company. When the latter died in 1913, the Tobey Furniture Company passed to a nephew, Arthur F. Shiverick. By 1939, when Tobey acquired the sixty-four-year-old Scholle Furniture Company, the company was owned by Shiverick's sons, Arthur and Francis Tobey, and their cousin, Jonathan Tobey Morley.

In 1888 the subsidiary Tobey & Christiansen Cabinet Company was organized by Frank Tobey and Wilhelm Frederick Christiansen (1847–1918) to manufacture high-quality furniture for exclusive sale by its own store. A Norwegian cabinetmaker who had come to Chicago in 1868, Christiansen had worked for John A. Colby & Sons before becoming superintendent of Tobey's factory. Furniture made in the cabinet shop, identified as Tobey Hand-Made Furniture by the use of metal tags after 1898, was distinguished by excellent craftsmanship and perfection of detail. Made from hardwoods like mahogany, maple, and oak, Tobey's pieces were finished on all sides, with as much attention lavished on the surfaces that stood against the wall as on the visible portions. In 1902 Tobey registered the trademark Russmore for use on mission style furniture and interior woodwork.

George F. Clingman (1857– ca. 1935), who joined the firm in 1888, served as head designer and, later, manager. Other Tobey designers included Wilhelm Christiansen's son, William, who worked for the firm from 1908 until 1915, and William Anderson, brother of Otto Anderson, the factory's chief carver. George Clingman's sons, George F., Jr., and J. Stuart, worked in the Tobey studios at the turn of the century. Both later became prominent furniture designers in Grand Rapids, Michigan.

Special designs for architects and interior designers were executed along with furniture designed by Tobey's staff for the store's customers and for stock. In 1905, a branch was opened in New York City that sold only Tobey Hand-Made Furniture. The company also made reproductions of Louis XIV XV, and XVI furniture finished in plain or powdered gold and created ornate Art Nouveau pieces modeled after those shown at the 1900 Paris Exposition. By the mid-1920s the Tobey factory was reproducing French Art Moderne living- and dining-room furniture in addition to more traditional patterns. The company also sold tall case clocks of its own make in addition to furniture by more than 200 other American and foreign manufacturers.

CLINGMAN VS. STICKLEY

Before long, Stickley's workshops were producing handmade leather goods, metalwork, and fabrics to accompany Craftsman furniture. Eventually he also designed Craftsman houses to contain the lot. Stickley's magazine carried building plans for his homes as well as instructions and materials for reproducing his furniture and textiles. For those fascinated with construction but not its actual practice, Stickley's products were available by mail. These had become popular enough in Chicago by 1902 to prompt Marshall Field & Company, the city's largest department store, to open a Craftsman showroom.

By this time the furniture was being referred to as "Mission furniture." The derivation of this term is confusing. Many who used the term related it to the severe oak pieces to be found in California's Spanish missions. Others drew its meaning from Gustav Stickley's assertion that the kind of furniture he designed *had* a mission. As Stickley himself described the situation: "If a chair be comfortable, well made and fine in structure, proportion, workmanship and finish, and if it harmonizes with its surroundings, it is everything that can be required of a chair, no matter what its style; and it is a thing that never will go out of fashion."[15] Although Stickley tried to identify his furniture by the trade name Craftsman, today the term "mission" is often used to designate all types of Arts and Crafts furniture.

Before long, Gustav Stickley's furniture had become so identified with the Arts and Crafts ideal and mode of life that Herbert E. Binstead's new book *The Furniture Styles*, published in 1909, asserted that Stickley was "entitled to the distinction of having originated and brought to recognition in the trade the one distinctly American school of design."[16] Publicity surrounding Binstead's book, the wide circulation of Stickley's catalogues (in which he called Craftsman furniture "the first original expression of American thought in furniture"),[17] and other claims in *The Craftsman* magazine fanned a dispute between Gustav and Leopold Stickley and George F. Clingman that must have been smoldering for many years. It erupted in the spring of 1911 in the form of a letter written by Clingman to Leopold Stickley in which he protested that "the claims that Gustave* Stickley makes are ridiculous" and stated that he, rather than Gustav Stickley, was the originator of American Arts and Crafts furniture.

Responding to a request from Leopold Stickley, George F. Clingman replied on May 26, 1911, with details concerning the purchase in July 1900 of the line that became the New Furniture and the sketching of the designs that Gustav Stickley soon had put into production. Clingman wrote:

At that time [1900] both Gustave and myself were stopping at Ottawa Beach. One afternoon on our way to Ottawa Beach I talked with Gustave about what he was making. I took a piece of paper out of my pocket, or in fact several pieces, and told him that if he was going to make a success of the furniture that he was making it would be necessary for him to make some more important pieces than he was making at that time. On this paper I drew out several large sofas with a square posts and flat arms with the loose seats and backs;

*Stickley dropped the "e" in his name around 1904.

some broad arm rockers and chairs, several styles of tables and one or two screens, and from these sketches Gustave Stickley made what he now claims to be the originator of, that is his so-called arts and crafts furniture.

To reinforce his argument, Clingman pointed out that:

the first simple plain piece of mission furniture that I know of having been made in this country I designed and our superintendent of the factory, Mr. Christiansen, executed for me when I was with John A. Colby & Sons in 1885. It was an absolutely plain, heavy square chair with broad wide flat arms and the seat was covered with Spanish sole leather with large oxidized nails. From that time on I made quite a number of pieces of furniture of this character, designs of which can be resurrected and testified to if necessary.[18]

Clingman's letter was accompanied by a clipping from the April 29, 1900, *Chicago Tribune* that illustrated a mission chair with square posts and rush seat and mentioned that tables and other pieces along these lines were also available.[19] "These are the facts and I have the documents, the various advertisements and various booklets that were published at the time to substantiate what I say" Clingman continued, "and instead of Gustave Stickley being the originator of this kind of furniture I claim the honor of being the first to introduce to the public generally this plain, simple kind of furniture."[20]

Gustav Stickley retains his fame, while George F. Clingman has been forgotten. To date, none of his sketches has been found and Tobey's records no longer exist. However, the basic facts outlined in Clingman's letter can be substantiated. He had indeed been a designer at John A. Colby & Sons in 1885 (see page 186). While there he worked with John E. Brower and Charles P. Limbert, two men who later became prominent designers of Arts and Crafts furniture in Grand Rapids. In 1888 he became head of the Tobey Furniture Company's special-order department and that year arranged for Wilhelm Christiansen to head Tobey's custom shop, a position Christiansen held at the time of Clingman's letter. His claim that the Norwegian cabinetmaker made mission furniture is also justifiable, since photos of Christiansen's own home show heavy, straight-lined bedroom furniture in use before 1901. As manager of the Tobey Company, Clingman had a considerable reputation. Frequent references to his talents, travels, and successes appeared in *Furniture World* and other trade publications. In 1897, for example, he was referred to as "a clever designer" with a "great reputation for knowledge" and one of the Midwest's best known and largest buyers.[21]

In print at least, Stickley ignored Clingman's accusations and continued to expand his Craftsman empire with undaunted zeal. Celebrating the opening of a large new Craftsman Building in New York City in 1913, he proudly recalled the founding of the Craftsman movement and the development, if not the origin, of his early furniture designs: "At first the furniture I made was on the usual conventional lines; but as the years went by and I experimented with the various forms of construction and design, I began to understand what good furniture and true craftsmanship meant. . . . I did not realize at the time that in making those few pieces of strong,

simple furniture I had started a new movement. Others saw it and pro-
phesized a far-reaching movement. To me it was only furniture; to them it
was religion. And eventually it became religion with me as well."[22] The
Craftsman movement ended abruptly three years later when Stickley was
forced into bankruptcy, having strained his resources by opening the
Craftsman Building and becoming involved in real-estate ventures, model
farming, and gardening. In 1917 Leopold, J. George, and Albert Stickley
purchased their brother's factory and organized Stickley Associated Cabinetmakers, with factories in New York and Michigan.

While George F. Clingman's claims are of historical interest and may
even have been true, in retrospect they appear rhetorical. Simple mission
or Arts and Crafts chairs were being made by more than one furniture
maker before Stickley's products appeared on the market. *The Decorator and
Furnisher* illustrated a severely plain oak settee made by Charles Rolfs of
Buffalo, New York, in 1888, while other pieces by him stained black, brown,
and green with pegs "much in evidence" were being shown at Marshall
Field & Company in Chicago as early as January 1900.[23]

Another New York furniture maker, Joseph McHugh, also claimed to
be the originator of mission furniture, citing as evidence the plain, rush-
seated chairs he had made for a San Francisco church as early as 1894.[24]
And, as mentioned in the previous chapter, mission style furniture was
being made by other Chicago craftsworkers by 1898. Nevertheless, it is true
that Gustav Stickley succeeded in making the Arts and Crafts style popular
with the American public. His work was then and is now considered by
many to be the finest commercially made Arts and Crafts furniture produced in America.

A broad leather strip suspended between dowels at front and back formed the seat of this oak lounge chair, illustrated in Tobey's New Furniture in Weathered Oak *catalogue ca. 1901.*
h: 34" l: 45½" w: 32"
CHS, Decorative Arts Fund, 1982
Photograph by Abramson-Culbert Studio

Despite the severing of the connection with Gustav Stickley, the Tobey Furniture Company continued to produce mission style furniture and went on to introduce two new lines. In 1901 it offered New Furniture in Weathered Oak, including chairs, settees, and bookcases, as well as tall case clocks and humidors, made from oak, ash, and even mahogany. Probably designed by George F. Clingman and made in the Tobey factory, the pieces were stained shades named Weathered Oak, Moss-Green Oak, Grey-Brown, or Silicified Ash, in evocation of the rich natural colorings found in the fields and forests. Except for incised designs on several Art Nouveau-inspired bookcases and cabinets, the pieces were free of decoration.

The *New Furniture in Weathered Oak* catalogue, whose cover showed a contented Puritan sitting in a new-style chair, offered something for every taste.[25] For a strong identification with the mission theme, the firm made a screen and a chair inset with leather panels painted with heads of monks; for those leaning toward the colonial theme, there was a simple bedroom set with oval mirrors supported by elongated S-scrolls. For the avant garde, the firm had chairs and settees with thin vertical slats resembling those being designed by Chicago architect Frank Lloyd Wright (see page 258), as well as a low-slung rectangular lounge chair in which the sitter reclined on

IMPROVING PUBLIC TASTE

a single strip of leather attached at crest and frontrail. Also new was the Tobey chair, a streamlined version of the adjustable Morris chair. Patented by Clingman, this piece featured a sliding seat and a reclining back that

Page from catalogue illustrating New Furniture in Weathered Oak, *ca. 1901.*

This table of dark stained oak attributed to the Tobey Furniture Company was illustrated in New Furniture in Weathered Oak, *ca. 1901.*
h: 29¾" d: 41"
Mr. and Mrs. William L. Porter
Photograph by Abramson-Culbert Studio

adjusted to the desired angle using a set of ratchets on the sides of the seat frame.[26]

During the summer of 1902 Tobey added Russmore furniture, a less expensive collection of rectilinear furniture designed "to meet the growing demand for a type of furniture of artistic simplicity in design, richness in finish, durability in construction, and of low price."[27] Made from wood treated a deep brown, it exhibited "a rich sheen" rather than the standard dull wax finish. The patented trade name Russmore was embossed on a copper medallion attached to each piece.

Frank B. Tobey, president of the Tobey Furniture Company, was a man of wide interests. Known for his support of progressive education, he encouraged John Dewey—then teaching at the University of Chicago and the experimental University Lab School—to bring teachers and students to the store to learn the fine points of furniture making. He also recruited for his staff talented and idealistic designers like Joseph Twyman, known as "foremost in this country in interpreting the art of William Morris."[28]

Active in promoting the latest British theories and products in Chicago since the 1870s (see page 190), Twyman had become an avid exponent of William Morris's social creed as well as a salesman for his goods after meeting him at Merton Abbey in 1883.[29] After 1898, as head of Tobey's decorating department, Twyman used his influential position to introduce customers to the type and styles of home furnishing advocated by Morris. An enthusiastic member of the Chicago Architectural Club and the Arts and Crafts Society, he frequently lectured on the moral effects of good furniture. In 1901, for example, he addressed a Milwaukee group on "the new movement which is resulting in such radical changes in the appearance of even ordinary homes."[30]

In September 1902, in conjunction with a showing of Morris & Co.

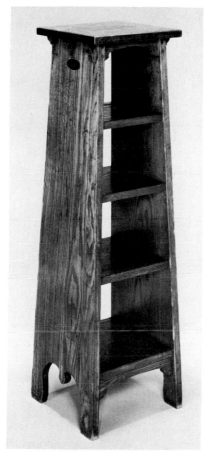

Oak side chair with cushioned seat bearing Tobey's Russmore trademark. h: 38¼" w: 20" d: 19"
Dr. and Mrs. James Fisch

Oak magazine stand with Russmore trademark of the Tobey Furniture Company, ca. 1902. h: 49" w: 14⅜" top: 13¾" x 14"
Mary and James McWilliams
Photograph by Abramson-Culbert Studio

products, Twyman set up a Morris Memorial Room at the store and furnished it with wallpapers, fabrics, textiles, stained glass, and furniture of Morris's design, including, he claimed, a few pieces from Morris's own house in England. To promote the exhibition, the company sponsored a public reception and a lecture series detailing Morris's work.[31]

In 1903 Twyman and two Hyde Park neighbors, Professors Richard Green Moulton and Oscar Lovell Triggs, founded the William Morris Society. Organized "to familiarize the public with the artistic and social ideals of Morris," the society planned to establish a museum and library devoted to his work. Professor Triggs, in turn, wrote booklets entitled *About Tobey Hand-Made Furniture* and arranged for a memorial exhibition of Twyman's furniture designs at the Art Institute following his friend's death in 1904.[32]

By the spring of 1902 the *Furniture Worker* was reporting that "Mission furniture has become a veritable craze . . . dealers can scarcely get enough to supply the demand." At first intended for use in dens, libraries, and dining rooms, the furniture was now available in forms suitable for every room in the house, as well as in shapes useful for schools, restaurants, and clubs. Men supposedly found "something very masculine" in its "comfortable solidarity and lack of frills."[33] Young adults, particularly women, found it daring and progressive, yet liked its strong associations with home and family. Commenting on the orders for mission furniture "pouring in" to manufacturers in 1906, *Furniture World* magazine attributed its widespread popularity to "the large numbers of young people who have set up their own homes and who have furnished almost entirely in mission goods."[34]

Young Chicagoans, in particular, embraced "the simple life," outfitting their bungalows with built-in cabinets and oak settles and furnishing their rooms with severe rectilinear tables and chairs, hand-loomed rugs, hand-wrought copper bowls and lighting fixtures, and monk's cloth or hand-embroidered linens. Rugs, baskets, and pottery made by American Indians or by Appalachian Mountain craftsmen showed their appreciation for other simple cultures. By the early 1900s, homes were indeed simpler than those of the previous generation, for in the words of cultural historian Gwendolyn Wright, "the aesthetic of 'New Art' sparseness had replaced Eastlake elegance as the latest moral domestic architecture."[35]

Although little concerned with the theoretical foundations of the Arts and Crafts movement, Chicago furniture manufacturers were quick to add lines of mission furniture. While pieces varied considerably from one maker to another, they shared common physical attributes that mimicked distinctive signs of handwork and capitalized on the popularity of the Arts and Crafts look. The best pieces were characterized by straight lines, solid construction, and a dull finish. The wood was strong-fibered and sturdy native white oak, often "fumed" to a dark shade using ammonia, or "weathered" to a gray-brown shade to suggest the look of age, and finished with wax to create a dull surface. Decorative binding straps, hinges, and escutcheon plates of brass, copper, or pewter displayed a "handwrought" hammer-marked surface. Seats were often of rush, or, if upholstered, usually of leather, nearly always in shades of red or brown.[36]

Continuing to praise the work of Gustav Stickley and other conscientious furniture makers, *House Beautiful* pointed out in 1902 that this new style of ready-made furniture was "very comfortable to sit on; its joints neither come unglued, or creak when a stout yokel sits upon it. Its lines are structural, frankly proclaiming their object to support weight in the simplest, most direct of ways."[37] Another writer, summarizing a commonly held view, stressed that mission furniture was "a heritage of which we may be proud—an American production, first made by native workmen, of native grown materials."[38] Others, however, would complain that it was too large, too heavy, and too clumsy, saying that it "represents the simple beginnings of furniture making, but only the a b c's of the craft."[39]

By 1902 S. Karpen & Bros. offered leather upholstered Spanish Mis-

Three-piece oak library suite made by
J. S. Ford, Johnson & Co. ca. 1902.
Used in the Highland Park home of
Ward W. Willits, for which Frank
Lloyd Wright was the architect. The
chairs have woven rush seats and
backs.
Chairs, h: 35¾" w: 29¼" d: 22"
Table, h: 29" w: 30" d: 24½"
CHS, gift of Dorothea F. Brown,
1974

sion oak chairs, and newly fashionable three-piece parlor suites composed of settees (designed for two people), an armchair, and a rocking chair. Chair manufacturer J. S. Ford, Johnson & Co. added a line of oak chairs with wide flat armrests, angled side slats, and seats of woven leather strips or fiber rush shortly after a chair of similar design was shown in the Chicago Arts and Crafts Society's 1901 exhibition. The firm combined an armchair, rocker, and table to form a "library set," the latest fashion among those furnishing new homes entirely in the mission style as well as an affordable alternative for those wishing to bring a touch of modernity into older homes.

The National Parlor Furniture Company, whose motto was "Makers of Sellers," followed suit, producing boxy oak library and parlor suites upholstered in leather in addition to their more than sixty varieties of Turkish chairs and heavily tufted couches. By 1909 the Valentine-Seaver Co., known for its "Pretty Parlor Pieces," was making plain oak chairs with leather seats along with colonial style sofas. Among local case goods manufacturers, L. Nonnast created massive square and round mission dining tables in dark stained oak, while the Schram Bros. Company specialized in tables, chairs, and sectional bookcases. In 1917 Schram Bros. offered dealers a plain, fumed oak library suite with a table and two chairs packed K. D. in a single 150-pound crate for the bargain price of $10.90.[40]

Library in the Lake Forest home of Mr. and Mrs. Van Wagener Alling in 1904. The Morris chair, Indian baskets, and embroidered scarves reflect the influence of the Arts and Crafts movement.
Mrs. Charles H. Brown

For several years, one new wholesale manufacturer, the Chicago Mission Furniture Company, specialized in supplying dealers exclusively with straight-line chairs and tables. This company had been formed in 1904 when Frederick P. Fischer, Jr., Arthur McDowell, Jacob Scherer, and John McLelland, all employees of the Balkwill & Patch Furniture Company, were out on strike. Fischer, the son of the foreman of Balkwill & Patch, had worked as a machine hand in the factory since the age of thirteen; John

McLelland had been a traveling salesman. Pooling their funds to rent a building on Wells Street, the four men began manufacturing mission furniture, then at the height of its popularity.

The new Chicago Mission Furniture Company was so successful that within three months it was able to expand its factory. By 1906 it had moved into a five-story building on Clybourn Avenue and employed 100 men. By

Mission rocker frame available from the factory of the Columbia Parlor Frame Company in 1905. From Seng Company's Good Fixtures *publication, August 1905.*
Francis A. Seng

The second photo shows "what a small amount of money and a large amount of taste" could accomplish in redoing a parlor in the mission style. From House Beautiful, *April 1905.*
The Newberry Library

then the company was producing rockers, tables, desks, dressers, and hall furniture noted for "artistic simplicity" and "strict adherance to Mission lines."[41] Six agents, including three in California alone, traveled throughout the South and Midwest selling its products.

Nearly every manufacturer of seating furniture offered his special version of the famous Morris chair, whose back reclined by adjustment of a rod in a series of notches or ratchets. Although a few copied the side spindles and two loose cushions of the original version designed by Phillip Webb in 1866, most were a far cry from Morris & Co.'s chair.[42] Attempting to create a unique product, manufacturers experimented with claw feet,

Advertisement for mission furniture in the Hartman Furniture & Carpet Co. catalogue, 1914.
I. H. Hartman, Jr.

lion's-head arms, machine-stamped ornaments, and spring-filled stationary cushions, creating models noted for their cheapness and novelty rather than honesty of construction. Reporting a run on Morris chairs at $1.50 apiece in 1898, when the Arts and Crafts movement was just getting under way, the editor of *Furniture World* despaired that he seemed "to hear the moaning of the oaks way out in the West, as they echoed back that price, Morris chairs at a dollar and a half. . . . Shade of William Morris, 'tis well thou art beyond the ken of such sacrilege!"[43]

Chicago-based mail-order houses like Sears, Roebuck & Company, Montgomery Ward & Co., and the Hartman Furniture & Carpet Co. introduced mission style furnishings to a remarkably large cross-section of American society. By 1904 Montgomery Ward & Co.'s catalogue showed double-page spreads of unornamented, straight-line Arts and Crafts and mission furniture for the den, library, and dining room in oak and ash available in weathered, golden oak, or Antwerp finishes at prices ranging from $0.35 for a leather-cushioned ash stool to $1.85 for a sturdy oak couch with large loose leather cushions.[44] At the same time, Sears offered its customers a nine-piece oak dining-room suite consisting of table, six chairs, sideboard, and china closet for $40.75. "The style of each piece is purely Mission, which has become very popular, because of its rigid simplicity," the catalogue assured its buyers.[45]

In 1912 the Hartman Furniture & Carpet Co., which specialized in time-payment mail-order sales, advertised massive four-piece mission library sets made of "thoroughly seasoned heavy oak" for $13.65. The same catalogue offered an "exceptionally fine" Morris chair in dark golden oak with broad arms supported by turned spindles and front supports embossed with florid scrolls above large claw feet. Rather than loose cushions, the back displayed a deeply tufted circular panel surrounded by "a very artistic ruffle."[46]

While plain, solid furnishings were often offered alongside the pseudo-mission goods, little distinction was made between the two in the advertising copy, for the goal was to sell merchandise, not to preach simplicity and improve morality. Mission furniture remained popular through the 1920s, when the traditional, historically based styles once more returned to favor with the population at large.

CHAPTER 15

A NEW PRAIRIE STYLE

1895-1917

In 1899 Professor Louis J. Millet of The Art Institute of Chicago stated his views on the future of furniture design and architecture as follows:

> I believe the day is dawning when a large part—yes, almost all—of the furniture in the house will be built for that building, and for no other. Then it will fit; then it will harmonize with the architectural design of the place and with the decorative scheme of coloring. . . . Of course, at present some articles of furniture, like sideboards and mantels, are built as permanent fixtures in the home, but ultimately this plan will include countless other articles. . . . I hope and believe the tendency to build low two-story houses, spread out over a large plot of ground, will increase in this country. I imagine that the American will think more of symmetry in the future and less of the picturesque in constructing his home.[1]

Millet undoubtedly had in mind the work of a number of Chicago architects whose designs for houses and furniture would later be characterized as belonging to the Prairie school. Influenced by Millet's contemporary and friend, the architect Louis H. Sullivan, these young architects were the American counterparts of the architect / designers of the British Arts and Crafts movement; the Deutsche Werkstätten and Deutscher Werkbund in Germany; the Wiener Werkstätte (or Secessionists) in Austria; and the Glasgow school in Scotland (see page 215).

What the older and younger generations of Chicago designers had in common was a desire to create a fresh approach to design based on organic relationships among the constituent elements. In the case of architecture, for example, this took into account the function of the building and its relationship to its site and emphasized the use of the most appropriate materials and technology available. The aim was, above all, to produce an original work expressive of contemporary needs rather than an imitation of spatially and temporally inappropriate styles. Sullivan believed that this ideal could be achieved only by "harmonious thinking."

In the early years of the twentieth century, Frank Lloyd Wright emerged as the most visible and influential member of this group. While each of the Prairie architects developed a personal style, their collective work was characterized by the bold use of abstracted forms and an understanding and use of natural materials. Free-flowing interiors with flexible open plans dictated the exterior forms of the houses, which were often sheltered under heavy, overhanging roofs and defined by horizontal lines and bands of leaded-glass or patterned wood mullion windows.[2] Discussing the work of Wright and his colleagues in 1908, a contemporary Chicago architect, Thomas E. Tallmadge, noted their preference for straight lines and horizontal planes, which he termed "an absolute result of the inspiration of the prairie."[3]

Like earlier architects who had pioneered new styles, Prairie architects were eager to apply their new design theories at every level, from structural shell to details of interior furnishings and fittings. At the time, few pieces of commercially made furniture were compatible with the clean-lined and uncluttered interiors they designed. Thus, like Chicago's Modern Gothic advocates of the 1870s (see page 157) and their protesting counterparts in Europe, the Prairie school architects found it necessary to design special furniture and accessories to function in harmony with the tightly controlled interiors of their houses.

When clients did not commission the architect to design all of the interior furnishings, Prairie architects usually convinced them of the importance of having specially designed pieces at least in such public areas as the dining room, living room, library, or hall. If the client did not desire or could not afford custom furniture, the architects recommended pieces from the workshops of Gustav Stickley or from those of his brothers, L. and J. G. Stickley.

Of the Prairie architects, the three best known for their innovative furniture designs—George Washington Maher, George Grant Elmslie, and Frank Lloyd Wright—began their careers in the 1880s in the office of Joseph Lyman Silsbee. An innovative residential architect, Silsbee had moved to Chicago from the East in 1882 to serve as the interior architect for Henry Ives Cobb's picturesque "castle" built for the Potter Palmers. All three later went on to work for the influential architectural firm of Adler & Sullivan.[4]

The first to leave and set up his own practice was Maher (1864–1926). At the time that he began to work on his own in 1888, he had already begun to reject the Queen Anne and picturesque revival styles. In their place he urged the adoption of a fresh, new architecture based on "original ideas." In 1886 he had told fellow members of the Architectural Sketch Club that "originality in American architecture rests to a great degree upon the basis of studying the necessities of labor and life, and meeting them without prejudice."

Suggesting that a building's function should be allowed to determine its design, Maher outlined the attributes of an ideal interior. Many of these would be incorporated in later Prairie style houses and in their less expensive counterpart, the bungalow:

This is the right idea of a residence, to have it speak of its function. . . . The true path toward an original style is to follow the dictation of necessity and then to improve upon detail. The interior of this class of building presents comfort in every form. Large, old-fashioned fireplaces, ease of stairs, nooks with settees; heavy oak beams leave the impression of solidarity; low ceilings convey the idea of privacy; all contribute to make life a matter of ease. This style of building suits the taste of the better class of American people, and if encouraged will develop into a style that speaks of home and comfort.[5]

Implementing his ideas, Maher employed what he called a "motif rhythm theory," in which a geometric shape was combined with a stylized floral form to create a dominant motif that was rhythmically repeated throughout interior and exterior to create visual unity. This theory, Maher explained, "completely harmonizes all portions of the work until in the end it becomes a unit in composition . . . since each detail is designed to harmonize with the guiding motif which in turn was inspired by the necessity of the situation and local color and conditions."[6] Like Elmslie and Wright, Maher selected a flower native to the area because, in his words, "the leading flower of a neighborhood is nature's symbol of the spirit out-breathed there."[7]

The dining room of "Pleasant-Home," the Oak Park residence of John Farson, designed by George W. Maher in 1897.
Violet Wyld and Philip B. Maher

Maher put his theory into practice in 1897, when Chicago lawyer John Farson asked him to design a large country house and stable in the western suburb of Oak Park. For "Pleasant-Home" (whose name derived from its location at the corner of Pleasant and Home) Maher combined the motifs of a honeysuckle and a lion's head. In addition to such standard built-in furniture as a buffet and hall seats, Maher designed a dining-room table with large, high-backed chairs ornamented with lions' heads. In the library, lions' heads appeared on the thick legs of the large central table and on the molding of the bookcase.[8]

In 1901 Maher was given the opportunity to refine and develop his "rhythm motif theory" when James A. Patten, known as the "Wheat King" of Chicago, commissioned him to design and totally furnish a residence in Evanston. For the Patten mansion on Ridge Avenue, Maher chose a motif combining the thistle, which grew wild on the site, and the octagon. Patten particularly liked the thistle, one Evanstonian recalled, because it symbolized his Scottish ancestry and "the frugality of habit" on which he prided himself.[9] Frugality, however, hardly was evident in the opulent edifice that Maher designed and Louis J. Millet decorated for the ebullient Patten.

As in other houses designed by Maher, the floral theme predominated, while the geometric element—the octagon—was more subtle. For example, it might appear as a frame for the thistle, as the form for a table leg, or even in the shape of a room. In sum, the various elements combined to produce an awe-inspiring effect. Writing in 1938, when the mansion was about to be razed, one reporter noted:

> To one who enters by the massive front gate, climbs the two flights of stone steps, passes through the leaded glass front door and stands in the great hall, the most striking feature of the silent mansion is the endless repetition of the thistle motif. . . . Stand in the hall and look about. There is the thistle blazoned on stained glass on the doors and on all the windows, giving bright color to the tiled floors of the lobby and card room, and again finding a setting in the walls, along the moldings, and on the framework of the massive pieces of furniture. . . . Even the grandfather clock, seven feet tall, made for the home,

bears the Scottish emblem in the woodwork surrounding the face. It is repeated in the dining room table and chairs, stolidly placed beneath a brass chandelier wrought with thorns. . . . All the furnishings, like the home itself, awe the observer through sheer size. Everything seems to have been designed to withstand an earthquake.[10]

George Washington Maher in his office, ca. 1901.
Violet Wyld and Philip B. Maher

Standing in the hall, one could look into the major public rooms. In the dining room, a band of incised thistles formed an apron on the square mahogany table supported by four heavy legs banded at the top with an octagon of thistles. The chairs, simpler than in the Farson house, had plain straight legs but their back-curving stiles bore octagons of thistle ornament. In the music room, a grand piano sported octagon-shaped legs carved with thistles; the table in the octagonal breakfast room was supported by similar legs, while the chairs were plain upholstered forms with backs that were modified octagons.

In 1902 Maher designed a large Glencoe country estate for lawyer Harry Rubens in which a simple band treatment enclosing a stylized hollyhock formed the dominant motif. For the F. N. Corbin house in Kenilworth (1904) and Charles Winton's residence in Wausau, Wisconsin (1905), he used a straight-line and poppy motif, while a tulip and tripartite arch repeated rhythmically in the Wausau home of Hiram Stewart (1906). Maher later used the poppy again in the C. J. Winton house in Minneapolis, Minnesota (1910), and the J. H. Hager house, Waukon, Iowa (1913).[11]

By the time Maher designed the Stone and Stewart houses, his motifs had become more delicate and increasingly geometrical. In 1906, when he

CHICAGO FURNITURE

served as architect for the Ernest J. Magerstadt house in the Kenwood neighborhood of Hyde Park, for example, the dominant floral motif, a poppy, bloomed serenely in the stained glass and exterior stone pillars while the

The music room in the James A. Patten house, Evanston, ca. 1903. From Architectural Record, *April 1904.*

furniture was reduced to simple geometric forms free of curves or carving. This shift toward simplicity may have been hastened by criticisms directed at his earlier work. It is more likely, however, that it stemmed from Maher's exposure to Frank Lloyd Wright's work, as well as from a visit to the St. Louis World's Fair in 1904, where he had seen the fluid forms of contemporary Austrian, British, and German designers. After that, H. Allen Brooks theorized, Maher turned to contemporary European design for inspiration.[12]

Like Maher, George Grant Elmslie (1871–1952) was an enthusiastic propagandist for originality in American architecture as well as a designer of distinctive furniture. As Louis H. Sullivan's chief draftsman between 1894 and 1909, Elmslie had been responsible for detailing and supervising the famous architect's last important commissions. This included designing built-in as well as free-standing furniture, draperies, and other accessories for the home of entrepreneur Henry B. Babson in Riverside, Illinois, in 1907.[13] For the main banking floor of the National Farmers' Bank (now Northwestern National Bank) in Owatonna, Minnesota (1906–8), Elmslie created simple, free-standing oak desks with ornamental bases whose carvings echoed the forms executed in stencils, stained glass, and terra cotta.[14] Elsewhere in the bank, as in the Babson house, plain oak furniture had been selected from the Craftsman designs of Gustav Stickley.

Elmslie's last project in Sullivan's office was the furnishings for the Harold C. Bradley house in Madison, Wisconsin (1909), where, working with Mrs. Bradley, he designed furniture, decorative accessories, leaded windows, and the interior detail.[15] For this house, Elmslie created a set of elegant dining-room chairs whose rectangular backs featured a central V-shaped splat pierced with an intricate motif of interlaced floral and geometric forms. He liked the effect so much that he created variations of these chairs for several of his clients as well as for his own home.

Oak dining table and four chairs with fret-sawn floral motif in the splats, designed by George G. Elmslie for his wife Bonnie in 1910.
Photograph courtesy of David Gebhard

In 1909, when he left Sullivan's employ, Elmslie joined William Gray Purcell (1880–1965) and George Feick, two young Minneapolis architects, to create the firm of Purcell, Feick and Elmslie. Purcell, who had grown up in Oak Park and had worked in Sullivan's office in 1903, had been collaborating with Feick in Minnesota for three years. While Purcell and Feick continued to work in Minneapolis, Elmslie took charge of the firm's Chicago commissions.[16] Purcell, who remained Elmslie's partner until 1922, remembered his friend as "a man of quick imagination; his mind in architecture was highly articulate, succinct and competent. He was not a long distance talker, but he was by no means a silent person. . . . He kept his mind open to current thought and salted his good talk with Scottish humor and repartee."[17]

Purcell and Elmslie worked together so closely that it is often difficult to attribute specific designs to either one. Both wanted to be involved in every phase of the design, believing that "the task of building was not that of a lone genius, but the coordinated effort of a number of men."[18] Nevertheless, many of the firm's furniture designs reveal Elmslie's hand.

Leather-upholstered oak side chair designed by George G. Elmslie for the Charles A. Purcell house, River Forest, in 1909.
h: 50" w: 21¼" d: 20⅜"
The Art Institute of Chicago, gift of the Antiquarian Society through Mrs. William P. Boggess II Fund

Tall case clock with brass inlay designed by Purcell and Elmslie for the Henry Babson house, Riverside, in 1912. The mahogany case was made by Niedecken-Walbridge in Milwaukee, Wisconsin; the gold face was executed by Chicago metalsmith Robert R. Jarvie.
h: 88" w: 15½" d: 24¾"
The Art Institute of Chicago, restricted gift of Mrs. Theodore D. Tieken

Although some of Purcell and Elmslie's furniture—for example, the pieces designed for the Edison Shop in Chicago in 1912—was clearly right-angle geometrical, much of their work exhibited lyrical ornament derived by combining an abstracted plant motif with a precise linear pattern—a carry-over from Elmslie's work with Sullivan. The resulting design, realized in fretwork in furniture as well as in interior woodwork, was also repeated in stained glass, stenciled on textiles, and wrought in metal to create a harmonious design. As Purcell and Elmslie explained in 1913: "The ornaments themselves represent the expansion of a single germinal idea, and may be severe, restrained, simple, or as elaborately evolved as desired for place and circumstance. After the motif is established the development of it is an orderly procession from start to finish, it is all intensely organic, proceeding from main motif to minor motifs, interblending, inter-relating and to the last terminal, all of a piece. It is the play work in the architect's day, his hour of refreshment."[19]

This organic approach is most clearly reflected in Purcell and Elmslie's chairs. Employing V-shaped back splats pierced with floral fretwork reminiscent of the splats in the Bradley house, Purcell and Elmslie designed similar chairs for Elmslie's wife, Bonnie, in 1910; for Purcell's father, Charles A. Purcell, who lived in River Forest in 1909; and for Purcell's own home in Minneapolis in 1913. The dining-room chairs for Elmslie's wife display pierced wooden backs incorporating a highly stylized tulip; those for Edna Purcell show simple upholstered backs capped with vertical rectangles inset with delicately leaded stained glass.

In 1912, when Purcell and Elmslie were working on the Edison Shop for the Babson Bros.' phonograph business, Henry B. Babson engaged them to design eight pieces of furniture for his house in Riverside (on which Elmslie had worked in 1907 while employed by Louis Sullivan). Most striking of the pieces—which included square armchairs, tables, and chairs—was a slender, tall case clock inlaid with narrow bands of brass and topped with a pair of airy geometric finials created for Babson's entrance hall.[20]

Purcell and Elmslie, like George Maher, established reputations as innovative architects who drew clients from other Midwestern states, including Wisconsin, Iowa, and Minnesota. However, despite their significant contributions to architecture and the decorative arts, they are relatively unknown outside the Midwest. It is Frank Lloyd Wright's name that became synonymous with the Prairie style and it is his work that is celebrated throughout the world.

After Frank Lloyd Wright (1867–1959) left Adler & Sullivan's office in 1893, he established an independent practice in the office complex known as Steinway Hall. Other architects with offices in the same building were Dwight Perkins, Robert Spencer, Jr., and brothers Irving and Allen Pond. Like Wright, they were among the founders of the Chicago Arts and Crafts Society in 1897. Sometime around the following year, Wright added a studio to his house in Oak Park to which he attracted a coterie of young architects, including Marion Mahony, William Drummond, Walter Burley Griffin, and Barry Byrne, among others. By 1902, when his work was accorded the place of honor in the annual Chicago Architectural Club Exhibition, Frank Lloyd Wright was already recognized as the leader and chief spokesman for the "radical" Prairie school and was well on his way to becoming one of America's best known architects.

In designing furniture, Wright followed the organic principle that formed the basis of his architecture. As he explained in his *Autobiography:* "The 'grammar' of the house, is its manifest articulation of all its parts—the 'speech' it uses. . . . When the chosen grammar is finally adopted (you go almost indefinitely with it into everything you do) walls, ceilings, furniture, etc. become inspired by it. Everything has a related articulation in relation to the whole and all belongs together because all are speaking the same language."[21]

As an integral part of the total design, Wright's furniture, like his houses, exhibited Spartan simplicity that reflected not only his admiration for Japanese culture (he was an avid collector of Japanese prints) but also his progressive ideas for a new architecture based on pure designs derived from abstract, geometrical principles.

Built-in furniture was one of the characteristics of Wright's interiors. As he explained, "The most truly satisfactory apartments . . . are those in which most or all of the furniture is built in as part of the original scheme."[22] Concerning himself with the overall unity of effect rather than individual pieces, Wright wanted to control the interior environment by eliminating free-standing furniture.

The Frederick C. Robie house, 5757 Woodlawn Avenue, designed by Frank Lloyd Wright in 1909.

In addition to built-in hall seats, Wright designed chairs and perhaps other furnishings in 1894 for the William H. Winslow house in River Forest, his first independent commission after leaving the firm of Adler & Sullivan. During the winter of 1896–97 Wright and Winslow, an amateur printer as well as a prominent iron manufacturer, published a limited edition of William C. Gannett's *The House Beautiful*, featuring type hand-set by Winslow and ornamental borders drawn by Wright. The philosophy of

Gannett, a Unitarian minister and family friend, was close to Wright's own, for both believed that the creation of gracious and beautiful homes would foster an atmosphere of love, hospitality, and repose.[23]

Dining room in the Ward W. Willits house, Highland Park, ca. 1902. Burnham Library, The Art Institute of Chicago

When Wright expanded his home in Oak Park in 1895 to meet the needs of his growing family, he converted the kitchen into a dining room and began to create his first "unified" interior. Plain, natural wood molding and paneling, window-ledge shelves, straight-lined oak furniture and geometric leaded-glass windows in an abstract plant design, all functioned to create an "organic whole." Viewing the room a few years later, Alfred H. Granger wrote in *House Beautiful:* "One's first impression of the dining room is of its simplicity—no rugs, no curtains, and only the necessary furniture, which, however, is in perfect harmony with all the room. One entire end of the room opposite the fireplace is practically all of glass, laid in leading of a very delicate design, which was evidently inspired by the lotus flower. . . . The oak woodwork, which is carried round the room to the height of the window sills, is designed to emphasize the horizontal line, a very wise thought in a small room."[24] (See color plate.)

The simple room ensemble with its plain rectangular table and high-backed dining chairs set forth a basic format repeated in many of Wright's later designs. With plain upholstered seats (no cushions), the chairs had backs shaped like vertical rectangles inset with rows of long narrow "twisted spindles." The spindles were later replaced by sturdier square slats. By 1899, when Wright designed similar chairs for the Joseph Husser house, the slats extended down the entire back of the chair and the stiles flared slightly at top and bottom, creating a more geometrical effect.[25]

Around the same time, Wright designed a "cube" chair for his home and studio that reflected his interest in reducing furniture and, indeed, all utilitarian objects to their basic geometric forms. Exhibited at the 1902 Chicago Architectural Club Exhibition, the chair displayed a rectilinear boxlike

Oak armchair designed by Frank Lloyd Wright for the Ward W. Willits house ca. 1902.
h: 34" w: 32" d: 23"
CHS, gift of Cameron Brown, 1969

Oak side chair made for the Willits dining room ca. 1902.
The Metropolitan Museum of Art, Purchase, Mr. and Mrs. David Lubart; gift in memory of Katharine J. Lubart (1944–1975), 1978

frame with wooden seat and absolutely no ornamentation. Wright later designed armchairs based on squares, octagons, and circles with upholstered seats and often with vertical slats for the interiors of his early commissions, including the homes of Joseph Husser, Chicago (1899); B. Harley Bradley and Warren Hickox, Kankakee (1900); Ward W. Willits, Highland Park (1902); Susan Lawrence Dana, Springfield (1902); Francis W. Little, Peoria (1903); Robert Evans, Longwood (1908); Avery W. Coonley, Riverside (1907–8), and Frederick C. Robie, Chicago (1909).[26] In 1912, when he designed a dining-room set for his lawyer, Sherman M. Booth, the chair backs were simple vertical rectangles with square seats, inset with machine-woven cane.

Tables, cabinets, desks and other case pieces designed for Wright's early houses exhibited "carefully calculated horizontality."[27] Broad, flat planes of wood formed the tops of tables and cabinets, recalling the extended cantilevers of the exterior roofs. Plain, square legs supported tables and chairs, meeting tops and stretchers at crisp right angles. Between table legs and across the backs and sides of chairs, rows of square vertical spindles created a screen effect, giving a sense both of privacy and of airiness. Dining-chair seats were usually covered with leather. On window seats, settles, and chairs, loose cushions upholstered in velour or linen softened contact with hard wooden surfaces while preserving geometric lines.

Side view of oak dining chair designed by Frank Lloyd Wright for the Joseph Husser house ca. 1899.
h: 52¼" w: 17¼" d: 16¼"
Mrs. Lynn Kearney

Back of oak dining chair designed by Frank Lloyd Wright for the Joseph Husser house ca. 1899.
h: 52¼" w: 17¼" d: 16¼"
Mrs. Lynn Kearney

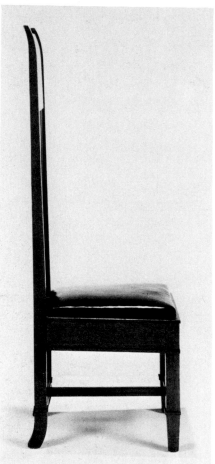 

Construction details were usually not visible, and each element was finished with equal care, so that the pieces could stand free like sculpture. Then, linear strips of wood were often nailed or glued onto the flat horizontal and vertical surfaces to bring the furniture and architecture into harmony. Since the architect was concerned with furniture as part of a total design rather than as a handcrafted product, pieces by Wright, as well as by other Prairie architects, gave the appearance of "studied simplicity" rather than massive quaintness, as was often the case with Arts and Crafts products. Progressive in form and harmonious in design and material, these hard, geometric forms were, however, more often soothing to the eye and mind than to the human physique. As Wright himself confessed: "I found it difficult . . . to make some of the furniture in the 'abstract.' That is, to design it as architecture and make it 'human' at the same time—fit for human use. I have been black and blue in some spot, somewhere almost all my life from too intimate contact with my own early furniture."[28]

Although Wright designed all types of household furnishings, he showed a decided preference for dining rooms, which he perceived as "always a great artistic opportunity."[29] In 1909, for the dining room of the Frederick C. Robie house near the University of Chicago campus, he created one of his most spectacular productions. In the long spacious room, six tall thronclike chairs surrounded a long rectangular table whose cantilevered top was visually enclosed by four thick vertical corner piers each topped by Japanese-style art glass lamps. The vertical and horizontal thrusts of the powerful ensemble repeated the lines of the built-in buffet; the diamond pattern of the art glass lamps repeated the pattern of the window panes.

Walnut sewing table with inlaid measuring standard designed by Frank Lloyd Wright for the Avery Coonley residence in Riverside ca. 1908. Executed by Niedecken-Walbridge, Milwaukee, Wisconsin.
h: 28" d: 18" w (extended): 46"
CHS, gift of Mr. and Mrs. Wilbert Hasbrouck, 1978

Birch side chairs with cane backs and seats designed by Frank Lloyd Wright ca. 1912 for the Glencoe house of his lawyer, Sherman M. Booth.
h: 31" w: 16" d: 17"
CHS, gift of Mr. and Mrs. Julius Abler, 1978
Photograph by Abramson-Culbert Studio

Wright actually continued to design furniture until the end of his life, usually for clients whose residences he had designed. However, as early as 1904 Wright had designed metal office furniture for the Larkin Company

Administration Building in Buffalo, New York, and as late as 1955 he created three lines of domestic furniture for the Heritage-Henredon Furniture Company of North Carolina. By then, the "radical" designs for a favored few had become available to the many, as *House Beautiful* noted in November 1955, hailing "the entry of [Wright's] great talents and principles into the important commercial field of home furnishings available for all to buy."[30]

OTHER PRAIRIE ARCHITECTS

Wright's influence on the furniture designed by architects who had at one time or another worked in his office is not hard to discern. Nevertheless, these architects, including Marion Mahony, her husband, Walter Burley Griffin, William Drummond, and Barry Byrne eventually developed their own versions of the Prairie school idiom. Working under Wright's direction, Marion Mahony (1873–1961), a gifted artist known for her beautiful Japanese-style renderings, helped design furniture, art glass, lighting fix-

Conference room in the office of Barry Byrne, 1915, showing furniture designed by the architect.

tures, and glass mosaics for Wright's commissions during the fourteen years she was associated with his studio.[31] After Wright left Chicago for Europe in 1909, she produced designs for furnishings in conjunction with Herman

Von Holst, who took over Wright's practice, and later in conjunction with her husband, Walter Burley Griffin.

The work of William E. Drummond, who served as Wright's chief draftsman and project manager from 1899 until 1909, tended to be crisper and more angular than Wright's; however, it is frequently mistaken for that of his mentor. In 1909–10, when Drummond constructed a home for his family in River Forest, he used built-in window seats, fireplace seats, and cabinets to complement boxy armchairs and straight-backed side chairs of the type designed by Wright for clients. The best known of Drummond's furniture designs are the chairs with vertical-slanted backs and protruding seats created in 1911 for the Brookfield Kindergarten, one of three structures created for Queene F. Coonley, wife of Avery Coonley, one of Wright's most affluent clients, and an enthusiastic promoter of the Montessori method of education.[32] Drummond occasionally used lighter-toned woods than Wright, as in the furniture and cabinetwork he created in 1914 for Ralph S. Baker's Wilmette home, which he had designed in partnership with Louis Guenzel.[33]

Birch armchair with cane seat and fret-sawn back designed by Barry Byrne for his office ca. 1915.
h: 37" w: 20" d: 20⅛"
CHS, gift of Annette C. Byrne, 1980

The conference table and chairs designed around 1915 by former Wright employee Francis Barry Byrne (1883–1967) show a highly individual style. Made of light-toned birch, they are embellished with fret-sawn ornament in a geometric motif. Byrne eventually went on to specialize in ecclesiastical architecture, often working in conjunction with Chicago artists Alfonso Iannelli and Edgar Miller.[34]

The few furniture designs attributed to Dwight H. Perkins, Pond & Pond, and Howard Van Doren Shaw reflect these architects' admiration for simplified medieval forms and their early involvement with the Arts

Interior view of American School of Correspondence, Chicago, designed by Pond & Pond, 1912.
American School of Correspondence

Oak bench designed by Pond & Pond and executed by F. C. Jorgeson & Co. for the American School of Correspondence in Chicago, 1912.
American School of Correspondence

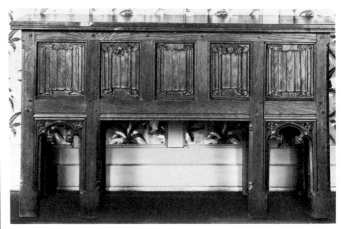

Architect Howard Van Doren Shaw designed this oak sideboard with Gothic detailing for the dining room of his house, "Ragdale," in Lake Forest. h: 39" w: 66" d: 18⅞"
Alice Ryerson

and Crafts movement. Perkins, whose primary interest was educational architecture and city planning, only rarely designed residential furniture, although he is known to have created special designs for the preacher's room and library of Hitchcock Hall at the University of Chicago around 1901 and a pair of settles for the Evanston home of his brother-in-law, Edwin F. Walker, in 1911.[35] Around 1912, handsomely carved Arts and

Crafts style desks and chairs were created for the classroom of the American School of Home Correspondence in Chicago by the Pond brothers, who were responsible for much of the architectural work at Hull-House. To the north in Lake Forest, furniture and interiors preserved in "Ragdale," the rambling home of architect Howard Van Doren Shaw, still recall the days when, in the words of Wright, "good William Morris and John Ruskin were much in evidence in Chicago intellectual circles."[36]

At first view, Prairie style furniture gave the illusion of simplicity; in fact it was quite complex. While its relatively straight lines allowed the use of modern woodworking machinery, a great deal of additional handwork was also required. Indeed, its execution called for a cabinetmaker who not only possessed the skill to translate the working sketches into a final product but who also had the patience to make pieces of unfamiliar design. While the city was filled with professional cabinet- and furniture makers, not many were willing to undertake such unconventional, time-consuming, and, thus, for the most part, financially unrewarding work.

None of the Prairie architects is known to have executed his own furniture. It is likely that some had their designs executed by custom shops like the one operated by the Tobey Furniture Company, which stressed its close collaboration with architects. Many went to factories that made furniture as well as mantels and woodwork. Frank Lloyd Wright, for example, turned to a woodcarver and millworker named John W. Ayers, who had operated a small furniture factory in Salem, Massachusetts, before moving to Chicago in 1887. In Chicago, Ayers operated shops at various addresses and with various partners from 1890 until his retirement in 1913.[37]

Wright-designed furniture executed by Ayers and shown in the 1902 Chicago Architectural Club Exhibition included the dining chairs, hall table, and reception-room chairs for "Glenlloyd," the B. Harley Bradley house in Kankakee; the dining-room table and chairs for the Warren Hickox house in the same city; and a group of "Office Chairs." In 1905 furniture for the Frank L. Smith bank in Dwight, Illinois, was executed by Ayers. Although little is known about the Wright-Ayers relationship, Irma Strauss and David Hanks, who have made a study of Wright's decorative arts, speculate that it was successful because Ayers "respected Wright's design ideas and was apparently willing to carry them out without imposing his own will."[38]

In 1907 Wright turned to a Milwaukee firm, the Niedecken-Walbridge Co., to have his furniture made. One of the owners, George M. Niedecken, had worked in Wright's studio after studying decorative design with Louis J. Millet before returning to his home town to open his own interior design firm. Under Niedecken's supervision, the F. H. Bresler Co., a Milwaukee firm that specialized in making picture frames, executed furniture for the Avery W. Coonley and Frederick C. Robie houses designed by Wright.

After 1910, when Niedecken-Walbridge established its own custom workshop, the company executed furniture for the Hauberg House in Rock Island, Illinois, designed by architect Robert C. Spencer, Jr., and his partner, Horace S. Powers. It also made the mahogany tall case clock and other furniture designed by Purcell and Elmslie for the Henry K. Babson house in Riverside in 1912. Around the same time, Niedecken-Walbridge executed furnishings for the Avery Coonley School in Downers Grove, Illinois, designed by Perkins, Hamilton and Fellows, and for the Brookfield Kindergarten designed by William Drummond.[39]

Furniture for Irving and Allen Pond was made by showcase manufacturer F. C. Jorgeson & Co. on North Anne Street in Chicago. Louis J. Millet designed and executed the art glass, glass mosaic, and frescoes in the Patten house for George W. Maher.[40] However, the contractors for Maher's many furniture commissions remain unknown.

ARCHITECTS AND THE ARTS AND CRAFTS

Why did Prairie architects turn to commercial manufacturers when the city was filled with Arts and Crafts exponents whose furniture manifested the same concern for simplicity, native materials, and honest construction as their own work? Probably because the two groups interpreted the Arts and Crafts philosophy differently. While the architects viewed furniture as one element in their plan to create a new environment, many Arts and Crafts furniture makers believed that the artist and the craftsman should be the same person. But this was not acceptable to the Prairie architects, who wanted to retain control of the design.

The second point of contention revolved around the use of machinery in the construction of the furniture. The majority of the Arts and Crafts furniture makers were opposed to the use of machinery except, according to the Chicago Arts and Crafts Society's constitution of 1897, "in so far as it relieves the workman from drudgery." But from the very beginning, Frank Lloyd Wright asserted that the machine was useful not only as a means of easing and hastening production but as a tool for achieving artistic expression. He first made this point at the meeting at which the constitution of the Arts and Crafts Society was adopted. Later he expanded on it in his famous lecture "The Art and Craft of the Machine," which he delivered at Hull-House in 1901 and which the Chicago Architectural Club and the National League of Industrial Art published the following year. In it he pointed out that woodworking machines "have placed in the hands of the designer a means of idealizing the true nature of wood harmoniously with man's spiritual and material needs without waste and within the reach of every one."[41]

Wright attempted to design furniture that would take advantage of modern machine technology. "The furniture takes the clean cut, straight-line forms that the machine can render far better than would be possible by hand," he explained in "The Cause of Architecture" in 1908. "Certain facilities . . . of the machine . . . are taken advantage of; and the nature of the materials is usually revealed in the process."[42]

Other Arts and Crafts Society members, such as Professors Charles Zueblin, who had organized the Northwestern University Settlement in 1891, and Oscar Triggs (see p. 229) attempted to humanize the production process by restructuring the workplace. They hoped that by promoting model workshops that combined art and industry, they would create a system that would restore dignity to the worker and merge art with everyday life. But their ideal systems were based on the human hand and not the machine. Arts and Crafts furniture workers, anxious to revive handicraft techniques, on the whole accepted this view.

Such divergent viewpoints undoubtedly prompted Prairie architects to seek out craftsmen who were skilled machinists to produce their "machine age" furniture designs. However, a 1907 *Architectural Record* article by architect Myron Hunt's partner, Elmer Grey, suggests that their avoidance of utopian craftsmen may have been prompted as much by economic as by philosophical considerations. "The architect must be at the head in all attempts to bring his work and that of the craftsmen closer together," he wrote. "All such attempts should begin on the working basis of the co-operation of an architect's office with a practical (but not with a visionary) craftsman's shop."[43]

From an architect's point of view, the ideal furniture maker was a dependable, well-trained craftsman who could translate a sketch into a three-dimensional object without interjecting his own prejudices regarding design or construction, complete the job within a specified time, and charge the lowest possible price. These objectives could most easily be met by professional cabinetmakers whose shops were equipped with labor-saving and cost-cutting woodworking machinery and whose location was easily accessible to the architects desirous of checking on the progress of the work. Arts and Crafts shops offering handmade furniture were rarely able to meet these requirements. Located in hard-to-reach suburban areas, staffed with idealistic and often self-taught craftsmen, and equipped with few labor-saving devices, these shops were not notable for efficiency, so that their products were often disproportionately expensive.

If the view of Wright and many of his colleagues differed so widely from those of other members of the Chicago Arts and Crafts Society, what was their debt to the Arts and Crafts movement? Answering this question, H. Allen Brooks pointed out that the acceptance of the Arts and Crafts philosophy helped foster the idea of a regional or national architecture, while its emphasis on the decorative arts and its appeal to the layman helped create a climate in which architects and clients were willing to engage experimental architects interested in designing a total environment.[44] Art historian Paul Sprague has made the point that the very existence of the Chicago Arts and Crafts Society made it easier for Wright and his fellow architects to convince their clients of the need for specially designed furniture and accessories. Indeed, according to Sprague, the architects themselves may have been inspired to start designing furniture for their integrated environments because of their involvement with the Society.[45]

By 1909, when Wright left Chicago for Europe, the influence of the Prairie school had begun to decline. By the time of America's entry into World War I, neither the Prairie architects nor the Arts and Crafts movement could claim strong support in Chicago. Among other reasons, many of the leading figures in both movements had moved away or died. Arts and Crafts proponents Oscar Triggs, Louis B. Easton, and D'Arcy Gaw had moved to California, and Ida Burgess and John Dewey to New York. Joseph Twyman and Madeline Yale Wynne had died. Frank Tobey had retired. Of the Prairie architects, Marion Mahony and Walter Burley Griffin were working in Australia, while Myron Hunt and Elmer Gray had moved to California.

After 1905 the Chicago Arts and Crafts Society had ceased sponsoring exhibitions and had become primarily a social group, with most of its lectures devoted to the topics of city planning or public school art.[46] In 1910 Chicago lost the publication of *House Beautiful* to New York, where that magazine filled its pages with illustrations of English and European-inspired period furnishings. Gustav Stickley's *The Craftsman* ceased publication in 1916 as a consequence of its publisher's bankruptcy.

Reviewing the exhibit of the Chicago Architectural Club in 1917, when colonial and Beaux Arts predominated, Thomas E. Tallmadge lamented:

> What is even more to be regretted is the absence of any evidence that the "Chicago School," as a potent style of architecture any longer exists. . . . Clients, the wives of whom at least, have received their architectural education in magazines edited in Boston and New York, now have turned back to pretty Colonial or fashionable Italian. Where are Sullivan, Wright, Griffin, and the others? The absence of the work of these men has removed from the show the last vestige of local color.[47]

By now these architects were no longer in the vanguard. America's involvement in the war interrupted the construction of housing and furniture, and by the time peacetime conditions were restored, it was the modernistic styles of European designers that captured the attention of those who had formerly patronized the Prairie architects.

PART IV

MODERNISM TO MIES

1918-1983

INTRODUCTION

The years between the end of World War I and the 1980s were marked by dramatic changes in Chicago's furniture industry. Expansion in the 1920s was followed by decline during the next decade, brought on first by the Great Depression and, after 1941, by America's involvement in World War II. In the postwar years many of the larger manufacturers relocated their factories in the South in search of cheaper labor and lower overhead costs. Nevertheless, the city retained a prominent position in the industry, though as a result of design and marketing innovations rather than volume of production.

As in the nineteenth century, architectural styles—particularly modern and international—once again exerted a strong influence on furniture, with several Chicagoans playing key roles in the evolution of modern furniture designs. Chapter 16 discusses some of the designers and manufacturers who popularized modernistic furniture between the two wars. Chapter 17 deals with Chicago's role as the Great Central Market during the same period and traces the establishment of several new enterprises, including ones engaged in what would become a major trend—the manufacture of metal and plastic furniture.

A striking development of the early postwar years in Chicago was the organization of a great variety of small furniture-making firms by European refugees and returned servicemen, often in collaboration with other members of their families. While many of these companies proved highly successful, only a relatively small number escaped absorption into larger concerns, especially during the 1960s and 1970s. Chapter 18 discusses overall directions in the city's furniture industry, including the revitalization of several old firms under new ownership and management, and the development of contract furnishings designed for commercial and institutional premises. The book concludes with an epilogue dealing with current Chicago furniture makers.

CHAPTER 16

WHAT IS MODERN?

1918 · 1945

In all ages, designers who expressed their own ideas rather than imitating models from the past considered their work "modern." Yet the term took on new meaning after World War I, when innovators in the plastic arts responded to vastly changed social conditions and new technology by creating objects whose forms and materials seemed to symbolize the spirit of their time.

Frank Lloyd Wright and other Chicagoans had urged for some time that buildings and interior furnishings be designed to reflect life in the twentieth century. It was not until after 1925, however, when the Exposition Internationale des Arts Décoratifs et Industriels Modernes held in Paris focused worldwide attention on the work of contemporary European designers, that furniture made in Chicago took on the striking characteristics commonly described as Art Moderne, Modernistic, and, more recently, Art Deco.

Rather than referring to furniture of recent construction, the term "modern furniture" came to be applied only to those pieces that were novel in form or in material and were not copies of historic styles. "In the decoration of our present-day interiors the past is dead, for the things of the past are out of harmony with the life of to-day," wrote Viennese-born New York furniture designer Paul T. Frankl, who, in his 1928 publication *New Dimensions,* explained how new attitudes as well as new surroundings were necessary to survive in a radically changed world full of new pressures and new technologies.

"Both our industries and our arts have undergone great changes due to invention and machinery," Frankl told his readers.

There is a great difference between the handicraft of today and that of the peasant of old. The main difference between these two is a difference in character. One is quite personal while modern work is almost impersonal. The old is complicated and fully carved and embellished with design, while modern work is severe and simple and gains its effects from its flat planes, sharp contrasts, angles, light and shadow. These aesthetic differences are differences in form. Yet the spirit and the individual touch are the same in both.[1]

The characteristic features of modern furniture were flat and unornamented surfaces, moldings (if used at all) sharply cut, and legs (previously treated as separate supports) running in an unbroken line from floor to hip and often to the top of the piece. Arms and legs of chairs flowed in one continuous sweep, with the back frame often becoming the rail. Upholstered furniture was low and deep and often had loose cushions. Plain, untufted surfaces accented line and fabric, and, with the base of the piece resting on the floor, legs were frequently eliminated. Tables were also lower, lighter, and smaller, geared for smaller-scaled rooms and for increasing informality. Wood was frequently finished with only a coat of wax, although cabinet pieces were often treated with paint or lacquer in brilliant primary colors, white, or black. Besides creating strong contrasts, the new furnishings reflected a growing awareness of other cultures, made possible by more rapid and widespread travel. This was accompanied by greater access to new materials, both natural and man-made.

The brilliant Oriental colors, primitive forms, and sharp contrasts advocated for modern interiors first made their appearance in Cubist and Futuristic paintings, and next in theater sets and costume and the world of fashion. The modern shapes in furniture, Frankl contended, were directly inspired by machine-age architecture, particularly its most visible manifestation, the modern skyscraper. "The skyscraper is certainly the monument of American business and enterprise . . . [that] has struck the keynote of our civilization," he wrote in *New Dimensions*.[2] To prove his point, he illustrated "skyscraper" bookcases and desks of California redwood with towers and set-backs that clearly echoed the urban skyline.

Thomas E. Tallmadge, asked by *House Beautiful* in 1929 to debate "Will This Modernism Last?," took an affirmative stance. Citing the New York Telephone Building and Number 333 North Michigan Boulevard in Chicago as examples of modern art, Tallmadge noted that this new movement was destined to succeed because it was sponsored by "the Brahmins." In his words: "With Europe and New York behind it, it will go over the top. Look about you and you will see it in our shops, hotels, clubs, and even now you can hear it knocking on our doors and prying open the windows of our homes."[3]

In 1929, when Tallmadge wrote his article, a number of architects and designers were already at work in Chicago creating modern furniture and interiors. Some, like early Arts and Crafts advocates Wright, Irving K. Pond, and Barry Byrne, continued to promote an integrated approach to design with an intensity that rarely wavered over the years. A few, like John Wellborn Root and Philip B. Maher, were sons of architects who had been considered progressive in their day. Others were newcomers, like Robert Switzer, Abel Faidy, and Hal Pereira, who designed furniture and interiors with an international ambiance and a theatrical flair or who, like Rue Win-

1920s MODERNISTS

terbotham Carpenter, Lucy Blair Linn, and Marianne Willisch, were among the leading female interior decorators of their day.

As in New York and Los Angeles, the first totally modern interiors were one-of-a-kind productions created by architects and decorators for new public spaces—offices and hotels, restaurants, clubs, and specialty shops—or the city apartments of the adventurous and avant garde. The influences of contemporary European and, in particular, French design were often evident, for many of the interior and furniture designs had been created by designers who traveled frequently to Europe or drew inspiration from publications illustrating the work of their celebrated Parisian counterparts. Their clients were also a cosmopolitan group—self-confident entrepreneurs who associated the new designs with a progressive image, or socialites who combined involvement in the arts with a taste for novelty and luxury. In the late 1920s imports from France and China, the latest from New York, and locally made interpretations of modernistic were, as one participant later observed, "all shaken together and served up . . . like some of those amateur early prohibition cocktails."[4]

During the 1920s most of the local experiments in the style were luxurious interpretations of modern French decorative art. One of the most stylish was commissioned in 1927 by women's clothier Stanley Korshak, who wanted to open a store modeled after New York's fashionable Bergdorf Goodman. Hiring Philip B. Maher, he took the architect to New York to see that installation, and then, accompanied by dress designer Hattie Carnegie, aboard the liner *Ile de France,* a floating exposition of modernism then in New York harbor. Convincing Korshak to "go modern," Maher designed the Blackstone Shop, a handsome structure that opened at 840 North Michigan Avenue in 1929. Its sleek modern furniture of gray wood and green satin, with lines echoing eighteenth-century pieces in the French Directorate style, had been designed by the architect and executed by Watson & Boaler.

The son of George W. Maher, Philip Maher (1894–1981) shared his father's belief in the value of ornament and kept abreast of the latest European trends. During the 1920s Maher frequently traveled abroad, touring England, the Continent, and Scandinavia. He pointed out that the majority of his clients during these years preferred their residences styled along classic European lines.[5] When called upon to design furniture, Maher skillfully blended clean lines and smooth surfaces with classical detailing.

Modern furniture was also a specialty of Holabird & Root, one of the first large architectural firms to maintain a staff of architects who designed interiors and furnishings. During the 1920s, when this department was headed by Johns Hopkins, the firm designed some of the city's most celebrated modern buildings, including the Chicago Board of Trade on LaSalle Street, the Palmolive (later the Playboy) Building, and the now demolished Diana Court at 540 North Michigan Avenue.

John Wellborn Root, one of the senior partners, had inherited his father's interest in unifying interior and exterior. Root "used to hover over the interior design department," recalled Harold Reynolds, who began designing furniture for the firm in 1924 and later headed this department.[6] In 1929, when Root was invited to prepare a model room for the landmark

"American Industrial Art, An Exhibition of Contemporary Design" at New York's Metropolitan Museum of Art, Reynolds assisted him in designing the furnishings for his entry, a woman's bedroom in soft tones of gray, blue, and pewter. Furniture designed by the firm was later put into pro-

The Blackstone Shop, ca. 1929.

The office of Philip B. Maher, 157 East Erie, in the 1920s showing armchairs designed by the architect and side chairs designed by his father, George W. Maher.
Violet Wyld and Philip B. Maher

duction by the Kroehler Mfg. Co. and distributed by Montgomery Ward & Co. Root's own apartment was furnished in crisp, sharp-edged modern style of gleaming chrome and glass.

In December 1927, two young Chicago architects, Robert Switzer (b. 1901) and Harold O. Warner, formed Secession Ltd., the first shop in the city to sell only modern decorative arts. Earlier that year Switzer, then employed by Holabird & Root, had accompanied Warner to Europe to study museum architecture preparatory to working on a proposal for renovation of The Art Institute of Chicago. Traveling by airplane, in itself an adventure, the two went to Vienna, visited the Bauhaus in Germany, and toured Scandinavia. Everywhere they were exhilarated by the modern decorative arts. "We bought so much stuff in Europe we had to go into business to pay for our trip!" recalled Switzer at eighty-two. "It was two weeks before Christmas when we sent out the invitations to the opening of our shop. They were all handwritten by Mrs. John R. Winterbotham and Mrs. Parmalee McFadden. They invited all of their friends—they were very well connected in artistic circles—and we sold out immediately. We started out with a bang!"[7]

To replenish their stock, Switzer started designing modernistic furnishings. With the assistance of three or four German cabinetmakers who lived in his North Side neighborhood, he created simple, geometric furniture. "Everything suggested the modern spirit," a student visiting the shop affirmed in 1929, drawing attention to numerous pieces that displayed an unmistakable "skyscraper influence." "A large cabinet, partially for display purposes was built in set-back formation. It was enameled in blue and white, the pattern suggesting the angularity of its structural form. . . . A large screen was constructed in set-back fashion."[8]

That year Switzer had a challenging commission that epitomized the new design ideas taking hold in the city and their rapid acceptance among the young. When Oak Park resident Walter S. Carr decided to move his family into the city, he hired Switzer to merge two apartments in the Lake Shore Drive Hotel into two separate but equal units, connected through

Advertisement from The Chicagoan, *July 14, 1928.*

Dining room in the apartment of Margaret Carr Sampsell, ca. 1934. The dining table and buffet of black lacquer and chrome was accompanied by twelve chairs, six upholstered in red silk, the remainder in white. The ceiling was bright blue.

their dining rooms. Carr and his wife resided in one of the apartments, which they furnished with pieces from their Oak Park home. Their son, Robert, and daughter, Margaret, lived in the other apartment, which was outfitted with new furniture custom designed by Robert Switzer.

In 1934 Switzer assisted Margaret Carr in furnishing her own apartment at 150 East Superior Street, following her marriage to Marshall G. Sampsell. A pioneer aviatrix and at the time editor of Marshall Field & Company's publication *Fashions of the Hour*, the stylish Mrs. Sampsell used furnishings designed by Secessionist Interiors in her living room and commissioned a dining-room ensemble from another young modernist, Robert Breckenridge. An interior designer who operated a shop at 840 North

Michigan Avenue, Breckenridge created a black lacquered table supported by tubular steel pillars that could be extended by the use of two smaller, matching tables. A black lacquered cocktail cabinet with a slight set-back formation held red glass tableware with bold black monograms. Furnished with scalloped-backed chairs—six white and six red—the room was "a model for the admirers of the modern manner in home furnishing," claimed the fashion editor for the *Chicago Daily News.*[9]

As might be expected, some of the most dramatic interiors of the late 1920s were devised by architects who specialized in theatrical or commercial design. One of the best known was Hal Pereira, who in 1929–30 created

Dining room in the apartment of Mrs. James M. Hopkins, 1530 North State Parkway, designed by Hal Pereira ca. 1929. The ebonized table and chairs are inlaid with stylized leaf blades of pewter.
Photograph by Hedrich Blessing

an exotic interior scheme for the sixteen-room apartment of Marjorie (Robbins Goodman) Hopkins, who had recently married railway supplies manufacturer James M. Hopkins. For their new duplex at 1530 North State Parkway, Mrs. Hopkins had assembled an eclectic mix of Chinese, French eighteenth-century, and modern furnishings. Robert Switzer had been involved in the first stage of the decoration of the apartment: "I was working up in the apartment for a long time, and Mr. Hopkins let me know he was tired of what he called this 'artsy' made-to-order work. One day I had an iron man up there doing special railings, and Mr. Hopkins got mad and wouldn't pay him. The iron man put a lien on the entire building. That's when I got fired."[10]

Hal Pereira, who worked for Granger & Bollenbacher and occasionally designed interiors for the movie palaces of Balaban & Katz, took over from there. Working together, Mrs. Hopkins and Pereira designed an entrance hall and dining room that was a dazzling symphony in ebony, silver leaf, pewter, and chartreuse.

Armchair of ebonized wood inlaid with pewter and upholstered with silver leatherette from the dining room of Mrs. James M. Hopkins.
h: 38" w: 17" d: 20"
CHS, gift of Mrs. Robert D. Graff, 1976

Telephone stand with ebonized banding from a suite designed by Abel Faidy for the Charles and Ruth Singletary apartment in 1927. The cabinet on top houses a telephone; the bottom door is the back of a slide-out chair.
h: 50¼" w: 18½" d: 14½"
CHS, purchase, 1979
Photograph by Abramson-Culbert Studio

The main table and side tables that could be used as adjuncts of it were Chinese in form with reedlike plant motifs extending up each leg to unfold in a stylized blossom near the apron. The tops of the tables and chair backs were inlaid with gracefully intersecting stylized leaf blades of pewter, modeled after the magnified plant forms popularized by recently published drawings and photographs of horticultural specimens. Silver leatherette, a new synthetic material, covered the chair seats, a folding screen with a scalloped top, and the half-round wooden rods that flanked the windows. Chartreuse walls were banded by a pewter dado etched with a hunting scene. Angular V-shaped wall fixtures and a pair of gray-toned paintings by Spanish modernist Pablo Pruna completed the scene.

"Mother saw the room as a stage set," explained Mrs. Hopkins's daughter; "she had a fairly theatrical sense of design."[11] The widow of playwright Kenneth Sawyer Goodman at the time of her marriage to James Hopkins, Mrs. Hopkins had often helped her first husband with the staging of his plays. "She was not a social butterfly type at all," said a friend, "but her friends meant a good deal to her and when she entertained them she really went all out. She was a bug on getting everything coordinated. Her favorite colors were a light chartreuse and a sort of grape-juice shade. She would concoct centerpieces out of green seedless grapes and eggplants. She had a zebra-skin rug on the black marble hallway floor, and when she gave big parties the waitresses had to wear black uniforms with zebra-patterned aprons, caps, and cuffs."[12] Pleased with the setting, Mrs. Hopkins maintained the apartment much as originally designed until her death in 1971. Pereira, with his brother, William, went on to design the Esquire Theatre (1937) before moving to Los Angeles, where he became a set designer for United Artists.

Another memorable Jazz Age ensemble was that designed by Abel Faidy (1894–1965) in 1927 for Charles and Ruth Singletary's small penthouse apartment at 1244 North Stone Street. The president of the Western Distributing Company, which he had founded in 1910 to handle subscription books, Singletary had recently married Ruth Palmer, a musician whose activities as a voice teacher and accompanist kept them active in artistic and musical circles.

The suite comprised a dining table and a breakfast table, each accompanied by four chairs, a settee, an armchair, a bookcase, a telephone stand, and a music cabinet. Carefully constructed of figured maple and satinwood veneer, and banded with black, the case pieces were based on a trapezoid form, while the backs of the dining chairs and settee assumed the jagged ziggurat shape becoming familiar in the forms of the city's new skyscrapers. Perhaps Faidy, like Paul Frankl, believed that the lines of the furniture in a modern apartment should harmonize with the cityscape visible through its windows.

To make the furniture fit comfortably into what was essentially one large room, Faidy used every inch of space. Each table base was fitted with cabinets and drawers; a low-backed chair merged into the base of the cabinet telephone-stand; and a cabinet, sectioned and grooved to hold sheet music, hung on the wall. The upholstered pieces, while more stylish than comfortable, pulled easily away from the tables to form groupings suitable for social activity.

A Swiss-born architect who had studied in England and Germany, Faidy had migrated to the United States in 1914. After four years in San Francisco, he moved to Chicago and spent the next nine years designing commercial interiors for the Guttmann Store Fixture Company and Taussig & Flech. After 1926, when he became a free-lance designer, he created interiors for showrooms, offices, and stores and supplied furniture designs to the city's major manufacturers, including S. Karpen & Bros. and the Howell Company, a producer of modern metal furniture.[13]

During the 1920s, luxurious modern interiors with a strong French accent were also the forte of Mrs. John Alden Carpenter and Mrs. Howard Linn, two of the city's best known interior decorators in the days when few society women worked. The daughter of manufacturer John H. Winterbotham and wife of a well-known composer, Mrs. John Alden Carpenter (1879–1931) combined modern furnishings adapted from Directorate and Empire models with bold contrasts of black and white when in 1928 she decorated the interior of The Casino, a private club on East Delaware Place, and developed a similar scheme for the Arts Club, then located in the Wrigley Building at 410 North Michigan Avenue.

Dining room of Mrs. Howard Linn at 55 East Cedar Street, in the 1920s. Mrs. Linn headed Au Paradis. The chairs are upholstered in leopard-design fabric; the table top is of an exotic burled wood; and the sideboard is of black lacquer. Mirrors form the panels of the accordion-pleated screen to the left.

A member of one of Chicago's pioneer families, Lucy McCormick Blair (1891–1978) operated an interior design firm called Au Paradis for several years after her marriage to realtor Howard Linn. A founder of The Casino and of the Chicago Junior League, Mrs. Linn was an accomplished horsewoman, an amateur actress, and one of the city's best-dressed women. In 1929 Mrs. Linn created what was described at the time as a "brilliant but unusually gracious" modern interior in black, pink, and silver for the "900," a restaurant in a new North Michigan Avenue apartment building. Notable among the furnishings, which had been largely purchased in France, were black lacquered dining chairs with pink leather seats whose backs had the number 900 entwined in a silver cipher.[14] Mrs. Linn's own dining room at the time was furnished with French furniture with accents of leopard skin.

Making their appearance in the modern interior by 1928 were simple handcrafted furniture and accessories imported from Sweden and Austria. That year, following an exhibition of contemporary Swedish art at The Metropolitan Museum of Art in New York, the Swedish Association of Arts and Crafts opened a retail shop in Chicago. This served as an outlet for the mellow wooden furniture of Carl Malmsten, then Sweden's foremost designer, along with glass, pewter, weavings, and other crafts whose simple patterns and graceful forms would soon be imitated by American manufacturers.[15]

Products of the Austrian Werkbund, Austria's semiofficial artists' guild, also became available in 1928 when Marianne Willisch began bringing annual exhibitions of that country's modern craft work to the United States. A young Austrian artist who had manned the Werkbund's shop in Vienna, Willisch had been invited to bring the crafts to America two years earlier when she assisted Chicagoans Mr. and Mrs. John Alden Carpenter in promoting Carpenter's "Skyscraper Ballet" in Vienna. The Carpenters had come to know Willisch when she served as their interpreter and contact with that city's cultural leaders. Impressed both by the young woman and by the Werkbund crafts, Mrs. Carpenter arranged for Willisch's Friends of the Austrian Werkbund to travel to the Arts Club of Chicago. This led to invitations from arts clubs and museums throughout the United States.[16]

In 1930 Willisch moved to Chicago, where she joined a group of artists and architects in organizing the Chicago Workshops, a cooperative modeled after the Austrian Werkbund. Opening a shop in Diana Court at 540 North Michigan Avenue, she began to sell modern furniture and crafts designed by members of the group as well as European imports. Gradually, as more and more clients asked her to furnish their interiors, she herself began to design and supervise the construction of furniture.[17] After working briefly with a Scandinavian cabinetmaker from Watson & Boaler, Willisch was associated for some fifty years exclusively with Alfred Mattaliano and later with his son, Frank, at Wells Furniture Makers.

Although experiments in modern design were just getting under way in 1927, the new philosophy was already causing controversy. In November of that year artists and architects gathered at the Palmer House to debate whether contemporary artists should completely discard the forms of the past and work only in the spirit of the modern movement. Modernists, represented by architect Irving K. Pond, sculptor Alfonso Iannelli, and Frank Sohn, president of the Art Directors Club, held their own against three of the city's most popular interior decorators, Marian Gheen, Maximilian H. Schackner, and James A. Kane, who pleaded the case of the conservative, historic styles.[18]

Although antiques and their contemporary adaptations continued to prevail in both the custom and mass markets (see page 299), the new movement made considerable headway during the next two years when a series of well-publicized competitions and exhibitions focused attention on modern work being produced by American designers and manufacturers. In Chicago the cause had been taken up by the Association of Arts and Industries, an organization founded in 1922 by artists and manufacturers to promote the training of industrial designers. After recession set in in 1927, furniture makers and retailers alike showed new interest in modern styling, seeing in the new movement an opportunity to stimulate lagging sales.

Serving as a catalyst was Adolph Karpen, head of S. Karpen & Bros. and a long-time supporter of modern industrial art. In 1901 his firm had been one of the first manufacturers to put Americanized versions of Art

Nouveau furniture into production (albeit with carving machines) after seeing the new designs displayed in Paris in 1900. In 1927, having viewed new European designs at the 1925 Exposition, Karpen once again led the way by donating $5,000 as prizes in a national Living Room Furniture Design Competition sponsored by the Art Alliance of America and by offering to put the winning designs into production. Entries, the rules stipulated, were to be original creations that embodied "beauty, utility and suitability for the American home."[19]

Sharing first prize in the contest, which drew over 400 entries, were J. B. Peters (Art Director for Famous-Players-Laskey film studios in Hollywood) and New York designer Richard Harrilland Smythe. Smaller awards were given to Kem Weber, set designer for the Paramount Motion Picture Corporation of Los Angeles, and modernist Paul Frankl. Despite the aura of Hollywood, most of the designs, *Good Furniture* reported, were characterized by straight lines and unornamented surfaces that possessed neither the "severity of the mission style" nor the "freakish and bizarre" aspects of pieces shown at the 1925 Exposition.[20] Most important, the contest brought designers in closer contact with industry. In fact, the *American Magazine of Art* even called the event "the first and constructive step towards interesting American designers to interest themselves in furniture design, a field hitherto neglected by creative designers due to the fact that the period motif held sway."[21]

During the winter of 1928–29, modern furniture available from American manufacturers was presented to the public in a well-publicized Expo-

Display of modern furnishings at Marshall Field & Company in 1929. Reproduced from Mildred May Osgood's thesis, "The Influence of the Skyscraper Upon Modern Decorative Arts," 1929.

sition of Arts and Industries held in conjunction with Mandel Brothers' department store. Accompanied by contemporary ceramics, textiles, and glass, the pieces were displayed in model rooms depicting a suburban home, a studio apartment, a modern elevator, and other typical interiors.[22] Modeled after similar exhibitions taking place at the Metropolitan Museum of Art, the American Designers' Gallery, and department stores in New York, the Chicago displays drew record crowds and, in the words of a *Good Furniture* reporter, proved "something of a revelation." Earlier that fall Mandel Brothers' had installed a gallery of model rooms featuring modern furniture available from American manufacturers designed by Paul Frankl and other celebrated designers.[23] A competitor, Marshall Field & Company, had begun exhibiting modernistic furnishings imported from France and Austria in the fall of 1927.

So successful were the exhibitions that the Association of Arts and Industries began raising funds for a long-talked-about School of Industrial Art.[24] S. Karpen & Bros., meanwhile, had put into production a whole line of modern furniture created for the firm by some of the country's most prestigious modern designers, including Kem Weber, Eugene Schoen of New York, and Edwin Josselyn of Boston. In 1929, commenting on a love seat designed by Schoen, *House Beautiful* pointed out that the piece "carries Mr. Schoen's initials and will be advertised as a Schoen piece."[25] The Kroehler Manufacturing Co. later followed suit, mass producing designs by Holabird & Root and New York industrial designer Gilbert Rohde.

Despite the growing interest in modern furniture in Chicago and other large urban centers, the majority of the country's manufacturers remained cautious. In September 1928, describing modern pieces displayed at the midsummer furniture market, *Good Furniture*'s correspondent reported: "The furniture and textile manufacturers have been watching the new-fangled designs from Europe and from American shops, waiting to see whether the American public would show enough interest to warrant taking the innovation seriously as a manufacturing proposition." But, he added: "Those who have given the matter serious thought feel that the new style is here to stay. . . . it gives every evidence of being a permanent development in America and one that will exercise a lasting influence on furniture."[26] This prediction was soon to be proven correct at A Century of Progress Exposition.

1930s MODERN

Held on the hundredth anniversary of the founding of Chicago, the 1933 World's Fair, known as A Century of Progress Exposition, celebrated the remarkable achievements that had taken place during the past century through the theme "Application of Science to Industry." The amazing developments in transportation, communication, electricity, and agriculture were shown in a setting of stark, modern buildings whose materials and designs, like the exhibits they housed, embodied the latest in architectural theory and technology.

While nearly all world's fairs had model houses glorifying the past or the future, A Century of Progress surpassed all previous ones in the number and scope of such houses. When the fair opened in 1933, there were thirteen model houses demonstrating the use of various building materials including lumber, brick, masonite, glass, and steel. A year later, when it reopened for a second season, the number had increased to twenty. Included among the dwellings were recreations of historic sites—Lincoln's boyhood home and Fort Dearborn—as well as glimpses of the way people would eventually live in the twelve-sided House of Tomorrow or the all-glass Crystal House, both designed by Chicago architect George Fred Keck, assisted by his chief draftsman, Leland Atwood.

Living room of George Fred Keck's House of Tomorrow in 1933 at A Century of Progress Exposition showing furniture designed by Leland Atwood. The wooden furniture was executed by Tapp, DeWilde & Wallace; metal pieces were executed by the Howell Company.
Photograph by Hedrich Blessing

Interiors were as diverse as the types of materials, ranging from rough-hewn furniture in the Cypress Log Cabin to the spare and shiny forms of steel and glass in the ultramodern Crystal House. Most, however, were assemblages of wood and metal, with straight-lined modern furnishings and graceful chairs of tubular steel designed by some of the country's best known modernists. Gilbert Rohde created furniture for the Design for Living House, while Wolfgang Hoffmann's work was shown in the "Lumber Industries House." Robert Switzer decorated the Common Brick House, and Marianne Willisch's Chicago Workshops created special furniture for the Steel House erected by General Houses in 1934.[27] The Kroehler Manufacturing Co. provided furniture designed for the Florida Tropical House, while Bowman Brothers and the Howell Company supplied tubular steel furniture for many of the houses and pavilions at the fair.

The simple, tasteful furniture and interiors shown at A Century of Progress created a whole legion of new disciples for modern design. Whereas previously only the luxury trade had been able to afford the best designs emanating from Paris, now the average American was being exposed to "modern" furniture that was mass-produced and therefore affordable. As Emily Genauer, author of *Modern Interiors Today and Tomorrow*, explained in 1939:

Up to the time of the Chicago exhibit, the consciousness of America's millions had not been appreciably dented by modern decoration. It had been little more than a phrase suggesting the arty ateliers of Paris and New York . . . beyond application to one's own normal scheme of living.

And it is for history now that they found modern decoration good. For the country-wide popularity of the new style dates from the time they came upon it accidentally in Chicago, admired its simplicity, its directness, its straight simple lines and chunky forms, and most of all, its patent livableness.[28]

By the end of the first season it was clear that a new era in furniture design had begun in the Chicago area. "Chicago . . . has come in for a heavy wave of enthusiasm for modern furniture since the Fair opened last summer," *Arts & Decoration* reported in June, 1934; ". . . State Street is taking modern decoration very, very seriously, with Marshall Field leading."[29]

Chrome-plated tubular steel chair designed by Leland Atwood and executed by the Howell Company for the House of Tomorrow at A Century of Progress Exposition, 1933.
h: 29" w: 19¾" d: 18½"
Elvehjem Museum of Art

Mahogany Classic Modern dining chair executed by Tapp, Inc. ca. 1940.
h: 36" w: 20" d: 18½"
CHS, gift of Jerry Gordon, 1983

At the time Marshall Field & Company was promoting what it called Livable Modern, a selection of contemporary furniture pieces from American manufacturers that were streamlined versions of traditional or classic forms. Executed in light-toned woods or combinations of wood, metal, and glass, they featured crisp, clean lines but lacked the severity of "pure" modern. In 1934, when *Arts and Decoration* published an article entitled

Tapp, DeWilde & Wallace, Inc. 2337 St. Paul, 1920–23; 1740 Arcade, 1924–35. **Tapp, Inc.** 1740 West Arcade, 1936–47; 2814 West Twenty-sixth, 1943; 314 North Michigan, 1949.

The company organized by Johan C. Tapp (1888–1939), Jack DeWilde, and William Wallace gained an enviable reputation for producing high-quality furniture inspired by eighteenth-century English designs. It also reproduced eighteenth-century French styles and, during the 1930s, introduced contemporary designs that were conservative in style and fabricated from light woods. Most sales came through the showroom the company operated in the Merchandise Mart between 1932 and 1942, although a large business was done in executing custom designs for architects and interior decorators.

Chicago businessman Alfred Vernon Jannotta became a partner in 1936. Following Tapp's death, Jannotta ran the firm and functioned as designer until America's entry into World War II, when he joined the Navy. He then sold the factory to designers Ben Davis and Jack Gladman, who merged it with a firm in Musoda, Wisconsin, that operated until 1949.

"The Modern Sweeps the Corn Belt," its writer conveniently identified the various furniture forms available through the department store: Classic Modern (simplified neo-classic forms), Chinese Modern (with enameled surfaces and Oriental details), Provincial Modern (made from native woods), Pure Modern, and far-out Modernissimus.[30] Classic Modern and Swedish Modern in blond woods soon became the forte of Art Institute graduate Edward J. Wormley, a Chicagoan who served as chief designer for the Dunbar Furniture Company, as well as of Tapp, Inc., which began offering designs by Ben Davis and Eleanor Forbes from San Francisco in addition to its fine reproductions of antiques.[31]

A subtle blending of old and new was also evident in interiors and furniture designed by architect Samuel A. Marx (1885–1964) at the peak of his career in the 1930s and 1940s. Sensitive to both modern and traditional expressions, Marx evolved a sophisticated style that was sleek yet sumptuous, personal yet contemporary. It both met the needs of his clients and reflected his personal philosophy. A *House Beautiful* editor who had interviewed Marx wrote:

> The Modern movement is constantly torn between what Mr. Marx terms intellectualized design—sharp, rational, and functional—and an opposing inclination toward traditional forms and manners. Sensitive to both expressions, Mr. Marx makes his style of architecture one that draws from both schools of thought. Pure Modernism he finds too naked and barren, too often lacking in quality. Pure traditionalism he finds outworn, repetitious, and dull. But his work is predominantly contemporary in that he employs a broad range of materials and is schemed to serve modern living needs.[32]

Like his Parisian counterpart Jean-Michel Frank, Marx eschewed cold steel and glass in favor of a richer range of natural and man-made materials. Combining old and new, he created uncluttered interiors in muted harmonies of cream, beige, and gray by bringing together such disparate ingredients as parchment, sharkskin, marbelized and tortoise-shell papers, lucite, mirror, hand-woven wool, and silver leaf. To blend dark-toned eighteenth- and nineteenth-century European antiques into his neutral color schemes, Marx often bleached the wood to make it lighter, a technique that came to be widely used as lighter toned "blonde" woods associated with contemporary Swedish furniture came into fashion.

Furniture used in a Marx interior was almost always specially designed, for most of his commissions consisted of elegant commercial spaces—like the Pump Room restaurant in the Ambassador East Hotel in Chicago, which he refurbished in 1937–38—or the homes and apartments of civic leaders and patrons of the arts who were unhampered by inadequate budgets. Shapes were straight-lined and geometric, with broad flat surfaces and cubic or circular silhouettes. Some were airy constructions of clear lucite, or supple combinations of exotic veneers and glass. Others were simple forms with unique surface treatments that, upon closer inspection, could be anything from lacquered paper to sharkskin. "What they are evolving is a sort of unctuous ornate Modernism that leans heavily on oriental ornament, mirrors and rare woods, and is undeniably handsome and effective," summed up *Interiors* in 1941.[33]

Furniture designed by Marx and his associates, Noel Flint and C. W. Schonne, was executed in the Near North Side shop operated by William J. Quigley, where as many as fifty craftsmen turned out reproductions of

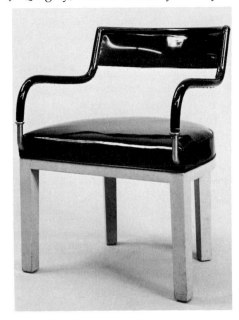

Armchair with black plastic upholstery and blond veneer legs designed by Samuel Marx and made by the William Quigley Co. for the Leigh B. Block apartment in 1944.
h: 30⅜" w: 23⅛" d: 17¾"
The Art Institute of Chicago, gift of Leigh B. Block

Veneered end table with glass top designed by Samuel Marx and made by William J. Quigley, Inc. for the Leigh B. Block apartment in 1944.
h: 25¼" w: 17¹⁵/₁₆"
The Art Institute of Chicago, gift of Leigh B. Block

Pfanschmidt & Quigley. 4 Monroe, 1906.
William J. Quigley & Co. 121 North State, 1907–9; 621 North State, 1910; 1045 Rush, 1913–20; 115–19 East Delaware, 1922–30.
William J. Quigley, Inc. 115–19 East Delaware, 1931–57.

William J. Quigley, owner of one of Chicago's most celebrated custom shops, began his career at the turn of the century with Edward C. Pfanschmidt & Co., a window shade and drapery firm. He became a partner and in 1906 president of the company. A year later Quigley started his own interior decorating firm, designing and fabricating furniture and draperies. In the 1920s the firm employed as many as 100 men and women, including cabinetmakers, upholsterers, and drapers. In addition to executing custom designs for architects like Samuel A. Marx, Quigley made reproductions of English antiques and adapatations of period furniture, branding such pieces with the company's name.

After Quigley's death in 1946, the decorating business was carried on by several of his employees for several years, although little furniture was manufactured. In 1964 Quigley's head cabinetmaker, Marijan Srnak, opened his own shop at 1821 West Irving Park Road, where he executed custom furniture and colonial adaptations impressed with his surname until 1981.

fine eighteenth-century English and French antiques as well as modern pieces. "We worked from the architect's drawings, used only the best materials, and made everything by hand," explained Marijan Srnak, a third-generation cabinetmaker who joined the firm after emigrating from Croatia in 1945. "Marx would bring customers to us. . . . we did the finest work in the city. . . . it was furniture for generations, not just a day," Srnak reminisced as he leafed through a thick album filled with snapshots of special pieces.[34] In 1964, after Quigley's went out of business, Srnak opened his own shop at 1821 West Irving Park Road, where he continued making many of Quigley's most popular designs for a coterie of loyal customers.

One of the first architects in the city to adapt modern designs to the business office, Marx received considerable publicity for the modern scheme he developed for the La Salle Street brokerage firm of A. G. Becker & Company in 1928.[35] When new construction almost ceased as a result of the Great Depression, Marx, like most architects, turned to modernizing shops, restaurants, hotels, and offices for owners who optimistically believed that a fresh and efficient-looking modern interior would bring in more customers. Later, when the economy revived, the work remained quite profitable.

S. J. Campbell Company. 1335 Altgeld, 1931–57; 1750 Wrightwood, 1957–67. *Campbell Custom Craft.* 2023 Carroll, 1967–72; 1500 Ogden, 1974–78; 325 North Wells, 1978–82; 400 N. Wells, 1982 to the present.

A native Chicagoan, Samuel J. Campbell had been an employee of the Valentine-Seaver Company for twenty-six years—serving as its president after 1927, when it became a division of the Kroehler Manufacturing Co.—before organizing his own firm and taking several key employees (George Johnson and Ira Jones, among others) with him. A few years later he was joined by his sons, Ralph O. and Bruce, who later became partners in the business. In addition to filling orders from decorators, furniture retailers, and mail-order houses, the company offered several lines, including Beidermeir-inspired Transitional furniture designed by Harold Faris in 1932 and Cinema Creations by Hollywood designers Jack Moore and Dick Pefferle, the latter introduced in 1947. Other designs were purchased from architects and free-lance furniture designers.

During World War II the company operated a parachute factory in Madisonville, Kentucky, which later became a men's shirt factory. Campbell acquired the inventory and many of the employees of the H. Z. Mallen Company in 1942. During the 1960s Camp-

"My husband did a lot of rejuvenating," recalled Mrs. James F. Eppenstein, whose late husband opened an office in Chicago in 1933.[36] A graduate of Harvard University who later studied furniture design in Berlin, Eppenstein (1899–1955) had left his father's manufacturing business to study architecture at the age of twenty-nine. Returning to Chicago, he designed and decorated several residences—including a stunning renovation of his own graystone at 1432 North Astor Street—but found it more profitable to modernize commercial structures. Revamping large hotels like the Shoreland, Chicago Beach, and others, Eppenstein designed not only the interior spaces but all of the furniture as well. Working from his drawings, the Garland Furniture Company executed the upholstered pieces, attaching labels that read, "Designed by James F. Eppenstein, Chicago."

During the 1930s, economic necessity inspired a host of other young architects to try their hand at furniture design and manufacture. Among them was L. Morgan Yost (b. 1908), who prepared some drawings for modern furniture at the suggestion of a friend. Yost related: "I peddled those designs freelance to any manufacturer who would look at them. The finest who used my work—and asked for more—was S. J. Campbell Co., then in the Merchandise Mart. Also there were Johnson Chair Co., Clementson Co. (office furniture) and Clemco Desk and others. . . . For quality seating pieces S. J. Campbell was tops."[37]

In addition to designing upholstered furniture, including some popular "Cogswell" reading chairs, Yost prepared sketches of radio cabinets for the Anton Clementson Company, whose owners were trying to interest the Zenith Radio Corporation in purchasing cabinets from them. He also streamlined the firm's line of office desks and created a bold new "Clemco" trademark. When the construction business picked up again later in the decade, Yost shifted his talents from furniture design to the fabrication of homes. Like many architects, he continued to design built-in furniture, which was built by the millworkers or cabinetmakers who worked on the interior of the buildings.

Two Chicago architects, Monroe Bowman (b. 1901) and his brother, Irving, had just begun to acquire a reputation for work in what was becoming known as the International style in the early 1930s when lack of commissions encouraged them to make modern metal furniture. Bowman Brothers had furnished interiors in the Chicago Board of Trade Building with items made of bent aluminum tubing and flat bars fabricated by Hungarian metalworker Adolph Newman. These designs were so well received (and the process and materials so inexpensive) that the Bowman Brothers purchased bending machines, hired several craftsmen, including Newman, and began to design and fabricate aluminum chairs and glass-topped steel, bronze, and brass coffee tables in a small shop in Evanston. After furnishing several interiors at the 1933–34 A Century of Progress Exposition, they continued to manufacture metal furniture under the trade name "Metalune" through 1936, selling it retail through Marshall Field & Company and wholesale through their architectural firm.[38]

Another architect who designed furniture was Bertrand Goldberg (b. 1913), who had studied at Harvard University, the Bauhaus in Germany, and Chicago's Armour Institute of Technology before opening an office in the city in 1937. A slow economy was one reason that he had time to design furniture for his architectural commissions. His decision to design all of the furniture in his own house grew out of his personal philosophy. Looking at photographs of some of his furniture designs, he recalled: "I believed that an architect should design everything. . . . it was all meant to be an invention. . . . I was looking for new uses for new materials that would lead to a better life."[39] Convinced that an architect could play an important role in shaping urban society, Goldberg adhered to the Bauhaus tradition in which an architect also functioned as an industrial designer. Since that time his dynamic originality has found expression in projects as diverse as the development of plastic freight cars for the railroad industry and the design of Chicago's unique twin-towered Marina City, a residential-commercial-recreational complex whose interior spaces radiate from a central core like petals on a flower.

It was the dean of the School of Architecture at Harvard who encouraged him to study at the Bauhaus. Goldberg arrived there in 1932, the last year of its existence. Returning to Chicago, he put his theories to work

bell manufactured desks and acquired Niemann, Inc., a small firm making upholstered furniture.

In 1967 the S. J. Campbell Company merged with Custom Craft, Inc., and its woodworking subsidiary, Craftsman Cabinet. In 1971 the S. J. Campbell name and design rights were sold to Ralph Morse of Grand Rapids, Michigan, who marketed furniture using that trade name until about 1980.

In 1974 Ralph O. Campbell bought Campbell Custom Craft from his partners and operated a small upholstering business until 1978. Since then he and his wife have used the name for their office furniture supply house. The firm no longer manufactures but subcontracts work to other firms.

Architect Bertrand Goldberg's molded plywood chair, 1938.
Bertrand Goldberg

designing furniture constructed of plywood, steel, plastic, and other modern materials. In 1938, experimenting with plywood, he designed a gracefully scrolled chair and settee, executed in Mexico, for display at the 1939 World's Fair in San Francisco. Marianne Willisch, at whose Diana Court shop Goldberg had spent many hours discussing modern design, urged him to continue making his Bauhaus furniture designs.

Continuing his experiments with shapes and materials over the next two decades, Goldberg designed furniture for his architectural projects and eventually for every room in his house. "Twenty-five or thirty years ago I went through a bicycle spoke period, making legs out of metal spokes," he recalled, describing the metal and acrylic pieces he developed. The airy, cone-shaped legs provided "enormous stability with less material," he explained, "but, their production proved quite labor intensive." Like all of his furniture, the pieces had been designed to take advantage of—indeed, even glorify—the capabilities of the machine. "Contemporary industrialization *transforms* the nature of materials through the machine. . . . we deform material and achieve strength and space," he explained, discussing his preference for using curvilinear shapes rather than the cubist rectilinear volumes commonly associated with modern design.[40]

In 1938, when Goldberg was designing chairs made out of bent sheets of plywood, his furniture was considered ultramodern, even radical. Yet, that very year, a new school had opened in Chicago whose experiments with new processes and materials would have considerable impact on furniture designed in the city. Its founders also followed the principles formulated at the Bauhaus.

THE NEW BAUHAUS

At the end of World War I, a national school of design known as the Staatliche Bauhaus was established in Weimar, Germany, following the amalgamation of two arts and crafts schools under the directorship of architect Walter Gropius. During the 1920s, the geometric and unornamented tubular steel furniture and industrial products designed by Marcel Breuer, Ludwig Mies van der Rohe, and others at the school attracted international attention, as did its objective of teaching students that art and life could be integrated by striving for "Art and Technology—a New Unity." The Bauhaus aspired to teach a methodology, a way of thinking, not a "style." The new industrial designer trained by the Bauhaus would exercise the same control as that exercised by artist / craftsmen of the past, but he would use technical knowledge rather than his hands.

In the early 1930s, following harassment from the Nazi government, Bauhaus teachers and students dispersed to various countries. Gropius, Breuer, and Josef Albers among others, came to the United States. Others went to France, Switzerland, and England. László Moholy-Nagy, a Hungarian artist who had been one of the school's outstanding instructors, was living in England when, in 1937, members of Chicago's Association of Arts and Industries invited him to come to their city to organize a new school modeled after the German Bauhaus. Determined to organize an industrial arts school that would stress the application of modern technology, the Association approached Walter Gropius, then at Harvard University. Gropius suggested that Moholy-Nagy be invited to come to the United States to establish the Bauhaus tradition there.

Accepting the Association's offer, Moholy-Nagy arrived in Chicago in the fall of 1937 with his wife, Sibyl, to set up the New Bauhaus in a vacant Prairie Avenue mansion that had been offered by Marshall Field III. Assembled in record time, both faculty and students represented a potpourri of geographical and educational backgrounds. Several members of the original Bauhaus—designer Hin Bredendieck, sculptor Alexander Archipenko, and artist Gyorgy Kepes among others—joined teachers drawn from local universities. Students came from all parts of the United States, attracted by the vibrant personality of Moholy-Nagy and the controversial nature of the Bauhaus Idea.[41]

When financial problems forced the New Bauhaus to close in June 1938 after only one term, Moholy-Nagy persuaded several colleagues to teach without pay. Chicago businessman Walter P. Paepcke, president of the Container Corp. of America and still a loyal supporter, provided financial backing and arranged for the experimental school to move into a large loft at 247 East Ontario Street. Renamed the School of Design of Chicago (and later the Institute of Design), it operated in those premises and later on North State Street until the fall of 1946, when it took over the large granite building at the corner of Ontario and Dearborn streets that had formerly housed the Chicago Historical Society.[42]

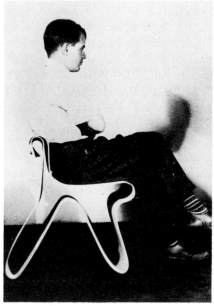

Molded masonite chair made by Donald P. Dimmitt while a student at the Institute of Design ca. 1950.
h: 32½" w: 19¼" d: 15"
Donald P. Dimmitt

Designer Charles Niedringhaus as a student at the School of Design sitting in an experimental chair of molded plywood made by Nathan Lerner ca. 1940.
Photograph by Nathan Lerner

Like the original Bauhaus, the School of Design attempted to unite art and industry by training a new kind of designer who had equal command of technology and form. To attain this objective, students took courses that emphasized learning by doing. Classes encouraged them to explore and combine color, form, material, and texture, while operating equipment gave them practical experience. "The Bauhaus Idea," explained Marianne Willisch, who taught evening classes in interior design at the school for twenty-five years, "was total design. It emphasized the equality of all creative designing. Its educational principles stressed a sensitive understanding of space and spatial relationships and a sound knowledge of materials. All arts—whether two-dimensional like painting or weaving—or three-dimensional like furniture and sculpture—were to be united in one harmonious whole within architecture, the master art."[43]

The same principles were to apply whether one was designing a matchbox, a chair, or a building. The end goal was machine art that was simple, impersonal, and functional. As Moholy-Nagy wrote in "Principles of Bauhaus Production" in 1926, "The Bauhaus workshops are essentially laboratories in which prototypes of products suitable for mass-production and typical of our time are carefully developed and constantly improved."[44] The ideal Bauhaus object was a functional unornamented form that could be mass produced using a minimum of material and labor. In the area of furniture design, that meant experimenting with new materials in order to create practical forms whose parts could be quickly and easily manufactured and assembled at a low cost. Moholy-Nagy believed that the design of one-piece objects (like molded chairs) that could be mass produced by machine would eventually eliminate the tedium of the assembly line and would thus improve conditions of work. Discussing chair designs, Moholy-Nagy explained: "The functional justification of a chair is seating. Its form, however, depends upon the materials, tools and skills. To wood, the industrial revolution added new materials: seamless steel tube, plywood and plastics and new means of production. Today we can produce new chair forms, such as seats using two legs instead of the usual four. Perhaps tomorrow there will be no legs at all—only a seat on a compressed air jet."[45]

In the realm of furniture design, students first put these principles into practice using plywood—a material that was strong, lightweight, and inexpensive—and the makeshift plywood-bending machine put together by two students. Curving wood, they found, gave it additional strength, while the large plywood sheets impregnated with thermoplastic glue offered more opportunity for experimentation than solid lumber. Used imaginatively, plywood could be curved into forms that eliminated joints, thus decreasing the time and cost involved in making chairs.[46]

When World War II broke out, Moholy-Nagy encouraged his students to draw upon their experiments with wood to assist local furniture manufacturers in developing substitutes for metal springs and other rationed materials. By 1942 his students had developed at least four types of "Z" and "V" springs using plywood and laminated wood that could be employed in making upholstered furniture.[47]

After 1938, when the Illinois Craft Project was established under the auspices of the Works Progress Administration (WPA) as a self-help program for unemployed artisans, School of Design students became regular workers in the shops that made furniture and related accessories for public buildings around the state. One of the first projects undertaken by the Craft Project (which was directed by John Walley) was the production, in conjunction with the Welfare Engineering Company, of molded plywood chairs and other furnishings for the Crow Island School in suburban Winnetka. Considered a radically modern building, the school had flexible classroom spaces, modular, movable seating, and other features inspired by the progressive educational theories of Carleton Washburne, superintendent of Winnetka's schools and promoter of the controversial Winnetka Plan for ungraded classes.

The furniture made for Crow Island School, like the building itself, was a product of collaboration among Washburne, the Chicago architectural firm of Perkins, Wheeler and Will (later Perkins and Will Partnership), and Eliel and Eero Saarinen, the Finnish architects who taught at the Cranbrook Academy of Art in Bloomfield Hills, Michigan. Lawrence Perkins, who inherited an interest in educational architecture from his father, Dwight Perkins, had initiated the collaboration, since his family had long been friends with the Saarinens.[48]

Together Eero Saarinen and Lawrence Perkins designed a chair for the school that consisted of a simple shell of molded plywood supported on legs of birch. Sturdy and comfortable, the chairs were easy to move around the room. But like many innovations, they were received with skepticism.

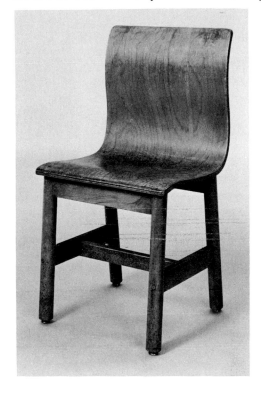

Molded and laminated birch chair designed for the Crow Island School, Winnetka, as part of a 1940 WPA Craft Project by architects Lawrence B. Perkins and Eero Saarinen.
h: 31⅝" w: 16" d:13"
The Art Institute of Chicago, gift of Crow Island School, Winnetka, Illinois

Reminiscing about these events in 1965, John Walley recalled "the crafts-men's disgust with the advanced design and techniques required for the furniture, which finally turned to pride when they were invited to the opening of the school and congratulated by appreciative parents and students who liked the results of all the work."[49]

Although the members of the Institute of Design were relatively few in number, their influence on the design of furniture manufactured in Chicago and elsewhere was considerable. Instructor James Prestini, best known for his classic, smoothly turned wooden bowls, won numerous awards for his designs in the 1940s and 1950s and later for his sculpture. Nathan Lerner, a New Bauhaus student who stayed on to head the school's Product Design workshop, achieved national recognition for the "Do-It-Yourself" designs and kits done for *Popular Home* magazine during the 1950s. Alumni Charles Niedringhaus and Donald Dimmitt later worked as designers, while Edgar Bartolucci, Jack Waldheim, Davis Pratt, and Harold Cohen all became furniture manufacturers in the 1950s. Donald Pettitt and Richard Schultz both went on to design furniture for Knoll International. In the decades after the war their innovative designs would find their way into the work-shops of many major manufacturers and would influence generations to come.

THE GREAT CENTRAL MARKET

1 9 1 8 - 1 9 4 5

The early postwar years were marked by some developments that would have long-range consequences for Chicago's furniture industry. First, new immigration laws cut off what had been a continuing source of woodworkers emigrating from Germany, Italy, Scandinavia, and the old Austro-Hungarian Empire. Second, the evolution of modernistic styles and the introduction of new materials like chromed steel and initial forms of plastic in the late 1920s and early 1930s began to bring about fundamental changes in style and production techniques. Before this line of development could reach full realization, however, the stock market crash of 1929 and the subsequent depression would put many manufacturers out of business. Although this led to a decline in the city's importance as a furniture manufacturing center, Chicago's role as a central market grew.

During the prosperous years of the 1920s, the output of Chicago's furniture factories increased dramatically, responding to a building boom that filled the city's downtown with new skyscrapers and encircled it with a ring of new residential, institutional, and commercial buildings. Meanwhile, the out-of-state market for Chicago furniture also expanded as the population of the Western region of the country—especially of California and the Southwestern states—grew steadily.

In 1920, some 250 furniture factories located in Chicago turned out as much as one-fifth of the furniture made in the United States.[1] Twice yearly—in January and July—wholesale furniture manufacturers offered new lines to retail dealers in markets sponsored by the Chicago Furniture Manufacturers Market Association. By then, at least fourteen buildings of various sizes could be found along Michigan and Wabash avenues housing samples of furniture made by factories located in a crescent formed around the lake by the states of Illinois, Michigan, Wisconsin, and Indiana.

While the number of buildings created plentiful choices, their scattered locations made it inconvenient and expensive for prospective buyers to visit every one of the showrooms. Since the 1890s various schemes to centralize the showrooms had been proposed, but none proved successful until 1922, when William H. Wilson, a Chicago furniture salesman, enlisted the help of investment banker Lawrence H. Whiting and his brother, Frank. Working with local furniture manufacturers, the men developed a plan to bring all of the city's wholesale furniture operations under one roof into a mammoth exposition center to be called the American Furniture Mart.

The huge Merchandise Mart, which opened in 1930, became an additional showcase for the city's furniture manufacturers as well as a source of competition for the American Furniture Mart.

The American Furniture Mart at 666 North Lake Shore, ca. 1926. The imposing tower with its blue tiled roof became the symbol of Chicago's preeminence in the furniture industry.
David R. Phillips, Chicago Architectural Photographing Company

Organized by Wilson and financed and managed by the Whitings, the American Furniture Mart was to be the world's largest building devoted to a single industry. Sixteen stories high and enclosing over a million feet of exhibition space, the huge terra-cotta and brick structure that rose at 666 North Lake Shore Drive between Huron and Erie streets covered an entire city block. When it opened in July 1924 it was 100 percent rented and housed 700 exhibitors from 31 states and 259 cities.[2] Within the first year 15,545 buyers registered to inspect and place orders for furniture.[3] Only two years later, a new addition with a thirty-four-story tower was completed, increasing the total floor space to nearly two million square feet.

The success of the American Furniture Mart, whose showrooms were

Butler Specialty Company. 1124 North Wood, 1930–32; 1714 North Damen, 1932–33; 1015 North Halsted, 1933–41; 8200 South Chicago, 1941 to the present.

The name Butler Specialty Company was first used in 1927 when Philip N. Daniels began manufacturing juvenile furniture under the trade name Kiddie Line. Three years later he was joined by salesman Martin Fainman (1903–1967), who suggested that the firm make novelty furniture. In 1933 Daniels sold his share of the company to Fainman and Harry Bergman (b. 1898), who had joined the company one year earlier.

Despite the depression, the company grew steadily during the 1930s under the direction of Bergman, who took over product design, and Fainman, who had charge of sales. At first the line consisted of wall racks, magazine baskets, and radio benches. During the late 1950s and early 1960s, the company gradually added larger pieces of accent furniture such as hall consoles and curio cabinets. Over the years Butler's mainstay has remained traditionally styled medium-priced furniture. Curio cabinets, consoles, and miscellaneous occasional pieces still make up the bulk of the firm's production, with combination lamp tables a relatively new addition. In 1982 the company began to market rattan furniture, which is executed in the Phillipines following its own designs.

Approximately 150 people are employed in Butler's factory and warehouse. A branch factory, opened in Paris, Illinois, in the 1960s, was closed

open year-round and not just during market months, established Chicago as the undisputed center of the country's wholesale furniture trade. Surveying the industry in 1925, the Chicago Association of Commerce reported: "The economy of centralization is obvious. It establishes the necessary contact cheaply, quickly and effectively. The buyer can get the most detailed information, the most useful suggestions and the most modern hints on merchandising. And he can pass on the effect of this contact to his trade." Noting that 65 percent of the country's furniture factories and more than 50 percent of its furniture retailers were located within 500 miles of Chicago, the report concluded that it was "safely estimated that 70 percent of the nation's furniture business is transacted in Chicago."[4] In 1928, manufacturers accounting for 90 percent of the country's furniture production were represented at the Chicago markets, where they did almost one-fourth of their total business for the year.[5]

The American Furniture Mart, complemented by local wholesale merchants such as Marshall Field & Company, Carson Pirie Scott & Co., and Butler Bros., offered the country's largest concentration of home furnishings samples available in a single city. Retail merchants could outfit an entire furniture or department store in the course of one trip to Chicago. Furthermore, they could have their goods delivered in record time. With forty railroad lines terminating in the city and over 2,500 freight cars leaving daily, furniture shipped from Chicago to the most distant parts of the United States could be expected to arrive in from three to nine days.[6] In 1926, for example, the Chicago Furniture Forwarding Company operated by the Chicago Furniture Manufacturers' Association loaded 3,324 railroad cars with furniture headed for the far West and Southwestern states. This area, with growing populations and agrarian economies, remained a major market, with 722 cars destined for California, 398 for Texas, and 271 for the Oregon-Washington area.[7]

Two years after the American Furniture Mart had opened, Lawrence Whiting began to promote a similar center for agriculture to be built on Wolf Point on the north bank of the river. Instead, Marshall Field & Company appropriated the idea and built a huge structure to house its own wholesale operations as well as offices and display areas to be rented out to other wholesalers of clothing and household goods. Covering two city blocks between Wells and Orleans streets, the eighteen-story Merchandise Mart opened in 1930. With four million square feet of floor space—the equivalent of ninety-three acres—it was the "biggest building in the world."[8]

The centralization of sales and distribution facilities helped manufacturers to distribute their products to all sections of the country while making it possible for retailers to receive their goods promptly, in good condition, and at reasonable cost. Within Chicago, however, furniture factories continued to be scattered throughout the city and differed widely both in size and in the types of products they manufactured. A survey conducted by the Chicago Association of Commerce in 1924 revealed that there were 294 furniture plants in Chicago, with a total of 15,715 employees. Of these firms, 49 made upholstered furniture, including 35 who made davenport (sofa) beds (named after a Boston upholsterer named Davenport) and 7 who made this item exclusively; 21 manufactured metal furniture; 19 made office furniture; 20 turned out case goods and dining-room furniture; and 65 made novelty furniture. In addition, 16 factories created rattan and reed goods, 8 made chairs, 7 manufactured tables, and 13 made only parlor frames.[9]

Although a few of the firms employed between 300 and 1,000 workers, the industry as a whole was still composed of a large number of small companies. Many were family businesses operated by a team of brothers or by more than one generation. As in the preceding century, the majority of the factory owners and most of their workers were foreign born. While most of the woodworkers were German, others had come from Italy, Lithuania, Holland, and Scandinavia. The upholsterers included large numbers of Poles, Scandinavians, Bohemians, and Germans. In contrast to earlier decades, however, a growing number of women were to be found in the ranks of the semiskilled and skilled, performing such tasks as assembling, upholstering, and finishing.

in 1982. Harry Bergman now serves as chairman of the board, while his son, Burton Bergman, is president. Burt Fainman, son of Martin Fainman, serves as executive vice-president, secretary, and treasurer.

Old-timers active in the furniture business in 1937, representing the following companies: (standing) Churchill Cabinet Co., Chicago Furniture Forwarding Co., S. Karpen & Bros., Lyon Furniture Mercantile Agency, and Valentine-Seaver; (seated) Columbia Feather Co., Kruissink Bros. and (unknown).
CHS, gift of the Chicago Furniture Manufacturers' Association

Beginning in 1921, a series of laws limiting immigration into the United States began to reduce the number of foreign-born workers entering the furniture industry, while the percentage of American-born workers grew as second-generation craftsmen began to take their fathers' places. "Among its polyglot citizenry are many artisans of the old world who have taught their craftsmanship to the younger generation," the *Furniture Journal* commented in 1922, adding that "as a reservoir for trained labor, Chicago stands unexcelled."[10]

In the larger factories, assembly-line procedures, combined with increasing automation, allowed the use of numerous semiskilled and unskilled workers. Many of the tasks, however, including the construction

Kruissink Bros. 273 South Canal, 1887–88; 29–31 North Jefferson, 1889–1906; 306–8 South Clinton, 1907–14; 3428 South LaSalle, 1915–53.

Ten years old when he arrived in Chicago from Holland in 1876, Martin J. Kruissink (1866–1960) worked in a sash, door, and blind factory before becoming a marker and scroll sawer at Clark Brothers chamber furniture factory, where his older brother, John, was also employed. When that firm closed, the two brothers went into business together making bookcases. John handled the bookkeeping and sales, while Martin took charge of production. During the period 1907–14 a furniture carver named Theodore Mack shared the rented space Kruissink Bros. occupied. Mack carved the famous Charlie McCarthy dummy for ventriloquist Edgar Bergen.

When orders for bookcases started to decline in the 1920s, the company turned to desks and, in the 1930s, occasional furniture. Working mostly in mahogany, it made wall shelves, tea carts, a variety of small tables, pier cabinets, and credenzas in traditional forms designed by Martin Kruissink. In 1928 Martin bought out his brother's interest in the company. His own two sons, Martin H. and John W., who had worked in the factory in spare time while in school, later joined the family business full time and gradually took over the firm. Martin handled materials and production, while his younger brother, John, was in charge of design and sales. During the 1940s their sister, Florence, joined the firm as treasurer.

At its peak, just after World War II, Kruissink Bros. employed fifty workers. However, as costs of labor and lumber increased, the company found it could not maintain its hallmark of original design and workmanship at competitive prices, and in 1953 it went out of business. The factory was later sold to the city and was demolished to make way for the Dan Ryan expressway. The company's products were unmarked.

of samples, the setting and operating of certain machines, and some of the finishing operations, still required a great deal of skill. Within the industry, wages varied greatly and were dependent upon sex as much as upon skill. In 1929, for example, the average weekly salary of a hand-carver was $42.66. A male cabinetmaker averaged $28.44, while a male upholsterer made $33.61 and a female upholsterer $16.93. Of all American furniture workers, those working in Illinois were the highest paid. In 1929 males averaged $30.21 per week while females received $21.17, nearly double the $17.61 paid to males and the $10.00 paid to females employed in factories in North Carolina.[11] However, the cost of living was also lower in that state and in the South in general. At the time, a loaf of bread cost only $0.07 and a standard Ford automobile $500.[12]

Furniture sales reached a peak in 1927, followed by a dramatic drop during the Great Depression. While many Chicago furniture makers went out of business, others managed to survive by reducing their work force, by instituting wage and salary cuts, and by modifying their lines to produce what people could afford. During the early 1930s the production of small inexpensive pieces of furniture and metal goods increased in importance, while sales of wooden case goods and hand-woven wicker declined. Novelty furniture (once called fancy cabinetware)—such as curio cabinets, magazine racks, baby cribs, and radio and phonograph cabinets—were turned out in record numbers, keeping hundreds of workers employed and maintaining Chicago's position as a major furniture producing center. By 1941 the city outranked all others in total pieces of furniture produced. That year Chicagoans made nearly three million pieces of furniture, averaging over 11,500 items each working day.[13]

Chicago's largest manufacturers relied heavily upon volume sales to retailers and upon "contract" sales to commercial enterprises, architectural firms, and mail-order houses to keep their prices competitive and their workmen steadily employed. Firms furnishing hotels, restaurants, theaters, and clubs dealt directly with factories, arranging for the production of durable, stylish furniture constructed to withstand commercial or institutional use. By the 1920s S. Karpen & Bros. and the Kroehler Manufacturing Co. had special departments to handle contract sales, while the output of a few of the smaller firms, like the Garland Furniture Company, consisted almost entirely of executing custom furniture for architects who specialized in commercial work. Similarly, custom "cuttings," or patterns, were created especially for the many mail-order houses with headquarters in Chicago.

Large upholstered pieces and case goods made for Sears, Roebuck & Company, Montgomery Ward & Co., Spiegel, and the Hartman Furniture & Carpet Co. were occasionally shipped to customers directly from the factory. In 1941, for instance, when Montgomery Ward & Co., introduced a new line of high-quality period adaptations called the Hallmark collection, one of the company's selling points was its "Ship-Direct plan."[14] By buying large quantities, the mail-order firm was able to offer the furniture at prices lower than those charged by retailers for similar pieces. Direct shipping also reduced the cost of overhead and handling, since customers paid the freight charges and unpacked the furniture themselves.

Between the two World Wars, the production of upholstered furniture was dominated by four large wholesale producers: S. Karpen & Bros., Fenske Bros., the Kroehler Manufacturing Co., and the Pullman Couch Company. Of this group, the firm with the largest factories and the longest history was S. Karpen & Bros. (see page 72).

Early in the century S. Karpen & Bros. had become one of the largest upholstered furniture makers in the United States as a result of innovative product design, efficient manufacturing techniques, and an effective marketing campaign that carried the Karpen name beyond the ken of furniture showrooms directly to the American consumer. During the next two decades, Karpen continued to initiate designs and marketing techniques that were imitated by other firms and soon became standard practice in the industry.

After World War I, the company developed a national network for the distribution of its furniture by building additional factories closer to major markets. While the Chicago and Michigan City factories continued to supply the Midwestern and Southern regions, a new factory erected in 1919 in Long Island City, New York, and another opened in 1927 in Los Angeles, California, gave the firm a competitive edge on the two coasts. Although retailers continued to order through catalogues or by visiting the Karpen Building, their orders could be filled in less time and shipped at less cost from the nearest Karpen factory.

Like the Karpen brothers, the family members operating Fenske Bros. exhibited considerable talent in both the manufacture and sale of furniture. Established in 1892 by upholsterer Ernst Fenske and his brothers, Albert, Fritz, Gustav, Otto, and Robert, the firm stressed value, durability, good design, and expert workmanship in its appeals to the trade. By 1923 the firm had three factories operating within the city and showed its samples

UPHOLSTERED FURNITURE

Pullman Sleeper made by the Pullman Couch Company ca. 1942. The wooden frame shows the influence of English Georgian styles, particularly those of cabinetmaker George Hepplewhite. Schnadig Corporation

in the new Fenske Building at 1315 South Michigan Avenue. In 1942, when the firm employed 160 men and 40 women, it was producing an average of 2,500 chairs and sofas a month, or 30,000 per year.[15] Despite such impressive figures, neither Fenske Bros. nor S. Karpen Bros. was able to regain its momentum after the war. Fenske Bros. went out of business in 1955; S. Karpen & Bros. became part of the Schnadig Corporation in 1952.

Both the Kroehler Manufacturing Co. and the Pullman Couch Company were substantial businesses by the late 1920s, due in large part to their owners' shrewdness in developing and marketing modern versions

Upholsterer completing an overstuffed armchair at the Pullman Couch Company in 1920. From Fort Dearborn National Bank Industrial Bulletin *no. 3.*

Louis XIV style chair with carved frame made in the Doetsch & Bauer factory ca. 1950. The needlepoint seat and back were worked by Mrs. Johanne Bauer; the upholstery was completed by the Chicago firm of Borgwardt & Ernst.
h: 44" w: 26²⁄₂" d: 22½"
Mr. and Mrs. Charles Bauer

of the patent folding bed lounge, the davenport bed. In 1909 Peter E. Kroehler, president of the Naperville Lounge Company, developed a foldable bed section with a removable mattress kept beneath the seat of a davenport. He brought out two models, calling the one that extended lengthwise the Unifold, and the other, which extended sidewise, the Duofold.[16] Foreseeing a widespread market for the cleverly hidden beds, Kroehler began to purchase companies holding similar patents. He had acquired four such firms by 1915, when he renamed his operation the Kroehler Manufacturing Co.

Over the next fifteen years, Kroehler bought other factories making upholstered furniture in California, Ohio, Michigan, and Canada to assure economical distribution. In 1927, to round out operations by offering furniture in all price brackets, Kroehler purchased the Valentine-Seaver Co. of Chicago, a firm that had been engaged in making high-quality parlor furniture since 1899. Manufacturing continued at Valentine-Seaver's Northwest Side plant until 1932, when operations were consolidated in Naperville. The company's main showrooms remained in the American Furniture Mart, where Kroehler had been the first to lease an entire floor.

The founders of the Pullman Couch Company—Jacob L. Schnadig and his brother-in-law, Julius Kramer—also attributed their success to the popularity of the davenport bed. As Schnadig later related, he and Kramer had made little profit in the upholstered furniture business until 1906 when they purchased the patent for a new "inner mattress" davenport whose seat revolved to reveal bedding in a box that formed the seat. After perfecting the mechanism and standard configuration, Schnadig and Kramer put it into production using a variety of popular innovations. "We have, undoubtedly, produced more improvements in the davenport bed field than all others," Schnadig wrote in 1927.[17] At the time, he could claim credit for putting on the market the "first successful inner mattress davenport bed, the first loose cushion overstuffed davenport bed, the first chair and rocker to match the davenport bed, and the first cane davenport."[18] Best known was the "Pullman Sleeper," introduced in 1936.

Other sizable firms manufacturing upholstered furniture for the mass market included the Continental Upholstering Co., the A. D. Gorrell Co., August Hausske & Co., Hollatz Bros. Co., International Furniture Co., Ketcham & Rothchild Co., H. Z. Mallen & Co., the National Parlor Furniture Company, and the Perfect Parlor Furniture Company.

While many of these manufacturers employed cabinetmakers who made frames for their sofas and chairs, the production of wooden frames and components remained a viable business. Zangerle & Peterson, still the city's largest producer of parlor frames, employed about 100 workers in its factory on North Clybourn Avenue. Next in size was the Doetsch & Bauer Company, operated by Joseph Doetsch, a former partner in the Northwestern Parlor Suit Co., and Carl Bauer, who had worked as a carver for the Kroehler Manufacturing Co. Located on Altgeld Street after 1914, the firm offered frames in a wide variety of forms ranging from traditional to modern. Elaborately carved components were still made by individual woodcarvers or establishments such as the American Wood Carving Company, operated by John P. Karowsky, which supplied carved birch legs, crests, and ornament for parlor furniture, pianos, and caskets.

Although modernistic styles from Europe were beginning to be emulated by the city's avant garde (see page 271), the largest proportion of the furniture made in Chicago's factories was in traditional styles like Chippendale, Queen Anne, or Louis XVI. After 1924, when the Metropolitan Museum of Art in New York opened its American wing displaying furniture in elegantly appointed room settings, interest in seventeenth- and eighteenth-century Early American furniture soared. The restoration of Colonial Williamsburg, Virginia, in 1926 and the creation of Greenfield Village in Dearborn, Michigan, in 1929 also brought examples of the furniture used by the country's earliest settlers to the attention of the average American.

The preference for good reproductions of period furniture, which had been limited to the style-conscious before World War I, now began to dom-

Doetsch & Heider Co. 816–26 Dunning (later Greenwood), 1907–9.
Doetsch & Bauer. 1534–44 North Greenwood, 1910–13; 1534 Altgeld, 1914–57.

A cabinetmaker who moved to Chicago in 1886, Joseph Doetsch (1855–1906) served as president of the Northwestern Parlor Suit Co. and the Columbia Parlor Frame Co. before establishing a factory to manufacture furniture frames with August Heider and Carl Bauer in 1907. When Doetsch died only a year later, Carl Bauer (1873–1947), a woodcarver who had come from Norway in 1899, bought Heider's interest. In the late 1940s Doetsch & Bauer started manufacturing Victorian and French Provincial occasional tables and wall shelves in solid maple and solid mahogany in addition to frames for upholstered furniture.

While Bauer headed the firm until his death, Doetsch's daughter, Anna, served as secretary-treasurer and also traveled in the East selling the company's frames. Bauer's son, Valentine, joined the firm in the 1920s and managed the office. A younger son, George, an architect, took charge of sales and assisted his father as designer. The company was operated after Carl Bauer's death by Valentine and George Bauer and Charles Bauer, Valentine's son. Frames made by the firm were impressed with the company name.

inate factory production. Reporting on style trends in the Chicago and Grand Rapids markets in 1931, *Good Furniture and Decoration* editor Athena Robbins noted the prevalence of "the continuously popular Georgian styles and the Early American," and their effect on upholstered furniture.

> This favor for the eighteenth century designs is appearing oftener than in former years in the displays of upholstered chairs and sofas. The characteristic shapes, fabrics and carvings of these historical periods are being developed often with admirable authenticity, even in those lines which have always had a distinctly commercial flavor. Here is a concrete indication of that large class of women who are becoming more enlightened concerning furniture periods and more insistent in their demands for correct styles.[19]

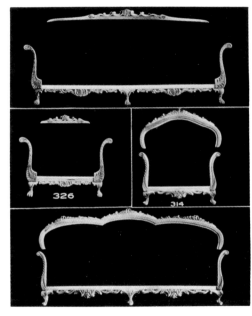

Hand-carved birch parlor furniture frames illustrated in the 1929 Trade Catalogue *of the American Wood Carving Company.*

Adaptation of a seventeenth-century English armchair made by S. Karpen & Bros. in the 1920s. The firm derived many of its designs from museum pieces.
h: 51½" w: 26" d: 20"
Dr. and Mrs. James Fisch

By the 1930s, the various historic revival styles had been categorized as Traditional or Provincial. Traditional styles, which drew their names from a monarch (Louis XVI), an epoch (the Renaissance), or a celebrated craftsman (Chippendale), had been defined as those classic designs associated with fine workmanship and wealth. Their colonial interpretations—which tended to be made by less skilled craftsmen using regional materials and cruder tools—made up the Provincial styles, whose names reflected geographical areas or the people who first produced them (French Provincial, Early American). Most popular were the eighteenth-century English styles grouped together as Georgian, and the various interpretations of American colonial design referred to as Early American.

Doing its best to clarify the terminology and educate furniture salesmen and their customers in the fine points of correct styling was the venerable Seng Company of Chicago, the country's primary manufacturer of furniture hardware and fixtures. In 1917 Seng had begun publishing a handy little reference book, *Seng Furniture Facts,* which described and illustrated the characteristics of the various historic styles. By 1938 some 50,000 copies were being distributed annually.[20] That year, celebrating its fiftieth anniversary, the Chicago Furniture Manufacturers' Association commended Seng on its contribution to education in design and pointed with pride to the medley of styles available from local manufacturers. "Today, Chicago furniture manufacturers borrow wisely from the past . . . reproducing in quantity distinctive French and English traditional pieces, fine Colonial adaptations, early provincial furniture from France and America, and even that which was best in the Victorian—the medallion-backed chairs, and sofas with carved fruit groups cresting their top rails."[21]

During the 1920s and 1930s, much of the upholstered parlor furniture made in Chicago factories combined carved wooden parts with period detailing and bodies that were "caned" or "overstuffed." If caned, backs and arms were inset with sheets of machine-woven cane, while the seats were upholstered with leather or fabric. Overstuffed pieces tended to be plump and massive, with rolled or flaring arms. Spring-filled seats and backs were deep, smooth, and broad, much like those found in the automobiles of the day.

The resemblance to motorcar seating may have been intentional rather than accidental, judging from A. D. Gorell Co.'s advertisements for "full automobile seat" parlor suites appearing in the 1920 *Furniture Journal.*[22] At the time, S. Karpen & Bros. was doing a brisk business supplying seats for buses and railroad cars through its Transportation Seating division. Looking back two decades later, the influential industrial designer Walter Dorwin Teague was to claim, "The automobile manufacturers have made, in the past few years, a greater contribution to the art of comfortable seating than chair builders had made in all preceding history."[23]

CASE GOODS AND CHAIRS

After 1900 the number of factories producing wooden cabinet ware in Chicago declined steadily as the cost of raw materials and labor increased. At the same time, changes in taste and technology modified the forms of furniture demanded by the public, hastening the demise of some specialty makers while stimulating the rise of others. During the 1920s the popularity of bridge playing, cocktails, the radio, and the phonograph led to the

Great Northern Chair Co. 2500 West Ogden, 1918–53.
Shelby Williams. 2500 West Ogden, 1954–67; 325 North Wells, 1968 to the present.

The Great Northern Chair Co., a firm specializing in inexpensive wire and bentwood chairs for restaurant and cafeteria use, was founded in 1918 by Joseph Silverman, previously president of the Great Northern Plating Works and a manufacturer of metal goods. The company was small at first, employing some thirty people in the production of Vienna-style bentwood chairs in its Ogden Avenue factory. Eventually the firm employed 175 workers and produced more than 100,000 chairs per year.

During the 1930s Silverman's son Rudy and his son-in-law, Saul Shapiro, took over the firm. In 1954 it was purchased by designer Sam Horwitz and Manfred Steinfeld, former manager of the Great Northern Chair Co. They changed the name of the firm to Shelby Williams and redesigned the company's line to offer more stylish seating furniture.

In 1963 the firm moved its manufacturing facilities to Morristown, Tennessee. In 1968 Shelby Williams was taken over by Coronet Industries, Inc., one of the country's largest carpet manufacturers. This firm, in turn, was acquired by RCA in 1970. Five years later RCA sold the Shelby Williams division to Manfred Steinfeld. Since 1978 Shelby Williams has made an average of one million chairs per year in factories located in Morristown, Tennessee, and Canton, Mississippi.

production of countless card tables, cocktail cabinets, and hostess carts, as well as the creation of console cabinets in a host of fashionable period styles. Smaller houses and apartments, complete with built-in closets, china cabinets, and buffets, made bulky wardrobes, hall stands, and sideboards obsolete. Although the National Retail Furniture Association did its best to convince architects and builders to plan wall space and rooms "sufficient to accommodate complete furniture suits,"[24] new architectural styles and increasing construction costs made it necessary to offer furniture that was smaller in scale, easier to move, and adaptable for use in more than one room.

After World War I wooden furniture continued to be made by more than 100 companies in forms that ranged from office desks to chairs. A few firms—such as Horn Bros., Louis Hanson, Johnson Chair, Kruissink Bros., and the Tonk Mfg. Co.—were now in the hands of the second or third generation. Others—like the Milano Furniture Company, Butler Specialty, and Storkline—were new specialty firms founded by entrepreneurs just entering the industry. Like the upholstered furniture makers, manufacturers of case goods and chairs turned out variations of popular period styles. Large-scale production and precarious economic times made experimentation with new designs seem unwise when sure profits could be had by supplying an established market with tried-and-true designs.

Bedroom and dining-room furniture was manufactured by at least twenty firms during the 1920s. J. D. Freese & Sons was producing walnut and gum bedroom suites in its new factory at 401 North Peoria in 1920, while making inexpensive oak and painted goods in its original location on Homer Street.[25] Within three years, however, both factories were turning out oak and gumwood dressers and walnut-veneered suites to meet the demand for inexpensive furniture in the popular period styles.[26] Horn Bros. Mfg. Co., located on West Superior Street since the 1880s, was still making bedroom furniture, while a much younger firm, Mascheroni & Miller, offered fine bedroom furniture with hand-carved details. Olbrich & Golbeck made dining-room suites as well as bedroom furniture in colonial and period designs. In business since 1881, Olbrich & Golbeck advertised in trade periodicals as an "old reliable company" but promised improvements in style and construction, along with fine hand-rubbed finishes.[27]

One of Chicago's pioneer furniture makers, the Louis Hanson Co., had been making bedroom furniture on the Northwest Side since 1869. Now, however, like many Chicago firms, it also turned out a line of radio and record cabinets. After 1923, when Louis Hanson died, his three sons, Martin, John, and Louis, Jr., carried on the business.[28]

By the early 1920s nearly 200 styles of tables could be seen in the factory of Louis F. Nonnast & Sons on North Halsted Street, while solid walnut dining-room sets with hand-carved details were available from the General Wood Turning Company. On North Rockwell Street, H. C. Niemann & Co. specialized in tables in "all Period and the Cheaper patterns" using solid as well as veneered mahogany, walnut, and oak.[29] By 1922 they were making chairs to accompany their dining tables, advertising "Sturdy lifetime Tables and Chairs built to last. Our suites are a perfect match."[30]

After World War I the Johnson Chair Co., still the largest chair manufacturer in the city, produced revolving office chairs and tablet-arm desks for offices and schools in its large factory on West North Avenue. Three

Upholstered easy chair illustrated in Valentine-Seaver Co.'s Trade Catalogue *of the mid-1920s.*
Prairie Archives Collection, Milwaukee Art Museum, gift of Mr. and Mrs. Robert L. Jacobson

Oak bentwood chair with veneered plywood seat by the Great Northern Chair Co. in 1939.
h: 34½" w: 17" d: 20½"
CHS, purchase, 1977

other sizable factories—the Herhold Chair Co., the Great Northern Chair Co., and the Heywood-Wakefield Co.—specialized in bentwood chairs of the type first made in the Thonet factory in Vienna, Austria. The oldest firm, the Herhold Chair Co., had been making "Vienna designs" since 1909.[31] In business since 1918, the Great Northern Chair Co. claimed to be turning out some 230,000 bentwood and semibentwood chairs and stools a year by 1942.[32] After 1939, when war broke out on the Continent, the firm stamped its chairs with the words "Made in U.S.A. Entirely with American Labor and Materials" to distinguish them from those being made in Austria, which had been annexed by Germany the previous year.

Bentwood chairs and theater seats (whose wooden parts were molded into shape using steam presses) were also produced in large quantities in the Chicago factory of the Heywood-Wakefield Co., which employed 674 in 1926.[33] One of seven factories located in various parts of the country, the plant on Arthington Street made wooden desks and chairs for schools in addition to rattan furniture, the company's original product.

While its chair departments made full use of power-driven machinery and assembly-line production, the Heywood-Wakefield Co.'s reed furniture division still relied upon craftsmen to weave the strips of pliable reed by hand to create the final form. Visiting the Chicago factory in 1926, the company president, Richard Greenwood, described this time-consuming process:

> The men work in individual stalls with long reeds lying on the floor or hanging from the walls—each stall the reed-worker's private domain. Stacks of frames stand in front of the weaver, and by his side is a pail of water into which the reed is dipped to make it pliable for weaving and to prevent splintering. The ends of the reed are pointed with a small knife so that they may be concealed when the piece is finished. Small benches with swivel forms help to hold the frame in position as the work progresses.[34]

Weaving reed furniture by hand at the Heywood-Wakefield Co.'s Chicago factory in 1920. From Fort Dearborn National Bank Industrial Bulletin *no. 3.*

Red painted child's chair with yellow stripes made by Heywood-Wakefield's Chicago factory ca. 1920.
h: 23½" w: 11" d: 11¾"
Erik Blucker

In the next room, a younger set of workers labored making chairs, settees, lamps, and baby carriages using a machine-woven fiber made from tightly twisted paper. Starting with the same frames that were used in making the more expensive reed furniture, sheets of the fiber were stretched over the wooden skeletons and held in place with tacks. The edges of the pieces were finished with woven braid. Hand-woven reed furniture was also made by the Chicago Reedware Mfg. Co., which advertised suites suitable for "sun-parlor, library, or living room" throughout the 1920s.[35]

While the slow process of hand-weaving recalled preindustrial production, the forms of the new reed furnishings were surprisingly modern.

"Woven furniture is being produced with marked success in *art moderne* designs," reported *Good Furniture* in 1928. "Sharp angularity of design, low chairs, deep cushions, vivid colors and futuristic fabrics are the outstanding features."[36]

By the mid-1920s several factories making wooden furniture had located in the new Central Manufacturing District (C.M.D.) developed on the city's Near South Side. One of these, the Martin Polakow Corporation, was a large producer of "occasional" furniture, as small pieces of novelty furniture such as curio cabinets, side tables, and wall shelves had come to be called. Made from maple, walnut, and mahogany, many of the pieces reflected the popularity of Early American style furniture. Others were painted and decorated with colorful floral or fruit motifs. By 1927 the firm was daily shipping three carloads filled with a total of 3,000 pieces of furniture.[37]

Assembling wooden chairs in the Chicago factory of Heywood-Wakefield in 1920. From Fort Dearborn National Bank Industrial Bulletin *no. 3.*

Walnut radio cabinet with handpainted interior made in the Milano Furniture Company in the mid-1920s.
h: 54½" w: 39" d: 18"
The Mattucci Family
Photograph by Abramson-Culbert Studio

Also in the Central Manufacturing District was the Milano Furniture Company, with its slogan of "Rain or shine, a daily new design."[38] Although the company's four owners admitted that a new pattern did not emerge every day, the large number of pieces offered by the firm in shapes ranging from plain, modern forms to Louis XVI and Chippendale reflected its versatility. At the time, Milano specialized in period adaptations that featured a good deal of hand-carving, fanciful marquetry, and hand-painted designs.

The owners of the Milano Furniture Company had all been born and trained in Italy, yet had met and become partners in Chicago. Frank Mazzukelly, the president, had first learned to carve in Milan. When he was about fifteen, there had been a debate as to whether he or his father should leave for America, where prospects were brighter and times more prosper-

Milano Furniture Company 922 New-ton, 1925; 2700 West Superior, 1926–27; 3311 West Forty-seventh, 1928–ca. 1971.

In business nearly fifty years, the Milano Furniture Company manufactured quality occasional furniture following traditional French and Italian designs. At its peak in the 1920s and 1930s, the company employed 100 to 120 workers and had eight to ten salesmen traveling throughout the country. For a while, dining-room and bedroom furniture and radio cabinets were also made. For many years the firm maintained a large showroom in the Merchandise Mart. Anthony O. Mattucci, who had attended the School of the Art Institute, served as the company's designer, while Angelo Belluomini took charge of purchasing and Louis Caracciolo supervised carving and veneer work. In the early 1950s, when Frank Mazzukelly retired, his share in the business was purchased by the other three partners. After Belluomini retired and Mattucci died, Caracciolo and his family operated the firm until 1971.

A MODEL FACTORY

ous. Finally it was decided that the young man should be the one to go, and so Mazzukelly left to join a relative in Pennsylvania. In Chicago by 1917, he worked for S. Karpen & Bros. and Mascheroni & Miller before joining cabinetmakers Louis Caracciolo and Angelo Belluomini to operate a carving school sponsored by the Chicago Furniture Manufacturers' Association.

During and after World War I, when the supply of skilled craftsmen was reduced—first by the draft and then by immigration quotas—hand-carvers became increasingly scarce. In 1921, for example, when striking members of the Carvers Union crippled local factories, the Chicago Furniture Manufacturers' Association resorted to sending an agent to Ellis Island, New York, to persuade Italian and Spanish carvers to come to work in Chicago "as they left the boats."[39] To train young immigrant boys, the manufacturers set up a carving school and hired Mazzukelly, Caracciolo, and Belluomini to run it.[40]

In 1926 the three were at 2700 West Superior, where the carving school paid the rent and allowed them to expand their own business, the Milano Furniture Company. Anthony O. Mattucci, who had been chief decorator at John A. Colby and later foreman of the Chicago Architectural Company, joined the team as a designer in 1925. Three years later, the firm moved into new headquarters in the Central Manufacturing District. There, in addition to performing administrative tasks, each partner continued to participate in the manufacturing process.

The Milano Furniture Company's new plant, employing more than 100 workers, was typical of factories producing wooden furniture in Chicago in the 1930s and varied little from firms manufacturing similar products today.

In 1934 David S. Oakes, a writer for the *Central Manufacturing District Magazine,* toured the three-story Milano plant and described its layout and operation. Contrary to the setup in many factories, Oakes noted, manufacturing in the Milano's workplace began in the basement (rather than on the first floor) of the building, where loads of kiln-dried hardwoods—mainly walnut, mahogany, and maple—were sawed into furniture components using high-speed labor-saving machinery.

On the first floor, furniture parts were shaped, carved, or veneered with rosewood, bubinga, harewood, or other exotic woods then in fashion. Commenting on the meticulous marquetry stars and diamonds decorating the tops of coffee tables and buffet doors, Oakes noted, "It is difficult to realize that these strips whose patterned graining here is indistinct and whose tints are dull with light dust beneath electric light, will come alive under treatment and be arranged into effects which glorify the art of cabinetmaking."[41] By the 1930s, improved woodworking machinery allowed the cutting and application of paper-thin veneers, which, in turn, encouraged the use of rare and strongly figured woods like coca-bola, bubinga, and zebrawood and made it economically feasible to ornament surfaces with intricate patterns and broad sheets of handsome veneer.

The large open loft space also housed the complex carving machines that formed the link between handicraft and mass production. "Here is the battery of carving machines whose uncanny multiplied fingers trace the reliefs we admire so much in fine furniture," Oakes explained, detailing the process by which duplicate carvings took shape as one operator slowly rotated a master of the piece. "We have come a long way in the mass production of wood carvings since David Salstrom, here in Chicago, perfected the ingenious devices here at work. They are the largest of their kind and they carve twenty-four pieces at a time."[42]

Nearby were the high-speed band and jig saws used to make patterns, to trim, and to miter. Workmen, however, still hand-turned spindles on the lathe to achieve the smoothest shapes. Intrigued by the turner's skill and accuracy, Oakes noted how "swiftly a gouge, under the lathe hand's accurate guidance, roughs out the diameter dimensions and then the smooth chisel deftly turns the beading, takes down the bevel and tidies up the corners. It is done so unhesitatingly and so surely that one forgets this man is working to caliper accuracy."[43]

On the second floor, cabinetmakers assembled the wooden parts into buffets, tables, commodes (low French cabinets), and cabinets. Along the north windows, where the light was constant, hand-carvers stood at benches giving final touches to the pieces. At the head was Frank Hoffman, a master craftsman responsible for making the "originals," or prototypes, of the pieces made in the factory. Here too was the drafting room, where Mattucci and Mazzukelly sketched designs and drafted working drawings.

Left to right: Anthony A. Matucci, Angelo Belluomini, Frank Mazzukelly, Louis Caracciolo.

Although a great deal of reducing, sanding, and polishing took place on the floor, there was little wood dust because a complete suction system carried it away to serve as fuel for the factory's furnace.

Finishing took place on the top floor, where thin coats of lacquer were applied to create a glossy finish. One workman carefully painted sprays of roses or lattice patterns on the curving fronts of commodes. "The French designs, of which the small commode is today's *dernier cri*, call for hand embellishments of color," Oakes wrote, having pointed out that the favorite models for tables were English forms.[44]

When dry, pieces were returned to the first floor, crated, and loaded onto the company's truck or in one of the five railroad cars standing on the private track that connected the factory with the Chicago Junction track and the city's major railroads. Milano's samples were displayed in the Merchandise Mart, where the firm dealt directly with representatives from the large department stores that were their major customers.

Novelty furniture was also produced in a host of revival styles by the American Furniture Novelty Company, which claimed to reproduce faithfully "the period designs of the old masters" in the library tables, tea wagons, and tables made in its factory.[45] Similarly, the Alonzi Furniture Company, founded in 1913 by Italian cabinetmakers Loreto and Carlo Alonzi and Savero Vignola, produced medium- and high-grade tables, desks, and curio cabinets, employing 140 workers by 1942.[46] Yet another manufacturer of novelty furniture was the Majestic Wood Carving Company, founded in 1929 by Thomas Montalbano.

Display of novelty furniture made by the Butler Specialty Company ca. 1940. From Butler Specialty Company's Spring Catalog for 1941. Butler Specialty Company

Newcomers in the novelty furniture field included the Butler Specialty Company, Storkline, and the United Table-Bed Company. Despite its founding on the eve of the Great Depression in 1930, the Butler Specialty Company grew steadily during the decade. By 1942, when it was located in a spacious factory on South Chicago Avenue, the company's 200 employees were turning out 450,000 wall shelves, valets, and curio cabinets a year.[47] The Storkline Corporation manufactured baby cribs and juvenile furniture, while the United Table-Bed Company produced the versatile

Mahogany Georgian Pier Cabinet made by Kruissink Bros. ca. 1938. h: 58" w: 25" d: 15"
Florence Kruissink Frazer

Alonzi Furniture Company. 453 North Carpenter, 1917–19; 1840 West Hubbard (Austin before 1937), 1920–79.

The Alonzi Furniture Company was operated by the three Alonzi brothers, Loreto, Carlo, and Anthony. Born in Sora, Italy, the three emigrated to Chicago during the years before, during, and after World War I. For sixty years the firm manufactured medium- to fine-quality novelty furniture in various period styles.

The Alonzis divided the work as follows: Loreto, president, was in charge of cabinetmaking and the machine room; Anthony, vice-president, handled shipping; and Carlo, treasurer, was responsible for the finishing room. Carlo's son and namesake joined the firm after World War II and became Loreto's assistant. Loreto's son Fritz ran the office, while Anthony's son Michael assisted in shipping.

In the 1950s and 1960s the company employed as many as 185 and was represented across the country by 20 salesmen. Goods were shipped to Canada, Mexico, Europe, and South Africa. As orders increased over the years, the firm made larger pieces of furniture, including desks, break fronts, and curio cabinets. The firm contracted out all of its machine carving, but employed many hand-carvers and painters to execute the more delicate work. Although the firm employed a staff designer, Nick Alonzo, it also used numerous free-lance designers.

Workshop of the Zangerle & Peterson Company from the firm's Catalogue No. 4, *1941–42.*
Prairie Archives Collection, Milwaukee Art Museum, gift of Mr. and Mrs. Robert L. Jacobson

"Ta-Bed." Resembling a modern dining table, the Ta-Bed's top flipped back to create a headboard, while apron, leaves, and legs extended to form a single bed. Like its predecessor, the patent folding bed, the Ta-Bed, in the words of its makers, "saves space, saves rent, perfectly combines in one piece of furniture the functions ordinarily performed by two."[48]

During the early 1930s, when there were few buyers for nonessentials like piano benches, bookcases, and parlor frames, three of the city's oldest specialty manufacturers—the Tonk Manufacturing Co., Kruissink Bros., and Zangerle & Peterson Co.—also turned to making novelty furniture. In 1932, under the leadership of Percival A. Tonk, son of the company's founder, the Tonk Manufacturing Co., by then the country's primary manufacturer of piano benches, added lines of living-room tables, children's high chairs, and music cabinets. By the early 1940s, the company was making as many pieces of novelty furniture as piano benches, of which they produced some 27,000 a year.[49] At the time, Tonk operated two factories, one on North Magnolia and another on Elston Avenue.

Walnut Italian Provincial side table made by the Tonk Manufacturing Co. ca. 1935.
h: 21¼" w: 19¼" d: 13¾"
Mr. and Mrs. Hampton E. Tonk and Family

This advertisement for Tonk piano benches was posted in the factory with a line added by management to encourage workers to produce their best.
Mr. and Mrs. Hampton E. Tonk and Family

Kruissink Bros., which had been making oak bookcases, added a line of small mahogany tables, tea carts, and wall shelves. The pieces were designed by Martin Kruissink, a Dutch cabinetmaker whose older brother, John, had founded the firm in 1882. Around 1942, by which time Martin's two sons—Martin and John—and his daughter Florence had joined him at the factory, the firm added period reproductions in maple. Similarly, parlor frame manufacturer Zangerle & Peterson began making fine tables, desks, and commodes. Now directed by Zangerle's sons, Arthur and Edwin, the company's 100 employees made an average of 24,000 frames and 36,000 pieces of occasional furniture by 1942.[50]

While Tonk, Kruissink, and Zangerle & Peterson managed to survive the depression by expanding their product lines, many other Chicago manufacturers were less fortunate. The Herhold Chair Co. failed in 1931; the Heywood-Wakefield Co. shut down its Chicago factory the following year. By 1942, case goods makers J. D. Freese & Sons, Horn Bros., and L. Nonnast & Sons had also closed their doors. However, although the furniture makers dependent upon wood and expensive hand-finishing felt the full force of the economic crisis, manufacturers of metal furniture flourished, for the most part because the components of their product were readily available from the numerous steel mills and foundries located in Chicago.

METAL FURNITURE

Metal had been used to make furniture as early as the 1890s by A. H. Andrews & Co., the Royal Metal Manufacturing Co., and the Tonk Manufacturing Co. (see p. 130). However, it was not until the 1920s that the W. H. Howell Company began to produce steel furniture in Chicago in stylish shapes suitable for use indoors as well as in the garden.

In 1924 Edward E. Ekvall and William McCredie purchased the W. H. Howell Company, a small foundry on the Fox River in Geneva, Illinois, which had been making irons, doorstops, and other cast-iron products since 1867. For the first year, the new owners continued to cast iron novelties, making drapery hardware, smoking stands, and supports for plants and aquariums that they lacquered black and gold, apple green, or Chinese red to harmonize with fashionable 1920s interiors. The following year, they began making brass-plated and lacquered wrought-iron tables with tops of marbleite or ornamental glass. Similar bases were upholstered for use as piano benches or radio benches (to be sat on while tuning the radio).[51]

By 1927 the Howell Company was showing its iron novelties in a large showroom in the American Furniture Mart and in its branch salesrooms in New York. Some of the pieces exhibited distinctive zigzag, ziggurat, hexagonal, and fluted shapes inspired by the well-publicized designs of European modernists. Others were conservative "reproductions of handcarved European-models" cast in iron. "By translating the beauty of handcarved wood into metal, we are able to produce these handsome pieces at a fraction of what the original models cost," Howell told potential customers in 1928.[52] The firm also introduced a selection of colorful garden furniture that included chairs with octagonal backs and seats composed of wedges of spring steel. Wrought-iron glass-topped tables and folding chairs completed the assortment of porch and patio wares. Weighing only half as much as cast iron, the new wrought-iron and steel products were well suited for volume production and soon replaced the earlier cast-iron products.

The Howell Company's line underwent a drastic change in 1929, when the company's owners first saw tubular steel chairs designed by Mies van der Rohe and Marcel Breuer (see page 338). Based on the cantilever principle, Mies's springy MR chair, as it was called, was made from a continuous tube of chromium-plated steel bent in graceful curves to support a one-piece seat and back of woven cane and to form a U-shaped support along

Brass-plated cast-iron stand with marble shelves made by the Howell Company ca. 1925.
h: 32" w: 18½" d: 14½"
CHS, gift of the Estate of William McCredie, 1981

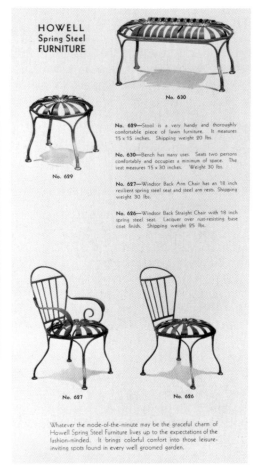

Illustration from the 1931 Howell Outdoor Furniture catalogue. Spring steel garden furniture was introduced by the Howell Company in the late 1920s.
CHS, gift of Emil Pfortmiller

the floor. Similar in design, Breuer's "Cesca" dining chair was more angular and employed strips of fabric to form the back and seat. Strong yet light, with frames requiring no welding, the tubular steel chairs had been designed for mass production.

Importing samples of the chairs from Europe, Howell employees adapted the designs for production by the firm. Within a year a series of chairs, armchairs, and settees had been added, with the tubular steel frames chrome-plated for indoor use and enameled for outdoor use. These Howell products "can probably be regarded as the important beginnings for tubular steel furniture in America," Murray Moxley, former vice-president of the company, explained, since up to this time, furniture of this type had been made exclusively in Europe.[53]

After perfecting variations of these highly popular chairs, the Howell

Tubular steel armchair with cane seat made by the Howell Company ca. 1928 after a design by German architect Ludwig Mies van der Rohe.
CHS, gift of the Estate of William McCredie, 1981

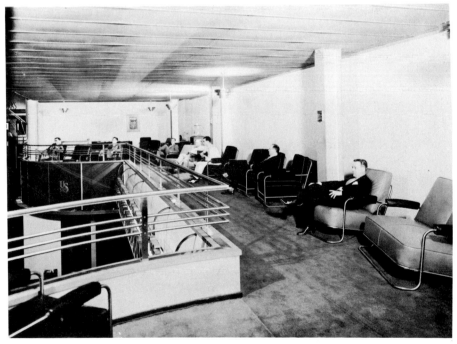

Chromsteel furniture made by the Howell Company in use in the U. S. Steel Building at Chicago's 1933 A Century of Progress Exposition. Murray Moxley, third from right, then an employee of the steel company, later became vice-president of the Howell Company.
CHS, gift of Murray Moxley

Company employed free-lance designers to create armchairs, sofas, tables, desks, and smoking stands made of tubular steel. By 1933, when the firm's Chromsteel furniture was used to furnish several of the model houses and exhibition buildings at Chicago's 1933 Century of Progress, the Howell line included items suitable for use in offices, showrooms, and residences.

The use of tubular steel furniture in 87 percent of the exhibition buildings at the 1933 World's Fair promoted the acceptance of metal furniture by the American public and helped establish it as an essential ingredient

Wolfgang Hoffmann, ca. 1936.
Mrs. Wolfgang Hoffmann

Prototype of a Howell Chromsteel serving cart designed by Wolfgang Hoffmann ca. 1935. Similar models were later put into production.
h: 26¾" w: 17½" l: 29½"
CHS, gift of the Estate of William McCredie, 1981

for a modern interior.[54] The fair also introduced William McCredie, president of the Howell Company, to the work of Wolfgang Hoffmann, who had designed the furniture and accessories for the Lumber Industries House at the Century of Progress and had assisted New York architect and theatrical designer Joseph Urban in developing the dramatic color scheme that caused so much comment at the fair. When McCredie asked Hoffmann to design exclusively for the Howell Company, the latter accepted and moved to Illinois.

The son of Viennese architect Josef Hoffmann, a founder of the Wiener Werkstatte, Hoffmann had studied architecture and furniture design at various schools in Vienna before joining his father's office. In 1925 the young Hoffmann and his wife, Pola, a textile designer and fellow student, had formed a design team and migrated to New York. After working briefly for Joseph Urban, who had formed an American branch of the Wiener Werkstatte, they opened an atelier on Madison Avenue, where they executed furniture, textiles, and decorative accessories whose "simple, direct colorful style" echoed the Werkstatte's penchant for geometric silhouettes and rich handcrafted materials.[55] In 1929 they joined Donald Desky, Paul T. Frankl, Bruno Paul, and other well-known modernists in organizing the American Designer's Gallery to promote contemporary industrial design. When Hoffmann exhibited his furniture in the gallery's second exhibition, the reviewer from *Good Furniture* commented that the designer's sensitivity to scale and function showed "real creative insight."[56]

From 1934 through 1942 Hoffmann was a "captive designer" for the Howell Company, creating complete lines of steel furniture that combined sleek flat bars or round tubing with wood, leather, or fabric to create pieces

Chromsteel "S" chair with red vinyl upholstery made by the Howell Company ca. 1935. Thousands of these chairs were sold for use in the kitchen. h: 33" w: 17½" d: 21"
CHS, gift of the Estate of William McCredie, 1981

Tubular steel "S" chairs being wrapped for shipment at the Douglas Furniture Novelty Co. ca. 1940. Douglas Furniture Corporation

that were modern in design yet suitable for mass production. Intended primarily for use in offices, showrooms, and commercial installations, Hoffmann's tables and desks featured plate-glass or glossy black Bakelite tops, while his chairs were upholstered in leather or fabric in clear primary colors to create a cheerful yet businesslike look. Commenting on this new furniture in 1934, a writer for *Architectural Forum* noted, "The awkward, angular, fantastic, objects with which the market was flooded during the early 'modernistic' craze, has given place to furniture which embodies grace as well as the maximum in scientifically determined comfort."[57] The Howell Company capitalized on the growing interest in modern design, featuring Hoffmann prominently in its catalogue and assuring prospective buyers, "Modern-minded men and women like the basic simplicity of functional styling found in Howell Chromsteel Furniture."[58]

In 1935, when the company installed equipment for applying synthetic enamel finishes in its new factory in St. Charles, Illinois, Hoffmann designed

Howell Company. Factory in Geneva, Illinois, 1924–35; in St. Charles, Illinois, 1936–ca. 1979. Showrooms in Chicago.

Around 1929 the Howell Company became the first American company to manufacture furniture in the modern mode using tubular steel. Between 1934 and 1942 Austrian-born modernist Wolfgang Hoffmann (1900–1969) was the company's designer, creating streamlined office, residential, and garden furniture exclusively for the firm. By the outbreak of World War II Howell was producing large quantities of office and institutional furniture, including upholstered chairs and restaurant booths, office desks, and dining tables and chairs. Tables were

topped with plastic laminates like Bakelite, Howellite, and linoleum. Seat coverings included cotton duck, woven cane, and synthetic vinyl fabrics like Fabrikoid and Fabrilite.

In the 1940s Howell's facilities were converted to the war effort. In the postwar years the company manufactured primarily dinette sets and institutional furnishings. By the 1960s, metal furnishings for cafeterias, auditoriums, and waiting rooms formed the greater proportion of its production.

The Howell Company was purchased by Acme Steel (renamed Interlake, Inc.) around 1954. Manufacturing continued under the Howell name when the firm was purchased by Burd, Inc. The company closed following a strike in 1979.

a new line described as "Summer Furniture," which included colorful lounge chairs, folding chairs, and chaises executed in enameled tubular or spring steel. He also created simplified versions of the "S" chair—as the classic cantilevered form came to be called in the trade—that lent themselves to mass production and generated high-volume sales. Especially suitable for use as dining chairs, clean-lined and inexpensive "S" chairs were soon paired with tables to create "dinette sets" whose durability and small size made them popular and practical for use in small apartment kitchens or the new combination living-room/dining-room areas that came to typify the modern house. So great was the demand for domestic and commercial dinette sets that they became the Howell Company's major product after World War II. During the war, when the Howell factory was converted for wartime production, Hoffmann left the firm to become a photographer, a career he pursued with considerable success until his death in 1969.

Responding to the demand for modern-looking metal furniture, other Chicago firms were quick to follow the Howell Company's lead during the 1930s. Given the large number of metalworking firms in the Chicago area which could supply the bent tubular steel components, it was fairly easy for manufacturers to begin assembling metal chairs. In 1933 the Royal Metal Manufacturing Company added tubular steel designs to its line of twisted-wire and metal furniture. Two years later, the Douglas Furniture Novelty Company switched from making wooden breakfast sets—which it had been producing at the rate of 100 a week—to tables and chairs with frames of tubular steel. A small manufacturing concern founded by the sons of retail furniture dealers Samuel and Libby Cohen, the company had begun making inexpensive breakfast sets in 1930, when Mrs. Cohen had noticed that the sets were the fastest selling items in their store. In 1939—with sales now averaging 500 sets a week—the firm replaced the enameled metal tops on its tables with sheets of a new plastic laminate called Formica, creating a dining ensemble that became a classic in the industry.[59]

Just as business was beginning to revive late in the 1930s, Chicago's furniture makers faced new challenges as World War II broke out in Europe. After America entered the war in December 1941, the "unlimited national emergency" cut through the ranks of Chicago's designers and craftsmen, sending some into the armed forces and others to work for new government agencies. At the same time, war restrictions froze the production of metal hardware, steel springs, upholstery tacks, feathers, down, and cotton webbing and rationed many other materials used in the manufacture of furniture.

To aid the war effort and secure government contracts that would enable them to keep their factories operating, members of the Chicago Furniture Manufacturers' Association producing wooden furniture organized the War Wood Industries Association in June of 1942. Composed of thirteen prime contractors and fifty-two potential subcontractors, the Association distributed a booklet describing the facilities and listing the machinery and personnel available in Chicago to agencies granting contracts for war work.[60]

Efficiently directed by upholstered furniture manufacturer A. D. Gorrell, the Association was instrumental in referring more than one million dollars worth of government contracts to local manufacturers. Between 1942

CHICAGO FURNITURE

and 1945, several Chicago factories devoted their entire production to goods required by the United States government and its allies. In 1943, for example, Butler Specialty Company supplied 12,000 bunk beds and 1,300 truck bodies and S. Karpen & Bros. built plywood chests and shelters for the Signal Corps.[61] Tapp, Inc. made control boxes, while the Tonk Manufacturing Co. manufactured wooden casings for lead-lined ammunition storage boxes.

Other contracts received by Chicago manufacturers required ingenuity rather than wood. When S. J. Campbell Company received a $500,000 contract to supply cargo parachutes to the U.S. Air Force, the firm converted an old tobacco warehouse in Madisonville, Kentucky, into a factory. Hiring local women as seamstresses and assemblers, they worked out such an efficient assembly line that the chutes were delivered ahead of schedule.

Workmen at the Seng Company loading and testing magazines for antiaircraft gun during World War II. Francis A. Seng

Indeed, the firm returned $60,000 to the government. "We didn't want to make a penny out of the war," proudly recalled Bruce Campbell, who coordinated the effort with his brother, Ralph, and his father, Samuel J. Campbell.[62]

When the war came to an end in 1945, Chicago manufacturers would find themselves with a pent-up demand for furniture—as well as new challenges involving shifts in population, the introduction of new materials, and new constellations of economic factors.

CHAPTER 18

THE POSTWAR YEARS

1946 - 1983

"The war means one of two things for Grand Rapids (and when I say Grand Rapids I mean the entire commercial furniture industry). It means a rebirth, or the end—the grand finale," wrote furniture designer T. H. Robsjohn-Gibbings in a letter to the editor of *Architectural Forum* in 1942.[1] Berating dealers and manufacturers who fed the public a diet of antiques and reproductions, the author of *Good-bye Mr. Chippendale* predicted: "There will be a hell of a lot of houses built between now and the end of the war—defense houses, I mean; and there will be even more of a hell of a lot after the war. And these houses won't be Cape Cod Colonial or English or French. They will be just plain, good American twentieth-century houses, and they will need good American twentieth-furniture to put inside them. It won't be Chinese 'modern,' or Colonial 'modern.' It will be good, down-to-earth, inexpensive *contemporary furniture.*"[2]

Although the omnipresent Chippendale outlived Robsjohn-Gibbings, the designer's prophecy for the commercial furniture industry would be fulfilled in the course of the next thirty years, but in Chicago rather than in Grand Rapids. When the war ended in 1945, the pent-up demand for housing and furniture would encourage the establishment of numerous companies offering new forms of modern furniture as well as assuring the continued existence of older firms producing familiar styles. Intense competition within the industry would later reduce Chicago's importance as a major furniture manufacturing center, at the same time that the city would take on a new role as center of the contract furnishings industry.

During the nineteenth century, ample timber supplies, cheap labor, and proximity to markets had been responsible for Chicago's supremacy in the furniture industry. After World War II, the absence of those advantages worked against the city's furniture manufacturers. The Southern states—still heavily forested and now the home of numerous military installations and the auxiliary populations they attracted—continued to draw new industry and population at the expense of older manufacturing centers in the Midwest and North. North Carolina, which had ranked fifth in furniture production in 1931, industrialized so rapidly that by 1956 it had become the premier furniture-producing state in the country. Illinois, following New York, ranked number three, with firms in the Chicago area producing 90 percent of the furniture made in the state.[3]

Although the Kroehler Manufacturing Co., the Howell Company, the Douglas Furniture Corporation, and several other Chicago-area firms were still expanding, many Chicago furniture makers, once leaders in their field, had gone out of business or were on the verge of shutting down. Specific reasons for closing varied from firm to firm, yet several common factors hastened their demise. Chief among these were the high costs of labor, energy, services, and taxes in Chicago, the problems inherent in sustaining family-owned businesses, and cut-throat competition.

"Furniture manufacturers could sell anything they could turn out right after the war," observed Philip E. Kelley, president of the Merchandise Mart and formerly head of Baker-Knapp & Tubbs, which has factories in Michigan and North Carolina. He went on to point out, however, that many Chicagoans were unwilling to make the "long-term capital investments necessary to meet the competition. They preferred to keep their profits by selling out or closing."[4] In contrast, furniture makers in Grand Rapids and the nearby communities of Zeeland and Holland, unable to compete with other manufacturers on price, had begun to assert leadership in highly styled case goods as early as the 1920s. Capitalizing on the high-level skills of their predominantly Dutch craftsmen, the firms hired top designers to produce pieces that justified the city's claim to being the Paris of furniture.[5]

While aging factories and outdated equipment tended to slow production, these proved less detrimental than the problems of a shrinking labor pool and aging management. Although many refugees from Europe settled in Chicago, few chose to work in furniture factories when higher-paying jobs could be found in other fields. Those who possessed woodworking or upholstering skills—as did many of the newcomers from Russia, Austria, Croatia, or Poland—often had to overcome the handicap of a language barrier and had to learn modern manufacturing methods.

More acute was the problem of management, since many of the firms founded at the turn of the century were reaching the end of their corporate life cycle. Several companies had closed or were up for sale because the owners had died, and no provision had been made for a successor to carry on. Other firms lost momentum in the hands of a second or third generation. "The furniture manufacturers who have gone out of business in Chicago in the last 12 to 15 years have all died on the vine, no competent management coming along to take over," wrote Charles H. Hanna, executive director of the Chicago Furniture Manufacturers' Association, to a member in 1959, going on to list "Fenske Bros., Johnson Chair Co., Louis Hanson Co., the old Karpen Bros., etc." as examples of attrition.[6]

Despite Richard J. Daley's claims during his long mayoralty that Chicago was "The City That Works," the city's leadership seemed unable to stem the furniture industry's flight to the South. By contrast, Southern legislators, mayors, and governors actively courted factory owners with attractive proposals of free land, minimal taxes, and a ready supply of cheap

American Picture & Novelty Co. 1934 Lake, 1911; 2006 Lake, 1912–15.
American Furniture Novelty Co. 2204 West Lake, 1916–20; 2601–2633 West Flournoy, 1921–71.

Emanuel B. Getzhoff (1882–1959) founded the American Picture & Novelty Co. in 1911 after working fifteen years as a salesman. Following World War II the firm employed 135 to 140 workers, making card tables, curio cabinets, lamp tables, and other occasional furniture. During busy seasons, some orders were contracted out to other firms and only assembled and finished in the company's factory, although all of the pieces were sold under the American Furniture Novelty Co.'s trademark, "Amfurnoco."

After Getzhoff's death in 1959, his wife, Mathilda, became company president. When she died only thirteen months later, her estate was left to several charities, and the company was sold in 1962 to Shelby Williams. The company operated under the name American of Chicago until the plant was liquidated in 1971, one year after Shelby Williams was acquired by RCA.

Furniture was identified only by a pattern number.

labor. In 1963 a depressed Charles H. Hanna, responding to the resignation of a member of the Chicago Furniture Manufacturers' Association who was moving his factory to the South, summed up the situation as follows: "It is a sad commentary on Chicago that furniture manufacturers have to move down South in order to produce furniture on a profitable basis and without the aggravation of producing in a big city. If any more firms leave Chicago for the South, I'll probably agree with Mr. Al Rota of the Upholsterers' Union, that it is unfair for the Southern communities to entice manufacturers down South with 'one dollar a year factory rent,' very low taxes, low wages, no fringes, no building inspectors, etc."[7]

Since wages accounted for 20 to 25 percent of the total cost of each piece of furniture, the high price of union labor in the Midwest became an important factor in the southern migration of the furniture industry. Even after minimal wage legislation went into effect in 1938, the differential between hourly rates in the Midwest and the South remained as high as 40 percent.[8]

Although large manufacturers of case goods and upholstered parlor furniture in Chicago had been unionized in the late nineteenth century, many of the smaller and newer factories were staffed with nonunion workers. Improved business conditions in the late 1940s, however, encouraged the Upholsterers' Union and the Brotherhood of Carpenters & Joiners (the successor to the Furniture Workers' Union) to try to organize the workers

Modern chair from the 1951 catalogue of Doetsch & Bauer. Also offered were frames in French Provincial, Victorian, and eighteenth-century styles that were reproductions of antiques.
Mr. and Mrs. John Erland

in these establishments. "My grandfather died of a broken heart after his parlor frame factory was unionized following World War II," related Charles Bauer, grandson of the woodcarver who had been co-founder of Doetsch & Bauer, one of the city's largest parlor frame factories. After carrying the firm's seventy-five employees at half-salary when there was no business during the Depression, Bauer was unable to prevent his workmen from joining the Brotherhood of Carpenters & Joiners when sales picked up again. When the union's labor negotiator insisted upon an increase of five cents per hour per employee, one half of the work force—whose average age was sixty-five—had to be let go when the proprietor and the union could not agree on terms for the contract. In 1950, not long after the senior Bauer's death, his sons and grandson decided to liquidate the firm rather than go bankrupt.[9]

"The union wasn't the only reason we decided to close our factory," Charles Bauer explained, "We weren't making any money. We were shipping frames that sold for $15 and paying $15 in freight. Since a frame is a hollow structure, we were paying for boxes of air. It was much cheaper for upholsterers to buy frames from a factory closer to their shop than to pay the price we had to charge in order to ship them from Chicago."[10]

Once the factory was closed, Bauer, like several other former manufacturers, remained in the furniture business as a manufacturer's representative, selling the products of several factories to buyers in the Midwest.

While old firms declined or died in the decade after the war, creative individuals and new firms emerged to offer new products or to cater to new markets. Realizing that modernization of facilities and new merchandising techniques were essential to compete in the mass market, a few local manufacturers—like Morris Futorian and Morton Cohen—opted for decentralization of manufacturing by moving their factories to the South. They invested in increased mechanization to raise productivity and in new designs to make their products more attractive. Others—such as Lawrence Schnadig and Manfred Steinfeld—created new firms by consolidating and revitalizing older companies like the bankrupt S. Karpen & Bros. and the Great Northern Chair Co. New firms like Marden Manufacturing, Inc., Interior Crafts, the Dresher Manufacturing Co., Parenti & Raffaelli, and the Gianni Furniture Company, as well as still viable firms like the S. J. Campbell Company, took advantage of the expanding market for custom furniture by offering high-quality products that were innovative in design and competitively priced.

"Those still in production in Chicago can attribute their success to three things: unusualness of their product, decentralization of facilities, or simplification of the basic design using assembly-line techniques," observed Bruce Campbell, co-owner of the S. J. Campbell Company and last executive director of the Chicago Furniture Manufacturers' Association. "There are only two kinds of markets: you have to go mass or custom."[11] The histories of the firms that remain in business today bear witness to the accuracy of that judgment.

"Back in the late forties we found a niche in the industry," related Morris Futorian, who in three decades went from being a non-English speaking refugee to being the owner of a furniture manufacturing empire with its headquarters in Chicago and its factories in the South. "No one was producing highly styled furniture by mass production methods so it could be sold at economical prices. We made a decision to locate a plant in Missis-

MECHANIZATION AND DECENTRALIZATION

sippi, and I was told by friends that I'd never find enough trained labor down there. . . . What they didn't understand was that I wasn't looking for trained labor. No one was producing furniture the way I wanted to do it. I wanted good people I could train in our methods."[12]

Inspired by a visit to an automobile assembly plant in Detroit, Futorian became the Henry Ford of the upholstered furniture industry. He built a new factory in rural New Albany, Mississippi, in 1947, which he named the Stratford Furniture Corporation (after the Chicago street on which he was living at the time), and put his plan into action. To speed the manufacturing process and to take advantage of unskilled labor, he standardized designs and broke the assembly-line process down into the minutest operations; to reach the consumer in record time and to keep warehousing and inventory costs low, he sold only in carload lots.

Sectional sofa from the catalogue of the Futorian Manufacturing Company, ca. 1945.
Morris Futorian

Working with a designer and cabinetmaker from the Futorian Manufacturing Company in Chicago, where he was making expensive custom-upholstered furniture, Futorian created a line of some two hundred models, hand-built the pieces, analyzed each step used in their construction, and then engineered assembly-line procedures.

To further decrease cost, each item was cut in large quantities and in a limited selection of fabrics and colors. Designs were modern yet "familiar," while the quality of materials and the construction methods used were almost identical to those being used to make custom furniture in Futorian's Chicago factory. Delivery to consumers was almost immediate, since they bought from retailers who carried a large inventory. Introduced at the January 1948 Chicago market, the Stratford line sold immediately because of its winning combination: the look and quality of expensive furniture and a surprisingly low price tag.

In 1948, when the Stratford Furniture Corporation introduced its first line, Morris Futorian was already proof that a person with ambition and foresight could still make the American dream come true. After arriving in Chicago with his parents and sister from Russia at the age of fifteen in 1923, he had spent a year learning English before going to work alongside his father in the Glabman Bros. furniture factory on Halsted Street, where he learned to be an upholsterer. Except for a brief fling at acting in Chicago's Yiddish Theatre when he was eighteen, Futorian worked in various furniture factories until 1935, when he started a small upholstering shop in his home. When the economy began to revive, he started making new furniture and gradually hired assistants. Each morning he upholstered; at noon he hit the road as his own salesman; in the afternoon he upholstered again. By 1947, when he came up with his new plan, he employed about seventy-five workers and was selling his modern upholstered furniture through showrooms in the Merchandise Mart.[13]

In 1952 Futorian applied his mass-manufacturing and mass-merchandising techniques to a specific product—reclining chairs—with the introduction of the Stratolounger, a line of stylish upholstered reclining chairs that sold for under $99, a price considerably below that of its competitors. "My goal was a reasonably priced, *well-made, well-styled* reclining chair that would appeal to the average consumer—a chair that wives would buy for their husbands, who, when they came home from work, would sit in it and feel like a king," explained Futorian, whose sensitivity to the deeper significance of furniture in the lives of his customers served him as well as did his skills as a businessman.[14]

After 1954, when Futorian stopped producing custom-made furniture in Chicago, he expanded his Southern operation to include three production and two supply factories in Mississippi and acquired two more factories in North Carolina specializing in a line of higher-priced Barcalounger reclining chairs. By 1964, Futorian-Stratford was the second largest manufacturer of upholstered furniture in the country—second only to Kroehler—and a leading producer of reclining chairs. It was at this point that the company was acquired by Mohasco Industries of New York, with Futorian staying on as president until his retirement in 1981.

Also competing in the mass market, the Douglas Furniture Novelty Company (renamed the Douglas Furniture Corporation in 1946) became the country's largest manufacturer of dinette sets by applying similar techniques in styling and production. During the war, when manufacture of metal furniture was prohibited, Douglas made metal goods for the War Department and turned out the limited quantity of wooden kitchen sets allowed under government regulations. However, these years gave Douglas the opportunity to test new products. When the artificial leather the company had been using for upholstery became unavailable, it turned to vinyl plastic, a new material that is now the most common upholstery material for seating furniture. When the company could not get cotton, it used foam rubber to pad its chairs. When the war ended, the company dropped wooden furniture entirely and began making only plastic-upholstered, foam-rubber padded, chrome-plated tubular steel chairs to accompany the Formica-topped metal tables it had introduced in 1939.

Douglas Furniture Novelty Co. 339 North Oakley, 1930 / 31–39; 1817 South Fifty-fifth, Cicero, 1939–45.
Douglas Furniture Corporation. 1817 South Fifty-fifth, Cicero, 1946–49; 5555 West Sixty-fifth, 1950–79; 5020 West Seventy-third, 1979 to the present.

In 1900 Samuel A. Cohen, a young businessman from Russia, started a moving and storage company with his wife, Libby, a merchandiser for the Boston Store. By 1921 the company, named after the Douglas Park neighborhood in which it was located, had evolved into a retail furniture store (Douglas Furniture House) as the Cohens found the sale of unclaimed furniture from their storage facilities profitable. Wooden dinette sets were selling extremely well in the late 1920s, and Samuel and Libby Cohen began making them under the name of the Douglas Furniture Novelty Co. in 1930, switching to tubular steel around 1935. In the 1960s and 1970s it often finished metal sets to resemble wood. (Recent demand has prompted the company to begin manufacturing wooden dining furniture again).

By 1949 freight costs had increased dramatically, and the company found it advantageous to acquire three California warehouses. In 1950 Douglas built its first West Coast factory, in Hawthorne, California. A second was added a few years later, in El Segundo, California. In 1980, the firm opened a new plant in Redondo Beach, California. The company employed 500 in the Chicago operation and 600 in the Redondo Beach plant in 1983. Each factory can produce more than 1,000 dining sets each day. The firm's annual output is half a million chairs, which are sold through wholesale showrooms in Chicago, Seattle, San Francisco, High Point, Atlanta, Minneapolis, and Dallas by a national sales force.

Today the Douglas Furniture Corporation is owned by Samuel Cohen's children and grandchildren. It is the world's largest producer of dinette and casual dining furniture, with markets across the country and in Europe, Africa, and in some Far Eastern countries.

Also taking its cue from the automobile industry, the company installed conveyor belts in its factory to speed production, started using staple guns, and later became a partner in a metal fabricating business to cut the costs of its basic materials. Emulating General Motors, Douglas began, in the words of its owners, to "make everything from Chevrolets to deluxe Cadillacs," including an expensive "Duncan Phyfe" dinette set that would prove

Showroom of the Douglas Furniture Corporation showing the Duncan Phyfe style dinette set (foreground) ca. 1948.
Douglas Furniture Corporation

a turning point for the firm. Fabricated from tubular steel, it featured a table whose legs curved inward and joined together to form a central pedestal rather than running straight to the floor like most breakfast table legs. As Morton Cohen, president of the company, explained:

> The Duncan Phyfe table design revolutionized the dinette and dining industry in the late 1940s because it took every retail store out of merchandising the so-called "low-end," basic, leg-style dining sets up to a super-deluxe set which retailed for about three times the amount of money. It became so popular, it was the start of grading-up style and quality in the industry. As a result of its introduction by Douglas, the company soon began selling 1,500 dinette sets a week, forcing the company to move to a larger factory in 1949. That's when Douglas moved to a factory on Sixty-fifth Street in the Clearing Industrial District.[15]

Around the same time, freight rates increased substantially and the company feared that it might lose its markets on the West Coast. As a result, it started warehousing in three locations in California and, in 1950, built a branch factory in Hawthorne, California, followed by another a few years later in El Segundo. Having outgrown all of its facilities by 1979, Douglas renovated a large factory on Seventy-third Street in the Chicago suburb of Bedford Park and at the same time moved into a new plant just south of Los Angeles.

"We make an almost generic product and put most of our effort into selling to dealers," explained vice-presidents Douglas Cohen and Stuart Applebaum, son and nephew, respectively, of president Morton Cohen. "You have to keep investing in new equipment to stay at the state of the art. We are able to compete from Chicago because it is still the hub of a core marketing area that extends for some 500 miles around the city in which the South has no advantage. We concentrate on sales in this area, while our California factory does the same for the West Coast."[16] Today, Douglas turns out 20,000 "S"-frame tubular steel Breuer style chairs a month. Each factory makes 1,000 casual dining sets a day.

During the 1930s, at least two ailing Chicago furniture factories were purchased by young men who combined effective business skills with their knowledge of the furniture industry to restructure their operations and redesign their product lines. Once such entrepreneur was Lawrence K. Schnadig, who revamped S. Karpen & Bros.; another was Manfred Steinfeld, who purchased the bankrupt Great Northern Chair Co. in 1954 and turned it into Shelby Williams Industries.

In 1952, when Lawrence Schnadig heard that a liquidating company had taken control of both S. Karpen & Bros. and the International Furniture Company, another Chicago firm that made upholstered furniture, he arranged with Sears, Roebuck & Company to buy them both on an equal-partnership basis to form the Schnadig Corporation. The son of Jacob L. Schnadig, co-founder of the Pullman Couch Company, he had worked for his father and uncle's firm after graduating from the Wharton School in Philadelphia. He was serving as president in 1951 when Julius Kramer's heirs, who held a controlling interest in the firm, decided to sell Pullman Couch to an outside buyer.

By the time Schnadig acquired Karpen and International, only the latter was still making furniture. But with Karpen he acquired a widely recognized and well-respected name and, between the two firms, a network of established factories located across the country that gave his firm an advantage over many of its competitors. Retaining the two trade names, Schnadig began to produce fine-quality upholstered furniture under the name of Karpen, and to market medium-priced upholstered furniture under the trademark of International.

Schnadig Corporation's administration offices and design facilities remained at the company's headquarters on West Belmont Avenue in Chicago. Woodworking operations located in Georgia and Texas manufactured wooden frames, which were shipped unassembled to other factories located in Pennsylvania, Indiana, Georgia, Texas, and California.

In 1966, when Schnadig and Sears wanted to buy each other out, Schnadig succeeded in acquiring the company with backing from a Chicago bank. Although his firm lost 40 percent of its orders as a result of Sears's withdrawal, the company regained most of its sales within a year when it became the first to market what was known as "Mediterranean" upholstered furniture to complement Spanish-style case goods that had just come on the market. Only four years after the break with Sears, the

Pullman Couch Company. 161 South Jefferson, 1906; 297–301 East Fulton, 1907–8; 515 West Kinzie, 1909; 1514 West Kinzie, 1910–11; 3759 South Ashland, 1912–54.

Schnadig Corporation. Executive offices, 4814 West Belmont, 1956; 4820 West Belmont, 1967 to the present.

In 1906 Jacob L. Schnadig (1876–1935) and his brother-in-law, Julius Kramer (1874–1932), purchased a small manufacturing business from a retail furniture dealer, naming it the Pullman Couch Company after the Pullman Building, where they planned the enterprise over lunch. The firm manufactured parlor suites and a few overstuffed rockers but soon acquired a patent for an improved folding davenport bed, which became its primary product. By 1927 the company employed 350 in its South Ashland Avenue plant and operated a branch factory in Long Island City, New York, making convertible sofa-beds and other upholstered parlor furniture.

In 1952 Lawrence K. Schnadig formed a partnership with Sears, Roebuck & Company to purchase S. Karpen & Bros. and the International Furniture Company, two Chicago parlor furniture makers that were in the hands of a liquidator. The new concern, called the Schnadig Corporation, retained the trade names Karpen and International to identify the upholstered furniture made in the five factories acquired as a result of the consolidation. Schnadig bought Sears' half-interest in 1967.

The Schnadig Corporation's executive offices and prototype shop remain in Chicago, while seven factories are located across the country. Woodworking takes place in Georgia and Texas; upholstering, in Indiana, Pennsylvania, Georgia, Texas, and California. Tables are manufactured in a factory acquired in 1980.

Schnadig now serves as chairman of the board, while his sons, Larry and Richard, are executive vice-president and corporate secretary, respectively; his son-in-law, Donald Belgrad, is president of the corporation.

Schnadig Corporation was producing 3,000 pieces of upholstered furniture a month. Over the next twelve years, its work force tripled, increasing from 500 to 1,440 workers.[17]

Another old Chicago firm that revived during the 1950s was the Great Northern Chair Co., which, under the direction of Manfred Steinfeld, became the foundation for Shelby Williams Industries. A refugee from Germany who arrived in Chicago in 1938 at the age of fourteen, Steinfeld served in the Army during World War II and graduated from Roosevelt University before going to work for Great Northern. He had worked his way up to vice-president by 1954, when he and furniture designer Sam Horwitz bought the nearly bankrupt firm. They changed its name to Shelby Williams ("just because the name sounded good") and redesigned the company's line.[18]

Convinced that American's would be traveling and eating out in record numbers in the postwar decades, Steinfeld and Horwitz concentrated on making wooden, metal, and plastic seating furniture for sale to the new hotels, motels, and restaurants that would be serving food to the public. In 1963, when it outgrew its Chicago factory, Shelby Williams Industries moved its manufacturing facilities to the new East Tennessee Valley Industrial Park in Morristown, Tennessee, leaving its administrative offices in Chicago. By 1981, four plants employed 1,000 workers turning out nearly one million chairs a year and Shelby Williams Industries was outfitting hotels and commercial installations in foreign countries as well as in the United States.[19]

SPECIALIZATION

While Futorian-Stratford, Douglas, the Schnadig Corporation, and Shelby Williams relied upon mass-production and mass-distribution techniques to make and sell their furniture, other companies were being formed to provide custom-made furniture in small quantities for very specialized markets. Marden Manufacturing, Inc. began to make upholstered and wooden furniture for commercial use, while Interior Crafts began to specialize in producing pieces for use in the home.

When the four Balonick brothers—Carl, Robert, Louis, and Melvin—started Marden Manufacturing, Inc. in a modest factory on Morgan Street in 1946, the customers for their upholstered furniture were primarily interior decorators. Over the next few years, however, they moved into the contract market, suiting their designs and construction to offices and hotel lobbies, schools, hospitals, and other public places. "Our furniture is really built too well for most people to use in their homes," said Robert Balonick, as he pointed out special construction techniques on samples displayed in the company's showroom.[20] Walnut conference tables, sculptured wood-framed upholstered chairs, and modular seating systems are manufactured by the company's seventy-five employees in its factory on North Ravenswood Avenue. Luxurious but heavy-duty textured wools, mohair plushes, and leathers featuring rounded, weltless seams ("welts show wear too quickly") distinguish the upholstered pieces.

The sons of a Chicago carpenter, the Balonicks had learned woodworking from their father and from an uncle who owned a furniture factory in LaPorte, Indiana. As in most family-run operations, the sons divided the tasks. From the beginning Melvin, a journeyman cabinetmaker, has been in charge of production, Carl has served as banker, while Robert and his son, Larry, and another partner, Dick Tremulis, have been responsible for design and sales.

Long Division, Marden's modular upholstered seating unit, designed by Robert Balonick in 1982.
Marden Manufacturing, Inc.

An upholsterer completing a chair in the Interior Crafts factory, 1983.
Photograph by Ellsworth H. Brown

Now the largest firm in the country producing custom-made household furniture, Interior Crafts, Inc., also started as a small upholstering business in the years just after the war. Working in an unheated loft above a bowling alley on Milwaukee Avenue, Jerry Seiff and Vito Ursini applied the skills they had learned while working for Tapp, Inc., where both had been employed before the firm went out of business. Buying good, heavy-duty equipment from other firms that went out of business during the 1950s, they gradually expanded their capabilities to include frame making, cabinetmaking, carving, wood finishing, and upholstering. Outgrowing two factories, they moved from their second—one of the old S. Karpen & Bros. plants in Cicero—to a new facility on West Cullerton Avenue on the city's Near South Side, where nearly two hundred craftsmen are employed. A master craftsman, Ursini supervises the factory operations, while Seiff takes charge of sales.

French Provincial wall unit made by Interior Crafts, Inc. in 1983.
Interior Crafts, Inc.

"Most of the good woodcarvers today are Italian, although we now have some excellent workmen from South America, Mexico, and Haiti," said Ursini, during a tour of the factory.[21] After showing how carving machines are used to rough out chair legs and other wooden components, he went on to describe how the hand-carvers finish each piece to provide the crisply carved details that have become a company trademark. In all parts of the factory, frame makers, cabinetmakers, carvers, gilders, upholsterers, and finishers were busy making furniture whose styles offered a panorama of the centuries. "About 30 percent of our work consists of reproductions of fine antiques, 20 percent is contemporary, another 20 percent is custom work for decorators and architects, and the remainder special orders. We have a line that changes from year to year, and also have Richard Himmel, Angelo Donghia, and Burt England create designs for us."[22]

Another GI who returned to Chicago and reentered the furniture business was Meyer S. Kaplan (b. 1914), who in 1942 invented the Sand-Rite sanding machine while working as foreman in the Lakeside Furniture Company operated by his uncle, Jacob Zake. When the firm received an order for 500 Chinese Chippendale style chairs, Kaplan worked in the evenings to develop a sanding machine with a flexible drum that could sand curved and round shapes and eliminate the tedious handwork. Patenting the machine, he developed a small business, which his wife continued while he was in the service during World War II. After the war, he continued to sell sanding machines. But, as he related, "My heart was in the furniture business and when on April 22, 1950, J. & S. Furniture Mfg. Co., a complete factory at 226 West Schiller, was put up for sale, I bought the whole place."[23]

Over the next thirty-three years Kaplan nursed the firm from "a run-down business with a fine reputation" into one making custom-upholstered furniture that was available in some 125 patterns in the 1960s. The firm filled orders from architects and interior decorators until 1983, when Kaplan sold it and returned to the sanding machine business, which had been in the hands of his son.

LaSalle Street Double Pedestal Desk from the S. J. Campbell Company catalogue, 1959.
Ralph O. Campbell

One of Chicago's premier custom furniture makers when the war ended in 1945, the S. J. Campbell Company experienced an upsurge in business just prior to the war (when it became a primary supplier for the Hallmark collection introduced by Montgomery Ward) and in the years immediately afterward when it put into production a new line of oversized furniture by Metro-Goldwyn-Mayer designers Jack Moore and Dick Pefferle called "Cinema Creations." "Moore and Pefferle believed that a few very large pieces of furniture would make a small room look larger, and the over-scaled upholstered pieces they designed for us were larger, deeper, and longer than most pieces then on the market," recalled Ralph O. Campbell, a partner in the firm. "We did a land-office business."[24]

Equally popular was the firm's line of reproduction and quasi-reproduction chairs and sofas, whose woodwork Campbell's cabinetmakers copied as exactly as possible from antiques or sourcebooks and whose seats and legs were adjusted to accommodate the larger modern figure. Pieces in their French Provincial line, for example, were made 30 percent larger in scale. "Our factory was located in the heart of the old German neighborhood," Campbell explained. "About 75 percent of our workers were highly skilled German or Bohemian woodcarvers or upholsterers."[25]

While those with upholstering skills made that type of furniture their specialty, others trained as woodworkers organized shops to provide custom cabinetry, reproductions of antiques, or special finishes. In this field, one of the most successful is the Gianni Furniture Company. Founded by Paul Gianni and his sons, Pat, Frank, and Dominick, in 1952, the firm specializes in making desks and office furniture.

Parenti & Raffaelli has been executing woodwork and furniture for residences, offices, and commercial structures since 1950. Its founders— Robert F. and Ronald Parenti and Silvo J. Raffaelli—had been cabinetmakers at the Northern Picture Frame Company, maker of gilded picture frames and high-quality, handcrafted furniture since the 1920s. When the firm closed in the late 1960s, the Parenti brothers' father, Peter, who had been a partner in Northern Picture Frame, came to work with his sons.

The company, which has executed some of the most elegant interior woodwork and furniture in the city, employs about forty craftsmen in its factory on North Noble Street. "All our tradesmen are union, the average employee has been employed by our firm over ten years, 70 percent are of European descent, and all are skilled in their trades," summed up Donald Parenti, Ronald's son, who with his brother Jim and cousin, Robert, Jr., are now learning the business.[26] Known for its special surface treatments, the company often works with exotic materials like goatskin and parchment and can make a painted wooden surface resemble anything from

Modern office interior in the Chicago headquarters of the Container Corp. of America on Dearborn Street in 1947. The interior designer was Maria Bergson; the wooden furniture was executed by the Woodwork Corporation of America.
Photograph by Hedrich-Blessing

sharkskin to malachite. The company uses polyurethane, polyester, vinyls, and lacquers in addition to more traditional finishes.

Unlike Parenti & Raffaelli, the Woodwork Corporation of America does not do residential work. It executes architectural woodwork, office furniture, counters, and other special furniture for banks, executive offices, hotels, or public buildings. Currently employing 275 cabinetmakers in its plant on West Twenty-first Street, the company was founded in 1913 by Hungarian cabinetmaker Joseph Kaszab but grew to its present size in the postwar years under the management of his son and now his grandsons, Robert F. and Joseph C. Kay. Like most firms specializing in interior finish and one-of-a-kind productions, the company executes the designs of others rather than offering its own line of furniture.

After the war, when metal once again became available, several new firms were established. Some made modern chromed steel and brass furniture; others manufactured metal frames or parts. One of the latter was the Stembridge Manufacturing Company, which supplied manufacturers with metal hardware and components. It was organized in 1945 when tool and die maker George N. Stembridge, who had operated a small plating business, went into partnership with his sons, George N., Jr., and Robert, after their return from wartime service in the U. S. Navy. Initially located in a factory on North Green Street for many years, the firm moved to the western suburb of Addison in 1976, where it continues to make stainless-steel, brass, and bronze bases for chairs and tables and, since its acquisition by Baker, Knapp & Tubbs, metal trim for a line of wooden furniture called "Mastercraft."

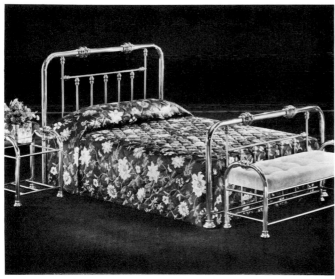

The Dresher Manufacturing Co. (now Dresher, Inc.) was the country's major producer of vinyl and velvet upholstered headboards in the 1960s when it added brass and metal bedsteads. The Newport model is one of a large selection of brass frames and accessories made by the firm in 1983.
Dresher, Inc.

Dresher, Inc., now the country's largest manufacturer of brass beds, was also founded in 1945, when German-born Max S. Dresher returned from military service and started to make hand-tied box springs and upholstered headboards in a store-front on Arthington Street. By the time he built a modern factory on Kostner Avenue in 1953, Dresher had expanded his product line to include wooden and plastic headboards, benches and divans, and even round beds. Nine years later, in 1961, he installed metal-working equipment and introduced brass bedroom furniture. By 1974, when Dresher moved into a highly mechanized factory in Bedford Park, brass bedsteads and accessories had become the firm's principal products.[27]

Another metal furniture maker, the JEM Furniture Corp., was organized in 1953 by Mark Tauber and his sons, Joseph and Edward (who combined the initials of their first names to create the company name). Starting out as a furniture retailer in the 1920s, Tauber became a wholesaler in the 1930s and later a manufacturer when he acquired a small factory that had been supplying his firm with furniture. Forming the JEM Corporation, the father-and-son team first made wooden furniture, then expanded into the metal furniture field and began making chrome, brass, and glass occasional tables, étagères, and tall-case clocks in contemporary styles. "We originate, improvise, redo, and borrow our styles," said one of the Taubers. "They are middle-of-the-road designs priced in the middle range."[28]

MODERN STYLING

When factories and shops returned to full-scale activity, many of the Chicago furniture designers and manufacturers put into production the modern styles that had begun to appear on the market prior to the outbreak of the war. Within a year, modern cantilevered chairs of tubular steel and tables topped with formica or glass made by the Howell Company, the Douglas Furniture Corporation, and other local firms were being purchased for kitchens and dining rooms. At the same time, S. Karpen & Bros., the Futorian Manufacturing Company, S. J. Campbell Company, and the Kroehler Manufacturing Co. were turning out boxy "sectional" sofas with three or four components to be clustered around free-form or kidney-shaped

Windows of the Baldwin Kingrey store, ca. 1952.
Photograph by Berko

coffee tables being made by such long-established firms as Zangerle & Peterson, the Milano Furniture Company, and the Tonk Manufacturing Co. In the typical postwar interior, these pieces would be supplemented by wall cabinets, bookshelves, and magazine racks made in the factories of Kruissink Bros., Butler Specialty Company, and the American Furniture Novelty Company.

While these pieces were often clean-lined and relatively inexpensive, they lacked what many young architects and designers considered to be "good design." Turning their talents to furniture design, this new generation became involved in enterprises to manufacture or market the domestic or commercial furniture whose high style or engineering reflected the spirit of the day.

Modern sofa bed designed by architect Harry Weese for the Baldwin Kingrey store ca. 1952.
Photograph by Harry Weese

"Harry [Weese] had the idea of setting up a Good Design Center where young marrieds could buy good modern furnishings that were inexpensive," explained his wife, Kitty Baldwin Weese, who, with interior designer Jody Kingrey, opened just such a store in March 1947.[29] Having secured a franchise in the Midwest to sell Finnish architect Alvar Aalto's fluid, laminated birch armchairs, serving carts, and stools, they secured a space in the Diana Court Building on North Michigan Avenue and organized Baldwin Kingrey to sell china, glassware, and fabrics along with the imported furniture. In addition to Aalto's pieces, the shop sold furniture designed by Bruno Mathsson and Borg Morgensen of Denmark. Among its bestselling items were "Womb" chairs and pieces designed by Eero Saarinen and manufactured by Knoll Associates and the high-style designs of architect Charles Eames and of sculptor Harry Bertoia recently put into production by Herman Miller. Among the first firms to manufacture only modern furniture, Knoll and Herman Miller played a key role in popularizing modern design.

Special pieces—metal lamps, adjustable bookcases, folding sofa beds, slatted benches ("anything we had calls for")—were designed for the store by Harry Weese and constructed by local craftsmen. "The sofa bed was one of our best sellers," Weese recalled, describing how the two rectangular foam rubber cushions that formed the starkly simple sofa could be arranged to make a double bed. Supported by a metal frame, the sofa's back cushion was held upright by a zigzag grid fabricated by a blacksmith in then-rural Barrington.[30]

A graduate of the Massachusetts Institute of Technology who had studied city planning at Cranbrook Academy, Chicagoan Harry Weese (b. 1915) tackled the design of furniture with the same concern for practicality, surrounding environment, and compatibility of old and new that would later distinguish his architecture.[31] Between 1937 and 1939 the architect and his brother-in-law and partner, Ben Baldwin, won a first prize and two honorable mentions in the International Low-Cost Furniture Competition sponsored by New York's Museum of Modern Art.

"The shop was always filled with artists and architects," his wife recalled, "and we started having art shows and exhibits to show the work of our friends and others. ID [The Institute of Design] (see page 288) was then flourishing and we often had shows of work by members of its faculty, including photographers Arthur Siegel and Franz Berko. We also imported exhibitions."[32] Jody Kingrey specialized in fabric selection and sales, Kitty Weese kept the books and did the ordering, and her husband created furniture and lamp designs and executed the graphics until 1958, when the store was sold to John Izume.

Not long after Baldwin Kingrey introduced the work of American and Scandinavian modernists to Chicago, Carson Pirie Scott & Company installed model rooms displaying Scandinavian furniture in its department store and Watson & Boaler imported the sophisticated chairs designed and marketed by Hans J. Wegner of Denmark. Hand-carved from solid teak or oak, and sculpted to fit the body, the "Classic chair" designed by the architect in 1949 featured a curving back that flowed into slender armrests and attached to four gently splayed legs. A hand-woven cane seat further enhanced its graceful look and provided comfortable seating. "In 1949, Watson & Boaler placed the first order, outside of Denmark, for the celebrated Wegner chair, copied in Chicago by the thousands," recalled John C. Murphy, former president of the firm, discussing the immense popularity that Danish modern enjoyed during the 1950s. "This style did not last long," he continued, "largely because the cost of fine handmade craftsmanship became prohibitively high."[33] By then, copies of Scandinavian styles were readily available from local manufacturers like S. J. Campbell or Shelby Williams.

The growing demand for comfortable household furniture with modern styling also encouraged Institute of Design instructors Edgar Bartolucci (b. 1918) and Jack Waldheim (b. 1920) to introduce their novel "Barwa" chair in 1946. An elongated, canvas-covered, rectangle supported by an angular tubular aluminum frame, the therapeutic "Barwa" tilted forward or backward to let its occupant sit up or recline. Explaining the metaphysics of the piece—described as "neither chair, couch nor resting board"—its inventors told readers of *The Chicago Sun:* "on the premise that centuries of upright position have failed to reconcile the human body to its defiance of gravity, the Barwa has been designed to follow the natural curves of the spinal column. . . . it allows rest and relaxation as nature intended."[34] The

Barwa was manufactured in Chicago by the two partners for several years and later by a firm in Los Angeles.

Bartolucci-Waldheim's Barwa chair as advertised ca. 1948. To shift from a sitting position to a reclining one, sitters were told to "simply press your weight backward."
Jack Waldheim

Tubular steel and orange nylon mesh lounge chair made by Designers in Production ca. 1955.
h: 29" w: 6" l: 14"
John Vinci

Another Institute of Design graduate and instructor, Davis J. Pratt (b. 1917), developed a comfortable and portable chair in 1948 by resting an inflated automobile tire inner tube slipcovered in heavy pile fabric on a ring-shaped metal frame, which could be folded flat for shipping. Entered in the Museum of Modern Art's International Low-Cost Furniture Competition in 1948, this design shared a second prize for seating units.[35] Between 1952 and 1957 Pratt and a former classmate Harold Cohen designed and manufactured household furniture under the name of Designers in Production. Among their best-known products were a series of metal-frame chairs and ottomans in which a tube of nylon mesh slipped over the frame to form a taut yet comfortable seat.

Sensible modern furniture that could be mass produced at affordable prices was also the objective of Henry P. Glass, an architect who spent a year in the New York office of industrial designer Gilbert Rohde after migrating from Vienna in 1939. Moving to Chicago after the war, he organized Henry P. Glass Associates in 1946. During the 1950s Glass patented a variety of reclining chairs before experimenting with the folding principle that led to the development of the award-winning "Cricket" chair of lightweight tubular aluminum and polyester mesh, put into production in 1979 by California manufacturer Brown-Jordan. In the mid-1960s Glass experimented with inexpensive plywood drums, out of which he fashioned a series of sculptured dining chairs called "Cylindra." Rounded plywood shapes also formed the basis for an upholstered group called "Intimate

Island" in which settee and chairs surrounded a glass-topped coffee table with an upholstered rim. "People will put their feet up on the furniture anyway," the designer told a *Tribune* reporter at the time. "You might as well invite them to."[36]

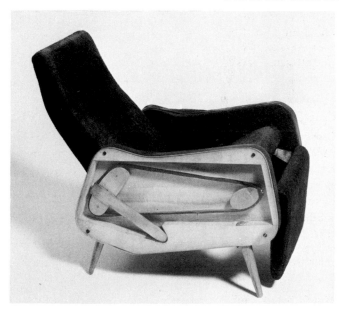

Model for Omega reclining chair patented by Henry P. Glass in 1959.
h: 7" w: 6" l: 14"
Henry P. Glass

Ludwig Mies van der Rohe leaning on an example of the Brno chair designed by him in 1930.
Photograph by Arthur Siegel

While Glass was designing practical furniture that made use of new materials, a young interior designer named Richard Himmel was acquiring a reputation both for creating novel effects and for forecasting the coming fashion. Like other mavericks entering the field, he offered new approaches to design and marketing. Himmel recalled:

> When I started in business in 1946 there was no furniture and very few fabrics. It was an era of recycling. We recycled everything. Almost immediately people began bringing in country antiques from England and we recycled those.
> Around 1950 I formed a company called Dods-Murdick [from the surname of Betty Dods, who ran the showroom, the name of his sister Muriel, and Himmel's own first name]. I got all of the Chicago workrooms to make a little something and we put it in the Mart in a showroom. I served as designer and Armand Lee, the Custom Furniture Makers, the Diebold Cabinet Shop, Bares & Rehak, Andrew Pakan, a retail dealer on North Ridge who made furniture above his store, and lots of others made the first Dods-Murdick furniture. It caused a furor in the trade.

One of the things I did was a beige silk tufted sofa adapted from one I found in an old Sears catalogue of the early 1900s. It had tufted sides, tufted arms, everywhere you looked it was tufted. To advertise it, we got a nude model to lie face down on it with her long blonde hair streaming over the edge. All the copy said was "Any Size." The editor of *Interior Design* will remember it well, since lots of readers canceled subscriptions. But it started a whole trend called Transitional furniture—pieces that were not that modern and not that traditional. We brought back the elegant touches and materials that Sam Marx and Jimmie Eppenstein had introduced before the war, and offered a fresh approach to upholstery.[37]

Himmel still designs for Dods-Murdick. In the late 1950s he created a line of transitional upholstered furniture for the Baker Furniture Company in Michigan and designed for numerous other manufacturers, and currently he serves as design consultant for Interior Crafts. Over the years Himmel has built up an international clientele of the caliber once enjoyed by Samuel Marx and James Eppenstein. In his Design Pavilion he offers everything from Chinese to Art Deco. "People keep forgetting that furniture is a fashion business," he says, "and the fashions come and go."[38]

Despite serious attempts by designers to develop popular demand for good contemporary furniture, the average consumer continued to prefer traditional styles. Thus furniture that was truly innovative in design and material came to be associated primarily with public and semipublic spaces like offices, banks, restaurants, hotels, and other interiors furnished by contract.

Within two decades after the war, architectural firms like Skidmore, Owings & Merrill (SOM) and the Perkins and Will partnership had grown from small offices into large "design factories" employing hundreds of architects, draftsmen, and clerical workers. Like Holabird & Root, they maintained staffs of architects and designers who developed or selected furnishings appropriate for the interiors of the commissions executed by the firm. Smaller firms were organized by architects or interior designers who specialized in space planning or contract work for office buildings and the various chain hotels, restaurants, and stores that had begun to spread out nationally, housing their enterprises in identically decorated quarters designed to convey a corporate image. By the mid-1950s the selection and commissioning of modern furniture in conjunction with office and business interiors had become such a lucrative business that *Interiors* magazine initiated a Contract Series and other publications, like *Arts & Architecture* and *Progressive Architecture*, began to report on these trends in the industry.

Even before the war had ended, Chicago's facilities for selling and distributing furniture had begun to draw firms with international clienteles for the modern furniture produced in their factories. Foremost among these were the Herman Miller Co., Knoll Associates (later Knoll International), and Steelcase, all of whom had factories in Michigan but major showrooms in Chicago. After 1949, annual Good Design exhibitions cosponsored by the Museum of Modern Art in New York and the Merchandise Mart called attention to the work of prominent architects and interior designers and reinforced the city's reputation as a center for innovative modern design.

One of the names most frequently associated with contemporary furniture was that of Chicago architect Ludwig Mies van der Rohe (1886–1969), mentioned earlier, who came to the city from Germany in 1938. As a youth, Mies van der Rohe had served an apprenticeship in the office of Bruno Paul, then Germany's leading furniture designer. Eventually Mies acquired his own reputation as an architect and designer and rose to be director of the Bauhaus. He was serving in that capacity when the school closed in 1933. While visiting the United States in 1937, he was invited to head the School of Architecture at the Armour Institute of Technology (later renamed the Illinois Institute of Technology), a position he assumed in 1938. Over the next two decades he developed the school's new campus. He also designed the Promontory Apartments on South Shore Drive (1949), twin apartment towers at 860–880 Lake Shore Drive (1951), the Federal Center (1964), and One IBM Plaza (1973) in the city's Loop. These and other crystal shafts with no-nonsense façades and uncluttered interiors inspired so many imitations that the predominant architectural mode of the post-World War II decades has often been styled "Miesian modern."

Lobby of apartment building at 860 North Lake Shore furnished with Barcelona chairs fabricated by the Wells Furniture Makers and Jerry Griffith ca. 1952.
Photograph by Hedrich-Blessing

The lobbies of Mies's buildings were furnished with chairs, couches, tables, and benches of steel, leather, and glass emulating the so-called Barcelona set he had designed for the German Pavilion at the 1929 International Exposition in Barcelona. A manifestation of Mies's oft-quoted motto, "Less is more," the sleek Barcelona chair consists of a pair of tufted leather cushions supported by a graceful "X"-frame formed by crossing two slim bars of steel. Convinced that "architecture belongs to the epoch, not to the individual" and that mankind needed "universal" rather than "special" solutions to its problems, Mies considered the impersonality of his furniture a virtue and did not find it necessary to design unique pieces for each commission. One of his favorite sayings was, "I don't want to be interesting, I want to be good."[39]

Epitomizing "good taste," the use of Mies's furniture in business and domestic interiors conferred status on its owners and testified to an awareness of what was appropriate in the age of highrise office blocks. To reproduce his designs Mies turned first to the Wells Furniture Makers, a custom shop founded by the late Alfred Mattaliano. An Italian cabinetmaker who had come to Chicago by way of French West Africa, Mattaliano had been

Vasarely chair upholstered in gray wool, designed in 1968 by Walter Netsch and Bob Peters, partners in the architectural firm of Skidmore, Owings & Merrill, for use in the Robie House at the University of Chicago. Executed by the Lakeside Furniture Company, Chicago.
h: 25¾" w: 50" d: 21"
Walter Netsch
Photograph by Abramson-Culbert Studio

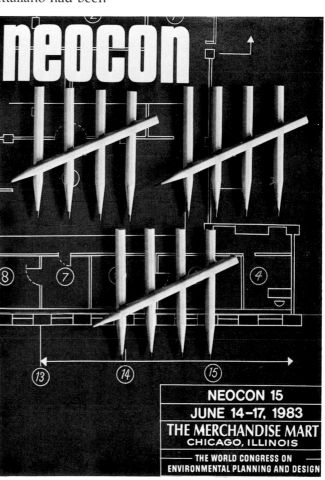

Poster for NEOCON, 1983.
CHS, gift of The Merchandise Mart

foreman of the cabinet shop operated by furniture retailer A. H. Revell & Company for several years before opening his own shop at 1335 North Wells Street in 1938. Working with architect Ed Duckett from Mies's office, Mattaliano shaped and upholstered leather cushions while metalworker Jerry Griffith fabricated metal frames. "The original Barcelona chairs were made out of cold rolled steel that was then plated with chrome. In the United States Mies used stainless steel," Frank Mattaliano recalled. The shop's current owner, he first began to help his father make furniture when he was nine years old. "The only difference between our chairs and those made by Knoll is in the X-frame," he continued. "Ours have a sharp corner where the pieces cross. Knoll's have a rounded corner."[40]

By 1955, when Knoll put Mies furniture into production, the demand for contract furniture had spawned a whole industry that specialized in providing durable, functional, high-style furniture. In 1969 commercial furniture accounted for such a large share of the market that the Merchandise Mart, in order to maintain leadership in the industry, began sponsoring the National Exposition of Interior Contract Furnishings (NEOCON), the Chicago equivalent of the "market" for residential furniture held in High Point, North Carolina, each year. By the 1980s NEOCON was drawing worldwide participation and offering week-long lecture series, exhibitions, and award presentations, indicative of Chicago's position as the international center for contract furnishings.

While modern furniture took on the characteristics of an international style, the local industry was also losing much of its regional identity. During the 1960s and 1970s small firms were acquired by larger ones, while larger manufacturers became part of syndicates or conglomerates that made more than one type of furniture or a variety of nonfurniture products. For example, as noted earlier, in 1964 the Futorian Corporation was sold to the New York-based Mohasco Corporation, whose subsidiaries produce a variety of home furnishings. In 1967 the S. J. Campbell Company merged with Custom Craft, another Chicago firm making upholstered furniture, and operated under the name Campbell Custom Craft until 1971, when the S. J. Campbell name and designs were sold to Ralph Morse of Grand Rapids. In 1977 Marshall Cogan and Stephen Swid purchased Knoll International from Walter E. Heller & Company, a Chicago commercial finance company, which had owned the firm since 1967.

In 1962 the American Furniture Novelty Company was acquired by Shelby Williams, which in 1968 was taken over by Coronet Industries, which in turn was purchased by RCA Corporation. Manfred Steinfeld purchased the Shelby Williams division from RCA in 1975. In 1972 the Baker Furniture Company of Michigan, a subsidiary of the North American Phillips Corporation, merged with Knapp & Tubbs, a furniture distributing firm that for over half a century had represented the major Grand Rapids manufacturers in Chicago. Baker - Knapp & Tubbs acquired the local Stembridge Manufacturing Company in 1981. After experiencing large financial losses in the 1970s, the Kroehler Manufacturing Co. was taken over in 1981 by the ATR Group of Northbrook, which has put its remaining three factories up for sale. While some mergers were due to financial problems, others were arranged to insure the continuity of the firm and to provide security for its employees.

As the industry decentralized and consolidated and manufacturing facilities and markets shifted to the South and Southwest, major furniture manufacturers found it necessary to open additional showrooms in High Point, North Carolina; Dallas, Texas; and Los Angeles, California, as well as in other cities. As a result, attendance at the American Furniture Mart's annual shows declined and tenants began to move out of the building. In 1979, the structure was sold to developers for conversion into luxury condominiums. The previous year, the Chicago Furniture Manufacturers'

Association, its membership reduced to twenty-nine, had merged with the Midwest Industrial Management Association and turned its archives over to the Chicago Historical Society.

Nevertheless, a number of factories large and small as well as countless individuals keep the city's tradition of furniture making alive by continuing to design and manufacture finely crafted furniture for a select clientele and for the mass market. The epilogue introduces some of the most active of these newcomers.

EPILOGUE

Listening to present-day furniture makers, designers, and distributors, one realizes that the city continues to attract and harbor furniture designers and makers with innovative ideas.

In 1983, the mood of the city's artistic community in some ways recalls that of the 1870s, when a variety of architectural styles was emerging and an ever-widening circle of artisans was beginning to make art furniture. In other ways, what is being made is closer to the taste of the 1920s, when innovations in architecture and interior design were matched by experiments with the shapes, colors, and materials of furniture. Now, as then, the new furniture designers are architects, interior designers, and craftsmen who are making a conscious effort to create furniture that embodies their ideals of functional beauty.

In many ways, the renewed interest in furniture design shown by contemporary architects reflects a widespread reaction against the conformity of taste and expression imposed by international modernism, not only in Chicago but in cities throughout the world. The search for new forms of artistic expression was already evident a decade ago, when British historian Ann Ferebee acknowledged: "With the introduction of new energy sources, satellite communications and computer controlled information networks, we are now embarking on a second industrial age and the articulation of a new esthetic. Punctuated by these developments and by the death of its great form-givers—Corbusier, Mies and Wright—Modern design, as we have known it for more than a century, slips into the past."[1]

In 1983 the diagonally sliced roofs, neoclassical detailing, varied textures, and set-backs of new skyscrapers rising in the city proclaim the end of the Mies van der Rohe era of repetitive flat-roofed highrises that began in Chicago in the 1950s and continued a decade beyond that architect's death in 1969. Glimmerings of this post-modern attitude first attracted media attention in 1976 when four local architects, displeased with the traditional rendition of "100 Years of Architecture in Chicago" being mounted for the

Bicentennial, organized a counter-exhibit called "Chicago Architects" that challenged the traditional interpretation of the city's architectural development with its emphasis on Frank Lloyd Wright and Mies. Afterward, the four agitators—Lawrence Booth, Stuart Cohen, Stanley Tigerman, and Benjamin Weese—formed the "Chicago Seven" with the addition of Thomas Beeby, James Freed, and James Nagle. They proceeded to hold art shows and competitions and were instrumental in reviving the Chicago Architectural Club in 1979. Two years later, when an exhibition called "New Chicago Architecture" opened in Verona, Italy, and Chicago, the work of the fifteen architects featured demonstrated that, as the subtitle of the show suggested, the city had indeed moved "Beyond the International Style."[2]

Helmut Jahn, a partner in the firm of Murphy/Jahn, who has designed some of the city's most sophisticated new skyscrapers, noted in the catalogue for the exhibition that architects had moved beyond utopian universal solutions to a new era stressing synthesis. "Our work is based on the belief that the modern movement is not dead and its principles can be extended and continued. We look to our immediate past which now has become a tradition and also to our remote past for inspiration. We see a 'new synthesis' not of an abstract nature, not of a technological utopia, nor looking back to borrow from history, but as a recomposition of classical and modern elements of the building arts leading to a 'historical continuum' based on conceptual relationship. Its strength can lie in the tensions and transformations it provides between old and new, art and craft, technology, abstraction, and meaning."[3]

"Furniture designed by architects is conceptualized as an extension of their architecture—it is literally an extension of space," says Stuart Cohen,

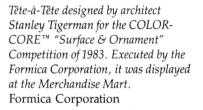

Tête-à-Tête designed by architect Stanley Tigerman for the COLOR-CORE™ "Surface & Ornament" Competition of 1983. Executed by the Formica Corporation, it was displayed at the Merchandise Mart.
Formica Corporation

who works in partnership with architect Anders Nereim.[4] Corporate and institutional clients most frequently commission furniture, while individual homeowners are still cautious about having a whole room full of architect-designed furniture, lest the pieces turn out to be uncomfortable or fail to meet their needs.

Stanley Tigerman, one of the most outspoken of the post-modern contingent, contends that "if dualism is what life is all about then that is what architecture should be about" and designs furniture and buildings that reflect the fashions of the time.[5] Frequently designing furniture and household accessories for both manufacturers and private clients in collaboration with his wife, Margaret McCurry, Tigerman most recently created a Formica "Tête-à-Tête" consisting of a pair of facing lounges whose wavy pink and blue awning-striped forms showed to good advantage both his concept of dualism and the Formica Corporation's new plastic surfacing material, COLORCORE™.

Tigerman was among ten designers invited to submit a furniture design to the company's Surface and Ornament Design Competition. The contest, whose winners were announced during the 1983 NEOCON held at the Merchandise Mart, drew 700 entrants and was afterward christened "the American Memphis" by one pundit who saw obvious similarities between these furniture designs and the radical "Memphis" collection of colorful geometric furniture and accessories introduced by a cooperative of designers and architects at the Milan, Italy, furniture exposition in 1981.[6]

In addition to COLORCORE™ Formica and a new dense form of chipboard called Medite, a host of more traditional surface treatments like lacquer, leather, paint or exotic veneers are being used in Chicago to create unique pieces of furniture often called "functional art." Adventurous in shape and frequently laminated, inlaid, or ablaze with color, the new art furniture runs the gamut from handcrafted chairs and tables in mellow woods to bizarre geometric confections in pale pastels or bold combinations of purple, fuschia, and pink. Made in limited editions, signed by the artist, and frequently dated, the new art furniture pays homage to fine handcraftsmanship while glorying in new materials.

Interest in furniture as art and in furniture design in general has been stimulated by competitions such as those sponsored by the Formica Corporation or the American Society of Interior Designers, and *Progressive Architecture,* as well as by the exposure offered by such local art galleries as Phyllis Needlman, Hokin/Kaufman, Frumkin & Struve, and the Hyde Park Art Center, all of which are promoting the work of local furniture makers. Selling only to architects and interior designers are showrooms such as the one operated by Roz Mallin in the Merchandise Mart, which specializes in furniture and accessories inspired by designers popular from the 1920s through the 1950s. Niedermaier, a Chicago-based manufacturer of store display merchandise, opened a showroom in the Mart to promote its new line of avant-garde furniture in 1982.

Reflecting the revival of interest in early twentieth-century furniture, Interior Crafts, Chicago's largest custom furniture maker, introduced French Art Nouveau reproductions a few years ago, followed by a large Art Deco collection in 1982. Chairs, tables, and cabinets by such well-known French

Interior Crafts, Inc. 805 Milwaukee, 1951–53; 2114 West Carroll, 1953–58; 1321 South Fifty-fifth Court, Cicero, 1958–68; 2513 West Cullerton, 1968 to the present.

Now the largest custom furniture house in the country, Interior Crafts was founded by Jerry Seiff and Vito Ursini, both former employees of Tapp, Inc.

Interior Crafts's facilities and work force have grown considerably since Seiff and Ursini began upholstering furniture in a loft above a bowling alley on Milwaukee Avenue. By the mid-1950s, when they acquired the former S. Karpen & Bros. plant in Cicero, they employed 100 workers. Since 1968, the number of employees has increased to 200.

At first the company upholstered frames purchased from other factories. It now has facilities for executing frames, case goods, and special finishes, and it makes all types of furniture. Recently the company introduced reproductions of French Art Nouveau designs, followed in 1982 by an Art Deco line that includes replicas of the work of Jacques-Emile Ruhlmann of France and Samuel Marx of Chicago. Interior Crafts specializes in reproductions of antique French, English, and Chinese furniture. Prominent interior decorators—Angelo Donghia, Burt England, and Richard Himmel—serve as consulting designers.

Interior Crafts maintains two showrooms in the Merchandise Mart and exhibits its products in New York City, Dallas, Houston, Miami, Los Angeles, San Francisco, and Washington, D.C. Their furniture is identified by a metal tag.

designers as Louis Majorelle, Jules Leleu, and Emile-Jacques Ruhlmann and tables by Chicago architect Samuel Marx are part of the new line, which includes pieces made of exotic Macassar ebony or finished in glistening black lacquer or silver leaf. Others display surfaces resembling tortoise shell or crushed ostrich eggs, or coverings of goatskin or leather. While not inexpensive, these pieces and the new designs shown in local salesrooms and galleries provide bold and colorful alternatives to the more subdued international style furniture traditionally selected for commercial or luxurious residential interiors.

Wishbone console by Jules Leleu, reproduced in 1982 in olive ash and brass by Interior Crafts for its Classics Circa Nineteen Twenty-five collection.
l: 60" w: 43" d: 25"
Interior Crafts, Inc.

Not only architects but interior designers—Gary Lee, Cal Spitzer, Jon Cockrell, to name only three—have been creating art furniture. Lee, formerly creative director of Niedermaier, often relies upon unusual color, trim, and detail rather than form to create furniture designed for shock appeal. As he told a *Sun-Times* reporter: "If we did a six-legged console table in mahogany, instead of in lacquer and red leather, it would have a very classic character. It wouldn't be that outrageous. Almost any single piece can be interpreted in a variety of ways and take on a variety of characters." Judy Niedermaier, owner of the firm, described her company's furniture as having "a flamboyance and a style that is applicable to both residential and contract settings."[7]

Building store displays for Niedermaier gave Cal Spitzer practical experience and some insight into marketing products in the home furnishings field. Spitzer, who had been trained at The Art Institute of Chicago, and his wife, Patti Gilford, formed Netto Design Works in 1980 and began to make furniture. "*Netto* is an Italian word that means clean, distinct, and exact," explained Gilford, who also has a background in fine arts. "We're not doing New Wave or Memphis furniture—ours is built for use. You might call it 'audience participation art,' sculptural perhaps, but always

functional."[8] High-gloss black or dark surfaces created by covering wood with lacquer or Formica, nontraditional multipurpose shapes, and bits of bright color, often in the form of thin bands, have become Spitzer's trademark.

Another Chicagoan known for colorful lacquered finishes and dramatic effects, Jon Cockrell uses rich materials and angular shapes that reflect his admiration for designs of the 1920s as well as a penchant for new materials. "The Art Deco period was furniture's highest hour," Cockrell asserted, "but today there are so many wonderful new materials and new ways of dealing with old problems."[9] Cockrell's designs make use of lacquer in cool pastels as well as rich, deep purples or reds. Sharp angles, arcs, and strong contrasts recall Art Moderne styling, while arrangement and material make a contemporary statement.

A few artists who usually paint or sculpt have also joined the ranks of the art furniture makers. Of these, Klindt Houlberg and George Suyeoka both create whimsical carved or painted furniture whose forms and ornamentation reflect their maker's personal points of view and transcend the traditional boundaries between art and craft. Houlberg, for example, hand-carves chairs, beds, tables, and other useful objects whose basic shapes are familiar but whose wooden heads, carved figures, and painted images make them more akin to folk art than furniture. "Each piece is a collaboration of an image and a function," he explained to a reporter. "The ideas, I hope, are humorous, shapely, strong, good-looking, and have nice personalities."[10] An associate professor of art at the University of Illinois at Chicago Circle, Houlberg took up furniture making after visiting Nigeria, where he was struck by the realization that non-Western art often takes the form of

Radical Modern Gothic chairs, table,
bud vase, and flower created by Klindt
Houlberg out of wood.
Phyliss Needlman Gallery

functional objects. In addition to his painting, he took up making quilts, hooking rugs, and eventually carving and painting furniture. "All of my quilts and rugs and furniture have a certain humor to them and a kind of imagery that is almost lyrical or poetic—like a fantasy. . . . I make them usable, but they are art."[11]

Hawaiian-born George Suyeoka, a free-lance illustrator, has been sculpting animal figures that function as furniture for the past eleven years. His "zoo" includes a variety of animal forms—hippos, ostriches, baboons, and cats, among others—that unfold or open to provide storage or work-space. "Bushman," a smiling gorilla modeled after a celebrity at Chicago's Lincoln Park Zoo, now preserved at the Field Museum of Natural History, turns into a chaise lounge when its back is folded down. A baby hippo can serve as a footstool or ottoman. Other figures, particularly those with human forms, are tongue-in-cheek allusions to current political conditions. Among the most playful in several senses is "The Bureau of Indian Affairs," which consists of an almost life-size Indian figure in full headdress whose torso sports a chest of drawers.

Over the last decade a number of designer/craftsmen working exclusively in wood have been making names for themselves in the field of custom furniture. Among these are Joseph Agati, Glenn Gordon, Howard Kavinsky, Mark Levin, David Orth, Lloyd Schwan, R. Thomas Tedrowe, Jr., and Lee Weitzman.

Trestle Table by R. Thomas Tedrowe, Jr., 1981. The elm top is supported by legs resembling I-beams held in a pearlwood truss. A series of stacking chairs with

"diamond plate" seats and backs made of cherry and holly also mimic metal. Table, h: 30" w: 55¾" d: 37" R. Thomas Tedrowe, Jr.

In addition to executing ecclesiastical furnishings, Joseph A. Agati's six-year old firm Agati Designs, Inc., now offers several collections of conference / dining tables and chairs finished in polyurethane enamels of white, gray, burgundy, or turquoise whose intriguing names (the Wing Table Collection, the Pin Stripe Collection, the Knife Edge Collection, etc.) allude to their decorative detailing. One set, the Petro Collection, a black enameled table with triangular legs and barrel-backed chairs, highlighted with thin

Black lacquered dining table and chairs, called the Petro Collection, designed and executed by Agati Designs, Inc., 1982.
Table, h: 29¼" w: 40½" d: 40½"
Agati Designs, Inc. Photograph by Michael Tropea

stripes of red and yellow, has received two of the furniture industry's most prestigious awards: the 1982 IBD product award and, in 1983, the Hardwood Institute's "Daphne" citation for Limited Productions, the equivalent of the film industry's "Oscar."

A designer/craftsman who says he acquired his basic woodworking skills "in a somewhat utopian co-op at North and Sheffield avenues," Glenn Gordon has been making one-of-a-kind pieces since 1970.[12] Using domestic hardwoods like cherry, oak, or maple, he accents his pieces with rarer woods like ebony, pearwood, or myrtle to create pleasing contrasts and to draw attention to the hand-cut joints and exposed tenons that have become his signature. Among his most recent pieces are tall stools with slender legs and tapered seats that call attention to beautifully grained wood and elegant joinery.

Walnut, oak, and glass Prairie table designed and executed by Glenn Gordon, 1982.
h: 20¾" w: 30⅛" d: 24"
Glenn Gordon. Photograph by Abramson-Culbert Studio

Model for wood and lacquer desk designed by Lloyd Schwan in 1982.
Hokin/Kaufman Gallery

A woodworker known for his supersmooth, hand-rubbed, glossy surfaces, Howard Kavinsky has been making furniture for ten years. Like most of this new generation of furniture makers, he takes full advantage of modern woodworking tools and techniques and saves his patience and energy for the creative processes of design and finishing.

Mark S. Levin, who has been in business since 1975, says that he doesn't have any "complicated theories" about what he does, "I just like to work wood."[13] Quite a few of Levin's linear desks and cabinets have found their way into Chicago's executive suites. Many of his best known designs, however, exhibit sensuous curves and tendril-like legs sculpted from blocks formed by laminating together several layers of wood. Pieces, first shaped by machine and then by hand, often assume leaf and flower forms. A series of lily pad and lotus leaf tables and desks, for example, display fluid rippled edges.

Bent and laminated display stand of cherry and padauk designed and executed by Mark S. Levin, 1980.
h: 56"
Mark S. Levin

Three generations of Diebold cabinetmakers (left to right): Richard A.; his sons, Richard G. and John P.; and his father, Richard O. Diebold.

In the midst of this new movement, Chicago remains home to a large number of traditional furniture makers. Numerous small firms continue to execute custom furniture and special finishes for interior designers or other furniture makers. Two of the oldest—Diebold's Cabinet Shop and Grand Wood Carving—were founded in the 1930s and are now operated by the third generation of the founding family. Located on North Springfield Avenue, Diebold's Cabinet Shop was established in 1936 by Richard O. Diebold, who still comes in to work alongside his son, Richard A., and grandsons, Richard G. and John. The shop executes furniture, does refinishing, and supplies many of the local upholsterers with wooden frames for chairs and sofas. Similarly, the children and grandchildren of Stanley F. Motyka, who opened the Grand Wood Carving shop on North Wolcott in 1939, continue to carve legs for pianos and tables and make other components for furniture in addition to carving figurines of horses and other animals.

In business since 1929, Thomas Montalbano founded the Montalbano Majestic Wood Carving Company on North Maplewood Avenue. Born in Chicago, he went to work for the Artistic Wood Carving Company at the age of twelve. Having learned his trade as a carver there, he went on to establish his own business in his garage, enlisting the help of his wife and sister. Eventually, his two sons, Richard and Bob, joined the business.

The firm moved into its current quarters in 1942, having purchased an existing factory with equipment for every stage of furniture making, from kilns to dry the lumber to shipping facilities. Starting out by making tables the company expanded its scope to include curio cabinets, bedroom and dining-room furniture and, in 1983, frames for upholstered furniture.

Traditional styles remain popular, as can be seen from this elaborately hand-carved furniture, including marquetry inlay and hand-rubbed finish, made by the members of the Montalbano family since 1929.
Montalbano-Majestic Wood Carving Company

The founder's training and skill as a carver determined the specialty that has come to be associated with the company's products. Inspired by Thomas Montalbano, who still appears for work daily, later generations of woodcarvers have continued to fashion the intricately carved, inlaid, painted, and hand-finished French Provincial style furniture for which the company is known.[14]

Other custom furniture makers include LeRoy J. Simon Assoc., whose owner has been designing and executing furniture for interior designers since 1952, and Frederick C. Boger of F.C.B. Designers, who has been working in wood, stone, and metal since 1951. Formerly employed by Watson & Boaler, Boger makes use of this training in architecture and product design to create a wide variety of unique household furnishings. Kiyoshi Tanouye has been executing fine furniture for numerous architects since 1955. Newer firms specializing in custom cabinetry include Jean Jacques Bernard (1978), and Wooden Horse Cabinetry (1978), operated by Andrew H. Pawlan and Stephen Gleich. Franz Pfeifer, owner of Creative Woodcraft Co. (1975), was certified as a master cabinetmaker in Germany; Sev Kemper, who specializes in executing architectural commissions, came to Chicago a decade ago from Poland.

Two of the fastest growing new furniture factories in the city produce seating furniture especially for contract interiors. Founded in 1963 by Jerry Saviano and Irving Cohen, the Regal Mfg. Company on West Twenty-first Street produces metal dinettes and bar stools. On West Ogden Avenue, System Seating makes upholstered wooden dining chairs in over 100 styles.

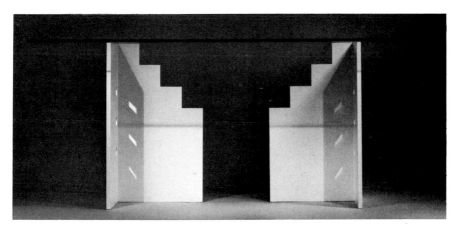

Organized in 1977 by David Wilson, who emigrated from Ireland in 1956, the firm has grown from three to forty employees in just six years.

Working with pliable vines of rattan rather than wood, the Novotny brothers—John, Louis, and Joseph—weave bassinets, chairs, chests, buggies, church collection plates, and caskets at the Artistic Reed & Willow Company at 420 South Kolmar Avenue. They learned to weave from their father, John, who started the company in 1920, thirteen years after emigrating from Czechoslovakia. Bassinets, modeled after their father's fifty-year-old design, are their principal product. But the Novotnys, who claim that they can translate any sketch into rattan, also build gondolas for a hot air balloon firm in South Dakota, making about 100 of these each year.

Marden Manufacturing, Inc. 1215 South Morgan, 1946–48; 615 North Aberdeen, 1948–53; 1015 North Halsted, 1953–67; 5823 Ravenswood, 1968 to the present.

Marden Manufacturing, Inc., makers of contract furniture, was organized by Carl and Melvin Balonick when they returned from military service after World War II. Within a short time two other brothers, Louis and Robert, joined them in the Morgan Street factory. Each of the Balonicks had had some experience in furniture making, having worked with their father, a Chicago carpenter/cabinetmaker, and in the factory of S. Karpen & Bros.

The company specializes in durable, modern furniture for use in schools, hotels, hospitals, or offices. In addition to upholstered work, it makes wooden conference and occasional tables, upholstered cane chairs, and wooden-framed sofas, chairs, and modular seating. Sold primarily through architectural firms and interior designers, its products are displayed in showrooms maintained in Chicago, Detroit, Minneapolis, Houston, Dallas, Denver, Los Angeles, Seattle, Atlanta, and Washington, D.C.

Marden remains a Balonick family business. Carl is president of the firm and Melvin is in charge of production, assisted by Robert's son, Brad. Robert and his son, Larry, and Homer and Demetrius Tremulis are responsible for design and graphics.

After three years of recession, Chicago's furniture makers agree that business is slow. However, there are varied opinions concerning current and coming trends. From the vantage point of his thirty-seven years in business, John C. Murphy of Watson & Boaler, dean of the city's interior designers, observed: "Except for those in the avant garde, who remind me of those in the twenties who embraced Swedish Modern and Art Moderne, the vast majority have remained thoroughly conservative in their homes. The smartest interior today is eclectic: a mixture of antiques, period reproductions, and contemporary accents."[15]

Designer Richard Himmel also sees many similarities between today's trendsetters and the tastemakers of the 1920s. He considers post-modern "a legitimate fashion statement," but not one he plans to adopt. "Things keep being restated to fit current times," he says. "I'm not an innovator; I'm an adaptor who knows how to look. I started bringing in Art Deco from France sixteen years ago when I saw that people were moving toward interiors that were simpler and more personal. Now I'm buying small-scale Louis XVI furniture because I think it fits the mood of the people and the size of the space they have to live with."[16]

More attuned to contemporary than antiques, architect Norman deHaan, whose firm Norman DeHaan Associates and its subsidiary, Interior Distributors, specialize in contract furnishings, commented that furniture of the 1970s had been "spare and scaled down," in harmony with the prevailing look of "white tile, butcher blocks, Swedish ivy, and homemade bread. . . . Now, in the eighties," he exclaimed, "it's overstuffed and developing tail-fins!"[17]

Robert Balonick, designer for Marden Manufacturing, Inc., makers of contract furniture, explained that his firm "doesn't jump on trends," but tries to create "a strong signature" by building furniture "the best way we know how." Where does he get his inspiration? From his hometown. As he puts it: "I even like the weather. In the winter, I'm a hibernating creature. In the spring, I can feel my blood starting to run and the pencil jumps into my hand. . . . Chicago is still a place that exudes energy. It's a breeding ground, a place where things happen and everyone runs to see."[18]

And so, one hundred and fifty years after James Reed and his fellow cabinetmakers first advertised their handcrafted wares in the city's only newspaper, one can still find furniture makers at work in Chicago, both in large factories and small workshops, suiting the needs and tastes of a broad range of clients throughout the United States.

OTHER CHICAGO DESIGNERS AND MANUFACTURERS

CCD = Chicago City Directories
CFMA = Chicago Furniture Manufacturers' Association
CTD = Chicago Telephone Directories

Acanthus Wood Carving Co.	Member CFMA in 1938.
Acers-Renfrow Cabinet Co.	Store and office fixtures and special cabinet-work for soda fountains, 1904–5. CCD
Acme Cabinet Works	Store and office fixtures. Founded by Frederick Bletzinger in 1914.
Acme Mfg. & Upholstering	Upholstered furniture, 1960–70. CTD
Acme Novelty Furniture Co.	Novelty furniture, 1936–39. CTD
Acme Spring Bed Co.	Iron and brass beds, mattresses. The Acme Hygienic Couch and Acme Easy Chair, 1891–1916. Name changed to Acme Co. by 1903. CCD
Adams, Francis W.	Manufactured Adams Chair & Sofa, 1896–ca. 1929. Renamed Adams Chair Bed Co. ca. 1923. CCD
Advance Furniture Mfg. Co.	Chrome furniture, 1950–55. CTD
Aetna Cabinet & Fixture Co.	Bank, store, and office fixtures, 1911–ca. 1918. CCD
Aetna Parlor Furniture Co.	*American Cabinet Maker and Upholsterer* (June 11, 1898) noted that the company "is sending to the trade a new catalog just issued. The . . . trade in cheap couches made it necessary for this firm to enlarge its force of employees."
Ahrens, George	Cabinetmaker, 1862–66. CCD
Albert, F. A. Furniture Mfg. Co.	Manufacturer, 1939–44. CTD

Alexander Parlor Frame Co.	Modern and Lawson style chair frames and sofa beds, 1929–70. CTD
Allen, J. M. & H. M.	Bureaus and bureau washstands, 1869–ca. 1876. Established by John M. and Henry M. Allen. Company carried on by Mrs. Nellie Allen 1874–75. CCD
Allen Parlor Furniture Mfrs.	Custom upholstered furniture, 1939–60. CTD
Allied Chair Corp.	Formica-top dinette sets and chrome chairs, ca. 1950. CTD
Allied Furniture Mfg. Co.	Novelty furniture specialties, specializing in tables, 1955–60. CTD
Al's Novelty Furniture Co.	Contract wood furniture, 1936–ca. 1955. CTD
Alsberg, Samuel	Ottomans, 1894–ca. 1903. Patented support for stools, chairs, etc. on Sept. 5, 1899. CCD
Altman's Modern Woodwork	Custom furniture, ca. 1950. CTD
Alvin Industries	Chromium pedestals, chair frames, and tubular parts, ca. 1950. CTD
Ambrosino, V. & Co.	"Custom built furniture for the trade," 1936–70. Name changed to Ambrosino Furniture Mfg. in 1950. CTD
American Chrome Co.	Chrome furniture, 1939–43. CTD
American Church & Chapel Furniture Co.	Church furniture, 1939–44. CTD
American Desk & Seating Co.	Office furniture, 1887–95. CCD
American Furniture Frame Co.	Frames, 1943–55. CTD
American Metal Ware Co.	Brass bedsteads, costumers, cuspidors, 1899–ca. 1908. Adolf Hartman was president in 1899. CCD
American Office Fitting Co.	Office furniture, 1891–94. CCD
American Parlor Frame Co.	Parlor frames, 1887–1939. CCD, CTD
American Parlor Furniture Co.	Parlor furniture, 1920–29. CCD
American Seating Co.	Seating for schools, theaters, churches, buses, etc. Began as Grand Rapids School Furniture Co. in 1886. Name changed in 1899 when they acquired eighteen concerns of public seating manufacturing. In 1951 acquired assets and patents of S. Karpen Bros. Transportation Seating Division. Chicago headquarters but manufactured in Buffalo, NY, Grand Rapids, MI, Racine, WI, and Manitowoc, WI.
American Store Stool Co.	Store, office, church, library, public hall, lawn and steamboat stools, 1868–85. CCD
American Wall Bed Co.	Folding beds, 1915–17. CCD

American Wood Carving Co., Inc.	Frames, furniture carvings, novelty furniture, 1910–50. CCD, CTD
American Wood Products Co.	Kitchenette and dinette sets, 1936–44. CTD
Ames & Frost	Manufacturer of spring beds, cots, folding beds, and bicycles, ca. 1872–ca. 1899. Charles L. Ames and A. H. Frost. Established branch house in Philadelphia in 1877. Numerous patents for bed springs, wire-coiling machines, and folding beds assigned to company, 1873–96. Bought out Boyington Folding Bed Co. after failure in 1888. CCD
Anderson Specialties	Lecterns, ca. 1970. CTD
Andres, John	Chair seats, ca. 1929. CCD
Annesley & Ferris	Manufacturers of furniture, picture frames, looking glasses, and Findley's Patent Screw Bedsteads, 1847–52. CCD
Apex Parlor Furniture Mfg. Co.	Parlor furniture, 1939–44. CTD
Arndt & Lange	Manufacturer, 1880–81. John Arndt, 1885–97. CCD
Arneson & Co.	Parlor furniture and chamber sets, 1871–73. Operated as Arneson & Trosterund, 1873–79. CCD
Arnold, Casper	Cabinetmaker at Hasey's, 1847–53; 200 Van-Buren, 1861–66. CCD
Arnold, George A.	Office desks, showcases, and cabinetmakers in general, 1859–65. CCD
Arrow Parlor Frame Co.	Frames, ca. 1943–70. CTD
Art Bedstead Co.	Brass and iron beds, Adams chair/bed, 1894–1919. F. W. Adams. CCD
Art Furniture Shop	Operated by Michael Bernstein and Morris Karpen, 1923. CCD
Art-Bilt, Inc.	Frames, ca. 1950–65. CTD
Art-Craft Parlor Furniture Mfg. Co.	315 West Hubbard, ca. 1950–70. CTD
Artistic Wood Turning Works	Pedestals, stands, novelties, and specialties in oak and mahogany, ca. 1908–ca. 1923. CCD
Ashbrook, Shirley W.	Manufacturer, 1908–11. CCD
Atco Furniture Co.	1509 North Halsted, ca. 1950–70. CTD
Atlas Furniture Mfg. Co.	Living-room furniture, 1940–55. CTD
Atlas Glass and Mirror Co.	Mirrored furniture designed by Robert Frederics in 1941. Founded 1916.
Atlas Parlor Furniture Co.	Frames, 1900–ca. 1904. Anthony A. Polka and James F. Brabec. CCD
Austrian, Leo & Co.	Mirrors, hatracks, "Illinois" folding bed, ca. 1888–97. CCD

Authentic Furniture Products	Early American dinettes and captain's chairs, 1965–70. CTD
Automatic Folding Bed Co.	Operated by Christian Bostad and Olaus O. Krabol, 1892–96. CCD
Ayers, John W.	Mantels and custom furniture, 1887–1909; Ayers-Ransom-Bauerle Co., 1910–11; Ayers-Cihlar-Ransom Co., 1912–50. John W. Ayers (1850–1914). CCD, CTD
Balkwill, John F. & Co.	Chamber and hotel furniture, 1888–94. Balkwill & Patch, ca. 1895–1923. John F. Balkwill and William Patch. CCD
Bamboo Manufacturing Co.	Bamboo furniture, 1890–93. CCD
Bares-Rehak Furniture Co.	828 North Wells, ca. 1950; Rehak Furniture Co., 1955–60. CTD
Barnes, H. R. Co.	730 North Franklin, ca. 1955–65. CTD
Barnhart & Hunt	Art furniture, ca. 1886; Barnhart & Spitz Mfg. Co., 1887–89; Barnhart & Wright Mfg. Co., 1890–91. CCD
Barth, Hermann & Co.	Parlor suites, lounge and patent rocking chairs, 1884–98. Successor to Dietsch & Barth. Hermann Barth and Frederick Frederickson, owners. Bankrupt in 1898.
Bast, Jacob S.	Art furniture, 1877–85. J. S. Bast & Son, 1884. E. E. Bast, 1885. CCD
Eli Bates Settlement House	Exhibited furniture in the 1918 Applied Arts Exhibition at The Art Institute of Chicago.
Bauerle & Stark	224–30 West Ohio, 1874–1907. CCD
Baumgart, F. G. & Co.	Upholstered furniture, 1908. *Directory of Furniture Manufacturers.*
Beauchamp, Joseph	Cabinetmaker, 1848–63. CCD
Bechyne, Vincent	Tables, 1888–95. CCD
Beck, Edward	Patentee and manufacturer of Beck's combination sofa bed and lounge (patent 407,151 in 1883.), 1883–86.
Becker, L. A. Co.	Saloon and drug store fixtures, ca. 1899. Louis A. Becker, Charles F. McLean, and William A. Barnes.
Beckley Cardy Co.	School furniture, ca. 1907–82. CTD
Behnke-Fink Mfg. Co.	Novelties, 1917–39. CCD
Beiersdorf, Jacob	Parlor and patent furniture. J. Beiersdorf & Co., 1860–84; Sugg, Lozier & Beiersdorf (Northwestern Furniture Mfg. Co.), 1868–71; Sugg & Beiersdorf, 1871–91. Also partner in the Rocker Spring Company.
Bel-Aire Creations	Armchairs, settees, breakfast nooks, 1950–70. CTD

Bent, John W.	Refrigerators, iceboxes, and furniture. Patent 166,679 for extension table on August 17, 1875. Manufacturer of Osgood's Patent Improved Extension Table in 1873.
Berg & Borgensen	Office desks, 1880. In 1881 became Thompson & Borgenson at same address. CCD
Berger, W. H. Mfg. Co.	Manufacturer, 1890–1910. CCD
Bishop, Samuel	Chairmaker, 1849–52. CCD
Biver Ernster & Co.	Parlor furniture, 1888–90. CCD.
Blackmer Bros. & Co.	Manufacturer, 1892–1901. CCD
Bleier, Charles & Co.	Upholstered furniture, 1907–11. CCD
Bliss, Jacob	Cabinetmaker at Jacobus, 1847. J. Bliss & Co. cabinet wareroom and shop, 1848–51. CCD
Blom, Geo. & Son	Antique furniture reproductions, 1939. CTD
Blonder Bros.	Manufacturer of brass and iron beds, 1903–6. CCD
Bodach, Frank	Parlor furniture and lounges, 1892–1910. F. Bodach & Sons, 1936–65. CCD, CTD
Bodach, Robert	Parlor furniture, 1943–70.
Boericke, R. & Co.	Manufacturer, 1887–93. CCD
Boesch, John O.	Manufacturer, 1886–91. CCD
Boese, Frederick & Bro.	Manufacturer, 1866–75. CCD
Borgwardt & Ernst Co.	Upholstered parlor furniture, church and club furniture, 1887–ca. 1950. CCD, CTD
Bosley, D. W. & Co.	Furniture carvings, 1872. CCD
Bostelmann, Christ & Co.	Chamber suites and bedsteads, 1874–84. Succeeded by Bostelman & Ladenburger in 1885. CCD
Bostelman & Ladenburger	Chamber suites and bedsteads, 1885–87. CCD
Bouc, Otto	Handmade period furniture, ca. 1950. CTD
Bowles & Bates	Center tables and "fittings for banks, offices and dwellings," 1871–73. CCD
Boyington Folding Bed Co.	Patent folding beds, 1872–ca. 1888. Levi C. Boyington, founder. Bought out by Ames & Frost in 1888. Levi C. Boyington received numerous patents for bed springs, cabinet beds, and spring bed bottoms, 1874–85.
Boynton, E. S.	Brackets. Successor to E. J. Lewis & Co., manufacturer of fancy cabinet ware, 1888.
Brethart (Britchard), Frederick	Cabinetmaker, 1851–61. CCD
Brett(s), William	Cabinetmaker, 1849–65. CCD
Brink Mfg. Co.	Upholstered furniture, 1939–44. CTD
Brody, B. Seating Co.	Chrome dinette sets, ca. 1950–ca. 1976. Harry Brody president in 1965. CFMA

Brody Brothers Furniture	Parlor sets, booths, nooks, 1944–60. CTD
Brown, George	Chair factory, 1839–50. CCD
Bruns & Collins Inc.	Metal furniture, 1936–39. CCD
Bruske Co., F. O.	Successor to Illinois Parlor Furniture Co. in 1921.
Budrick Brothers Furniture Manufacturers	Manufacturer, 1944–65. CTD
Buhmann & Hansen	Parlor furniture, 1887–95. CCD
Bukoi Mfg. Co.	Manufacturer, 1950–70. CTD
Brudett, Chair Mfg. Co., The	Chairs, 1897–98. CCD
Burhop, Henry	Parlor furniture, 1894–95. CCD
Burhop, Mahnke & Walter	Parlor furniture, 1887–89. Burhop & Mahnke, 1890–93. CCD
Burt, Larock & Zarndt	Manufacturer of People's Folding Bed, 1884–86. CCD
Busack, Christian	Manufacturer, 1864–73. CCD
Buschert, Sebastian	Church furniture (esp. Catholic), 1881–ca. 1886. Partner in Buschert & Gramer, 1879–81. CCD
Buschmeyer, H. & Co.	Manufacturer, 1882–85. CCD
Busse, F. & Co.	Bedsteads, tables, and washstands, 1861–75. CCD
Bussey, J. E.	Manufacturer, 1897–1908. Bussey & Briggs, 1909–11. CCD
Butera, Samuel & Sons	Upholstered furniture, 1955–70. CTD
Butzow & Brother	Bureaus and washstands. Butzow & Brother, 1859–69; J. Butzow & Co., 1870–79; became Kraus, Butzow & Peters in 1879. Christian Butzow. CCD
Cahn & Buschmeyer's Furniture Manufactory	French bedsteads, center tables, chamber sets, 1872–75. Cahn & Berg, 1877. Henry Cahn & Co., 1878–81. CCD
Capitol Furniture Mfg. Co.	Made-to-order furniture frames, ca. 1950. CTD
Cardelli Wood Carving Co.	Member CFMA in 1938.
Carlton Inc.	Manufacturers, 1950–55. CTD
Carpenter Bros. Mfg. Co.	"Cane and solid suits/also odd chairs and rockers," 1907–21.
Carsley, Frank E.	Art furniture, 1878. Carsley & East Mfg. Co., manufacturers of "Fine interior finish," 1886–93. Became Carsley Mfg. Co. in 1893. CCD
Carter, H. S.	Parlor furniture, 1856–61; Joslin & Carter, 1865–66; H. S. Carter & Company, 1867–95. Patented and manufactured folding lounges in 1870s; employed seventy in 1877.
Casey, Patrick	Manufacturer, 1888–91. CCD

Central Parlor Frame Mfg. Co.	Frames, 1929–60. John Marcek, president. CCD
Central Union Parlor Furniture Co.	Labor unrest at company mentioned in January 29, 1920, *Furniture World.*
Century Parlor Furniture Co.	School furniture and office fixtures, 1906–23. CCD
Century Seating Co.	School furniture, tables, and office fixtures. Became Century Parlor Furniture Co. in 1906. CCD
Chain, W. A. Couch Co.	Couches and Morris chairs, 1906–9. William A. Chain. CCD
Champion Table Slide Co.	Extension table slides and cabinet work benches, 1890–93. CCD
Chase, J. L. Co.	Chairs, 1936–60. CTD. Purchased by Schnadig Corp. in 1960.
Chicago Cane Seating Co.	Chairs, 1895–98. Michigan City and Chicago factories.
Chicago Carpet Co.	Furniture and upholstery manufacturer and retailer, 1883–98.
Chicago Chair Co.	Chairs, 1889–91. See Francis F. Eggleston. CCD
Chicago Chair & Wheel Co.	Wheel chairs. Was the Geo. F. Child and Physicians' National Supply Co. Established 1887 by George F. Child, who was succeeded by B. F. Hales in 1897.
Chicago Combination Folding Bed Co.	Folding beds, ca. 1888. CCD
Chicago Desk Mfg. Co.	Manufacturer of desks and the "Chicago" folding bed, 1880–91. Successors to Skielvig, Peterson & Co. in 1880.
Chicago Fancy Furniture Co.	The *Furniture Journal* (November 1921) noted that there had been a fire in the company's plant at 21–25 South Hoyne.
Chicago Furniture Makers	535 North Broadway, 1950–55. CTD
Chicago Furniture Mfg. Co.	The *Furniture Journal* (June 1922) noted that company had taken lease on a seven-story building at Blackhawk and Cherry.
Chicago Hassock Co.	Manufacturer of hassocks, footstools, ottomans, and commodes, 1882–1908. CCD
Chicago Iron Bedstead Mfg. Co.	Iron bedsteads and children's cribs, ca. 1873–1900. CCD
Chicago Iron & Brass Bed Mfg. Co.	Metal beds, 1898–1903. CCD
Chicago Lounge Co.	Upholstered lounges, 1896–1904. CCD
Chicago Mission Furniture Co.	Wooden furniture, 1904–27. Frederick P. Fischer, Jr., Arthur McDowell, Jacob Scherer,

	and John McLelland. After 1918 produced library, parlor, and end tables in quartered oak and later in mahogany.
Chicago Novelty Furniture Co.	Novelties, 1923–39. CTD
Chicago Parlor Furniture Co.	Parlor goods, couches, and library furniture, 1880–1923. Began manufacturing own frames in 1902. CCD
Chicago Parlor Set Manufacturing Co.	A cooperative factory, 1877–80.
Chicago Rattan Co.	Rattan and reed furniture, 1882–94. Name changed to Chicago Rattan & Reed Co. by 1882; became Chicago Rattan & Reed Works in 1890. CCD
Chicago Reedware Mfg. Co.	3127 West Chicago, 1922–23. CCD
Chicago Upholstered Furniture Co.	Incorporated in 1911 by partners in National Parlor Furniture Co. (Frank Cumming, J. K. Deimel, and A. P. Stephens); 1911–14. CCD
Chicago Willow & Rattan Works	Reed furniture, 1888–1905. CCD
Chicago Wire Chair Co.	Steel wire chairs, stools, fancy tables, etc. 1900–1908. CCD
Chicago Woodworkers, Ltd.	Wall systems, desks, fixtures, 1978–present. Roselle, Illinois.
Chicago Wood Carving Co.	High-grade artistic furniture, 1907–ca. 1918. CCD
Chicago Wood Novelty Co.	Novelty furniture, ca. 1950. CTD
Child, Geor. F. Adjustable Chair Co.	"Parlor, Invalid & Physicians' Chairs, Earth Closets and All Kinds of Invalid Furniture," 1887–1917. CCD.
Chrom Furniture Works	Metal furniture, 1936–39. CTD
Chromade Corp.	Metal furniture, ca. 1936. CTD
Churchill Cabinet Company	Cabinetmakers, ca. 1905–ca. 1976. O. Gullicksen and Spencer Gullicksen officers in 1936; W. A. Gullicksen president in 1976. CFMA
Clarin Mfg. Co.	4640 West Harrison, 1965–70. CTD
Clark, Elisha	Cabinetmaker, 1848–62. CCD
Clark, W. H.	Manufacturer of "Heath's Patent Reclining Chair and Invalid Bed," ca. 1873.
Clark Brothers & Co.	Chamber furniture and desks, 1869–86. Henry M. Clark. CCD
Clemco Desk Manufacturing Co.	Clemco desks. Founded by Dante A. Raggio (1873–1945).
Clementsen Company, Anton	Office furniture, 1890–present. In 1918 changed production to special cabinets and wood specialties; Anton Clementsen (1859–1936). John A. Clementsen president in 1976. CFMA

Cloyde, John	Upholsterer, 1847; turning shop, 1848–50. CCD
Cockrell, Jon	Designer, 1977–present.
Coe, Thomas	Cabinets and chairs, 1843–44. Coe & (Henry) Mills, 1847–50. CCD
Colby, Joseph H. & Co.	Manufacturer, 1887–1905. CCD
Colonial Chair Company	Dining, office, and bedroom chairs in period and colonial patterns, 1906–ca. 1936. CCD
Columbia Furniture Mfg.	Manufacturers, 1939–43. CTD
Columbia Lounge Co.	Parlor furniture, couches, and leather upholstered furniture, 1906–12.
Columbia Parlor Frame Co.	Parlor, lounge, couch, odd chair, Morris chair frames, 1894–1917.
Columbian Adjustable Table and Desk Co., The	Folding tables and table desks, 1892. CCD
Comfort Bed Spring Co.	Juvenile, kitchen, and restaurant furniture, 1939–70. Name changed to Comfort Lines, Inc., 1950. CTD
Commercial Furniture Co.	Office desks, 1888–ca. 1936. A. H. Stringe, Harry Stringe, and A. R. Stringe were officers in 1936. CFMA
Conrad, Andrew	Chairmaker, 1848–51. CCD
Consolidated Metal Products Co.	Furniture frames, 1960–70. CTD
Continental Mfg. Co.	Frames for parlor furniture and couches, 1879–1923. CCD
Continental Upholstering Co.	Mike and Ed Havlik, 1936–40. CTD
Cook(e), Horatio	Chairmakers, 1848–51. Horatio, Jr., George H., and John. CCD
Cookie, Louis J.	Novelty furniture, ca. 1944. CTD
Coopercraft Mirrored Furniture	3122 West Lawrence, 1955; name changed to Coopercraft Industries, Inc., 1960. CTD
Corona Furniture Co., Inc.	"Designers and builders of fine furniture—tables, chairs, corner cabinets, mantelpieces, etc.," 1936–ca. 1970. CTD
Cortland Parlor Furniture Co.	Parlor furniture, 1943–65. CTD
Cottage Steel Folding Bed Co.	Founded by L. N. Bachaud to manufacture folding beds in June 1900; name changed same year to Sanitary Steel Folding Bed Co.
Courtesy Upholstery and Mfg. Co., Inc.	3062 West Armitage, 1965–70. CTD
Cowen Furniture Co., Inc.	Occasional furniture, 1936–55. L. D. Cowen, officer. CTD
Cozy Nooks Seating Co.	Custom booths and nooks with removable spring seats, 1955–70. CTD

Creative Woodcraft	Custom furniture, 1975–present. Franz Pfeifer.
Crest Upholstering & Mfg. Co.	Upholstered furniture, 1936–39. CTD
Crocker, Ansel L.	Manufacturer and wholesale dealer, 1866–80. CCD
Crockett, E. Jr.	"Bureau looking glass frames and parlor tables," 1867–73. CCD
Croft, E. H.	"Designers & Mfrs of Special Furniture," 1903–4. CCD
Crossman & Sturdy	Decorators & Furnishers, ca. 1898. Abner Crossman and J. F. Sturdy. Formerly Crossman & Lee.
Cudell & Meissner	Custom furniture and interior woodwork. Adolph Cudell (1850–1910) and Robert F. Meissner, 1844–85; Cudell & (Alfred A.) Lehmann, 1886–88; Cudell & (August) Blumenthal, 1889–91; A. Blumenthal & Co., 1893–96.
Custard, Morris B.	Fancy cabinet ware, 1885–ca. 1890. Successors to Lutwyche & Lentz in 1885.
Custom Furniture Mfrs.	Custom upholstered furniture, 1944–65.
Custom Special Furniture Mfg. Co.	156 West Walton, 1955. CTD
Customline Mfg. Co.	903 North Spaulding, 1965–70. CTD
Dargatz Parlor Frame Co.	Parlor furniture frames, 1906–8. CCD
Dauber & Spachman	Edward Dauber and James J. Spachman, 1897–1905. CCD
Davidson Limited	Manufacturer, 1936–60.
Davis & Horwich	Brass and iron beds, 1894–1905. Successor to Horwich Iron Folding Bed Co., founded by H. J. Horwich in 1892. Operated as Davis, Horwich & Steinman 1905–17. CCD
Dean & Company	"Decorative Furniture in Bamboo & Hardwood," 1889–92. CCD
Decor Mfg. Co.	Brass and iron special furniture and wood and marble wall consoles, 1960–65. CTD
Deimel & Bros., R.	Parlor furniture, lounges, and rockers, 1875–90. Rudolph, Simon, and Joseph Deimel, co-partners. Employed 162 in 1883.
Deimel Sofa Bed Fixture Co.	Incorporated August 1907 by Rudolph and Joseph Deimel to handle fixtures for beds manufactured by National Parlor Furniture Co.
Demme & Dierkes	Bedroom furniture, 1886–94. CCD
Demme & Fredericks	Chamber furniture, 1880–85. CCD
Design Presentations	Custom cabinetry, 1970–present. William I. Spiegel, president; Joseph Getzinger, vice-president. Skokie, Illinois.

Deutsch Bros., Inc.	Upholstered furniture, 1936–73. Eugene, Leonard, and Ethel Deutsch. CTD
Dibblee Co., The Henry	"Fine Mantels, Sideboards, Hall and Library Furniture From Special Designs Only," 1891–94. CCD
Dietsch & Barth	Patent rocker frames, 1879–82. Anton Dietsch and Herman Barth. CCD
Dimnent & Martin	Bedsteads and chamber furniture, 1873–77. CCD
Doe, Pettersen & Co.	Bureaus and bureau handles, 1872–80. Iver Doe and John Pettersen. Employed forty in 1873. Succeeded by Iver Doe Furniture Co., 1881–95. CCD
Dones, P. A. Furniture Co.	Upholstered furniture, 1939–ca. 1970. CTD
Donnelly & Barnes	Painted cottage furniture, 1877–83. CCD
Downey, Joseph	Chairs and cabinet furniture; carving, turning, and general machine work, 1873–75. CCD
Dunn, John A.	Chairs, reed furniture, reed baby carriages, 1893–1923+. CCD
Economy Chrome Mfg. Co.	Chrome furniture, 1955–60; Economy Dinette Mfg. Co., 1960–70. CTD
Edelman-Jankow Co., Inc.	Settees, booths, lounges, 1955–70. CTD
Ehman, Charles & Bro.	Pier and mantel frames, 1873–88; Ehman & Simon Mfg. Co., ca. 1889–ca. 1898. CCD
Empire Parlor Bedstead Co.	Cabinet combination bedsteads, 1872–93. David A. Titcomb and Elbridge S. Pratt. CCD
Empire Table Company	Organized 1934 to manufacture porcelain-top breakfast sets. Began making chrome furniture in 1952. 1936–ca. 1960. CCD, CTD
Empire Works	Wrought-iron furniture, 1955–60. CTD
Englewood Desk Co.	Office desks and typewriter desks. Founded by Ellis G. Durkee in 1914.
Enterprise Parlor Furniture Co.	Parlor furniture, 1906–29. CCD
Esmay, Abram S.	Gilt Edge Lounge, 1880–82. CCD
Eureka Parlor and Furniture Mfg.	Parlor furniture and tables, 1918–62 (in 1943 eliminated "Parlor" from name). CTD
Everill, William H.	Parlor furniture, 1882–88. CCD
Everson, Henry L. D.	Cabinetmaker and furniture repairer, 1863–74. CCD
Excel Furniture Mfg. Corp.	2509 West Cermak, ca. 1950. CTD
Exclusive Wrought Iron	9112 South Chicago, 1965–70. CTD
Fabian Otto & Co.	Chairs, 1873–88. CCD
Fairbank, L. G. & Co.	Lemuel G. Fairbank. Patent 166,516 for combined reading and writing desk on Aug. 10, 1875. Manufacturer, 1877–79. CCD

Faultless Chair Co.	Faultless Automatic Morris Chair, ca. 1909.
Federal Parlor Furniture Co.	Hand-carved mahogany frames, ca. 1922.
Federal Woodcarving	Occasional furniture and furniture frames, 1939–ca. 1970. Name changed to Federal Wood Industries, 1960. CTD
Fellman, J. Francis	Chairmaker, 1843–49. CCD
Ferring Co.	Court and church furniture, 1901–ca. 1929. CCD
Fenske Brothers	Upholstered living-room furniture, 1936–55. CTD
Fischbeck, F. & Co.	Patent lounges, 1869–90. Frederick Fischbeck. Patent 169,978 for sofa bedstead on November 16, 1875 (others followed through 1885).
Fischer Furniture Co.	Occasional furniture and case goods, 1936–39. E. P. Fischer and Fred Fischer. CTD
Florence Wood Working Co.	Sewing-machine cabinets, 1936–70. CTD
Florentine, Francisco and Albert	Cabinetmakers and woodcarvers, 1873–76. CCD
Ford, Johnson & Co. J. S.	Chairs: commercial, domestic, institutional, 1872–1905. Ford & Johnson, 1906–14.
Foulke, W. H. & Co.	Church and school furniture, mantels and tile work, 1880–96. CCD
Framke & Sievers	Tables, 1888–1912. Reinhold Framke and August Sievers. Kraft & Framke, 1878; Kraft, Framke & Sievers, 1879; Tarnow, Framke & Co., 1880; Framke, Sievers & Rohn, 1882–87; Framke & Sievers, 1888–1912. CCD
Fredin, Auguste	Manufacturer and cabinetmaker, 1859–68. CCD
Freedman Bros. & Co.	Upholstered parlor suites, 1897–1916. CCD. *Furniture Journal* (June 25, 1907) noted H. Freedman had been awarded a medal at the World's Columbian Exposition, 1893.
Freese & Co.	Chamber furniture, 1874–76; John D. Freese & Co., 1877–78; Freese & Hamline, 1879–84; J. D. Freese & Sons, 1903–32. CCD
Friedson & Dahl, Inc.	Custom-built living-room furniture, 1950–70. CTD
Gannon & McGrath	Parlor furniture and mattresses, 1878–85. CCD
Garden City Stool Co.	Piano, organ, and office stools, 1886–99. CCD
Garland Furniture Co.	Upholstered and special furniture, 1936–72. Joseph and A. A. Liederman. CTD
Garvey & Company	Cottage steel folding beds, couches, divans, and steel cots, 1898–1913. CCD
Gassman Bros. & Troemper	Manufacturers, 1887–94. William Gassman. Gassman Parlor Furniture Company, 1895–96. CCD

Geis(s), Conrad	Cabinetmaker, 1847–62. CCD
General Chair Co.	1308 North Elston, 1950–55. CTD
Gen-O-Craft, Inc.	Brass and glass serving carts, 1960–65. CTD
Giffert & Lane	Manufacturers, 1891–94. CCD
Giffert, William	Upholstered parlor furniture, 1867–99. CCD
Gilberg, Liefman & Larson	Office desks. John Gilberg, Niels Liefman, Peter Larson, ca. 1880. CCD
Gill, A.	Willowwork stands, chairs, and rockers, 1863–73. CCD
Glabman Bros. Inc.	Upholstered furniture, ca. 1936–70. CTD
Glass Novelty Co., The	Cribs, bassinets and juvenile furniture. The Stork Line, ca. 1922.
Glick, John	Cabinetmaker, 1849–62. CCD
Globe Cabinet Co., Inc.	Novelty furniture, 1950–70. CTD
Gobel & Gloeckler	Manufacturers, 1875–77. CCD
Gohst, Henry	Saloon fixtures, 1862–89. CCD
Goldner Specialty Co.	2301 West Wabansia, 1936–44. CTD
Goode, Sarah E. (Mrs.)	Patent 322,177 for cabinet bed on July 14, 1885. Furniture manufacturer, 1884–86. CCD
Goodhue, Stephen W.	Parlor frames, 1873–76. CCD
Gordon, Charles G.	Furniture and store and office furnishings, 1871–83. Also owner of Western Furn. Co. CCD
Gordon, Glenn	Designer/craftsman/woodworker, 1970–present.
Gordon, T. E. & Son	Vertical cylinder desks, secretaries, bookcases, and office furniture to order, 1875–80. CCD
Gordon Parlor Furniture Co.	Member CFMA in 1938.
Gorrell, A. D. & Co.	Upholstered furniture, ca. 1903–39. CCD, CTD
Graef, Jacob	Cabinetmaker, 1859–74. CCD
Gramer, Valentine	Church furniture, 1881–1903. CCD
Grand American Furniture Co.	1812 West Hubbard, 1950–60. CTD
Grand Wood Carving	Carved component parts: legs, aprons, decoys, etc.; also completed finished figurines of horses, 1939–83. Stanley F. Motyka; now operated by Lawrence Motyka.
Great Northern Dinette Mfg. Co.	2607 West Monroe, ca. 1955. CTD
Green Mfg. Co.	Parlor furniture, frames in white, couches, and odd chairs, 1897–1960. CTD
Greenfield, Charles	Bedsteads and chamber sets, 1879–80. CCD
Greenpoint Metallic Bed Co.	3622 South Morgan, 1911–17. CCD
Grosfeld, Albert, Inc.	600 North Wabash, 1936–50. CTD
Gross, E. J.	Furniture factory at 7457 Railroad damaged by

	fire, according to *Furniture World* (April 29, 1897).
Guild-Craft Furn. Mfg. Co.	131 North Green, ca. 1965. CTD
Haerle, A. & Co.	Adolph Haerle, 1880–86. CCD
Hafner Furniture Co.	Upholstered parlor furniture, 1893–1915. Formerly Hafner & Schoen Furniture Co. CCD
Haggard & Marcusson Co.	Spring beds and couches, 1897–1921. John D. Haggard and Henry H. Marcusson. CTD
Hallman, Clemens F.	330–38 North Wood, 1889–95. Partner in: Hallman, Wagner & Waarich, 1889; Hallman, Wagner & Co., 1890–91; Hallman, Ennesser & Co., 1892–93; Hallman Furniture Mfg. Co., 1894–95.
Halvorsen & Bredshall Co.	Folding beds (Columbia folding bed), 1892–97. CCD
Halvorson, Harold L.	Manufacturer, 1936–65. CTD
Halvorson, Johnson & Co.	Sideboards, bookcases, and chamber furniture. 1875–79. H. Halvorson, 1881–89. CCD
Hambrook Mfg. Co., Richard T.	"School, church and fine house furniture, cylinder and office desks a specialty," 1873–82. Patent 204,216 for refrigerator-sideboard on May 28, 1878. CCD
Hamlin Furniture Frame Co., Inc.	1633 North Hamlin, 1939–70. Name changed to Western Furniture Corp., 1950.
Hamline, L. M. & Co.	Chamber furniture and desks, 1889–95. CCD
Handmade Furniture Shop	Founded by Albert Weinhardt (d. 1914); operated ca. 1914–39. CTD
Hanke Bros.	Parlor desks, sideboards, china closets, bureaus, washstands, and chamber suits, 1882–1907. Succeeded Jost & Hanke in 1882. Albert, Herman, and Charles Hanke came to Chicago from Germany in 1869.
Hanson-Brockman Co.	Furniture frames, 1939–44. CTD
Harlen Co., Inc.	Parlor frames, 1936–39. CFMA, CTD
Harris-Hub Bed & Spring Co.	Bed frames, cots, bunk bed springs, cabinets, and metal outdoor furniture. 1943–70. Listed as Harris-Hub Co., Inc., 1970. CTD
Harrison & Jones	Chair- and cabinetmakers, 1847–51. CCD
Hartmann, Malcolm Co.	Furniture frames, 1943–50.
Hassewer, Jean (John) B.	Reproductions of antique furniture, 1901–16 (Hassewer Fine Art Furniture Mfg. Co., Hassewer Table Co.). CCD
Hausske, August & Bros.	Parlor frames, church and lodge furniture, 1880–1936. Augustus, Robert, and Adolph Hausske. CCD
Helene Curtis Chrome Furniture	Chromium-plated furniture, 1939–44. CTD
Hellum, Peter E.	Manufacturer, 1896–1913. CCD

Henry, Frank	Manufacturer, 1882–90. CCD
Herhold Chair Co.	Chairs, 1868–1931. Herhold, Johnson & Borgmeier & Co. (Frederick Herhold, Adolph Borgmeier, Andrew P. Johnson), 1868–70; Herhold, Johnson & Co., 1871–74; Herhold, Lenz & Co., 1875; Niemann, Lenz & Co., 1876–78; F. Herhold & Co., 1880–86; F. Herhold & Sons, 1887–1906; Herhold Chair Co., 1908–31. CCD, CTD
Hermanson Desk Co.	454 North Armour, ca. 1970. CTD
Hewlet & Wilson Parlor Frame Mfg. Co.	Frame manufacturer, 1936–43. CTD
Hi-Art Wood Carving Shop	Frame manufacturer, 1939–44. CTD
Hilgus, A. & Son	708 North Carpenter, 1943–55. CTD
Hodkinson, H.	Chairmaker, 1847–49. CCD
Hoffman-Carpenter Co.	Parlor frames, ca. 1903–4. Hoffman Co., 1905–19. CCD
Hoffman & Demlinger Co.	Tables, 1939–55. Became Hoffman Table Co. in 1943. CTD
Hoffman-Ivers Art Mfg. Co.	2220 North Wayne, 1950. CTD
Hollatz Bros.	Upholstered parlor furniture, 1896–ca. 1976. Name changed to Hollatz Furniture Co. in 1964. William and A. E. Hollatz, officers in 1936; E. H. Ehlert, president ca. 1976. CTD, CFMA
Holmquist-Swanson Co.	Children's furniture, 1936–55. CTD
Homer Bros.	Upholstered furniture, 1909–present.
Howard Parlor Furniture Co.	Upholstered furniture, 1939–70. Also listed as Howard Premiere in 1965. CTD
Hughes Rattan Works	Wicker furniture and baskets, 1880–86. Luke Duffy Hughes.
Hunter & McCue Mnfg. Co.	Parlor furniture, 1887–1900.
Ideal Furniture Co.	Parlor furniture, 1936–50. Name changed to Ideal Parlor Furniture Co., 1943. CTD
Ideal Furniture Mfg. Co.	Kitchenette and dinette furniture, occasional tables, TV chairs, 1950–65. CTD
Ideal Products	Iron furniture and ornamental specialties, ca. 1955. CTD
Illinois Bedding and Mattress Co.	Upholstered furniture, 1950–76. CTD
Illinois Chair Co.	Chairs, 1892–93. CCD
Illinois Furniture Co., The	Parlor furniture frames, 1877–89. Moritz Schreiber and Henry Knaak.
Illinois Moulding Co.	Novelty furniture and occasional tables, 1939–76. CTD
Illinois Rattan Co.	Rattan furniture, ca. 1897–ca. 1904. Factory at Joliet Prison.
International Furniture Co.	Upholstered furniture 1898–1951; Adolph

	Cohn, Leo Weber, and Philip W. Pelts. Originally named International Parlor Furniture Co. Purchased by Schnadig Corp in 1951.
Islander, Charles F.	Cabinetmaker, 1873–75; exhibited writing desk and parlor table at 1873 Exposition.
J C Furniture Mfg. Co.	Kitchenette and dinette sets, 1950–present. CTD
J D Furniture and Upholstering	Restaurant furniture, ca. 1965. CTD
J & M Furnitgure Mfg. Co.	4538 South Marshfield, 1936. CTD
J & S Furniture Mfg. Co.	Upholstered parlor furniture, 1917–82. Founded by Joe Volen and Mr. Soren; purchased by Meyer S. Kaplan in 1950; sold to Caledonian, Inc., Winnetka, January 1983.
Jacobson, N. & Co.	Parlor suite frames, 1878–87. Niels Jacobson. CCD
Jacobsen & Hansen	"Sideboards, china closets and panel work a specialty," 1902–3. CCD
Jahn, August	"Designers and Manufacturers of Special Furniture," 1896–1901; Jahn Cabinet & Interior Finish Co., 1903–5. CCD
James, Thomas Christmas	Cabinet- and patternmaker, 1843–51. CCD
JEM Furniture Corporation	Metal and glass furniture, 1953–present. Mark H., Joseph B., and Edward S. Tauber, founders.
Jensen & Rosberg	Manufacturer, 1888–1911. CCD
Jo-Aire Wood Products, Inc.	Furniture frames, ca. 1960. CTD
Johnson & Arneson	Chamber sets, bookcases, and sideboards, 1880–83. CCD
Johnson & Ellerson	Center tables and sideboards, 1877–84. CCD
Johnson, Enochson & Co.	Manufacturers, 1891–93. Became Johnson & Strick in 1893. CCD
Johnson, J. D. & Co.	"Cabinet Work, Stair Builders and Manufacturers of Patent Adjustable Chairs," ca. 1895. CCD
Johnson, Nelson & Co.	Parlor furniture, 1886–88; Johnson, Nelson & Moller, 1888–89. CCD
Johnson & Olaison	*American Cabinet Maker* (February 7, 1880) noted that company was commencing business with a line of center tables; "a leading designer" was furnishing them with styles.
Johnson & Paulson	Furniture manufacturers, 1878–81. CCD
Johnson, Peter	Wardrobes, cupboards, tables, and cradles, 1903–23. CCD
Johnson-Randall Co.	Reed furniture, 1936–39. CTD
Jones, D. A. and E. M.	Cabinet and chair manufacturers, 1839–ca. 1848. CCD

C. E. Jorgenson	Chamber furniture, 1883–1921. CCD
Jost & Hanke	Bureaus, 1870–81. Succeeded by Hanke Bros. in 1882. CCD
Judkins & Co.	Folding beds in oak and imitation mahogany, 1894–1911. CCD
Julin, John Furniture Co.	Breakfast nooks, formica tables, etc., ca. 1955. CTD
Just-Rite Wood Products	Manufacturer, ca. 1955–75. CTD
K C Wire Shop (K C Wire Products, Inc.)	Wrought-iron furniture, 1955–76. CTD
K & K Manufacturers	Wrought-iron, chrome-plated, marble and formica-top and juvenile furniture, 1970–76. CTD
Kappes & Eggers	Office and store fittings, 1872–84. CCD
Katz Bros.	Parlor furniture, 1920–ca. 1931. Solomon Katz. Mattress maker, 1907–15; retail furniture dealer, 1915–20. CCD
Kaye Chrome Products	Breakfast nooks and custom formica tops, ca. 1955. CTD
Kaydee Metal Products Corp.	Furniture frames, 1965–68. CTD
Keck, Buhmann & Hansen	Parlor furniture, 1885–86; J. M. Keck & Co., 1887–95. CCD
Keller, Strum & Co.	Fancy cabinet ware, 1878–80; Keller & Co., 1883–89. CCD
Kemmeth (John) & Co.	Upholsterers, 1894–1917. John & Charles Kemmeth and William Wiand. CCD
Kenna, Joseph W.	Inventor of numerous folding chairs, springs, etc., 1880–88. Assigned to J. W. Vail and Charles P. Kenna.
Ketcham & Rothschild	Wholesale upholsterers and manufacturers of parlor furniture, 1880–1939. Ira P. Ketcham and William S. Rothschild. CCD, CTD
Kies & Fromm	Furniture designers, 1888–91. Nicholas Kies and George Fromm. Nicolas & D. Kies patent 312,721 for table on February 24, 1885.
Kimball & Chappell Co.	Brass and iron beds, 1897–1917. Founded as Kimball & Johnson Metal Bedstead Co.; renamed Kimball & Chappell Co. by 1899. Charles H. Kimball & J. D. Chappell. CCD
Klein, Mathias	Iron beds and Wilson Adjustable Iron Chair, 1877–78. CCD
Kleinhenz, M.	Chair factory, 1849–51. CCD
Klewer Bros.	Parlor frames, 1879–94. Emil and Otto Klewer. CCD
Knaak, Knaak, Schick & Co.	Parlor frames, 28 Indiana, 1887–89. Henry F. Knaak, 1890–95. CCD
Knaus & Green Mnfg. Co.	Manufacturers, 1891–96. CCD

Kniblo, William	Cabinetmaker and carver, 1848–51. CCD
Knoche Bros.	Manufacturers, 1897–1901. Charles Knoche. CCD
Kochs, Theo. A. Co.	Beauty and barber shop furniture, ca. 1880–ca. 1936. Theo. A. Kochs and A. R. Schwarzkofe, officers. CFMA
Koenig & Jahncke	Manufacturer, 1875; Koenig, Frederick & Bowell, 1876–78. CCD
Koenig, P. E.	Cylinder desks and bedsteads, 1878–79. CCD
Kolb, Jacob	Cabinetmaker, 1859–75. CCD
Koppmeyer (Koppmeier), John	Manufacturer, 1873–92. CCD
Koral Fine Furniture Co.	2319 West Devon, 1955–72. CTD
Kramer & Ibach Co.	Upholstered furniture, 1880–85. CCD
Krol, B. F.	Children's furniture, 1936–70. CTD
Kraus, John	Bedsteads, chairs, cabinet ware. Also general carving, scroll-sawing, and planing business. 1857–78. Kraus, Butzow & Peters, 1879–83; Kraus & Peters in 1884. CCD
Krause, W. J.	Manufacturer, 1858–73.
Kroeber, Phillip & Adam	Store fixtures, 1862–76. CCD
Kroll Bros. Co.	Children's furniture and baby carriages, 1939–55. Also known as Chicago Baby Carriage Co. CTD
Kron, Francis	Manufacturer, 1868–74. CCD
Kuhn, Frederick & Co.	Children's furniture, 1896–1902+. *Furniture World* (March 20, 1902) noted they were "now confining themselves to the making of music cabinets and ladies desks."
Lakeside Furniture Mfg. Co., Inc.	"Upholsterer of custom and contract furniture—catering to architect's designs," ca. 1939–present. Jacob Zake, president; William Zake, vice-president in the 1960s. Factory at 1218 North Wells burned in 1981.
Landsidel, Wicki & Co.	Chamber sets and sideboards, 1872–78; 1884–85. CCD
La Rose Upholstery Shop	4888 West Armitage, 1955–70. CTD
Larsen, Eric(K)	Manufacturer, 1877–85. CCD
Larsen & Munson	Parlor furniture, 1876–86. CCD
Larson, Peter	Desks, 1884–91. CCD
Laser, M. T. & Co.	Furniture frames, 1955–72. CTD
Lask Woodworking Co. (I & R Chair Co.)	1528 West Armitage, ca. 1960–83. CTD
L'Atelier Fine Furniture	Custom furniture, 1955–60. CTD
Lauer, Jacob	Manufacturer, 1872–78. Proprietor of Northwestern Planing Mill, 1869–74. Lauer & Niemann, 1959–61. CCD

Leganger, E. & Co.	Fiber, rattan, and reed furniture, 1936–55. CTD
LeMoyne Parlor Frame Co.	Frames, 1929–60. John and Stanley Kleszyk, officers in 1936. Became LeMoyne Wood Industries in 1955. CTD, CFMA
Liberty Cabinet Furn. Co.	2120 West Grand, 1939–present. CTD
Liebenstein & Co., J. & A.	Cabinet hardware, upholstery goods, undertakers supplies, 1859–78. Bought by Chicago Furniture Supply Co. in 1879.
Liebenstein, Henry & Co.	Henry Liebenstein & Joseph Speigel, ca. 1860–92. CCD
Lutwyche & Lentz Mnfg. Co.	Fancy cabinet ware, 1883–84.
McAvoy, Frank B.	Art furniture, curtain poles, and cornices, 1881–85. CCD
McCabe, Wilkins & Spaulding	Parlor furniture, 1865–73. CCD
McDonough, Price & Company	Upholstered parlor furniture, 1867–76; McDonough, Wilsey & Co., 1877–78; Eastman & Wilkins (Samuel G. Wilkins and Frank L Eastman), 1883–84; S. J. Wilkins & Co., 1885–93; Wilkins, Ketcham & Rothschild, 1894–95; Ketcham & Rothschild, 1896–1940. See also Ketcham & Rothschild.
McKay Co.	McKacroft Metal Furniture, chairs, gliders, tables, etc., 1936–68. CTD
McLelland, John	Manufacturer, 1898–1904. CCD
Magerstadt, Fred	Cabinetmaker, 1868–75. CCD
Mallen, H. Z.	Frames and upholstered parlor furniture, 1877–1942. H. Z. Mallen, 1877–83; H. Z. Mallen & Co., 1884–1942. Herman Z. Mallen and son Herman W. Mallen (1856–1932). Made frames until 1911, when began to manufacture sets of upholstered parlor furniture. Factory on St. John's Place, 1887–1942.
Marcek Furniture / Div. of Central Parlor Frame Mfg. Co., Inc.	Modern and traditional tables, 1950–60. CTD
Marsh Bros.	Cabinetmakers. "Largely engaged in manufacture of sofas." 1859–61. CCD
Martin, Arthur D.	"Cheap oak chairs," 1895–1904. Dealer in prison-made goods.
Martin Bros.	Manufacturers, 1886–90; Mrs. Ellen Martin, 1894. CCD
Martins (Martens), Charles	Manufacturer, 1866–73. CCD
Masterkraft Parlor Furniture Mfrs.	Living-room furniture, 1950–68. CTD
May, Bernard H.	Willow furniture, 1885–93. CCD
May Plywoods, Inc. (May Wood Industries)	Frames and wood parts, 1960–present. CTD

Meilahn Bros.	"Special Designed Tables & Furniture for Schools & Public Buildings," 1885–present. Frederick Meilahn (1866–1950) and two sons, Fred, Jr. and Harold. CCD, CTD
Meissner Furniture Mnfg. Co.	Manufacturer, 1872–75. Julius F. Meissner, Robert F. Meissner, and William Longe. Meissner, Stock & Co., 1881; Meissner & Tonjes, 1883–84; Robert F. Meissner patent 277,046 for folding bedstead on May 8, 1883; 270,327 for wardrobe bedstead on January 9, 1883.
Melchior Bros. Furniture Co.	Barber supplies and store fixtures, 1889–99. Edward and Fred Melchior patents for barber's chairs in 1888, 1889, and 1895. CCD
Metal Bedstead Co.	Incorporated by H. Y. Johnson, James W. Patterson, and John J. Beilman in 1897.
Metallic Folding Bed Co.	Metal beds, 1899–1917. CCD
Metz, J. L. Furniture Co.	Dining-room suites, 1905–70. Factory moved to Hammond, Indiana.
Meyenschein, Frederick A.	Furniture designer associated with S. Karpen & Bros., H. Z. Mallen Co., and the Windsor Furniture Company between 1895 and his death in 1939.
Mick Novelty Co.	Novelty furniture, 1950–60. CTD
Mid-City Upholstered Furniture Co.	Frank and S. S. Lesner, officers, 1936. CFMA
Midland Wood Products Co.	Manufacturer of novelty furniture, 1936–50. CTD
Midwest Folding Products	1414 South Western, 1965–83. CTD
Midwest Furniture Mfg. Co., Inc.	3423 West Ogden, 1939; 3700 West Roosevelt, 1950–55. CTD
Midwest Parlor Furn. Co.	Furniture frames, 1936–50. CTD
Mikkelsen & Bendtsen	Manufacturers, 1881–87. Edward Mikkelsen.
Miller, Edward D.	Office desks and store fittings, 1869–76. CCD
Miller & Fritsch	Folding beds, 1880–88. CCD
Millman & Stern Inc.	Chrome dinettes, 1950–55. CTD
Miltz, William L. & Co.	Manufacturer, 1876–82. CCD
Minardi & Co. Inc.	Occasional furniture, 1850–69. CTD
Mirrored Furniture Stylists	6327 North Broadway, 1950. CTD
Modern Craft Juvenile Furn.	Children's table and chair sets, ca. 1965. CTD
Modern Parlor Furniture Co.	Patent bed davenport, 1910–29. CCD
Modern Trends, Inc.	410 North Wells, 1955–76. CTD
Modern Upholstering Mfg. Co.	5139 West Diversey, 1960–69. CTD
Molinelli, A.	Furniture and fine interior work, 1874–84. CCD
Molter Bros.	Chamber suites and extension tables, 1872–95. Christian and Henry A. Molter. CCD

Mueller, Gloeckler & Co.	Fancy cabinet ware, 1865–78. John Gloeckler. CCD
Mularski Parlor Frame Co.	Frames, 1950–60. CTD
Munago Co. Inc.	1015 North Halsted, 1936. Name changed in 1922 from International Art Furniture Co. CTD
Mylan Furniture Co.	Manufacturers, 1950–65. CTD
Nardi, V. Inc.	Manufacturer of ready-to-paint furniture, 1960. CTD
National Chrome Products	Chrome furniture, 1950–68. Became National Dinette Furniture Co. in 1965. CTD
National Parlor Furniture Co.	Upholstered parlor furniture, 1891–1910. Rudolph and Joseph Deimel, founders. Succeeded by Chicago Upholstered Furniture Co.
Nelson & Moller Co.	Upholstered furniture, 1890–93. CCD
Nelson, Nicholas B.	Manufacturer, 1889–92. CCD
Nerad, Frank & Co.	Upholstered parlor furniture, 1885–1917. CCD
Neuberger, A. J. & Bros.	Parlor, chamber, and office furniture, 1865–87. Abraham J., Ferdinand, and Frederick Neuberger. CCD
Neuberger, H. & M.	Parlor and chamber furniture, 1866–84. CCD
Nifti-Nook Mfg. Co.	3716 North Cicero, 1950–present. CTD
Nord & Co.	3516 North Clark, 1950–65. CTD
Northern Picture Frame Co.	Custom furniture, ca. 1903–ca. 1960. CTD
Nottelmann, Otto	Bedsteads, 1863–82; with John Nottleman, 1866–68. CCD
Novelty Wood Works	Bank, office, store, sewing-machine cabinets, 1869–73. F. R. Wolfinger. CCD
Noyes, Charles	Parlor furniture and mattresses, 1875–93. CCD
Noyes, LaVerne	Dictionary holders, ca. 1879–99. CCD
Oberbeck & Holts	Chamber furniture, 1879–81. Oberbeck Brothers, 1885–ca. 1891. Louis and Frederick Oberbeck. CCD
Olach-Hanze Furn. Co. Inc.	Parlor frames, 1936–50. CTD
Olaison & Johnson	Library and parlor tables, 1879–91. Paul C. Olaison and Louis Johnson (d. 1881). CCD
Olbrich & Golbeck & Co.	Bureaus and washstands, 1879–1950. CCD, CTD
Olsen, O. C. S. & Co.	Office desks, 1890–1943. O. C. S., Chester, and U. R. Olsen, officers. CFMA, CTD
Olsen, Reinhard	Desks, 1884–93. CCD
O'Mara Parlor Frame Co.	Parlor furniture frames, 1890–ca. 1943. John F. O'Mara. CCD
Ovitt, A. W. & Co.	Extension and parlor tables, 1877–84. Alonyron W. Ovitt. CCD
Owen Bros.	Benjamin F. & E. L. Patent 373,599 for folding bed on November 22, 1887. Manufacturers of folding beds, 1887–88.

Paidar, Emil J.	Barber chairs and beauty industry fixtures, ca. 1909–72. Emil Paidar, F. J. Paik, R. C. Schultz, officers. CFMA
Palmer Specialties	Chrome tables and chairs, 1939–50. CTD
Parenteau Studios	Upholstered furniture, 1959–present. Paul Parenteau.
Parenti & Rafaelli	Custom woodworking; commercial and residential furniture, 1950–present. Robert F. and Ronald Parenti and Silvo J. Raffaelli.
Parquin Industries	Breakfast nooks, dinettes, wrought-iron furniture, 1950–55. CTD
Parthier, F.	Reed and rattan goods, 1888–ca. 1903. CCD
Patch & Balkwill	Tables and stands, 1882–87. William Patch and John Balkwill. CCD
Peerless Upholstering & Furniture Co.	6822 North Oakley, 1921–67. CTD
Perfect Parlor Furniture Co. Inc.	1532 North Elk Grove, 1936–55. Ad says "manufacturers of quality furniture since 1919." CTD
Perfection Parlor Furniture Co.	2267 North Clybourn, 1936–44. CTD
Peters, Theodore G.	Furniture maker, 1872–90. CCD
Peters, William Morgan	Furniture designer, 1888–89.
Peterson, A. & Co.	Desks, 1879–ca. 1907. Anton Petersen. CCD
Peterson, George L. Co.	Mantels, sideboards, bookcases, 1883–94. CCD
Peterson, Martin	Manufacturer, 1862–75. CCD
Peterson & Oveson	Manufacturer, 1886–97. CCD
Pfeiffer, Robert	Parlor tables and novelties, 1900–4. CCD
Phoenix Parlor Frame Co.	Parlor furniture, 1901–7. CCD
Pilgram & Greenfield	Parlor and chamber furniture, 1871–78. CCD
Pirrung Mnfg. Co.	Manufacturer of rockers and lounges, 1880–93. George and Felix Pirrung patent 477,449 for bed lounge on June 21, 1892.
Pitcher, Carroll	Custom furniture, 1955–70. CTD
Platt Mfg. Co.	Dinette sets, 1936–55. CTD
Poehlmann, John	Cabinetmaker and upholsterer, 1858–75. CCD
Poland & Whitman	Carriages and reed furniture, 1886–94. CCD
Poths & Co.	Parlor frames, 1879–87. CCD
Pottle, Wm.	Willowware and rattan ware, 1861–ca. 1886; Pottle & Pierpont; Chicago Rattan & Reed Co. CCD
Poulsen, Hans	Office desks, 1886–89. Poulsen & Johnson, 1883–85. CCD
Preston Furniture Mfg. Inc.	Manufacturers, 1955–68. CTD
Pries, Lohse & Company	Chamber furniture, 1873–81. Successor to Pries & Wichman, 1868–72. CCD

Quality Furniture House	Custom furniture, 1965–70. CTD
Quality Chrome Co.	Dinette sets, 1950–75. CTD
Rann, Jacob P. & Son	Manufacturer, 1906–17. CCD
Rasmussen, Geo. L.	Saloon and store fixtures, 1893–1913. Rassmussen & Johansen, 1884–87. CCD
Rauch Manufacturing Co.	Chamber furniture, desks, wardrobes, 1866–1904. CCD
Raulf, Joseph	Manufacturer, 1906–13. CCD
Reese Furniture Service	Custom furniture, 1950–55. CTD
Reinken & Co.	Custom furniture and interiors, ca. 1920–ca. 1970. Howard William Reinken.
Reliable Furniture Mnfg. Co.	Manufacturer, 1917–70. Harry Stein listed as officer, 1936. CCD, CTD, CFMA
Revell, Alexander H. & Co.	Manufacturer and retail dealer, 1876–ca. 1931. Alexander Hamilton Revell (1858–1931).
Rhoads, Samuel S.	Center tables, 1877–89. CCD
Rhoner, Frank & Co.	Rocking chairs and parlor furniture, 1878–89. CCD
Rice, C. F.	Pier and mantel mirrors, frames, brackets, stands, and tables, 1879–88. CCD
Rieckenberg, Frederick R.	353–59 West Randolph, 1882–84; Rieckenberg & Clarke, 1884–86. CCD
Riley, Eugene J.	Parlor furniture and lounges, 1869–91. CCD
Roberts, Claude J.	Manufacturer, 1876–77. CCD
Rocker Spring Co.	Manufactured B. & B. Patent Rocker Spring, 1882–91. William Bunker and Jacob Beiersdorf.
Rock-Ola Mfg Corp.	Occasional pieces, bars, desks, and upholstered furniture, 1939–83. CTD
Rohn & Kolberg	Parlor frames, 1884–89. CCD
Roos Mnfg. Co.	Novelty furniture and cedar chests, 1914–ca. 1942. Listed in 1942 in Forest Park. Ed Roos.
Roosevelt Furniture Mfg. Co.	Manufacturers, 1936–76. CTD
Rubee Furniture Mfg. Corp.	Sofa lounges and sofa beds, 1960–70. CTD
Rudolph, John	Extension dining tables, 1858–89. CCD
Rudy Furn. Shops, Inc.	3042 West Chicago, 1936–44. CTD
S & W Manufacturing Co.	Furniture frames, 1950–60. CTD
Sabath Desk Co.	Office furniture, 1909–30. Rudolf Sabath. CTD
Salter & Bilek	Fancy cabinet ware, 1879–91. Salter Manufacturing Company, 1900–23. CCD
Schafer, Joseph J.	"Manufacturer of all kinds of furniture ornaments," 1901–8. CCD
Schaub & Strehl	"Wood and fancy turners; house and office furniture," 1866–71. CCD
Schenk Lumber Co.	Furniture frames, 1943–74. CTD
Scheubert, C.	Center tables and whatnots, 1879–82. CCD

Schieferstein, A. & Bro.	Upholstered parlor furniture, 1860–73. CCD
Schmidt, A. C. & Co.	Upholstered parlor furniture, 1882–1908. Albert Schmidt. CCD
Schmidt & Bros.	Willow chairs and cribs, 1869–ca. 1873. CCD
Schoen Lounge Co., John A.	Lounges, 1894–96. Patent 170,403 for sofa bedstead on November 23, 1875. CCD
Schomer, Henry	Metal beds, 1888–ca. 1922. CCD
Schram Bros. Company	Music cabinets, 1871–ca. 1919. Louis Schram (1844–1919).
Schuette & Hauschildt	Parlor furniture, 1882. Schuette Bros., 1883–92. CCD
Schultz Bros.	Parlor and chamber suites, 1857–95. CCD
Schultz, Gobel & Co.	Parlor furniture, 1867–74. CCD
Schultz, John F.	Exhibited Revolving Self-Waiting Dining Table at 1873 Inter-State Industrial Exposition.
Schwenn, E.	Lounge frames and woodturning, 1869–73.
Sidway Manufacturing Co.	Adjustable bedside and utility tables, 1893–1902.
Sleemakers Inc.	Couches and sofa beds, 1955–70. CTD
Smalley Mfg. Co.	Frames and novelties, 1896–99. Frederick G. Smalley. CCD
Smyth, John M. & Co.	Retail furniture dealer since 1867. John M. Smyth (1843–1909). John McDonnell Smyth became president of company in 1917.
Sohn, Morris	1037 West Roosevelt, ca. 1944–55. Sohn Bros., 1950–74. CCD
Sorem Furniture Mfg. Co.	Manufacturer, 1936–70. CTD
Sorensen, John & Bro.	Sideboards, 1883–89. CCD
Spak & Natovich	Office furniture, 1943–70. CTD
Spiegal & Cahn	Retail furniture house that made furniture to order from original designs, 1877.
Stachura, Thos. B.	French period furniture, 1939–60. CTD
Stafford, E. H. & Bros.	Manufacturer, 1900–23. CCD, CTD
Stahl, John C.	Manufacturer, 1861–75. CCD
Stampen, Lee & Co.	Lounge frames, 1878–86. CCD
Standard Parlor Furniture Co.	Parlor furniture and couches, 1899–1917. CCD
Stanford & K Dinette Mfg. Co.	3644 West Sixteenth, 1950–55. CTD
Statlin Bros. Furniture Co.	Furniture frames, 1943–55. CTD
Steiger's Upholstery & Furniture	4922 North Lincoln, 1970–83. CTD
Stephani, Monheimer & Hart	Billiard table manufacturer, 1865–ca. 1873. CCD
Sterling Furniture Mfg. Co.	Furniture frames, 1909–55. CTD

Stone, B. F.	Chamber furniture, 1870–73. CCD
Storagewall	Modular structural storage system designed by architect George Nelson in 1945. Manufactured under franchise by Chicago architect Robert Picking and Henry Wright; factory in Indiana.
Storkline Furniture Co.	Juvenile furniture and baby carriages, 1919–ca. 1960. Founded as Glass Novelty Co. by A. G. Feldman in 1916.
Stotz, Woltz & Co.	Office furniture, 1863–93. John W. Stoltz and John Woltz. CCD
Strahan & Diez	"Fine furniture made to order," 1881–83. CCD
Straight, George W.	Folding beds, 1881–96. CCD
Stram, Thovald	Tables, 1882–88. CCD
Stubb, Jacob	Manufacturer, 1879–86. CCD
Strum & Speigel Furniture Co.	Cabinet furniture and mantels, 1887–94. CCD
Style-Craft Seating	Chrome chairs, stools, settees, 1950–76. CTD
Style Master Dinette Co.	1355 West Addison, 1950–76. CTD
Stylemaster Bedding, Inc.	Holiday House furniture, 1960–70. Became Stylemaster Furniture, Inc. in 1970. CTD
Superior Furniture Co.	Upholstered parlor furniture, 1923–present. CTD
Superior Parlor Frame Co.	Parlor frames, 1929–39. CCD, CTD
Superior Sleeprite Co.	Bedroom furniture, including the patented "Sleeprite 3-in-One Chair," 1943–76. CTD
Sutor Furniture Co.	Upholstered furniture, 1963–83. Ernst Sutor.
Swiney, D. M. & Bro.	Bank, store, and office furniture and fixtures, 1867–75. Later in business on own: Dennis M. Swiney, 1877–1923; Edward E. Swiney, 1876–1907. Brothers born in Ireland.
Szumy, Anton & Sons	Furniture frames, 1936–70. CTD
Tallman Robbins & Co.	Office furniture, 1943–74. CTD
Tarnow, Charles	Manufacturer, ca. 1864–75. CCD
Tauber, Maurice & Co.	Parlor furniture, 1907–ca. 1939. CCD, CTD
Thompson & Borgenson	Office desks, 1880–84. CCD
Thorman, Henry	Manufacturer, 1864–77. CCD
Thorson, Andrew	Manufacturer, 1876–94. CCD
Thorson, Christian	Lounges, 1882–88.
Thorson, Thorwald	Manufacturer, 1893–1900.
Tomlinson & Carsley	Manufacturers of fine interior finish and furniture from special designs, 1883–ca. 1886. I. Tomlinson and F. M. Carsley.
Tri-Lo Products	Upholstered chairs and headboards, 1965–present. CTD
Tunk, Richard	Bamboo furniture, 1893–98. CCD

Turk & Voss	Manufacturers, 1888–94. CCD
Turner Mfg. Co.	Occasional furniture, 1950–76. CTD
U. S. Parlor Frame Mfg. Co.	Frames, 1890–95. CCD
Universal Specialty Manufacturing Co.	Morris chairs and mission furniture, 1906–9. Mrs. M. L. Nelson, president, succeeded husband after his death.
Utility Wood Specialty Co.	Hassocks, seats, and backs for chrome furniture, 1965–76. CTD
Valentin-Seaver Co.	Upholstered parlor furniture, 1899–1927. Louis Lincoln Valentine (1866–1940) and Andrew E. Seaver. Subsidiary, Century Parlor Furniture Company, organized in 1906. Sold to Kroehler Manufacturing Company in 1927.
Vendome Parlor Furn. Co.	Morris chairs and upholstered parlor suites, 1906–12. Ben and A. Blumenthal. CCD
Venice Furniture Novelty Mfg. Co., Inc.	Living-room tables, 1936–84. CTD
Victory Upholstered Seating Co.	Manufacturers of seating, booths, and nooks for hotels, restaurants, etc., 1955–83. CTD
Visconti, Fortunato	Cabinetmaker and repairer of antique furniture, 1889–ca. 1905. CCD
Vollon & Peterson Furniture Mfg. Co.	230 West Huron, 1943–65. CTD
Waco Products, Inc.	Chrome furniture, 1950–70. CTD
Wagner, H. V. & Co.	Manufacturer, 1882–86. CCD
Wales, Bruce & Co.	Aluminum lawn furniture, 1955–present. CTD
Walter, Christian	Manufacturer, 1892–1908. CCD
Walters, C. & Co.	Horn furniture, 1893. CCD
Warnecke, Conrad H.	Office furniture, 1865–ca. 1876. CCD
Wascher, Louis C. F. & Co.	Special upholstered furniture, 1899–1906. CCD
Weber Bros.	Store fixtures, billiard tables, and pianos, 1871–ca. 1910. Became Weber Furniture Co. ca. 1910.
Wells Furniture Makers	Custom cabinet and upholstered furniture for architects and interior decorators, 1938–present. Founded by Alfred Mattaliano (d. 1965). Now operated by founder's son, Frank Mattaliano, and his sons, Frank, Jr., and Michael, and daughter, Nancy.
Wenderoth Bros.	Manufacturers, 1884–93; Frank Wenderoth & Co., 1882–83. Richard J. Wenderoth, 1896–98. CCD
Western Furniture Co.	Dressers, 1896–98. Herman Barth and family. CCD
Wester Parlor Frame Co.	Parlor furniture frames, 1896–1905. CCD
Western Table Co.	Tables, 1950–74. Became Western-Stickley, 1970. CTD

Westman, Jack Co.	441 North Franklin, 1939–55. Westman Shops, 1960. CTD
Wetzler, Charles	Patent folding bed lounges, 1868–77. CCD
Whittlesey & Peters	Woven-wire mattresses and Peerless Cabinet Bed, 1870–79. CCD
Wilkins, S. G. & Co.	Parlor furniture, including the Hartley Reclining Chair, 1885–93. Wilkins, Ketcham & Rothschild, 1894–95. CCD
Windsor Folding Bed Co.	Dining-room, library, and hall furniture, 1885–ca. 1929. Became Windsor Furniture Co. in 1914. CCD, CTD
Wippo, Charles & Co.	Parlor, chamber, dining, and office furniture, 1853–74. CCD
Wolfinger, Francis R. (Novelty Wood Works)	Manufacturer of sewing-machine cabinets, 1873–79. Office, store, and bank fittings, 1879–84. CCD
Woodcraft Novelty Mfg. Co.	Manufacturers, 1936–39. CTD
Woodwork Corporation of America	Custom desks, credenzas, and occasional furniture for banks, hotels, offices, and public buildings, 1913–present. Joseph Kaszab, founder. Present officers, Robert F. Kay, Joseph C. Kay, Jr., and Bruce F. Stulik.
Wullweber, O. L. & Co.	Parlor furniture and moldings, 1880–93. CCD
Zeller, A.	Billiard Table Manufactory, 1867–73. CCD

NOTES

CHAPTER 1

1. Harry Edward Pratt, "Biographical Sketch of John Dean Caton, 1812–1895," p. 51. Typescript memoirs. Chicago Historical Society (hereinafter CHS). A similar version appears in Harry E. Pratt (ed.), "John Dean Caton's Reminiscences of Chicago in 1833 and 1834, *Journal of the Illinois State Historical Society* 28 (April 1935):10–11.
2. Pratt, "Caton's Reminiscences," p. 49. Danville and other cities in the valley of the Wabash River supplied Chicago with produce and lumber during the mid-nineteenth century. Wabash Avenue recalls this early trade.
3. *Chicago Democrat*, December 31, 1833, through March 18, 1834.
4. Election Returns, vol. 21, p. 3, line 72. Illinois State Archives, Springfield, Illinois.
5. *Chicago Democrat*, June 11, 1834.
6. *Chicago Democrat*, March 3, 1834.
7. *Chicago Weekly American*, June 8, 1835. Since many of Chicago's earliest records were destroyed by the Fire of 1871, it is difficult to trace the lineage of many early settlers. The 1850 U.S. Census for Illinois lists James Rockwell, 38, birthplace Connecticut, living in nearby Kane County in 1850. Mrs. J. N. Rockwell, J. N. Rockwell, and J. F. Rockwell, also Connecticut born, were residents of Cook County in 1850.
8. *Chicago Democrat*, March 23, May 18, May 19, June 8, October 5, 1836.
9. Dennis S. Dewey was in Lake County by August 2, 1841, when he was a candidate for county commissioner. Dewey, 42, birthplace New York, is also listed in the 1850 U.S. Census for Illinois.
10. *Chicago American*, September 27, 1839; September 18, 25, 1840; January 6, 1842.
11. *Chicago American*, September 17, 25, 1840.
12. *Chicago Express*, October 24, 1842.
13. John A. Kouwenhoven, *The Arts in Modern American Civilization* (New York: W. W. Norton & Co., 1967), pp. 19–20. Originally published under the title *Made in America* in 1948.
14. The sudden leap from home economy to mechanized production in the areas of agriculture, manufacturing, and homemaking are discussed in Siegfried Giedion, *Mechanization Takes Command* (New York: Oxford University Press, 1948; rpt. ed. New York: W. W. Norton & Co., 1969). Describing the mechanization of agriculture, Giedion notes: "England forms the hub of the movement during the eighteenth century, the American Middle West during the latter half of the nineteenth. Here begins what is perhaps a new chapter in the history of man: a changed relation to the soil and the uprooting of the farmer" (p. 6).
15. For common practices in the Eastern furniture industry, see Jan Seidler, "Transitions in New England's Nineteenth-Century Furniture Industry: Technology and Style, 1820–1880," in *Tools and Technologies: America's Wooden Age* (Burlington, Vermont: Robert Hull Fleming Museum, University of Vermont, 1979), pp. 64–79.
16. Changes in shop organization are discussed in Charles F. Hummel, "The Business of Woodworking: 1700 to 1840," in *Tools and Technologies*, pp. 43–63.
17. See William J. Cronon, "To Be the Central City: Chicago, 1848–1857," *Chicago History* 10 (Fall 1981):130–40.
18. By 1845 circular saws, woodworking tools, mahogany veneers, and cabinet trimmings were readily available at the Hardware and Tool Store operated by W. F. Dominick, who appealed to "Country Cabinet Makers" in the *Chicago Democrat*, July 23, 1845. An advertisement for the Joliet Woolen Factory appeared June 25, 1845.
19. *Chicago Democrat*, February 9, 1842.
20. The Classic Revival in Illinois is described by Betty I. Madden, "Greek Temples and Gothic Spires," *Art, Craft, and Architecture in Early Illinois* (Urbana: University of Illinois Press, 1974), pp. 137–58.

21. John J. Halsey, *History of Lake County, Illinois* (Philadelphia: R. S. Bates, 1912), p. 24; U. S. Census 1840, Illinois, p. 99; also U. S. Census 1830. James H. McClure and his brothers, Thomas, Charles, John and William were born in Ireland, although the family was of Scottish lineage. Immigrating to Illinois, the brothers settled in Lake County, where they became farmers and cattlemen. James died before 1857, when his widow Bertha and his sons Robert, a carpenter, and William, an undertaker, returned to Chicago and were listed in that year's directory.

22. Pratt, "Caton's Reminiscences," pp. 64–65.

23. Dewey: *Chicago Democrat*, May 18, June 8, 1836; Weir: *Laws & Ordinances of the City of Chicago*, 1839.

24. Letter from Lambert Hitchcock, Chicago, October 27, 1835, quoted in John Tarrant Kenney, *The Hitchcock Chair* (New York: Clarkson N. Potter, 1977), pp. 308–10.

25. A. T. Andreas, *History of Chicago, 1871–1885*, vol. 3 (Chicago: A. T. Andreas Company, 1886), p. 735.

26. *Norris Chicago City Directory for 1847–8* (Chicago: J. H. Kedzie, 1847), p. 4.

27. *Seventh U. S. Census for 1850; Schedule 5: Products of Industry*, Illinois, Cook County, Chicago, Charles Roberts, p. 395, line 5. Illinois State Archives, Springfield.

28. S. S. Schoff, *The Glory of Chicago—Her Manufactories: The Industrial Assets of Chicago* (Chicago: Knight & Leonard, 1873), p. 71.

29. See Ronald W. Pilling, "Plank Bottom Chairs," *The Antiques Journal* 36 (December 1981):26–28, 48.

30. Andreas, *History of Chicago*, 3, p. 737.

31. *1850 Industrial Census*, John Phillips, p. 395, line 17.

32. Andreas, *History of Chicago*, 3, p. 741.

33. Ibid. See also Polly Ann Earl, "Craftsmen and Machines: The Nineteenth-Century Furniture Industry," *Technological Innovation and the Decorative Arts* (Charlottesville: University Press of Virginia, 1974), pp. 307–29.

34. Andreas, *History of Chicago*, 3, p. 736.

35. Letter from Henrietta Hamilton McCormick to Martha Ann Hamilton, Chicago, December 3, 1848, as quoted in "Leander James and Henrietta (Hamilton) McCormick: Brief Note on the Hundredth Anniversary of their Arrival in Chicago, November 20, 1848." Typescript. CHS. The letter, incorrectly dated 1838, is quoted in Caroline Kirkland's *Chicago Yesterdays* (Chicago: Daughaday & Company, 1919), pp. 36–38, and Thomas E. Tallmadge, *Architecture in Old Chicago* (Chicago: University of Chicago Press, 1941; rpt. ed. 1975), p. 53.

Chapter 2

1. "The Rail-Roads, History and Commerce in Chicago," *Annual Review of Trade and Commerce 1852–1860* (Chicago: Daily Democratic Press, 1860), 1854, p. 57.

2. "Annual Review of the Commerce, Manufactures, Public and Private Improvements of Chicago, Up to the Year 1855," *Annual Review*, 1855, p. 43.

3. *Chicago Democrat*, November 13, 1850.

4. A. T. Andreas, *History of Chicago, 1871–1885*, vol. 3 (Chicago: A. T. Andreas Company, 1886), p. 738. *Industrial Schedules for Illinois (8th Federal Census)*, 1860, Cook County, Chicago, D. &

F. Hanson, 6th Ward, p. 2, line 15. Illinois State Archives, Springfield.

5. *Annual Review*, 1856, pp. 34–36.

6. *Annual Review*, 1854, p. 57. Successors in 1853 to the firm of Annesley & Ferris, which had been in business since 1849. Thomas R. Ferris was the senior partner in both firms.

7. Ibid., 1855, p. 43.

8. Obituary for Mrs. Cornelia A. Clark (Mrs. Elisha Clark), *Chicago Tribune*, January 29, 1887, p. 4, col. 7. *Industrial Schedules for Illinois (8th Federal Census)*, 1860, Cook County, Elisha Clark, p. 396, line 21.

9. *Udall & Hopkins' Chicago City Directory for 1852–53* (Chicago: Udall & Hopkins, 1852), p. 276.

10. *Annual Review*, 1857, p. 41.

11. Ibid.

12. S. S. Schoff, *The Glory of Chicago—Her Manufactories: The Industrial Assets of Chicago* (Chicago: Knight & Leonard, 1873) p. 63.

13. *Industrial Schedules for Illinois*, 1860, John Schuyler, 10th Ward, p. 8, line 10.

14. Ibid., Robert George, 10th Ward, p. 7, line 9; John Poehlmann, 10th Ward, p. 3, line 12; Conrad Geis, 10th Ward, p. 2, line 7.

15. *D. B. Cooke & Co.'s Chicago City Directory 1859–60* (Chicago: D. B. Cooke & Co., 1859), p. 376.

16. *Smith & Du Moulin's Chicago City Directory 1859–60* (Chicago: Smith & Du Moulin, 1860), p. 376.

17. *Chicago Daily Democrat*, September 11, 1860: "Horses wanted/ We will pay in furniture for ten-fifteen good horses/ Shearer, Paine & Strong, No. 203 Randolph Street."

18. Telephone conversation with Leonard B. Shearer, Paine Furniture Company, Boston, Massachusetts, 1981; letter from Jonathan C. Shearer, president, Paine Furniture Company, November 12, 1981. CHS. See also *Annual Review*, 1860, p. 3 for discussion of southern trade.

19. Chicago city directories, 1857–1870; *Daily Museum and Chicago Hotel Register*, March 1, 1865. W. W. Strong, May 2, 1872. Illinois vol. 30, p. 280, R. G. Dun & Co. Collection, Baker Library, Harvard University Graduate School of Business Administration.

20. Andreas, *History of Chicago*, 3, p. 734.

21. "Charles Tobey," *Biographical Sketches of Leading Men of Chicago* (Chicago: Wilson & St. Clair, 1868), p. 421. Andreas, *History of Chicago*, 3, p. 734.

22. *Chicago Journal of Commerce*, October 17, 1869. Newspaper clipping "Builders of Chicago (25)" by Caleb, n.d., Clipping File, Printed Collection, CHS.

23. Interview with Frank B. Tobey conducted by Charles S. Sweet, secretary to Robert Todd Lincoln, December 10, 1907, Robert Todd Lincoln Papers, Illinois State Library.

24. Ibid. The furniture frames may have been made by Mitchell & Rammelsburg of Cincinnati, who advertised their factory in Chicago publications. A chair similar in pattern to the Lincoln suite bearing the label of Michael Schreiber of New York is described in Edward J. Stanek and Douglas K. True, "Belter, Meeks or Schreiber?," *The Antique Trader Weekly*, April 22, 1981, pp. 85–87.

25. *Chicago Tribune*, April 22, 1900, p. 14.

26. "Tuthill King" pattern parlor suite, CHS accession 1928.6, gift

of Mrs. George Henry High, granddaughter of Tuthill King. "Rosalie" pattern suite, CHS accession 1955.19, 1955.20, and 1969.1361, gifts of Mrs. Howard Linn, granddaughter of William Blair. A three-drawer rosewood bureau (1969.1364) made by Alexander Roux of New York also came from the home of Blair.

27. "Fourth Annual Review of the Commerce, Manufactures, and the Public and Private Improvements of Chicago for the Year 1855," *Annual Review*, p. 34.
28. "Twelfth Annual Review of the Trade and Commerce of the City of Chicago for the Year 1860 as Published in the Chicago Daily Tribune January 1," *Annual Review*, p. 39.
29. *Industrial Schedules for Illinois (7th Federal Census)*, 1850, Cook County, Knauer & Son, p. 383, line 16.
30. "Annual Review of Commerce Up to 1855," *Annual Review*, p. 44; "Annual Review for 1855," *Annual Review*, pp. 41–42.
31. "Annual Review for 1855," *Annual Review*, p. 41.
32. Van Allen Bradley, *Music for the Millions: The Kimball Piano and Organ Story* (Chicago: Henry Regnery Company, 1957), p. 37.
33. Ibid., pp. 38–41.
34. *Halpin & Bailey's Chicago City Directory for the Year 1862–63* (Chicago: Halpin & Bailey, 1862), p. 1.
35. *Halpin's Chicago City Directory 1864–65* (Chicago: T.M. Halpin, 1864), p. 261.
36. Schoff, *Glory of Chicago*, p. 73.
37. Andreas, *History of Chicago*, 3, pp. 733, 742.
38. *Industrial Schedules for Illinois (9th Federal Census)*, 1870, H. S. Carter, 1st Ward, p. 3, line 6.
39. Andreas, *History of Chicago*, 3, p. 737.
40. *Industrial Schedules*, 1870, C. C. Holton, City, p. 8; McDonough, Price & Co., City, p. 3, line 2; E. A. Jacobs, 20th Ward Supp., p. 1, line 4; A. B. Fiedler, City, p. 7, line 7.
41. Ibid.: J. F. Rapp, p. 5, line 3; McCabe & Wilkins, City, p. 7, line 1; Schieferstein & Bro., 3rd Ward, p. 3, line 6; W. W. Strong, City, p. 6, line 10.
42. Interview with June Hanselman, granddaughter of George Hanselman, 1975.
43. *Norris' City Directory for 1847–8*, p. 13.
44. McDonough, Price & Co. *Seventeenth Semi-Annual Price List, Sept. 1, 1874* (Chicago: J. C. Drake, 1874), pp. 22–37. CHS.
45. *Industrial Schedules*, 1870, John Koenig, City, p. 8, line 6; Anton Matuska, City p. 9, line 2; Pries & Wichman, 9th Ward, p. 2, line 7; Charles Tarnow, 8th Ward, p. 3, line 2; F. Mayer, 9th Ward, p. 4, line 8; and see Schoff, *Glory of Chicago*, pp. 62, 65, 70. For a detailed description of the use of the woodworking machinery mentioned, see Michael J. Ettema, "Technological Innovation and Design Economics in Furniture Manufacture," *Winterthur Portfolio* (Summer/Autumn 1981):207–15.
46. Andreas, *History of Chicago*, 3, p. 741.
47. *Industrial Schedules*, 1870, John Phillips, 15th Ward, p. 4, line 10; Phillips & Liebenstein, 18th Ward, p. 5, line 4.
48. Ibid.; Herhold Johnson, 15th Ward, p. 1.
49. "Chicago," *Cabinet Maker* 2 (October 28, 1871):196.
50. Ibid.; and Schoff, *Glory of Chicago*, p. 61.
51. "Chicago," *The Cabinet Maker* 2 (October 28, 1871):196.
52. For description see *The Land Owner: An Illustrated Newspaper* 5 (January 1873):7.

53. Schoff, *Glory of Chicago*, pp. 63, 64.
54. Ibid., p. 64.
55. Jacob Beiersdorf, November 14, 1870, Illinois vol. 30, p. 280; November 18, 1871, vol. 30, p. 281; March 21, 1874, vol. 32, p. 229. R. G. Dun & Co. Collection, Baker Library, Harvard University Graduate School of Business Administration.

INTRODUCTION, PART II

1. See *The Inter-State Exposition Souvenir* (Chicago: Van Arsdale & Massie, 1873); see also Perry R. Duis and Glen E. Holt, "Chicago's Last Exposition," *Chicago History* 26 (July 1977):72–74, 190.
2. S. S. Schoff, *The Glory of Chicago—Her Manufactories: The Industrial Assets of Chicago* (Chicago: Knight & Leonard, 1873).
3. Advertisement, Palmer House, *The Advance Guide-Book* (Chicago: C. H. Howard, 1875), inside front cover.
4. *The Palmer House Illustrated* (Chicago: J. M. Wing & Co., 1876), p. 9.
5. Ibid., p. 30.
6. Ibid.
7. Ibid., p. 32.
8. *American Cabinet Maker* 3 (June 7, 1873):4.
9. "The Exposition Visitors," *The Land Owner* 5 (October 1873):179.
10. *Industrial Chicago: The Building Interests*, vol. 2 (Chicago: The Goodspeed Publishing Company, 1891), p. 493.
11. See Gwendolyn Wright, *Moralism and the Model Home: Domestic Architecture and Cultural Conflict in Chicago* (Chicago: University of Chicago Press, 1980).
12. "Furniture," *The Inland Architect and Builder* 1 (May 1883): 54.

CHAPTER 3

1. See Alfred DuPont Chandler, Jr., *The Visible Hand: The Managerial Revolution in American Business* (Cambridge, Massachusetts: The Belknap Press of Harvard University Press, 1977).
2. A. T. Andreas, *History of Chicago, 1871–1885*, vol. 3 (Chicago: A. T. Andreas Company, 1886) p. 733; *The Furniture Interests of Chicago* (Chicago: American Furniture Gazette, Fall Extra, 1884), p. 2; *The Wood Worker* 13 (January 1895):35; Bessie Louise Pierce, *A History of Chicago, 1871–1893*, vol. 3 (Chicago: University of Chicago Press, 1957), pp. 534, 535.
3. "The Furniture Industry," *The Industries of a Great City* (Chicago: The Little Chronicle Co., 1912), p. 63.
4. Andreas, *History of Chicago*, 3, p. 734.
5. "Advantages to Working in Chicago," *American Cabinet Maker* 18 (November 16, 1878).
6. *Furniture Interests*, pp. 2–3.
7. *American Cabinet Maker* 16 (November 24, 1877):20.
8. "Innovations in Furniture Decoration," *American Cabinet Maker* 14 (March 3, 1877):4.
9. Ibid.
10. *The Trade Bureau* 29 (December 1, 1888):17.
11. Chicago Furniture Manufacturers' Association, Typewritten manuscript, 1891, p. 25. CHS

12. Novelty Tufting Machine, Advertisement, *American Cabinet Maker* 60, 10 (June 24, 1899):14.

13. "Woods Used in Furniture," *Furniture World* 13 (August 15, 1901):5.

14. *Industries of a Great City*, p. 65.

15. "A Summary of the Furniture Business," *The Furniture Worker* 33 (January 10, 1899):39.

16. *Furniture Interests of Chicago*, p. 2.

17. "Hand vs. Machine Labor," *The Furniture Worker* 34 (January 25, 1900):12.

18. Ibid., p. 11.

19. *The Cabinet Maker* 1 (December 23, 1871):258.

20. *American Cabinet Maker* 15 (June 9, 1877):20.

21. *Vobote*, July 1, 1876. For an analysis of the German furniture workers, see H. Keil and J. Jentz, eds. *German Workers in Industrial Chicago: 1850–1910: A Comparative Perspective*. Papers delivered at the Chicago Project Conference, October 9–12, 1981 (DeKalb, Ill.: Northern Illinois University Press, forthcoming) and J. Jentz, "Skilled Workers and Industrialization: Chicago's German Furniture and Metal Workers, 1800 to 1900." Chicago Project Publication; see also Hartmut Keil and John Jentz, "The Chicago Project; A Study in Ethnicity," *American Studies International* 20 (Summer 1982):22–30.

22. Pierce, *History of Chicago*, 3, p. 534.

23. See Richard Schneirov, "Chicago's Great Upheaval of 1877," *Chicago History* 9 (Spring 1980):2–17.

24. For contemporary accounts of the Haymarket Affair see Mrs. Lucy E. Parsons, *Life of Albert R. Parsons* (Chicago: The author, 1889) and Paul C. Hull, *The Chicago Riot* (Chicago and New York: Belford, Clarke & Co., 1886).

25. Dyer D. Lunn, "The Eight-Hour Movement," *Mass Violence in America* (New York: Arno Press and the New York Times, 1969), p. 13.

26. "The Labor Question," *The Trade Bureau* 24 (April 24, 1886):23.

27. Ibid.

28. Ibid. For an overview of the Haymarket Riot see Pierce, *History of Chicago*, 3, pp. 273–87.

29. "Hours and Wages," *The Trade Bureau* 24 (May 22, 1886):17.

30. "Chicago," *The Trade Bureau* 24 (June 12, 1886):15.

31. *The Trade Bureau* 32 (May 31, 1890).

32. "The Rise and Fall of Wages," *The Furniture Worker* 31 (November 11, 1898):10.

33. Series D-737, Consumer Price Index, *Historical Statistics of the United States Colonial Times to 1970* (U.S. Government Printing Office: Bureau of Census, 1976).

34. "That New Enterprise," *American Cabinet Maker* 15 (September 22, 1877):22; December 6, 1877, p. 19.

35. *American Cabinet Maker* 20 (April 24, 1880):18.

36. Ibid., 13 (October 7, 1876):2.

37. Minute Books, Chicago Furniture Manufacturers' Association. CHS.

38. "About Drummers," *The Trade Bureau* 20 (August 18, 1888):28.

39. *Furniture Trade Journal* 6 (April 1879):47.

40. *Furniture World* 5 (April 22, 1897):19.

41. *American Cabinet Maker* 17 (October 2, 1878):5.

42. Minutes, Chicago Furniture Manufacturers' Association, September 14, 1909. CHS.

43. "A Flying Trip to the Chicago Furniture Exposition," *The Furniture Worker* 38 (January 10, 1902):22.

44. "A Summary of the Furniture Business," *The Furniture Worker* 33 (January 10, 1899):39.

45. "Anent the Chair Consolidation," *Furniture World* 9 (May 25, 1899):4.

46. Chicago Furniture Manufacturers' Association, *NEWS* 2 (October 1952):2.

CHAPTER 4

1. *American Cabinet Maker* 19 (September 3, 1879):14.

2. *The Furniture Interests of Chicago* (Chicago: *American Furniture Gazette*, Fall Extra, 1884), pp. 3, 4.

3. A. T. Andreas, *History of Chicago, 1871–1885*, vol. 3 (Chicago: A. T. Andreas Company, 1886), p. 742; "Zangerle Mnf. Co.," *Furniture Interests*, p. 12; *American Cabinet Maker & Upholsterer* 60 (June 24, 1899):33.

4. "Zangerle Mfg. Co.," *Furniture Interests*, p. 12.

5. Ibid.

6. *American Cabinet Maker* 19 (June 14, 1879):17.

7. "Chicago Reports," *The Trade Bureau* 14 (June 4, 1881):42.

8. H. W. Mallen, "A Story of Chicago," (Typed manuscript, n.d.), Addena. CHS.

9. Ibid.

10. Ibid.; J. Seymour Currey, "Herman Z. Mallen," *Manufacturing and Wholesale Industries of Chicago* (Chicago: Thomas B. Poole Company, 1918), p. 189; Andreas, *History of Chicago*, 3, p. 742.

11. *American Cabinet Maker* 19 (June 14, 1879):24; 20 (December 6, 1879):19.

12. "Chicago Reports," *The Trade Bureau* 14 (January 29, 1881):14.

13. *Good Fixtures and Supplies for Furniture Manufacturers* 2 (October 1903):n. p. Published by The Seng Company.

14. "August Hausske & Co.," *American Cabinet Maker & Upholsterer* 60 (June 24, 1899):50.

15. Charles L. Eastlake's *Hints on Household Taste in Furniture, Upholstery and Other Details* was reprinted numerous times after 1868. See *Eastlake-Influenced American Furniture, 1870–1890* (Yonkers, N.Y.: The Hudson River Museum, 1973).

16. "Correspondence," *American Architect and Building News* 1 (April 22, 1876):134.

17. *American Cabinet Maker* 16 (April 13, 1878):18; 19 (May 17, 1879):1.

18. "Gannon & McGrath," *Furniture Interests*, p. 11.

19. Wallach, Theresa, "Solomon Karpen," *Fifty Forward Years 1888–1938* (Chicago: Chicago Furniture Manufacturers Association, 1936), p. 10.

20. Chicago Furniture Manufacturers' Association, *Karpen 1880–1930: 50 Years* (A Testimonial Dinner on the Occasion of the Fiftieth Anniversary of the Founding of S. Karpen & Bros., 1930), n. p. CHS.

21. "S. Karpen & Bros.," *American Cabinet Maker & Upholsterer* 60 (June 24, 1899):12.

22. Ibid.

23. *Furniture World* 8 (December 15, 1898):16.

24. *American Cabinet Maker & Upholsterer* 60 (June 24, 1899):12.

25. Advertisement, S. Karpen & Bros., "A Revolution in Carving Machines," *The Furniture Worker* 39 (April 10, 1902):656.

26. The motto was adopted in 1897. *Chicago Upholstery Journal* 1(1897):22. High Point Furniture Library.

27. *Furniture World* 11 (June 11, 1900):18.

28. *Furniture World* 5 (May 6, 1897):19.

29. Chicago Furniture Manufacturers' Association, *Karpen 1880–1930.*

30. "Karpen's New Factory," *The Furniture Worker* 34 (March 25, 1900):32–33. "S. Karpen — Brothers New Plant," *Furniture World* 10 (Dec. 14, 1899):17.

31. "Modern Methods to Meet Modern Demands," *The Furniture Worker,* 35 (December 10, 1900):64.

32. Chicago Furniture Manufacturers' Association, *Karpen 1880–1930.*

33. Delmar and Kenneth Kroehler, *Our Dad: His Career and His Philosophy* (Privately printed, 1941), pp. 18, 25. Property of Kenneth Kroehler.

34. "Style," *The Cabinet Maker* 2 (May 13, 1871): 1.

35. Kenneth L. Ames, "Sitting in (Néo-Grec) Style," *Nineteenth Century* 2 (Autumn 1976):52–53.

36. *Book of Illustrations of Lounges, Parlor Furniture* (Chicago: McDonough, Price & Co., 1876), p. 12. State Historical Society of Wisconsin.

37. Joseph Zangerle & Co., *Illustrated Catalogue of Jos. Zangerle & Co., Manufacturers of Parlor Furniture and Lounge Frames* (Chicago: Joseph Zangerle & Co., 1881), p. 38. Similar Dog or Student chairs also illustrated in O. L. Wullweber & Co., ca. 1881), p. 12 and Gannon & McGrath, *Parlor Furniture, Easy Chairs & Lounges* (Chicago: Gannon & McGrath, 1883), p. 25. All, Warshaw Collection of Business Americana, National Museum of American History.

38. McDonough, Price & Co., *Book of Illustrations,* pp. 15, 29, 27, 31.

39. *American Cabinet Maker* 14 (December 30, 1876):11.

40. *American Cabinet Maker* 14 (October 28, 1876):2; similar chairs were exhibited in 1879 Exposition, *American Cabinet Maker* 19 (September 20, 1879):15.

41. *American Cabinet Maker* 23 (October 1, 1881):11.

42. "Furniture," *Inland Architect and Builder* 1 (May 1883):54.

43. "Art Notes," *Inland Architect and Builder* 2 (November 1883):136.

44. Wolf, Sayer & Heller, *Illustrated Catalogue* (Chicago: Wolf, Sayer & Heller, ca. 1893). CHS.

45. Broadside, J. R. Sheridan & Co., (ca. 1885). CHS.

46. *Illustrated Catalogue of Furniture Manufactured by A. J. Neuberger* (Chicago: A. J. Neuberger, ca. 1881), p. 23. Warshaw Collection of Business Americana, National Museum of American History.

CHAPTER 5

1. "Chicago Trade Reports," *Trade Bureau* 9 (July 27, 1878):26.

2. The author wishes to thank Betty J. Blum for compiling an index of furniture-related patents granted to Chicagoans between 1860 and 1890.

3. Barger, U. S. Patent 481, 358, August 23, 1892; Cardona, U. S. Patent 341,222, May 4, 1886; Brown, U. S. Patent 435,376, September 30, 1890.

4. Siegfried Giedion, *Mechanization Takes Command* (New York: Oxford University Press, 1948; rpt. ed. New York: W. W. Norton & Co., 1969), pp. 395–96.

5. Rodris Roth, "19th Century American Patent Furniture," *Innovative Furniture in America* (New York: Horizon Press, 1981), p. 31.

6. Henry T. Williams and Mrs. C. S. Jones, *Beautiful Homes* (New York: Henry T. Williams, 1878), p. 116; also quoted in Ellen and Bert Denker, *The Rocking Chair Book* (New York: Mayflower Books, 1979), p. 83.

7. *American Cabinet Maker* 16 (March 30, 1878):21.

8. Giedion, *Mechanization Takes Command,* p. 393.

9. Denker, *Rocking Chair Book,* p. 84.

10. *American Cabinet Maker* 24 (February 4, 1882):7.

11. J. Beiersdorf, *26th Annual Illustrated Catalogue* (Chicago: J. Beiersdorf, September 1883). Warshaw Collection of Business Americana, National Museum of American History.

12. U. S. Patent 131,031, September 3, 1872.

13. *The Inter-State Industrial Exposition Souvenir* (Chicago: Van Arsdale & Massie, 1873), p. 118.

14. Giedion, *Mechanization Takes Command,* p. 415.

15. Elmer E. Barton, "Wilson & Bayless," *A Business Tour of Chicago* (Chicago: E. E. Barton, 1883), p. 177.

16. See Giedion, *Mechanization Takes Command,* pp. 420–21.

17. *Inter-State Exposition Souvenir,* p. 118.

18. Ibid.

19. Barton, *A Business Tour,* p. 177.

20. Advertisement, *A Business Tour.*

21. "Invalid Furniture," *The Furniture Worker,* May 25, 1902, p. 40.

22. Williams and Jones, *Beautiful Homes,* p. 256.

23. *American Cabinet Maker* 14 (August 4, 1876):7.

24. U. S. Patent 83,949, November 10, 1868.

25. See David A. Hanks, *Innovative Furniture in America* (New York: Horizon Press, 1981).

26. *The Cabinet Maker* 2 (May 13, 1871):1.

27. *American Cabinet Maker* 14 (March 31, 1877):20.

28. Advertisement, H. S. Carter & Co., *Western Furniture Trade* 3 (August 1876), n.p.

29. *The Cabinet Maker* 2 (July 22, 1871):88.

30. Advertisement, *The Decorator and Furnisher* (January 1884):154.

31. Conversation with N. I. Bienenstock, former editor of *Furniture World,* at The Furniture Library, High Point, North Carolina, July, 1981.

32. Empire Parlor Bedstead Co., *Illustrated Catalogue of the Empire Parlor Bedstead Co.* (Chicago: Empire Parlor Bedstead Co., 1875), Introduction. CHS.

33. *The Chicago Magazine of Fashion, Music and Home Reading* 3 (June 1872):68.

34. Empire Parlor Bedstead Co., *Illustrated Catalogue.* CHS.

35. *The Chicago Magazine* 3, p. 68.

36. "Union Wire Mattress Co.," *The Furniture Interests of Chicago* (Chicago: *American Furniture Gazette,* Fall Extra, 1884), pp. 20–23.

37. A. T. Andreas, *History of Chicago, 1871–1885,* vol. 3 (Chicago:

A. T. Andreas Company, 1886), p. 739; "L. C. Boyington," *Furniture Interests*, p. 17.

38. "L. C. Boyington," *Furniture Interests*, p. 17.

39. Jno. E. Land, *Chicago: The Future Metropolis of the New World* (Chicago: The author, 1883), p. 115.

40. Andreas, *History of Chicago*, 3 p. 742.

41. A. H. Andrews & Co., *The Andrews Upright Cabinet and Parlor Folding Beds* (Chicago: A. H. Andrews & Co., ca. 1887), pp. 16–17. CHS.

CHAPTER 6

1. *The Furniture Interests of Chicago* (Chicago: *American Furniture Gazette*, Fall Extra, 1884), p. 2.

2. Ibid.

3. S. S. Schoff, *The Glory of Chicago—Her Manufactories: The Industrial Assets of Chicago* (Chicago: Knight & Leonard, 1873), p. 61.

4. Ibid. See also "Furniture Factory for Sale," *American Cabinet Maker* 16 (April 20, 1878):17.

5. *American Cabinet Maker* 13 (May 20, 1876):12.

6. Sugg & Beiersdorf, *Illustrated Catalogue* (Chicago: Sugg & Beiersdorf, 1882). Winterthur Museum, Winterthur, Delaware.

7. A. T. Andreas, *History of Chicago, 1871–1885*, vol. 3 (Chicago: A. T. Andreas Company, 1886), p. 736.

8. "Chicago Reports," *The Trade Bureau* 14 (June 18, 1881):20.

9. *American Cabinet Maker* 14 (March 17, 1877):21.

10. *Furniture Trade Journal* 6 (April 1879):7; J. Koenig & Co., *Illustrated Catalogue* (Chicago: J. Koenig & Co., 1875). State Historical Society of Wisconsin.

11. "The Chicago Exposition," *American Cabinet Maker* 15 (September 15, 1877):18.

12. Jno. E. Land, *Chicago: The Future Metropolis of the New World* (Chicago: The author, 1883), p. 150.

13. See "Hanke Bros.," *American Cabinet Maker & Upholsterer* 60 (June 24, 1899); Andreas, *History of Chicago*, 3, p. 735; Broadside, Jost & Hanke. State Historical Society of Wisconsin.

14. Advertisement, *Furniture Trade Journal* 6 (April 1879):66.

15. "August Wichman," *Furniture Interests*, p. 9.

16. *American Cabinet Maker* 18 (January 25, 1879):18.

17. "Wichman," *Furniture Interests*, p. 9.

18. Harriet Prescott Spofford, *Art Decoration Applied to Furniture* (New York: Harper & Bros., 1878), p. 39.

19. *American Cabinet Maker* 14 (April 7, 1877):22.

20. Henry T. Williams and Mrs. C. S. Jones, *Beautiful Homes* (New York: Henry T. Williams, 1878), p. 10. For a discussion of similar Grand Rapids chamber furniture see Kenneth L. Ames, "Grand Rapids Furniture at the Time of the Centennial," *Winterthur Portfolio* 10 (1975): 23–50.

21. Louis Schultze, *Illustrated Catalogue of Louis Schultze* (Chicago: Louis Schultze, 1875); Broadside, F. Mayer & Co., November 1, 1872. Both, CHS.

22. *American Cabinet Maker* 15 (November 3, 1877); 17 (September 28, 1878):18.

23. *American Cabinet Maker* 16 (January 4, 1878):19; 19 (May 17, 1879):1; 23 (August 27, 1881):11; 24 (February 11, 1882):13; (March 4, 1881):11.

24. "Furniture," *Inland Architect and Builder* 1 (May 1883):54.

25. *American Cabinet Maker* 14 (December 16, 1876):5; 21 (November 6, 1880):13.

26. "Furniture," *Inland Architect*, p. 54.

27. *The Builder and Wood-Worker* (September 30, 1880): 178.

28. "Chicago Trade Reports," *The Trade Bureau* 15 (July 9, 1881):20.

29. F. Mayer & Co., *The Illustrated Catalogue of Furniture Manufactured by F. Mayer & Co.* (Chicago: J. L. Regan Printing Co., 1887). CHS.

30. "Furniture," *Inland Architect*, p. 54.

31. Helen Campbell, "Household Art and the Microbe," *House Beautiful* 6 (October 1899):218.

32. "The Adams & Westlake Co.," *American Cabinet Maker & Upholsterer* 60 (June 24, 1899):60.

33. Charles H. Kimball, "The Making and Care of Metal Beds," *Furniture* (July 1909):39.

34. Advertisement, *American Cabinet Maker & Upholsterer* 46 (January 7, 1893):74.

35. *Furniture Journal*, 26 (March 25, 1907):65; see also *Furniture Journal*, 27 (December 23, 1907):5; "Adams & Westlake," *Decorator & Furnisher* 21 (February 1893):165.

36. "Adams & Westlake," *American Cabinet Maker* 60 (June 24, 1899):60.

37. *Furniture World* 4 (July 9, 1896).

38. "Miller Hall & Son," *American Cabinet Maker & Upholsterer* 60 (June 24, 1899):33.

CHAPTER 7

1. A. T. Andreas, *History of Chicago, 1871–1885*, vol. 3 (Chicago: A. T. Andreas Company, 1886), p. 740.

2. *Industrial Chicago: The Manufacturing Interests*, vol. 1 (Chicago: The Goodspeed Publishing Company, 1891), p. 748; "Chicago's New Furniture Factories," *The Furniture Journal* 31 (October 9, 1909):84. A. E. Strand (ed.)., "Johnson Chair Company," *A History of the Norwegians in Illinois* (Chicago: John Anderson Publishing Co., 1905), pp. 241–44.

3. Advertisement, *Furniture Trade Journal* 6 (April 1879).

4. *Industrial Schedule for Illinois (10th Federal Census)*, 1880, Cook County, Chicago, p. 95.

5. See *American Cabinet Maker* 22 (March 19, 1881):19.

6. Advertisement, *Chicago Journal of Commerce*, October 14, 1869, p. 1.

7. *Furniture Trade Journal* 6 (April 1879); "Johnson Chair Co.," *The Furniture Interests of Chicago* (Chicago: *American Furniture Gazette*, Fall Extra, 1884), p. 14.

8. *Industrial Schedule*, 1880, p. 95.

9. Jno. E. Land, *Chicago: The Future Metropolis of the New World* (Chicago: The author, 1883), p. 91.

10. Andreas, *History of Chicago*, 3, p. 740; "F. Herhold & Sons," *American Cabinet Maker & Upholsterer* 6 (June 24, 1899): 48.

11. *American Cabinet Maker* 18 (March 22, 1879):14.

12. "Items," *American Cabinet Maker & Upholsterer* 46 (April 22, 1893).

13. Advertisement, *The Furniture Worker*, 33 (January 10, 1899):36.

14. Advertisement, *Furniture Interests*, p. xv.

15. Advertisement, *Furniture Trade Journal* 6 (April 1879); "Manu-

facturer and Pioneer is Dead," *Chicago Tribune*, April 23, 1905, in Harpel Scrapbook, p. 123. CHS.

16. "Phillips & Leibenstein," *Furniture Interests*, p. 15.

17. "J. S. Ford, Johnson Co.," *Furniture Interests*, p. 13; Andreas, "J. S. Ford, Johnson & Co.," *History of Chicago*, 3, p. 735.

18. Andreas, *History of Chicago*, 3, p. 735.

19. Ibid.; *Illustrated Catalogue of J. S. Ford, Johnson & Co., Manufacturers of Chairs* (Chicago: R. R. Donnelly & Sons, ca. 1887).

20. "J. S. Ford, Johnson Co.," *Furniture Interests*, p. 13.

21. Andreas, *History of Chicago*, 3, p. 735.

22. Ibid.

23. See Dr. Nick Scrattish, *Historic Furnishing Study, Ranch House (HS-1) and Bunkhouse (HS-2) Grant-Kohrs Ranch National Historic Site, Deer Lodge, Montana* (Denver Service Center, U. S. Dept. of the Interior, 1981). See also John Albright assisted by Peter Snell and Paul Gordon, *Historic Resource Study and Historic Structure Report, Kohrs and Bielenberg Home Ranch, Grant-Kohrs National Historic Site, Montana* (Denver: National Park Service, 1977).

24. S. S. Schoff, *The Glory of Chicago—Her Manufactories: The Industrial Assets of Chicago* (Chicago: Knight & Leonard, 1873), pp. 176 77.

25. *American Cabinet Maker* 15 (November 10, 1877):20.

26. Ibid.

27. Richard Saunders, *Collecting & Restoring Wicker Furniture* (New York: Crown Publishers, 1976), p. 22.

28. Ibid.

29. Andreas, *History of Chicago*, 3, p. 736.

30. "C. W. H. Frederick," *Furniture Interests*, p. 15; Andreas, *History of Chicago*, 3, p. 736.

31. "Chicago Rattan & Reed Company," *Furniture Interests*, p. 13.

32. Ibid.

33. Richard N. Greenwood, *The Five Heywood Brothers (1826–1951): A Brief History of the Heywood-Wakefield Company During 125 Years* (New York: Newcomen Publications, 1951), pp. 17–18; also quoted in Saunders, *Wicker Furniture*, pp. 29–30. Greenwood gives a date of 1884 for the beginning of Heywood Brothers's manufacturing operations in Chicago. *A Completed Century, 1826–1926: The Story of Heywood-Wakefield Co.* (Boston: Printed for the company, 1926) written twenty-five years earlier, explains how manufacturing began in 1886.

34. Clark Bros. & Co. went out of business at the end of 1887, when the factory was sold. The Heywood Brothers & Wakefield Company owned the factory until 1902, when it was sold to Richard Curran. *The Furniture Worker* 38 (April 10, 1902):36.

35. Advertisement, C. W. H. Frederick, *Furniture Interests*, p. xv.

36. *The Trade Bureau* 28 (February 25, 1888):15.

37. "Gov. Altgeld's Prison Policy and Rattan Goods," *Wooden and Willow-Ware Trade Review* 10 (October 25, 1896):29; *Furniture Journal* 23 (September 25, 1905):39; *Furniture World* 4 (October 1, October 8, 1896); 40 (December 31, 1914):43.

CHAPTER 8

1. Bessie Louise Pierce, *A History of Chicago*, vol. 3 (Chicago: University of Chicago Press, 1957), pp. 397, 544, 381.

2. For a discussion of the Chicago school of architecture see Carl W. Condit, *The Rise of the Skyscraper* (Chicago: University of Chicago Press, 1952); Condit, *The Chicago School of Architecture* (Chicago: University of Chicago Press, 1964); or Perry Duis, *Chicago: Creating New Traditions* (Chicago: CHS, 1976), pp. 13–37.

3. *Industrial Chicago: the Manufacturing Interests*, vol. 1 (Chicago: The Goodspeed Publishing Company, 1891), p. 168; also quoted in Condit, *Rise of the Skyscraper*, p. 18.

4. For a discussion of the evolution of specialized chairs, see Siegfried Giedion, *Mechanization Takes Command* (New York: Oxford University Press, 1948; rpt. ed. New York: W. W. Norton & Co., 1969), pp. 396–422.

5. U. S. Patent 3,057 (design), May 26, 1868; 5,282 (design), September 26, 1871; 68,680, September 10, 1867.

6. S. S. Schoff, *The Glory of Chicago—Her Manufactories: The Industrial Assets of Chicago* (Chicago: Knight & Leonard, 1873), p. 64.

7. A. T. Andreas, *History of Chicago, 1871–1885*, vol. 3 (Chicago: A. T. Andreas Company, 1886), p. 740; *Industrial Chicago*, 3, pp. 761–62.

8. Elmer E. Barton, *A Business Tour of Chicago* (Chicago: E. E. Barton, 1883), p. 92; Jno. E. Land, *Chicago: The Future Metropolis of the New World* (Chicago: The author, 1883), p. 203.

9. U. S. Patent 82,061, September 15, 1868.

10. Advertisement, *Lakeside Annual Directory of the City of Chicago* (Chicago: Donnelley, Loyd and Company, 1878–9), p. 1356.

11. *American Cabinet Maker* 21 (October 2, 1880):17; 13 (October 14, 1876):5.

12. "A. H. Andrews & Co.," *Inland Architect and Builder* 6 (November 1885):90.

13. *American Cabinet Maker* 20 (December 27, 1879):19.

14. E. R. Garczynski, *Auditorium* (Chicago: Exhibit Publishing Company, 1890) n. p. CHS.

15. A. H. Andrews & Co., *Guide to Church Furnishings* (Chicago: A. H. Andrews & Co., 1876). Library of Congress.

16. Advertisement, *The Bon Ton Directory* (Chicago: Blakely, Brown & Marsh, 1879–80), p. 210.

17. Albert Nelson Marquis, *Marquis' Hand-Book of Chicago* (Chicago: A. N. Marquis & Co., 1885), p. 312.

18. *The Inland Architect and Builder* 6 (November 1885):90

19. *Commercial Furniture* (Chicago: A. H. Andrews & Co., 1886). CHS.

20. *American Cabinet Maker* 24 (March 11, 1882):14; 21 (October 16, 1880):16; 23 (May 21, 1881):14; 23 (July 23, 1881):12.

21. Andreas, *History of Chicago*, 3, p. 735.

22. Ibid.; *Marquis' Hand-Book of Chicago*, p. 311.

23. *Commercial Furniture*, p. 75.

24. James K. Nesbitt, "Craigdarroch Castle" (British Columbia, Canada: Society for the Maintenance and Preservation of Craigdarroch Castle by the Provincial Government of British Columbia). Pamphlet.

25. Letter from William R. Fritze to Susan Schollwer, Chicago Public Library, April 16, 1980.

26. Andreas, 3, p. 871.

27. *American Cabinet Maker & Upholsterer* 46 (December 17, 1892):16.

28. *Furniture Journal* 27 (July 10, 1907):98.

29. Barton, *A Business Tour*, p. 86. See also A. E. Strand (ed.), "The Central Manufacturing Company," *A History of the Norwegians of Illinois* (Chicago: John Anderson Publishing Company, 1905), pp. 245–46.

30. Andreas, *History of Chicago*, 3, p. 736.
31. *American Cabinet Maker & Upholsterer* 60 (June 24, 1899):32; Andreas, *History of Chicago*, 3, p. 741.
32. A. Petersen & Co., *Illustrated Catalogue* (Chicago: A . Petersen & Co., 1886). CHS. *American Cabinet Maker & Upholsterer* 60 (June 24, 1899). Strand, "A. Petersen & Co.," *Norwegians*, pp. 246–ff.
33. S. S. Schoff, *The Glory of Chicago—Her Manufactories: The Industrial Assets of Chicago* (Chicago: Knight & Leonard, 1873), p. 63.
34. Barton, *A Business Tour*, p. 141.
35. *American Cabinet Maker* 17 (October 19, 1878):18.
36. Andreas, *History of Chicago*, 3, p. 734.
37. Jno. E. Land, *Chicago: The Future Metropolis of the New World* (Chicago: The author, 1883), p. 128.
38. U. S. Desk: *Marquis Hand-Book of Chicago*, 1885, p. 309; Mikkelson & Bendtsen: *A Business Tour*, p. 139; Weber Brothers: Andreas, *History of Chicago*, 3, p. 737.
39. "William A. Amberg," *The Book of Chicagoans* (Chicago: A. N. Marquis & Company, 1905), p. 21.
40. Andreas, *History of Chicago*, 3, p. 742.
41. Andreas, *History of Chicago*, 3, p. 740.
42. Chicago Furniture Manufacturers' Association, "Chicago Furniture Exposition, 1891," p. 5 (Typed manuscript) CHS; Andreas, *History of Chicago*, 3, p. 733.
43. Chicago Furniture Manufacturers' Association, "Exposition," p. 32.
44. Ibid.
45. Group 90, Furniture of Interiors, Upholstery and Artistic Decorations, *Official Catalogue World's Columbian Exposition 1893* (Chicago: W. B. Conkey Company, 1893), Part 8 (H), pp. 22–25.
46. *Chicago Upholstery Journal* 2 (1897):21, High Point Furniture Library.
47. *American Cabinet Maker & Upholsterer* 46 (January 7, 1893):28.
48. Ibid., 46 (October 29, 1892):14.
49. Ibid., 46 (January 8, 1893):28.

CHAPTER 9

1. Henry T. Williams and Mrs. C. S. Jones, *Beautiful Homes* (New York: Henry T. Williams, 1878), p. 175.
2. *Illustrated Catalogue of Stadtfeld & Wolf's Center Table Manufactory* (Chicago: Matthias Schram, ca. 1875). CHS.
3. *American Cabinet Maker* 18 (April 26, 1879):21; 22 (December 4, 1880):17.
4. Ibid., 17 (July 27, 1878):7; 17 (August 24, 1878):3.
5. A. T. Andreas, *History of Chicago, 1871–1885*, vol. 3 (Chicago: A. T. Andreas Company, 1886), p. 742.
6. Ibid.
7. "R. E. Pohle," *The Furniture Interests of Chicago* (Chicago: American Furniture Gazette, Fall Extra, 1884), p. 8.
8. *Illustrated Catalogue* (Chicago: R. E. Pohle, ca.1885). Warshaw Collection of Business Americana, National Museum of American History. Advertisements, *American Cabinet Maker*, 1878–80.
9. Andreas, *History of Chicago*, 3, p. 736.
10. *American Cabinet Maker* 21 (June 19, 1880):13.
11. "Neimann, Weinhardt & Co.," *Furniture Interests*, p. 8.
12. *American Cabinet Maker & Upholsterer* 60 (June 24, 1899):34.
13. "Niemann, Weinhardt & Co.," *Furniture Interests*, p. 8.
14. "H. Niemann & Co.," *American Cabinet Maker* 60 (June 24, 1899):44–45.
15. Andreas, *History of Chicago*, 3, p. 736.
16. "Schuebert Bros.," *Furniture Interests*, p. xxiii.
17. Advertisement, *Furniture Trade Journal* 6 (April 1879):n.p.
18. Elmer E. Barton, *A Business Tour of Chicago* (Chicago: E. E. Barton, 1883), p. 170.
19. "Chicago's New Furniture Factories," *Furniture Journal* 31 (October 9, 1909):86; "Head of Hanson Company Passes Away," *Furniture Journal* 53 (July 1923):47.
20. "Louis F. Nonnast," *American Cabinet Maker* 60 (June 24, 1899).
21. Williams and Jones, *Beautiful Homes*, pp. 11–12.
22. Ibid., pp. 6, 12.
23. Arthur Hope, *A Manual of Sorrento and Inlaid Work for Amateurs, with New and Original Designs* (New York: O. P. Putnam's Sons; Chicago: J. Wilkinson, 1880).
24. As quoted in Russel Lynes, *The Tastemakers* (1955; rpt. ed. New York: Dover Publications, 1980), p. 114.
25. Williams and Jones, *Beautiful Homes*, p. 4.
26. Harriet Prescott Spofford, *Art Decoration Applied to Furniture* (New York: Harper & Bros., 1878), p. 224.
27. *American Cabinet Maker* 15 (July 14, 1877):23; see also 21 (July 31, 1880):11; 15 (July 14, 1877):23.
28. See Michael J. Ettema, "Technological Innovation and Design Economies in Furniture," *Winterthur Portfolio* (Summer/Autumn 1981):220–21.
29. *Furniture Trade Journal* 6 (April 1879):39.
30. *American Cabinet Maker* 19 (September 30, 1879):16.
31. "F. Wenter," *Furniture Interests*, p. 24.
32. Arthur S. White, "Recollections of an Onlooker," *The Furniture Manufacturer and Artisan* 2–4 (October 1911):489; "Frank Wenter," *Prominent Democrats of Illinois* (Chicago: Democrat Publishing Co., 1899), pp. 330–31.
33. *The Inter-State Industrial Exposition Souvenir* (Chicago: Van Arsdale & Massie, 1873), p. 110.
34. *American Cabinet Maker* 14 (November 11, 1876):8.
35. Ibid., 15 (November 3, 1877).
36. Ibid.
37. Ibid.
38. See Andreas, *History of Chicago*, 3, 739; Salter & Bilek, *Manufacturers of Fancy Cabinet Ware* (Chicago: Salter & Bilek, 1886). CHS.
39. Barton, *Business Tour*, p. 152.
40. *Lakeside Directory of Chicago*, 1891, p. 2705.
41. "E. J. Lewis," *Furniture Interests*, p. 22.
42. *11th Annual Catalogue of Fancy Cabinetware, Etc.* (Chicago: Edgar S. Boynton, ca. 1887). CHS.
43. "Old Chicago," *American Furniture Gazette* (Spring Extra, 1883), p. 6.
44. Ibid., p. 6.
45. Ibid., p. 17.
46. Ibid., p. 14.

47. Ibid., p. 20.
48. Ibid.
49. "Furniture Fancies," *The Trade Bureau* 30 (March 16, 1889):24.

CHAPTER 10

1. "Our Furniture: What it Is, and What it Should be," *The New Path*, April/May, 1865. Burnham Library, Art Institute of Chicago (hereinafter AIC).
2. Ibid., 2 (May 1865):68.
3. P. B. Wight, "The Development of New Phases of the Fine Arts in America," *The Inland Architect & Builder*, 4 (December 1884):63.
4. Sir John Summerson, "Viollet-le-Duc and the Rational Point of View," *Viollet-le-Duc* (London: Academy Editions, 1980), p. 8.
5. Sara Gradford Landau, *P. B. Wight: Architect, Contractor, and Critic, 1838–1925* (Chicago: Art Institute of Chicago, 1981), pp. 30–43, "Obituary: "Asher Carter," *American Architect and Building News* 2 (February 27, 1877):31; Donald Hoffmann, *John Wellborn Root* (Baltimore: Johns Hopkins University Press, 1973), p. 6.
6. William LeBaron Jenney, "A Reform in Suburban Dwelling," *Inland Architect* 1 (February 1883):2–3; also in Jenney *Scrapbook*, pp. 33–34. CHS.
7. For biographical sketch see Theodore Turak, "William LeBaron Jenney: A Nineteenth Century Architect," Ph.D. Dissertation, University of Michigan, 1966. Microfilm, CHS.
8. For discussion of furniture designed by James Renwick, Jr., and Alexander Jackson Davis see Marion Page, *Furniture Designed by Architects* (New York: Whitney Library of Design, 1980).
9. Ibid., pp. 71, 72.
10. P. B. Wight, "Concerning Furniture," *American Architect and Builder* 2 (May 26, 1877):164.
11. Jenney, "Reform," pp. 2–3. For views on use of building materials, see Sanford E. Loring and W. L. B. Jenney, *Principles and Practice of Architecture* (Chicago: Cobb, Pritchard & Co., 1869). AIC.
12. Jenney, *Scrapbook*, p. 54.
13. *Chicago Tribune*, May 23, 1875, p. 7.
14. Harriet Prescott Spofford, *Art Decoration Applied to Furniture* (New York: Harper & Bros., 1878), p. 191.
15. Ella Rodman Church, *How to Furnish A Home* (New York: D. Appleton & Company, 1882), p. 72.
16. "Department of Household Art at the Exposition," *Chicago Tribune*, September 26, 1875, p. 3.
17. "Household Art in Chicago," *The Art Journal* 2 (1876):19.
18. Ibid. See also "Fine Arts," *Chicago Tribune*, September 5, 1875, p. 7.
19. "Department of Household Art," *Chicago Tribune*, September 26, 1875, p. 3.
20. "Household Art in Chicago," *The Art Journal* 2 (1876):19.
21. "Obituary: Asher Carter," *American Architect and Building News* 2 (February 27, 1877):31.
22. Asa Lyon lived at various addresses in Chicago and Evanston between 1872 and 1884, when he moved to Grand Rapids,

Michigan, and became a furniture designer. Information supplied by Dr. Barbara Buchbinder-Green, Evanston.
23. "The Inter-State Exhibition," *American Architect and Building News* 1 (September 30, 1876):319.
24. Ibid.
25. Ibid.
26. *The Patent Gothic Star Chairs* (Chicago: F. W. Krause, 1876), pp. 3–4, 5, 7, 9, 12. CHS.
27. *Lakeside Directory*, 1874–5, p. 1271; for biographical sketch see David A. Hanks, *Isaac E. Scott: Reform Furniture in Chicago* (Chicago: Chicago School of Architecture Foundation, 1974). For Scott's contribution to Chicago ceramics, see Sharon S. Darling, *Chicago Ceramics & Glass* (Chicago: CHS, 1979), p. 49.
28. "Household Art in Chicago," *The Art Journal* 2 (1876):19.
29. "Sideboard," *American Cabinet Maker, Upholsterer and Carpet Reporter* 20 (January 3, 1880):13. Sketch, p. 12 supplement.
30. Ibid. See also *Chicago Tribune*, May 23, 1875, p. 7.
31. "Correspondence," *American Architect and Building News* 1 (April 15, 1876):126.
32. *Handbook of the Bric-a-Brac Collection*, Inter-State Industrial Exposition (Chicago: 1877), p. 88. CHS.
33. Frances Glessner Lee to her son, John Glessner Lee, 1961, quoted in Hanks, *Isaac Scott*, p. 6.
34. Hanks, *Isaac Scott*, p. 17.
35. *American Cabinet Maker* 13 (October 28, 1876):2.
36. *Presented by A. Fiedler & Co., Designers and Manufacturers of Artistic Furniture* (Chicago: A. Fiedler & Co., 1877), pp. iii, 6, 11, 12, 25. CHS.
37. "The Chicago Exposition," *American Cabinet Maker* 15 (September 15, 1877):17.
38. Ibid.
39. Chicago Board of Trade. *Origin, Growth and Usefulness* [its leading members and representative businessmen in other branches of trade. An epitome of Chicago's history, and the prominent points of interest]. (New York: Historical Publishing Co., 1885–86), p. 356; Illinois vol. 39, p. 130, R. G. Dun & Co. Collection, Baker Library, Harvard University Graduate School of Business Administration.
40. Frederick William Goodkin, *The Chicago Literary Club: A History of its First Fifty Years* (Chicago: The Chicago Literary Club, 1926), p. 33.
41. *American Architect and Building News* 1 (August 19, 1876):271.
42. *Edward's Directory of Chicago*, 1873, p. 920; S. S. Schoff, *The Industrial Interests of Chicago* (Chicago: Knight & Leonard, 1873), p. 70; A. T. Andreas, *History of Chicago, 1871–1885*, vol. 3 (Chicago: A. T. Andreas Company, 1886), pp. 734–35.
43. Sheets 108, 112, and 116, Peter B. Wight Collection, Burnham Library, AIC.
44. "Department of Household Art," *Chicago Tribune*, September 26, 1875, p. 3.
45. "Correspondence," *American Architect and Building News* 1 (April 15, 1876):126.
46. Paul Blatchford Diary, 1876. Private Collection.
47. "Decorative Fine-Art at Philadelphia: American Furniture," *American Architect and Building News* 2 (January 13, 1877):13.
48. "State of Trade," *American Cabinet Maker* 15 (September 8, 1877):22.

49. John W. Root, "Architectural Freedom," *Inland Architect* 8 (December 1886):65, quoted in Hoffmann, *John Wellborn Root*, p. 9.

50. *Industrial Chicago: The Manufacturing Interests*, vol. 1 (Chicago: The Goodspeed Publishing Company, 1891), p. 308.

51. *Inter Ocean*, December 30, 1883, in Jenney *Scrapbook*, p. 64.

CHAPTER 11

1. "Studies of the Great West III—Chicago," *Harper's New Monthly Magazine* 76 (May 1888), as quoted in Bessie Louise Pierce, *A History of Chicago: The Rise of a Modern City, 1871–1893*, vol. 3 (New York: Alfred A. Knopf, 1957), p. 467.

2. Arthur Meeker, *Prairie Avenue* (New York: Alfred A. Knopf, 1949), p. 3.

3. Thomas E. Tallmadge, *Architecture in Old Chicago* (Chicago: University of Chicago Press, 1941 (rpt. ed. 1975), p. 184.

4. *Lakeside Annual Directory of the City of Chicago* (Chicago: Donnelley, Loyd and Company, 1877–8), p. 1183.

5. *The Elite Directory and Club List of Chicago, 1881–82* (Chicago: The Elite Publishing Co.), p. 111.

6. *Lakeside Directory*, 1877–8, p. 1183.

7. J. Seymour Curry, "The Decorators Supply Co.," *Manufacturing and Wholesale Industries of Chicago*, 2 (Chicago: Thomas B. Poole Company, 1918), pp. 344–46.

8. A. T. Andreas, *History of Chicago, 1871–1885*, vol. 3 (Chicago: A. T. Andreas Company, 1886), p. 741. Advertisement, *The Furniture Worker* 33 (February 25, 1899):29.

9. Advertisement, *Interior Decorator* 4 (October 1893), p. 291.

10. "Chicago," *Furniture Trade Review* 16 (February 10, 1896):45.

11. "The Western Eagle Screams," *The American Carpet & Upholstery Trade*, 8 (October 1890):967.

12. *Industrial Chicago: The Building Interests*, vol. 2 (Chicago: The Goodspeed Publishing Company, 1891), p. 710.

13. For descriptions of the work of Healy & Millet see David A. Hanks, "Louis J. Millet and the Art Institute of Chicago," *Bulletin of the Art Institute of Chicago* 67 (March–April, 1973):13–19; Sharon S. Darling, *Chicago Ceramics and Glass* (Chicago: CHS, 1979), pp. 104–8. See also Louis J. Millet, "Interior Decoration: Its Development in America," *The Inland Architect and Builder* 1 (February 1883):3; Millet, "Decoration in America," *Inland Architect* 1 (March 1883):18.

14. Chicago Board of Trade, *Origin, Growth and Usefulness*, p. 386; Jno. E. Land, *Chicago: The Future Metropolis of the New World* (Chicago: The author, 1883), pp. 184–85.

15. Adreas, *History of Chicago*, 3, p. 741.

16. John Drury, *Old Chicago Houses* (Chicago: University of Chicago Press, 1941), p. 341.

17. Thomas E. Tallmadge, *Architecture in Old Chicago*, p. 118.

18. "Colby & Peabody," Illinois, vol. 34, p. 55, R. G. Dun & Co. Collection, Baker Library, Harvard University Graduate School of Business Administration; Andreas, *History of Chicago*, 3, p. 740; *Furniture Trade Journal* 6 (April 1879):46; *American Cabinet Maker* 18 (March 1, 1879):19; 18 (March 8, 1879):14.

19. Eliza Voluntine Rumsey, *Recollections of a Pioneer's Daughter* (Pasadena, California: The Castle Press, 1936), p. 46.

20. Ibid., p. 44.

21. *Furniture Trade Journal* 6 (April 1879):46.

22. "Graduates from John A. Colby's Chicago Store," *Furniture World* 22 (January 18, 1906):47.

23. *Who's Who in Chicago: Book of Chicagoans* (Chicago: A. N. Marquis & Co., 1931), p. 196.

24. "Recent Deaths; John E. Brower," *Grand Rapids Furniture Record* 28 (June 1914):424.

25. "Graduates," *Furniture World*, p. 47.

26. Andreas, *History of Chicago*, 3, p. 734.

27. *Furniture World* 9 (June 8, 1900):17.

28. "Trademark Habit Contagious," *American Cabinetmaker and Upholsterer* article quoted in Sara E. Traut, "A Study in American Material Culture: The Tobey Furniture Company Advertising and Stylistic Eclecticism, 1898–1905," Unpublished manuscript,1980, p. 15.

29. *Tobey Hand-Made Furniture* (Chicago: The Tobey Furniture Co., 1904), p. 3. Strong Museum, Rochester, New York.

30. Advertisement, *The Furniture Worker*, November 10, 1900, as quoted in Traut, "Tobey Furniture Company," p. 17.

31. Advertisement, "A Little Bit About Tobey Hand-Made Furniture," *Home Economics*, quoted in Traut, "Tobey Furniture Company," p. 9.

32. "An Exhibition of Wallpaper," *American Architect and Building News* 5 (March 8, 1879):79; "Art Notes," *Inland Architect & Builder* 2 (November 1883):136.

33. George T. B. Davis, "The Future of House Decoration," *House Beautiful* 5 (May 1899):260–61.

34. "The Victorian Age in Furniture," *The Furniture Worker* 37 (May 10, 1901): 18. See "The Work of Joseph Twyman," *Architectural Record* 18 (December 1905):453–59.

35. "Styles for the Coming Season," *Interior Decorator* 5 (January 1894):114. See also *Furniture World* 12 (March 14, 1901):19.

36. Interview with William F. Christiansen, 1976.

37. *Furniture World* 2 (March 14, 1901):19.

38. *Upholstered Furniture* (Chicago: S. Karpen & Bros., 1906), p. 31. CHS. A sofa from the suite is illustrated in *The Upholsterer* 26 (June 15, 1901):30. See also Diane Chalmers Johnson, *American Art Nouveau* (New York: Harry N. Abrams, 1979), p. 284–86.

39. *Upholstered Furniture*, 1906, p. 31.

40. Ibid.

41. *The Furniture Worker* 36 (February 25, 1901):38.

42. *The Furniture Worker* 34 & 35 (May 10, 1900):40; "A Revolution in Carving Machines," *The Furniture Worker* 39 (April 10, 1902):66.

CHAPTER 12

1. "Roaming the Chicago Furniture Industry," *The Furniture Worker* 34 (February 10, 1900):30.

2. "Mechanical Art," *Sketch Book of the Inter-State Exposition*, 1883. CHS.

3. Jno. E. Land, *Chicago: The Future Metropolis of the New World* (Chicago: The author, 1883), p. 152.

4. "Our Illustrations," *Inland Architect and Building News* 3 (March 1884):23. See also "Chicago Reports," *The Trade Bureau* 20 (March 22, 1884):40.

5. *Industrial Chicago: The Building Interests*, vol. 2 (Chicago: The Goodspeed Publishing Co., 1891), p. 739; Advertisement, *The*

Elite Directory and Club List of Chicago, 1888–89 (Chicago: The Elite Publishing Co.).

6. *Industrial Chicago,* 2, p. 740.

7. Advertisement, Chicago Interior Decorating Co., *The Architectural Record,* 5 (July–September 1895):4.

8. A. T. Andreas, *History of Chicago, 1871–1885,* vol. 3, (Chicago: A. T. Andreas Company, 1886), p. 738.

9. Margaret Jones Williams, "And They Came to America," unpublished manuscript. CHS.

10. *Furniture Journal* 27 (December 10, 1907):122.

11. Advertisement, Chicago City Directory, 1882, p. 1403.

12. "Joseph Dux," *Chicago on the Eve of the Twentieth Century* (Chicago: Mercantile Advancement Co., 1900), p. 132.

13. "Gensch & Hartmann," *Chicago on the Eve,* p. 130.

14. "American Made Furniture at the Fair," *Interior Decorator* 4 (August 1893):204.

15. Catalogue, Chicago Architectural Sketch Club, 7 (May 1894), AIC. An advertisement for Visconti appears in *The Sketch Book* 6 (November 1906):xii.

16. "An Ideal Colonial Dining Room," *Fine Arts Journal* 26 (January 1912):46.

17. See Rodris Roth, "The Colonial Revival and Centennial Furniture," *The Art Quarterly* (Spring 1964):57–81. Gwendolyn Wright, *Moralism and the Model Home* (Chicago: University of Chicago Press, 1980).

18. W. L. Kimerly, *How to Know Period Styles of Furniture* (Grand Rapids, Michigan: Periodical Publishing Co., 1917), p. 137. See also Howard P. Hildreth, "Selling the Idea of Period Furniture," *Furniture Journal* 48 (December 1918):140–141.

19. Advertisements, *House Beautiful* 5 (March 1899):v; 8 (September 1900):xiii; 8 (August 1900):xi.

20. Ibid., 8 (November 1900):706, 710.

21. J. Seymour Currey, "The Chicago Wood Carving Company," *Manufacturing & Wholesale Industries,* vol. 3 (Chicago: Thomas B. Poole Co., 1918), pp. 331–33.

22. Ibid.

23. Samuel McClintock, unpublished history of Marshall Field & Company, p. 107. Marshall Field & Company Archives, Chicago.

24. Home Furnishings Scrapbook, October 1902. Marshall Field & Company Archives.

25. Advertisement, *Architectural Record,* April 1912, in Home Furnishings Scrapbook, p. 30.

26. John C. Murphy, "Notes on Furniture Making and Interior Decoration and Design in Chicago," unpublished manuscript, 1980. CHS.

27. June Hill, "Old-guard firm sees you in its new lofty idea," *Chicago Tribune,* November 29, 1981, section 13, pp. 1–2.

28. "William Kennett Cowan," *Who's Who in Chicago: Book of Chicagoans* (Chicago: A. N. Marquis & Co., 1917), p. 156.

29. Advertisements, *House Beautiful* 5 (March 1899):iv; 13 (December 1903):xxvii; 16–17 (June 1904):24.

30. George T. B. Davis, "A Talk About Colonial Furniture," *House Beautiful* 6 (June 1899):20.

31. Advertisement, *The Sketch Book* 6 (December 1906):xiii.

32. Advertisement, *The Furniture Journal* 31 (October 25, 1909):67.

33. "David Zork," *Who's Who in Chicago,* 1931, p. 1086; "Frank Joseph Wagner," p. 1007.

34. Lee S. Arthur, "David Zork's Store is Most Beautiful One," *The Furniture Journal* 54 (December 1921):186–87.

35. Edith Weigle, "Work of Master Designer Will Live After Him," *Chicago Tribune,* March 26, 1939. Clipping File, CHS.

36. Ibid.

37. Elsie de Wolfe, *The House in Good Taste* (New York: The Century Co., 1913), p. 24.

CHAPTER 13

1. Florence Morse, "About Furnishings," reprinted in Mrs. Candace (Thurber) Wheeler (ed.), *Household Art* (New York: Harper & Bros., 1893), pp. 180, 181, 193, 187. University of Chicago.

2. The Central Art Association, a Chautauqua-like organization founded in Chicago in 1894 by philanthropist Mrs. T. Vernette Morse, novelist Hamlin Garland, and sculptor Lorado Taft, attracted 3,000 members within four years in its campaign for "the promotion and dispersion of Good Art among the People."

3. "Fancies in Furniture," *The Furniture Worker* 30 (April 25, 1898):12.

4. Oscar L. Triggs, *The New Industrialism* (Chicago: National League of Industrial Art, 1902), p. 54. Overviews of the British and American Arts and Crafts Movements include Robert Judson Clark (ed.), *The Arts and Crafts Movement in America* (Princeton, NJ: Princeton University Press, 1972); Clark (ed.), "Aspects of the Arts and Crafts Movement in America," *Record of the Art Museum,* Princeton University, no. 34 (1975); Gillian Naylor, *The Arts and Crafts Movement* (Cambridge, MA: The MIT Press, 1971); Lionel Lambourne, *Utopian Craftsman: The Arts and Crafts Movement from the Cotswolds to Chicago* (Salt Lake City: Perigrine Smith, 1980).

5. See *C. R. Ashbee & the Guild of Handicraft.* An Exhibition organized by Cheltenham Art Gallery and Museum. (Cheltenham, England: The Gallery, 1981). For Ashbee's influence on Chicago metalwork see Sharon S. Darling, *Chicago Metalsmiths* (Chicago: CHS, 1977), pp. 33–34.

6. "Art Life in Chicago," *Chicago Inter-Ocean,* March 27, 1898, p. 26 in AIC *Scrapbook,* 1898, vol. 9, p. 149.

7. "Hull-House Shops," *Hull-House Bulletin* (Autumn 1904):15.

8. "Art Life in Chicago," p. 26.

9. Constitution, *Catalogue of the Chicago Architectural Club,* 1898, p. 118; also "Chicago Arts and Crafts Society," *Hull-House Bulletin* 1 (December 1, 1897):9.

10. AIC *Scrapbook,* 1898, vol. 9, p. 149.

11. T. Vernette Morse, "Arts and Crafts," *Arts for America* 7 (April 1898):491.

12. "At the Art Institute," *The Furniture Worker* 30 (April 10, 1898):22.

13. Morse, "Arts and Crafts," p. 491.

14. AIC *Scrapbook.* Also E.K., "The Arts and Crafts Exhibition," *House Beautiful* 3 (May 1898):101–5.

15. See George M. R. Twose, "Successful Houses," *House Beautiful* 6 (October 1899):208–17 for description of Higginson's house.

16. "Chicago Manual Training School," *Inland Architect* 4 (August 1884):2.

17. "Art Editorials: Art Industries," *Arts for America* 7 (January 1898):300.
18. J. Seymour Currey, *Chicago: Its History and Its Buildings,* vol. 1 (Chicago: The S. J. Clarke Publishing Co., 1912), p. 301.
19. H. H. Windsor, *Mission Furniture: How to Make It,* 3 vols. (Chicago: Popular Mechanics Co., 1909, 1910, 1912), rpt. ed. Dover Publications, 1980.
20. Katherine Louise Smith, "Women in the Art Crafts," *Brush and Pencil* 5 (November 1899):76.
21. P. B. Wight, "Architecture and Decorative Art at the Art Institute of Chicago," *Inland Architect and News Record* 27 (July 1896):52. In 1896, for example, sixty-seven women and eight men enrolled in Millet's three-year course.
22. W. M. R. French, "The Art School of the Art Institute of Chicago," *The Sketch Book* 2 (July 1903):10.
23. *Industrial Chicago: The Building Interests,* vol. 2 (Chicago: The Goodspeed Publishing Company, 1891), p. 576. See also Decorative Arts Society papers, CHS.
24. *American Cabinet Maker* 14 (August 9, 1879):15.
25. Group 96: Carvings in Various Materials, Woman's Building, *The Official Directory of the World's Columbian Exposition* (Chicago: W. B. Gonkey, 1893), p. 1054.
26. Morse, "Arts and Crafts," *Arts for America* 7 (April 1898):491.
27. "At the Art Institute," *The Furniture Worker* 30 (April 10, 1898):22.
28. "Holiday Gifts," *House Beautiful* 9 (December 1900):5.
29. For an overview of Wynne's metalwork see Darling, *Chicago Metalsmiths,* pp. 63–67.
30. Harriet Monroe, "An Easter Bride's Chest," *House Beautiful* 11 (May 1902):365–66. See also Madeline Yale Wynne, "Brides and Bridal Chests," *House Beautiful* 6 (September 1899):159–164.
31. John W. Patterson, "An Artist's Vacation Work," *Brush and Pencil* 9 (November 1901):87–92.
32. AIC *Scrapbook,* February 19, 1899, vol. 10, p. 124.
33. "Holiday Gifts," p. 4.
34. B[essie] Bennet, "The Crafts Shops of Chicago," *The Sketch Book* 1 (March 1902):10.
35. Advertisement, *House Beautiful* 13 (December 1902):xxiv.
36. Bennet, "Crafts Shops," p. 10.
37. Ibid.
38. Ibid., p. 8.
39. See Mabel Tuke Priestman, "History of the Arts and Crafts Movement in America," *House Beautiful* 20 (November 1906):15; Perry Duis, *Creating New Traditions* (Chicago: Chicago Historical Society, 1976), p. 116; Max West, "Revival of Handicrafts in America," *Bulletin of the Bureau of Labor,* no. 55, November 1904, Washington, D.C., p. 1603.
40. "Evanston An Art Center," *Times-Herald,* April 16, 1900; "A Garden of Genius," *Boston Herald,* June 4, 1900; "New Art School for Evanston, *Record,* April 1900. Clipping File, Evanston Historical Society, Evanston, Illinois.
41. *Chicago Architecture Club,* 1908, n.p.; AIC, *Catalogue of Arts and Crafts Exhibition,* 1907, pp. 66–67.
42. Priestman, "History," p. 15.
43. "Louis S. Easton," in *California Design 1910,* ed Timothy J. Anderson, Eudorah M. Moore, Robert W. Winter (Pasadena: California Design Publishing, 1974), pp. 122–23.

44. Ibid.
45. AIC, *Catalogue of the Arts and Crafts Exhibition,* 1902, p. 27; also Elizabeth Emery, "Some Recent Work," *House Beautiful* 3 (February 1904):38.
46. "Arts and Crafts Exhibition," *The Sketch Book* 2 (February 1903):14.
47. "Easton," *California Design 1910,* p. 127; "The Home of a Craftsman on the Pacific Coast," *House Beautiful* 15 (May 1904):373–74.
48. "Arts and Crafts Exhibition," *The Sketch Book* 2 (February 1903):14.
49. Anne McD. Powers, "The Quisisana Furniture," *House Beautiful* 11 (February 1902):194.
50. Oscar L. Triggs, "The Industrial Art League," *House Beautiful* 11 (February 1902):198; see also Priestman, "History," p. 15.
51. Oscar Lovell Triggs, *Chapters in the History of the Arts and Crafts Movement* (Chicago: The Bohemia Guild, 1902).
52. "The New Industrialism," *Craftsman* 3 (November 1902):100, quoted in Gwendolyn Wright, *Moralism and the Model Home* (Chicago: University of Chicago Press, 1980), p. 128.
53. "Triggs to Head New School," *Chicago Tribune,* July 1, 1904, p. 7.
54. Advertisement, *To-Morrow* 1 (March 1905):8.
55. Elizabeth Emery, "Some Recent Work," *House Beautiful* 15 (February 1904):138; see also, "The Arts and Crafts Exhibit at the Art Institute of Chicago," *The Sketch Book* 3 (December 1903):99–101.
56. W.M.R. French, "Practical Problems of an Art School," *Brush and Pencil* 10 (July 1902):233.

Chapter 14

1. "Notes," *House Beautiful* 3 (February 1898):103.
2. Bertha Lynde Holden, "Tenement Furnishings," *House Beautiful* 7 (April 1900):307–12.
3. See Sara Traut, "A Study in American Material Culture: The Tobey Furniture Company, Advertising and Stylistic Eclecticism, 1898–1905." Unpublished manuscript, 1980.
4. Advertisement, *Harper's Monthly Magazine* 97–98 (1898); quote from 101 (October 1900):58.
5. Advertisement, *Chicago Tribune,* April 29, 1900, p. 14.
6. *Chicago Tribune,* October 7, 1900, p. 10; reproduced in David Cathers, *Furniture of the American Arts and Crafts Movement* (New York: New American Library, 1981), p. 37; also *House Beautiful* 9 (December 1900):vi–vii.
7. *Chicago Tribune,* October 7, 1900, p. 10.
8. Gustav Stickley *New Furniture* catalogue, courtesy of William Porter.
9. Advertisement, *House Beautiful* 8 (October 1900):vi–vii; 9 (November 1900):vi–vii.
10. Margaret Edgewood, "Some Sensible Furniture," *House Beautiful* 8 (October 1900):653–55.
11. *American Cabinet Maker and Upholsterer* (December 22, 1900), as quoted in Cathers, *Arts and Crafts Furniture,* p. 38.
12. Leopold Stickley Memoirs, unpublished manuscript. Stickley collection, The Edison Institute, Dearborn, Michigan.
13. Advertisement, "Holiday Suggestions from Catalogue of the

'New' Furniture," *House Beautiful,* chiefly 10 (November 1901):vi–viii.

14. *Stickley Craftsman Furniture Catalogs* (New York: Dover Publications, 1979), p. iii.

15. Gustav Stickley, *Chips from the Craftsman Workshop, Number One,* pp. 24–25.

16. J. Newton Nind, "Mission or Craftsman's Furniture," chapter 13 in Binstead's *The Furniture Styles* (Chicago, 1909), as quoted in John Crosby Freeman, *The Forgotten Rebel* (Watkins Glen, New York: Century House, 1966), p. 47.

17. Gustav Stickley, *Craftsman Furniture,* 1909, p. 4.

18. George F. Clingman, The Tobey Furniture Company, Chicago, to Lee [Leopold] Stickley, Fayetteville, New York, May 26, 1911, 3 pp. Stickley Collection, The Edison Institute, Dearborn, Michigan.

19. *Chicago Tribune,* 5 (April 29, 1900):14.

20. Clingman to Stickley, May 26, 1911.

21. *Furniture World* 5 (April 29, 1897):7.

22. Gustav Stickley, "The Craftsman Movement: Its Origin and Growth," *The Craftsman* 25 (October 13, 1913):23.

23. *Decorator and Furnisher* 12 (June 1888):78; Charlotte Moffitt, "The Rolfs Furniture," *House Beautiful* 7 (January 1900):81–85.

24. *American Cabinet Maker and Upholsterer,* June 1918, quoted in Cathers, *Arts and Crafts Furniture,* p. 15.

25. Tobey Furniture Company, *New Furniture in Weathered Oak* (Chicago: Barnes-Crosby Co., ca. 1901). CHS.

26. Advertisement, "The Tobey Adjustable Chair," *Furniture Journal* 36 (October 10, 1901); U. S. Patent 71, 675, 1902.

27. Advertisement, *House Beautiful* 12 (1902): xxv.

28. *Inland Architect and News Record* 45 (April 1905):29.

29. Joseph Twyman, "The Art and Influence of William Morris," *Inland Architect and News Record* 62 (January 1904):43–45.

30. "Talks of Good Furniture," *The Furniture Worker* 36 (February 25, 1901):16.

31. Isabel McDougall, "A William Morris Room," *House Beautiful* 13 (February 1903):169–77; Rho Fisk Zueblin, "The Production of Industrial Art in America," *The Chautauquan* 36 (March 1903):627.

32. Oscar L. Triggs, *About Tobey Hand-Made Furniture* (Chicago: The Press of Metcalf, 1906). CHS.

33. "Country House Furniture," *The Furniture Worker* 39 (April 25, 1902):22.

34. *Furniture World* 22 (March 8, 1906):30.

35. Gwendolyn Wright, *Moralism and the Model Home* (Chicago: University of Chicago Press, 1980), p. 130.

36. For contemporary descriptions, see "Mission and Kindred Styles," *Grand Rapids Furniture Record* 6 (January 1903):141–46; Fred Bull, "Fads in Furniture," *Grand Rapids Furniture Record* 6 (May 1903):530–31.

37. Coleman, "Ready-Made Furniture," *House Beautiful* 12 (November 1902):386.

38. Lida T. Drennan, "Mission Furniture," *House Beautiful* 19 (January 1906):31–32.

39. Mary J. Quinn, *Planning & Furnishing the Home* (New York: Harper & Bros., 1914), p. 71.

40. Advertisement, *Furniture Journal* 47 (December 25, 1917):125.

41. Advertisements, *The Furniture Journal,* 1909; J. Seymour Currey, "The Fischer Furniture Co.," *Manufacturing and Wholesale Industries of Chicago,* vol. 2 (Chicago: Thomas B. Poole Company, 1918), pp. 203–5.

42. See Elizabeth Aslin's *Nineteenth Century English Furniture* (London: Faber and Faber, 1962), p. 55. She points out that the Morris chair is "basically a rural type found in Sussex" and that it is almost certain that William Morris never designed any furniture.

43. *Furniture World* 8 (January 13, 1898):7.

44. Montgomery Ward & Co., *Catalogue No. 73,* 1904–5, pp. 966–67, 968–69.

45. Sears, Roebuck & Co., *Catalogue No. 114,* 1905, p. 631.

46. Hartman Furniture & Carpet Co., *Catalogue,* 1912, p. 68. CHS.

CHAPTER 15

1. George T. B. Davis, "The Future of House Decoration," *House Beautiful* 5 (May 1899):266.

2. There developed many variations on this theme. For examples see H. Allen Brooks, *The Prairie School* (New York: W. W. Norton and Co., 1972), and issues of *Prairie School Review* (quarterly: 1964–ca. 1982, 15 vols.). Published by Prairie School Press at Prairie School Bookshop, Chicago.

3. Thomas E. Tallmadge, "The Chicago School," *Architectural Review* 15 (April 1908):72.

4. The author wishes to thank Timothy Samuelson for calling her attention to a list of Adler & Sullivan's employees prepared by George Elmslie, ca. 1946, in the Purcell & Elmslie Papers, Northwestern Architectural Archives, University of Minnesota.

5. George W. Maher, "Originality in American Architecture" *Inland Architect,* 1886, reprinted in *Prairie School Review* 1 (First Quarter, 1964):12, 15.

6. George W. Maher, "Art Democracy," *Western Architect* 15 (March 1910):30, quoted in Brooks, *Prairie School,* p. 67.

7. Arthur C. David, "The Architecture of Ideas," *Architectural Record* 15 (April 1904):379.

8. "Pleasant-Home," portfolio, CHS; Exterior illustrated in George W. Maher, "A Plea for an Indigenous Art," *Architectural Record* 21 (June 1907):431.

9. "James A. Patton Mansion Going to the Wrecking Crews," *Chicago Herald & Examiner,* Sept. 4, 1938, p. 5. Clipping File, Evanston Historical Society. See also "Studio-Talk," *The Studio* 30 (Oct. 1903):82; "Description of Mr. James A. Patten's House, Evanston, Illinois," *Inland Architect and News Record* 42 (August 1903):6; David, "Architecture of Ideas," pp. 375, 382.

10. "Patton Mansion Going to Wrecking Crews."

11. See *Prairie School Architecture in Minnesota Iowa Wisconsin* (St. Paul: Minnesota Museum of Art, 1982).

12. Brooks, *Prairie School,* p. 105.

13. Bedroom illustrated in Montgomery Schuyler, "A Departure from Classical Tradition: Two Unusual Houses by Louis Sullivan and Frank Lloyd Wright," *Architectural Record* 30 (October 1911):338; see also Marion Page, *Furniture Designed by Architects* (New York: Whitney Library of Design, 1980), pp. 112–15; Milwaukee Art Center, *The Domestic Scene (1897–1927):George M. Niedecken, Interior Architect* (Milwaukee: Milwaukee Art Center, 1981), pp. 33–43.

14. Paul E. Sprague, "The National Farmer's Bank, Owatonna,

Minnesota" *Prairie School Review* 4 (Second Quarter, 1967), pp. 5–21.

15. Gordon Orr, "The Collaboration of Claude and Starck with Chicago Architectural Firms," *Prairie School Review* 12 (Fourth Quarter, 1975):7. David Gebhard, "Louis Sullivan and George Grant Elmslie," *Society of Architectural Historians Journal* 19 (May 1960):62–68.

16. See Gebhard, "Purcell & Elmslie Architects," and Gebhard, "A Guide to the Architecture of Purcell & Elmslie," *Prairie School Review* (First Quarter, 1965)—issue devoted to their work.

17. As quoted in Gebhard, "Sullivan and Elmslie," p. 62.

18. As quoted in Page, *Furniture*, p. 114.

19. "The Statics and Dynamics of Architecture," *The Western Architect* 19 (Jan 1913): plate 14; also quoted in Page, *Furniture*, p. 115.

20. As quoted in Page, *Furniture*, pp. 93–94.

21. As quoted in Edward Lucie-Smith, *Furniture: A Concise History* (New York: Oxford University Press, 1979), p. 162.

22. As quoted in Page, *Furniture*, p. 94.

23. Robert C. Twombly, *Frank Lloyd Wright, An Interpretive Biography* (New York: Harper & Row, 1973), p. 38–39.

24. Alfred H. Granger, "An Architect's Studio," *House Beautiful* 7 (December 1899):36–37.

25. Irma Strauss, "Husser House Dining Room Set," *The Frank Lloyd Wright Newsletter* 2 (First Quarter, 1979):5–9.

26. See David A. Hanks, *The Decorative Designs of Frank Lloyd Wright* (New York: E. P. Dutton, 1979); Craig R. Miller, "Frank Loyd Wright and Modern Design: An Appraisal," *The Frank Lloyd Wright Newsletter* 3 (First Quarter, 1980):1–6.

27. Donald Kalec, "The Prairie School Furniture," *Prairie School Review* 1 (Fourth Quarter, 1964), pp. 5–13.

28. Frank Lloyd Wright, *Autobiography* (New York, London, and Toronto: Longmans, Green and Co., 1932) p. 145.

29. As quoted in Hanks, *Decorative Designs*, p. 107.

30. Hanks, *Decorative Designs*, p. 188.

31. David T. Van Zanten, "The Early Work of Marion Mahony Griffin," *Prairie School Review* 3 (Second Quarter, 1966):5–23.

32. Suzanne Garnschinietz, "William Drummond: Talent and Sensitivity," *Prairie School Review* 6 (First Quarter, 1969):5–19; "Partnership and Obscruity," *Prairie School Review* 6 (Second Quarter, 1969):5–19.

33. Kalec, "Prairie Furniture," p. 9.

34. Sally Kitt Chappell and Ann Van Zanten, *Barry Byrne, John Lloyd Wright: Architecture and Design* (Chicago: CHS, 1982).

35. Interview with Lawrence B. Perkins, son of Dwight Perkins, March 2, 1983; Albert Tannler, "The Creation of Charles Hitchcock Hall 1900–1902," *The University of Chicago Library Society Bulletin*, Fall, 1975, p. 28.

36. Frank Lloyd Wright, *A Testament* (New York: Horizon Press, 1957), p. 17.

37. Hanks, *Decorative Designs*, pp. 201–2.

38. AIC, *Catalogue of Exhibits, Chicago Architectural Club*, 1902, pp. 6–7, and Hanks, *Decorative Designs*, p. 202.

39. Milwaukee Art Museum, *Domestic Scene*, pp. 33, 43.

40. "Description of Patten House," *Inland Architect* 42 (August 1903):7.

41. Frank Lloyd Wright, "The Art and Craft of the Machine," *The New Industrialism* (Chicago: National League of Industrial Art, 1902), p. 94.

42. Quoted in Frederick Gutheim (ed.), *Frank Lloyd Wright on Architecture: Selected Writings, 1894–1904* (New York: Grossett & Dunlap, 1941), p. 42.

43. Elmer Grey, "The Architect and the Arts and Crafts," *Architectural Record* 21 (June 1907):132–33.

44. H. Allen Brooks, "Chicago Architecture: Its Debt to the Arts and Crafts," *Journal of the Society of Architectural Historians* 306 (December 1971):312–7.

45. Paul E. Sprague, "Book Review: *The Prairie School: Frank Lloyd Wright and His Midwest Contemporaries* by H. Allen Brooks in *Prairie School Review* 8 (Fourth Quarter, 1971):14–18.

46. "With the Societies," *Handicraft* 3 (August 1910):180–89.

47. Thomas E. Tallmadge, "The Thirteenth Annual Architectural Exhibit in Chicago," *The Western Architect* 25 (1917):27, as quoted in Leonard Eaton, *Two Chicago Architects and their Clients* (Cambridge, MA: MIT Press, 1969), p. 229.

Chapter 16

1. Paul Frankl, *New Dimensions* (New York: Brewer & Warren, 1928), pp. 18, 23, 38.

2. Ibid., p. 44.

3. Thomas E. Tallmadge, "Will This Modernism Last?" *House Beautiful* 65 (January 1929):44.

4. Joseph Aronson, *The Book of Furniture and Decoration, Period and Modern* (New York: Crown Publishers, 1936):155.

5. Interview with Philip B. Maher, April 14, 1980.

6. Interview with Harold Reynolds, May 14, 1983.

7. Telephone conversation with Robert Switzer, May 25, 1983.

8. Mildred May Osgood, "Observations Made at Secession Decorators—Dearborn Street, April 27, 1929," in "The Influence of the Skyscraper upon Modern Decorative Arts" (M. A. diss., University of Chicago, 1929), p. 48.

9. "Little Journeys to Chicago Homes," *Chicago Daily News*, December 28, 1935.

10. Celia Hilliard, "Castles in the Sky," *Chicago* 27 (November 1978):180.

11. Telphone conversations with Marjorie Goodman Graff, 1976 and 1980.

12. Hilliard, "Castles," p. 182.

13. After 1947, when Faidy began to study the work of Le Corbusier, his work acquired an increasingly geometric look as he came under the spell of the ancient theory known as the Golden Section. See M. W. Newman, "Abel Faidy's lonely voyage into design formulas," *Sun-Times*, Jan. 11, 1981; Nory Miller, "If I Can't Solve This, I'd Rather Die: Abel Faidy's Extraordinary Design Quest," *Inland Architect* (Spring 1971): 8–13. Jean Davidson, "Decades Later, Abel Faidy is Recognized at Last," *Chicago Tribune*, May 8, 1983, p. 7; Chicago Chapter, American Institute of Architect Foundation, *Villa Dionysos and Estate*, 1981.

14. "Two Modern Restaurants," *Good Furniture* 32 (May 1929):223.

15. *Good Furniture* 30 (July 1928):23; also Philippe Gardner, *Twentieth-Century Furniture* (New York: Van Nostrand Reinhold Company, 1980), pp. 164–65.

16. Interview with Marianne Willisch, May 11, 1983.
17. Ibid. Edna Wright "Newest Art Center Opens with a Flourish," *Chicago Evening Post Magazine of the Art World,* November 4, 1930, p. 8.
18. *Chicago Evening Post Magazine of the Art World,* October 25, 1927, p. 1; *Chicago Daily News,* November 5, 1927, p. 7.
19. Martin Battersby, *The Decorative Twenties* (New York: Walker and Company, 1969), p. 154; "Art Modern Furniture Design in America," *Good Furniture* 29 (October 1927):179.
20. "Living Room Furniture Design Competition," *Good Furniture* 29 (July 1927):40.
21. As quoted in Battersby, *Decorative Twenties,* p. 154.
22. "Modern Art Exposition in Chicago," *Good Furniture* 20 (December 1928):321; 31 (September 1928):116; "Manufacturers Seek Modern Designs," *Chicago Evening Post Magazine of the Art World,* September 25, 1928, p. 3.
23. "Modern Rooms in New York and Chicago," *Good Furniture* 31 (December 1928):311–17.
24. Lloyd C. Engelbrecht, *"The Association of Arts and Industries: Background and Origins of the Bauhaus Movement in Chicago"* (Ph.D. diss., University of Chicago, 1973), p. 86.
25. *House Beautiful* 65 (February 1929):154.
26. "Art Moderne at the Midsummer Markets," *Good Furniture* 31 (September 1928):118.
27. Marianne Willisch, "General Houses' Steel House Interior Furnishings," *Homes and Furnishings* (Chicago: A Century of Progress Exposition, 1934), pp. 64–69; Leland Atwood, "The Crystal House," p. 36–43.
28. Emily Genauer, *Modern Interiors Today and Tomorrow: A Critical Analysis of Trends in Contemporary Decoration as Seen at the Paris Exposition of Arts and Techniques as Reflected at the New York World's Fair* (New York: Illustrated Editions Company, 1939), pp. 11–12, as quoted in Englebrecht, "Arts and Industries," p. 166.
29. G. A. Young, "Modernist's Dilemma," *Arts and Decoration* 41 (June 1934):23.
30. "The Modern Sweeps the Corn Belt," *Arts and Decoration* 41 (May 1934):51.
31. "Swedish Modern in the U.S.A.," *American Home* 22 (July 1939):24.
32. "Meet Samuel Marx," *House Beautiful* 87 (November 1945):120.
33. "Snapshots: Samuel A. Marx," *Interiors* 101 (September 1941):41. See also "Connoisseur's Modern: S. A. Marx Apartment, Chicago," *House and Garden* 79 (April 1941):34–37.
34. Interview with Marijan Srnak, October 3, 1980.
35. "Decorating the Business Office," *Good Furniture* 31 (September 1928):135.
36. Interview with Mrs. James F. Eppenstein, March 3, 1983.
37. Letter from L. Morgan Yost to Mrs. Irma Strauss, May 27, 1981. CHS.
38. Interview with Monroe Bowman by Betty J. Blum, July 28, 1983; telephone conversation with Monroe Bowman, August 9, 1983.
39. Interview with Bertrand Goldberg, February 22, 1983. See "Bertrand Goldberg," in Paul Heyer, *Architects on Architecture* (New York: Walker and Company, 1978), pp. 49–54, and in John Wesley Cook and Heinrich Klotz, *Conversations with Architects* (New York: Praeger, 1973), pp. 122–46.
40. As quoted in Cook and Klotz, "Bertrand Goldberg," *Conversations,* p. 126.
41. See Richard Koppe, "The New Bauhaus, Chicago," *Bauhaus and Bauhaus People* (New York: Van Nostrand and Reinhold, 1970), pp. 234–42. Dorothea Moholy-Nagy, *Moholy-Nagy: Experiment in Totality* (New York: Harper, 1950); Hans M. Wingler, *Bauhaus* (Cambridge, Massachusetts: MIT Press, 1969).
42. John Chancellor, "The Rocky Road from the Bauhaus," *Chicago* 2 (July 1955):28–35.
43. Interview with Marianne Willisch, May 11, 1983.
44. As quoted in John Heskett, *Industrial Design* (New York and Toronto: Oxford University Press, 1980), p. 101.
45. Laszlo Moholy-Nagy, "New Trends in Design," *Interiors* 102 (April 1943):49.
46. Interview with E. Raymond Pearson, March 26, 1983; interview with Nathan Lerner, August 3, 1983. Furniture illustrated in Laszlo Moholy-Nagy, *Vision in Motion* (Chicago: P. Theobald, 1947), pp. 46, 88, 89.
47. "The New Springs," *Interiors* 102 (December 1942):34–35.
48. See Betty Williams Carbol, *The Making of a Special Place: A History of Crow Island School* (Evanston, Illinois: Advance Reproductions, 1980), interview with Lawrence B. Perkins, March 2, 1983.
49. Clark Sommer Smith, "Nine Years of Federally Sponsored Art in Chicago, 1933–1942" (M.A. diss., University of Chicago, 1965), p. 51.

CHAPTER 17

1. "Chicago Leads in the Manufacture of Furniture," *Fort Dearborn Magazine* (May 1920), p. 19.
2. *Survey of the Furniture Trade* (Chicago: Chicago Association of Commerce, 1925), p. 6. After the American Furniture Mart was organized, the Chicago Furniture Market Association turned over its comprehensive *Buyers' Book* to the managers of the Mart, who enlarged it to include all of the furniture wholesalers represented in the building. Local manufacturers also helped organize the Furniture Club of America in 1923 to improve relations among those working in the furniture industry.
3. *Survey,* p. 6.
4. "Construction Starts on Furniture Mart Building," *American Furniture Mart News* 1 (January 27, 1923); Lee S. Arthur, "Furniture Mart World's Largest Building," *Furniture Journal* 52 (June 1923):3–11; "Furniture Group Sets Own House in Order," *Central Manufacturing District Magazine* 13 (March 1929):18–23.
5. *Survey,* p. 6.
6. "Furniture," *Encyclopedia of the Social Sciences* (The Macmillan Company, 1931), p. 540.
7. *American Homes Bureau Reference Book* (Chicago: American Homes Bureau, 1925), p. 243.
8. Chicago Furniture Forwarding Company, "Comparative Statement of Traffic Handled for Year Ending Sept. 30, 1926," Chicago Furniture Manufacturers' Association Minute Books. CHS.
9. Frank F. Sengstock, "World's Largest Building Can House 90,000," *Public Service Magazine* (June 1930):101; Joseph Engel-

hub, "Furniture Hub of Country is Chicago's Boast," *Chicago Tribune*, January 6, 1952. CHS Clipping File.

10. Prepared by the Chicago Association of Commerce Anniversary Committee on the Furniture, Household Utilities and Musical Industries of Chicago.

11. *Furniture Journal* 51 (April 1922):20.

12. "Furniture," *Encyclopedia of the Social Sciences*, p. 541.

13. *Facts on Chicago Made Furniture* (Chicago: Chicago Furniture Manufacturers' Association, 1941), n.p.

14. Montgomery Ward & Co., *Hallmark Quality Furniture* 1 (1941):1; 2 (1942):1. Courtesy of Montgomery Ward & Co.

15. *Chicago War Wood Industries Association* (Chicago: Chicago War Wood Industries Association, 1942), pp. 38–39.

16. Delmar and Kenneth Kroehler, *Our Dad: His Career and His Philosophy* (Privately printed, 1941), pp. 25–26. Courtesy of Kenneth Kroehler.

17. J. L. Schnadig, "Pullman Couch Active for Past 20 Years," *Central Manufacturing District Magazine* 11 (January 1927):50–51. In 1916 the Pullman Couch Company, S. Karpen & Bros., and Kroehler Manufacturing Company turned the patents they held for davenport beds over to the Seng Company, which had been manufacturing the various metal folding mechanisms used in making all of the beds. Since each firm had developed a slightly different mechanism, Seng supplied each with its own design and paid the firms a royalty when its patented design was used by another firm.

18. Ibid.

19. Athena Robbins, "Furniture Goes to Market," *Good Furniture* 36 (February 1931):93.

20. *Fifty Forward Years* (Chicago: Chicago Furniture Manufacturers' Association, 1938), p. 16.

21. Ibid., p. 17.

22. Advertisement, *Furniture Journal* 50 (December 1920):24.

23. Walter Dorwin Teague, as quoted in Stephen Bayley, *In Good Shape* (New York: Van Nostrand Reinhold Company), p. 13.

24. *Furniture World* 62 (January 29, 1925):1549.

25. *Furniture Journal* 50 (October 1920):162.

26. *Furniture Journal* 53 (December 1923):85.

27. *Furniture Journal*, 1920–23.

28. *War Wood Industries*, p. 51; "Head of Hanson Company Passes Away," *Furniture Journal* 53 (July 1923):47.

29. Nonnast: "The New Nonnast Factory," *Furniture Journal* 31 (October 9, 1909):88, 90; H. C. Niemann: *Furniture Journal* 48 (May 1919):28.

30. *Furniture Journal* 52 (July 1922):108.

31. "Changes in the Furniture Exchange," *Furniture Journal* 31 (October 9, 1909):102.

32. War Wood Industries, p. 45.

33. *A Completed Century, 1826–1926: The Story of Heywood-Wakefield Company* (Boston: Printed for the company, 1926), p. 98.

34. Ibid., p. 98.

35. Advertisement, *Furniture Journal* 51 (March 1922):84.

36. "Art Moderne at the Midsummer Markets," *Good Furniture* 31 (September 1928):119.

37. "Novelty Furniture Firm Locates in C.M.D.," *Central Manufacturing District Magazine* 11 (June 1927):61.

38. David S. Oakes, "Design for Living," *CMD Magazine* 18 (April 1934):8. Revisions of this article appear as Mary D. Schopp,

"The Milano Tradition," 41 (September 1957):11–17 and A. J. Blair, "Tradition in a Mass Production Age," 34 (April 1951):11–19.

39. "Consolidated Report of the Industrial Committee, Annual Meeting Held October 18, 1921," Minute Books, 1921, p. 5, Chicago Furniture Manufacturers' Association Papers. CHS.

40. Interview with E. C. Snyder, 1976.

41. Oakes, "Design for Living," p. 11.

42. Ibid., p. 14.

43. Ibid.

44. Ibid.

45. Telephone conversation with Abe Rosen, 1983. Advertisements in *Furniture Journal*, 1920–23.

46. *War Wood Industries*, pp. 14–15; "Loreto P. Alonzi Rites Set," *Chicago Sun-Times*, December 19, 1973.

47. *War Wood Industries*, pp. 26–29.

48. Advertisement, *Furniture Journal* 50 (May 1921), inner front cover.

49. *War Wood Industries*, p. 80.

50. "Newsreel," *Interiors* 101 (May 1942):55; "Thumbnail Sketches: Martin Kruissink," *Furniture World* 153 (October 19, 1950):8; interview with Florence Kruissink Frazer, May 24, 1983; Zangerle & Petersen: *War Wood Industries*, pp. 86–89.

51. *Decorative Iron Furniture* (Geneva: W. H. Howell Company, 1928). Courtesy of Lisl Ekvall.

52. Ibid., p. 10.

53. Interview with Murray Moxley, May 1981.

54. *Furniture World* 130 (January 17, 1935):85.

55. "Pola Hoffmann's Designs," *Good Furniture* 31 (September 1928):142; Hazel Appleton Read, "Twentieth-Century Decoration; the Modern Note as Exemplified by American Craftsmen," *Vogue* 72 (September 1, 1928):108, telephone conversation with Mrs. Wolfgang Hoffmann, February, 1983. For biographical sketch of Hoffmann see N. I. Bienenstock, *A History of Modern Furniture* (New York: N. I. Bienenstock, 1970), p. 141.

56. Vogelgesang, "Contemporary Industrial Design," *Good Furniture* 32 (May 1929):229; "Exhibit of American Designers' Gallery," *Good Furniture* 32 (January 1929):45.

57. "Modern Furniture and Decoration," *Architectural Forum* 60 (June 1934):457.

58. *Modern Chromsteel Furniture*, catalogue no. 19 (St. Charles: The Howell Company, 1938). CHS.

59. Interview with Douglas Cohen and Stuart Applebaum, Douglas Furniture Corporation, April 5, 1983; Joseph Englehof, "Furniture Hub of Country is Chicago's Boast," *Chicago Tribune*, January 6, 1952.

60. *Chicago War Wood Industries Association* provided information concerning facilities, financial position, personnel, and product.

61. Notebook, 1942, Chicago War Wood Industries Association, Chicago Furniture Manufacturers' Association Papers. CHS.

62. Interview with Bruce Campbell, December 1983.

CHAPTER 18

1. T. H. Robsjohn-Gibbings, "Declaration of Independence," *Architectural Forum* 77 (August 1942):28.

2. Ibid.

3. William Clark, "Chicago Sits High as Maker of Furniture," *Chicago Tribune*, May 14, 1954. Federal Reserve Bank of Chicago, "Furniture—Stronghold of Small Business," *Business Conditions*, June 1956, p. 10.

4. Conversation with Philip E. Kelley, April 6, 1983.

5. Federal Reserve Bank, "Furniture," p. 11.

6. Letter from Charles H. Hanna, Executive Director, Chicago Furniture Manufacturers' Association, to Leon Davis, B. Brody Seating Co., July 28, 1959. Chicago Furniture Manufacturers' Association Papers. CHS.

7. Letter from Charles H. Hanna to Manfred Steinfeld, Shelby Williams Manufacturing Inc., May 27, 1963. Chicago Furniture Manufacturers' Association Papers. CHS.

8. Federal Reserve Bank, "Furniture," p. 11.

9. Interview with Charles Bauer, June 2, 1983.

10. Ibid.

11. Interview with Bruce Campbell, December 1982.

12. As quoted in Len Brodsky, "An interview with Morris Futorian," *Home Furnishings Daily*, April 22, 1974, p. 6.

13. Interview with Morris Futorian, July 27, 1979; "The Story of Futorian Strattord: Mass Manufacturing, Mass Marketing," prepared by Joseph W. Ketcham, Harshe-Rotman, Inc., Aug. 21, 1958; "Stratford Furniture Corp. cuts production costs with new techniques, *Upholstering* (October 1940): 62–66.

14. Interview with Morris Futorian, July 27, 1979.

15. Typewritten company history prepared by Douglas Cohen, Douglas Furniture Corporation, April 5, 1983.

16. Interview with Douglas Cohen and Stuart Applebaum, Douglas Furniture Corporation, April 5, 1983.

17. Interview with Lawrence Schnadig, Schnadig Corporation, March 4, 1983; Schnadig Corporation Policy Manual PBI–1–4/70; Dan Rottenberg, "Chicago's Invisible Economy," *Chicago* 31 (August 1982): 129–33; John H. Grun, "Every Executive Has a Say in Running Schnadig," *HFD–Retailing Home Furnishings*, Sept. 7, 1981, section 1, p. 12.

18. Edwin Darby, "Chairmaker Presides over Seat of Success," *Chicago Sun-Times*, July 17, 1983, Business section, p. 62.

19. "Shelby Williams Industries, Inc.," typewritten company history, 1983.

20. Interview with Robert Balonick, Marden Manufacturing Company, March 17, 1983.

21. Interview with Vito Ursini and Jerry Seiff, Interior Crafts, March 21, 1983.

22. Ibid.

23. Interview with Meyer S. Kaplan, February 24, 1983.

24. Interview with Ralph O. Campbell, June 21, 1983.

25. Ibid.

26. Letter to prospective customers from Donald Parenti, 1983; interview with Robert Parenti, February 10, 1983; see also June Hill, "Crème de la Crème Cabinetwork Designed to Fit that Castle in the Air," *Chicago Tribune*, July 19, 1981, section 13, pp. 1–2.

27. "The Dresher Story," Dresher, Inc., n.d.; interview with Max S. Dresher, November 17, 1983.

28. Telephone conversation, June 20, 1983.

29. Interview with Kitty Baldwin Weese, June 7, 1983.

30. Ibid.

31. See Paul Heyer, "Harry Weese," *Architects on Architecture* (New York: Walker & Co., 1978), pp. 41–47.

32. Interview with Kitty Weese; telephone conversation July 20, 1983.

33. John C. Murphy, "Further Notes on Interior Decoration and Design in Chicago," 1980. Typewritten manuscript. CHS.

34. Alice Nelson, "New Type of Reclining Chair Styled for Complete Relaxation," reprint from *The Chicago Sun*, 1946. Courtesy of Jack Waldheim. See also "Industrial Design," *Interiors* 105 (July 1946): 86–95.

35. David A. Hanks, *Innovative Furniture* (New York: Horizon Press, 1981), p. 106. See also "Designers in Production," *Furniture Forum* 3 (September 1952): 83.

36. The "Cricket" was awarded a First Place Casual Furniture in 1979 by the Pacifica Awards Resources Council Inc. See Edward K. Carpenter, *Industrial Design 25th Annual Design Review* (New York: Whitney Library of Design, 1979), p. 76. Nancy Poore, "Chicagoan Has Latest Word on Design," *Chicago Tribune*, February 21, 1956, section 2, p. 5.

37. Interview with Richard Himmel, June 16, 1983.

38. Ibid.

39. Various clippings in CHS clipping file, including: David L. Shirley, "Mies the Master," *Newsweek* (September 1, 1969); Mies van der Rohe: Disciplinarian for a Confused Age," *Time* (August 29, 1969); M. W. Newman, "Mies: The Man and the Legend," *Daily News*, August 23–24, 1969; "Mies the Man: The Life and Times of an Old Master," *Daily News Panorama*, April 27, 1968; Edward Barry, "Mies' Space Age Striking in Institute," *Chicago Tribune*, April 26, 1968; "Architect Still is Designing for a Future Civilization," *Chicago Tribune*, February 18, 1968; M. W. Newman, "In the Land of Mies, 5 Years after His Death," *Daily News Panorama*, August 17 & 18, 1974; Robert Feder, "A Documentary Builds on the Mies van der Rohe Genius," *Chicago Sun-Times*, October 10, 1980; Ruth Moore, "Mies van der Rohe—The Conscious of Chicago Architecture," *Chicago Sun-Times*, June 19, 1966.

40. Telephone conversation with Frank Mattaliano, Wells Furniture Makers, June, 1983.

EPILOGUE

1. Ann Ferebee, *A History of Design from the Victorian Era to the Present* (New York: Van Nostrand Reinhold Company, 1970), Preface.

2. Museu Di Castelrecchio, Verona and Graham Foundation, Chicago, *New Chicago Architecture: Beyond the International Style* (New York: Rizzoli, 1981).

3. Ibid, p. 141.

4. Interview with Stuart Cohen, May 15, 1983.

5. Stanley Tigerman, *Versus: An American Architect's Alternatives* (New York: Rizzoli, 1982), back cover. Interview with Stanley Tigerman, May 16, 1983.

6. Nancy Adams, "A Design Contest's Winners are called an 'American Memphis,'" *Chicago Tribune*, June 26, 1983, section 14, p. 4.

7. As quoted in Michael Walsh, "Niedermaier: The Empire Branches Out," *Chicago Sun-Times*, September 2, 1982, p. 64.

8. Interview with Patti Gilford, Netto Designs, February 24, 1983.

See also Natalie Block, "Furniture Gives Avant Garde Art a Leg to Stand on," *Skyline,* August 26, 1982.

9. Interview with Jon Cockrell, February 10, 1983.

10. As quoted in Judith Neisser, "Radical Sleek," *Chicago* 31 (August 1982): 122.

11. As quoted in Nancy Adams, "Straddling the line between function and fantasy," *Chicago Tribune,* January 16, 1983.

12. Interview with Glenn Gordon, January 13, 1983.

13. Interview with Mark Levin, January 13, 1983.

14. Interview with Richard Montalbano, September 20, 1983.

15. John C. Murphy, "Further Notes on Interior Decorating and Design in Chicago," typewritten manuscript 1980. CHS.

16. Interview with Richard Himmel, June 16, 1983.

17. Interview with Norman DeHaan, January 28, 1983.

18. Interview with Robert Balonick, March 17, 1983.

SOURCES

Few business records and little correspondence documenting the activities of Chicago designers and manufacturers have survived to the present. Therefore, most of the information for this publication has been compiled from city directories, periodicals and newspapers, exhibition and trade catalogues, interviews with designers and manufacturers and their descendants, and careful study of the artifacts. The Chicago Historical Society (CHS) is the primary source for such materials, although rich collections of printed materials are found at The Art Institute of Chicago, the Illinois State Library, Northwestern University, The University of Chicago, the Grand Rapids Public Library, the High Point Furniture Library, the New York Public Library, and the Library of Congress.

PART I: Primary sources for the study of Chicago's pioneer furniture manufacturers are the city's earliest newspapers, the *Chicago Democrat* and the *Chicago American*, and city directories, published annually between 1843 and 1929. Statistics published in the *Chicago Tribune's Annual Review of the Trade and Commerce of Chicago, 1853–1871* are useful in determining production and distribution patterns. Biographical sketches of leading nineteenth-century manufacturers can be found in A. T. Andreas, *History of Chicago, 1871–1885*, vol. 3 (Chicago: A. T. Andreas Company, 1886) and *Biographical Sketches of the Leading Men of Chicago* (Chicago: Wilson & St. Clair, 1868). Personal accounts include "John Dean Caton's Reminiscences of Chicago in 1833 and 1834," edited by Harry Pratt; *Journal of the Illinois State Historical Society* 28 (April 1935), based on an unpublished biography at CHS; and "Leander James and Henrietta (Hamilton) McCormick: Brief Notes on the Hundredth Anniversary of their Arrival in Chicago, November 20, 1848," also at CHS. Census records, particularly Schedule 5: Products of Industry, for the years between 1850 and 1880 provide valuable comparative information.

General background information on nineteenth-century Chicago was drawn from various surveys, the most important of which are Bessie Louise Pierce, *A History of Chicago*, 3 vols. (New York: Alfred A. Knopf, 1937–40; Chicago: University of Chicago Press, 1957); Harold M. Mayer and Richard C. Wade, *Chicago: Growth of a Metropolis* (Chicago: University of Chicago Press, 1970); and Paul Gilbert and Charles Lee Bryson, *Chicago and its Makers* (Chicago: Felix Mendelsohn, 1929). Other studies include Elmer A. Riley, "The Development of Chicago and Vicinity as a Manufacturing Center Prior to 1880" (Diss., University of Chicago, 1911) and William J. Cronin, "To Be the Central City: Chicago 1848–1857," *Chicago History* 10 (Fall 1981).

General studies of nineteenth-century furniture manufacturing that helped place the Chicago industry in context include Charles F. Hummel, "The Business of Woodworking: 1700–1840" and Jan Seidler, "Transitions in New England's Nineteenth Century Furniture Industry: Technology and Style, 1820–1880," both in *Tools and Technologies: America's Wooden Age* (Burlington, Vermont: Robert Hall Fleming Museum, University of Vermont, 1979); Polly Anne Earl, "Craftsmen and Machines: The Nineteenth-Century Furniture Industry," *Technological Innovation and the Decorative Arts* (Winterthur Conference Report, 1973); Wendell P. Garrett, "The Matter of Consumers' Taste," *Country Cabinetwork and Simple City Furniture* (Winterthur Conference Report 1969; Charlottesville: University Press of Virginia, 1970); and Anthony N. B. Garvan, "Effects of Technology on Domestic Life, 1830–1880," in *Technology in Western Civilization* (New York: Oxford University Press, 1967). Andrew Jackson Downing's *The Architecture of Country Houses* and J. C. Louden's *Encyclopedia* of 1833, the latter reprinted as *Furniture for the Victorian Home* (Watkin's Glen, New York: American Life Foundation Study Institute, 1978), remain standard sources for the period, while Alan Gowan's *Images of American Living: Four Centuries of Architecture and Furniture as Cultural Expression* (New York: Harper & Row, 1976) and Betty I. Madden, *Art, Craft, and Architecture in Early Illinois* (Urbana: University of Illinois Press, 1974) successfully discuss furniture in relation to other arts.

PART II: Material on the development of furniture manufacturing and distribution in nineteenth-century Chicago is to be found in various trade publications: *American Cabinet Maker & Upholsterer* (New York, 1870–1919, when it merged with *Furniture World*); *American Furniture Gazette* (Chicago, ca. 1880–1902); *Central Manufacturing District Magazine* (Chicago, 1916–48); *Decorator and Furnisher* (New York, 1882–98); *Furniture Record* (Grand Rapids, 1892–1940); *Furniture Journal* (Rockford and Chicago, 1888–1931); *The Furniture Worker* (Cincinnati and Chicago, 1883–1922); *Furniture World* (New York, 1895 to the present); *Good Furniture and Decoration* (Grand Rapids, 1913–31); and *The Western Furniture Trade* (Chicago, 1874–ca. 1879). In addition, catalogues, broadsides, and price lists of various wholesale, retail, and mail-order houses have been indispensable.

Profiles of furniture manufacturers and their firms can be found in *A Business Tour of Chicago* (Chicago: E. E. Barton, 1883); *Origin, Growth and Usefulness of the Chicago Board of Trade* (New York: Historical Publishing Co., 1885–86); J. Seymour Currey, *Manufacturing and Wholesale Industries of Chicago*, 3 vols. (Chicago: Thomas B. Poole Company, 1918); *Industrial Chicago: The Building Interests*, vol. 2 (Chicago: The Goodspeed Publishing Company, 1891); Jno. E. Land, *Chicago: The Future Metropolis of the New World* (Chicago: The author, 1883); *Majestic Chicago: Chicago or the Eve of the Twentieth Century* (Chicago: Mercentile Advancement Co., 1900); *The Merchants and Manufacturers of Chicago* (Chicago: J. M. Wing & Company, 1873); S. S. Schoff, *The Industrial Interests of Chicago* (Chicago: Knight & Leonard, 1873); and Algot E. Strand, *A History of the Norwegians of Illinois* (Chicago: J. Anderson Publishing Co., 1905). Brief overviews of the city's furniture industry are "The Furniture Industry," in *The Industries of a Great City* (Chicago: The Little Chronicle Company, 1912) and *Fifty Forward Years, 1888–1938*, a pamphlet published by the Chicago Furniture Manufacturers' Association in 1938.

The Minutes books and files of the Chicago Furniture Manufacturers' Association, 1892–1978, provide valuable insight into the day-to-day operations of Chicago's factories and contain information regarding numbers of employees, average wages, freight rates, and labor relations. Two important studies of the social and geographic mobility of the city's German furniture workers are H. Keil and J. Jentz (eds.), *German Workers in Industrial Chicago, 1850–1910: A Comparative Perspective* (De Kalb, Illinois: Northern Illinois University Press, forthcoming) and J. Jentz, "Skilled Workers and Industrialization: Chicago's German Furniture and Metal Workers, 1800 to 1900," published by The Chicago Project of the American Institute of the University of Munich, Germany.

Technological innovations that revolutionized the furniture industry are ably discussed in Michael J. Ettema, "Technological Innovation and Design Economics in Furniture Manufacture," *Winterthur Portfolio* 16 (Summer/Autumn 1981) and John A. Kouwenhoven, *The Arts in Modern Civilization* (originally *Made in America* [New York: W. W. Norton & Co., 1967]). Siegfried Giedion's *Mechanization Takes Command* (New York: W. W. Norton & Co., 1948; rpt. ed. 1969) and Rodris Roth's "Nineteenth-Century American Patent Furniture," in David A. Hanks, *Innovative Furniture in America from 1800 to the Present* (New York: Horizon Press, 1981) are excellent discussions of patent furniture.

Contemporary domestic guides dealing with the selection and arrangmenet of furniture abound. Among the most useful are Ella Rodman Church, *How to Furnish a Home* (New York: D. Appleton & Company, 1882); Clarence C. Cook, *The House Beautiful* (New York: Scribner, Armstrong & Co., 1878); Julia Darrow Cowles, Artistic Home Furnishing for People of Moderate Means (New York: F. M. Lupton, 1898); Harriet Prescott Spofford, *Art Decoration Applied to Furniture* (New York: Harper & Brothers, 1878); Almon C. Varney, *Our Homes and Their Adornment* (Detroit, Michigan: J. C. Chilton & Co., 1884); and Henry T. Williams and Mrs. C. S. Jones, *Beautiful Homes* (New York: Henry T. Williams, 1878). Studies stressing the role of furniture in Victorian society include Kenneth L. Ames, "What is the NEO-GREC?," *Nineteenth Century* 2 (Summer 1976) and "Sitting in (Néo-Grec) Style," *Nineteenth Century* 2 (Autumn 1976) and Leslie A. Greene, "The Late Victorian Hallstand: A Social History," *Nineteenth Century* (Winter 1980).

PART III: Advertisements for and references to Chicago art furniture makers can be found in society handbooks such as *The Elite Directory and Club List of Chicago* (Chicago: The Elite Publishing Co.), beginning in the 1870s, and in periodicals such as *Inland Architect and News Record* (Chicago, 1883–1908) and *American Architect & Building News* (Boston and New York, 1876–1938). Other rich sources are publications issued in conjunction with expositions, such as *The Inter-State Industrial Exposition Souvenir* (Chicago: Van Arsdale & Massie, 1873); the *Sketch Book of the Inter-State Exposition* (Chicago: R. R. Donnelly & Sons, 1883); and the *Official Catalogue, World's Columbian Exposition 1893* (Chicago: W. B. Conkey Company, 1893).

Several articles published in the 1870s record the heyday of Modern Gothic furniture in Chicago. Four of these are "Household Art in Chicago," *The Art Journal* (1876); "Department of Household Art at the Exposition," *Chicago Tribune*, September 26, 1875; "The Chicago Exposition," *American Cabinet Maker* 15 (September 15, 1877); and "The Inter-State Exposition," *American Architect & Building News* (September 30, 1876). Drawings reproduced in the reprint of Bruce J. Talbert's *Gothic Forms Applied to Furniture, Metal Work and Decoration for Domestic Purposes* (1867) and *Examples of Ancient and Modern Furniture, Metal Work, Tapestries Etc.* (1876) (Watkins Glen, New York: American Life Foundation for the Athenaeum Library of Nineteenth Century America, 1978), proved helpful in comparing stylistic characteristics of locally made furniture, as did those appearing in Charles L. Eastlake's *Hints on Household Taste in Furniture, Upholstery and Other Details* (New York: Dover Publications, 1969; rpt. of 1878 ed.). "The Eastlake in Furniture," *American Cabinet Maker* 15 (July 23, 1877) and Mary Jean Smith Madigan's *Eastlake-Influenced American Furniture* (Yonkers, New York: The Hudson River Museum, 1973) reflect the widespread influence of the British tastemaker on furniture at the time.

The growing influence of "period" furnishings and reproductions of antique styles, as well as other trends in interior decoration, are evident in popular manuals like Elsie de Wolfe, *The House in Good Taste* (New York: The Century Company, 1913); Lucy Abbot Throop, *Furnishing the Home of Good Taste* (New York: McBride, Nast & Company, 1912); and Edith Wharton and Ogden Codman, *The Decoration of Houses* (New York: Arno Press, 1975, first published ca. 1897); W. L. Kimerly's *How to Know Period Styles of Furniture* (Grand Rapids; Periodical Publishing Co., 1917); and the annual volumes of *Seng's Furniture Facts* prove useful in understanding contemporary terminology.

Several studies of Chicago's cultural life at the turn of the century depict the local circumstances that encouraged and supported the making of art furniture. Herbert E. Fleming, *Magazines of a Market-Metropolis* (Chicago: University of Chicago Press, 1906) discusses the emergence of *House Beautiful* as an arbiter of taste, while Perry Duis, *Chicago: Creating New Traditions* (Chicago: CHS 1976) and Gwendolyn Wright, *Moralism and the Model Home: Domestic Architecture and Cultural Conflict in Chicago, 1873–1913* (Chicago: University of Chicago Press, 1980) compare the interrelationships between reformers and innovators in various fields. Illustrations of Chicago houses and interiors appear in Julian Cavalier, *American Castles* (South Brunswick and New York: A. S. Barnes & Co., 1973); David Lowe, *Chicago Interiors: Views of a Splendid World* (Chicago: Contemporary Books, 1979); John Drury, *Old Chicago Houses* (Chicago: University of Chicago Press, 1941); Mabel Tuke Priestman, *Artistic Houses* (Chicago: A. C. McClurg & Co., 1910); Herma Clark, *The Elegant Eighties, When Chicago Was Young* (Chicago: A. C. McClurg & Co., [1941]); and Thomas E. Tallmadge, *Architecture in Old Chicago* (Chicago: University of Chicago Press, 1941).

Although numerous publications have appeared in the past decade, the standard reference on Arts and Crafts furnishings remains *The Arts and Crafts Movement in America* (Princeton, N.J.: Princeton University Press, 1972), prepared by Robert Judson Clark and others. Various Chicago publications—*House Beautiful, Arts for America, The Sketch Book, Brush and Pencil, Fine Arts Journal,* and exhibition catalogues and bulletins of The Art Institute of Chicago—as well as national periodicals such as *The Chautauquan* and *The Craftsman*—featured work by Chicago furniture makers. Basic to an understanding of the American movement is Max West, "The Revival of Handicrafts in America (U.S. Department of Commerce and Labor; Bulletin of the Bureau of Labor, no. 55 (November 1904), which traces developments in a number of cities, including Chicago. Also important are Mabel Tuke Priestman, "History of the Arts and Crafts Movement in America," *House Beautiful* 20 (November 1906); Gustav Stickley, "The Craftsman Movement: Its Origin and Growth," *The Craftsman* 25 (October 1913); and Oscar Lovell Triggs, *Chapters in the History of the Arts and Crafts Movement* (Chicago: The Bohemia Guild, 1902). Current perspectives are gathered in "Aspects of the Arts and Crafts Movement in America," a special issue 34, no. 2, 1975 of the *Record of the Art Museum,* Princeton University.

Studies of Arts and Crafts furniture makers who had links with Chicago include David M. Cathers, *Furniture of the American Arts and Crafts Movement* (New York: New American Library, 1981), a study of Gustav Stickley's work; John Crosby Freeman, *The Forgotten Rebel: Gustav Stickley and his Craftsman Mission Furniture* (Watkins Glen, New York: Century House, 1966); Deborah DeVall Dorsey Norberg, "Charles P. Limbert, Maker of Michigan 'Arts and Crafts' Furniture," *The Herald* (Henry Ford Museum, October 1976); *California Design 1910* (Pasadena: California Design Publications, 1974); and *The Domestic Scene (1897–1927); George M. Niedecken, Interior Architect* (Milwaukee Art Museum, 1981). Gillian Naylor's *The Arts and Crafts Movement: A Study of Its Sources, Ideals and Influences on Design* (Cambridge, Massachusetts: MIT Press, 1971); *C. R. Ashbee and the Guild of Handicraft* (Cheltenham Art Gallery and

Museum, 1981); and Lionel Lambourne, *Utopian Craftsmen: The Arts and Crafts Movement from the Cotswolds to Chicago* (Salt Lake City: Peregrine Smith, 1980) proved particularly helpful in interpreting the British Arts and Crafts movement.

Since Hull-House was a center of craft activity, the writings of Jane Addams, especially *Twenty Years at Hull-House* (New York: Macmillan Company, 1910) and *Forty Years at Hull-House* (New York: Macmillan Company, 1935) are important sources. The weekly *Hull-House Bulletin* contains notices of craft classes and programs of the Chicago Arts and Crafts Society. The December 1, 1897, *Bulletin* contains the organization's constitution. Lawrence Cremin's *The Transformation of the School: Progressivism in American Education, 1876–1957* (New York: Vintage Books, 1964) discusses the evolution of the manual training movement. Oscar Lovell Triggs outlined his philosophy in "Industrial Art," an essay in *The New Industrialism* (Chicago: National League of Industrial Art, 1902), which also contains a reprint of Frank Lloyd Wright's "The Art and Craft of the Machine."

Material on interiors and furniture designed by Chicago architects can be found in numerous periodicals, especially *Inland Architect, Arts and Decoration, Architectural Record, Architectural Review, House Beautiful, Ladies' Home Journal,* and *Western Architect,* as well as in the annual exhibition catalogues of the Chicago Architectural Club at The Art Institute of Chicago. H. Allen Brooks, *The Prairie School: Frank Lloyd Wright and His Midwest Contemporaries* (New York: W. W. Norton & Co., 1972) is vital to an understanding of this artistic movement and the city's cultural milieu. Individual Chicago architects are profiled in issues of the *Prairie School Review* and the *Journal of the Society of Architectural Historians,* as well as in: The Milwaukee Art Center's *The Prairie School Tradition* (New York: Whitney Library of Design, 1979); Narciso G. Menocal, *Keck & Keck, Architects* (Elvehjem Museum of Art, University of Wisconsin-Madison, 1980); and Sally Kitt Chappell and Ann Van Zanten, *Barry Byrne, John Lloyd Wright: Architecture & Design* (Chicago: CHS, 1982).

The work of Frank Lloyd Wright, George W. Maher, and George G. Elmslie are treated in Marion Page, *Furniture Designed by Architects* (New York: Whitney Library of Design, 1980); Wright and Shaw are compared in Leonard K. Eaton, *Two Chicago Architects and Their Clients: Frank Lloyd Wright and Howard Van Doren Shaw* (Cambridge, Massachusetts: MIT Press, 1969). Two other useful sources illustrating Wright's work are David A. Hanks, *The Decorative Designs of Frank Lloyd Wright* (New York: E. P. Dutton, 1979) and the *Frank Lloyd Wright Newsletter* published by the Frank Lloyd Wright Association, Oak Park, Illinois.

PART IV: Information on Chicago's modern furniture designers and manufacturers was obtained primarily from conversations with architects, artisans, workers, and officers of the companies or from their families, as well as from clippings, sketches, photographs, catalogues, and other materials that they made available.

In addition to the records of the Chicago Furniture Manufacturers' Association, the *Survey of the Furniture Trade* conducted in 1925 by the Chicago Association of Commerce and Industry and "Furniture—Stronghold of Small Business," a review published by the Federal Reserve Bank of Chicago in June 1956, proved particularly useful in studying business conditions. George Marshall's summary of the furniture industry in the *Encyclopedia of the Social Sciences* (New York: The Macmillan Company, 1931) helped place the local industry in perspective. John C. Murphy's "Notes on Furniture Making and Interior Design and Decoration in Chicago," (Unpublished manuscript, 1980) provided an overview of the local scene from the 1920s to the present.

Publications concerned with modern styling are particularly plentiful. Paul T. Frankl's *New Dimensions* (New York: Brewer & Warren, 1928) and periodicals, particularly *Interiors, Architectural Forum, Arts and Decoration, Good Furniture,* and *Pro-*

gressive Architecture, present design theories prevalent between the two world wars. Developments in Chicago are recorded in four Master's theses completed at the University of Chicago: Mildred May Osgood, "The Influence of the Skyscraper upon Modern Decorative Arts" (1929); Ethel Dixon Reynolds, "Trends in the Use of Color and Texture in Interior Decoration in the United States from 1927 to 1937" (1938); Marguerite Smith, "Modern Design in American Domestic Furniture, 1925 to 1945" (1947); and Clark Sommer Smith, "Nine Years of Federally Sponsored Art in Chicago, 1933–1942" (1965). Model homes and furnishings at A Century of Progress Exposition, the 1933 Chicago World's Fair, are illustrated and described in *Homes and Furnishings* (Chicago: M. A. Ring Company, 1934). Recent interpretations of these decades are Martin Battersby, *The Decorative Twenties* (New York: Walker and Company, 1969) and Martin Grief, *Depression Modern: The Thirties Style in America* (New York: Universe Books, 1975).

A definitive history of the New Bauhaus, later the Institute of Design, has yet to be written. However, aspects of its work are treated in Laszlo Moholy-Nagy, *Vision in Motion* (Chicago: P. Theobald, 1947); Dorothea (Sibyl) Moholy-Nagy, *Noholy-Nagy: Experiment in Totality* (Cambridge, Massachusetts: MIT Press, 1969); John Chancellor, "The Rocky Road from the Bauhaus," *Chicago* 2 (July 1955); Richard Koppe, "The New Bauhaus, Chicago," in *Bauhaus and Bauhaus People* (New York: Van Nostrand Reinhold Co., 1970); Roslyn Newman, "The Development of the Department of Architecture Begun at the Bauhaus and Its Continuation in the Illinois Institute of Technology," (Master's diss., Northwestern University, 1971); and Lloyd C. Engelbrecht, "The Association of Arts and Industries: Background and Origins of the Bauhaus Movement in Chicago (Diss., University of Chicago, 1973). A protagonist point of view is expressed in Tom Wolfe, *From Bauhaus to Our House* (New York: Farrar, Straus & Giroux, 1981).

Studies that mention the work of Chicago architects include Edgar Kaufmann, Jr., *Prize Designs for Modern Furniture from the International Competition for Low-Cost Furniture Design* (New York: The Museum of Modern Art, 1950); Charles D. Gandy and Susan Zimmerman, *Contemporary Classics: Furniture of the Masters* (New York: McGraw-Hill Book Company, 1981); David A. Hanks, *Innovative Furniture in America from 1800 to the Present* (New York: Horizon Press, 1981); and Clement Meadmore, *The Modern Chair; Classics in Production* (New York: Von Nostrand Reinhold Co., 1979). The contemporary scene is described in Stuart E. Cohen, *Chicago Architects* (Chicago: The Swallow Press, 1976); Oswald W. Grube, Peter C. Pran, and Franz Schulze, *100 Years of Architecture in Chicago* (Chicago: J. Philip O'Hara, 1973); *Chicago Architects Design* (The Art Institute of Chicago and Rizzoli International Publications, 1982); and Maurizio Casari (ed.), *Beyond the International Style: New Chicago Architecture* (Chicago: Rizzoli, 1981); and Chicago Architectural Club, *The Chicago Architectural Journal* 2 (1982) (New York: Rizzoli International Publications).

INDEX

Green, Zola, 67
Greene, R.G., 26
Greenwood, Richard N., 120, 304
Griffin, Walter Burley, 256, 262, 263, 267
Griffith, Jerry, 338, 339
Gropius, Walter, 288
Grueby Faience Company, 234
Guenzel, Louis, 263
Guide to Church Furnishing, 164
guilds, 225-31
gum, 50
Gunlocke Co., 114

Hafner, William H., 67, 70, 85
Hafner & Schoen Furniture Company, 66, 70, 136
Hager, J. H., 252
Hagmayer, Albert, 212
haircloth, 11
Haka, Clifford and Susan, 77
Halbach, Frederick A., 181-82
Hale & Bros., A. L., 34, 38
hall furniture, 153-54
Hallman, Clement F., 146
Halstrick, William F., 206-7
Halvorson, H., 98
Hambrook, R. T., 132
Hamline, L. M., 98, 136
hand-carved furniture, 197-205
Hanke, Albert, 98
Hanke, Charles, 98
Hanke, Herman, 98
Hanks, David, 265
Hanna, Charles H., 319, 320
Hanselman, June, 31, 32
Hanselman, Mr. and Mrs. George, 31, 32
Hanson, Daniel P., 18
Hanson, Franklin S., 18
Hanson, John, 148
Hanson, Louis, 144, 148, 302
Hanson, Louis, Jr., 148
Hanson, Martin, 148
Hanson Co., Louis, 148, 302
harewood, 306
Harrilland, Richard, 280
Harrison, John, 124
Hartley, DeBert, 87
Hartley Mfg. Co., 87
Hartley Reclining House Chair, 87-88, 88
Hartman, I. H., Jr., 62, 246
Hartman Furniture & Carpet Co, 63, 246, 247, 296
Hartmann, John, 201
Hasbrouck, Mr. and Mrs. Wilbert, 261
Haskins, G. W., 198
Hasselgren, Rudolph, 209
Hasselgren & Co., R., 209
Hasselgren Studios, 209
Hauberg House, 265
Hausske, August, 67, 136
Hausske, Robert, 67
Haymarket Affair (Mary 4, 1886), 54, 55
Hazenplug, Frank, 218, 220
headboards, 101, 207
Healy, George P., 182
Healy, Phyllis (estate of), 207
Healy & Millet, 181, 182
Heider, August, 299
Henry Dibblee Company, 198-99
Henry Liebenstein & Co., 29
Henry P. Glass Associates, 335
Herhold, Frederick, 15, 111, 112-13, 143
Herhold, Johnson & Borgmeier, 111, 112, 113
Herhold, William, 113
Herhold & Co., F., 113

Herhold & Sons, 136, 137
Herhold Chair Co., 303, 311
Herhold Johnson Chair Factory, 33
Heritage-Henredon Furniture Company, 262
Herman Barth & Co., 67
Herman Miller Co., 337
Herrmann, William, 66
Herter Brothers, 181
Heywood, George H., 121
Heywood, Henry, 121
Heywood, Levi, 119
Heywood and Morrill Rattan Co., 120, 121
Heywood Brothers & Company, 119, 120, 122
Heywood Bros. and Wakefield Company, 62, 120, 122
Heywood-Wakefield Company, 120, 303-4, 311
Hickox, Warren, 259
Higginson, Augustus, 218, 220
Higginson, Frances, 218, 220
Hildreth, Charles H., 90
Himmel, Richard, 328, 336-37, 345, 354
Hints on Household Taste, Upholstery, and Other Details (Eastlake), 69, 80
History of the Norwegians of Illinois, The (Strand), 133
Hitchcock, Lambert, 13
Hitchcock, Reuben H., 114
Hitchcock Chair Company, 114-15
Hjort, Glenn C., 224
Hoffman, Frank, 307
Hoffmann, Josef, 314
Hoffmann, Paula, 314
Hoffmann, Wolfgang, 282, 314-15
Hokin/Kaufman, 345
Holabird & Root, 272, 281, 337
Hollatz Bros. Co., 299
Holton, C. C., 67
Holton & Co., C. C., 29, 34
Hompe, Alexander W., 184, 186, 187
Hoover Universal, 85
Hope, Arthur, 146
Hopkins, Anson S., 199
Hopkins, James M., 275
Hopkins, Julius, 272
Hopkins, Mrs. James M., residence of, 275-77, 275, 276
Horman, August, 144, 146
Horn, Jacob M., 98, 102
Horn, John C., 97-98, 102
Horn Bros. Manufacturing Co., 97-98, 102, 302, 311
horn furniture, 77, 78-79
Hornug, Anton N., 90
Horwitz, Sam, 302, 326
Hotel Metropole, 181-82
Hough, Mary Pat, 147
Houlberg, Klindt, 347-48
House Beautiful, 106, 156, 158, 191, 206, 210, 217, 220, 223, 224, 225, 226, 227, 229, 230, 232, 233, 235, 242, 245, 258, 262, 268, 271, 281, 284
House Beautiful, The (Gannett), 257
House in Good Taste, The (de Wolfe), 213
House of Tomorrow (model home at A Century of Progress Exposition), 282, 283
How to Know Period Styles of Furniture (Kimerly), 206
Howell Company, W. H., 277, 282, 283, 311-17, 319, 332
Hubbard, Elbert, 228
Hull-House, 216, 217
Hull-House Shop, 218, 220
Hunt, Myron, 268
Hunt, Richard Morris, 179

Husser, Joseph, 259
residence of, 260

Iannelli, Alfonso, 263, 279
Illinois Craft Project, 290
Illinois Furniture Company, 67
Illinois Trust & Savings Bank, 127
Illustrated Catalogue (Schultze), 101, 103
Illustrated Catalogue of Furniture Manufactured by F. Mayer & Co., The, 105
Illustrated Catalogue of Stadtfeld & Wolf's Center Table Manufactory, 140, 141
immigrants, 53, 54, 295, 296
immigration laws, 292, 295
immigration quotas (1921), 53
Improved Housing Association, 233
Industrial Arts League, 155, 229, 230
Industrial Chicago, 42, 123, 182, 199
Inland Architect & Builder, 43, 56, 60, 78, 102, 126, 198
installment buying, 62, 63
Institute of Design, 291, 334, 335
Interior Crafts, 321, 326, 326-28
Interior Decorator, 194, 201
interior decorators, 181-83
Interiors, 284, 337
International Furniture Co., 299
International Studio, 217
Inter-State Exposition Souvenir, The, 38, 86
Inter-State Industrial Exposition (1873), 37-38, 37, 40, 86, 89, 93, 126, 130, 155
Inter-State Industrial Exposition (1875), 161-62
Inter-State Industrial Exposition (1876), 163-64, 171
Inter-State Industrial Exposition (1883), 197
Inter-State Industrial Exposition (1884), 93
iron beds, 106-9
Izume, John, 334

Jacobs, E. A., 29
Jacobson, Mr. and Mrs. Robert L., 303, 309
Jacobson, Nils, 67
Jacobus, Augustus, 17, 18
Jacobus, David A., 15
Jacobus, David L., 9, 17-18, 22
Jacobus, D. & A. L., 18
Jacobus, D. L. & Bro., 18
Jacobus, James, 18
Jacobus, Steele & Co., 18
Jahn, Helmut, 344
Jannotta, Alfred Vernon, 212, 284
Jarvie, Robert R., 255
JFM Furniture Corp., 332
Jenney, William Le Baron, 158, 159-60, 161, 166, 176
John A. Colby & Co., 209
John A. Colby & Sons, 184, 185, 186-87, 188, 202, 203, 206, 207, 237
Johnson, Andrew P., 111-12, 113
Johnson, Arthur, 113
Johnson, Henry W., 114
Johnson, James A., 204
Johnson, Joseph, 114
Johnson, L. B., 207
Johnson, Nels, 113, 114
Johnson, Olaf, 113
Johnson, Walter, 114
Johnson & Co., 51, 62
Johnson & Co., A. J., 136
Johnson & Co., A. P., 110, 112, 113
Johnson Chair Co., 112, 112, 113, 136, 137, 286, 303
Joliet Prison, 122
Joliet Woolen Factory, 11
Jones, D. A., 9
Jones, Edward Burne, 9, 15, 160